3705

LOWDEN OF ILLINOIS

Matzene Studio

Frank O. Lowden about 1904

LOWDEN OF ILLINOIS

The Life of Frank O. Lowden

VOLUME I: CITY AND STATE

By William T. Hutchinson

PRESTON AND STERLING MORTON
PROFESSOR OF AMERICAN HISTORY
THE UNIVERSITY OF CHICAGO

THE UNIVERSITY OF CHICAGO PRESS

219

Fall '62

F
546
L92

Library of Congress Catalog Number: 57-6274

The University of Chicago Press, Chicago 37
Cambridge University Press, London, N.W. 1, England
The University of Toronto Press, Toronto 5, Canada

© *1957 by The University of Chicago. Published 1957*
Composed and printed by The University of Chicago
Press, *Chicago, Illinois, U.S.A.*

TO FRANCES

923
H97

FOREWORD

When the present century opened, Frank O. Lowden was at approximately the mid-point of his eighty-two years of life. Back of him lay his youth in frontier Minnesota and rural Iowa; ahead, his titles of governor, Republican elder statesman, and "Sage of Sinnissippi." During his crowded career he shared in many of the events and developments whereby the United States of Civil War days became the United States of World War II.

The story of his boyhood and early manhood is merely one version of the familiar American saga about how a gifted country lad, after winning his way through college and law school, rose within a single decade "by pluck and luck" from penury to a comfortable fortune and assured social position in Chicago. Thereafter, thanks to his own considerable income and the even larger resources of his wife, Florence Pullman, he engaged for several years in the creation and management of industrial corporations and for the rest of his life in experimental husbandry upon a large Rock River estate in Illinois and cotton plantations in Arkansas. As a farmer-planter he had to face most of the difficult problems besetting midwestern and southern agriculture after World War I.

Lowden's political career divides into three fairly distinct periods. At its outset he served a twelve-year apprenticeship amid the hurly-burly of partisan striving for the control and reform of Chicago's City Hall. After launching his state-centered phase by a dramatically unsuccessful effort to become governor of Illinois, he represented his rural district in Congress for five years. Following an equal span in virtual retirement, he emerged in 1916 to serve a highly creditable term as chief executive of his state during World War I and for two years after the Armistice. Building upon the wide reputation gained by his achievements in this office, he opened the longest and final chapter of his political story by a near-miss of the Republican presidential nomination in 1920. Subsequently, he refused a half-dozen offers of high appointive positions and continued in his role of a leading spokesman for the midwestern wing of his party. By declining its vice-presidential nomination in 1924 and "seceding" from its Kansas City convention as a presidential candidate four years later, he angered many of his fellow Republicans, even while he convinced them that the advancement of policies rather than the attainment of offices was his principal concern. From then until his death in

1943, high-ranking Democrats as well as leaders of his own party often sought his counsel. Measured in terms of the number of governmental posts he had held, his record was surpassed by many of his contemporaries. Yet, in the duration and scope of his influence, he was one of the outstanding public men of his generation.

During his last twenty-five years of life he was best known, and probably will be longest remembered, for instituting at Springfield, Illinois, a widely copied program of state administrative reforms and for unwearyingly advocating farmers' co-operatives, the equalization fee, reforestation, and government subsidies for soil conservation as a means of reducing crop surpluses. Few men have dedicated themselves with equal earnestness to the cause of making rural folk happy and prosperous as the best means of safeguarding American democracy, the best offset to economic and political radicalism, and the best insurance against shortages of food and fiber in the not-distant future. To him, these words carved on the pediment of the Union Station in Washington, D.C., needed no modification, "The Farm: Best Home of the Family, Main Source of National Wealth, Foundation of Civilized Society, the Natural Providence."

Prior to 1921, Lowden's associations with urban-industrial life largely shaped his course in politics and his convictions about the proper function of government in American society. After that year, on the other hand, the distressed condition of agriculture supplanted the city and big business as the major force molding his views and his career. It was his fate to be called ultra-conservative by progressives in the earlier period and an agrarian radical by the standpatters of the Harding-Coolidge-Hoover era. Although these labels did him considerable injustice, they tersely signified his basic dilemma in politics. Indeed, his own party, at the same time, faced the similar and ever more difficult problem of preserving the alliance between northern farmers and businessmen which had given it birth on the eve of the Civil War. Lowden managed in his private life to unite agriculture harmoniously with heavy investments in business corporations, but he failed after 1920, except in his own state and Iowa, to attract as much political support from the cities as from the countryside.

Any account of his public career would be meaningless if divorced from its context of Illinois Republican politics at the local and state levels, its machinery and how it operated, the mode of starting and sustaining a campaign for office, the always baffling problems of patronage and getting out the vote on election days, the ceaseless friction between factions, and the interplay of the Chicago metropolis and the downstate and of the so-called "state crowd" and "federal crowd." Although the political chapters of this biography furnish something of a history of the Republican party in Illinois for about thirty years after the early 1890's, their main purpose is to follow Lowden as he gradually developed from a Chicago ward leader of reforming tendencies into a member of the inner group at the top of the national party.

His unusually large circle of friends in every walk of life included some who believed that he was never at his best in the arena of practical politics. In their judgment he rendered his most notable services as lawyer, administrator, conciliator of men at odds in a common cause, dynamic head of many public service enterprises, and effective bridge between political scientists and government officials, economists and businessmen, and agricultural college professors and farmers. Moreover, a few of his closest associates, without discounting the significance of his achievements, insist that he was, above all, a magnetic personality, a stimulating companion who often talked more eloquently about the virtues of his purebred cattle and his deficiencies as a golfer than about issues of national moment. He was continually a surprise to them. They knew him as both sentimental and coldly analytical, modest and vain, kindly and harsh in judgment, gracious and abrupt in manner, slow to make up his mind and quick in decision, buoyant and depressed, and unwilling to drive himself hard, yet tireless in his energy. Whatever his mood, he remained loyal to his friends and ceaselessly drew new ones to him. Among the very few whom he eventually alienated, Mayor William Hale Thompson of Chicago most adversely affected his political career. Among the public men with whom he at first sharply disagreed but later became closely reconciled, former President Herbert Hoover was the most distinguished.

If his biography were ever to be written, wrote Lowden in 1924, "it can be done just as well after . . . [I am] . . . dead, thus saving . . . [me] . . . much trouble." Rarely thinning out his files during his lifetime, he left behind an extraordinarily large mass of source materials. His correspondence, copies of speeches and articles, scrapbooks, and bundles of newspaper and magazine clippings are now in the William Rainey Harper Memorial Library of the University of Chicago. Certain family papers, including his investment records and the invaluable diary of Mrs. Lowden, are either in the office of Sinnissippi Farm at Oregon, Illinois, or in the possession of Dr. and Mrs. C. Phillip Miller of Chicago. They opened these manuscripts to my unrestricted use and aided my research in many other ways. Without their co-operation, this biography could not have been written.

Governor Lowden's sisters, Mrs. Herbert M. Sammis, Mrs. Eva Sheldon, and the Misses Isabel and Eleanor Lowden, kindly shared their memories with me. Equally generous in this regard were Mrs. Joseph T. B. Bowen, Mrs. Albert G. Simms (Ruth Hanna McCormick), Miss Margaret Enders, and Miss Mary Humphrey, and the Messrs. Earl D. Babst, Martin T. Baldwin, Frank Bane, Archibald L. Bowen, Charles G. Dawes, George B. McKibbin, Charles E. Merriam, John R. Morron, Gordon A. Ramsay, Henry C. Taylor, Leslie P. Volz, and Roy O. West. For background material on life seventy-five years ago in Hardin County, Iowa, and at the University of Iowa, I am indebted to Mrs. Laenas G. Weld, J. R. Bahne, Wendell S. Clampitt, Clifton C. Coldren, and especially to the Misses Ada and Delia Hutchinson and Laurence T. Kersey. At Sinnissippi Farm, Miss Nell M. Hanley and Mr. and Mrs. William Hewitt made my research the more pleasant and rewarding by their friendliness. Following the transfer in 1950 of most of Lowden's manuscripts from the farm to Harper Library, the head of its Department of Special Collections, Robert Rosenthal, extended to me many courtesies in the continued use of these papers. Miss Bessie L. Pierce, Walter Johnson, and Donald F. Lach, of the Department of History, University of Chicago, as well as other scholars in the fields of history or political science, including Mrs. Gayle Smith, Howard K. Beale, Vaughn D. Bornet, Allan W. Bosch, Howard S. Greenlee, Lawrence J. R. Herson, Richard Lowitt, David M. Pletcher, Harrison J. Thornton, and Alfred P. Tischendorf, thoughtfully sent me references to Governor Lowden in the source collections engaging their attention. The generosity of the Social Sciences Research Committee of the University of Chicago furthered the preparation of the manuscript for the press. In this connection Miss Imogene Sumner and Albert U. Romasco were especially helpful. For over two years I greatly benefited from the expert assistance of Mrs. Shirley A. Bill. She brought as much persistence and enthusiasm to the project as though it had been her own and relieved me of many office chores beyond the scope of her assignment.

WILLIAM T. HUTCHINSON

TABLE OF CONTENTS

VOLUME I

TABLE OF CONTENTS

CHAPTER I

A BOY IN TWO BACKWOODS

A century ago Sunrise City was a little cluster of shanties and cabins in Chisago County on the eastern edge of Minnesota Territory about fifty miles north of St. Paul. By exploiting the timber and fish, trading for furs and deerskins with the Chippewa Indians, and harvesting grain on the rich land between the cranberry and tamarack marshes, the home-makers expected their settlement quickly to justify its ambitious name. Pioneers on other American frontiers indulged similar roseate hopes during the few years preceding the panic of 1857. Fated to remain unimpressive, Sunrise City was one of the many stunted offspring of the first Minnesota land boom. Nevertheless, by greatly increasing the population, this boom advanced the territory to statehood before the decade closed.

Among the first settlers of Sunrise City were Lorenzo Or(r)en Lowden, Isaac Parmenter, and his sister-in-law, Nancy Elizabeth Breg(g). The records and recollections of these distant years are scanty and conflicting, but Lorenzo probably reached Taylors Falls on the St. Croix River in 1854 and moved the fifteen miles to Sunrise City about two years later. He and Nancy Breg were married on March 16, 1856.[1] How and when they first met and where they wed are not known. The problem of providing themselves with food and shelter necessarily dwarfed their interest in genealogy, even granting that they knew the meaning of the word or the names of their ancestors farther back than their own grandparents. Their children, however, have furnished them with lineages running deep into America's past.

Among the Puritans reaching Boston harbor in 1638 during the "Great Migration" of that decade, were Richard Lowden, probably from Scotland, and Joseph Loomis, a woolen draper of Essex County, England. Richard ventured no farther than Charlestown, Massachusetts, before making his home, but some of his descendants settled in New Hampshire and, still later, in Vermont.[2] Soon after arriving in the New World, Joseph Loomis moved to Connecticut, where his offspring lived until the Revolution. One of them,

---

1. *History of Hardin County, Iowa* (Springfield, Ill.: Union Publishing Co., 1883), p. 304.

2. George F. Black, "The Surnames of Scotland, Their Origin, Meaning, and History," *Bulletin of the New York Public Library*, XLIX, No. 6 (June, 1945), Part XX, 474–75. See also F. O. Lowden's correspondence with Mrs. Henry Burrell, of Freeport, Illinois, between Dec. 14, 1908, and Apr. 5, 1911. Hereafter in these footnotes "FOL" will stand for Frank O. Lowden.

John Loomis, served in the patriot army and married Elizabeth Standish of Ashfield (North Adams), Massachusetts. She traced her direct ancestral line to the redoubtable Captain Miles Standish of Pilgrim fame. Among their children was Jerusha (1809–47), who became the wife of Or(r)en Lowden (1809–68), a descendant of the Richard Lowden already mentioned.

In 1832, three years after their marriage, Jerusha and Oren settled in Riceville on Oil Creek in northwestern Pennsylvania. There he tilled his small farm and served his neighbors as a blacksmith. A tall, swarthy man, addicted to Scotch snuff, he fashioned nails and horseshoes, shared in the Millerite hysteria, and never wearied of upholding Jacksonian principles and his fellow Pennsylvanian, James Buchanan. Soon after Jerusha's death, Oren trekked to the new state of Iowa. In Pleasant Township of Hardin County he broke the tough prairie sod and devoted the last twenty years of his life to his farm.[3]

Left behind in the East at the time of his migration was Oren and Jerusha's son, Lorenzo Or(r)en Lowden, then fifteen years of age. Under circumstances and for reasons unknown, the boy spent four years in Wyoming County, New York, and attended an academy there. Returning to Riceville in 1852, he briefly followed in his father's footsteps as a blacksmith. Many years later, he was remembered as a skilled workman who welcomed children to his forge and enjoyed discussing politics and religion with his neighbors. It was he who caught the Minnesota "fever" in 1854 and the fancy of Nancy Breg shortly thereafter.

Nancy reached Sunrise City by a quite different trail whose American portion was probably shorter than her husband's. One of her grandfathers, George Elliott of Pelham near Amherst, Massachusetts, came from English stock, but she also had Dutch and French folk among her forebears. Descendants of George Elliott followed the usual westward course from New England to central New York. After Eleanor Elliott of Auburn married William Breg, they moved to Steuben County, just north of the Pennsylvania border. Breg gained some little prominence in local politics before a falling tree brought his life to an abrupt close. Among his eight children, the youngest was Nancy Elizabeth, born October 8, 1836. For three years in her late teens she turned her academy training to good account by teaching school. When her brothers-in-law, Isaac Parmenter and I. B. Warner, sought better health and fortune in the Minnesota wilderness, she gladly joined in their adventure.[4] Perhaps she expected to introduce the three R's to the numerous children in the north woods. If so, Lorenzo Lowden intervened to change her plans not long after her arrival in Sunrise City.

Life in this little community formed a pattern well known to any frontier clearing in Michigan, Wisconsin, or Minnesota a century ago. In their old age Lorenzo and Nancy remembered the Sunrise settlers as a closely knit group of a few congenial families. Coming most readily to mind were the

3. E. J. Smith, Los Angeles, California, to FOL, Apr. 19, 1921.

4. W. R. Breg, Washington, D.C., to FOL, Aug. 28, 1941; Miss Isabel Lowden, New York City, to Mrs. C. P. Miller, Chicago, Oct. 20, 1945.

Parmenters, Warners, Ringers, Starkeys, Starkweathers, Runyans, and Vosses. They worked, worshiped, and played together. With them, the Lowdens shared in barn- and house-raisings, sewing and singing circles, planting, harvesting, husking, hunting and fishing, dancing and other "frolicking." A few Scandinavian "foreigners" lived among, but were not of, this self-sufficient coterie. During the early years the Chippewas outnumbered the whites. Deemed a nuisance, these Indians always were viewed with suspicion and sometimes with fear. The pioneers preferred co-operative efforts to individual striving, but they remained clannish and barred redskins and unwanted whites from the circle of their social democracy.

Although Lorenzo's and Nancy's congeniality assured them of friends, their firm resolve to preserve their liking for good books and serious conversation might have gone for naught if their tastes had not been shared by some of their neighbors. To subdue, rather than to be subdued by, the frontier demanded not only hard manual labor but also a stubborn refusal to let cultural interests die. The Lowdens belonged to a literary society whose members read and discussed the works of Shakespeare, Emerson, and Longfellow. Lorenzo helped to build the one-room schoolhouse where Stella Parmenter, his wife's niece, taught the rapidly growing number of children. He nourished his own inclination toward the law and politics by studying the few legal treatises available for his use. Soon, as justice of the peace, he found a welcome outlet for his learning and his skill in arbitrating disputes. Of independent mind and not afraid to differ with his neighbors, he stood up in a church meeting to let them know that he rejected every religious creed. Thereafter, until his death, he declined to become a member of any denomination. Nancy apparently followed her husband's lead.[5]

Blessed with good health and friends and surrounded by a bountiful nature, Lorenzo had no fear of starving or freezing on the Minnesota frontier, but he was puzzled to know how he could mount the economic ladder. Money was scarce and hard to come by. Even though he produced farm crops or lumber beyond the needs of his own family, he could not haul them profitably over almost non-existent roads to the distant St. Paul market. An obvious expedient, although one seldom calculated to bring wealth quickly, would be to furnish a service required by the community or by families newly arrived from "the States." More artisan than farmer, he had brought his blacksmith's tools with him from Pennsylvania. Thanks to these, he soon competed with the smithy of Henry Voss in supplying the many iron articles used by lumbermen, boatmen, farmers, and house-builders.[6] Before long, he moved Nancy and the two babies from their shanty to a clapboard house which he had

5. C. W. Ringer, typed "Sketch of Early Life of Frank O. Lowden" (date and place of writing not shown, but probably Minneapolis, 1920). *Brainerd* (Minn.) *Journal-Press,* Feb. 13, 1920. Conversation of the author, Dec. 29, 1945, with three sisters of FOL—Mrs. Alice L. Sammis and the Misses Isabel and Eleanor Lowden.

6. Interview with FOL reported in *Chicago Daily News,* Mar. 2, 1920; F. H. Wolf, Harris, Minnesota, to FOL, Jan. 2, 1920.

erected on "a rise of ground" about two miles outside the village. Here on January 26, 1861, Frank Orren Lowden was born.

The care of the new home and her steadily enlarging family probably explains why Nancy found no time to teach school.[7] With her husband away every weekday in his shop, the farmwork fell largely upon her shoulders. Even after Lorenzo lightened the demands of his forge by making I. B. Warner his partner, he relied upon Nancy to milk the cow, swill the pigs, and help in the fields. Furthermore, her friends soon discovered that she had a "way" with the sick. As soon as she could trust May Adele, her oldest daughter, to tend the babies, Nancy frequently spent days at a time in her neighbors' homes as a practical nurse. Long afterward, Frank always thought of May as his "little mother." She kept him scrubbed and out of mischief and walked him to Stella Parmenter's school at the age of four.

"The sparks of my father's blacksmith shop are mixed with my earliest memories," wrote Frank Lowden many years later. He also said repeatedly that, although he had "very pleasant" recollections of his childhood in Sunrise City, they were, in all honesty, "very meager." In their middle age his former playmates told somewhat conflicting stories about him as a lad. If they can be believed, he led them in play and outshone them in the classroom.[8] He challenged their accuracy when they recalled a precocious toddler dressed in homespun, walking to school barefoot or in copper-toed boots, with his head always bent over a book. As he remembered himself, he was a shy, towheaded, sunburned youngster of stocky build, who joined, but never excelled, in outdoor sports. Throughout his life his head always served him better than his hands. Although they were well shaped and excellently fashioned for graceful gesturing, they lacked dexterity. Even as a very young lad he had farm chores to do, but both then and later the spur to their performance was duty rather than love.[9]

Less than three months after his birth, Fort Sumter surrendered to Confederate troops. Minnesota shared in the economic good times of the North during the Civil War, but its farms suffered from a labor shortage after men enlisted in the armed forces. Lowden family tradition tells of Lorenzo answering one of the governor's first calls for volunteers and becoming a major in the Eighty-fourth Minnesota Infantry. Nevertheless, so the story goes, he could not pass the medical examination because of varicose veins in his legs. No contemporary evidence supports any part of this tale. No doubt the war enthusiasm during the late spring and early summer of 1861 might even have led a man with a farm, a blacksmith shop, a wife, and three babies to offer his services. Majors' commissions were sometimes given to locally

7. May A. Lowden was born Feb. 5, 1857; Eugene W., June 25, 1858; Eva D., June 29, 1862; Caroline E., Oct. 3, 1863; and Alice L., Oct. 14, 1865. Five other children were born later.

8. MSS of FOL's speeches at St. Paul, Feb. 12, 1918, and at North Branch, Minnesota, Mar. 2, 1920; *Brainerd* (Minn.) *Journal-Press,* Feb. 13, 1920. FOL to Mrs. A. A. Sandahl, San Jose, California, Feb. 21, 1939.

9. MS of FOL's speech at North Branch, Minnesota, Mar. 2, 1920.

prominent or popular men of no military experience. The story, however, arouses the more skepticism because in the following year, during the Sioux uprising, Lorenzo Lowden patrolled the woods of Chisago County as a humble Fourth Sergeant in Captain James Starkey's Ranger Company.[10] During those anxious months, when the settlers feared lest the Chippewas put aside their ancient enmity toward the Sioux and join them on the warpath, Nancy Lowden took her babies with her to the pasture where she milked the cow every morning and evening.[11] Deaths occurred in the Lowden family during the Civil War, but illnesses rather than Indians were the cause.[12]

Several years after the close of the conflict, the nation's farmers entered an extended period of hard times. For a while longer the forty families of Sunrise City, contrary to actuality or any reasonable hope, continued to call their settlement "a growing town." Two stores, two grist mills, and one sawmill made up its entire business inventory. Every blessing which would have fostered its life had passed it by. The federal land office was in Taylors Falls, the nearest post office at North Branch, and the county seat at Chisago City. As a climax of ill luck the Superior Railroad, crossing the county from north to south, came no closer to Sunrise City than North Branch, about ten miles away. The entire county in 1868 had fewer than three thousand people and scarcely that many acres under cultivation. At the November election in that year, the county mustered only 655 voters. Of these, 538 supported General U.S. Grant for the presidency and 117 his opponent, Governor Horatio Seymour.[13] Whether the staunch Democrat, Lorenzo Lowden, cast one of these ballots is unknown. That autumn he was much occupied with selling his farm and shop and making ready for the long journey to Hardin County in central Iowa. He had found it a pleasant land on his visit there in the late summer after hearing of his father's death.[14] During his twelve years in Sunrise City, he had done well, when measured by its modest gauge of success. Now in the prime of life and eager to forge ahead, he knew the time had come to leave a community which had failed to gain the means of progress.

In mid-autumn, he and Nancy bade goodbye to their kinsfolk and other friends, loaded their few possessions into a wagon, and, with their three daughters and two sons, headed south on the corduroy road to St. Paul. Arriving at its Merchant's Hotel two days later, Frank gaped at the crowds, the busy railroad traffic, and the magnificent river boat "War Eagle" which carried the Lowden family down the Mississippi to Dubuque. From there

10. Minnesota Board of Commissioners, *Minnesota in the Civil and Indian Wars, 1861–1865* (St. Paul, 1890), p. 813. The Rangers served without casualties from mid-August to early November, 1862.

11. Conversation of author with Mrs. Eva Lowden Sheldon, June 19, 1945. The center of the uprising was about 100 miles west of Sunrise City.

12. A son, Eugene W. Lowden, died Jan. 25, 1862, at the age of three and a half years, and a daughter, Caroline E. Lowden, Oct. 29, 1865, at the age of two years.

13. J. W. McClung, *Minnesota as It Is in 1870* (St. Paul, 1870), pp. 204–5, 279–81.

14. Oren Lowden died Aug. 22, 1868, and was buried at Point Pleasant, Iowa.

they went by train to Eldora, hard by their destination at the tiny settlement of Point Pleasant.[15] Once again, as in Pennsylvania and Minnesota, Lorenzo set up his forge and anvil. They provided a small income until he felt enough at home in the neighborhood to buy land with the money gained from the sale of his Sunrise City properties.

At the start, separated by long miles from the beloved Parmenters and Warners and surrounded by people who spoke only German or, being Quakers or Methodists, frowned upon dancing and other diversions, Nancy was homesick. She wrote nearly forty years later: "I do not think I felt any older when I came to Iowa than I did at 20. How I did love to Dance, and your Father and Mother were said to be the best Dancers that attended Partys [sic] in Sunrise but we never done [sic] very much frolicking after reaching Iowa. What a terrible Back Woodsy Puritanical Plaice [sic] that was to bring up a family in."[16] Although contemporary sources suggest that, in retrospect, she exaggerated her discontent, they also stress her eagerness to revisit Sunrise whenever her slender purse permitted. In July, 1886, Frank accompanied her, enjoying his first ride in a Pullman car. With one exception, thirty-four years later, it was his only pilgrimage to his native heath.[17]

"Backwoodsy" as a descriptive term for central Iowa in the 1860's is not literally accurate. The Lowdens had come from a forested frontier to one where lumber for buildings and timber for fence rails were hard to find. Around Point Pleasant the open prairie, lush with grass and flowers during the long, hot summers, stretched to the horizon, unbroken except by low, tree- or brush-covered hills along the gently flowing streams. Frank Lowden once remarked that the monotonously level land made it hard for a boy to find a long and fairly steep slope to coast down in winter.[18] The leaping trout of the Sunrise River gave place to pickerel, suckers, and bullheads. There were no deer. When, in 1869, a cougar was caught in a mink trap, the editor of the *Eldora Ledger* voiced the hope that it would be "the last of the cantankerous catamounts" ever to bother the neighborhood. Unlike Minnesota, rattlesnakes were a nuisance, but at Point Pleasant, as at Sunrise, the Lowdens could combine sport with community service by joining in a wolf drive.[19] Although the settlers often supplemented their home-grown fare with ducks, geese, rabbits, and squirrels, these wild creatures were eclipsed by the prairie chickens in Lowden's nostalgic recollections of boyhood hunting. Both their eggs and their flesh provided delectable food. Because of the abundance of the fowl, stalking them with a setter was usually rewarding, not only as a sport but also as a means of saving the grain from their

15. MS of FOL's speech to Iowa Bankers Association, Fort Dodge, June 25, 1919.

16. Mrs. L. O. Lowden to FOL, Apr. 16, 1907.

17. *Eldora* (Iowa) *Ledger,* July 1 and 22, 1886.

18. FOL to Harvey Ingham, Des Moines, Iowa, Dec. 29, 1930; MS of FOL's speech at Hubbard, Iowa, Dec. 21, 1921.

19. *Eldora Ledger,* Feb. 13, 1869. During that year this paper often noted the $5.00 bounty paid for wolf scalps. Even ten years later, community wolf hunts were still in vogue around New Providence.

ravages. Their distinctive calls and antic lovemaking in spring etched themselves deeply on the memory of Frank Lowden and many another "son of the Middle Border."[20]

When the Lowdens moved to Hardin County, ten thousand people already lived there, and more were arriving every month. Quakers from Indiana and North Carolina, distinctive in garb, speech, and manner of worship, had been among the earliest settlers.[21] Instead of the Scandinavians of Sunrise City, the foreigners in Hardin were fresh from Germany. They kept much to themselves and usually followed the lead of their conservative Lutheran pastors. To folk like the Lowdens, unwilling to use a church as their community center, the Noble Order of the Patrons of Husbandry, better known as the "Grange," served as a welcome medium of social expression and an outlet for economic discontent.

In 1868, however, unaware of the imminent depression, the Hardin County settlers believed they were on the threshold of a prosperous era. A decade of rivalry for the county seat between Eldora, Point Pleasant, and Iowa Falls, marked by expensive litigation and the erection of at least one building designed, but never used, for a public purpose, was just ending. Eldora emerged the victor. Point Pleasant, with its "White Ghost" saloon and Lorenzo Lowden's smithy, eventually reverted to a cornfield.[22]

For the farmers near that crossroads, the loss of the county seat was not overwhelming, since Eldora lay only eight miles to the east and Iowa Falls sixteen to the north. The *Eldora Ledger* soon congratulated its readers upon the number of buildings going up in the village and the acreage of new land being broken in the neighboring countryside.[23] Above all else, the summer of 1868 witnessed the completion of a spur railroad from Eldora to Ackley, seventeen miles away, where it joined the east-west track between Dubuque and Sioux City. No wonder the *Ledger* on August 1 abandoned all restraint in rhapsodizing about the town's good fortune: "Eldora Exalted! The Supreme Court Declares It the County Seat!! Grand Ratification Meeting! The Engine Among Us! Bully for the Eldora Railroad! Flags Flying and Bonfires Burning. One Hundred Guns Fired." Something of the spirit of the West, as well as of joyful extravagance, is illustrated by a toast drunk by the city fathers in honor of the occasion: "The Star Spangled Banner, the best flag in the World; the Eldora Railroad, mother of the Iowa River Railway Co., and father of the Grand Route from St. Paul to St. Louis; Eldora the golden tinged Eden of Iowa." Frank Lowden was one of the neighborhood boys who marveled at the big labor force being used to level off the bed and lay the track. The "Grand Route" would eventually be completed, but the

20. FOL later called hunting prairie chickens his "most fascinating" boyhood sport. In it, he used an Irish setter, which always thereafter was his favorite breed of dog.

21. *Eldora Ledger,* Aug. 26, 1870; F. T. Clampitt, *Some Incidents in My Life: A Saga of the Unknown Citizen* (Ann Arbor, Mich., 1935), pp. 2–6.

22. *History of Hardin County,* pp. 241–43, 396–403; *Eldora Herald,* Feb. 13, 1920.

23. *Eldora Ledger,* Apr. 10, 1869, and Apr. 22, 1870.

long depression of the 1870's delayed the work far beyond the expectations of the jubilant citizens of Eldora on that midsummer day in 1868.[24]

Frank Lowden arrived too late that year to share in the August celebration, but other red-letter days impressed themselves indelibly upon his memory. Among the closest friends of his youth were Frank Kelley and Thomas and Matthew Kennedy, the son and stepsons of John Kelley, whose farm adjoined Lorenzo Lowden's land.[25] With these youngsters and others, Frank hunted and fished, swam and skated, wrestled, played baseball, pitched horseshoes, and feuded with "Bill" Mitterer and his gang. Long afterward, when he had reached an economic and social status far different from that of his youth, he assured an audience that he had once been "the plainest of plain folks you ever saw." He always looked back with pride and pleasure upon his humble, rural upbringing and treated his boyhood friends without intentional condescension.[26] For him, "Iowa" was a magic word as long as he lived.

The high days came when his parents took him to a circus, a Fourth of July celebration, a county fair, a political mass meeting, or a lyceum. In 1870, Van Amburgh and Company's menagerie visited Eldora with "Seigrist's great French Circus, Lowanda's Brazilian Circus and Kingcade's United American Circus" joined to it "under the largest tent in America." Five years later, Cooper, Bailey, and Company's Great International Circus performed in the same town with "Ten Great Lady Performers, four female Gymnasts," and "Living Representations of All the Rare, Wonderful, and Remarkable Types of the Zoological and Ornithological Kingdoms."[27] Troupes like the Enoch Arden Comedy Company and Kendall Comedy Company made two-night stands in Porter and Moir's Hall in Eldora. There, too, Susan B. Anthony spoke in 1875 and Vice-President Schuyler Colfax in the following year.[28]

Rain could hardly dull the great Centennial Independence Day celebration of 1876. The Eldora Artillery wakened the people at sunrise with a hundred-gun salute fired from a twenty-pounder Parrott gun, bought especially for that purpose. Later in the day came the parade in "three grand divisions with color bearers, silver cornet band and brass band"; with thirty Potawatomies and Winnebagos led by their chief, Captain Jack; with Civil War veterans in their faded blue uniforms; with fifty young ladies garbed in red, white, and blue and enough others with banners to symbolize every state in the Union. The grand marshal and his mounted aides, including Lorenzo Lowden, kept

24. FOL's speech at Hubbard, Iowa, Sept. 21, 1921, reported in *Eldora Herald*, Sept. 29, 1921 (*History of Hardin County*, pp. 506–14).

25. For the location of L. Lowden's farm see A. T. Andreas, *Illustrated Historical Atlas of the State of Iowa* (Chicago, 1875).

26. MS of FOL's speech on Oct. 3, 1906, at Amboy, Illinois.

27. *Eldora Ledger*, Sept. 23, 1870; *Eldora Herald*, Sept. 1, 1875.

28. *Eldora Reform-Herald*, Feb. 17, 1874; *Eldora Herald*, Mar. 24, 1875, and Feb. 16, 1876.

back the cheering crowd "of 3,000" people from the line of march. After reaching Snyder's Grove, the Indians thrilled the spectators with a war dance and horseback "ride." There was even a balloon ascension. A proper amount of Fourth of July oratory followed the reading of the Declaration of Independence. If the weather had held good, the festivities would have been rounded off with evening fireworks.[29] For such a gala day as this, Frank hoarded his pennies to buy firecrackers at ten cents a bunch. These patriotic rituals, dominated by Union soldiers and the long shadow of the martyred Lincoln, shaped his outlook upon his country's history. He never forgot the lessons.

The autumn fairs of the Hardin County Agricultural Society provided other memorable occasions for Frank and his companions. Established in 1856, this organization limped along precariously until its reorganization sixteen years later. Lorenzo was one of its nine directors who helped Eldora acquire a permanent fairgrounds. Within its fenced inclosure were a ticket office, race track, judges' stand, stables and pens, Fruit Hall, Floral Hall, and other buildings. Although the society had no reason for existence except to stage the yearly fair, the solicitation of competitive exhibits and money for prizes was no easy task.[30] "In my boyhood," Frank Lowden told the American Association of Fairs and Expositions in 1919, "for days and weeks we looked forward to the county fair. Mother prepared the best dinner of the year to take as a picnic."[31]

This autumn fair provided every sound, smell, and sight that a boy's heart could desire, the jargon of the barkers at the side shows, the whistle and aroma of the peanut and corn roasters, the "pop" of opening soda-water bottles, the music of the merry-go-round, barrel organ, and band, the bursting of breath-filled paper bags, the crash of the maul on the weight-lifting machine, and even the haze of dust over the race track as the horses thudded by with the wind whipping the bright blouses of the jockeys. Probably it was at one of these fairs that Frank Lowden marveled at Charles Strothers' Shorthorns, the first purebred cattle he had ever seen.[32]

No wonder that in after years he disagreed with "realistic" novelists who portrayed life in the Iowa back country of the 1870's as drab and mentally deadening.[33] Not that there was no monotonous drudgery. Every day brought chores for all members of the family except the toddlers and the sick. But the holidays, picnics, shows, and fairs could be more keenly antici-

29. *Eldora Herald,* May 10, June 7, and July 5, 1876.

30. *Eldora Reform-Herald,* Oct. 3, 1873; *History of Hardin County,* pp. 489, 501–2.

31. Speech at Chicago, Dec. 3, 1919.

32. *Ibid.*

33. FOL thought that Hamlin Garland, in his *A Son of the Middle Border,* overstressed mud, dust, heat, flies, mosquitoes, barn smells, and toil. He said in a speech at Hubbard, Iowa, Sept. 21, 1921: "They were good old days in Iowa. . . . My life then was full and rich and real. No one had money, and so there were no invidious comparisons. They were among the best years of our lives despite their ruggedness."

pated and enjoyed because they came as infrequent breaks in the routine of rural living.

Frank Lowden loved the countryside as intensely as he disliked the labor required to till its soil. During his adult years he never firmly decided whether his boyhood had provided more of pleasure or of pain. His youthful experiences became an inexhaustible well from which he drew diverse and sometimes contradictory illustrations attuned to the ear of his audience and the demands of his instant theme. Thus, when he wished to emphasize the blessing conferred upon farm lads by the invention of the mechanical corn harvester, he could say vividly and with complete accuracy:

When I was a boy, the only implements used for this were a simple corn cutter, usually constructed out of a broken scythe, and a hickory husking peg. . . . I wish to testify that to the half-grown boy who follows the wagon, his nether garments wet and heavy and cold, and who, with fingers numb and bruised, with no other aid than the little husking peg, plucks the ear of corn from out of its covering of ice and husk, the poetry of the scene dissolves as rapidly as does the same brilliant frost before the ascending sun.[34]

But at other times he lingered in retrospect over "the poetry of the scene." By all accounts, he was a sensitive lad when in his teens, prone to daydreaming in the midst of his work. He naturally found it easier to idealize farm life after he had left it than when it hedged him about. With conscious hyperbole, but also speaking from the heart, he won applause from a Des Moines audience in 1900 by eulogizing "this noble state of Iowa,"

whose undulating plains fringed with woods painted in richest colors by October frosts, all mellowed by a genial glow, a nebulous haze which came from out the sky to enfold the earth with a mother's tenderness. It was at this glorious time that the great masters in literature first spoke intelligibly to me, for they but gave utterance to the prodigal beauty which was all about me. . . . I can recall, even at this day, having husked several million bushels [of corn] myself. . . . The milk that I myself have . . . wrung from the patient cow would have whitened all the waters of the Mississippi.[35]

Although these quotations suggest that husking corn and milking cows impressed young Lowden the most, his casual reminiscences, interpolated into many a speech or letter, also mentioned plowing, planting corn by hand, raking and shocking wheat, threshing grain, and cutting and carrying stove wood. Wheat and pork, rather than corn, comprised the chief cash crops of Hardin County when he was a boy.[36] Giving little attention to rotation, farmers felt lucky when they harvested an average of from ten to fifteen bushels of wheat an acre. Threshing crews, often bitter rivals, traveled from farm to farm in late summer, expecting each housewife and her daughters

34. MS of speech entitled "The Value of Education to the Farmer," given before the Ogle County Farmers' Institute, at Mount Morris, Illinois, Jan. 30, 1902.

35. MS of speech entitled "The Mississippi Valley—the Cradle of the American Race," delivered before the Grant Club of Des Moines, Apr. 27, 1900.

36. MS of speech at Watertown, South Dakota, Feb. 21, 1920.

to provide Gargantuan meals but also bringing much laughter and a budget of local news. As soon as he grew old enough to help with the harvest, Frank Lowden took over the grimy, itchy job of keeping the "tail" of the threshing machine clear of straw and chaff. After this tough initiation, he "was promoted to the dignity of band-cutter and was very proud . . . to stand up as a boy alongside the feeder and cut the bands of the sheaves." When the busy season came to an end on his father's farm, he often earned pocket money by hiring out to a neighbor for a half-dollar a day or its equivalent in farm produce.[37]

Balls, bats, knives, fishhooks, and firecrackers took some of his hard-won silver, but, unlike most of his companions, he invested a portion of it in books. From the time that he could first spell out the words, he was an avid reader. In later years, when he held up Lincoln as the greatest of all Americans, he probably overdrew the parallel between young Abe's and his own willingness to walk miles in order to borrow a book. However this may be, young Lowden read and reread his small supply of classics until he knew them almost by heart.[38] Poetry, fiction, biography, and history especially attracted him, and he liked to juggle a mathematical problem in his head without resorting to pencil and paper. Memorizing with unusual ease, he delighted his parents and teachers by reciting, with appropriate gestures, verse after verse of poetry and long passages of prose from McGuffey's readers.[39] Skill in debate was fostered by his father, who never felt happier than when arguing any proposition either practical or theoretical. He and his son, aged twelve, engaged in public debate in the Tipton Creek (Dean) schoolhouse, upon a subject long since forgotten.[40] A year or two later the boy delivered a Fourth of July oration in a grove near New Providence. Perhaps as a sure way of winning a controversy, his father once switched him for being "too uppity" in manners and speech. Frank's feelings on this occasion are not on record, but later, when advocating the retention of corporal punishment in the grade schools, he affirmed that "no whipping ever left a scar on my soul." In his young manhood, Frank and his father customarily adjourned to the parlor after supper, where, enveloped in a haze of cigar smoke, they discussed any topic inviting a difference of opinion.[41]

At the age of eight, when he entered the Rough Woods district school at Point Pleasant, he was ready for the fifth reader. Both there, in the person of Miss "Lizzie" Young, and during 1872–73, under Miss "Nannie" Blair at the Dean School, he had tactful and stimulating teachers. From one of them he

37. FOL to B. B. Clarke, Madison, Wisconsin, Feb. 3, 1927; MSS of FOL's speeches of Feb. 5, 1920, at Michigan Agricultural College, and of Sept. 21, 1921, at Hubbard, Iowa.

38. MS of FOL's speech, Aug. 24, 1908, at Stephenson County (Ill.) Old Settlers' picnic.

39. FOL to Mark Sullivan, Jan. 24, 1927.

40. Memorandum of FOL, Feb. 10, 1936, made after talking with J. T. Boylan; Mrs. Sarah Boody, Eldora, Iowa, to FOL, Apr. 12, 1920.

41. Conversation of author with three sisters of FOL; *Byron* (Ill.) *Express Record,* Aug. 13, 1908, reporting FOL's speech at Oak Grove School.

received a copy of Jacob Abbott's *Rollo's Garden* as a reward for excellence in his studies. On this little volume, the first prize he had ever won, he continued to lavish much sentimental affection, even as late as 1934. When the cover of the book became shaky, he had it handsomely rebound.[42] Frank Lowden was a precocious youngster, but, fortunately for his reputation among his schoolmates, he was not a prig. He often muddied his clothes or mussed his hair at play, although he felt uncomfortable when disheveled and relied upon his older sisters to repair the damage quickly after he reached home. Being the only surviving son in a large family, he was continually surrounded by girls and came to like and expect their attention. Perhaps the fastidiousness of his attire during his adult life derived from their coaching.[43]

On an autumn day, probably in 1874, Frank and May Lowden, Andrew J. Hunter and his three sisters, and James F. Cady and John T. Boylan arrived at Lemuel Moore's door in New Providence, eight miles south of Point Pleasant. Besides a few household effects, they brought a store of food which their parents replenished each Sunday thereafter. Under Mrs. Moore's chaperonage, the four boys occupied one room on the second floor of her home and the four girls another. As the seniors, Hunter and Cady had real beds, while Lowden and Boylan bunked together on a narrow "push-in" lounge, its tick stuffed with wheat straw and rosinweed. In this fashion, Frank began his first stay away from home.[44]

The children were about to begin the twelve weeks' term at New Providence Academy. It had been established five years before by the Honey Creek Quarterly Meeting of the Society of Friends, so that "our young men and women can acquire a more thorough education than they can get at our common schools." The four faculty members taught about seventy boys and girls in the ground-level classrooms of a rectangular brick building whose second floor was a hall used by the Quakers for their Wednesday morning hour of worship. Frank Lowden occasionally attended these services. His presence, it may be hoped, reflected a desire to share in the period of silent meditation or to profit from the words of Jonathan Hockett, whose spirit often stirred him to speech, rather than to witness the annoyance of the soberly clad congregation at the birds perching dangerously on the overhead bracerods or at the chipmunks disturbing the solemnity of the meeting whenever the windows were open.[45]

42. FOL to W. J. Abbott, Boston, Massachusetts, Jan. 12, 1934.

43. F. D. Tomson's MS, "The Story of an Iowa Farm Boy" (1920), based on recollections of childhood playmates of FOL. In a letter of Jan. 13, 1931, to C. W. Whitney, of Hubbard, Iowa, FOL questioned the accuracy of Whitney's statement—"You'd cry if you couldn't get your lessons, and we'd cry if we had to get ours."

44. Conversations of the author with L. T. Kersey of Chicago; see J. T. Boylan, "Early Days on the Tipton: Pioneer Days in Hardin County," *Eldora Herald,* June 3, 1926.

45. L. T. Kersey's MS, "New Providence Academy, New Providence, Iowa," quoting from the *Minute Book* of the Honey Creek Quarterly Meeting of the Society of Friends, June 2, 1866; also, Kersey's MS, "Sauntering over Boyhood Trails and Beyond"; and *Eldora Ledger,* Aug. 5, 1870; *Eldora Reform-Herald,* Nov. 11, 1873.

Why Frank Lowden went to the academy, how long he stayed, and what, besides history, he studied there are unknown. If he had continued until graduation, he would have been eligible to give instruction in a country school. Apparently he had already decided to earn enough money by teaching to go to college as a preparation for becoming a lawyer.[46] Certain it is, however, that his experience at New Providence left him with a lasting respect for the Society of Friends and a real affection for two of the academy's faculty, Miss Hannah Moore and Mrs. Anna C. Hoag.

By his fourteenth birthday Lowden had mastered all that the district school could offer. Independent study at home and attention to the recitations of the more advanced pupils in the one-room schoolhouses enabled him to forge far ahead of most children his own age. School-board regulations prescribed that no one could teach without passing a qualifying examination after reaching at least the age of seventeen. To make ready for that test, he applied himself to algebra and other required subjects in which he had had no formal instruction. Late in 1875 he asked friends of his family to persuade the county superintendent to waive the minimum age limit for his benefit. With this initial excursion into "politics," the earliest period of Lowden's education came to its close.[47]

In the meantime, Lorenzo Lowden had also become a loyal Iowan. Even if his wife Nancy preferred Minnesota, she and her husband had several congenial neighbors, as well as other friends living farther away whom they occasionally "dropped in upon" for visits lasting several days. In the mid-1870's, the Lowdens were among the most active members of a newly formed literary society.[48] The little schoolhouse was a social focus for its district. There, of an evening, parents and their older children vied with one another in a "spelldown." Time could not have hung heavily on Nancy's hands as baby followed baby in almost regular procession. Their illnesses and those in families nearby made frequent demands upon her nursing skill. Lorenzo and she buried three of their own children during their first fifteen years in Iowa.[49] These graves helped to strike the parents' roots deep into the land. And, too, by 1880 they were beginning to count their grandchildren.

The scanty records permit only an uncertain tracing of Lorenzo Lowden's business affairs. During the first four years after his arrival at Point Pleasant, he and his family apparently lived in a farmhouse less than a mile northwest of the crossroads. After acquiring the village blacksmith shop and opening a country store, he was soon sufficiently busy to employ an assistant. The El-

---

46. FOL to Miss Florence Pullman, Dec. 17, 1894. Here he says that "over twenty years ago" he decided to become a lawyer but did not confide his hope to his parents because its attainment seemed impossible.

47. Interview with FOL reported in *East St. Louis* (Ill.) *Daily Journal,* Feb. 8, 1920.

48. MS of FOL's speech at Hubbard, Iowa, Sept. 21, 1921 (*Eldora Herald,* Jan. 20, 1875).

49. Arthur B. (Nov. 8, 1870–Aug. 9, 1871); Walter (Apr. 24, 1873–May 4, 1873); Ina Isabel (July 24, 1875——); Bertha Eleanor (Nov. 5, 1877——); Edie (Apr. 5–Apr. 15, 1883).

dora weekly mentioned him for the first time in the spring of 1869 by noting his civil suit against "Eaton & Percival" in the district court. Neither the cause nor the outcome of this action is known. About a year later, he joined R. C. Kyte and A. Mitterer, probably the father of Frank's "enemy," to form "Prairie Lea," a cemetery association at Point Pleasant.[50] Whatever may have been the outcome of this venture, it at least symbolized the dying state of the village, now that Eldora had gained both the county seat and the railroad.

Probably it was in early 1873 that Lorenzo gave up storekeeping, sold his smithy to his helper, and bought a farm on Tipton Creek about four miles west of Point Pleasant and twice that distance from Eldora. During the first year in the new location, the Lowdens lived in a log cabin, where Frank, as he later recalled, spent the warmest winter of his boyhood. For nearly a decade thereafter, Lorenzo was a Tipton Township farmer, reading law in his spare time, serving often on juries, and occasionally making local news as an auctioneer or as a lay attorney appearing in court on behalf of a client. Press notices of his activities increased from year to year. At long last, in October, 1881, he gained formal admittance to the bar. Although nearly fifty years of age, he was still called "a promising gentleman."[51]

In the spring of that year he moved with his family to the eastern outskirts of the new and growing railroad town of Hubbard, six or seven miles by road to the south of his farm. At Hubbard, he took as his junior law partner, James F. Cady, who had been Frank Lowden's fellow student at New Providence Academy. This partnership, however, soon ended, and Lorenzo thereafter practiced alone, supplementing his small income from legal fees by selling insurance and real estate and collecting debts. His fellow townsmen elected him to their school board, and he served for several years as its president.[52] But, for the third consecutive time, he had chosen as his place of residence a village which failed to fulfil its early promise.

His local prominence arose in large degree from his fluency of tongue, his penchant for public discussion, his craving for political office, and his habit of promoting new enterprises. He was a crusader of causes. He divided his energies between so many endeavors that he achieved no great success in any of them. On the other hand, his contemporaries in Hardin County respected his honesty and courage.[53]

Soon after coming to Iowa he deplored the widespread and flagrant violations of the state's temperance law. In 1871, as a vice-president of the Eldora Temperance Society, he organized a vigilante committee to help en-

50. *Eldora Ledger,* Mar. 16 and Apr. 10, 1869, June 3, 1870.

51. *Eldora Herald,* Oct. 19, 1881. Because he paid a $65.45 tax on his 120-acre Tipton Township farm in 1881, the *Herald* (Apr. 26, 1882) called him "one of the heavy tax payers" of Hardin County. But the bill seems small compared with the $453.35 paid by William F. Andrews of New Providence.

52. *History of Hardin County,* pp. 304–5, 895.

53. W. M. Boylan, Carthage, Missouri, to FOL, Apr. 25, 1942.

force the statute in his own neighborhood. Three years later, when spiritual-ism briefly attracted him, the *Eldora Reform-Herald* announced that "Rev. L. O. Louden [*sic*] will speak at Point Pleasant Church . . . on 'Christ as a Spiritual Medium, Moses and the Burning Bush, the Salem Witchcraft' and a few other leading illustrations of spiritualism."[54]

Not temperance or spiritualism, however, but party politics and the Pa-trons of Husbandry brought him most often to public attention. Almost an-nually during the 1870's he sought some local office, but, except for the post of clerk of Tipton Township, he lost all his election campaigns.[55] While Iowa was establishing its national reputation for staunch Republicanism, Lorenzo remained a Democrat and a "left-winger" at that. Most Hardin County voters viewed an outspoken member of that party with suspicion, as possibly still tainted by Civil War Copperheadism. German Lutherans and Catholics, taking their cues from their pastors, looked askance at any protest movement, whether in economics or in politics. As a rule, the few families of considerable wealth in Hardin County threw their influence against both the Grangers and the Democrats. Under these circumstances, a restless man like Lorenzo Lowden was fated to gain notoriety rather than public office.

Hardin County politicians interspersed the serious business of campaigning with much fun and satire. The gossipy cut-and-thrust of Eldora's rival news-papers was spiced with an earthy humor which often left its victim in doubt whether to join in the merriment at his expense or sue the editor for libel. An editorial entitled "Fortitude," in the *Ledger* on Oct. 13, 1871, illustrates this rural wit:

Ellis Parker, present mayor of Eldora, is a man of some moral determination or stubbornness. Twenty-five years ago he lost his wife and though many attractive Abigails offered, has remained true to his deceased wife. For fifty-two years he chewed tobacco incessantly, and for several years swallowed most of the juice, seldom or never squirting it about in yellow jets. He desired to quit the nasty practice three years ago, and succeeded in breaking loose from the filthy habit.

In the campaign of that autumn, having been easily defeated for the clerk-ship of the district court the year before,[56] Lorenzo Lowden tried unsuccess-fully to supplant the popular Frank Moore as county superintendent of schools. He ran behind the rest of the Democratic slate and carried only Tip-ton of the fourteen townships in his county.[57] Undiscouraged, he devoted much of his time for the next eight years to the Grange and various political protest groups. The first of these styled itself the "Anti-Monopoly Party." It joined with the Democratic organization to operate as the People's or Inde-pendent party in 1875 and most of 1876. For about a year thereafter, during a rift in this alliance, the Anti-Monopolists called themselves the "Inde-

54. *Eldora Ledger,* Jan. 16, 1871, Feb. 3 and 10, 1874.

55. *Ibid.,* June 16, 1871, and Jan. 12, 1872.

56. *Eldora Ledger,* Oct. 21, 1870.

57. *Ibid.,* Sept. 1, 1871.

pendent Greenback Party." Following a few months of political chaos, it maintained for about two years a new but shaky entente with the Democrats. By 1879 the worst of the long economic depression was over, and Lorenzo Lowden, evidently surfeited with protest, gladly rejoined his old party when it broke loose for the second and last time from its dying ally.[58] In the meantime, under an Anti-Monopoly, Greenbacker, Fusionist, or Democratic banner, he served on many political committees and ran once for the office of county supervisor and thrice for the state assembly.[59] As lecturer of the Hardin County Patrons of Husbandry, he repeatedly braved the ridicule of the *Eldora Ledger* by denouncing the barbed-wire and agricultural-machinery monopolies, exorbitant freight and grain-elevator rates, the hard-money policy of the Republican party, and the shameful corruption and misrule of the Grant administration.[60] After a decade of defeat in his numerous efforts to win public office, he was a somewhat "tired liberal" by the time of his admission to the bar and move to Hubbard in 1881.

Frank Lowden grew to young manhood in this rural environment of simple living, economic discontent, and political protest. Farming and politics continually surrounded him. Judging from his father's example, he should strive to become a lawyer, even if twenty years of effort were required to win a license to practice. He witnessed the rise and fall of ineffective third parties and the cost of political irregularity. From his many discussions with his father, he acquired a persuasive tongue, a ready wit, and a considerable knowledge of practical politics at the local level. As a chart of the way to succeed, however, Lorenzo's "scattered" career mainly traced paths to avoid rather than to follow.

In after years, although he always spoke of his father with liking and respect, he reserved his terms of deepest affection for his mother. Apparently she knew nothing of politics and cared less, but she enveloped him with love and protection, laughed at his pranks, and took pride in his record at school. As her only son to survive childhood illnesses and as a lad of high promise, he occupied a special place among her numerous offspring. His older sisters also danced to his tune. By the mid-1870's the time had come to test whether he could stand alone and move forward without their help.

58. *History of Hardin County,* pp. 354–58.

59. *Eldora Reform-Herald,* Oct. 3, 1873; Jan. 6, Feb. 17, June 10, 17, Aug. 5, and Sept. 13, 1874; Sept. 8, 22, and Oct. 13, 1875; Apr. 26 and Oct. 18, 1876; July 11 and Aug. 22, 1877; Sept. 10, Oct. 3, 8, and 22, 1879. In 1881 he tried in vain to be Democratic nominee for state senator.

60. *Eldora Ledger,* Mar. 17, 1871, and Jan. 5, 1872; *Eldora Reform-Herald,* Dec. 2, 9, and 16, 1873; Feb. 3, Apr. 1, and June 10, 1874; Jan. 13, 1875.

CHAPTER II

FROM "ROUGH WOODS"
TO MICHIGAN AVENUE

Lorenzo Lowden's political activities threatened to handicap his son in gaining permission, while still under age, to take the qualifying examinations for a teaching certificate. Besides trying to prevent the re-election of the county superintendent of schools in 1871, Lorenzo attended the state Granger convention two years later, which adopted resolutions deploring the condition of public education in Iowa and recommending that three examiners in every township replace the office of county superintendent.[1] By good fortune, in late 1875 Lorenzo's political foe, Frank A. Moore, resigned the headship of the Hardin County schools. His successor was L. S. McCoy, a Civil War veteran and genial friend of all aspiring youth. Among these he counted Frank Lowden, who also shared McCoy's enthusiasm for poetry and history.[2]

When John T. Kersey, a district schoolteacher, strongly supported Frank's plea to disregard his tender years and grant him a certificate, McCoy finally yielded, but with the proviso that he make a perfect score on the qualifying examinations. Although Lowden easily met this requirement, his alarmingly young appearance made the local boards wonder whether he could keep order among children, five years old and upward, crowded into a one-room schoolhouse. Indeed, a few pupils would be his seniors in age. As Lowden once remarked, a main prerequisite for success as a teacher in rural Iowa was the ability "to keep from being thrown out of a window" by an obstreperous and muscular boy.[3] Over the protest of several of its members, the Meeker district board finally offered him $100 to teach during the winter term of three months beginning in December, 1875. He hastened to accept. Being hard pressed for money, he also took on the janitor's job at an additional $1.00 a month.[4]

1. *Eldora* (Iowa) *Ledger,* Sept. 1, 1871; *Eldora Reform-Herald,* Dec. 16, 1873.

2. MS of FOL's speech of Nov. 2, 1922, before the Iowa State Teachers' Association, at Des Moines; also article by J. T. Boylan in *Eldora Herald,* June 3, 1926.

3. MS of FOL's speech on Oct. 2, 1906, at Pawpaw, Illinois.

4. Interview with FOL, reported in *East St. Louis* (Ill.) *Daily Journal,* Feb. 8, 1920. In 1875 the 59 male teachers in Hardin County averaged $33.98 a month and the 154 "schoolmarms," $29.38. The length of the school year was 7½ months (*History of Hardin County, Iowa* [Springfield, Ill.: Union Publishing Co., 1883], p. 311).

The three or four miles from his home to the Meeker school were too far to walk in the dead of winter. Expediency also led him to accept the offer of Asa Meeker, chairman of the board, to furnish a term's board and lodging for $40.00. Arising betimes every weekday morning and carrying his lunch along with the textbooks, he reached the schoolhouse an hour or more before the opening bell. He had to sweep the floor, wash the blackboard, and make the stove glow with heat early enough to have the room tolerably warm before the children arrived. And yet, as a fellow teacher recalled, the sides of the room were often so cold that "the pupils' spit froze on their slates."[5]

Even under most favorable conditions, the first months of teaching would have been difficult for a boy. Frank's troubles included big "Bob" McBride. Obliged to recite to a former schoolmate, he did his best to make his teacher's life miserable. Frank solved the problem by following a course which proved effective under similar circumstances in his later schools. Enduring the "persecution" until he won the liking of the other pupils, he waited for a particularly flagrant instance of Bob's offensiveness. By then the miscreant believed that the teacher dared not punish him. Taking him completely off guard, Frank switched him soundly, while the rest of the class applauded. Thereafter McBride gave no more trouble and later became Lowden's good friend.[6] Thus, upon a miniature stage, he discovered the efficacy of vigorous action by a leader who had the force of public opinion to back him.

When the Meeker school term ended in late March, 1876, Frank was about $60.00 in pocket. Incidentals had cost him only the amount of his pay as janitor. He intrusted his savings to his father for safekeeping as a nest egg toward the cost of a college education. To his mother he returned the handbell which she had rung when a teacher in New York State over twenty years before. Young Lowden used it to open school and close recess until he was appointed to a building with a belfry. His characteristic sentiment led him to treasure the old bell as long as he lived.

He always admired the district school boards for their "foxiness" in ending each of the two terms of a year at just the season when farmwork became heavy, so that the children could help with the spring plowing and sowing, the late-summer haying and harvesting, and the autumn planting and husking. This shrewd arrangement, however, affected him advantageously as a teacher, because he could supplement his small salary by laboring in the fields.[7]

The autumn of 1876 found him in the first of his three terms at the Rough Woods district school which he had attended as a small boy. Faced by a larger proportion of older pupils than at Meeker, he had much occasion to use his favorite mixture of strategy and switch, but he thoroughly enjoyed

5. F. T. Clampitt, *Some Incidents of My Life: A Saga of the Unknown Citizen* (Ann Arbor, Mich., 1935), p. 15.

6. Interview with FOL, reported in *East St. Louis Daily Journal*, Feb. 8, 1920.

7. MS of FOL's speech at Amboy, Illinois, Oct. 3, 1906.

his role. Assured by Superintendent McCoy that he was making good, he gained self-confidence rapidly. Before the school year ended, he enhanced his local reputation by taking a leading part in the evening programs of the Rough Woods lyceum and literary society.[8] His feeling of well-being was nourished by boarding with Mrs. Fred Boody, his father's loyal Methodist ally in temperance work. Helping with her evening chores, he won her affection, and she treated him as her own son.[9]

The superintendent expected every Hardin County teacher to attend, at his own expense, the monthly meetings of the county teachers' association each winter and also the "normal institute," lasting for two or three weeks every summer. In 1877, at Steamboat Rock, Lowden was among the hundred teachers instructed by schoolroom demonstrations and "distinguished lecturers" at one of these institutes. Early the next year, when teaching at the Point Pleasant school and living at home, he shared in the program of two successive teachers' association meetings. At the first he made "many practical suggestions" for stiffening and grading written examinations, while at the other he lectured on "Applications of Percentage."[10] By then, Superintendent McCoy was bestowing special attention upon this unusual young man, who could coach his elders in mathematics, win the affection of most of his pupils even as he held them to high standards of performance, and view teaching as merely an interlude before going to college. In McCoy's behalf, on the other hand, Lowden engaged in what he later called his first political activity. Traveling over the county and telling influential farmers about McCoy's superior virtues as an educator, he helped to re-elect his boss for another term as superintendent of schools.[11]

Letters written to Lowden by former pupils many years afterward furnish glimpses of his classroom methods. He regarded these notes as the most gratifying testimonials he ever received. After making allowance for the authors' probable wish to associate themselves with, and have autographed replies from, a man who had become nationally well known, they still make clear that Frank Lowden had indelibly impressed them as a skilful teacher. His amazing memory, his insistence upon thoroughness rather than speed, his eloquence, and his ability to bring the readings in McGuffey dramatically to life were his qualities most often recalled.[12] One former student remembered how he obliged a fourth-reader class to spend two weeks on a single "piece" in McGuffey until every pupil had the pronunciation and inflection letter-

8. This school was about six miles west of Eldora. See *Eldora Herald,* Feb. 6, 1878, and Jan. 8, 1879.

9. Mrs. Sarah Boody, Eldora, Iowa, to FOL, Apr. 12, 1920.

10. *Eldora Herald,* Aug. 29 and Sept. 12, 1877.

11. *Ibid.,* Feb. 20, 1878.

12. In acknowledging on Nov. 25, 1935, the gift of a reprinted and autographed set of McGuffey's readers from Henry Ford, FOL wrote: "I not only learned to read from . . . [them], but later as a school teacher I used all of them in my teaching. . . . I find in them a perfect medium for reviving memories of the long ago."

perfect. Another never forgot that she cried when he recited "The Death of Little Crystal" and that the year's closing exercises "were like a funeral" because he would not return to that school in the fall. Still others wrote to thank him for his valuable instruction in mental arithmetic and for suggesting as a useful lifetime habit the copying in a notebook, under appropriate headings, of original thoughts or apt quotations about various subjects.[13] These letters came as a welcome, if belated, offset to the poor pay and monotonous paper-grading associated with teaching.

Having saved a little money by the autumn of 1878, Lowden enrolled for a ten weeks' term of study at the Iowa State Agricultural College at Ames. As all sources agree that he had determined considerably before that date to become a lawyer, his registration in the "Agricultural Curriculum" is difficult to explain. Fifty years later he wrote that "those brief months" at Ames were

my first excursion into the world and I recall . . . [them] . . . more vividly than most things which have occurred at a later date. . . . I changed from there to S.U. [State University of Iowa] only because I got it into my mind that I preferred a classical course. When I left Ames that fall I fully intended to return some time later and complete my course. I wasn't able, however, to go back the next year and finally decided on S.U. instead. I do remember that I took the exams. which would have qualified me to enter the sophomore class if I had returned to Ames the next year.[14]

He attended classes in botany, animal physiology, horticulture, composition, criticism, and geometry. His final grades, course by course, ascended in that order.[15]

The sole anecdote about his experience at Ames smacks more of fiction than of truth. Perhaps, as this story insists, Lowden arrived on the campus "the rawest thing that ever came off the stakes." And yet he could hardly have seemed greener than many another farmer lad in the Freshman class. He may have been naïve enough, or, more likely, "cocky" enough, to have attracted the Sophomores as an especially choice victim to haze in their mock court. Where the tale becomes too good to be true, however, is in its account of this "country bumpkin" abashing his tormentors by his legal knowledge and dumfounding them by his eloquence. The reminiscence fittingly closes by noting that his remarkable exhibition of poise and ready wit immediately made him an object of admiration rather than of derision.[16]

Shortly after returning from Ames and resuming his teaching in a district

13. Letters to FOL from Marie Seamans, Helena, Montana, Aug. 4, 1921, and Marcella C. Hadley, Tucson, Arizona, May 27, 1928. "The Death of Little Crystal" should probably be Charles Dickens' "Death of Little Nell," in W. H. McGuffey's *New Sixth Eclectic Reader* (Cincinnati, 1857), p. 78.

14. A composite from FOL's letters of Jan. 5 and June 7, 1927, and Jan. 25, 1928, to Thomas C. Burke of New York City.

15. Mrs. Gayle S. Smith kindly furnished the author with a list of FOL's courses and grades. A perfect mark was 4. FOL received 3.48, 3.55, 3.60, 3.71, 3.95, and 3.96, respectively, in the courses in the order given above.

16. T. C. Burke and J. S. Dewell, "A Reminiscence," *Alumnus of Iowa State College,* XXIII, No. 4 (November, 1927), 92–93.

school, he and several of his sisters were stricken with diphtheria. Lowden's life was despaired of for several days, and his convalescence extended over many weeks. Not until June, 1879, had he sufficiently recovered to serve as Superintendent McCoy's substitute in visiting "some of the fair school teachers of Tipton and Pleasant townships."[17] At the close of that year, the county teachers' association meeting at Eldora named him one of a committee of three to foster in each township a schoolteachers' organization which should propose a uniform curriculum and strive to elevate the standards of performance expected from teachers and pupils alike.[18]

By then he was teaching at the Fairview School, a few miles southwest of New Providence, and rooming with the farmer-scholar, Miles Reece. After graduating from Penn College at Oscaloosa, Reece had been one of Lowden's instructors at New Providence Academy, and now tutored him in the Latin he would need for entrance to the state university. Lowden also found time that winter to share in the weekly programs of the literary society at the neighboring village of Midland. His tenure at Fairview ended his apprenticeship in a one-room district school. Shortly thereafter he became principal of a school twice that size at New Providence.[19] There, too, he roomed in the home of the influential Quaker, William F. Andrews, the biggest taxpayer in Hardin County. Lowden's ability and personality brought from his host an offer to stake him financially to whatever further education he might desire.

In September, 1881, Lowden passed the examinations in six subjects required for admission to the classical course of the state university at Iowa City. Its undergraduate college was housed in five buildings, including "Old Capitol," which had been the meeting place of the state legislature until 1855. Many of the two dozen teachers of undergraduates chafed under the allegedly dictatorial and inefficient administration of President Josiah L. Pickard.[20]

Probably of more concern than faculty politics to Lowden and his classmates were the efforts then being made to raise the moral tone of Iowa City. Unless these succeeded, some of the students, at least, would disappoint the hopes of the university administration as stated in its catalogue: "Students are expected to comply with the requirements of morality, propriety, and courtesy . . . for the attainment of those ends the Faculty have always relied chiefly on the self respect and honor of the students, with the happiest results."[21] Although the undergraduate began his recitation day with an obliga-

17. *Eldora Herald,* June 25, 1879.

18. *Ibid.,* Jan. 7, 1880.

19. *Ibid.,* Nov. 3, 1880, and Apr. 6, 1881. The length of FOL's stay in each of his teaching positions cannot be stated with certainty because the sources are in conflict.

20. The student paper, the *Vidette-Reporter,* Oct. 1, 1881, p. 3. W. C. Lang, "A History of the State University of Iowa: The Collegiate Department from 1879 to 1900" (unpublished Ph.D. dissertation, University of Iowa, 1941; in university library), pp. 37, 62–64, 88–96, 101–6; hereafter cited as "Lang."

21. *Catalogue of the State University at Iowa City, for 1881–1882,* p. 41.

tory chapel service and might elect courses on moral science and "Evidences of Christianity," he was tempted by the thirty saloons and three breweries of Iowa City. Tobacco-chewing as well as drinking showed an alarming increase, but the Board of Regents, perhaps fearing to offend many of the town's businessmen, advised the faculty not to share in a "clean-up" crusade. Disregarding this admonition, Professors N. R. Leonard and S. N. Fellows joined vigorously with some of the students in a temperance movement.[22] Contradictory evidence makes it impossible to determine Frank Lowden's share, if any, in this drive. At least on one occasion he debated in defense of the national Prohibition party. In later years he mentioned no saloon in Iowa City but spoke nostalgically of Madame Noel, a shopkeeper whose banter enticed many students to buy her candy, Jamaica oranges, and fried oysters.[23]

During his college days he necessarily adjusted his appetite for food and fun to his slender purse. Tuition at $25.00 a year and board and lodging at $4.00 a week seemed high to a student whose resources totaled only a few hundred dollars. Doing odd jobs provided a little pocket money, but Lowden rarely permitted outside chores to embarrass his studies and social life.[24] Since the university lacked dormitories and a commons, the undergraduates roomed in town, a dozen of them often forming an eating club. It employed a housekeeper to buy, prepare, and serve its meals in her home. She furnished the food while Lowden and his fellows added the hilarity and song to assist in its digestion. If fresh subjects of merriment played out, the club members could always fall back upon their moth-eaten joke of asking the housekeeper when Phineas T. Barnum would send his next supply of chickens for their table—remarkable fowl with numerous wings, necks, and backs but neither breasts nor legs.[25]

The Iowa River provided a ready means of swimming, fishing, boating, and skating. Lowden often walked with his friends to the stone quarries between Observatory Point and the Old Mill in order to watch and sometimes to help with the blasting.[26] The social high-water mark of many a week was an evening spent in the Hutchinson home near the campus. The master of the house had been a "Forty-niner" but had returned from the gold fields to make a more comfortable living out of Iowa City real estate. Frank Lowden and his companions would remember Mrs. Hutchinson almost as gratefully for her tolerance of their noise and nonsense as her daughters for their wit and vivacity. Among these daughters, Delia and Sophie were the particular lodestones which drew Frank and his fellows so frequently to the Jefferson

22. Lang, pp. 40–41, 96, 326.

23. J. B. Noel, Clinton, Iowa, to FOL, Dec. 24, 1926, and his reply, Jan. 6, 1927.

24. C. C. Coldren, Chicago, to J. A. Hemenway, Boonville, Indiana, May 28, 1920, and to the author, July 23, 1945.

25. Letters to FOL from J. B. Weaver, Des Moines, Iowa, Dec. 18, 1937, and Jan. 10, 1940, and from W. A. Warner, Dubuque, Iowa, Dec. 5, 1919.

26. J. B. Weaver in *Iowa Alumnus* (State University of Iowa), October, 1914, pp. 7–8; J. B. Weaver to FOL, Oct. 8, 1914.

Street parlor that it became almost an informal clubroom. The Hutchinson house faced St. Mary's church. To the initiated, the stock phrase "going to St. Mary's" had no religious connotation whatsoever. Frank's hearty laugh, his skill in repartee, his seemingly inexhaustible store of remembered poetry, and his liking for group singing made him one of Sophie's favorite callers. Until her death in 1924 he occasionally sent her a copy of a literary masterpiece, handsomely bound, to remind her of the mutual interest in good books which had helped to make them friends during his undergraduate days.[27]

Hospitality of this kind was difficult to repay. Even if the rules of propriety had been less rigid, the university and town afforded few resources for entertaining a young lady. College dances were prohibited; there were no fraternity houses and few intercollegiate athletic contests. An intramural baseball or football game between class teams might draw some of the "coeds." John Corlett's livery stable had buggies, surreys, and sleighs for hire. Occasionally during the winter the Opera House attracted such star performers as Oscar Wilde, Rose Eytinge, Minnie Maddern, and Callender's Minstrels.[28] There, too, the Zetagathian or the Hesperian Society held its annual oratorical and debating "exhibition." On Saturday nights the Shakespeare Club or some other literary society occasionally arranged for a "sociable" between the close of its formal program and the ten o'clock curfew.[29]

Lowden did not attain the extraordinary distinction in scholarship and student leadership claimed for him by some of his friends long after his graduation, but he was popular and shared prominently in a few activities. In the autumn of 1881 after the Freshman class unanimously elected him to be its historian, the *Vidette-Reporter* commented that "a better choice could not have been made. Mr. Louden [*sic*] is a young man of ability, and is well worthy of the work he is called upon to perform."[30] Thereafter for the rest of his Freshman year the student paper made no further mention of him. Even this single reference may have mainly reflected his fellow membership with the editor of the paper in the Zetagathian Society.[31]

Lowden's experiences in this literary club were probably the most valuable and enjoyable of his college career. From the standpoint of the future, however, his initiation into the Beta Theta Pi fraternity produced ties of more lasting influence. The Zetagathians had for rivals the members of the Hesperian Society and the Irving Institute. Each club occupied separate quarters

27. Conversation of author with the Misses Delia and Ada Hutchinson, June 22, 1945. FOL to Dean Emeritus C. R. Brown, Yale Divinity School, Oct. 30, 1941.

28. C. R. Brown, New Haven, Connecticut, to FOL, Jan. 8, 1936: ". . . we used to go sleigh riding sometimes from Iowa City to Mt. Vernon or to Cedar Rapids for an Oyster Supper. . . ."

29. *Vidette-Reporter,* Oct. 28, 1882, and advertisements therein, 1881–85; Lang, pp. 332, 338, 364.

30. *Vidette-Reporter,* Oct. 22, 1881.

31. Theodore A. Wanerus, *History of the Zetagathian Society of the State University of Iowa* (Iowa City, 1911), p. 74.

on the top floor of Old South Hall. The "Zets" boasted of a gilt-frescoed room equipped with curtains, gas lights, rostrum, a marble-top table for the secretary, another for the "critic," and cherry-colored chairs arranged in concentric semicircles upon an ornately flowered Brussels carpet. The main business of each society was to determine, by means of orations and debates between its own members, who should represent it in its contests with its two competitors and at the annual "exhibition."[32] The winners then engaged in oratorical battle with teams from the state universities of Illinois, Ohio, Indiana, and Wisconsin for the prizes offered yearly by the Northwestern Inter-State Collegiate Association.[33]

Although the annals of the Zetagathian Society mention Lowden a half-dozen times, he did not hold forth from its rostrum as often as his friends in later years liked to believe. He elected the course in declamation in each of the three terms of his Sophomore year and a course entitled "Oration" in one term when a Senior. The grade of S, signifying somewhat above average performance, was all that he received for this work in each term.[34] He apparently never served as an officer of the Zetagathians, he won no university prize in oratory, and he did not represent the student body in any intercollegiate debate. On the other hand, he shared in a few intra-club contests, he appeared twice on the program of the annual "exhibition" of the "Zets," and he may have been on their panel in one debate with the Irving Institute team.[35]

Not until his Sophomore year did Lowden make the news as a debater. Hardly had he arrived back on campus in September, than he profited from his Democratic upbringing by upholding the negative of the proposition that the Republicans in Congress were justified in enacting a Rivers and Harbors Bill. Lowden and his partner outpointed their opponents.[36] Perhaps as a reward for the strength of his argument in this contest, the "Zet" society picked him and three others to speak at its annual exhibition in the following March. At this meeting, on the question whether Congress should restrict immigration further, he argued extempore so forcibly in the affirmative that the *Vidette-Reporter* remarked upon the great applause and how much he had "added . . . to his high reputation as a debater." Although he made a strong case for excluding aliens, unfitted by their backgrounds to share in America's political life or to prosper in its highly competitive society, he and

32. *Ibid.,* pp. 81–83; *Vidette-Reporter,* Sept. 23, 1882.

33. Lang, p. 361. In 1901, FOL gave twenty-five shares of National Biscuit Company stock to the university in trust for the Northern Oratorical League, as this association was called after 1891. It provided about $175 a year for prizes, and he supplemented it later with an annual gift of $150. Eventually he presented the State University of Iowa with $5,000 as an endowment whose yield would provide $50 annually for debating prizes and awards of $25 in each of five other subjects.

34. Registrar's Office, State University of Iowa, *Record Book No. 1, Beginning 1871,* p. 39.

35. Wanerus, *op. cit.,* pp. 127, 211, 229.

36. *Vidette-Reporter,* Sept. 23, 1882.

his associates lost the debate.[37] Absence from campus during his Junior year prevented him from sharing in the oratorical contest reserved for members of the third-year class. When he was a Senior, he delivered before the Zetagathians the oration, already mentioned, in defense of the Prohibitionists. At the society's annual exhibition late in February, 1885, he contended that a parliamentary system with a responsible ministry was better than a government in which the chief executive could balk the people's will as expressed through their representatives in Congress.[38]

Lowden brought to the university a liking for baseball as well as debate. By 1882 the Pickard administration had satisfied the growing student demand for athletics to the extent of designating a field for baseball and football, providing a small, poorly equipped gymnasium in the boiler house, and tolerating intramural games.[39] In that year, with the president's tacit consent, the Juniors and Seniors formed a university athletic association. Although they dedicated it to the promotion of "physical culture" in general, they mainly confined its early activities to gymnastics. There were, however, class teams in football and baseball, as well as less formal ones glorying in such names as the "Fleshly Livers" and the "Oscar Wildes." Lowden's partiality toward baseball far exceeded his skill as a player. When he was a Sophomore, he failed to make the class team, but his big share in organizing a class baseball association won him its presidency.

To this point in the story of Lowden's college years, emphasis has been given to those matters which he usually thought of before all others when he looked back upon his undergraduate days. Good times with close friends dominated his recollections and largely accounted for his lifelong loyalty as an Iowa alumnus. Lack of a chapter house may explain why the Beta Theta Pi's figured so little, as a group, in his memories of college, although he was an unusually devoted member of that fraternity to the end of his days.[40] In like manner he always supported the YMCA, and, as a Freshman, had helped to form a branch of it on the Iowa campus. Perhaps Professor L. F. Parker's Sunday Bible class, which Lowden attended, was under "Y" auspices.[41]

In after years Lowden liked to tell how he and his fellow students had lived in an "ideal democracy," animated by a carefree spirit of co-operation and a belief that all problems admitted of solution, but he was not always so complimentary when he mentioned the faculty. He held several of them, including Leonard F. Parker (history), Thomas H. Macbride (botany), and Samuel Calvin (geology), in high esteem[42] and readily acknowledged that

37. *Ibid.,* Oct. 28, 1882, and Mar. 17, 1883.

38. *Ibid.,* Dec. 20, 1884; Feb. 21 and 28, 1885.

39. Lang, pp. 339–40.

40. FOL was initiated into the fraternity on Feb. 10, 1882. He was a member of its national senate in 1934.

41. Lang, p. 368. For many years, FOL sent a check annually to the YMCA at the state university, and also to the "Y's" of a half-dozen other colleges or towns near his home.

42. FOL later contributed to gift or portrait funds for these and other professors.

the greatest reward of college life was "the direct personal relation between the student and the soul of the gifted teacher," but he deplored the cloistered unworldliness of some of his instructors.[43] This adverse criticism apparently did not occur to him during his years in Iowa City. After his graduation, however, he often deprecated the scholar who divorced his subject from reality, encouraged a feeling of "Weltschmerz" on the part of his students, or advocated utopian doctrines in the realms of economics and politics. "The atmosphere of college," said Lowden accusingly, "is peculiarly congenial to contemplative moods in which the world dissolves into dreams."[44]

About half the courses in the classical curriculum, for which Lowden enrolled, were obligatory. They included eight terms of Greek, four of Latin, and basic instruction in mathematics, history, English literature, "mental science" (logic), astronomy, geology, physics, and chemistry. In the Freshman year, when no electives were permitted, each term focused wholly upon Latin, Greek, and mathematics. Thereafter, a student's free choice of electives was hedged by classifying them into groups, from each of which he must select one or, at the most, two. Lowden registered for more courses in Latin, Greek, and history than his major required and also did work in declamation, oration, rhetoric, evidences of Christianity, political economy, international law, botany, and zoölogy.[45] Being a classical major, he was exempted from military training. For one term of his Senior year, however, he donned a dark-blue uniform, with a red stripe on each trouser leg, and served in the battery of field artillery.

His commendable scholastic record by no means warranted an overly enthusiastic friend's later effusion that it was of "the highest rank ever made up to that time at the State University of Iowa."[46] In twenty-seven of his courses he received an *H* grade and in the remaining seventeen, *S*. The quality distribution of his grades suggests that he did as well in the sciences and social sciences as in the humanities.[47] Interestingly enough, his highest grades came in his Junior year, when he was not in residence, but met the full requirements by passing examinations on ten courses after independent study. The Phi Beta Kappa Society admitted him to membership at the time of his graduation.

His summer earnings from teaching in the Iowa Reform School at Eldora and the Iowa Falls High School were too small to permit his return to the university in the autumn of 1883. The school board of Hubbard, including his father and his friend John T. Kersey, made him the principal of the town's high school. After a happy year of teaching, supervising three other

43. MS of FOL's speech at Knox College, Galesburg, Illinois, Feb. 15, 1902.

44. MSS of FOL's speeches at Michigan Club banquet at Detroit, Feb. 22, 1899, and before Beta Theta Pi convention, Chicago, July 28, 1895.

45. State University of Iowa catalogues, 1881–85; Registrar's Office, *Record Book No. 1, Beginning 1871*, p. 39.

46. C. S. Sweet, MS, "Sketch of Frank O. Lowden" (undated, but written in 1920).

47. Registrar's Office, *Record Book No. 1, Beginning 1871*, p. 39.

instructors, and living at home, he felt complimented by an appointment to the staff of the Hardin County Normal Institute.[48] During its three weeks' session at Eldora, he was chosen to present, after appropriate remarks, a gold watch to County Superintendent Howard Fuller. It may have been a matter of interest to Lowden that Francis W. Parker, the distinguished schoolman of Quincy, Massachusetts, witnessed the presentation; but it was far more important for the young man's future that the dynamic Leigh Hunt had directed the institute. Falling under the spell of each other's forceful personalities, Hunt and Lowden began a lifetime friendship of considerable moment to both men.

At the close of the summer, Lowden still lacked enough money to finance his Senior year at the university. Desperately eager to graduate with his own class, he finally sought the aid of William F. Andrews of New Providence. The Quaker gladly fulfilled his earlier promise of help by extending a loan guaranteed only by his faith in Lowden's future. Thereupon, the *Vidette-Reporter* announced in its issue of September 27, 1884, that "F. O. Louden [*sic*] has returned to graduate with '85."

He always remembered his graduation day "with a thrill."[49] As class valedictorian, he followed thirteen other Senior speakers on the Commencement program and brought the undergraduate portion of the exercises to a close. After several of his predecessors at the rostrum had deplored the "irreverence and restlessness generated in our overcrowded cities," the influx of ignorant and penniless foreigners "clogging the wheels of progress," the extreme utilitarianism of the present age, with its overstress upon the "practical" and "its tendency to destroy the cultural unity of society and divide men into discordant classes"; after others had extolled the individual conscience as "the proper criterion for human action," Job over Prometheus, Cromwell over the Levellers, Gladstone over Disraeli, and a scientific over a classical education, Frank Lowden arose. Probably to the relief of a satiated audience on a hot day in late June, his oration on "Social Tendencies" was "pointed and brief."

Lowden aimed to demonstrate that "Yes" was the correct answer to his introductory question, "Must the Great Mass of Men Always Be Toilers?" He blamed Plato and certain leaders of the French Revolution for "that fallacious theory of man's absolute equality" with which too many demagogues in the United States sought "the plaudits of the vulgar crowd." Interference by government lessened the happiness and prosperity of society. "All tendencies toward socialism are toward the rule of mediocrity. Reform can not come through legislative enactments; it must come from within. Such as we are the Gods can not help us. Each of us must help himself because government can not do so." Thus he declared his faith in nineteenth-century individualism and laissez faire. Following an address by a Master's candidate on

48. *Vidette-Reporter,* Sept. 15, 1883, and May 10, 1884.

49. FOL to J. H. Pohlman III, Clinton, Mississippi, May 22, 1939.

"Modern Biography and Its Abuses," Lowden and thirty-four other Seniors filed by President Pickard and received their Bachelors' diplomas.[50]

Even as late as graduation day, Lowden had not decided what his next move would be. His ultimate goal was the law. To enrol in a law school required money; to repay his debt to Andrews demanded a larger sum more quickly than the pitiful salary of a lawyer's clerk would provide. And yet his quandary could hardly have been greater than that of his biographer, who tries to reconcile the conflicting accounts of his course of action during the spring and summer of 1885. The *Eldora Herald* of April 29 announced that he had been "elected principal" of the Burlington, Iowa, High School at a "fine salary." The word "principal" should have been "teacher of Latin and mathematics," but otherwise the statement squares with what he became that autumn.[51] In later years, however, he sometimes attributed his first interest in Burlington to a conversation with W. W. Baldwin at a Beta Theta Pi "get-together" on the state university campus immediately after the Commencement exercises in late June. Baldwin, then president of the Burlington school board, repeated this story many times before his death in 1936.[52] Lowden strongly implied that he did not decide to go to Burlington until a telegram reached him in midsummer from his friend Laenas G. Weld, of its high-school staff, urging him to take the competitive examinations for determining who should have the appointment. Weld's wire, declared Lowden in 1929, "changed the entire course of my life; no one knows or ever will know, whether for better or worse."[53]

Much, but not all, of the doubt about what actually happened would disappear if the Baldwin conversation and the examinations occurred prior to April 29 rather than later. In other words, the notice in the *Herald* could hardly have been a product of the editor's imagination, but Lowden and others might easily have jumbled the time sequence when they told the story many years later. Even if these episodes did take place in the early spring, Lowden either long delayed his acceptance of the position after placing first in the examinations or, more probably, at some time during the summer heartily regretted his decision and was held to it only by the persuasiveness of Weld or Baldwin, or both. Shortly after Commencement he attended a normal institute in Des Moines.[54] While there, he explored the possibility of becoming a law clerk in that city. His fruitless inquiries may have reinforced the counsel of his friends not to throw away the monthly salary of

50. *Vidette-Reporter,* suppl., June 24, 1885.

51. See also *ibid.,* May 16, 1885; and *Burlington* (Iowa) *Daily Hawkeye,* Sept. 3, 1885.

52. George B. McKibbin, of Chicago, kindly furnished the author with a typed "Memorandum *re* Frank O. Lowden, 1885–86," recounting the story which he had repeatedly heard from his uncle, W. W. Baldwin, who was then the district land commissioner at Burlington of the Chicago, Burlington, and Quincy Railroad and later one of its vice-presidents.

53. FOL to H. Ingham, Des Moines, Iowa, Dec. 13, 1929.

54. MS of FOL's speech to Iowa State Teachers' Association, Des Moines, Nov. 2, 1922.

$100 offered by Burlington. It would be by far the highest pay he had ever received.

A combination of fortunate circumstances made his ten months in Burlington one of the happiest periods of his life. He boarded in the home of a Mr. Newman and found much to laugh about with his brood of children. One of them reminded him twenty years later that he had been "the genial and affable inmate of our old home, who enlivened us with eloquence and poetry. I even remember, 'Water! Bright Sparkling Water!' . . . and how I resented your pulling my ears!"[55] Thanks to his talent for quickly making friends, he soon was reading law under the kindly guidance of Judge John C. Power. The *Daily Hawkeye*, the leading journal of this busy Mississippi River town, rarely mentioned the high school but noted many local events in which Lowden probably shared during 1885–86. Classes suspended for two days in mid-September to enable the faculty and students to attend the fair of the Des Moines County Agricultural Association with its exhibit of Shorthorn and Holstein cattle. The political campaign that autumn brought to Grimes Opera House Lowden's friend of later years, Senator William B. Allison, as well as the rival gubernatorial candidates, William Larrabee and James B. Weaver. In early June Lowden and his faculty colleagues shepherded the members of the graduating class aboard the river boat "John Taylor" and regaled them with a party at Picnic Point.[56] Lowden had in his classes Anna L. Burdick and Harriet Connor, perhaps the ablest students he ever taught. Later in life he rejoiced when they fulfilled his confident expectations.[57]

Above all, that year, Lowden enjoyed his companions on the high-school staff—Laenas G. Weld, Charles J. Reed, and the principal, Dr. Ewald Poppe. Another kindred spirit was Charles C. Clark, whom Lowden replaced on the faculty when Clark resigned in order to study law. It was a remarkable group. Weld, an able mathematician, would soon be summoned to teaching and administrative posts with his alma mater in Iowa City. Reed, a promising chemist, joined the laboratory staff of Thomas A. Edison at Menlo Park, New Jersey, and later struck out on his own as an engineer in California. Clark became a successful Burlington lawyer.[58]

In 1885–86, however, it was Dr. Poppe, nearly twice the age of any of the others, who drew them together into a congenial band. German-born and a graduate of the University of Breslau, he had reached the mid-point of his almost sixty years as a teacher of Latin and German at Burlington. His

55. Mrs. Frank (Mabel Newman) Dauterman, Pittsburgh, Pennsylvania, to FOL, Sept. 6, 1906.

56. *Daily Hawkeye,* Sept. 5, 17, 26, and Oct. 30, 1885; June 10, 11, 17–19, 1886.

57. Mrs. Harriet Connor Brown, or "Cheddie" as FOL always called her, won the *Atlantic Monthly* Prize in 1929 for her volume, *Grandmother Brown's Hundred Years.* For Anna L. Burdick, see *School Life* (U.S. Office of Education, Washington, D.C.), XXV, No. 2 (November, 1939), 34.

58. Weld became professor and dean at the State University of Iowa (1886–1910) and later (1911 to his death in 1919) the first principal of the Pullman Free School of Manual Training in Chicago.

interests were catholic, and he read omnivorously. He seemed childlike or professor-like in his business naïveté and absent-mindedness, but he touched many subjects with humor and insight. Something of his "flavor" can be gained from a note written over twenty years later to "my dearest friend," Frank Lowden, who was ill:

Wish I could come and help you. Oh, I am a good nurse. I should make it so quiet, so still around you, nothing should come to you, but now and then an innocent joke, for you cannot live without this food, which you used to fabricate masterly in old times. Will we ever laugh again, as we did? What miserable cigars we enjoyed in those happy days! How little is needed for happiness![59]

These good companions met in reunion whenever possible over the years, occasionally in Chicago and often in Burlington or Iowa City. Until Dr. Poppe's death at the time of World War I, he and Lowden exchanged letters frequently, continuing the discussions of their halcyon days in Burlington and sprinkling their correspondence with comments about their reading. They levied upon the wisdom of Plato and Cicero, Shakespeare and Goethe, Mommsen and Ferrero, Trevelyan, Tagore, and many other authors to bolster their points of view about contemporary problems.[60] Every Christmas, Lowden sent Dr. Poppe a box of his favorite cigars and in 1910, on his eightieth birthday, joined the many other devoted friends of the old master to ease his declining years with a purse of $5,200.

Although Lowden could hardly have been more contented, he counted his year in Burlington as merely an interlude of money-saving and watchful waiting for an opportunity to advance toward the practice of law. He inclined, first of all, toward a law-office clerkship in a small city giving promise of rapid growth. After almost deciding that Sioux City, Iowa, fully met this specification, he accepted W. W. Baldwin's invitation in June, 1886, to introduce him to Wirt Dexter, the general counsel of the Chicago, Burlington, and Quincy Railroad. Although Dexter's firm of Dexter, Herrick, and Allen in Chicago employed only full-fledged lawyers as clerks, the senior partner thought well enough of Lowden to offer him a job, provided that he promise to attend law school at night.

Upon returning to Burlington, Lowden faced the hard alternative of continuing in its high school with his salary advanced to $1,600 a year or becoming a very junior employee of a big law firm at a wage of $8.00 a week—about what the Rough Woods district school board had paid him ten years before. After arguing out the problem with his Burlington companions, his folks at home, and James B. Weaver, a Des Moines attorney and old college friend, Lowden wired his acceptance to Dexter. Already twenty-five years of age, it was high time that he made a start, however humble, upon the road which had long been his choice.

59. E. Poppe to FOL, June 5, 1909. For a brief sketch of the first eighty years of Poppe's life see *Burlington Daily Hawkeye,* Sept. 11, 1910.

60. As examples, see E. Poppe to FOL, Feb. 2, 1913, and Jan. 23, 1914; FOL to E. Poppe, Jan. 27, 1916.

And so, on a Monday morning in August, 1886, Lowden closed his decade as farmhand, schoolteacher, and college student by entering the offices of the Dexter firm in the heart of Chicago's business district at the corner of Washington and Dearborn streets. The day before, not a little homesick in his cheerless hall bedroom, he attended the service in Central Church on Michigan Avenue. There he heard the redoubtable Dr. David Swing denounce the anarchists, so much in the thoughts of good Chicagoans that summer, and quote Holy Writ in support of respect for the established law.[61] Frank Lowden had struck the same note, although less eloquently, in his valedictory at the State University of Iowa. Evidently, the American city as well as the countryside, however much their people might differ about some important issues, stood as one in their determination to defend a common political and economic heritage against assault by radicals. To do this was the obligation of every American both as a citizen and as a Christian.

This, furthermore, was peculiarly the duty of a lawyer—such a lawyer, for instance, as Wirt Dexter, who, with other Chicago leaders, attended Central Church. More than any other group, the members of the bar had in their charge the upholding of the Constitution and statutory law. This mission lifted their work from merely a respectable means of making a living into a profession worthy to rank alongside that of the clergy or physicians. These were prime tenets of young Lowden's faith and helped shape his thought and action as long as he lived. In the summer of 1886, he determined to master his homesickness and longing to be again in the country—feelings to which he would often surrender in later years—in order to join as soon as possible this highly dedicated profession of the law.

61. The Haymarket Riot occurred on May 4, 1886.

CHAPTER III

HALL BEDROOM TO "CASTLE REST"

Even the imagination of Horatio Alger hardly contrived a success story more improbable than that of Frank Lowden's first ten years in Chicago. Good luck was on his side, but luck would have availed little if he had not attracted it by talent, hard work, eloquence, sociability, a generous fund of wit and information, and a readiness to conform whenever he could do so without loss of self-respect. Luck in the shape of heredity deserved some of the credit for his fine presence. He was not unmindful then, nor would he ever be, of his handsome, ruddy face with its wide, sensitive mouth, prominent well-shaped nose, deep-blue eyes, and high forehead crowned by a mass of wavy blond hair. His handclasp was firm and his gaze direct. He impressed his acquaintances by his sincerity, wholesomeness, and enthusiasm for living and learning. Even as a lawyer's clerk he was unabashed by the business leaders of Chicago who frequently came to his employer's office. Whenever they invited it, they found him ready to exchange banter or talk seriously on equal terms. People who were misled by his erect carriage thought him taller than his five feet, eight inches. His sturdy torso seemed somewhat too heavy for his short legs and small feet adequately to support. He had trained them, however, to a swinging stride which served him well on his long walks for exercise. In so far as his slender funds permitted, he tried to be carefully and correctly groomed at all times. In later years he would be obliged to curb his liking for starchy foods, but in 1886, when a thirty-cent meal was an extravagance, he had no reason to worry about overweight.

Wirt Dexter told him shortly after he reached Chicago that whenever he learned to write more legibly he could keep the office docket or daily journal of the firm's business. Although hardly a promotion, this task would entail some little responsibility and be a welcome supplement to the humdrum work of typing letters and legal documents. A night-school course at the YMCA, whose aid he gratefully acknowledged later by many donations, improved his penmanship sufficiently within a few weeks to bring the docket to his charge.[1] He would never write with Spencerian clarity, but his handwriting thereafter was easy to read. The tall, angular letters of these early days, so wasteful of paper and ink, gradually compressed themselves into more moderate compass without, however, changing much in their shape.

1. MS of FOL's speech on behalf of the YMCA War Fund, Nov. 14, 1917.

In September, 1886, he enrolled in evening courses at the Union College of Law, then under the joint management of Northwestern University and the first University of Chicago. Helped by his considerable background training, he was able after examination to confine his work for the degree to the last year of the two-year curriculum. With a full-time job every day, a tight schedule of evening classes, and hardly enough money to buy a square meal, he found the months until June, 1887, among the most arduous of his life. On the other hand, they brought gratifying rewards. After his election to the legal fraternity, Phi Delta Phi, he was chosen to speak for the students at a banquet in honor of Judge Thomas M. Cooley, distinguished teacher at the University of Michigan Law School, author of standard treatises on constitutional law and history, and soon to be the first chairman of the Interstate Commerce Commission. Moreover, at Commencement, Lowden was the valedictorian of his class. Following his speech, he was informed by Dean Henry Booth that he had won the fifty-dollar prize in oratory and an award of equal amount for excellence in scholarship.[2] The money came like manna from heaven. As he said later, his other cash resources amounted to exactly forty cents. "Oyster stew and coffee," served up in "hash houses," had been his principal diet for many weeks.[3]

In July, 1887, he passed the Illinois bar examinations and shortly thereafter was admitted to practice. With his salary rising to $65 a month, he thus became a full-fledged lawyer on the staff of a firm with which any young attorney would feel fortunate to be associated. Better still, Wirt Dexter made him his personal aide. Faithful in his attendance at Central Church, he was an occasional guest at Sunday dinner in Dr. Swing's home.[4] All in all, he had good reason to be satisfied with his progress during his first year in Chicago.

Lowden always thought of Wirt Dexter as his "best friend" in the city during these early days.[5] Treating him as a social equal, Dexter introduced him to many of Chicago's best-known citizens. Besides the Burlington Railroad, the clients of his firm were mostly banks, public utility companies, and men connected with the senior partner's large interests in lumber. Lowden could hardly have been better placed to gain at least a nodding acquaintance with those who held the keys to economic and social success in Chicago. On returning to his boarding house from a day at the office or an evening in Dexter's home, he regaled his neighbor, William May Garland, a teller in the Illinois Trust and Savings Bank, with humorous descriptions of what he had seen and heard. These good companions and Frank H. Smith had their meals

2. FOL to John H. Wigmore, Evanston, Illinois, July 1, 1937; *Chicago Legal News,* May 2, 1896, pp. 289–91.

3. Interview with FOL, reported in the *Freeport* (Ill.) *Journal,* Feb. 15, 1908.

4. MS of FOL's speech in Orchestra Hall, Chicago, Dec. 15, 1935. When Dr. Swing died in 1894, FOL was one of the pallbearers. He was soon a trustee of Central Church and served until 1906. In 1930 he accepted the office again.

5. FOL to Mrs. (Stanley) Katharine Dexter McCormick, Washington, D.C., Feb. 25, 1919.

together in the "modest little dining room of Mrs. York" at 1812 Michigan Avenue, and sometimes spent an evening playing poker.[6]

Lowden's own work during the three years following his graduation from law school merged anonymously with the business of his employer. The published records of the lawsuits in which the firm of Dexter, Herrick, and Allen was counsel do not identify the members of its staff who appeared in the courtroom. Besides its corporate clients, the firm occasionally handled the suit of an individual against a business concern, as when Charles D. Lathrop, a Chicago tea and coffee merchant, won damages in the Illinois Supreme Court because the Postal Telegraph and Cable Company had caused him financial loss by garbling his telegram or when the same court ordered the Merchants' National Bank of Chicago to return to the executor of Nathaniel K. Fairbank's will some shares of stock deposited as security for a loan. By helping to prepare briefs and interrogate witnesses, Lowden gained a rich experience in civil cases involving public and private contracts, licenses, wills, bankruptcies, and claims for damages against railroads and streetcar companies on account of personal injuries.

His thesis at the Union College of Law dealt with "Combinations of Masters and Workmen at the Common Law." Apparently no suit in which he was the counsel furnished an outlet for his special knowledge of this subject. In a closely packed essay of thirty pages he traced sequentially the leading decisions of British and American courts relevant to his topic. At the close he summarized unemotionally the status of the matter in 1887:

> If workmen combine merely for the purpose of raising their wages, that combination is not *per se* criminal. Those who are members of such a combination, however, must not violate a *contract* of service. Any combination of masters or workers to lower or raise the wages of *others* or to curb their freedom by coercion, is indictable. A threat of strike or lockout, if it has the effect of coercion, may be *indictable*. . . . The key question always is, was the combination formed for the *bona fide* purpose of better protecting its members by legal means or was it to *injure others?* . . . The present enlightened view is that any man or set of men is the best judge of their own interests and to allow them to pursue these interests by any method short of violence or fraud best serves the public weal.[7]

Nothing that Lowden wrote in this matter-of-fact dissertation could offend even the most conservative of Chicago's businessmen.

By rigorous thrift during these financially lean years, he was able to attend the annual banquets of his fraternity and visit his folks in Hubbard, Iowa, at Thanksgiving and Christmas time. On January 3, 1888, for example, he spoke to his brothers in Beta Theta Pi on "The Chapter as the Student's

6. *Lakeside Annual Directory* for each year between 1887 and 1891 lists FOL's frequent changes of address. Garland moved to California in 1890, where he found good health and fortune. He became president of the Los Angeles Realty Board and president of the California Chamber of Commerce.

7. This MS dissertation is dated June 23, 1887. In it, English cases are traced to the 1870's and American from the memorable New York case of *People* v. *Fisher* in 1835.

Home" at their second annual banquet in the Grand Pacific Hotel. At this banquet he sat between William B. Keep (Beloit, 1873), whose law practice was said to have made him a millionaire, and John C. Smith, a former lieutenant-governor of Illinois.[8] Overlooking his poverty, his friends and relatives in Iowa already pointed to him with pride as a model for other young men to emulate. Not only had he performed a feat, unusual for a country lad in his day, of graduating with high honors and as the valedictorian from both a university and an urban law school, but he was demonstrating his ability to more than hold his own in competition with young men bred to the life of a great city. But he still liked to associate with his boyhood friends, and they occasionally resumed their well-loved sport of hunting prairie chickens. During his homecomings he slipped back into the family circle without conscious effort, singing and whistling as had always been his wont, teasing his younger sisters, and pleasing them with little gifts from the big Chicago stores.

As the months went by, his work for Dexter, Herrick, and Allen centered more and more upon assisting its ailing senior member, who made him his protégé and, to a considerable extent, his confidant. For these reasons, Dexter's death in 1890 severed Lowden's chief professional and personal bonds with the firm.[9] He had gained the respect of those Chicago men of affairs who had retained the partnership as their counsel chiefly because of Wirt Dexter's membership in it. Since they offered to turn some of their business Lowden's way, his potential assets had become greater than Herrick and Allen were willing to reflect in his salary. Therefore, by the summer of 1890, it was to his professional advantage to seek a new position. He had built up enough good will to be an acceptable junior partner of some Chicago lawyer on the lookout for more clients. Although Lowden could bring no financial capital to such an association, he could offer a surprising amount of credit. In the long run his credit would produce ample fees.

Emery S. Walker, a favorably known but not a leading Chicago attorney, quickly recognized this asset. On July 1, 1890, Frank Lowden transferred his few lawbooks to the Marine Building at 154 Lake Street and proudly entered an office door marked "Walker and Lowden." It was a fortunate move. His income greatly increased and his local reputation widened, now that he appeared oftener in courtrooms and acted on behalf of his own clients. His leisure hours became more enjoyable because he could indulge his liking for the companionship of men of his own age. Among the most congenial were Frederick A. Delano, superintendent of the Burlington Railroad, Walter Herrick, son of one of his former employers, and the attorneys Kenesaw M. Landis and Edgar A. Bancroft.[10]

8. *Chicago Tribune,* Jan. 4, 1888.

9. *Chicago Legal News,* May 2, 1896.

10. F. A. Delano, an uncle of President Franklin Delano Roosevelt, died on March 28, 1953. In 1892 K. M. Landis was an assistant on the faculty of Northwestern University Law College, as the Union College of Law was called from 1891 on. E. Bancroft came to

One of Lowden's most difficult cases at this time had no connection whatsoever with the Walker partnership. In the late 1880's, Lorenzo and Nancy Lowden were stunned when told by a lawyer representing Samuel P. Withrow that he rightfully owned their 200-acre farm on the outskirts of Hubbard, Iowa. When Lorenzo had purchased the land and buildings about ten years before, the seller had assured him of a clear title. Lorenzo had improved the property, kept the taxes paid on time, and made it into a comfortable home for his wife and younger children. In it, he had sunk the major part of his life's savings. Withrow, on the other hand, could show that in 1857 he had acquired the farm in settlement of a debt. Unknown to him at the time, so he claimed, there had been a mortgage on the land which was foreclosed four years later—also without his knowledge. The validity of Lorenzo Lowden's deed depended upon the legality of this foreclosure. Withrow, of course, insisted that his title took precedence over Lowden's. Although Withrow's case was weakened by his long delay in asserting his ownership and by undisturbed, adverse possession of the property by others for nearly thirty years, it was sufficiently strong to make Lorenzo sick from worry and to gray his hair. The expense alone was frightening, especially after Withrow, a man of considerable wealth, declared that, if need be, he would carry his cause to the highest court in Iowa. Frank Lowden came to Eldora, the county seat, to join with a firm of local attorneys as counsel for the defense. After losing before a jury in the Hardin County court, Withrow appealed to the state supreme court at Des Moines. Once again Lowden hurried to his father's assistance. On January 24, 1891, he won the battle when the highest tribunal of Iowa sustained the decision of the lower court on the ground that Withrow had waited too long before asserting his claim. The issue had been nip and tuck, and Frank Lowden often referred to it as one of his hardest-fought contests at law.[11]

At this time in Chicago he often appeared at the bar of a court. His reputation was already so high that older lawyers came to hear him question witnesses, challenge opposing counsel, and address juries. The *Chicago Legal News* commented upon his skill in argument, the breadth of his scholarship, and his popularity among his brother attorneys.[12] By then he had left his dark hall bedroom far behind. As one of the directors of the Calumet Club at the corner of Twentieth Street and Michigan Avenue, he kept bachelor's quarters in probably the most exclusive clubhouse for men in Chicago.[13] The initiation fee of $100 and the $80 annual dues were an investment rather than

Chicago from Galesburg, Illinois, and was an attorney for the Atchison, Topeka, and Santa Fe Railroad. He is best remembered as United States ambassador to Japan. Walter Herrick died suddenly of heart disease in 1905.

11. *S. P. Withrow* v. *L. O. Lowden,* 82 Supreme Court of Iowa Reports, Appendix, 717.

12. *Chicago Legal News,* Apr. 30, 1892, Feb. 18 and 25, 1893; *Chicago Tribune,* July 10, 1890. Interview with John J. Knickerbocker reported in the *Dixon* (Ill.) *Telegraph,* Nov. 20, 1903.

13. In 1891, FOL also joined the Sunset Club and the Union League Club.

an extravagance. Among the four hundred members were many of the most substantial citizens of the city, including George M. Pullman, Marshall Field, Philip D. Armour, T. B. Blackstone, Levi Z. Leiter, A. C. Bartlett, and John H. Hamline. Thirteen other bachelors besides Lowden made their home in the clubhouse. Several of these, like Robert H. Fleming, John R. Morron, J. B. Goodman, and John J. Knickerbocker, notable as a lawyer and a leader of movements for civic reform, were his close friends. These men and others—"heavy thinkers and heavy drinkers" in the words of one of the congenial band many years later—smoked their postprandial cigars and talked of current affairs and books while seated under the club's famous collection of Civil War portraits and battle scenes or at their round table in the dining room.[14] At about this time Lowden and one of his best friends, Frank Hamlin, enjoyed a boat trip along the New England coast in the craft of Hamlin's brother Hannibal, of Maine. Many years later Lowden recalled it nostalgically as "the famous yachting cruise."[15]

John J. Knickerbocker's brother, Probate Court Judge Joshua C. Knickerbocker, was the first judge before whom Lowden appeared as an attorney. Two years after the jurist's death in 1890, Chicago named a public school in his honor, and Lowden delivered the dedicatory speech.[16] His address on June 24, to an audience of school children and adults, was the first of many similar ones he would make during the next few years. One cannot read it today without wondering why the audience applauded so enthusiastically. The romantic patriotism of the 1890's and the magnetic presence of the young orator are alike gone. Flowery metaphors and similes no longer appeal. But Lowden could be certain of handclapping when he told his listeners that "the first lesson in colors I would have the child receive should be read in the lustrous folds of his country's flag." A generation which viewed the Supreme Court as the embodiment of wisdom expected to be reminded that "the court of judicature is the sum of civilization. It is the point of contact between the people and organized society. In it the functions of man 'show likest unto God.' " Many people, however, would still agree with the leading theme of his speech, set forth after he had completed his eulogy of Judge Knickerbocker: "I can not too deeply impress upon you to-day the great truth that the first and last duty of every loyal American is to yield implicit obedience to the laws of the land. . . . The rights or supposed rights of a single individual must yield when they come in conflict with the existence of society." Lowden's recognition of a possible antithesis between individual rights, even though not exercised by fraud or violence, and the higher

14. Statement of John R. Morron to the author on Dec. 29, 1945.

15. FOL to H. E. Hamlin, Ellsworth, Maine, May 24, 1922, and Nov. 28, 1933. In the latter, FOL dates the cruise as "forty-one years" ago. The Hamlins were sons of the vice-president of the United States, 1861–65. When Frank Hamlin died in May, 1922, FOL wrote: "There is no one in Chicago to take his place in my affections."

16. MS of address of dedication of Knickerbocker School, June 24, 1892.

rights of society marked a significant shift of emphasis from that of his vale-dictory at Iowa City in 1885.

Shortly before making this speech, he and Walker went their separate ways, and Lowden for the next sixteen months was the junior law partner of William B. Keep. The reasons for this change are not clear. Although Walker lacked unusual ability and aggressiveness, he and Lowden remained good friends, and their association had been mutually profitable. When Walker suffered broken health and fortune about fifteen years later, Lowden came quickly to his financial assistance.[17] Probably an expectation of larger fees mainly accounts for Lowden's move. The wealthy and socially prominent Keep, with several railroads and public utility companies among his clients and a luxurious suite of offices in the "Temple" at the corner of La Salle and Monroe streets, could not fail to attract a young lawyer "on the make."[18]

Lowden was not disappointed. He soon became a familiar figure at the bar of the Federal District Court and the Supreme Court of Illinois. Keep and he garnered a rich harvest of fees from clients like the Chicago and Erie Railroad Company, the West Chicago Street Railway Company, the North Chicago Street Railway Company, the International Loan and Trust Company, and the Waukesha Hygeia Mineral Springs Company. Somewhat against his preference, for, above all, he enjoyed matching wits with opposing counsel and sharing in the drama of a suit in criminal law, he was drawn more and more into litigation where the matters at issue involved statutes regulating partnerships and corporations—their charters, stocks and bonds, trade marks, and liability for injuries suffered by their employees and customers.[19]

Lowden's prominence in the various associations of lawyers within Chicago both reflected and enhanced his professional standing. Early in 1893 he and Wallace Heckman helped to organize the Law Institute, or "Law Club," as it soon became. Apparently, no one thought Lowden presumptuous when he announced his candidacy—unsuccessful, as it turned out—for election to its first board of managers in competition with such well-known attorneys as Cyrus Bentley, Frank H. Scott, and John M. Harlan.[20] Later in the same month of January, 1893, he made the principal speech at the first annual banquet of the Chicago alumni chapter of Phi Delta Phi. He kept that appointment and attended the regular monthly dinner of the Law Club several evenings later with some difficulty because he had lost most of his personal possessions in the Calumet Club fire a few nights before. According to the

17. E. S. Walker to FOL, May 20, 1907; FOL to E. S. Walker, May 14, 1912. The Keep-Lowden partnership began in May, 1892.

18. *Chicago Legal News,* XXIV (1891–92), 279.

19. *Ibid.,* Oct. 8, 1892, p. 51; Dec. 24, 1892, p. 152; Oct. 7, 1893, pp. 48–49; *Chicago Tribune,* Apr. 13 and May 3, 1893.

20. *Chicago Legal News,* Dec. 3, 1892, p. 124; *Chicago Tribune,* Jan. 7 and 8, 1893.

Chicago press, the cry of "Fire" at 5:30 in the afternoon of January 17 found Lowden in his room

clad only in his undergarments as he rested before dressing for dinner. Thus thinly clad he rushed out of the burning building into the biting wind of Michigan Avenue and took refuge in a house next door to the Club. One hour later he was rescued by a friend who brought him a suit of clothes. That is why he appeared at the Lexington Club last night in a suit not made for him.[21]

The blaze which compelled Lowden to buy a new wardrobe may have suggested to his ready imagination the metamorphosis he had undergone in more significant ways since his unnoticed coming to the city less than seven years before. By 1893, besides making his first venture into politics,[22] he had attracted more clients than he could well accommodate and no longer needed the prestige of an older associate to bring him business. For this reason the firm of Keep and Lowden dissolved on September 1, and the junior partner opened his own office in the "Temple."

Although happy and prosperous, Lowden was driving himself too hard. "If labor were the penalty of man's first sin," he told the students of the Northwest Division High School of Chicago on Washington's Birthday, 1894, "a divine justice has declared that it shall be the open door through which he may return to Paradise."[23] Persistent application had no doubt helped to lift him swiftly up the ladder of his chosen career, but his friends cautioned him that excessive toil would eventually blunt the keen edge of any man's talent, no matter how great, and injure his health, no matter how sound. In their judgment he merited a vacation. Without a partner, however, to carry on for him while he was away, he felt less able to close his desk than at any time since he had become a lawyer. Moreover, in the spring of 1894, the University of Iowa's Law Department greatly pleased him by its invitation to make the Commencement address in June. Realizing that the audience would include his former professors and many friends of his college days, he prepared his speech with particular care.

They received him with a warmth exceeding his fondest hopes. His remarks, entitled "The Lawyer's Allegiance to the Law," was published in full by the university and in the *Chicago Legal News*. Under the caption, "Forensic Ethics," lengthy extracts of it appeared in the *Brief*, an English barristers' journal printed in London.[24] The agrarian and labor unrest of the mid-1890's suggested to Lowden his theme and permitted him appropriately to

21. *Chicago Tribune,* Jan. 18 and 19, 1893. During the rebuilding, FOL lived at the Union League Club.

22. See chap. v.

23. This statement was one of FOL's favorites as long as he lived. He sometimes appended to it: "The problem is not how to avoid work but how to find joy in it." He rarely spoke so epigrammatically, and yet, in so far as the present author knows, he did not plagiarize this adage. Its precept, of course, is one of the themes stressed in McGuffey's readers.

24. *Chicago Legal News,* XXVI, 402; XXVII, 37; *Brief* (London), I, No. 9 (Sept. 15, 1894), 255 ff.

repeat the conclusions already quoted from his Bachelor's dissertation at the Union College of Law. Above all, however, he emphasized the duty of the legal profession and the courts, amid the "clash of classes," to play a neutral and conservative role in American society. The "lawyer's allegiance to the law" was his greatest social service as a citizen, because the very existence of his country depended upon maintaining the supremacy of the law. Rule by majority voice could be as tyrannical as dictation by an autocrat. The "vox populi" might be the voice of the Devil rather than of God. The federal Constitution itself represented "a confession by the people of their distrust in themselves." How fortunate America, that it had not been led by doctrinaires like Jefferson but by lawyers with reverence for history and wise precedent! The judges belonged to "the priesthood of patriotism" and held the scales of Justice steady. Indifferent to inflamed public opinion, they impartially weighed against the norm of the law the actions of individuals, corporations, and labor unions. In terms of the happiness and security of Americans, the contributions of Chief Justice John Marshall exceeded those of all the presidents between 1800 and 1850. Wisely and rightfully the Fourteenth Amendment, made by lawyers, was being interpreted so as to protect the property of individuals and corporations against the intemperate regulatory acts of certain state legislatures.

These views of Lowden were commonplace among the lawyers of that day and, in fact, among those of a half-century before. For this reason and since Lowden was an excellent speaker, he "was surrounded by an admiring crowd of grey-haired judges and attorneys" at the close of the Commencement exercises, if the *Iowa City Citizen* can be believed.[25] Upon his return to Chicago after a brief visit with his parents, he discovered that his remarks had been given wide currency because of their timeliness during the bloody Pullman strike. Six years later his comments about this historic clash included:

It does not matter what the merits of the controversy were; a large body of men were in open rebellion against the constituted authorities. . . . At this crisis I visited my old home in Iowa. I found there that men of all classes, with the spirit of "sixty-one" still pulsing in their veins, would have hailed with joy an opportunity to march into Chicago and rescue the jewels of law and order from hands which only tarnished them.[26]

In the summer of 1894, Frank Lowden found it hard to sympathize with striking workmen. He was living more comfortably than ever before in a suite of two rooms at the new Calumet Club. On chilly evenings he could read by his own hearthstone. His windows afforded a wide outlook over Lake Michigan and the busy traffic of Michigan Avenue. Close at hand were the mansions of George M. Pullman and many other captains of transporta-

25. Issue of June 13, 1894. The prime importance of an "independent judiciary" as the cornerstone of the Constitution was a favorite lifetime theme of Lowden.

26. MS of FOL's speech before the Grant Club, Des Moines, Iowa, Apr. 27, 1900. The Pullman strike extended from mid-May to late July, 1894, with its most violent phase about July 7.

tion or industry who had shared in making Chicago the second largest city of America, vibrant with restless and sometimes ruthless wealth.[27] Lowden's close friends included several sons of these powerful businessmen. Their fathers were usually too preoccupied with more important matters to join the nightly get-togethers of the younger generation in the restaurant, bar, and lounges of the Calumet Club, but the weight and inspiration of their success were always present.

On one such midsummer's evening, so the story goes, Frank Lowden and a few of his companions were discussing the merits of French cooking. In a jovial mood, either he or Walter Herrick suggested that they go as soon as possible to Paris to "chase French chefs to their lair."[28] Perhaps it was in this spirit of levity that Lowden finally consented to take a vacation. If so, it was an ironic prelude to the most fateful journey of his entire life.

Herrick and Lowden sailed for Paris and London on the "Normandie," leaving New York before sunrise, Saturday, August 4. Later that morning at breakfast, Herrick called his friend's attention to Miss Florence Pullman, whom Lowden had never seen before.[29] That evening on deck in the rain he was presented to her, and they exchanged the usual words of courtesy. Thereafter for the remainder of his vacation—and, in fact, for the rest of his life—she was rarely absent from his thoughts. On her part, she at least remembered his name long enough to list it in her little diary among the people whom she had met on board that day. Miss Pullman, unlike her mother, who accompanied her, was not a good sailor and kept to her stateroom on Sunday until early evening. At that time, because the wind and sea were moderating, she went on deck "for several hours and found Mr. Herrick and Mr. Lowden very agreeable companions."[30] During the rest of the passage they were often together, playing cards in Mrs. Pullman's stateroom, reading to each other on deck, or standing at the stern of the ship, "watching the great white billows of foam that followed in our wake."[31] Although Lowden and his conversation impressed both Mrs. Pullman and her daughter, the latter's willingness to be so frequently in his company may be partially explained by her diary entry of August 6: "Our fellow passengers do not appear to be very interesting and are mostly foreigners."

Disembarking at Le Havre on the morning of August 12, Herrick and Lowden helped Miss Pullman celebrate her twenty-fourth birthday by sightseeing until mid-afternoon, when they boarded the train for Paris. Once there and under her expert guidance, the two vacationers toured the city.

27. In the census of 1890, Chicago's population for the first time exceeded Philadelphia's.

28. MS, "Sketch of Frank O. Lowden" (unsigned and undated, but probably written in 1920).

29. For the period Aug. 4–18, the vacation story is based mainly upon the diaries of Mrs. George M. Pullman and Miss Florence Pullman. That FOL, contrary to some stories, had never seen Miss Pullman before Aug. 4 is made certain by her letter to him of Aug. 5, 1895, her diary entries of Aug. 5, 1903, and Aug. 4, 1934, and his letter to her of Jan. (?), 1895.

30. Florence Pullman's diary, Aug. 5, 1894.

31. Florence Pullman to FOL, Aug. 5, 1895.

Together they visited Napoleon's tomb, Notre Dame and St. Eustache, attended mass at the Church of the Madeleine, ascended the Eiffel Tower, and dined at the Café d'Armenonville in the Bois to the accompaniment of the "wild, beautiful music" of a Hungarian orchestra.[32] On the evening of the eighteenth, as Lowden was about to leave the Hôtel Continental for his trip to London, he included within a gift of flowers to Miss Pullman a note telling her, "Everything I have seen is blended with your face . . . and the confusion has made it all the more beautiful. We go tonight and shall sail [for home] about the Twenty-fifth; I to struggle along the lines of one of my ambitions, and to despair, I fear, of the attainment of the other. But at any rate, you will permit me to come to see you when you return."[33]

Lowden's impetuous frankness and lack of finesse must have been a new experience for Florence Pullman, running counter to the social code in which she had been carefully trained at exclusive schools in Chicago, New York City, Fontainebleau, and Potsdam.[34] Since 1890, when she and her younger sister Harriett had made their debuts,[35] she had conformed to the standards and shared prominently in the activities expected of young women born to great wealth. Her diary in the winter of 1894, for example, is crowded with notations about teas, dinners, dances, benefits, dolls' bazaars, and calls upon the other families who could afford to live in huge graystone houses in the Prairie Avenue neighborhood of Chicago's Near South Side. For some weeks each winter she accompanied her mother to Ormond Beach, Florida, and in summer to the family-owned islet amid the Thousand Islands of the St. Lawrence River, at "Fairlawn" in Elberon, New Jersey, or on a brief visit to the old home of the Pullmans at Albion, New York. Wherever she traveled in the United States there were private Pullman cars to carry her and a retinue of servants at her beck and call. A long trip abroad was almost a routine part of her annual schedule. She felt no embarrassment in a company which spoke only French, German, or Italian. What she did and what she wore had been subjects of newspaper comment ever since her birth. During the five years since her debut, speculations about whom she would marry had been a favorite topic in the society columns of the metropolitan press. As early as 1890, the *Chicago Post* ventured to prophesy: "No foreign jackanapes of a nobleman will marry her, it may safely be said. She has wonderful coolness and self-possession."[36] Rumors of her engagement had been frequent—now to Prince Leopold of Isenberg-Birstein of Germany, then to King Alexander of Serbia, and later to the Marquis de Lorme, a Spanish grandee who came to the Columbian Exposition in the suite of the Princess Eulalia. While in

32. FOL to Florence Pullman, Aug. 14, 1895. Her birthday was really Aug. 11.

33. FOL to Florence Pullman, Aug. 18, 1894.

34. She attended "Les Perches" school at Fontainebleau in 1882, graduated from Anne Brown's School for Girls in New York City in 1887, and studied music in Potsdam in 1890.

35. *Chicago Post,* May 16, 1890. An article in the *Chicago Tribune,* Jan. 21, 1896, stressed her personal attention to philanthropic work of many kinds. Seven years earlier, she and others had organized the Visiting Nurses Association of Chicago.

36. *Chicago Post,* May 16, 1890.

France in the late summer of 1894, she was reported inaccurately to have promised to marry one Du Chanois, to whom she introduced Frank Lowden in Paris but who cannot now be identified.[37]

The strenuous social whirl in which she lived, as well as her long and frequent absences from Chicago, reflected in large degree the will and the whims of her restless, vivacious, and pleasure-loving mother. She and a half-dozen other women were the social arbiters of Chicago society. Anyone similarly absorbed in her own little world fell easily under the spell of her wit and boundless energy and marveled at her complete devotion to a business-centered husband, who did not always treat her with consideration. Even though, characteristically, Mrs. Pullman needed more than a year to discover that Lowden's name was not "Lowdon," she liked him from the outset and soon became his ally. His drive and sense of humor attracted her, while her gift of persiflage met its match in his own. She found him a good partner at cards and appreciated, but never shared, his "down-to-earthness" and sure sense of economic values.[38]

Florence Pullman inherited a measure of her father's business talent and firmness of will. Her persistence in the pursuit of her goals resembled his, but she used tact and excellent timing, while he relied upon the blunt force of his vast financial resources. Given to outbursts of monumental anger, George M. Pullman required skilful handling, an art which she had mastered. At the same time they were devoted to each other, and he never felt happier than when in her company. He regarded her with an almost fierce possessiveness. On his long business jaunts over the railroads of the land in his luxurious private car, she was sometimes his sole companion, reading to him by the hour and listening to his soliloquies about men and affairs. Like other daughters of her generation, she promised her father that she would not engage herself to marry until he had given his consent.[39] She recognized that he let his imperious will and pride in achievement mask a real concern for the social welfare. She was one of the few who knew about his large, anonymous gifts to Chicago charities. But, to his bitterness, the whole world had heard of the Pullman strike and how, after providing his workmen with a "model village," they rose against him, only to be crushed by federal troops and his own hard hand. For his unbending conduct on that occasion, significantly unmentioned by Mrs. Pullman and her daughter in their diaries, he was pilloried in sermons and editorials and portrayed as the personification of heartless capitalism.

Against this background Florence Pullman received at Aix-les-Bains the farewell note in which Frank Lowden, after a two-week tourist friendship, thinly disguised his hope of eventually becoming her husband. In her reply

37. *New York Commercial Advertiser,* Jan. 21, 1896; Miss Pullman's diary, Aug. 22, 1894; FOL to Florence Pullman, Sept. 12, 1895.

38. Mrs. G. M. Pullman's diary, 1894–96, *passim.*

39. Florence Pullman to FOL, July 19 and Sept. 26, 1895. This paragraph, however, is based mainly upon her diary and that of her mother, 1894–98, and upon statements to the author by Miss Margaret Enders, a close friend of the family.

she thanked him and Walter Herrick "for many happy hours" and invited them to call "as soon as we reach Chicago." By saying that she would be for some time at the Hôtel du Nord in Aix-les-Bains she implied that he might write to her again. Archly, she added: "I hope . . . that your voyage home will be as smooth as the one coming over. I'll not say that I hope you will enjoy it more for I am selfish enough to hope that you will not!"[40] To Lowden, who was doing his valiant best to visit in less than a week all the places worth seeing in London, her letter resembled "manna from Heaven"—"a bit of delirium has come into my life."[41]

He was back in his office by early September, 1894, but six weeks more went by before the Pullmans returned to Chicago. Although he confined his October calls upon Florence Pullman to Sunday afternoons, she favored him with a half-dozen weekday evenings during the following month. Beginning late in November, he wrote to her frequently, not expecting as many replies but eager to tell her how the inspiration of her friendship was tripling his output of work and greatly adding to his effectiveness as a lawyer and an orator.

Upon his elevation at this time to the presidency of the Second Ward Republican Club, he hastened to assure her that he would resist pressures from machine politicians and not use his position "for personal gain or power." Indeed, he amazed and disturbed the spoilsmen of his party that winter by publicly attacking their methods, prosecuting cases of alleged fraud at the recent autumn elections, urging that the ward committeemen be shorn of most of their power, and pleading with apathetic "good citizens" to get out and vote.[42] Evidently he pictured himself as a modern Sir Galahad performing good deeds for the sake of his fair lady. In by far his best speech up to that time, delivered before the Sunset Club at the Grand Pacific Hotel on February 28, 1895, he minced no words in describing how Chicago was misgoverned. He called upon his listeners to recognize that venal politics in city administration overshadowed in importance all other issues. Let every honest man support the appointment of a non-partisan Civil Service Commission and work his hardest to end conditions whereby "offices become not a public trust but a party steal."[43] Although on this occasion he added to the force of his indictment by keeping clear of personalities, he threw restraint aside during the mayoralty campaign of the following spring. With Edgar Bancroft and other "young reformers," he supported the victorious candidacy of George B. Swift against Mayor Hopkins, whom he denounced for consorting

40. Letter of Aug. 19, 1894.

41. Letter from Hotel Victoria, London, to Florence Pullman, Aug. 23, 1894.

42. FOL to Florence Pullman, Nov. (?), 1894, Dec. 3 and 8 (?), 1894; MSS of FOL's speeches of Nov. 15, 1894, at a banquet of the Two Million Club, and of Jan. 6, 1895, at a banquet of the Review Club.

43. *The Sunset Club, Chicago: The Meetings of 1894–95* (Chicago, n.d.), pp. 239 ff. In this speech, he trained his guns upon both political parties, charging that many of the ward committeemen "have studied political economy only over the bar of the saloon of which they have been the proprietor."

with "Frenchy the Gambler, Kid Harris, Big Ed Hennessey, Red Davis, and the Hon. Hinky Dink." To his great satisfaction, the voters of Chicago authorized the application of a merit test to many office-holders, in accordance with the option recently extended to the city by the state legislature.

Politics, however, were largely beyond Florence Pullman's horizon at this time, but she recognized that Lowden, unlike most of her suitors, had won a place of leadership among his fellows by his own merits.[44] Although nearly thirty-five years of age, he still had the dreams and enthusiasm of youth. She believed that he wooed her with more speed than discretion, but she welcomed a suitor who did not fawn upon her and was not ashamed to quote poetry or talk about the masters of literature. Above all, he appealed to her heart. From the time of their first meeting, they were at ease in each other's company, almost like old friends. Merely to read or talk together made an evening altogether enjoyable. In his letters to her, he frankly admitted the wide social and financial gulf between them, but he wrote to her as to his equal. He convinced her that she and not her wealth had won his complete devotion.[45]

By early January, 1895, they had reached a secret understanding and wrote back and forth in terms of endearment. Mrs. Pullman was abroad from January 10 to April 5, and, for once, her daughter did not go with her. To Lowden's despair, however, she left Chicago with her father for many weeks. It was also an unhappy time for Florence Pullman. When she told her father in February of her love for Frank Lowden, he reminded her of her promise not to become engaged without his prior consent and admonished her to see and write to the young lawyer far less frequently.[46] She dutifully acquiesced. Following Mrs. Pullman's return from abroad and before her departure with her family in late June for the Thousand Islands, she braved her husband's displeasure by arranging occasional meetings between Lowden and her daughter. The latter refused to go to greater lengths in defiance of her father and persuaded the reluctant Lowden to accept her "wait and hope" strategy. But he found the inaction a torture—a seemingly unsolvable personal problem which aggravated the strain of his unusually heavy law practice. Becoming nervous and depressed, he was urged by Florence Pullman and others of his friends to go abroad for a rest.[47] After visiting his parents in Iowa over the Fourth of July, he and three companions booked their passage for Le Havre on the S.S. "St. Louis," sailing from New York on August 7. Before leaving Chicago for the East Coast, he ushered at Kenesaw M. Landis' wedding and spoke at the annual dinner of the Beta Theta Pi fraternity.

44. Florence Pullman to FOL, Sept. 10 (?), 1895: "It makes me far happier to think of your attaining the place you now occupy alone and unaided, than if you had been born to wealth and influence and distinction."

45. Frequent entries in her 1895 diary and his many letters to her early in that year.

46. By letter of Apr. 11, 1895, FOL reminded her that the evening before had been the first time in seven weeks that he had been permitted to see her. He asked forgiveness for the sharp words he had spoken to her about her father.

47. Her letter to him of July 19, 1895, and his letters to her of July 27, Aug. 1 and 4, 1895.

On the eve of his embarkation, he called upon Florence Pullman at her parents' seaside home in Elberon, New Jersey. As keepsakes, she gave him one of her handkerchiefs and a copy of Ian Maclaren's *Beside the Bonnie Briar Bush,* with passages marked for his special enjoyment. He left with her a volume of sermons and essays by their beloved Dr. David Swing. They also devised a brief cable code which served them thereafter for life. The word "eternal," for example, meant to them alone "I send you all the love a human heart can hold." Although they agreed that neither would mail a letter to the other oftener than once a fortnight, they further agreed that each might write to the other every day and let the sheets accumulate. As a result, one of Lowden's epistles ran to forty-three pages![48]

"For sentiment's sake," he revisited in Paris the restaurants and historic sites where Florence Pullman had been his guide and interpreter the year before. Above all, however, he enjoyed what was for him a veritable pilgrimage to Scotland, the home of Burns, his favorite poet, and Scott, his favorite novelist. As always when abroad, he was an indefatigable and romantic tourist, seeking to see every important place mentioned in the Waverley cycle, as well as Scott's home at Abbottsford and Burns's birthplace at Ayr. Reveling in the moods of melancholy or exaltation that came over him as he stood upon soil hallowed by important events, he tried to describe his emotions in his letters. His companions accused him of being "blasé" because he declined to go with them to the London variety shows. But he assured Florence Pullman that he was determined to become more worthy of her by devoting every moment of his trip to self-improvement. On the return passage, when the books at hand repelled him because they dealt with the "mean and sordid in life," he talked politics with Charles R. Crisp, Democratic speaker of the House of Representatives, and Senator James Smith, Jr., of New Jersey.[49]

As soon as his ship docked at New York, he hurried to Elberon to spend a week end with the Pullmans. Whatever of mental and physical relaxation the voyage had brought him was destroyed by the cold formality of the master of the house. Lowden went there in high hopes that the appropriate time had come to ask Mr. Pullman for his daughter's hand in marriage. But the words remained unspoken because the father's attitude left no doubt about what his answer would be. To add to Lowden's bitterness as he boarded his train for Chicago, he knew that Florence Pullman had been forbidden to write to him.[50]

Later that month Mr. Pullman lifted the ban to the extent of obliging her

48. FOL to Florence Pullman, Aug. 7–14 and Aug. 14–17, 1895; her wire to him, Aug. 4, 1895; Mrs. G. M. Pullman's diary, Aug. 6 and 7, 1895.

49. FOL to Florence Pullman, Aug. 21–28 (?) and Sept. 1–6 (?), 1895. Between Aug. 15 and 19, he was in Le Havre, Paris, Versailles, and Trouville; on Aug. 20 and 21 and between Aug. 28 and Sept. 1, in London and Oxford; and between Aug. 21 and 27, in Scotland.

50. Mrs. G. M. Pullman's diary, Sept. 7–11, 1895; FOL to Florence Pullman, Sept. 11 and 15, 1895.

to send Lowden what was probably the most painful letter she ever wrote or he ever received. Her confession to her father of her secret engagement led him to declare that his confidence in her integrity would be restored only if she asked Lowden formally to release her from her pledge. She wrote:

> I know my own disposition so well, and what a slave I am to my conscience, that my fear is that I could not overcome the consciousness that I had failed to atone for my fault, and it might lead to unhappiness between us. Above everything else I want my husband to have absolute *trust* and confidence in me, and also to know that I am strong enough to make sacrifices. . . . Don't think . . . that my love for you is not greater at this moment than it has ever been. . . . I have a strong feeling that the moment I have submitted to Papa's stronger will . . . he will feel that his position has been maintained with dignity, and that there will be nothing then he will not do to promote my happiness.[51]

Lowden, of course, gave her the release she so little desired and sought to comfort her as much as the unhappy situation permitted. Instead of expressing bitterness against her father, he took the full blame for not cultivating his good will more tactfully. Nevertheless, "weary and broken," he would go to his parents' home to "find peace." Having been "too proud and self reliant," he welcomed this "dark vale" of suffering because it would "chasten and soften" his spirit and mold him into a "better man." "My love for you came without my bidding," he assured her. "It will not go at my bidding. . . . My cross is that I have made you unhappy when my one aim in life was to make you happy."[52]

Florence Pullman's forecast that her father would veer around as soon as he had had his own way began to come true late in October. From then until Christmas he permitted Lowden to visit her on Wednesday and Sunday evenings of each week. In mid-December, as he was walking the four blocks from the Pullman home to the Calumet Club, he fell on the ice and sprained his ankle so badly that he could not leave his room for several days. Family tradition has it that, after limping to the Prairie Avenue home on one of his semiweekly calls, he and Florence Pullman were told by her father that their engagement had his blessing. No more welcome Christmas gift could have been bestowed.[53] The Chicago papers on January 9, 1896, included a rumor of their betrothal, although ten more days went by before the formal announcement appeared. The highly complimentary press notices ironically reported that Mrs. Pullman and not her husband had opposed the match.[54] Both he and his daughter received many letters from complete strangers, expressing satisfaction that an upstanding American citizen and not an effete

51. Florence Pullman to FOL, Sept. 26, 1895: "I am being punished for not doing what I honestly thought would be better delayed"—that is, telling her father of her "understanding" with FOL.

52. FOL to Florence Pullman, Oct. 1, 1895.

53. Conversation of the author with Mrs. C. P. Miller; entries in Mrs. Pullman's diary between Oct. 27 and Nov. 6, 1895.

54. The Jan. 9, 1896, issues of *Chicago Post, Dispatch, Evening News,* and *Journal.*

European nobleman was the lucky man. "You have displayed most excellent judgment," a Texan wrote, "in discarding the constitutional and intellectual imbeciles of aristocracy and the pampered paupers of dead dynasties who are seeking only to augment their perishing fame and fortune by swapping titles for ducats."[55]

Γo Frank Lowden, who had lived for so long as his own master, the many new social and financial demands occasioned by his engagement and approaching marriage came as a shock.[56] By late February, the wedding date had been fixed for April 29. Although the chief burden of the elaborate preparations fell upon the willing shoulders of Mrs. Pullman and her daughter, Lowden discovered that much was also expected of him. "With you, precious," he wrote half-seriously, "I can see in luminous light the advantages of an elopement. The modern conventionalities which painfully lead up to and then hedge about the wedding ceremonies are almost in restraint of marriage."[57] There were a house to rent, redecorate, and furnish, ushers to arrange for, gifts to buy, invitation and announcement lists to prepare, a wedding trip to plan, stag dinners to attend, and many social and business appointments where he and Florence Pullman must appear together. The "modern conventionality," however, which drew from him the most satirical comment, was his obligation to call alone upon the "first families" of Chicago whom he had never met but who had written to Florence Pullman upon the announcement of her engagement. During much of this time she was in Florida or in New York City assembling her trousseau. Although he felt lonely during her absence, he at least could write or wire her now to his heart's content.

Florence Pullman and Frank Lowden were wed in the drawing room of her home at eight o'clock on the evening of April 29. Her uncles, the Rev. James M. Pullman, of Lynn, Massachusetts, and the Rev. Royal A. Pullman, of Baltimore, read the Episcopal marriage service. About two hundred people witnessed the ceremony, and nearly one thousand more came in later for the reception. The guests in whom the bridegroom took the most pride were his father and mother,[58] but the newspapers gave more emphasis to the Andrew Carnegies, the John D. Rockefellers, the Henry Flaglers, the Stephen B. Elkinses, Supreme Court Justices Brown, Field, and Harlan, General and Mrs. Nelson Miles, former President and Mrs. Benjamin Harrison, the Mar-

55. R. H. Edwards, Farmersville, Texas, to Florence Pullman, Mar. 24, 1896.

56. In a speech to the Chicago Jewelers' Association on the evening of Jan. 9, 1896, after quoting almost no end of poetry mentioning jewels, FOL ruefully continued, ". . . may not the poet be called the jeweler of literature, or, better still, the jeweler be called the poet of trade—though . . . when I received a bill from a jeweler just after Christmas, poet was not the word I used . . . but poesy and piracy are akin."

57. FOL to Florence Pullman, Feb. 26, 1896.

58. FOL to Florence Pullman, undated but early August, 1895: "I think I am as proud of my parents, though *their* life . . . has always been simple and commonplace, as though I were sprung from royal lineage. And I know that my Mother, the opportunity given, would have been a Queen anywhere."

shall Fields, the Robert Lincolns, the Philip Armours, the Shelby Culloms, Mrs. James G. Blaine, Mrs. Ulysses S. Grant, Mrs. Philip H. Sheridan, Mrs. John A. Logan, and many other notables. Together, they made the occasion "one of the most brilliant in many years."[59]

Late that evening Mr. and Mrs. Frank O. Lowden left the Union Station in the "famous private car of the Car King" for a ten-day stay in Washington.[60] Not long afterward they visited the Thousand Islands, where the bridegroom had his first glimpse of "Castle Rest," the Pullmans' summer home. Its towers, rising from a rocky island with the blue St. Lawrence as its moat, made it seem like a real castle to Lowden, so recently from an Iowa farm. He at last had won his princess.

59. *Chicago Evening Post,* Apr. 29, 1896; *Chicago Chronicle,* Apr. 30, 1896; *Chicago Legal News,* May 2, 1896.

60. Mrs. Pullman's diary, Apr. 29, 1896: "Everything passed off splendidly." *Chicago Legal News,* May 2, 1896: "Too many eager gapers at the Union Station sent the blinds of the . . . [car] . . . down with a bang."

CHAPTER IV

A CAREER AT ITS TURNING POINT, 1896–1902

At the time of his marriage Frank Lowden was known about Chicago as an able lawyer with an ever lengthening list of corporation clients. He was a leading Republican soldier of "Hamline's reform brigade" in municipal politics and an able speaker—perhaps even too ready to accommodate with remarks, grave or gay, scholarly or flamboyantly oratorical, to fit any occasion. The city's frothy night life attracted him not at all, but his happiness demanded the companionship of men of his own tastes. Both then and later he found it hard to resist an invitation to join a club or society, whether political, literary, fraternal, or recreational in its aim. Even before his marriage, appointments had crowded his days and many of his evenings.[1] Thereafter, his time was invaded by a host of new demands—so many, in fact, that he soon had to choose a main channel for his career. Both Mrs. Lowden and he found it a most difficult decision to make and one which would largely shape the whole of his future.

Lowden did not exaggerate when he told Florence Pullman in the summer of 1895 that "professional success has now come to me in much larger measure than I ever expected or hoped for. . . . I have just begun to taste the sweets of an honorable and not ordinary place in my profession."[2] The Chicago press remarked upon his "deserved popularity with his fellow lawyers," his "handsome professional income," "his luxurious offices in the Temple Building," and his leading position among the "young lawyers of the Chicago bar."[3] He was determined to become "the greatest lawyer" of his generation and was "fired with a desire," he assured Florence Pullman, "to be of some service to my time and kind." To this she gravely replied, "We will work together, sweetheart, for the best and most honorable place the world can give you."[4]

If his career were not to be submerged under the title "husband of Flor-

1. The *Chicago Legal News,* Feb. 14, 1899, p. 203, lists thirteen clubs of which he was a member.

2. This quotation combines a sentence from each of two letters by FOL to Florence Pullman, one on Aug. 1 and the other on Aug. 4, 1895.

3. *Chicago Inter-Ocean,* June 23, 1895; *Chicago Post,* Jan. 9, 1896; *Chicago Legal News,* May 2, 1896.

4. FOL to Florence Pullman, Feb. 21 and Sept. 15, 1895. Florence Pullman to FOL, Sept. 10(?), 1895.

Frank O. Lowden, Senior at the State University of Iowa,
1885.

Frank O. Lowden, Schoolboy

Frank Lowden's Parents and Sisters about 1890. From left to right, upper row: May Lowden Hammer, Isabel Lowden, Frank Lowden, Alice Lowden Sammis, Eva Lowden Sheldon. From left to right, lower row: Lorenzo O. Lowden, Eleanor Lowden, Nancy Breg Lowden.

Frank O. Lowden about 1896

Mrs. Frank O. Lowden about 1896

Lieutenant Colonel Frank Lowden, First Regiment, Illinois National Guard, about 1900.

The Wayne MacVeagh House at 1710 Massachusetts Avenue, Washington, D.C., where Mr. and Mrs. Lowden Lived from 1908 to 1911.

Mr. and Mrs. Lowden's House (extreme left of picture) *at 1912 Prairie Avenue, Chicago, from 1899 to 1906.*

Frank Lowden, Shorthorn Breeder, and "Ceremonious Archer," about 1905

Frank Lowden, President of the Holstein-Friesian Association of America, 1921–30

Mrs. Lowden and Her Children, 1904. From left to right: *Florence Lowden, Frances O. Lowden, Mrs. Lowden, George M. Pullman Lowden, Harriet E. Lowden.*

The Original House at "Sinnissippi" Farm

"Castle Rest," Alexandria Bay, New York

Sequel to the "Deadlocked Convention" of 1904, as Portrayed by John T. McCutcheon.
(*By permission of the* Chicago Tribune.)

The Lowden House at "Sinnissippi," Built in 1906

The Executive Mansion, Springfield, Illinois, in 1917

Moffett Studio

Frank Lowden, Candidate for Governor of Illinois, 1916

Governor Lowden, Former Speaker of the House of Representatives, Joseph G. Cannon, and Mr. Justice James H. Cartwright of the Supreme Court of Illinois, about 1920.

Governor Lowden Astride "Iowa"

ence Pullman," he would have to be conspicuously successful. Although she brought him no dowry, she soon had an annual income which dwarfed his $15,000 or $20,000 from legal fees. During their life together, he served as her principal business adviser, investing her surplus and managing some of her properties. When he acquired real estate of his own, the account books distinguished what was his from what was hers, but the lack of differentiation in spirit remained far more important. No controversy seems ever to have arisen between Frank and Florence Lowden over a matter of money. Following the death of her father and mother, the trust departments of two Chicago banks cared for her life-interest in the large bequests to her. Except for these, she and her husband were equal partners who virtually pooled their incomes, however unequal, for their mutual use and happiness.

Lowden's familiarity with the world of big business necessarily deepened and widened after he became the son-in-law of George M. Pullman. The unhappy incidents of the days of his courtship were quickly forgotten, and each man soon admired and trusted the other. Even two months before the marriage, Pullman asked his daughter to send his love to Lowden whenever she wrote to him.[5] By the autumn of 1896 the influence of his father-in-law and the investments of his wife were drawing him further than ever before into the affairs of corporations. His legal career thereupon entered a new and, unknown to him, its final phase.

Edgar Lee Masters recalled nearly forty years later that "about 1895," at the Calumet Club, he witnessed a "saturnalia" where "champagne flowed like a mountain stream" as the "Moore brothers of Rock Island Railroad fame," with the Fields, Pullmans, and "corporation lawyer" Lowden among their guests, celebrated "their absorption of Diamond Match."[6] This may have happened, although if Masters meant by "absorption" the cornering of much Diamond Match Company stock, the date was 1896 and the banquet a premature crowing over a victory which was never fully won.

Two Chicago lawyers, William H. Moore and his younger brother James, had organized this corporation about seven years before. By consolidating nine factories and several soft-wood timber companies and by securing more capital, they had made the concern by 1896 a huge and profitable enterprise with an international clientele.[7] On the strength of this and other similar feats, including the formation of the New York Biscuit Company, the Moores became Chicago's outstanding promoters of business mergers. William was president of the biscuit company and first vice-president of the match company, while James served as second vice-president of each. They had gained large wealth and, better still, an excellent credit rating with Chicago bankers and leading entrepreneurs, including Philip D. Armour and George M. Pullman.

5. Florence Pullman to FOL, Mar. 1, 1896.

6. Edgar Lee Masters, "Introduction to Chicago," *American Mercury,* January, 1934.

7. *New York Times,* Aug. 5, 1896.

Thus in 1896, when the Moores and a few others set out to make "a killing" by skyrocketing the market value of match and biscuit stocks through heavy purchases of them on margin, they could rely upon eminently respectable bankers and businessmen to accept these securities as collateral for large advances of cash.[8] Fortunately for these lenders, they limited their accommodations to what the stocks were normally worth rather than the "aerial height" to which the brothers pushed them by manipulating the market. Without formal authorization by the boards of directors, the Moores also used money from the surplus funds of each company to buy in its stock on the company's behalf.[9] Within a short time these securities almost doubled in market value. The mad speculation in them comprised much of the business of the Chicago stock exchange during the summer of 1896.

This frantic trading came to an abrupt and shocking end on August 4, when the heavily overextended Moores defaulted on their contracts and threw themselves upon the mercy of their creditors.[10] To ward off a financial panic, or at least so drastic a collapse of the match and biscuit securities as to injure severely the two innocent companies along with the creditors of the speculators, the stock exchange closed its doors for three months. Wall Street brokers derided the financial naïveté of their Chicago counterparts.[11]

During this period a complicated readjustment, unnecessary to detail here, pooled the paper losses, as well as the actual losses, among the principal parties in interest. Large investors in the two companies agreed not to drive down the market value of the securities by unloading their own. Probably it speaks much for the business ethics of the 1890's that the Moore brothers, notwithstanding their responsibility for the crash and their narrow escape from being prosecuted for criminally misusing Diamond and Biscuit funds, received such tender consideration that they soon were able to resume their operations. Although they had to resign their positions, their voices still carried weight in shaping the policies of the two companies. As a result of the reorganization, George M. Pullman became the owner of sufficient New York Biscuit Company stock to have Frank Lowden in January, 1897, named general counsel of the corporation and one of its directors.[12]

Following a price war earlier in the decade, this firm forced its principal rivals, the American Biscuit Company and the United States Biscuit Company, into a price-fixing and division-of-sales-territory compact.[13] The two latter firms reopened the conflict more aggressively than ever in the late summer of 1896, evidently believing that the forays of the Moores had sufficiently damaged New York Biscuit Company's prestige in the Chicago area

8. *Chicago Tribune,* Aug. 5 and 9, 1896; *Economist* (Chicago), Aug. 8, 1896, p. 154.

9. *New York Times,* Aug. 5 and 7, 1896.

10. *New York Tribune,* Aug. 5, 1896.

11. *New York Times,* Sept. 19, 1896; *Chicago Tribune,* Nov. 5, 1896.

12. *Bankers, Merchants, Manufacturers* (Chicago), Oct. 31, 1896; *New York Times,* Aug. 7, 1896, and Feb. 4, 1897.

13. *Chicago News,* Sept. 16, 1897.

to make it an easy victim. The attorney of the American Biscuit Company was Adolphus W. Green of Chicago, a foeman worthy of Lowden's steel and one who eventually became his good friend. But for the moment they led opposing forces and couched their correspondence in martial language. Each was "throwing hot shot into the camp" of the other. Lowden had financial backers whose stubbornness as fighters was almost proverbial in the world of business. They stood ready, until their enemies cried for mercy, to cover New York Biscuit Company deficits resulting from selling its products at below-cost prices. "We are in war," wrote Lowden and his associates in the early spring of 1897, "and we will use our entire assets, if necessary, to win. . . . The American Company is being hurt in the fight more than we are. We are willing to confer with one or both Companies but the conference must be in Chicago."[14]

Even while these firms outwardly engaged in deadly battle—incidentally providing consumers with crackers at sacrifice prices—their attorneys conferred behind the scenes about a permanent settlement of their differences.[15] By the early summer of 1897 it was common knowledge among stockbrokers that Pullman and Armour had been mainly responsible for the erratic fluctuations in cracker prices during recent months and were trying to form a "pool" so as to control the entire business of cracker-baking and selling.[16]

William H. Moore, Adolphus Green, and Frank Lowden devoted much time in the autumn of 1897 and early winter of 1898 to discovering how to convert the three competing companies into one gigantic biscuit-making concern, how to raise the twelve million dollars probably needed to buy out stockholders averse to the contemplated merger, how to bring other bakeries into it, and how to finance plant expansion and the underwriting of new stock. Helped by the emergence of the nation's economic life from the prolonged depression following the panic of 1893, the promoters' money-raising efforts in Chicago and eastern seaboard cities were markedly successful.[17] By early December, Philip Armour, a man hard to please, expressed satisfaction to Lowden that the favorable outlook warranted higher cracker prices but urged a speedy completion of the merger. To effect this, he recommended that stock subscriptions be solicited, above all, from "big men" whose purchases would "act as cheese on the platter to the little fellows."[18] Just before Christmas, Lowden came back from New York feeling sanguine of an early victory. By that time, one hundred and thirty-eight bakeries had consented to join. Every one of these small, independent concerns pledged to raise its prices to whatever level the promoters might dictate.[19]

14. G. H. Webster, C. Buckingham, FOL, and H. J. Evans, to "?" but probably to the stockholders of the New York Biscuit Company, Mar. 29, 1897.

15. FOL to E. N. Blake, Arlington, Massachusetts, Apr. 12, 1897.

16. *New York Sun* and *Chicago News,* each of June 4, 1897.

17. FOL to Mrs. Lowden, Sept. 13, 15, 16, 29, 1897.

18. P. D. Armour to FOL, Dec. 4, 1897, and Jan. 17, 1898.

19. *Chicago Post,* Nov. 22, Dec. 3, 4, and 18, 1897, and Feb. 9, 1898; *Chicago Inter-Ocean,* Dec. 6 and 23, 1897, and Jan. 1 and 18, 1898.

The new business giant, the National Biscuit Company, gained a New Jersey charter on February 3, 1898. Practically all its $25,000,000 of preferred stock and $30,000,000 of common had been subscribed for.[20] Benjamin F. Crawford, of Mansfield, Ohio, was its president, Lowden its second vice-president and one of its fifteen directors, and Adolphus W. Green its principal attorney. The *New York Times* estimated that it controlled 90 per cent of the commercial biscuit-baking in the United States. For their services, the four chief promoters, including Lowden, apparently received blocks of common stock worth $1,590,000 on the market. Whether each man pocketed an equal amount is unknown, but Lowden's portion, no doubt, seemed very large when compared with his customary legal fees. The *Chicago News*, in line with its usual hostility toward the doings of the Pullman family, observed that he would most likely "make a success of his new business and his friends will look for pronounced improvements in the dainty white hats and jumpers all cracker bakers wear. Mr. Lowden will probably bake for the Pullman buffet cars."[21]

For the next eight years he continued to hold his offices in the National Biscuit Company and regularly attended the directors' meetings in New York City. As a member of its executive committee, he persuaded the management to stop taking rebates from railroads. In accomplishing this, he was much aided by the threat of the attorney-general of Ohio to institute suit under its antitrust law. Adolphus W. Green, who became the chairman of the board of directors, relied heavily upon Lowden for support, calling him a "tower of strength" and so trustworthy in counsel that "when I can not bring you around to my opinion . . . I am pretty well convinced that . . . [it] . . . is not the right one."[22] The company's general policy was to add to its capital at need and "secure the largest volume of business at the smallest percentage of profits consistent with conservative business methods." When, in 1899, it first put its "Uneeda Biscuits" on sale and shortly thereafter its "Uneeda Jin Jer Wafers," it could not keep pace with the eastern demand and curtailed its advertising until it could build, or otherwise acquire, enough ovens to supply the fast-growing market. Even before this expansion took place, the company sold sixty-five million packages of biscuits and wafers in one year. During Lowden's association with the company, it averaged a 7 per cent quarterly dividend on its preferred stock and, after 1899, 4 per cent quarterly on its common. At the time of his resignation in 1906, he commented to Green, "I am proud of the Biscuit Co. and proud to have been connected with it."[23]

A smaller promotional venture, but one which probably brought Lowden even greater satisfaction because he undertook it almost alone, was the reorganization of the American Radiator Company in late 1898 and early

20. *Chicago Record,* Feb. 7, 1898. The Pullman estate was said to have taken $500,000.
21. *Chicago News,* Feb. 4, 1898; *New York Times,* Feb. 4, 1898.
22. A. W. Green, Chicago, to FOL, Mar. 23, 1899.
23. FOL to A. W. Green, May 18, 1906.

1899. Green had presided at its birth about six years before, and his friend-ship brought Lowden into a profitable connection with it.[24] By the close of 1898 its rapidly mounting sales of steam- and water-heating equipment ex-ceeded the capacity of its factories. At this juncture Lowden carried through the underwriting of new stock sufficient to increase the capital of the com-pany to $10,000,000. He also drew under its aegis the Standard Radiator Company of Buffalo, the Titusville Iron Company of Titusville, Pennsyl-vania, and the St. Louis Radiator Company. He effected all this with sur-prising ease because the eagerness of a few wealthy businessmen and bank-ers to participate led to a large oversubscription of the new stock on the first day it was offered. The owners of the three rival concerns, mentioned above, sold out to the reorganized company for blocks of its stock rather than for cash. Thereby, the American Radiator Company's control of the national market for its line of products increased from about 50 to about 75 per cent.[25]

Among its fourteen directors besides Lowden were Clarence M. Woolley, secretary and soon president, and Charles H. Hodges, treasurer. These three men became lifelong friends. Indeed, all the members of the small group con-trolling the company remained unusually close-knit and congenial. Once again, Lowden's associates heeded his plea against rebates. For some years they paid no dividends on the preferred stock and inconsequential ones on the common, because they plowed back most of the profits into the busi-ness. Under Woolley's able leadership, the company grew apace and opened branch factories in France and Germany. The New York City *Fi-nancial Review* declared that Lowden, in his relationship to the company, had "an enterprising spirit, tenacity, and considerable progressiveness."[26] When he resigned as a director in 1906, his record led Woolley to comment:

> The splendid service you rendered in the initial work of bringing our company into existence did not cease when this was accomplished. Your counsel, born of a heart-interest in the enterprise, and a firm conviction that it would win the right to be recognized as one of the substantial industrial institutions of the country, exerted a powerful influence in helping us to achieve our purpose in this regard. Your advice was ever on the side of conservatism but it did not lack the vigorous elements of progressiveness and enterprise.[27]

Long after he severed his connection with the company, he received from Woolley detailed accounts of its growth and prosperity. Whenever Lowden was in Europe, he used its branch offices as his mailing addresses and en-joyed getting together with the overseas staff.[28]

Lowden's third and last excursion into the field of big-business promotion

24. *Chicago Times-Herald,* Feb. 12, 1899.

25. Mrs. Lowden's diary, Feb. 11, 1899; *Journal of Commerce* (N.Y.), Feb. 14, 1899.

26. *Financial Review* (New York), Mar. 28, 1900.

27. C. M. Woolley, Chicago, to FOL, Aug. 21, 1906.

28. FOL to C. M. Woolley, Apr. 11, 1910; Woolley to FOL, Apr. 8 and 15, 1910.

caused him more worry than the other two combined. At its close he felt a deep sense of relief that, after many narrow squeaks, he had managed to carry the enterprise through with fair success and even make a little profit for himself. In 1899, the two-year-old Shelby Steel Tube Company, operating under a Pennsylvania charter with its central office in Cleveland, was one of about fifteen firms in the United States engaged in the manufacture of seamless steel tubing. Although its day of prosperity seemed to be waning as the bicycle "craze" gradually subsided, the company owned valuable patents. Furthermore, its product should find an increasing sale for many other uses besides bicycle frames.[29] With a decline in business as its short-term outlook, however, its majority stockholders wished to offset the shrinking market by combining with rival concerns. If this were done, the price of tubing might hold steady or even rise. A merger would also lower managerial costs, reduce the expense of competitive advertising and selling, and lessen the outgo for patent royalties. Furthermore, a "reorganization . . . [will] give an opportunity to influential people, who will help to extend the business . . . to acquire . . . stock . . . [which if distributed widely] will more readily have a market value." The income resulting from victories in patent infringement suits against outside manufacturers would be a welcome by-product of a merger.[30]

After Lowden had convinced about a dozen rival firms that they would gain by uniting, he organized them into a new Shelby Steel Tube Company, incorporated in early February, 1900, under a New Jersey charter. Its capital, comprising $6,000,000 worth of preferred stock and $9,000,000 worth of common, was over double that of its predecessor.[31] Compared with the latter's annual output of 57,000,000 feet of tubing, the new firm could produce about 85 per cent more in the same time. Signifying the financial tieup between it and the big American Bicycle Company, its principal customer, three of the directors of the latter were also associated with Lowden on the twelve-man directorate of the Shelby concern. How much stock he received for his services is unknown.[32]

Although the new company paid a small quarterly dividend on its preferred stock during the early months of its operation, it was adversely affected from the outset by the Morgan-Rockefeller-Carnegie battle, leading, in April, 1901, to the birth of the United States Steel Corporation. In this conflict, one of Morgan's companies, backed by his unrivaled resources of cash and credit, was the National Tube Company of Pittsburgh. When

29. *Chicago Tribune,* Feb. 10, 1900; *New York Commercial,* Feb. 15, 1900.

30. *Iron Trade Review,* Mar. 22, 1900, p. 9; *Iron Age,* Mar. 29, 1900, p. 4.

31. Mrs. Lowden's diary, Feb. 9, 1900; *New York Commercial Advertiser,* Feb. 6, 1900; *Boston Transcript,* Feb. 10, 1900.

32. F. J. Carolan, FOL's brother-in-law, was also a director. A financial statement of the company in the *Chicago Daily News,* Feb. 10, 1900, says that $1,305,900 worth of common stock had been used for "fees, expenses, organization, etc." Hidden in this, no doubt, was FOL's remuneration.

Lowden was canvassing for purchasers of stock in the new Shelby firm, he prophesied that it would virtually monopolize the seamless steel-tubing business because National Tube's output consisted mainly of wrought iron.[33] This quickly proved to be a mistaken forecast. Consequently, Shelby Company stock sagged, and the holders soon began to dump it on the market. To slow up this decline and to bolster the waning confidence of investors in the new concern, Lowden put more and more of his own money into its stock.[34] These purchases seemed the more advisable because, in late 1900, J. P. Morgan and Company began to nibble for the acquisition of Shelby Tube. To better its own buying position, the House of Morgan subjected Shelby to the cutthroat competition of the National Tube Company. By early April, 1901, however, rumors that the newly formed United States Steel Corporation wished to purchase Shelby Tube favorably affected the market value of its securities.[35]

During the preceding six months Lowden had frequently visited Cleveland and New York City on Shelby business. He confided to his wife that he found the matter "an awful burden" which he would be lucky to unload without financial loss.[36] Not until June 22 were the general terms agreed upon for the sale of the company to United States Steel. Two months more went by before all the details of the transfer could be ironed out. The United States Steel Corporation gave one share of its preferred stock for every two and two-thirds shares of Shelby turned in and exchanged the common stock in the ratio of one for four. This arrangement yielded some Shelby stockholders a small profit on their investment.[37] To Frank Lowden the entire episode had been so fraught with toil and worry that, unlike his work as an architect of the National Biscuit Company and the American Radiator Company, he rarely mentioned it in later years.

These were only the more outstanding business enterprises in which he participated prominently between 1896 and 1902. Among his trusteeships or directorships were the Pullman Company, the Pullman Loan and Savings Bank, the Kansas City, Pittsburg, and Gulf Railroad, the Goodrich Lake Transportation Company, the National Bank of the Republic, the Parmelee Passenger and Baggage Transfer Company, and the London Guarantee and Accident Company, Ltd. For several years he served as president of the Pullman Loan and Savings Bank, and in April, 1902, he declined the presidency of the Chicago Title and Trust Company.[38]

A short time before, he had helped to organize a company designed to

33. *New York Times,* Mar. 4, May 19, 26, July 13, 1899, and Aug. 5, 1900.

34. Mrs. Lowden's diary, between April, 1901, and July, 1901, *passim; Chicago Record-Herald,* Feb. 10, 1900.

35. *Chicago Record-Herald,* Apr. 6, 1901.

36. FOL to Mrs. Lowden, undated, but late May, 1901.

37. *New York Commercial,* June 25 and Aug. 17, 1901; *Iron Trade Review,* June 27, 1901; *Iron Age,* Aug. 29, 1901, p. 18.

38. Mrs. Lowden's diary, Apr. 5, 1902; *Chicago Inter-Ocean,* Apr. 10, 1902.

provide Chicago with a "permanent exposition building." Thanks to the efforts of this group, the huge Coliseum at Wabash Avenue and Fifteenth Street opened its doors in the summer of 1900. At the dedicatory exercises during Grand Army Week, Lowden spoke for the stockholders in "presenting" the building to Mayor Carter Harrison, Jr., for public use.[39] In similar fashion two years later, he joined with Harold F. McCormick, Daniel H. Burnham, Bryan Lathrop, and others to buy land on Michigan Avenue as a site for the home of the Chicago Symphony Orchestra. On Christmas Eve, 1904, he and Mrs. Lowden attended their first concert in the new building.[40]

The carrying-through of these two semicivic projects, as well as his association with banks and other corporations, deeply impressed Lowden with the importance of credit in the nation's economic life. Addressing an audience of Chicago bankers in the spring of 1902, he adorned his thought about this subject by saying:

It is credit, not money, which makes the sea white-winged with commerce. It is credit which whispers to the spindles in the factory until they sing the simple song of contented industry. It is credit that fills the earth with hope and makes all seasons Spring. . . . If you think the banks of this city exist only to lend money, you are mistaken. If this were their object they would not rise in dignity above the pawnshop.

Most of this business highly interested and financially rewarded Frank Lowden, but it distracted him from the practice of law. For about two years after his marriage he continued to appear frequently in court on behalf of his clients, even while he met the growing demands of his other more complicated affairs. Finally, on March 1, 1898, he gained some relief in his legal work by becoming senior partner in the firm of Lowden, Estabrook, and Davis. Henry D. Estabrook, forty-four years of age, had come from Omaha two years before and quickly gained a reputation in Chicago as an able lawyer and an unusually eloquent public speaker. Herbert J. Davis, four years younger than Estabrook and equally stalwart in his Republicanism, had been his associate in both Omaha and Chicago.[41] Until June, 1902, when the partnership dissolved because of Davis' ill-health and Estabrook's decision to become chief counsel of the Western Union Telegraph Company, the firm was busy with important cases in civil and criminal law before the state and federal courts, including the Supreme Court of the United States.[42]

Although Lowden believed that the outstanding attorneys of the future would be specialists in some particular compartment of the law, he continued to engage in general practice. Frauds, wills, contracts, personal injuries, patents, copyrights, and bankruptcy suggest the variety of business on his

39. *Chicago Times-Herald,* Nov. 23, 1897, Aug. 12 and 26, 1900; *Chicago Tribune,* Aug. 26, 1900.

40. *Chicago American,* Dec. 6, 1902; *Chicago Post,* Feb. 13, 1903.

41. Mrs. Lowden's diary, Feb. 28 and Mar. 1, 1898; *Chicago Tribune,* Jan. 7, 1901.

42. Following the dissolution of the partnership, FOL's law office continued to be in the Temple Building, 184 La Salle Street.

office docket. Here was none of the monotonous routine for which he would always have so much aversion. "I am absolutely satisfied," he assured his wife in July, 1898, "that no other work will ever give me the pure intellectual joy which I derive from the Law. Probably this is because I have worked harder at it than anything else."[43] At that time he had just been elected president of the Law Club of Chicago and was composing a witty speech on "The Lawyer Out of Court" for use at the annual banquet of the Illinois State Bar Association.[44] Early in the next year he, John Barton Payne, J. H. Hamline, and others on a committee of the Chicago Bar Association prepared for introduction in the state legislature a bill to revise the procedure and jurisdiction of the police courts.[45]

During the autumn and winter of 1899–1900, a few months after his election as president of the Alumni Association of the Northwestern University Law School, he delivered there at least seventeen lectures on federal jurisprudence. The skeletal outline of this series, devoid of his personality, elaborations, and asides, is not impressive. Students wrote long afterward, however, to tell him how much they had profited from his instruction.[46] In October, 1902, among the ceremonies attending the installation of Edmund J. James as president of Northwestern University was the dedication of its new law building at the corner of Lake and Dearborn streets. In recognition of Lowden's donation of fifteen hundred dollars toward its books and furnishings, the assembly room bore his name. Associate Justice Oliver Wendell Holmes of the United States Supreme Court made the main address at the dedication. Following Holmes's speech, Lowden had him inscribe his name with a diamond-pointed stylus on a small plate of glass to be set in the ornamental mantel in Lowden Hall.[47] For the next fifteen years, although the University of Iowa retained his primary loyalty, he shared prominently in the activities of the Northwestern University Law School Alumni Association and counted the dean of the school, John H. Wigmore, among his closest friends.[48]

A minor evidence of Lowden's growing reputation was the frequency with which reporters asked his opinion about all sorts of subjects. In 1900, for example, the *Record* invited him and other "prominent Chicagoans" to comment upon whether a young man could succeed by merit alone. Lowden's lawyer-friend, Clarence Darrow, categorically answered that merit

43. FOL to Mrs. Lowden, July 13, and an undated letter of early September, 1898. As long as he lived, he continued to say that he had been happiest as a lawyer and was sorry he had given up his practice.

44. FOL to Mrs. Lowden, July 13, 15, and 17, 1898.

45. *Chicago Tribune,* Jan. 15, 1899.

46. T. S. Chapman, Chicago, to FOL, May 30, 1940.

47. The $1,500 donation may have been his salary as lecturer in 1899–1900. At least in a speech at Watseka, Illinois, Apr. 25, 1901, he said he had asked that his honorarium be used to purchase lawbooks.

48. In June, 1937, FOL gave the university 30 shares of International Harvester Company preferred stock to endow two Lowden-Wigmore prizes of $100 each.

did not guarantee success unless accompanied by "money, pull, and luck." Lowden characteristically took the opposite view. The increase in the number of big businesses meant more opportunities for bright beginners than ever before, because "a young man's chance to rise in a corporation is measured only by his ability."[49] About a year later he extended these remarks by comparing law and industry as fields for a career. He pointed out that changes in the industrial structure of the country worked to the great disadvantage of the general practitioner. Most of the ablest lawyers, he believed, would soon be found in the exclusive employ of big corporations. The number of lawyers, however, would decline. The consolidation of rival business firms reduced the amount of litigation. Title-guaranty companies and insurance companies of various types indemnified against risks formerly requiring the services of attorneys. People were no longer so prone to sue for slander or libel as in the past. "Today men litigate as a rule only when it may be profitable, and every lawyer will confess that litigation rarely ever pays pecuniarily—except to the lawyer." A generation ago, concluded Lowden, law was a more attractive career than business, but, for the reasons stated, the reverse had become true. In both pursuits, however, "there is always room at the top."[50]

Following his marriage, Lowden worried lest someone accuse him of resting on his oars because he had entered a family of great wealth. Determined to avoid an identification with the "idle rich" and to demonstrate that, even if his wife had been penniless, he could support her in luxury on his own income, he worked harder than ever before. He had abundant self-pride. Alert to the danger of being called a snob, he took special pains to cherish the friends of his leaner days. In the autumn of 1899 he was interrupted in his office so often when preparing his Northwestern law lectures that he stayed at home in the quiet of his library for several mornings in order to finish them. But, as he confessed to his wife, he felt much embarrassed to walk to the Loop in the forenoon because his acquaintances might conclude that he had grown lazy.[51]

Mrs. Lowden fully sympathized with his resolve to prove that he could forge a distinguished career for himself without the aid of the Pullman name or fortune, but she felt anxious lest his strenuous schedule undermine his health. She encouraged him in his favorite diversions and tactfully led him to add some new ones. She indulged his liking for historical novels by giving him expensively bound sets of his favorite authors and helped him collect out-of-the-way books about early Illinois and Abraham Lincoln.[52] They continued to read aloud to each other whenever a free evening permitted. The halting interest in card-playing of his bachelor days at the Calumet Club was

49. *Chicago Record-Herald,* Sept. 22, 1900.

50. The MS in the Lowden papers is dated July 5, 1901.

51. FOL to Mrs. Lowden, Sept. 8, 1899: "I know this is foolish weakness but I am so likely in my position to be misunderstood that it is perhaps pardonable."

52. Mrs. Lowden's diary, Mar. 23, June 26, and Nov. 27, 1898; Apr. 2, 1900.

nurtured after his marriage by lessons from an expert, but the time was still far in the future before he would be a persistent and formidable devotee of auction, and later of contract, bridge. During the first three winters of his early married life he proved to the satisfaction of himself and his tutor that a will to learn French, unaccompanied by any aptitude for it, profited little. "My French teacher is taciturn and rarely says anything complimentary," he confided to his wife. "But tonight he admitted he was surprised at my progress. If I make progress, I am sorry for those who make less. But I will keep at it until I can speak a little, although I confess to you I will never try to learn another foreign language."[53]

And then there was golf! Using Mrs. Pullman's clubs in the summer of 1897, until he could buy a set of his own, he enthusiastically played against Leroy Fuller, Wallace Kirk, or Walter Herrick on the links of Washington Park, the Chicago Golf Club at Wheaton, or the Onwentsia Club in Lake Forest. "Of course I was beaten," was his usual report to Mrs. Lowden. Both the enthusiasm and its disappointing outcome summed up, with fair accuracy, his lifetime of golf. Although some of the best professionals in the country coached him and he practiced assiduously, he never attained a mastery of the game. From his avid and prolonged pursuit of it he derived much relaxation and exercise and countless opportunities to joke about his own shortcomings as a golfer.

During the decade in Chicago before his marriage, Lowden rarely found an opportunity to indulge his boyhood liking for horseback riding, hunting, and fishing. After 1896 he let hunting remain a pleasant memory of his youth, but he gratified the other two hobbies more than ever before. Mrs. Lowden shared his enjoyment of the saddle and of driving a matched pair of thoroughbreds. Her diary of these years frequently tells about their rides together in Lincoln or Washington Park in their victoria, landau, brougham, or hansom cab behind "Fearnaught," "Starlight," "Pilot," or "Maximus." In the autumn of 1900, at a horse show in the Coliseum, with Charles G. Dawes the most active member of its committee on arrangements, the Lowdens won a first and a second prize for their entries.[54] As for fishing, the waters of the St. Lawrence provided bass and pickerel in abundance. A fish fry on Pitch Pine Point after a day of sport in their launch often contributed to the happiness of a summer vacation at "Castle Rest."[55]

The winter, too, brought its diversions. To Lowden, who never relished the formalities of "high society," the quiet evenings at home with his wife were the best of all, but they appeared frequently together at the opera, theater, and symphony concerts. Helped by a butler, a cook, and two maids,

53. FOL to Mrs. Lowden, Sept. 21, 1898.

54. *Chicago Tribune,* Oct. 21, 1900; *Chicago Post,* Oct. 31, 1900; *Chicago Inter-Ocean,* Nov. 4, 1900.

55. In 1902, at "Castle Rest," the Lowdens bought the steam yacht, the "Venice," for $25,000. It was about 100 feet long, could go 20 miles an hour, and needed an eight-man crew. From its skiffs, FOL did much fishing.

Mrs. Lowden's household tasks were mainly ones of planning and supervising. Fine needlework and knitting occupied many of her leisure hours. Her sure sense of what was appropriate in the furnishings of her home and in its hospitality elicited the admiration of her friends. The loyalty and affection of her personal maid and of the other servants bore witness to her skill in housekeeping. But she had many outside interests as well. Clarence, the coachman, often drove her to meetings of the Antiquarian Club and Dilettante Club or to the headquarters of one of the many social service organizations which benefited from her membership. Of these, the Auxiliary Board of St. Luke's Hospital, where a children's ward bore her name, was probably the chief.[56] When her husband had a director's meeting in New York, she usually accompanied him. They regularly stayed at the Holland House and, if his schedule permitted, spent two or three days attending the theater, shopping for their home or, separately, for the costly gifts which marked their birthdays, wedding anniversaries, and Christmases. During the winters he often went with her for a week or two to Ormond Beach, Florida, Thomasville, Georgia, or Hot Springs, Arkansas.

On most Sunday mornings when in Chicago they listened to Dr. Newell Dwight Hillis of Central Church or, after he left in 1899 for a Brooklyn pastorate, to the equally eloquent, but more scholarly, Dr. Frank W. Gunsaulus. The trustees of Central Church comprised such notable businessmen as Erskine Phelps, Lyman Gage, Harry Selfridge, Adolphus Bartlett, Ferdinand Peck, and Lowden. When the advance of trade obliged the pulling-down of the Marshall Field Building and the adjacent Central Music Hall, where the church had had its home for over twenty years, Lowden took the lead in organizing a ten-man company to acquire another Michigan Avenue site. On it they planned to erect a twelve-story structure in which to house the Central Church, the Chicago Symphony Orchestra, and probably the Hamilton Club as well. The project failed to work out entirely as planned, but the congregation moved to Orchestra Hall upon its completion in late 1904.[57]

His prominence in these three organizations and his efforts to cover them with one roof strikingly illustrate one facet of his outlook and that of other wealthy men toward society. They believed a cordial alliance existed, and always should be fostered, between culture, education, Republican politics, and the Protestant faith. As a trustee of the symphony orchestra (1898–1911), he helped to meet its annual deficit with a sizable check and to explain its financial needs to the audiences during the intermissions of the last concerts of the season. With many of his fellows, he held that the platforms and policies of the Republican party, supported by the Hamilton Club, furnished the best guide to what self-government should be and do. A democratic and a Christian society were one and the same thing.

Earnest but not narrowly sectarian in his religious views, Lowden believed

56. In April, 1902, William Hewitt began as coachman and continued in that capacity or as chauffeur for the rest of Mr. and Mrs. Lowden's lives.

57. Mrs. Lowden's diary, Dec. 19, 1898, and Nov. 18, 1901; *Chicago Post,* Sept. 13, 1900; *Chicago Tribune,* Apr. 29, 1901.

that public school education and Christianity ought to be closely in tune. Disagreeing with many of Thomas Jefferson's political and constitutional ideas, he nevertheless echoed the Virginian's insistence that free schools must form the cornerstone of any political structure providing for popular government. The educational system, he said, should be "enfolded in the soft atmosphere of religion," but he left this phrase vague. Thus in a speech entitled "The University of the Twentieth Century," prepared for delivery in January, 1901, at the semicentennial celebration banquet of Northwestern University and substantially repeated about a year later at Knox College, Lowden remarked:

> Religion has proven in America that it, like the individual, flourishes better under absolute freedom. . . . No nation without religion can survive. . . . It is the function of the university of the future to listen to all that science says, and then compel science to confess that there is a Greater than all men may know. . . . The old supposed conflict between religion and science has reached its ebb-tide. That conflict has produced this result: religion has learned a new humility and science admits its limitations. The scientist explains phenomena until he reaches a point where he says God is still necessary to explain the universe. . . . Religion without intolerance, liberty without license, democracy without demagoguery.[58]

This passage, like any which brings into conjunction "liberty," "democracy," "religion," "science," and "education," bristles with ambiguities and seems to confine God to the diminishing area where scientists have not yet penetrated with their research. However this may be, the Lowdens generously supported the work of their church, contributed to worthy humanitarian enterprises of secular origin, and joined religion with education in the upbringing of their own children.

During their first three years of married life they lived at 53 East Twentieth Street in Chicago. In this rented home their first two children were born —George M. Pullman Lowden on January 20, 1897, and Florence Lowden on May 4, 1898. The two babies, attended by a trained nurse and two other nurses, required so much room that the parents began to look for a larger house. As early as July, 1897, an erroneous news item reported that Mr. Pullman, who lavished affection upon his grandson and namesake, had bought the Wirt Dexter residence, immediately north of his own, in order to give it to the Lowdens.[59] Not until November, 1898, however, did they purchase, for $57,500, the Byron Moulton brownstone house at 1912 Prairie Avenue. As values then stood in that fashionable neighborhood, this figure was not high, but they almost doubled it by altering and redecorating the interior, building a considerable addition, enlarging the stables, and landscaping the lawn.[60] When they spent their first night there in early June, 1899, the work

58. FOL was a trustee of Knox College from 1916 to 1929.

59. *Economist* (Chicago), XVIII (July 10, 1897), 43.

60. Mrs. Lowden's diary, Nov. 21, 1898. The property was 55 feet in width and 177 in depth. The house reportedly cost $200,000 when erected a few years before. It was flanked by the homes of S. W. Allerton and Edson Keith.

of renovation was still going forward, and October came before all members of the Lowden family could gather in the new home.

During the weeks of impatient waiting, Mrs. Lowden gave her personal attention to all that the workmen did, including the installation of a large pipe organ in the hall. Her husband wrote with pride in September: "There will not be another house in Chicago the equal of this in real elegance, my clever old wife."[61] At long last, over three years after their marriage, they had a home arranged and furnished exactly as they wished it to be. Here on August 7, 1900, Harriet Elizabeth Lowden was born, and Frances Orren Lowden on December 16, 1903. The residence permitted the Pullmans and Lowdens with their children and servants, to the number of about fifty in all, to continue the family custom of singing carols around the lighted tree at Christmas time. There was even room for eight hundred callers to move along the receiving line and have refreshments at the annual New Year's reception—the principal and most strenuous example of Lowden hospitality during each winter season.[62]

Over a year before the Lowdens purchased their new home, the sudden death of George M. Pullman on October 19, 1897, brought sorrow and new responsibilities into their lives. Mrs. Pullman remained inconsolable for months thereafter.[63] Even after she regained her usual good spirits, she depended more than before upon her daughter Florence. For this reason, Mrs. Lowden felt a special obligation to leave her husband alone in Chicago for weeks at a time while she stayed with her mother at Elberon or "Castle Rest." Lowden had come to like Mr. Pullman as a man who was "frank, candid, and did not deal in mysteries." Following the funeral, he and several other Chicagoans tried to rehabilitate the car magnate in public esteem. The harshness with which he was commonly misjudged, if Lowden can be believed, arose from the "dastardly part" played by the newspapers during the Pullman strike. Granting that truth demands a more favorable appraisal, it still waits upon a scholar to make it.[64]

The terms of Mr. Pullman's will created difficult business problems for Lowden as well as the executors, Robert T. Lincoln and Norman B. Ream. Mrs. Lowden and her sister, Harriett P. Carolan, were each bequeathed the income from $1,000,000 and ultimately about $3,000,000 from the residual estate. Pullman, however, cut off his two sons, who had not fulfilled his hopes, with $3,000 a year, apiece. Besides the home at Eighteenth Street and

61. FOL to Mrs. Lowden, Sept. 7, 1899.

62. The strenuous character of a New Year's reception may be indicated by ten days of blank diary following the one in 1901. For the one in 1902, Mrs. Lowden sent out 1,100 invitations. Eight hundred people came in 1903, when there were a dozen people in the receiving line from 4:00 to 7:00 P.M.

63. Mrs. Pullman's diary for late 1897 and early 1898.

64. FOL to Mrs. Lowden, July 19, Sept. 9 and 18, 1898; *Chicago Legal News*, Oct. 23, 1897. K. M. Landis, Judge Christian Kohlsaat, Thomas B. Bryan, president of the Union League Club, Rev. N. D. Hillis, and others tried to have Mr. Pullman remembered as a humane gentleman with a strong sense of social responsibility.

Prairie Avenue, the widow inherited $50,000 in cash and the income from $1,250,000. About $300,000 were divided among other relatives and friends; $130,000 equally among twelve charitable organizations and the Chicago Historical Society; and $1,250,000 was set aside for a "free manual training school." "Castle Rest" became the property of Mrs. Lowden exclusively, subject to certain provisos, and with an endowment of $100,000 for its maintenance.[65] The worth of the whole estate remained problematical, but in 1900 the *Chicago Inter-Ocean* reported $17,500,000 as the approximately correct figure, or nearly double the estimated total value when the will went to probate.[66]

With the concurrence of her two daughters, Mrs. Pullman protested that her husband had done less than justice to her two sons. In July, 1898, after many conferences with her family, the executors, and her lawyers, she formally renounced all bequests made to her in the will and asserted her dower right to one-third of Mr. Pullman's personal property and a one-third interest for life in his real estate. By thus reducing her daughters' shares as residuary legatees and increasing her own income from the estate, she could provide adequately for the sons. Her action also transferred the title of her Prairie Avenue home, for the most part, to her two daughters, but they, of course, accorded her the full and free possession of it. The displeasure of several collateral relatives over the terms of the will, the heartburning within the immediate family because of the bestowal of "Castle Rest" upon Mrs. Lowden alone, and the making of satisfactory arrangements for the support of the sons, especially after one of them married unhappily in late 1898, gave rise to a succession of delicate issues.[67] During his entire career, Frank Lowden frequently helped bring people of discordant views together by finding a common platform upon which all could stand. His effective work as a family peacemaker for two years after Mr. Pullman's death led Mrs. Lowden to assure him on September 6, 1899:

The more I think of the sweet influence you have exerted this summer in bringing different elements into harmony, the more grateful I am to you. It was something that without you, beloved, I never in the world could have accomplished. So much of the cheer and good feeling at Castle Rest came because of what you are and do. You have done more than anyone else to carry out Papa's ideas and wishes, and I feel sure he knows and rejoices that you are all he could have wished for in a son.

The most valuable single portion of Mr. Pullman's estate comprised forty thousand shares of stock in his profitable company. Robert T. Lincoln, its acting president, Norman B. Ream, and Marshall Field were its leading directors for several years. Under their guidance the Pullman Company absorbed

65. *Chicago Legal News,* Oct. 30, 1897, p. 86.

66. *Chicago Inter-Ocean,* Dec. 27, 1900. The executors' fees were $425,000; the state inheritance tax paid by Mrs. Pullman and her two daughters was $46,000.

67. Mrs. Lowden to FOL, July 11 and Sept. 3, 1899.

the $20,000,000 Wagner Sleeping Car Company before the close of 1898. Because Pullman Company stock advanced about 35 per cent on the market between October, 1897, and the following midsummer, the sale value of these forty thousand shares increased $2,000,000.[68] Who would succeed Mr. Pullman as president of the company aroused much speculation in financial circles. Lowden as *de facto* head of the family was often mentioned in the press, both as a contender for the position against Lincoln and Ream and as their rival for the control of the stock. Nothing in the manuscript sources lends support to these rumors. In 1901 Lincoln became president of the corporation and Lowden one of its directors. Among his co-directors were William K. and Frederick K. Vanderbilt and J. Pierpont Morgan. Lowden resigned from the board in 1906.[69]

One of the weightiest and by all odds the longest-lasting problem arising from Mr. Pullman's bequests centered about his gift of $1,250,000 to erect, maintain, and endow "a free school of manual training for the benefit of the children of persons living or employed at Pullman," Illinois. By the terms of the will, Lincoln, Lowden, Ream, and four other men were to be its directors or trustees. Taking the long view, it seems fortunate that the donor did not clearly define what he had in mind. In the late 1890's, however, this ambiguity caused the trustees to disagree about their proper course, especially since there was no successful manual-training school in the United States to serve them as a model.[70] Having been associated with President William Rainey Harper of the University of Chicago in several civic enterprises, including his educational extension work in the Stock Yards district, Lowden turned to him for advice in the summer of 1898. Always eager to experiment and to extend the "frontiers" of the new university's influence, the dynamic president manifested great interest and a desire to help. Although he counseled delay in starting the school until the endowment had benefited from accumulating Pullman Company dividends, he foresaw a mutually advantageous affiliation between the University of Chicago and the proposed institution. It could be made a unique and important project in technical training and, incidentally, a recruiting ground for University of Chicago students. Lowden came away from the conference much encouraged.[71]

Perhaps he evinced the more interest in manual training because of his own inability to fashion useful or beautiful objects or to operate machinery of any kind. He read whatever he could find upon the subject of industrial education and soon published an article about its value.[72] In the summer of 1899 he joined with Clarence Darrow, Wallace Heckman, James Westfall Thompson, Louis H. Sullivan, and others to form the Illinois Industrial Arts

68. *Chicago Tribune,* July 23 and Oct. 14, 1898.

69. *Chicago Record-Herald,* Oct. 18, 1901. FOL was again a director, 1912–17.

70. *Chicago Chronicle,* Dec. 12, 1899.

71. FOL to Mrs. Lowden, July 14 and 18, 1898.

72. "Value of Manual Training," *Chicago Tribune,* July 15. 1900.

League. President Harper soon lent to this movement the prestige of his name. Lowden served as its president from the time of its organization until 1903. It aimed to provide "guilds of artists and craftsmen" with workshops, tools, libraries, a periodical, and an exhibition and salesroom for the products of their skill. Its motto was Ruskin's, "Life without industry is guilt, and industry without art is brutality." By 1902 it had a bookbindery and two furniture shops in Chicago and financially aided the Jewish Manual Training School, of which Lowden was also the president and Emil G. Hirsch the secretary. The four hundred members of the league, besides those already mentioned, included Mrs. Potter Palmer, Mrs. Emmons Blaine, George E. Vincent, and Hamlin Garland. It more and more tended to become fashionable and "arty" rather than utilitarian in its emphasis. In 1901 its members apparently sensed no incongruity in royally entertaining Prince Peter A. Kropotkin, author and anarchist. The following year Lowden presided at the first national convention of the industrial arts movement. Speeches by Archbishop Ireland, Elbert Hubbard, Frank A. Vanderlip, and Emil G. Hirsch attracted many listeners.[73]

All this, however, except in name, was a far cry from providing facilities for training the children of Pullman in the manual arts. And yet, at the close of 1899, Lowden and his co-trustees of the non-existent school felt sanguine that it could be erected and begin operation within a year. When a canvass of the families living in Pullman revealed that 644 boys and 649 girls hoped to attend such an institution, the trustees suddenly realized how greatly they had underestimated the size of their problem. The yield of the endowment plainly could not provide the buildings, equipment, and salaries of enough faculty members to have one instructor for every twenty students. At this time, the trustees relied heavily upon their secretary, Duane Doty, for their views as well as their facts. He contended that Mr. Pullman's intent would not be violated if the potential student body was kept small by means of high scholastic entrance requirements, a formidable course of studies, and the charging of fees for the use of laboratory and shop materials. When the donor used the term "manual training," continued Doty, he did not mean handwork only but a broad curriculum of technical or industrial education comparable with the best afforded overseas.[74] According to him, the "car king" had wished to emancipate American manufacturers from dependence upon skilled craftsmen from abroad. "Our shops are filled with European artisans. Our continued industrial prosperity seems to demand that we do as much for our boys as Germany does for hers."[75] Uncertain how to proceed, the trustees merely formed themselves into an Illinois corporation in the summer of 1900, elected Lowden its president, and then marked time, in so far as constructing a school building was concerned.

73. *Chicago Record-Herald,* Sept. 29, 1902; *Chicago Inter-Ocean,* Oct. 5, 1902.

74. D. Doty, Pullman, Illinois, to R. T. Lincoln, Feb. 17, 22, and 23, 1900.

75. D. Doty to R. T. Lincoln, Mar. 1, 1900.

He wrote to his friend, Laenas G. Weld, dean of the Graduate College of the State University of Iowa, asking whether he would like to be a candidate for the headship of the Pullman school. Fearing lest he "sink gradually into helpless fossilism" at Iowa, Weld was receptive and came to Chicago for a conference with President Harper. To Weld's entire satisfaction, Harper proposed that the technical school maintain its separate identity but that its teachers have faculty status at the University of Chicago and occasionally offer courses there. Harper also suggested that the Pullman curriculum extend for six years and in its breadth and depth be equivalent to high school and the first two years of college; that its general courses in humanities, social sciences, and science be taught by University of Chicago graduate students in order to give them experience as instructors; that fees be charged at Pullman for the obligatory courses in nonvocational subjects and in its proposed summer school for students preparing to teach manual training; and that the Pullman entrance requirements be raised gradually until a high-school diploma became a prerequisite for admission. By all these means, according to Harper and Weld, the interests of the Pullman school and the University of Chicago would be equally served. The endowment income of the former, freed from a heavy levy for teachers' salaries and supplemented by student fees, would be sufficient to cover the annual costs. Before deciding about the curriculum, Weld hoped that the trustees would send him abroad to study technical education in Sweden, Germany, Switzerland, and the Netherlands.[76]

Long after President Harper's death in 1906, a small fragment of this plan became an actuality. In 1900, however, and from time to time thereafter, the trustees regretfully concluded that their financial resources were too small to provide an independent school of the highest quality. It was 1908 before they acquired a building site in Pullman; 1912 before they enabled Weld, whom they had named principal the year before, to go overseas to observe industrial education there; 1914 before the donor's only grandson, Pullman Lowden, laid the cornerstone of the first building; and 1915 before the first classes began. During all these years, the investing of school funds, the mollifying of people disgruntled over the long delay, and eventually the making of contracts for the construction of the building demanded no little of Frank Lowden's time and thought.[77]

His association with William Rainey Harper led him to admire the forceful president under whose leadership the University of Chicago had "leaped to the front in hardly more than a decade."[78] A number of his friends were deeply involved in its affairs. Franklin MacVeagh and Adolphus C.

76. L. G. Weld, Iowa City, Iowa, to FOL, Nov. 10, 1900.

77. The school opened in October, 1915, with 72 boys and 34 girls enrolled. Weld looked ahead to a student body, 500 strong. There were 590 in 1938. Weld died on Nov. 28, 1919, and was succeeded by Urban G. Willis. For some years Willis had been its dean, and, before that, the tutor of the Lowden children.

78. Wire of FOL to Jesse A. Baldwin, Feb. 19, 1907.

Bartlett were trustees; Wallace Heckman, university counsel and business manager; and Harry Pratt Judson, head of the Department of Political Science and dean of the faculties of arts, literature, and science. Under these circumstances it was not surprising that Lowden accepted election as a trustee in the autumn of 1905. Although he felt uncomfortable because he could not attend many meetings of the board, he continued to serve for five years.

President Harper's long illness terminated in his death on January 10, 1906. With a lowering sky emphasizing the solemnity of the occasion, the lengthy funeral service took place in Mandel Hall four days later. Accompanied by his wife, Lowden attended as one of the honorary pallbearers. Although the trustees appointed Dr. Judson as acting president almost at once, they required over a year of search and discussion before conferring the full title upon him. Lowden chafed under this delay. When the issue came to a head in mid-February, 1907, he sent a long telegram from Washington to one of his fellow trustees urging the choice of Judson on the score of his scholarship, administrative ability, "sanity," and long familiarity with the problems of the university. "I confess," he continued, "that if I were present, to vote for him would be as plain a duty as I have ever discharged."[79] Immediately upon his election, Judson was assured by Lowden that he now had "no fear of the future of the Chicago University." His confidence in the new president was the greater because he was a staunch Republican and liked to fish.[80]

Often called upon for gifts of money both large and small in aid of the university, Lowden's contributions ranged in size from his annual dues of $3.00 to the Reynolds Club for students to $2,500 toward a library building in memory of President Harper. Professor J. Laurence Laughlin's efforts in the Department of Political Economy "to train men to think accurately on socialism, labor, money and banking, taxation and railways" especially appealed to Lowden. He also made donations to the Institute of Sacred Literature and for the publication of the *Classical Journal*.[81] Following Judson's elevation to the presidency, Lowden wished to resign his trusteeship because he had "only waited for" that event before doing so, but his friend persuaded him to continue on the board three more years.[82] During the rest of his life he watched the growth of the university with much interest, at no time more so than after Robert Maynard Hutchins became president in 1929.[83]

If Lowden ever reviewed the varied and important ways in which the death of his wife's father affected his own life, bringing to his family so many perplexities as well as much money, he must have been impressed by

79. FOL's wire to J. A. Baldwin, Feb. 19, 1907; Baldwin's wires to FOL, Feb. 18 and 19, 1907.

80. FOL's wire to H. P. Judson, Feb. 21, 1907.

81. J. L. Laughlin to FOL, Mar. 1, and FOL's reply, Mar. 16, 1907.

82. FOL to H. P. Judson, Mar. 16 and 21, 1907, and Judson to FOL, Mar. 18, 1907.

83. See p. 639.

their contrast with the very simple problems occasioned by the death of his own father. After vainly searching for better health by living for a time in Stuttgart, Arkansas, Lorenzo returned with Nancy to their farm at Hubbard but soon moved a few miles north to a new home in Iowa Falls. There his life closed on January 15, 1899. "I inherited nothing from . . . [him] . . . ," Frank Lowden said several years later, "except things not represented by money. But am I not prouder of him though I got no money[,] because of the fact that no man said of him that he did any man wrong[,] than if he had left me one hundred thousand dollars?"[84] Perhaps he was thinking of George M. Pullman when he uttered these words.

After his father's death Lowden did all in his power to make his mother happy and comfortable during the few remaining years of her life. She came several times to stay in his home, and he went to see her in Iowa Falls at least once a year. He enabled her to fulfil her dream of visiting her daughter Alice, who had moved with her husband to West Seattle, Washington. Medical specialists could do no more than retard the advance of the heart disease from which Nancy Lowden suffered. When seventy-two years of age, she died at Iowa Falls on May 16, 1908.[85]

From that time forward, his two aged aunts, several cousins, five sisters, and sundry nieces and nephews regarded him as the head of the Lowden clan. This position was more than an honorific one. They often sought his advice and sometimes his financial aid. He advanced them money at low interest rates, or at no interest whatsoever, and did not press for repayment. Loans never returned, monthly allowances, and cash gifts at Christmas or in emergencies amounted to a considerable total outlay over the years. Two of his sisters and their children had hard going on Dakota farms, while a third found life only a little less difficult in the Far Northwest. His other two sisters, Isabel and Eleanor, remained unmarried and made careers of their own. Eleanor was a much-liked professor of English literature at Grinnell College, and Isabel founded the Music Education League in New York City, wrote musical plays for children, and produced pageants for their elders.[86]

Lowden had enjoyed his annual pilgrimages to his mother the more because she lived in rural Iowa. "I love the country—its every phase and mood—better than anything on earth," he told Florence Pullman in 1894. She shared his feeling and apparently agreed that some day they "must have a farm."[87] Not long after their marriage he found strong practical reasons to bolster the desire which hitherto had been little more than the romantic dream of a

84. MS of FOL's speech at Amboy, Illinois, Oct. 3, 1906; *Eldora* (Iowa) *Herald,* Jan. 18 and 25, 1899.

85. Mrs. Lowden's diary, May 11–20, 1908; *Cedar Rapids* (Iowa) *Times,* May 18, 1908; *Des Moines* (Iowa) *Capital,* May 18, 1908.

86. For a summary of Isabel Lowden's career see *Who's Who in America,* XXVI (1950–51), 1670. Eleanor Lowden, Ph.B. and (Hon.) L.H.D. from Grinnell, and A.M. and Ph.D. from the University of California, taught at Grinnell from 1919 until her retirement as Professor Emeritus in 1942.

87. FOL to Florence Pullman, Dec. 8 (?), 1894, and Sept. 12, 1895.

young man in love. When his wife was away for weeks on end in the summer at "Fairlawn" and "Castle Rest" with her two children and her mother, the home in Chicago became for him merely an empty house where his law practice condemned him to stay. He felt lonesome and desolate almost to the point of illness. He poured out his feelings in long letters to Mrs. Lowden, sometimes writing several in one day. These effusions, customarily ending with an apology for his "stupid" or "scrawny little note," rarely told much about his work but set forth with many variations in phrase, "I love you and miss you more than I can really tell you!"[88]

Mrs. Lowden and he both realized that some way must be found to bring these long separations to an end. In the autumn of 1897 he let her know that "I am beginning to look upon a summer home near Chicago, where it is just as good for you and the baby—or babies—as at the seashore, with a good deal of favor."[89] As the result of Mr. Pullman's death a few weeks later, his widow needed her daughter's company in the East during the following summer more than ever before. This three months' absence convinced Lowden that a country place had become a necessity. He vainly hoped that Mrs. Pullman might grow to like it as much as Elberon or the Thousand Islands.

During the following winter his "confidential man" kept on the alert for a farm property combining beauty of landscape with accessibility to Chicago. Mrs. Lowden succinctly recorded the outcome of this search in her diary on May 15, 1899: "Frank and I have been on a farm-hunting expedition today," she wrote. "We went in the private car at 8:30 A.M. to Oregon, Ill. to look at a very beautiful farm of 600 acres on the Rock River. We were most pleased and made an offer. Rain. Home, 10:30 P.M." Even in the rain the old Hemenway property, known as "The Oaks," with its farmhouse on a knoll a few hundred feet from Squaw Rock at a bend of the river, seemed idyllic. The dwelling had been built of heavy, native stone over fifty years before by Luke Hemenway, a pioneer from New Hampshire. Its beams and paneling were of black walnut, and its floors of quarter-sawed oak set in mosaic patterns.[90] The rolling land, fringed on the north by the island-dotted river, was beautiful to look upon. Grassy meadows, cleared fields, and stands of hardwoods invited relaxation, as well as diversified farming and the raising of livestock. About five miles to the north on the Burlington Railroad was Oregon, the county seat of Ogle County. Nearly one hundred miles to the east lay Chicago. To the Lowdens the farm seemed so well qualified to make their dream come true that only five days after their visit they purchased its 576 acres for $27,500.[91]

88. FOL to Mrs. Lowden, Sept. 19, 1897: "I feel absolutely lost. I have been completely transformed during the last sixteen months, and the years that lie before me are only attractive so far as they shall be spent with you."

89. FOL to Mrs. Lowden, Sept. 25, 1897.

90. Forrest Crissey, "The Oaks," *Chicago Evening Post,* June 17, 1899; planotyped booklet by Urban G. Willis, *The Story of Sinnissippi Farm.*

91. MS, "Real Estate Record" at Sinnissippi Farm, Oregon, Illinois. FOL (really Mrs. Lowden) purchased the farm, May 20, 1899, from Lorenzo D. Kneeland and wife of Chicago.

In preparation for their occupancy, they enlarged and modernized the house with telephone, gas, electricity, plumbing, a laundry, a furnace, and wide porches with pressed-brick floors. An all-weather road, three-quarters of a mile long, replaced the dusty or muddy lane which led through the woods to the Oregon turnpike. The repaired and enlarged barns and stables were big enough to accommodate carriage and saddle horses, purebred cattle, and the children's ponies. Lawns were leveled and seeded, numerous trees cut down or moved, and shrubs and flowers planted. These improvements required careful planning with the architects Pond and Pond of Chicago and took many months to complete. Mr. and Mrs. Lowden occasionally visited the farm for a few hours to inspect the work, but it was June 29, 1900, before they, Mrs. Pullman, the two children, their three nurses, a cook, a coachman, and several maids arrived at the Oregon station in Mrs. Pullman's private car for a two weeks' stay. The villagers had gossiped much about the extravagant operations in progress at "The Oaks," but the size and complexity of the Lowden caravan outran their imagination. Their smiles would have been broader or their bewilderment the greater, if they had known that Mrs. Lowden wrote in her diary that evening: "Our first day on the farm a great delight to all. We expect to lead a very simple and wholesome life here and keep early hours which will do us all good."

Within a few years Lowden would point out that he had bought the property because "I had farm in my blood and . . . my children were coming on, and I wanted them to be raised where life was simple, where the real thing appeals to one, and not the artificiality and glamour of metropolitan life."[92] The first of these reasons, interpreted to mean love of the countryside rather than of farmwork, was undoubtedly true. The second came largely as an afterthought, reflecting what Mrs. Lowden and he soon recognized to be a fact. One of his sisters recalled her own and her mother's incredulity when they first heard of this purchase, in view of his boyhood aversion for labor in the fields and barn.[93] He immediately made it clear, however, that he intended at "The Oaks" to provide himself with every possible urban convenience, to extract all the pleasures from rural living and avoid its drudgery, and to indulge his liking for planning and experimentation. Nevertheless, he also declared that he would do some real farming. Years went by before some of his skeptical friends and all his political opponents used "Farmer" Lowden as a sobriquet of merited honor rather than of scornful irony.[94]

During the first year at the farm, he built the "largest and finest" stock barn in Ogle County, at a cost of $10,000. Its interior walls were of polished oak and its mow accommodated three hundred tons of hay. The prize-win-

92. MS of FOL's speech at Pawpaw, Illinois, Oct. 2, 1906. This quotation must be read in the context of an appeal for rural votes.

93. Statement of Mrs. Eva Lowden Sheldon to the author, June 19, 1945.

94. For sneering references to FOL as a farmer see *Ogle County Republican* (Oregon, Ill.), Nov. 14 and Dec. 11, 1902, and *Rockford* (Ill.) *Republic,* Oct. 30, 1902.

ning Shorthorn cattle luxuriated in forty-four double stalls equipped with feed carriers, running water, and electric lights.[95] Lowden's livestock partners, W. J. Baker and son, assembled this herd and exercised general management over the farm's operations. In the autumn of 1901, eight of the Shorthorns, when exhibited at the International Live Stock Show in Chicago, won two second prizes—a forerunner of much better success in the future.[96] The new stables became the summer home of "Papoose," "Blackhawk," and the ponies, "Nip," "Tuck," and "Midget." The grooms required thirty-six hours to bring them out over the poor roads from Chicago. The carriage barn housed a growing number of vehicles adapted to country use—a trap, Goddard buggy, omnibus, surrey, phaeton, buckboard, and sleigh. After the manager's house, a guesthouse, and servants' houses were ready for use by the spring of 1901, the *Oregon Reporter* scarcely exaggerated when it called the farm-center a "veritable village."[97]

Before the close of the next year, as a result of several purchases of adjoining land, the acreage had more than doubled. At some earlier time the Lowdens changed the name of their property to "Sinnissippi," the Indian word for the Rock River.[98] During 1901, twenty-five miles of woven-wire fence were put up, and fifty men, working with ten teams of horses, completed about eight miles of roads within the farm.[99] That autumn, Justice James H. Cartwright and other Oregonians and the local congressman, Robert R. Hitt of Mount Morris, witnessed the little ceremony attending the raising of a flagpole, a hundred and fifty feet high, on a low hill beside Squaw Rock at the water's edge not far from the residence.[100]

This party illustrated the efforts made by the Lowdens to win the confidence and liking of their neighbors. It was no easy conquest. The economic gap remained wide and ineradicable. To be "accepted" was the more difficult because "Sinnissippi" quickly became a show place. An increasing throng of visitors, drawn by idle curiosity or genuine interest, arrived during summer week ends to tramp over the lawns, gather flowers, picnic near the house, stare annoyingly at the family, or wander through the barns, often with lighted pipe or cigar. These neighborhood sightseers required tactful handling if they were not to be alienated. Summer campers along the river had to be kept within bounds, and hunters warned that gunning was prohibited. With so much woodland and brush, fire was always a hazard. In mid-spring,

95. *Oregon Republican,* Sept. 6, 1900; *Oregon Reporter,* May 22, 1901.

96. The *Drovers' Journal* (Chicago) of Nov. 9, 1901, and Jan. 10, 1902, noted that the Shorthorn herd numbered 85.

97. Issue of May 22, 1901; *Freeport* (Ill.) *Journal,* Feb. 6, 1902.

98. MS, "Real Estate Book." 670 acres in three parcels in 1901; 270 acres in two parcels in 1902. These 940 acres cost $55,704. The name "Sinnissippi" was used at least as early as October, 1901 (see *Oregon Reporter,* Oct. 24, 1901).

99. *Oregon Reporter,* May 22, 1901. The *Oregon Republican,* Dec. 11, 1902, mentions 500 acres of blue-grass pasture, 120 Shorthorns, etc.

100. Mrs. Lowden's diary, Nov. 5, 1901; *Ogle County Republican,* Nov. 17, 1901.

1902, flames of undetermined origin swept over a considerable area of timber not far from the house.[101]

To foster good will, the Lowdens bought most of their farm supplies in Oregon and other nearby communities. A local lumber company provided the 150,000 shingles and other materials for the stock barn. An agency in Oregon handled the insurance on the farm buildings. The improvements almost always in train furnished employment to many men of the area. Lowden opened an account of substantial size at the local bank and later purchased some of its stock. In like manner he invested in the Schiller piano factory of Oregon and bought one of its instruments for "Sinnissippi."[102] The editor of the *Oregon Republican* showed his friendliness in 1900 by helping him organize a local "Yates-for-Governor Club," editorializing about his contributions to the economic life of the community, and advising sightseers at "Sinnissippi" how they should conduct themselves.[103] Mr. and Mrs. Lowden aided the public school and library in Oregon by giving pictures to the one and hundreds of books and magazines to the other. The librarian for many years was Miss Emily Cartwright, a sister of Justice Cartwright of the Supreme Court of Illinois. Lowden and the jurist quickly became warm friends. They shared a common interest in law, politics, and thoroughbred horses.

The Ogle County Farmers' Institute helped to win for Lowden the respect of the more progressive farmers in his neighborhood. He found it tactically wise to let them know of his rural upbringing, even while he disclaimed much knowledge about husbandry. Thus, in 1902, he addressed his fellow members on "The Value of Education to the Farmer." After referring briefly to his Iowa boyhood, he humbly added: "I must sit at your feet for some years yet before I shall be entitled to speak with authority upon any topic relating to agriculture." A farmer, he admitted, needed practical experience before he could use his land wisely and well, but the institute could help by making known the important agricultural aids provided recently by science and invention. As illustrations, he mentioned crop rotation, nitrogenous cover-crops, soil analyses, carefully selected fertilizers, scientific stockbreeding, and the probability that meteorology would eventually become of genuine service to farmers. "Agriculture," he said, "can hardly be any longer called a manual pursuit. . . . Science has conquered every other domain; it will surely conquer agriculture. . . . The most compelling reason why the farmer should be educated is that the destiny of this Republic is in his hands. . . . No nation has long survived the decay of agriculture or the decadence of its rural inhabitants." As an attentive listener, Mrs. Lowden believed it the best speech she had ever heard her husband make.[104] Her judgment may have been colored by the enthusiasm she had come to feel for "Sinnissippi" and country life.

101. *Rockford* (Ill.) *Republic,* Apr. 15, 1902; *Oregon Republican,* Apr. 17, 1902.

102. Mrs. Lowden's diary, May 29, 1901.

103. *Oregon Republican,* Sept. 6, 1900.

104. Mrs. Lowden's diary, Jan. 30, 1902.

One Ogle County group which the Lowdens immediately found congenial was the Eagle's Nest summer colony of Chicago folk on a hill overlooking Oregon. They included the families of Wallace Heckman, already mentioned, Lorado Taft, sculptor, and Charles F. Browne, painter. Hamlin Garland visited there frequently. He and Lowden looked back upon similar boyhood experiences on the "middle border," and each enjoyed chaffing the other about his lack of skill as a "dirt farmer." Finally, in early July, 1902, the lawyer challenged the author to a mowing contest with a scythe. Garland won the duel. If his own account in *Companions on the Trail* can be believed, his friend, looking "like an English earl," cut a ragged path through the clover, with its edges "a series of notches."[105] During the same summer, Lowden invited Judge Peter S. Grosscup of the United States Circuit Court and William J. Calhoun, a Chicago lawyer, to compete against him in a plowing match. The three referees included a general and another judge. After considerable hesitation in deciding which contestant had performed least poorly, they awarded the palm, in the form of a silver plow, to Calhoun.[106]

By 1902, Miss Margaret Enders, whose close friendship virtually made her one of the family, had dubbed Lowden, the "Squire of Sinnissippi." This title aptly suggested the position he was making for himself in the Oregon community. Even by that year, many of its members admitted, at least grudgingly, that he and Mrs. Lowden were helping their neighborhood. Others, however, questioned the disinterestedness of their aid and wondered when Frank Lowden planned to ask for votes in return. To do so would also befit his role of "Squire." He occasionally may have regarded the Rock River Valley as his future political constituency, but at this time he viewed it with more earnestness as his true home. Already Mrs. Lowden and he were asking themselves whether they should not follow the lead of their hearts and the wishes of their children by living the year around at "Sinnissippi." "I like to think of that beautiful and fertile spot," Lowden would say a few years later, ". . . as the place where my children and my children's children and their children after them will gather long after I have become dust, and in the shade of old trees my own hand has planted."[107]

During the late 1890's, as the next chapter will relate, Lowden became more and more enmeshed in politics. His speech-making spread beyond the limits of Chicago and drew him downstate for weeks at a time. Added commitments as a lawyer or businessman also obliged him to be away from home with increasing frequency. These pressures reached a climax in 1901, when Shelby Steel Tube problems greatly worried him. Mrs. Lowden suffered from much ill-health that year, including some days in May when her condition became critical.[108] Harried from all sides, her nervously tired husband

105. Hamlin Garland, *Companions on the Trail* (New York, 1931), pp. 154–55.

106. Mrs. Lowden's diary, June 7, 1902; *Dixon* (Ill.) *Telegraph,* June 10, 1902.

107. MS of FOL's speech at Pawpaw, Illinois, Oct. 2, 1906; statement of Miss Enders to the author, Dec. 29, 1945.

108. *Chicago American,* May 8, 1901; *Chicago Inter-Ocean,* May 9, 1901.

was almost at his wit's end. She felt that he could readily ease his overcrowded schedule by declining to make so many speeches. Since politics were outside the range of her experience, she viewed with distaste the roughhewn characters whose acquaintance he necessarily cultivated when he worked in a campaign. She wished him to find happiness by confining his career to law and business.[109] Try as hard as she could, she was unable to hide her feeling of possessiveness toward him or to conceal her regret because she had to share him with others. She found it difficult to echo his enthusiasm when he told her of the applause accorded his political speeches and of his growing influence in the councils of the Republican party in Illinois. She customarily packed his bag whenever he left for a trip and put a note in the pocket of his pajamas. In one of these letters, dated October 1, 1901, she well summarized her problem in these words:

If I had one half the sense I am credited with, I should rejoice to see the manifestations of affection people have for you, my darling, instead of making myself and you wretched on that account, and perhaps the day will come when I can show you that much of what we have gone through has been the result of physical rather than mental weakness. . . . It can't help being in your mind, my beloved, that much of your success or failure in a possible public career will depend upon my attitude, and I could not blame you for feeling now that the unfortunate disposition of which I have given evidence lately would be a serious hindrance to you; but I say to you, with all the sincerity of which I am capable, that I don't want you to consider that side of it, for I will overcome my weakness and try with all my mind and heart and strength to be the help and comfort to you that you ought to have.[110]

Between the summer of 1901 and the summer of 1902, when Frank Lowden was about forty years of age, he came to a crossroads in his life where he faced the hard choice between the paths of law, business, and politics. His stern experience with the Shelby Company made it easier for him to reject the road of business, especially since his investments and those of his wife provided him with plenty of work along that line. To decide between the law and politics, however, was most difficult. It was the more so because Mrs. Lowden clearly hoped that the latter would not be his preference. The dissolution of the firm of Lowden, Estabrook, and Davis occurred unexpectedly in June, 1902, and, fortunately or unfortunately, helped to turn him toward politics as his career. Thereafter, for a few years, he occasionally accepted a client, but he never again made the practice of law his main vocation.

Mrs. Lowden's recovery of better health helped to reconcile her quickly to her husband's decision. She admired him for his independence of mind. No one justifiably could say that the Pullman influence had led him into politics, even though the shadow of that influence would pursue him as long as he sought public office. Their deep and mutual liking for "Sinnissippi" pro-

109. Mrs. Lowden to FOL, July 2, 1897, Sept. 6, 1899, and May 3, 1901.
110. See also her letters to him of May 21, July 10, Sept. 30, and Oct. 2, 1901.

vided a new bond between them. The longer they stayed there each year, the more evenings they shared together. In contrast to life in Chicago, he could work at the farm without interruption and feel less tempted to accept speaking engagements in the city. In time, Mrs. Lowden became interested in politics, but until then she and her husband united joyfully in the work of making "Sinnissippi" mean progressive agriculture and, better still, their home.[111]

111. Mrs. Lowden's diary, Dec. 31, 1902: "This has been the happiest year we can remember." For "Sinnissippi" as an economic enterprise prior to 1917 see chap. x.

CHAPTER V

POLITICS AS AN AVOCATION, 1893–1903

Frank Lowden once said that if Iowa City had permitted university students from out of town to vote, he would have made the "grave mistake," in the first presidential election after reaching his majority, of supporting Grover Cleveland rather than James G. Blaine.[1] At some unknown time following his graduation but soon after coming to Chicago, he left the party of his father and became a Republican.

His new circumstances in the big city encouraged this shift and stimulated his interest in politics. Wirt Dexter and most of the other men whom Lowden met in his work were Republicans. Manufacturers claimed that they could not pay generous fees to their legal counsel unless high tariffs on imports continued. The Interstate Commerce Law, enacted under a Democratic regime, pleased railroad owners to the extent that it substituted a single set of regulations for the jungle of separate state laws, but its underlying principle, if broadened in practice, would menace free enterprise. Railroads and manufacturing concerns comprised the principal clients of Dexter, Herrick, and Allen, Walker and Lowden, and Keep and Lowden. If, by 1893, Lowden still had any lingering doubt about the political party to which he should belong, the panic of that year with the Democrats in the saddle at Washington and Springfield convinced him that sound reason had justified his conversion. In Chicago, Mayor Carter Harrison and his Democratic cohorts in the City Hall seemed to be flagrantly corrupt. Their meddling with the franchises and operating policies of the streetcar companies exasperated some of Lowden's most valued business acquaintances.

The Union League and Calumet clubs, to which he belonged, were largely Republican in membership. The Union League Club, born during and of the Civil War, had come to have political discussion and action as its chief reason for being. Its members fostered the spread of the myth, which thousands of voters believed by the 1880's, that the Republicans alone had won the Civil War, saved the Union, and abolished slavery. To Frank Lowden, the northern soldiers in that conflict, from the lowliest private up to General Grant, were heroes to be eulogized and cherished by a grateful people. His papers include an undated manuscript entitled "Good Reading at This Juncture." Although he probably wrote it during the campaign either of 1888 or of 1892, there is no evidence that he ever used it as a speech. Its theme is

1. MS of FOL's speech to the Michigan Club, Detroit, Feb. 22, 1899.

that, as long as the Republicans remain united, the Democrats can never win another presidential election because, as a result of the Civil War, the sons of Democratic fathers have grown up to be Republicans. "The curse of slavery has pursued the Democratic Party and has hounded it to its death. Therefore, let it die, and no lip will be found to say a prayer over the grass on its grave. . . . The public schools have slain the Democratic party with the textbook."

Not until 1893, however, were Frank Lowden's political activities even occasionally noted in the Chicago press. At that time he served on the Union League Club's Committee of Political Action and also on the Citizens' Committee. Both of these supported Samuel W. Allerton in his efforts "as a business man running on a non-partisan business platform" to unseat Mayor Harrison. The Committee of Political Action had as its more general goal the abolition of the spoils system at every level of government. Its chairman was the magnetic John H. Hamline, lawyer and former alderman, who had stimulated a group of young men, including Lowden, to unite in the cause of civil service reform. They often mentioned Theodore Roosevelt's work in its behalf as evidence of what energetic action could accomplish. Hamline's band assisted Allerton's Citizens' Committee in preparing a list of four thousand men, allegedly "colonized" illegally in the tenements of doubtful precincts for the purpose of voting for Harrison. Both committees provided poll watchers to challenge any one of these miscreants who might try to cast a ballot.[2]

In this campaign Lowden spoke at least six times in as many Chicago wards, helping to "warm up" audiences before Allerton arrived to deliver the main address. His maiden efforts as a politician were all in vain. In the April 5, 1893, election the Democrats retained control of the city offices. According to John H. Hamline, the "decent element was outnumbered"; but Harrison attributed his victory to the fact that most voters knew how unjustly he had been assailed as a spoilsman.[3] When, soon afterward, an assassin's bullet ended his career, the politicians added to the excitement of Chicagoans over their impressive Columbian Exposition by waging a new battle for the control of City Hall. In December another Democrat, John P. Hopkins, became Harrison's successor by defeating Acting Mayor George B. Swift in a special election.

The Republican party in Cook County and Chicago presented a united front only when fighting its rival in an election campaign. At other times it split into factions and unstable intra-party coalitions representing different districts of the city or leaders ambitious for more power. Although patronage rather than principles was chiefly at issue, a group of young men, including Lowden, living in the "silk-stocking" wards, annoyed the older politicians by pressing for honest elections, an extension of the classified civil service system over many city and county offices, and less partisanship in the gov-

2. Green P. Raum, *History of Illinois Republicanism* (Chicago, 1900), pp. 328–30.
3. *Chicago Tribune,* Mar. 30, 31, and Apr. 6, 1893.

ernment of Chicago. To the men in control of the "machine," on the other hand, civil service reform spelled the doom of the complicated but efficient organization whereby they chose candidates, fought campaigns, won elections, and rewarded service to the party. Without jobs to dispense, the chieftains believed all centralized control of strategy and the main incentive to work hard for party victory would be destroyed.

The mode of doling out patronage in Chicago had hardened into a system which ramified through the many city and county offices. Its basic unit was the party committee in each of the thirty-five wards and in each rural township of Cook County. The chairmen of these groups constituted the county central committee. These committeemen controlled the choice of delegates to the party's nominating conventions, the candidates named by them, and the selection of election officials. Following a victory at the polls, each committeeman went to the successful candidates for city and county offices to learn what subordinate appointive jobs his organization could fill. Thereupon, the local leader, in consultation with his committee, chose the lucky persons up to the limit of his quota. As a rule, the winner in an election could freely name his own secretary and treasurer, if any, but the remaining posts under his jurisdiction, whether clerks, laborers, policemen, or firemen, were allotted among the little Republican "machines" in the various wards and rural districts.

When Lowden first entered politics, the Republican organization included several ambitious and able young men who, for weal or for woe, would much influence his career. Charles S. Deneen, graduate of McKendree College and the Union College of Law, lived on the South Side of Chicago in the Englewood area. There he recently had met Roy O. West, a fellow Methodist and lawyer with a Bachelor's degree from DePauw University. In their boyhood they had lived within ten miles of each other in downstate Illinois. Their acquaintanceship soon ripened into a close personal friendship and political alliance, with "never a written understanding and never a misunderstanding" between them as long as Deneen lived.[4] In 1892 he began his one term as an assemblyman at Springfield. Two years later, as an assistant county attorney, West started to ascend a political ladder which eventually lifted him into President Coolidge's cabinet as secretary of the interior.

North and northwest of Chicago's central business district, known as the "Loop," Henry Hertz and James Pease each controlled the Republican party in the township of his residence, while in Hyde Park, south of the Loop, Dr. T. N. Jamieson ruled as boss. The doctor, however, had hitched his political wagon to the fast-ascending Near West Side star, William Lorimer.

Lorimer's rise to a position of influence had been no easy one. Of English birth and Scottish ancestry, he was brought to Chicago by his parents in the late 1860's. His father, a Presbyterian minister, died soon afterward, leaving a widow and six children in difficult circumstances. William, the eldest son, helped at the age of ten to support the family by working as newsboy and

4. Statement of Roy O. West to the author, Jan. 6, 1951.

bootblack and at other odd jobs. With no time for school, he was taught to read, write, and "figure" by his mother and his Sunday school teacher. Following the destruction of the Lorimer home by fire in 1874, he toiled for five or six years in the Union Stock Yards and felt grateful to his employers for their considerate treatment of him. Later, when his congressional district included the "Yards," he carefully sent the packers advance copies of all bills which might affect their business. About 1880 he started a five-year stint as a horsecar driver and conductor along West Twelfth Street, on the south edge of the Loop. This job afforded him an unusual opportunity to widen his circle of acquaintances at every economic level of society and among the varied ethnic groups in his home neighborhood. He organized a conductors' union and cultivated the friendship of Democrats as well as Republicans. Thereafter, for the rest of his career, his supporters never came wholly from, nor was his dispensation of favors ever confined to, the ranks of his own party. This bipartisan policy, usually unembarrassed by principles or issues, was known as "Lorimerism" to his foes. Whether helped by Republicans or Democrats, he repaid them with jobs or with contracts for the materials and labor so often needed by the fast-growing metropolis.[5]

Shortly after casting his first presidential ballot in 1884, he exchanged his conductor's uniform for a house-painter's overalls. At the same time he formed a political club in his precinct "to see to it that at the next election there would be enough Republican ballots held or peddled around the polling booth." Within two years, although his painting job collapsed and he derived only a precarious livelihood from selling real estate, he was Republican boss of his ward, a member of the Cook County Republican Central Committee, and a constable. His economic fortunes improved greatly in 1887, when Mayor Roche named him assistant superintendent of water-mains extension. For the next twenty-five years he rarely lacked a fairly lucrative political job. During 1889 a contract from the city kept fifty teams of horses busy under his direction. Two years later Mayor Hempstead Washburne made him head of the Chicago Water Department. The coming of the Democrats to power momentarily checked his rise, but in 1894 he began the first of his eight successive terms as congressman. As a profitable side line to politics, he organized the Murphy-Lorimer Brick Company and soon its natural ally, the Lorimer-Gallagher Construction Company. His brief and unhappy career as a La Salle Street banker was still in the future.

Lorimer's tirelessness as a worker and his good faith in abiding by his promises won him the grudging admiration of his political enemies and the firm loyalty of his supporters. Although his name came to be synonymous

5. Herman H. Kohlsaat, who from his long experience in the Chicago newspaper world could speak as an authority, defined "Lorimerism" as "the affiliation, co-operation, and cohesion of Democrats and Republicans for party pelf and for private pelf . . . a cohesion of the worst elements in one party with the worst in the other for the sake of spoils." He thus testified in the *Election of William Lorimer: Hearings before a Committee of the Senate Pursuant to Senate Resolution No. 60*, etc. (62d Cong., 2d sess. [1911–12]), Senate Doc. No. 484, I, 429; hereafter cited as "*Dillingham Committee Hearings*."

with "spoils," he never sullied it by vicious personal habits. Among his friends in the opposition camp, none was closer than Roger Sullivan, a Democratic boss in Chicago. They sent their sons to Andover Academy and sailed their boats together on Lake Michigan. Sailing was about the only recreation which Lorimer permitted himself to enjoy. He neither drank nor smoked, and his home life was exemplary. As he once said, "I don't go to theatres and I don't go out to dinners, with anybody."[6] By 1893 he controlled virtually all the Republican patronage in a half-dozen Chicago wards, including the one in which Lowden lived.

Following the special mayoralty election late that year, the Union League Club's Committee of Political Action continued to press for honesty in politics and civil service reform. When several policemen were charged with "kidnaping, assaulting, and falsely arresting two Republican election officials," Lowden led in their prosecution. The *Chicago Inter-Ocean*, owned by Herman H. Kohlsaat, declared that Lowden "represented the better elements [in the city], both democratic and republican." In his own Second Ward, as the spring elections of 1894 approached, he worked vigorously with the other "independents" to elect an alderman who supported a reduction in the price of gas and an elevation of the streetcar tracks in the business heart of the city.[7]

Insurgency of this kind did not endear Lowden to the "machine" Republicans. Although he usually voted for their mayoralty candidates, he often stated that local election campaigns should be non-partisan and have corrupt versus honest municipal government as their main issue. Shocked to discover that some prominent businessmen backed notorious spoilsmen, he bluntly told the Review Club of Chicago in early 1895 what Lincoln Steffens would point out thirty-six years later in his *Autobiography*. "Many otherwise good men," said Lowden in effect, "do not vote in the primaries because they want a bad Common Council which they can bribe. If public sentiment can not elevate the ethics of successful business and professional men, then criminal prosecution must. They must be taught that in the long run they lose by gaining privileges unlawfully."[8] To rescue his city from the grip of a venal machine and to create a public opinion as sensitive to the quality of Chicago's government as it was proud of her physical growth signified to Lowden "a

6. The best source known to the author for reconstructing the early life of Lorimer is the volumes of the *Dillingham Committee Hearings,* esp. VIII, 7639, 7646–67, 7821, 7851–57. The quotation in the text is from VIII, 7786. Lorimer's congressional district was west of the Loop and extended to the western limit of the city. As an extreme illustration of the devotion Lorimer inspired, John I. Hughes, secretary of Lorimer's Federal Improvement Company of Chicago (a general contracting company), testified: "To my mind he [Lorimer] is the greatest man that ever lived from the time of Christ." This quotation is on p. 35 of *Election of William Lorimer . . . a Copy of the Report of the Special Investigating Committee of the Illinois Senate, Douglas W. Helm, Chairman, in Regard to the Election of William Lorimer as United States Senator* (62d Cong., 1st sess.), Senate Doc. No. 45; hereafter cited as "*Helm Committee Hearings.*"

7. *Chicago Inter-Ocean,* Feb. 4 and Mar. 25, 1894.

8. MS of FOL's speech, Jan. 6, 1895.

holy cause . . . a battle for democracy itself." In his view the governing of a city, unlike the governing of a nation, was wholly a business problem. Therefore, in municipal elections, party politics became a harmful irrelevancy. At the national level, however, it was "the highest patriotism" to be a member of the Republican party. Only under its banner could the "centrifugal" domestic and "flabby" foreign policies of the Democrats be avoided.[9]

Lowden's thought often lacked clarity when he tried to distinguish between municipal government as a business and the government at Washington as not a business. Nor could he always maintain the differentiation. In 1895, for example, one count in his indictment of Mayor Hopkins was that he supported the Wilson-Gorman Tariff Law. On the other hand, the Second Ward Republican Club, of which Lowden was then president, concentrated upon city rather than national issues. In harmony with his principles, he resigned his office in this organization in 1896, when "after zealous labor" he failed to shift its focus of interest from the distribution of patronage to the promotion of honesty and efficiency at City Hall.[10]

Everywhere except in the southern states, the Republican party by 1896 was emerging from its lean years marked by populism, the second administration of Grover Cleveland, and a prolonged financial depression. Many farmers and businessmen in Illinois chafed under the "radical" rule of Governor John P. Altgeld, the first Democrat to occupy the Executive Mansion at Springfield since 1857. The energetic and able Charles Gates Dawes was working—successfully, as it turned out—to rally Illinois Republicans behind the candidacy of William McKinley of Ohio for the presidential nomination. Early in the preconvention campaign, Lowden wanted Senator William B. Allison of Iowa to be the party's nominee, but Congressman Lorimer and John R. Tanner, the Republican choice for governor, brought forward Senator Shelby M. Cullom as the state's "favorite son."[11] Largely through Lorimer's influence, the Cook County Republican convention nominated Charles Deneen for the office of state's attorney. He won the election in the autumn, along with the rest of the state ticket.

Although Lowden belonged to the Political Action Committee of the Union League Club in this red-letter year of American politics, he took almost no part in the stirring election campaign. His engagement, marriage, and wedding trip, as well as his law practice, left him little time for politics during the first half of 1896. Beginning in early August, typhoid fever confined him to his bed or kept him from undertaking any extra tasks for about six weeks. He was back at his desk by mid-September, but it was late autumn before he had fully recovered his strength. As his entire contribution to his

---

9. MS of speech, "The Patriot at the Polls," delivered before the Two Million Club of Chicago in mid-November, 1894 (see p. 44).

10. *Chicago Post,* Jan. 9, 1896; *New York Times,* Mar. 22, 1896.

11. Bascom N. Timmons (ed.), *Charles Gates Dawes: A Journal of the McKinley Years, 1893–1913* (Chicago, Ill., 1950), pp. 50–51, and *passim;* hereafter cited as "*Dawes Journal, 1893–1913.*"

party's hard-won victories in the state and nation, he could only point to his check for $1,000 and several speeches accusing Altgeld of plundering the public funds. If he had desired an appointive office, his meager share in the campaign would not have argued strongly in his favor. But he sought no position in government. Politics in 1896 and for a half-dozen years thereafter was merely one of his avocations.

In 1897, as soon as the Democrats chose the younger Carter Harrison as their mayoralty candidate, Lowden and the "Hamline brigade" tried to unite the Republicans behind Judge Nathaniel C. Sears, who promised, if elected, to enforce the proposed new civil service law and make streetcar companies pay liberally for a renewal of their franchises. Unfortunately, John M. Harlan and Washington Hesing, who similarly pledged themselves, refused to withdraw as independent candidates and leave Sears a clear field against Harrison.[12] Under these circumstances, reform groups like the Municipal Voters League denounced Harrison but declined to give their exclusive indorsement to any of his three opponents.

Lowden and his friends were further embarrassed when the Lorimer-Hertz Republican organizations and T. N. ("Doc") Jamieson, Republican national commiteeman of Illinois, came out for Sears and thus tagged him with the "machine" label. Thereupon, the *Daily News* called Lowden "a nobody except the son-in-law of George M. Pullman" and ridiculed him as a pseudo-reformer who supported the slate of the spoilsmen. The *Chicago Chronicle* declared that his best service to the cause of better government would be to abandon politics altogether, because his championship of municipal reform merely turned many workers against it.[13] He thus received his first, but by no means his last, warning that his Pullman affiliations would be a handicap if he should ever embark upon a political career. With the opposition split three ways, Harrison easily won in the April election.[14]

A forward step in the direction of cleaner politics was taken ten months later, when the state legislature enacted a new primary law. The Civic Federation's Committee on Political Action, of which Lowden was a member, shared in the framing of this measure and lobbied at Springfield in its behalf. As chairman of the similar committee of the Union League Club, he arranged for non-partisan exercises in every Chicago school on Washington's Birthday. At each student assembly a Union League Club speaker told the children about their patriotic duties as citizens, including the urging of their fathers to demand that the new law be so enforced as to bring cleaner and less machine-ridden city government.[15]

This law provided for a non-partisan board of election commissioners to divide Chicago into primary election districts and appoint the election clerks

12. *Chicago Inter-Ocean,* Mar. 24, 1897; *Chicago Chronicle,* Mar. 25 and 28, 1897. Harold Ickes was Harlan's campaign manager.

13. *Chicago Chronicle,* Mar. 25 and 28, 1897; *Chicago Daily News,* Mar. 27, 1897.

14. *Chicago Chronicle,* Mar. 31, 1897; *Chicago Inter-Ocean,* Apr. 21, 1897.

15. *Chicago Times-Herald,* Feb. 20, 1898; *Chicago Inter-Ocean,* Feb. 25 and 26, 1898.

and judges of each district from a list of nominees submitted by each party. Whether this innovation would break the control of the ward committee-men over nominations and assure an honest count of the ballots cast in the primaries would obviously depend upon the quality of the board and its election officials. The two political action committees already mentioned—the executive committee of the Civil Service Reform League, the Municipal Voters League, and, above all, the special Citizens' Committee of One Hundred, with Franklin MacVeagh as chairman and Lowden heading its sub-committee on organization—enlisted the help of clergymen, politicians, labor leaders, and employers in arousing a public demand for an honest application of the law. Lowden's subcommittee picked one Republican and one Democrat in each primary district to arrange for watchers at every polling place. The Committee of One Hundred offered rewards for information leading to the conviction of anyone "delaying, coercing, or bribing a voter."[16]

Momentarily only, this new system appeared to break the grip of professional politicians upon the nominations for city and county offices, but Lowden and his fellow crusaders could not feel at ease as long as Harrison was mayor. Beginning in the autumn of 1898, they temporarily redirected their energies toward exposing the inefficiency and financial waste which thwarted even honest and able officials as long as county, township, town, and city governments overlapped within Cook County. The growth of Chicago made this whole jerry-built structure absurdly anachronistic. Its only excuse for being, except that the Illinois constitution and statutes sanctioned it, was its generosity in providing many unnecessary offices for deserving party workers. Public lethargy and ignorance helped the machines of both parties to preserve what sound reasoning could not justify. By abolishing some and combining others of these governments, taxes could be reduced, duplicate jurisdictions and functions ended, and responsibility for dishonesty or incompetence more clearly fixed. If nothing was accomplished except to wipe out the useless townships within Cook County, it alone would be a considerable gain. But Lowden and other young leaders dreamed of a "Greater Chicago" comprising most, if not all, of the suburban communities and hence rendering unnecessary even the county government itself.[17]

Late in 1898 he made this reform a main item on the program of the Political Action Committee of the Union League Club. Early the next year, as a member of a Civic Federation committee, he helped draft a constitutional amendment embodying this blueprint for Cook County.[18] But his trips with others to Springfield in its behalf, as well as five more years of effort along the same line, achieved nothing. Unfortunately, the movement became entangled with the sharply divisive issue of the degree of power which the mayor and council should have over the street-railway lines. Many Cook

16. *Chicago Tribune,* Feb. 25, Mar. 6, 9, 11, 17, 20, 1898; *Chicago Record,* May 29, 1898.

17. *Chicago News,* Nov. 12, 1898; *Chicago Inter-Ocean,* Jan. 5, 1899. In 1901 the legislature provided for the consolidation of township governments within Chicago.

18. *Chicago Times-Herald,* Feb. 18, 1899; *Chicago Chronicle,* Nov. 16, 1899.

County assemblymen at Springfield, not to mention those from downstate, opposed any alteration in the structure of Chicago's government. Most of the little towns in the county retained their rural outlook and hence resisted absorption by the metropolis. Its own residents were usually apathetic, while the reformers themselves could not agree upon the most feasible procedure for carrying the proposed changes through to success. Lowden favored the amendment route. So much else was out of date in the Illinois constitution, argued others, that nothing less than a constitutional convention to draft a completely new organic law would be effective. This, to him, would cut away the past too suddenly. He insisted that a democracy must move forward by "evolution" rather than by "revolution."[19]

During the years ahead, Lowden came gradually to agree that a constitutional convention would provide the only means for modernizing Illinois's outworn fundamental law of 1870. Although he soon reversed his views about primaries and argued against them as vigorously as he had formerly spoken in their favor,[20] he continued to champion a business-like government for Chicago and civil service reform. In the early 1900's he worked mainly for the latter through the Civil Service Reform Association of Illinois, headed by Wallace Heckman. Late in 1902 he helped frame a bill to forbid the political assessment of office-holders, to make the Chicago civil service regulations less easy to evade, to provide a hearing whenever a civil service appointee was suspended by his superior, and to remove from the spoils system nearly every non-elective official in Illinois. He testified in favor of this measure before a joint committee of the legislature, but the labor of its advocates went for naught.[21]

To Lowden and his co-workers a "Greater Chicago" meant more than an expansion of its boundaries, the reform of its government, and the awakening of a "civic conscience" in all its citizens. Although these were fundamental, the sprawling city had become a "circle with a circumference but no center." By providing a cluster of ideals and measures which all good Chicagoans might gladly strive for, no matter in what part of the metropolis they lived, he dreamed of ending much of the bickering between its geographic "divisions" and many ethnic groups.[22] Furthermore, he hoped that beauty rather than ugliness might attend its rapid physical growth. To this end he indorsed the ambitious and far-seeing plan of Daniel H. Burnham for an orderly development of Chicago, with ample provision for parks, boulevards, playgrounds, and rapid transportation.[23]

Although Lowden first came to public notice in politics as a critic of Chi-

19. *Chicago Post,* July 11 and Oct. 31, 1901.

20. See pp. 244–46, 254–55, and 477–79.

21. MSS of FOL's speeches to Atlas Club of Chicago, Jan. 21, 1902, and to League of Cook County Women's Clubs, Nov. 15, 1902.

22. MS of FOL's speech on a "Permanent Exposition Building," before the Merchants' Club, Chicago, Dec. 10, 1898.

23. *Chicago Inter-Ocean,* Apr. 17, 1897.

cago's government and its residents for their customary indifference toward civic welfare movements, he was equally ready to speak in his city's praise. He shared in the Chicago Day exercises held annually on October 9, to commemorate the Great Fire of 1871 and the finer metropolis which arose almost magically from the ruins.[24] For this occasion in 1899, when President McKinley agreed to lay the cornerstone of the new Federal Building, Lowden headed a committee sent to Canada to invite its governor-general and prime minister to the ceremony.[25] Two years later, as one of three speakers on Illinois Day at the Pan-American Exposition in Buffalo, he admitted in a "short but brilliant address" that Chicago was smoky and noisy and lacking in polish and "repose." But, he continued, polish signified decadence, and repose, impending death. The city's crudities and restlessness exemplified her vigorous youth and guaranteed her a much greater future.[26]

No doubt the cosmopolitan audience in the exposition's Temple of Music expected him to speak in this lyric vein, but back in Chicago he often seemed much less certain that the crudities gave warrant for good cheer. In the late 1890's, for example, Charles T. Yerkes and his public utility companies sought to renew their franchises. Although his firms and others in the same line of business disagreed among themselves about what new terms to ask of the city council, Yerkes requested a ninety-nine-year extension at the lowest possible cost and with the maximum amount of freedom from governmental supervision.

When he turned to the state assembly in 1896 to secure the repeal of the statute forbidding franchise grants of over twenty years' duration, he precipitated the hottest issue in Chicago politics during the next two years. Its people were the more easily aroused because they had long endured overcrowded trolleys, high fares, and poor and hazardous service. In late March, 1897, a non-partisan mass meeting named a committee of 100 to thwart Yerkes at Springfield. In this group, besides Lowden, were many leading citizens, including J. P. Altgeld, J. M. Palmer, Graham Taylor, Victor Lawson, Potter Palmer, C. R. Crane, Leon Mandel, J. V. Farwell, Jr., H. H. Kohlsaat, F. MacVeagh, and J. H. Hamline. They succeeded in defeating the Humphrey Bill desired by Yerkes[27] but could not prevent the passage of the Allen Bill giving the city council almost complete freedom to make its own terms with any streetcar company, provided only that its franchise was for not over fifty years.[28] This, to Lowden and many another Chicagoan, meant an excess of local autonomy. They feared lest the aldermen "sell out" to the traction interests by granting franchises for the maximum term at too

24. He spoke on "The New Chicago" at the Marquette Club's Chicago Day banquet, Oct. 9, 1897.

25. MS of FOL's speech at Château de Frontenac, Quebec, Sept. 12, 1899.

26. *Buffalo News,* Oct. 7, 1901.

27. All Chicago newspapers except the *Inter-Ocean* opposed the Humphrey Bill. Yerkes called its narrow defeat, "a victory for the socialistic and anarchistic elements."

28. *Chicago Record,* May 21, 1897; *Chicago News,* May 29, 1897.

low a price. So great an uproar arose from both parties—even louder from the Democrats than from the Republicans—that the council withheld action and the chastened legislature replaced the Allen Bill with its original measure limiting public utility company franchises to a twenty-year maximum. Governor Tanner had alienated numerous Chicago Republicans, including Lowden, by signing the Allen Bill.[29]

Neither the citizens nor the street-railway interests were satisfied with the outcome. In an advisory referendum in April, 1902, the voters spoke emphatically for municipal ownership and operation of traction lines and of gas and electric light plants as well. Although Lowden continued to hold that a city should be administered like a business enterprise, he opposed this popular verdict. To him it threatened private "vested rights" and smacked of state socialism. Consequently, he found himself in the uncomfortable position of disagreeing with many of his reformer friends and working with the Lorimerites and the traction companies to defeat bills conferring upon Chicago's government an unbridled mastery over the whole public utilities field. Notwithstanding their stiff opposition at Springfield, they succeeded only in delaying until the late spring of 1903 the passage of the Mueller Municipal Ownership Law, whereby the government of Chicago had the option of issuing twenty-year franchises or, if the people approved, of buying out the traction companies. In April of the next year a huge majority of the voters again spoke in favor of municipal ownership and operation. Thereafter, a lack of money in the city treasury and delaying court actions by the private companies gained for Lowden and his friends what they had been unable to ward off at the capital in Springfield and in the City Hall.

The Yerkes affair of 1896–98 provided Lowden with a stark example of how a dishonest tie-up between big business and government could injure the public welfare. At the opposite pole, as he saw it, the tactics of the Pullman Company strikers and the "socialist" doctrines of Governor Altgeld were equally harmful and unpatriotic. Each extreme was "radical" in the sense that it menaced democracy. For organized wealth to manipulate government to its own ends would be as vicious as for organized labor to resist by violence a court injunction or to prevent a non-union man from holding his job. Democracy, however vague its boundaries, meant the middle road between plutocracy and mobocracy.[30]

As a corporation lawyer and the son-in-law of George M. Pullman, Lowden was at a marked disadvantage in advocating laws regulating trusts. His political opponents doubted his sincerity whenever he criticized big business or complimented workingmen's unions. To him, this suspicion resembled the unpatriotic demagoguery of certain Democrats like Bryan and Altgeld, who emphasized the class divisions within American society and apparently sought

29. E. B. Smith, "Street Railway Legislation in Illinois," *Atlantic Monthly*, XCIII (January, 1904), 109–18; Carter H. Harrison, Jr., *Stormy Years* (Indianapolis, Ind., 1935), *passim*.

30. MS of FOL's speech before U. S. Grant Club, Des Moines, Iowa, Apr. 27, 1900.

to line up the poor against the rich. This "socialistic" palaver alarmed him because he observed that more and more voters were accepting it as truth. In his judgment the public schools had a major responsibility to combat this heresy. In a democracy, he insisted, the basic distinction between man and man, whether rich or poor, must be on the score of character and achievement alone. Contrary to what agitators said in their inflammatory speeches, farmers and laborers were rapidly bettering their lot, capitalists had less influence in government than before, and honesty increased in the conduct of elections. No one could convincingly deny that the chasm between the very wealthy and the very poor had widened, but so also had "the spread between the extremes of intellectual, moral, and physical capacity. This divergence adheres in the very development of human nature." American government was not, as the Socialists said, a "despotism of the rich" but, on the contrary, permitted a maximum of individual freedom. Of course, Lowden continued,

the unreason and the unreasonableness of the discontented are no excuse for ignoring the reality of their distress; nor does their demand for a disastrous remedy warrant the neglect of their complaints. . . . Ways must be found to help the starving, honest, and capable laborer; but only by the use of constitutional methods and through an orderly development of our law. . . . Equality of opportunity must be preserved. . . . The Republican Party by its history is consecrated to right the wrongs of the men who toil.[31]

This brought poor comfort to underpaid wage-earners. And yet, admiring Abraham Lincoln more than any other American—with Alexander Hamilton or John Marshall a close second—Lowden quoted approvingly the Emancipator's dictum that the rights of labor deserved priority over those of capital. The *Daily Labor World* found him sufficiently forthright in support of unions and in advocating governmental curbs upon big business to merit the workingman's vote for any high office to which he might aspire.[32] Although his diagnosis of the ills of society was more persuasive than his prescription for curing them, he recognized the offenses of certain corporation officials and bluntly condemned them in his speeches.

In an address on "The Development of the Civic Conscience," delivered at the Central Music Hall in Chicago in March, 1897, he declared that "corporate interests must learn that every immunity or benefit dishonestly gained is a menace. Those who buy a franchise become suspect in all they do, and public officials will not even do the legitimate thing for them without a bribe." The voters must, like sentinels, he continued, be ever on the alert against malfeasance by those in the seats of governmental power. "The United States citizen is a paradox. He is magnificent in a crisis. In war he will give all to the state; in peace he expects all from the state and will give nothing in return. In war he dies heroically for his country; in peace he imperils its existence

31. MS of FOL's speech before the Marquette Club, Chicago, Oct. 9, 1897.

32. *Daily Labor World* (Chicago), Oct. 25, 1899; *Chicago Times-Herald*, Feb. 4, 1901; Mrs. Lowden's diary, Feb. 4, 1901.

by acquiescing in the corruption of its officials." Believing this, Lowden had been much pleased when, at his invitation, former President Benjamin Harrison addressed the Union League Club of Chicago on "The Obligations of Wealth" and admonished his propertied listeners against condoning or conniving at dishonesty in government.[33]

Quantitatively at least, Lowden had more to say about the obligations of big business to society than about the social responsibilities of labor organizations. "No corporation," he remarked in 1899, "unless it rests on a public franchise can acquire a monopoly in any other sense than that if it gives the public more for its money than individual enterprise can do, it will have most of the business. Apparently some trusts do." No big corporation, he believed, could survive if it tried to make a maximum profit by charging exorbitant prices for its commodities, but a "healthy combination, honestly managed, preserves the stability of prices and prevents panics."[34] On the one hand, he applauded as "clear and cogent" Judge Christian C. Kohlsaat's decision in early 1900, holding the Illinois antitrust law of 1893 unconstitutional because its exemption of farmers and stock-raisers from its provisions made it "special class legislation." But, on the other hand, he urged a stiffening of federal statutes in order to forbid the giving of rebates by firms in interstate commerce and to require them—and labor unions, as well—to publish annually a detailed report of their assets and liabilities. Furthermore, state laws should deny a charter of incorporation to any overly capitalized business group and penalize by forfeiture of charter any corporation accepting a rebate from a railroad. Although the heyday of the small merchant was past, the decline in cutthroat competition because of mergers between companies in the same line of business conferred benefits upon labor as well as upon consumers.[35] He took special pride in the fact that he preceded Theodore Roosevelt in distinguishing between "good" and "bad" trusts. On June 11, 1901, at the State University of Iowa, in a forceful Phi Beta Kappa address entitled "Some Phases of the Industrial Question," he brought together these views about capital and labor in relation to government. This speech probably received more widespread and favorable attention from the press than any he had delivered up to that time.[36]

The coming of the Spanish-American War in 1898 had temporarily weakened the impetus toward political and economic reforms. The issues of honest primaries and city officials, labor unions and corporations, were submerged by the tidal wave of emotional patriotism engulfing Chicago. Lowden helped to raise it and rode upon its crest. In a fifteen-minute speech at the Union League Club, he "electrified" his hearers by reviewing Spain's history of "blood, inhumanity, and misrule" in the Western Hemisphere. If he were

33. B. Harrison to FOL, Nov. 12, 1896; *Chicago News,* Feb. 22, 1897.

34. *Chicago Journal,* May 14, 1900; typewritten record of an interview with FOL, undated except "autumn, 1899."

35. *Chicago Tribune,* Jan. 30, 1900.

36. It was published in full in the *Iowa City Republican,* June 11, 1901. FOL to O. R. Zipf, Freeport, Illinois, July 16, 1906.

correct, her officials arranged for the U.S.S. "Maine" to be anchored above a mine. God willed that the United States as "the divine instrument" should achieve its splendid destiny by forcing Spain forever out of America. The Monroe Doctrine prevented any European power from engaging in this "holy mission"; therefore it was America's duty and high privilege. Nine other speakers, including H. D. Estabrook, the Rev. Newell Dwight Hillis, and Judge John Barton Payne, contributed to the torrent of eloquence on this occasion.[37]

The club enthusiastically named Lowden the head of a committee to raise and equip a Union League Club brigade of three regiments of volunteers, to have Governor Tanner allot National Guard armories in Chicago for their use, and to persuade President McKinley to dispatch the troops to Cuba or the Philippines. Although Lowden disclaimed any military ambition or experience, he had considerable trouble in warding off his election to command the brigade or at least one of its regiments. The Chicago newspapers greatly exaggerated the extent of his military training at the State University of Iowa. If the soldiers went to the firing line, he was willing, but not anxious, to go with them. On the other hand, he did not wish to don a uniform and merely sit out the war in a home camp.[38] When the administration at Washington was slow to recognize its need for the club's brigade at the front, Lowden visited the capital city in mid-July to urge prompt action. Thanks to the influence of Charles G. Dawes, comptroller of the currency, Lowden gained access to President McKinley and several of his cabinet. But his mission was all in vain. The fighting was almost over, and the Chicago volunteers saw no active service. By September, the Illinois National Guard regiments were returning home, and Lowden's chairmanship of the league's war committee came to an end.[39]

Early in 1899, the officers of the First Regiment, Illinois National Guard, rewarded Lowden's civilian war service by electing him its lieutenant colonel —second in command under Colonel J. B. Sanborn. The main duty of the lieutenant colonel of this proud and plush outfit had long been "to represent the regiment socially and before the public." Lowden, however, tried to make clear that he would be "no parlor orator or dress suit soldier" but stood ready to obey all commands of his superior officer and "share my hardtack with the needy."[40] Eating hardtack did not figure importantly in his four years of service, but he studied the army manuals, attended the evening drill periods faithfully, and endured the heat of the annual summer encamp-

37. MS of FOL's speech, "The War with Spain," Apr. 22, 1898; *Chicago Chronicle,* Apr. 23, 1898.

38. *Chicago Inter-Ocean,* Apr. 30, May 8 and 17, 1898; *Chicago Chronicle,* May 3, 1898. FOL wrote to his wife, July 14, 1898: "I do not think there is much danger of my going to the front. I think we are doing valuable work but I will not be sorry when relieved of war duties."

39. *Dawes Journal, 1893–1913,* p. 165, entry of July 17, 1898; undated letter of FOL to Mrs. Lowden in early September, 1898.

40. *Chicago Inter-Ocean,* Jan. 31, 1899; *Chicago Legal News,* Feb. 4, 1899.

ment and maneuvers at Camp Lincoln near Springfield. In July, 1899, during his first "tour of duty" there, he found his brother officers and Colonel Sanborn "considerate of my inexperience." "I received the Regimental parade last evening," he added, "and with the entire Regiment before me and five thousand spectators around, I was nervous enough, I tell you."[41] Although he was an excellent rider, his horse fell and rolled on him a few days later, denying him the excitement of sharing in the formal parade and review which brought the encampment to its climax and close. Better luck had attended him on Memorial Day of that year, when, in the absence of Colonel Sanborn, he led the regiment in parade on Michigan Avenue in Chicago.[42] In Washington a few weeks later, he had Dawes take him to the White House to see whether he could obtain a regular army commission for Philippine service. He "received some encouragement" but soon wired Dawes to let the matter drop.[43]

The chief service which Lowden hoped to render his regiment and other National Guard units in Chicago failed of accomplishment through no fault of his own. In 1899 the state legislature appropriated $100,000 for the construction of a big armory and parade ground in that city. The municipal and state officials approved of a lake-front site, north of Monroe Street in the heart of the main business area. Ever since its origin twenty-five years before, the First Regiment had been a favorite of Chicago's businessmen. They viewed it much more as a shield against labor unrest than as a protection against a foreign enemy. The heads of the traction companies, especially, cherished the troops as insurance against property loss in case of strikes. To have the new armory strategically well located was therefore of much importance. One of the armory commissioners, along with Lowden, was Colonel E. R. Bliss, a close business affiliate of the streetcar interests.

The commissioners, however, had not taken Montgomery Ward, "the watchdog of the lake front," sufficiently into their reckoning. He insisted that the building could be centrally located without putting it where it would mar the city's chief aesthetic asset. In answer to his petition, a court enjoined Lowden and his two colleagues from going ahead with their project. In response to their appeal the Supreme Court of Illinois upheld the ban,[44] and Lowden had doffed his uniform before the new armory was ready for use. When he resigned his commission early in 1903, his fellow officers presented him with a loving cup.[45] To many friends, he remained "Colonel" Lowden as long as he lived.

Besides diverting him from his work as a reformer, the Spanish-American War and its aftermath created issues which helped to draw him into a bigger

41. FOL to Mrs. Lowden, July 10, 1899; Mrs. Lowden's diary, Nov. 16, 1899; July 5 and Oct. 25, 1901; July 10, 1902.

42. Mrs. Lowden's diary, May 30, 1899; *Chicago Tribune,* May 31, 1899.

43. *Dawes Journal, 1893–1913,* pp. 195–96.

44. *Chicago Inter-Ocean,* May 14, 1899; *Chicago Chronicle,* May 30 and June 20, 1900.

45. FOL to Mrs. Lowden, Sept. 16, 1902; *Chicago News,* Jan. 10, 1903.

political arena than Chicago alone. His interest in civic betterment continued, but he supplemented and eventually overshadowed it by enlarging his participation in Republican party activities at the state and national levels. In this shift of focus, he followed the pattern of other middle-of-the-roaders like Theodore Roosevelt, whose career as a reformer and soldier Lowden much admired. The more he broadened his sphere of action, however, the more he became entangled in the party machinery, and the harder he found it to maintain his local reputation as a liberal and a reformer. The coming of the Republicans to power in 1896 at Springfield and Washington also deepened his conservatism. Until then, his role had been that of a prosecutor, charging the incumbent Democrats with sins of omission and commission. Thereafter, for seventeen years, loyalty to his party impelled him to defend most of what it did while at the helm of his state and the nation. As long as he sought no office, he could maintain a considerable independence of action. If, however, he ever decided to make politics his vocation, he would have to align himself with one or another of the Republican factions in Illinois.

The history of the Republican party in Illinois is a kaleidoscopic and often bewildering story of transitory rivalries and temporary bargains or compromises between unstable groups. Disagreements over platform issues were usually minor in importance when compared with contests between leaders, between areas downstate, between areas within Chicago, and between the so-called "federal crowd" and "state crowd." Simple at least in its main outline, this last-mentioned cleavage was merely a division or feeling of difference between the congressmen, senators, and federal office-holders, on the one hand, and the state office-holders, on the other. In some measure it reflected the desire of Republican state officials for positions in Washington or to be federal judges, marshals, postmasters, or collectors of internal revenue within Illinois. Already ensconced in many of the more desirable jobs, the "federal crowd" naturally had a semblance of unity. Because its members were Washington- rather than Springfield-centered, their interests could not be spoken for adequately by the state central committee of their party. With the exception of the two senators—and their terms of office were long—the federal officials were independent of the governor and state legislature. Often aspiring to be a United States senator as his next step up the political ladder, the governor occupied a difficult spot. To have a successful administration, he must co-operate with his fellow Republicans in the legislature; to attain his senatorial ambition, he usually needed help from the federal office-holders, with their entree at the White House.

Intra-party rivalry between Republican bigwigs living in different regions of the state largely meant a jostling for a "fair share" of the appointive offices. Leaving Cook County out of consideration and omitting exceptions for the sake of clarity, Illinois, like Gaul, was divided into three political parts— "Egypt," or the southern counties; a middle zone centering around Jacksonville, Springfield, and Bloomington; and the area west of the Illinois River. Egypt never furnished a Republican majority; the central area usually did, while northern Illinois remained staunch in the faith. The party members of this "rock-ribbed" section, which included Ogle County and "Sinnissippi," complained that their steadfastness worked to their injury. In other words, the party chieftains outside that region could depend upon its allegiance without apportioning it an equitable share of patronage or of the nominees chosen by the state party conventions. To make inroads upon the Democrats, southern and central Illinois Republicans received favors beyond their deserts.

State representatives and senators from these three areas, however, would fight shoulder to shoulder against bills for the benefit of Chicago at downstate expense. Only at this point in the factionalism did issues become as important as offices. Reflecting the deep-rooted distrust of urban folk by rural folk, the country assemblymen resisted measures to grant Chicago more home rule and a fairer allotment of representatives at Springfield. On the other hand, a bipartisan Chicago bloc opposed downstate politicians whenever they tried to modernize Illinois's antiquated tax system by obliging owners of stocks, bonds, and other "intangibles" to pay taxes in proportion to their yearly incomes.

The Republican factions in Chicago, although wrangling interminably between elections and allying frequently with one or another Democratic clique in a political "deal," normally managed to unite long enough to support a slate for the various elective offices in the city government. Their delegates, however, rarely voted as a unit at a state convention of their party. For this reason, as well as because of the downstate versus Chicago sectionalism, a Chicago Republican seldom became the party's choice for governor. An aspirant from the metropolis could not hope to be nominated unless a considerable number of rural delegates supported him as well as an almost solid Cook County contingent. His strongest card, although rarely decisive in his favor, was a financial one. The party's "war chest" depended heavily upon the purses of Chicago's businessmen. An unwritten rule of the game prescribed that, no matter how acrimonious the intra-party strife might be before a slate of candidates was decided upon, all contention must yield to an outward appearance of complete harmony during an election campaign.

District delegates meeting in convention chose the Cook County Central Committee. This convention also picked representatives from the state senatorial districts in the county to attend the annual Republican state convention. At this gathering the delegates from each of the twenty-two state senatorial districts designated one of their number to be a member of the Republican State Central Committee. The state convention elected seven more members at large. In a presidential year, this assemblage also appointed the delegates at large to the national nominating convention and, at least nominally, confirmed the other delegates who had been elected in the congressional districts. At the national convention this contingent selected a leading Republican to be the Illinois member of the Republican National Committee for the next four years. He co-ordinated and in some measure directed the campaigns within Illinois for elective federal offices. His patronage power over appointive jobs in the national government rarely amounted to much, in spite of his prestige.

The Republican State Central Committee named its own chairman, secretary, and treasurer. Like its national counterpart, it further organized itself by empowering its chairman to appoint an executive committee and separate committees on organization, finance, literature, press, judiciary, railroads, and speakers. As Lowden remarked, this body had "absolute charge of conducting the campaign after the nomination of the state ticket" at the state convention. "The funds for conducting the campaign," he added, "are raised in various ways. Each congressional committee [that is, the Republican committee in each congressional district in the state] is usually assessed $1,500, which is raised by the committeemen, and donations are received from Republicans throughout the state, office holders, etc."[46]

In this complicated structure of committees and conventions, Lowden began to take his place in the late 1890's. Thus in June, 1898, he gladly served as a delegate from his district to the Cook County Republican convention[47] and later that summer joined with Roy O. West, Edgar A. Bancroft, Walter L. Fisher, Merritt Starr, and other members of the Union League Club to form a "Roosevelt, 1904 Club." It proposed to work for the hero of San Juan Hill "on all occasions as a fearless, independent, Republican successor to McKinley."[48] Before the year closed, he and other members of a Hamilton Club committee presented Roosevelt in Albany with a bronze inkstand upon the occasion of his inauguration as governor of New York.[49]

Lowden agreed with the Rough Rider's vehement support of a large navy, a downright foreign policy, and the retention of the islands taken from Spain in the recent war. In his view, the New Yorker had that "audacity of genius" which explained why the Republican party served the nation so well during the Civil War, why the McKinley administration was making a memorable record, and why Republicanism and the highest patriotism were equivalents. In his first important political speech outside Illinois, he told his audience at the Michigan Club banquet in Detroit on Washington's Birthday, 1899, that the Democrats benefited their country only when out of power. By championing the antiquated doctrine of state's rights and other impracticable theories inherited from their overrated patron saint, Thomas Jefferson, they served as a useful spur to the Republicans, keeping them alert and forwardgoing with their program in fulfilment of America's proud destiny. After mentioning Lowden's "handsome face and graceful bearing" and noting that he employed no gestures, the *Detroit Free Press* complimented him upon "the prettiest speech of the evening" and one that flowed "as smoothly as the waters of the Detroit River." On the other hand, two Democratic papers

46. FOL to W. Grimes, Guthrie, Oklahoma, Jan. 7, 1907.

47. Mrs. Lowden's diary, June 8, 1898.

48. *Chicago Record,* Aug. 26, 1898.

49. *Ibid.,* Dec. 31, 1898.

of that city sarcastically expressed regret that he had not been alive a century earlier to warn the Fathers against Jefferson. One of them added: "We are indebted to Mr. Lowden of Chicago for the formal announcement of a rapprochement between Providence and the Republican Party."[50]

For a year before the national elections of 1900, there was little doubt about the names of the opposing presidential candidates or the outstanding issue of the campaign. McKinley and Bryan would be pitted against each other once more, and American imperialism, especially of the Filipino variety, would supplant the 1896 money question as the principal subject of debate. Lowden contributed nothing original in thought to the perfervid Republican oratory but, contrary to his recollection in his old age,[51] he enthusiastically defended American expansion across the Pacific Ocean. He debated before the Marquette and Hamilton clubs of Chicago on behalf of resolutions upholding "the march of the flag" into the distant islands of the Far East. Annexation of the Philippines, he declared, squared with "the logic of events" and America's duty to the civilized world. England or Germany would gobble up the Filipinos if they were cut adrift. They could not govern themselves, and only a few of them resisted American rule. Therefore, the charge that the United States had to dragoon a majority of the islanders into submission was untrue. Did President Jefferson, a Democrat, ask permission of the inhabitants of Louisiana territory before buying it from Napoleon? Aguinaldo and his meager band probably turned their arms against their deliverers from the Spanish yoke because Democrats and a few renegade Republicans beguiled them with unwarranted sympathy.

The opposition fallaciously charged, Lowden continued, that the annexation treaty violated the Declaration of Independence, the Constitution, and the Monroe Doctrine. As for the immortal Declaration, the United States followed its very essence by freeing thousands of the "little brown men" from tyranny. Although the Monroe Doctrine had never applied to the Pacific Ocean, it was a formula for national security and the expression of a hope, when announced in 1823, that all lands in the Americas would shake off their European yoke. For these reasons, the Spanish-American War and the treaty of peace harmonized with the Doctrine. Furthermore, the Constitution did not forbid territorial expansion. Precedent (the Alaskan purchase) and Supreme Court decisions supported an extension of the nation's boundaries beyond its continental limits. Ever since the birth of their party in the mid-1850's, the Republicans had insisted upon the sovereignty of Congress rather than of the Constitution in the territories. Hence there could be no doubt about the legality of a tariff on Puerto Rican and Filipino imports. Moreover, the islanders were not United States citizens.[52]

50. *Detroit* (Mich.) *Free Press,* Feb. 23, 1899; *Detroit Journal,* Feb. 23, 1899; *Detroit Tribune,* Feb. 24, 1899.

51. See pp. 490 and 732, n. 27.

52. MSS of FOL's Chicago speeches before the Hamilton and Marquette clubs (Oct. 27 and 28, 1899); before the Jewelers' Association banquet, Jan. 19, 1900; and before the Hamilton Club, Apr. 9, 1900.

One of Lowden's proudest moments during these months occurred on the evening of April 26, 1900, when as toastmaster at a Marquette Club banquet he introduced Roosevelt, who gave the final lecture in a series on "Expansion." Lowden reminded him that, looking forward to the White House four years later, the support of the club should bring him good fortune because it had been one of the first organizations to champion William McKinley for the presidency. According to the newspapers, Roosevelt seemed "supremely happy" and led the guests in singing "There'll Be a Hot Time in the Old Town Tonight."[53]

Lowden's active share in the election campaign of 1900 contrasted sharply with his insignificant role in the hectic battle of 1896. During the intervening years he had made a place for himself among the second-string leaders of his party in Illinois. Although he showed no public interest in running for office and seemed content merely to help the candidacies of other men, he was mentioned by the Chicago press from time to time as a possible mayor, congressman, attorney-general of Illinois, or governor.[54]

Early in 1900 the Cook County Central Committee, dominated by Lorimer, West, and Deneen, declared that Judge Elbridge Hanecy of their own faction should be the gubernatorial nominee. Governor Tanner unwillingly acquiesced after he discovered little enthusiasm for his own renomination or for his second choice, Congressman Joseph Cannon of Danville. The "federal crowd," led by Comptroller of the Currency Dawes, who supposedly acted under White House inspiration, brought forward the "dark horse," Richard Yates, eager for the race.[55] When all the anti-Tannerites, including Lowden, rallied to Yates's banner at the Republican state nominating convention in Peoria in May, the Lorimerites hopped on the band wagon. If the Lorimer faction could not have Hanecy, it at least wanted the credit of tipping the convention's scales in Yates's favor. Although Lorimer had fewer henchmen than before on the state central committee, he managed temporarily to keep control of the Cook County Republican organization. But even on his home grounds, the defection of Deneen, West, and others from his coterie soon weakened his leadership. Having been encouraged in their action by the Lawson-Noyes-Patterson newspaper triumvirate, the Deneenites seemed merely to exchange a control by one master for that by three others.[56]

Richard Yates possessed the usual characteristics of a compromise candidate. Few Republicans were enthusiastic about him, but all accepted him as preferable to a party schism. The son of Illinois's Civil War governor, he had

53. *Chicago Record,* Apr. 27, 1900.

54. *Chicago Journal,* May 26, 1899; *Chicago Eagle,* May 27, 1899; *Chicago Times-Herald,* Jan. 30, 1900. In his Detroit speech of Feb. 22, 1899, he said: "I have not held public office and there is no such spontaneity of desire on the part of my fellow-citizens to have me serve them as to induce the hope within me that I ever shall."

55. *Dawes Journal, 1893–1913,* pp. 210, 224–27; *Chicago Times-Herald,* July 14, 1900.

56. Frank Noyes of the *Chicago Record-Herald,* Victor Lawson of the *Chicago News,* and Robert W. Patterson of the *Chicago Tribune.* Noyes echoed the views of his employer, Lawson.

capitalized upon the magic of his father's name among veterans to assure himself a political career. For nearly twenty years before his gubernatorial nomination, he had been a favorite orator on national holidays and at GAR posts and encampments. An easygoing, affable gentleman, his impressive appearance and silver-tongued sentimentalities about Illinois, Grant, Logan, and Lincoln attracted votes as well as applause. In a candidate's role he had every qualification; but even some of his friends wondered whether he had enough force and originality to be a statesman-like governor.

Among the delegates whom Congressman Cannon led to the Republican national convention was Frank Lowden from the Third Congressional District.[57] On June 16, after parading with the Cook County Republican Marching Club down Michigan Avenue, he boarded his private car for Philadelphia. Like the rest of the coaches in Governor Tanner's special train, Lowden's was bedecked with "McKinley and Dolliver" banners on the gala trip eastward. Male quartets competed in song, a fifty-piece band often drowned out the vocalists, and Lowden, Deneen, and others readily supplied oratory whenever the music began to pall. Between the sessions of the convention, Lowden favored his friends with a ride to New Jersey seaside resorts.[58]

These evidences of good feeling, however, did not signify unity within the Illinois delegation either in its support of a nominee for the vice-presidency or in the choice of the Illinois member on the Republican National Committee. The Lorimerites and Tannerites wished Governor Tanner to have this latter post as a solace for his failure to win renomination. But Cullom, Dawes, Lowden, and others backed Graeme Stewart and eventually had their way. In similar fashion, but with a quite different alignment, two-thirds of the Illinois delegation, including the Chicago contingent, wanted Senator Dolliver of Iowa to be McKinley's running mate. Cannon and a dozen others rallied to the apparently unwilling Roosevelt. And yet, no sooner had the convention named the New York governor, than Lowden told reporters that the choice, like the "conservative and wise" platform, was "perfect." In his opinion Roosevelt could be vice-president without endangering his chances of entering the White House four years later. Although the weary Lowden had a severe cold when he arrived back in Chicago on June 24, he presided at the Hamilton Club's ratification meeting in Steinway Hall. Dawes and Dolliver were the featured speakers.[59]

The next four months found Lowden more active politically than ever before. Even his week in camp with his regiment was broken by a trip with Senator Cullom "in fearful heat" to Watseka, Illinois. There he delivered an oration as part of a typical county-seat observance of the Fourth of July, with parade, bands, businessmen's "floats," Indians, cowboys, "Deadwood" stagecoach, races, cakewalks, fireworks, and open-air speeches in the court-

57. *Chicago Chronicle,* May 22, 1900.

58. *Chicago Tribune,* June 15, 1900; *National Republic* (Chicago), June 23, 1900.

59. *Chicago Chronicle,* June 22, 1900; Mrs. Lowden's diary, June 24, 1900.

house square. In mid-July he led in organizing a Yates Club at Oregon and felt obliged to deny a rumor that Lorimer had picked him to contest Cullom's renomination as United States senator.[60]

As a member of the Committee of Notification of the Republican national convention, he journeyed to Canton, Ohio, in early August on a superfluous mission to inform William McKinley of his renomination. While there, however, he was "pleased and surprised" when the President invited him to be first assistant postmaster-general of the United States at an annual salary of $5,000.[61] This was the first of many offers of appointment to federal positions which Lowden received during his lifetime. Dawes and Stewart pressed him to accept "as a service to his party," but he hesitated to give up his new home in Chicago and a professional income of approximately $50,000 a year. After talking "long and hard" with Mrs. Lowden, he declined the invitation "for business reasons."[62] At this time she could not encourage him to launch upon a political career.

Apparently uninterested in holding any office, either elective or appointive, and uncommitted to any of his party's factions, Lowden was in the enviable position of being courted by all of them. In August, 1900, when Mark Hanna asked him to be on the national advisory committee for the duration of the campaign, he gladly accepted. This provided exactly the opening he had sought. It brought him into association with the top leaders of the party and placed him in an advantageous position from which to observe the management of a presidential contest.[63]

Beginning in late September and continuing until election day, six weeks later, he kept almost continuously on the road with the "Republican Legion." It was his first experience in political barnstorming—of day after day in the cramped quarters of a dusty train, of short rear-platform speeches at scores of small way stations, of voice-straining efforts in the open air of noisy picnic grounds and courthouse squares, and of competing with tobacco smoke and hecklers in the halls and opera houses of many Illinois towns. He found the work exhausting and exhilarating. The congenial companionship of men like Yates, Dawes, Cullom, Mason, Hanecy, and Lawrence Y. Sherman yielded a sufficient reward for all his exertion.[64] Lowden was an excellent mixer, no matter what the economic and social status of his audience. Its applause served as the best of tonics when he felt weary. But, like other politicians before his day, he discovered how much larger Illinois actually was than he had ever imagined it to be.

60. MS of FOL's speech at Oregon, Illinois, July 13, 1900. In this first address to his new neighbors he told why he was a Republican.

61. FOL was the third choice for the post, left vacant by the resignation of Perry Heath of Chicago (*Dawes Journal, 1893–1913,* pp. 237, 239, 243–44).

62. Mrs. Lowden's diary, Aug. 4 and 5, 1900; Postmaster-General C. Emory Smith to FOL, Aug. 13, 1900.

63. *St. Louis Republic,* Aug. 17, 1900; *Chicago Times-Herald,* Sept. 11, 1900.

64. FOL to Mrs. Lowden, Sept. 22, 1900.

The speeches of Lowden and his fellow travelers, delivered in many towns between Galena and Cairo, repeated over and over the same arguments in identical phrases. Each orator really had only one address. He launched upon it after a few prefatory remarks in compliment of the village where he was speaking and in support of the local Republican candidates for office. Any listener who read a newspaper must have attended a political rally only to share in the excitement, gaze upon the candidates, and note how closely each speaker could recite exactly what he had said elsewhere. In delivering these speeches, Lowden and his colleagues subjected their vocal cords and their consciences to far greater strain than their intellects. "Pointing with pride" and "viewing with alarm," interspersed with humor, flattery, and extravagant promises, comprised the standard ingredients of an effective address. To strike home, however, it had to be delivered with vigor and earnestness and with an air of appealing on a man-to-man basis of equality to the common sense of each listener. The speaker knew that his target was not the mind of the hearer but his funny bone, his emotions, and his relish for a well-turned phrase apparently embodying a profound truth.

Probably no politician in American history has drawn against himself a greater barrage of witty and wordy invective than William Jennings Bryan. By their use of it, the Republicans and "Gold" Democrats revealed their fear of his magical platform presence and the persuasiveness of his program. That Lowden shared in this strategy of ridicule is the more surprising because during his long political career he rarely attacked the personality or character of his opponent. As early as April, 1900, in an address before the Hamilton Club in Chicago on "Democracy and the Declaration of Independence," he gave free rein to an alliterative characterization of the Democratic presidential aspirant. He often repeated it during the rest of the campaign. Bryan, he said, was "the peerless leader of modern democracy whose hybrid organization flourishes on famine, prospers on panics, and breeds by virtue of bankruptcy"; "the raven of politics who hopes to be borne into office on the shoulders of discontent." He uses the "blatant palaver of a wandering political prophet"; he "juggles with words and performs with phrases" and "is the victim of a vocabulary who never flickers in his fluency, yet whose smooth sentences would break should they strike 'the rough edge of a thought.' "[65] "Which is sweeter to your ear, the hum of industry or Populist oratory, Democratic promises or Republican performances?" The Democratic party, insisted Lowden, had opposed civil service reform, assaulted the Supreme Court, acted dishonestly on the money question, arrayed class against class by demagogic offers of quack remedies, and fostered economic panics ever since Andrew Jackson's day. A vote for Bryan was a vote for a return of hard times. As for the Republicans, their administration had restored so much prosperity that the Kansas Populist, Mary Ellen Lease, now imported her gowns from Paris, and "Sockless" Jerry Simpson no longer deserved his

65. MS of FOL's speech at Hamilton Club, Apr. 9, 1900.

sobriquet. The protective tariff meant a "full dinner pail" for the industrial worker.[66]

In addition to all this, Lowden usually included some references to the "benedictions" attending the American flag wherever it had gone since 1776 and to the not-distant day when the "brown men of the Philippine Islands" would rise up to bless William McKinley as the Negroes revered Abraham Lincoln.[67] In the main, however, he confined his speeches to the domestic record of the Republican party. Rural or small-town audiences were more interested in the effects of the tariff and the gold standard upon their everyday life than in Aguinaldo and whether "the Constitution followed the flag."

By early October, when Mrs. Lowden joined her husband aboard "The Reindeer," the Fish Commission's boat, for his two days of speech-making in towns along the Illinois River,[68] his memory of the campaign was studded with place names like Metropolis, Golconda, Elizabethtown, Robinson, Sumner, and Mason City. Although he spoke in them all, no one of them had left a distinct impression. What he said and the circumstances attending his speech had everywhere been almost identical. Noise from cannon, fire bells, or factory whistles greeted his party upon its arrival. There followed an impromptu reception in a hotel lobby, with babies to admire, wives to flatter, and husbands to thank for "confidential" information of no great importance. The local reception committee primed the speakers about matters of neighborhood pride to mention in their remarks. With a band in the van, small boys frolicking close to its bass drum, and the "grown-ups" lining the sidewalks, if any, the speakers were escorted by the mayor and the local Republican club in carriages to the place of meeting.

A glee club or a throng of school children often opened the program with patriotic songs. The chairman then introduced the "warmer-upper," usually the junior among those scheduled to speak and the one whom the audience least wanted to hear. After he concluded, "Lem" Wiley ran through the melody of a "piece" on his cornet, a stereopticon flashed the words upon a suspended bed sheet, and everyone joined in the singing. Frequently it was a "hit" tune of the day with the lyric altered to suit the campaign. After the last of the two or three politicians had delivered his peroration and answered or humorously evaded questions from the audience, they underwent another ordeal of handshaking and being cordial.

As soon as the meeting adjourned, the procession re-formed to take the orators to their train or their hotel.[69] For them, there were too much to eat,

66. MS speech of FOL for use in autumn of 1900.

67. MS of FOL's speech at Watseka, Illinois, July 4, 1900. Whenever FOL or some other Republican speaker held forth in a town where the citizens regarded Stephen A. Douglas as the greatest of all Democrats, he portrayed him as an expansionist who would have deplored the timid position taken by his party in 1900.

68. Mrs. Lowden's diary, Oct. 1–4, 1900.

69. Mrs. Lowden's diary entries for late September and early October, 1900; also his daily letters and/or telegrams to her.

too much to drink, too much to smoke, too much to be said in a loud voice, and too little restful sleep. Near the close of the campaign of 1900, Richard Yates stated that in fifty days he had visited seventy-five of Illinois's one hundred and two counties, clasped two hundred and fifty thousand hands, and made a hundred and sixty addresses of from one to two hours in length. These did not include scores of "brief remarks." On one day he "orated" ten times. Lowden could not match this endurance record, but, by the time he once again reached Chicago in mid-October, he was hoarse and exceedingly tired.

His brief respite by his own fireside enabled him to catch his breath and recover his voice in preparation for the two final and most hectic weeks of the campaign. In accordance with precedent, the Republican politicians made Chicago the center of their effort when the contest neared its climax. Besides sharing in this metropolitan roundup of votes, Lowden was off to Oregon, Clinton, Nioga, and Anna in northern Illinois between October 22 and 26 and closed the Sangamon County campaign with a speech at Springfield on the eve of election day.

On October 27 the party staged its "Parade of Prosperity" in Chicago, with Mark Hanna in the reviewing stand. The Republicans claimed to have over thirty-five thousand men in line, although the *Chicago American* charged that many employers compelled their pro-Bryan workmen to share in the demonstration. However that may have been, there were contingents from all the leading industries and stores, as well as elephants and gaily decorated floats. The rank and file of the Republican marching clubs wore white uniforms, while their officers were resplendent in white and blue. "Brigadier General" Lowden, astride a horse, led the first brigade, with J. B. Sanborn as one of his "lieutenant colonels" and Roy O. West and Homer K. Galpin as two of his "lieutenants."[70] On the following day the weary candidate Richard Yates, having partaken of too much lemonade and lobster salad in the buffet car on his way from Galena to Chicago, was sick abed in Lowden's home. Thanks to the ministrations of his host's physician, Dr. Frank Billings, he recovered sufficiently to address a large crowd at the Auditorium on the evening of the twenty-ninth and to appear with Lowden at the Tenth Ward Wigwam earlier that night and again with Lowden and Deneen for a speech on the thirtieth at Fortschritt Turner Hall.[71]

How much at odds newspapers can be in their reports of political rallies is illustrated by their contrasting stories of Lowden's speech at the Chatterton Opera House in Springfield on the evening of November 3. A parade featuring a Negro drum corps, Greek fire, Roman candles, and red lanterns escorted him and his wife to the hall. If the *Springfield Journal* (Republican) can be believed, Lowden, "one of the most brilliant orators of the West," delivered "one of the best speeches of the campaign" in a crowded

70. *Chicago Tribune,* Oct. 27, 1900; *Chicago American,* Oct. 28, 1900.

71. Mrs. Lowden's diary, Oct. 27 and 28, 1900; *Chicago Tribune,* Oct. 29 and 30, 1900; *Chicago Inter-Ocean,* Oct. 31, 1900.

theater. On the other hand, the *Springfield Register* (Democrat) made known that his "weak speech," a tirade of abuse and ridicule two hours in length, elicited "feeble applause" from the small audience of not over eight hundred people, three-fourths of whom were women. "Lowden is a rather fine looking young man," continued the *Register*, "but one on whom high living has already set its mark, for he is already becoming beefy." In her diary, Mrs. Lowden agreed with the *Journal*.[72]

Lowden listened with high satisfaction to the state and national election returns as they came by telephone and telegraph to the Chicago Republican headquarters on the night of election day. McKinley and Yates carried Illinois, while Deneen won another term as state's attorney. "The election demonstrates," Lowden told a reporter of the *Chicago Record*, "that the people of America are still absolutely sane, and that they will be for safe and sound principles."[73]

Hardly was this contest over when the long-simmering Illinois senatorial kettle began to boil. Although President McKinley and Dawes supported Cullom for re-election, their will was resisted by many influential members of the party. These included Governor Tanner and Congressmen Hopkins, Vespasian Warner, and Robert R. Hitt, who aspired to the senatorship themselves. As long as the opposition split between so many candidates, Cullom felt certain of victory. Under these circumstances the Lorimerites tried to unite the field against him by persuading his four rivals to withdraw if Lowden would enter the race. Richard Yates, the governor-elect, prudently declared that he favored all the contestants equally.[74] When Lowden refused to be tempted, the "stop Cullom" movement suddenly collapsed in mid-January, and the Illinois legislature re-elected the veteran senator by an almost unanimous vote of its Republican members.[75] Earlier that month, Mr. and Mrs. Lowden witnessed Yates's induction into the governorship and danced a few moments at the crowded Inaugural Ball.

By that time, Lowden was finding the never ending game of politics irresistible in its fascination. Late in January, when he gave a stag dinner in celebration of his fortieth birthday, more political than business friends sat at his table.[76] The Republican leaders in Chicago, about to try once again to defeat Mayor Carter Harrison, Jr., for re-election, frequently mentioned Lowden as the man to do the job. But he manifested no more interest in going to the City Hall than to the Senate or the Post Office Department

72. *Springfield* (Ill.) *Register* and *Springfield Journal,* both of Nov. 4, 1900.

73. Mrs. Lowden's diary, Nov. 6 and 7, 1900; *Chicago Record,* Nov. 7, 1900. Samuel Alschuler of Chicago had been the Democratic gubernatorial candidate.

74. Yates took a neutral position only after he failed to persuade Dawes to come out against Cullom (*Dawes Journal, 1893–1913,* entries of Aug. 6, Nov. 18–19, Dec. 9, 11, 28, 1900; *Chicago Inter-Ocean,* Jan. 18, 1901).

75. *Journal of the House of Representatives of the Forty-second General Assembly of the State of Illinois* (Springfield, Ill., 1901), pp. 86–91.

76. Mrs. Lowden's diary, Jan. 26, 1901.

in Washington. His choice of an opponent to Harrison was William Hale Thompson, the young and popular alderman from the "silk-stocking" Second Ward. Nevertheless, at the Republican city convention on March 2, which Lowden attended as a delegate, Lorimer secured the nomination of Judge Elbridge Hanecy.[77] Friendship as well as considerations of party solidarity led Lowden to support the judge in speech after speech as a man whose election would end the "crime, vice, and corruption" associated with the Democratic administration. His efforts went for nothing. In Dawes's words, the outcome was "a Hanecy Massacre." Rebuffed by the re-election of Cullom and Harrison and further weakened politically by the death of his ally, former Governor Tanner, in late May, Lorimer's prestige sank to a low ebb. His enemies within his own party sought eagerly to profit from his faltering fortunes by driving him into complete political oblivion.

Among these enemies, none was keener for the chase than Charles Gates Dawes. If he reached his quarry, he would win a seat in the United States Senate in 1903 and end Lorimer's malevolent influence within the party at the same time. Political virtue and personal ambition joined in happy alliance. Strengthened by his close tie with the White House, he succeeded in ranging on his side, and hence against the Congressman, the forces of Cullom, Republican National Committeeman Stewart, and Lawrence Sherman, the speaker of the Illinois Assembly. In Chicago he could count upon the help of Deneen, West, Henry Hertz, and Fred Busse, the state treasurer.[78] Although Dawes probably would find Yates athwart his path, he did not consider him a redoubtable foe.[79] As for William Mason, whose Senate seat Dawes coveted, his unimpressive record at Washington included opposition to the administration's Filipino and Puerto Rican policies. He belligerently declared that he would seek re-election, but he could not have been sanguine of success.[80]

Mason's weakness and Lorimer's evident need to recover political status by backing a winner aroused much newspaper speculation about whom the "Blond Boss" would bring forward to oppose Dawes's senatorial ambition. If, as seemed probable by mid-1901, the Lorimer, Yates, and old Tanner factions were to combine behind one man, who would better fit their needs than Frank Lowden, often known as the "Chinese puzzle" or "dark horse"

77. *Chicago Journal,* Nov. 7, 1900; *Chicago Record,* Nov. 20, 1900; *Chicago Inter-Ocean,* Dec. 20, 1900; *Chicago Times-Herald,* Mar. 2, 1901.

78. Henry Hertz was United States collector of internal revenue for the Chicago district (*Dawes Journal, 1893–1913,* p. 273, under date of July 19, 1901). Dawes told the author on Nov. 7, 1947, that he came out for the Senate because certain Illinois politicians were trying "to knife McKinley."

79. During 1901, Yates drew closer to Lorimer, who opposed Dawes.

80. Mason was a Chicago lawyer (Mason and Ennis). After ten years in the Illinois legislature, he went to Congress in 1888 for two terms. In 1897 he defeated Altgeld for the Senate. He was an old-fashioned, "tub-thumping" orator with much good humor. He called Dawes a "carpetbagger" who had come to Illinois too recently to merit one of her senatorships (*Chicago News,* Apr. 13, 1901; *Chicago Tribune,* July 6, 1901; *Chicago Chronicle,* Oct. 3, 1901).

of Illinois Republican politics?[81] Neither the case-hardened newspaper reporters nor the professional politicians could fathom him. New to their experience was an ardent Republican who desired no office, joined no faction, made no effort to build one of his own, hobnobbed cordially with leaders in every camp, and worked for reforms certain to reduce his party's patronage power. After pondering about his unorthodox conduct, some columnists decided that "the Pullman millions" furnished the clue. Evidently he had enough astuteness to recognize that the wealth which enabled him to be an independent Republican also barred him from becoming a popular candidate for any elective office.[82]

It was common knowledge during 1901 that Yates and Lowden were close friends and frequently consulted William Lorimer. In late August and early September the Lowdens entertained Yates and his wife at "Castle Rest." On September 6, while on the golf links, the two men received a wire telling them that McKinley had been seriously wounded by an anarchist at the Pan-American Exposition in Buffalo. Following the President's death about a week later, they went to Washington together to attend the impressive state funeral.[83]

The assassination of McKinley greatly altered the senatorial outlook. To oppose Dawes would not offend the new President. Moreover, Theodore Roosevelt held Congressman Albert J. Hopkins, chairman of the Civil Service Committee of the House of Representatives, in high regard. Foiled in his effort to succeed Cullom in the Senate early in 1901, Hopkins now saw his great opportunity.[84] At the state fair at Springfield in October, where much "politicking" took place annually, the rumor was current that Yates and Lorimer relied upon Hopkins to defeat Dawes. The incumbent, Senator Mason, seemed to be forgotten by everyone except himself. To remind the public that he had not withdrawn, he opened campaign headquarters at the fair and distributed lapel buttons bearing his picture.[85] Before the end of the year Hopkins formally announced his candidacy, while Lorimer and Yates came out openly in his favor. Although Lawrence Sherman and others stubbornly continued to work for Dawes, he realized that his chance to win had been buried with McKinley. Temporarily disgusted with politics and determined to resist the lure of any elective office in the future, he turned to banking for a new career. With the help of Lowden and other wealthy friends, he incorporated the Central Trust Company of Chicago. When this four-million-dollar institution opened its doors on July 8, 1902, Lowden was one of its incorporators, directors, and stockholders.

In May of that year, the Yates-Lorimer-Cannon coalition pushed Hopkins'

81. *Chicago Record,* May 12, 1901; *St. Louis Republic,* July 22, 1901.

82. *Springfield News,* June 10, 1901.

83. Mrs. Lowden's diary, Sept. 6, 14, 16–17, 1901.

84. *Chicago Inter-Ocean,* Sept. 29, 1901; *Chicago News,* Oct. 3, 1901.

85. *Chicago American,* Oct. 1, 1901; *Chicago Chronicle,* Oct. 3, 1901.

nomination through the Republican state convention by a vote of over two to one.[86] Outwardly neutral in the contest, Lowden declared that he was interested only in preventing it from splitting the party. Political pundits, who professed to know his inmost thoughts, surmised that he either was working secretly for Hopkins or counted upon being the beneficiary of a deadlock in the Illinois legislature.[87] Indeed, by 1902, many signs indicated his readiness to run for some office, although for which one even he probably did not then know. In that year, as already mentioned, he ended his activities as a promoter of business corporations, dissolved his law partnership, reduced the number of his clients, and resigned his commission in the Illinois National Guard.[88] He assiduously cultivated his acquaintanceship with Theodore Roosevelt. In late January, 1902, while in Washington to attend the Gridiron Club dinner, he conferred with the President at the White House.[89] In several speeches on the tariff and the trusts he carefully attuned his views to those of the administration. In preparation for a visit by Roosevelt to Chicago in October, Lowden gladly agreed to head the committee on arrangements. Although his work in this connection went for naught because a minor ailment obliged the President to postpone the trip, Lowden served as toastmaster at the civic banquet in Roosevelt's honor the following spring.[90]

At this time Yates's confidential relationship with Lowden began to cool because he noted his friend's undue interest in the Executive Mansion at Springfield as a place where he would like to reside in the near future.[91] Could "love of rural life" wholly explain why he and his wife spent more and more time at "Sinnissippi"? To those reporters who discovered a studied purpose in every act of a politician, Lowden's newly acquired passion for pursuing "the wily potato bug to its lair" and teaching "the young bean to shoot" meant in reality "a cultivation of country votes." Deliberate and shrewd as always, according to this view, he was laying a deep rural foundation beside his urban one, in order to have a doubly strong base upon which to erect a political career.[92]

This interpretation did not altogether miss the mark. Beyond any doubt he earnestly sought the good will of influential people in the Thirteenth Congressional District, where his farm was located. Its representative at

86. *Chicago Inter-Ocean,* May 9, 1902.

87. MS of FOL's speech at Hyde Park Republican banquet, Chicago, Apr. 11, 1902; *Chicago Eagle,* June 12, 1902; *Chicago Inter-Ocean,* July 10, 1902.

88. In a letter of Sept. 16, 1902, to Mrs. Lowden, he commented: "I want this year to close out most of my quasi-public duties on the ground that I've done my part."

89. Mrs. Lowden's diary, Jan. 25–27, 1902.

90. MS of FOL's speech on "Hamilton and Reciprocity," Hamilton Club birthday banquet, Chicago, Jan. 11, 1902. The civic banquet for Roosevelt was in the Auditorium Hotel on Apr. 2, 1903.

91. *Chicago Chronicle,* Aug. 28, 1902; *St. Louis Republic,* Sept. 11, 1902. Congressman William Lorimer visited FOL at "Castle Rest" in September, 1902.

92. *Chicago Journal,* Aug. 15, 1901.

Washington was the aging and ailing Robert R. Hitt of Mount Morris. Perhaps "Farmer" Lowden hoped for Hitt's blessing as his successor in Congress in the not-distant day when he must retire. The editors of the *Freeport* (Ill.) *Journal* and *Ogle County Republican* of Oregon, Illinois, availed themselves of every opportunity to build up Lowden in that district, as though they expected him soon to need the votes of their subscribers.[93]

More than ever before except on the eve of an election, he traveled about the state, making speeches at GAR "campfires" and elsewhere, eulogizing Hamilton, Lincoln, Grant, McKinley, and Theodore Roosevelt and reiterating his great love for Illinois. Seeking to please every faction within his party, he spoke in Springfield, on May 23, at Governor Tanner's grave in Oak Ridge Cemetery, a few feet from Lincoln's tomb.[94] Mrs. Lowden entertained more politicians in her home in 1902 than in any previous year. Her diary entries of guests at meals read like a roster of the influential Republicans of Illinois— Governor Yates, Attorney-General H. J. Hamlin, Speaker of the House Lawrence Y. Sherman, Congressman Lorimer, Alderman William Hale Thompson, "Boss" T. N. Jamieson, Judges Hanecy, Grosscup, and Bethea, and many others.

On September 12, 1902, the Republicans opened the Chicago phase of their mid-term election campaign with a monster outdoor mass meeting and picnic in Sans Souci Park near the University of Chicago. On the battery of speakers were Lowden and Congressmen Hopkins, Lorimer, and Mann. The committee in charge provided so much entertainment in the form of fireworks and prizes, with free ice cream, cookies, lemonade, "penny-lickers," and red popcorn balls for the children that a force of one hundred policemen could not maintain order among the fifty thousand people who crowded into the grounds. Most of them unashamedly exhibited more interest in the free food and in pocketing spoons and tin cups as souvenirs than in the eloquence. The orators fought a losing battle against the crying babies and shouting children. To add to Lowden's discomfort, his voice was hoarse with a cold. He assured his wife that he never before had faced so large an audience or spoken amid such trying conditions.[95]

Among his remarks, he included the three or four main points to which he returned again and again until election day. The Democrats, said he, still talked about the obsolete currency and imperialism issues of the 1900 election. He insisted that the high rates of the Dingley Tariff were "reasonably good." To tamper with them would make businessmen so nervous that the economic prosperity might come to an end. The opposition, he admitted,

93. *Freeport* (Ill.) *Journal,* Jan. 8 and Feb. 7, 1902. The editor was J. R. Cowley, a member of the Republican State Central Committee and soon to become FOL's political aide and private secretary.

94. MSS of fifteen different speeches between October, 1901, and September, 1902, in Chicago and at least nine downstate towns.

95. FOL to his wife, Sept. 13, 1902. Professor Harry P. Judson, of the University of Chicago, presided over the speech-making.

stood on stronger ground when it spoke for a tightening and widening of the federal antitrust laws. Voters, however, should remember that these statutes bore a Republican label. The Democrats prated no end about the evils of big business but characteristically had done nothing to abolish them when in power in Washington. For Bryan and others to say that the high tariffs bred trusts was absurd. As a matter of fact, if business consolidations were fairly capitalized, honestly managed, and properly controlled in the public interest, they benefited laborers, consumers, and America's foreign trade. Under the Constitution, Congress could do little more to curb wrongful practices by the few predatory trusts until an amendment clearly conferred "plenary power" to regulate all corporations in interstate and foreign commerce. Lowden made clear that an amendment for that purpose would enlist his support.[96] Organized labor deserved credit for the enactment by Congress of the Chinese Exclusion Act and the anticontract labor law. Unions had influenced state legislatures to pass acts reducing the employment of children in industry and the hazards of all workmen. "This Republic," Lowden concluded, "can claim no more useful citizens in the working out of our great industrial problems than its Sargents, its Arthurs, its Gompers, its John Mitchells, its Morgans, [and] its Hannas."[97]

He felt no hesitation that autumn in backing Lorimer in his successful effort to win re-election to Congress. "I believe in the ultimate triumph of the right always," Lowden declared sententiously just before the balloting, "and William Lorimer is in the right." On the night of election day, after Mrs. Lowden had taken refuge at "Sinnissippi," he installed a telegraph instrument in his Chicago home and entertained fourteen Hyde Park politicians at a stag dinner. The evening was much the merrier because of the good news coming over the wires.[98]

Although several newspapers insisted that Lorimer felt unhappy about Hopkins' senatorial candidacy and expected to bring Lowden forward that autumn as the best man to succeed Mason, their story was probably sheer invention.[99] The West Side boss was too shrewd to risk a further loss of prestige by shifting his support to a candidate whose chance of success would be slight. Nor would Lowden gamble against such heavy odds when making his first bid for public office. In early January, at a political meeting at Rochelle, state Senator Charles H. Hughes of Dixon, near "Sinnissippi," declared that the time had finally come when northern Illinois could furnish the state with a Republican governor. Frank Lowden was the man.[100] In all

96. In the autumn of 1902, for the first time in his political career, he received an invitation from a Republican state committee to speak outside Illinois. This address was at Muscatine, Iowa, Oct. 23, 1902.

97. MS of FOL's speech in the Auditorium, Chicago, Oct. 29, 1902, under the auspices of the First Ward Roosevelt Republican Club. Also MSS of his speeches at Bloomington, Illinois, Oct. 14, and at Rockford, Illinois, Oct. 17, 1902.

98. MS of speech of Oct. 31, 1902; Mrs. Lowden's diary, Nov. 4, 1902.

99. *Chicago Eagle,* June 12, 1902; *Chicago Inter-Ocean,* July 10 and 11, 1902.

100. *Ogle County Republican* (Oregon, Ill.), Jan. 8, 1903.

likelihood he had asked his friend to send this "kite" aloft to test the strength and direction of the political wind. Thus he had reached a turning point in his career. At long last he was ready to make politics his vocation.

Two weeks after Hughes's speech, the Illinois legislature, by a unanimous vote of its Republican members, elected Hopkins to the United States Senate. The press of Chicago hailed this event as "a startling Lorimer victory," whereby he regained a controlling position in Illinois politics.[101] With Lorimer's star bright once more in the Republican sky, could Lowden avoid steering by it, now that he was ready to launch his own political bark?

101. *Chicago American,* Jan. 7, 1903; *Chicago Inter-Ocean,* Jan. 22, 1903; *Chicago Chronicle,* Jan. 25, 1903. All Chicago papers except the pro-Lorimer *Inter-Ocean* had opposed Hopkins' election.

CHAPTER VI

SPRINGFIELD OR WASHINGTON, 1903–6?

Early in 1903, when Lowden confided to a few of his friends that if conditions became auspicious he might seek the gubernatorial nomination, he recognized the seriousness of the factional strife within his party in Illinois. All the party leaders agreed that Theodore Roosevelt deserved another term in the White House, but even their unanimity on this point caused keen rivalry among them to gain his exclusive indorsement for some high federal or state office. On his part, the President limited his intervention to delivering little homilies about how much all this bickering damaged the Republican cause. Wishing the solid support of the Illinois delegation in the national nominating convention of 1904, he carefully kept every important clique vying for his favor.[1]

One phase of this intra-party conflict was the previously mentioned fight over the senatorship in January, 1903. After having been ousted from the speakership of the state House of Representatives as an episode in that contest, Lawrence Y. Sherman was in no mood to support any candidate of the Hopkins-Yates-Lorimer coalition who might seek the official backing of his party. An able lawyer, Lincolnesque in appearance, he was popular enough with the electorate to expect "compensation" for his lost post. On his advice, his followers in the Assembly bowed to the will of the Republican legislative caucus and voted for Hopkins, but they naturally disliked an outcome effected at their own expense. The congenial governor, Richard Yates, lacked great force as a leader and controlled only one wing of his party. Although he wished to be renominated, he knew that the heads of the other factions hoped to displace him in the Executive Mansion at Springfield. Sherman, among others, was receptive and could count upon Dawes's help. In May, 1903, thirty-nine members of the legislature called Sherman their candidate.[2]

Charles S. Deneen, state's attorney for Cook County and a South Side Chicagoan, believed that his own city should furnish the next Republican governor, and he wanted to be the man. With Yates, Sherman, and perhaps other leaders in the running, Deneen could not count upon the support of many downstate delegates to the Republican state convention, but he might be their second choice in case their favorites withdrew or deadlocked. Other

1. John McC. Davis, *The Breaking of the Deadlock* (Springfield, Ill., 1904), pp. 27–28; hereafter cited as "Davis."

2. *Chicago Chronicle*, May 17, 1903; *Dawes Journal, 1893–1913*, pp. 337–59, *passim*.

strings in his bow were his excellent record as a prosecuting attorney, his Illinois pioneer forebears, his downstate upbringing and education, and his recent break with Lorimer. To many a rural as well as urban voter, Lorimerism signified city politics at their worst. And yet the opposition of the "Blond Boss" meant that Deneen would not have the unanimous backing of the Chicago delegates. At best, he might win as many as two-thirds of them. No Chicago gubernatorial candidate in the past had ever been able to exceed that fraction. The metropolitan contingent would comprise about one-third of the total membership of the nominating convention.[3]

As compared with Lowden, Deneen at the age of forty was an experienced office-holder. For nearly fifteen years he had served at one time or another as alderman, assemblyman, state's attorney, and in several appointive positions. He was a veteran member of the Republican State Central Committee and had been a delegate to national nominating conventions. In view of this record, he deserved better than Lowden's patronizing attitude toward him in 1898. "I want to give a dinner to Deneen sometime this week," he informed Mrs. Lowden on September 19, ". . . I think an official such as Deneen, honest and faithful, though a politician in a sense, ought to be encouraged and sustained by the men whose respect he would so much like to have." At about this time, Bernard A. Eckhart, a rich and influential Chicago miller, began to make the political advancement of Deneen and Roy O. West his particular concern. In 1902, Percy B. Eckhart, Bernard's son, graduated from Harvard Law School and formed a law partnership with West which continued for over forty years. Their first office was the part of Lowden's suite in the Temple Building which he relinquished upon the close of his business association with Estabrook and Davis. Consequently, West and Lowden had neighboring doors and met frequently.[4]

Although William Lorimer played his usual "gumshoe" game by declining to make known whom he favored for the governorship, he certainly would not pick Deneen. By all logic, he should have helped Yates win a second term, but in recent months he had been drawing closer to Lowden. For many weeks after Hughes's speech at Rochelle, however, Lowden remained coy and reticent about his candidacy, if any. One Chicago newspaper ventured the opinion that, like several of the other gubernatorial aspirants, he hesitated to announce his entrance into the race lest Lorimer "jump on his bandwagon" and blast his hope of success.[5] Other editorial writers believed Washington rather than Springfield to be his target and that he planned to succeed or supplant Congressman Hitt in the Thirteenth Congressional District. How he could do this when his residence and place of voting were in Chicago remained in doubt, but at least the question posed the city-country

3. *Chicago Journal,* June 1, 1903. In Chicago, Deneen was favored by the "newspaper czars" already mentioned and by leading Republicans like Fred Busse, Henry Hertz, and Dan Campbell, the postmaster.

4. As stated to the author by Roy O. West, Jan. 6, 1951.

5. *Chicago Record-Herald,* July 21, 1903.

dilemma which bothered Lowden during much of his political career.[6] Because of his manner of living at "Sinnissippi" and his close affiliation with Chicago and big business, farmers often viewed him with suspicion. Contrariwise, his emphasis upon the needs of agriculture and his early identification of himself as a "farmer" invited city politicians—and even the spokesmen of corporations later in his life—to challenge his fitness to represent their interests.

Considerations of sound political strategy in 1903 led him to cultivate the favor of voters both in Chicago and downstate. No one could win the gubernatorial nomination by the backing of Cook County delegates alone. His trips to Springfield that spring on behalf of further civil service legislation and a greater measure of home rule for his city enabled him to become better known to influential downstate Republicans.[7] His Rock River farm and the growing discontent of northern Illinois members of his party because they had always been slighted in the distribution of offices were a fact and a feeling which he could exploit to his own advantage.[8] If he surprised Deneen by developing considerable delegate strength in the city, he planned to announce his candidacy in Chicago and employ Rock River Valley support as a useful supplement. On the other hand, if he garnered only one hundred or even two hundred of Cook County's more than five hundred delegates to the state convention, while capturing the favor of many from the rural areas, he would formally make known his candidacy at a meeting in Oregon and go before the convention primarily as a representative of the Illinois countryside.[9] Furthermore, by delaying this announcement, he would be spared the embarrassment of withdrawing in case he received too little encouragement to stay in the prenomination contest. If he realized his ideal, his candidacy would emerge from an apparently spontaneous public demand too insistent for him to resist. During the first half of 1903 he put himself in "the hands of his friends," outwardly doing as little as possible to call newspaper attention to his hopes.

Denying that he was a candidate, however, did not bar him from moving about northern Illinois in search of new friends, visiting Springfield to be introduced to members of the legislature, conferring with Sherman and other leaders of his party, and noting with satisfaction the articles about himself, his family, and "Sinnissippi" in the press.[10] On May 14, 1903, he held the first

6. *Joliet* (Ill.) *Republican,* Feb. 26, 1903; *Rockford* (Ill.) *Star,* Apr. 5, 1903; *Urbana* (Ill.) *Courier,* Apr. 23, 1903.

7. Mrs. Lowden's diary, Feb. 24–26, Mar. 9–11, Apr. 13 and 21–23, 1903.

8. *Chicago News,* Apr. 30, 1903; *Rockford Republic,* June 2, 1903.

9. *Chicago Journal,* Oct. 8, 1903: "The burning question of the hour is whether Frank Lowden will run from Cook County, Ogle County, Pullman, or Hawaii." In MS notes for an urban-centered acceptance speech, he wrote: "Deneen calls me a bogus farmer. I never claimed to be anything but a resident of Chicago. . . . The press refuses to print anything but derogatory things about me unless I pay them. So I will have to meet people personally."

10. *Dixon* (Ill.) *Telegraph,* June 19, 1903; *Peoria* (Ill.) *Star,* June 24, 1903; *Ogle County Reporter* (Oregon, Ill.), June 24, 1903; and *Calumet* (Ill.) *Record,* June 25, 1903.

of a long series of political meetings at his farm. At this "social" gathering, B. F. Shaw, a charter member of the Republican party and editor of the *Dixon Evening Telegraph;* James R. Cowley, editor of the *Freeport Journal;* former state Senator Charles H. Hughes of Dixon; and Ziba A. Landers, editor of the *Ogle County Republican* were four of his guests. A few days later, in order to hold the urban-rural balance even, he entertained at "Sinnissippi" Roy O. West, Victor Elting, Bernard Eckhart, and Brode B. Davis. Also with them on this occasion was Attorney-General Howland J. Hamlin, who would soon enter the gubernatorial free-for-all himself.[11] Whether Hamlin's purpose was merely to gather some downstate delegates for eventual delivery to Lowden or whether the latter was merely a "stalking horse" for Governor Yates raised questions of much interest to newspaper editors. On Chicago's South Side, "Doc" T. N. Jamieson and Professor Harry Pratt Judson made themselves unique among the Republican leaders of that area by opposing Deneen and viewing both Hamlin and Lowden with favor.[12]

Lowden kept as closely in touch with Congressman Lorimer as he did with many other leaders of his party. The Chicago boss disliked Hamlin and reportedly urged Congressman Vespasian Warner of Clinton to declare his candidacy as a means of undercutting Hamlin in his own district. If Lorimer preferred Yates above all others, he encouraged Lowden only in order to divide the strength of Deneen in Cook County so that the latter could not injure Yates. In his own interest, Deneen naturally insisted that Lowden was tarred with Lorimer's brush.[13] On the other hand, Lorimer hoped to get as many candidates into the running as possible. With a divided field, his own bloc of delegates might play a decisive role in the nominating convention. His prestige in Chicago suffered another blow in June when the Democrats defeated fourteen out of eighteen on his "slate" of candidates for Chicago's judicial offices. Among the vanquished was Judge Hanecy. This rebuff enabled Deneen and his supporters to give new emphasis to their earlier assertion that the Republicans would never come to power in Chicago as long as Lorimer dominated the party's organization.[14]

All important newspapers in that city opposed Lowden. In their columns and cartoons the publishers tied him to Lorimer's coattails, ridiculed his pretensions of being an Ogle County farmer, and portrayed him as a rich playboy who really should run for the vice-presidency, where his only duties would be "to eat, drink, and sign checks." In like fashion many rural editors made merry at his expense by alleging that he manicured the hoofs of his livestock, exhibited a stuffed two-headed calf in a Chicago store, and could not tell the difference between wheat and oats.[15] His was a rough initiation into the fraternity of Republican office-seekers.

11. Mrs. Lowden's diary, May 23, 1903.

12. *Chicago News,* June 10, 1903; *Chicago Tribune,* June 18, 1903. On Sept. 27, 1903, FOL wrote to his wife: "Hamlin tells me much that even the editors don't know."

13. *Springfield* (Ill.) *News,* Dec. 4, 1903.

14. *New York Times,* June 3, 1903.

15. *Chicago Tribune,* June 17, 1903; *Chicago News,* July 16, Sept. 21, and Oct. 21, 1903; *Chicago Journal,* Aug. 29, Sept. 2, Oct. 20, and Dec. 12, 1903.

In the summer of 1903 nearly a year had still to go by before the meeting of the Republican nominating convention, but the gubernatorial campaign was already in almost full swing. So many country delegations visited "Sinnissippi" that a brief lull in their comings and goings led Mrs. Lowden to comment in her diary, "I've been rather glad to see no politicians about for a change."[16] Judging from her husband's little speeches to these guests and his press releases, his candidacy was never mentioned. On the contrary, these high-minded gentlemen concerned themselves only with effecting a solidarity of policy among the Republicans of northern Illinois and ending the intra-party factionalism throughout the state. Having harmony as his dominant theme, Lowden evidently cast himself in the role of a peacemaker whose lofty mission it was to draw all discordant elements together. The opposition press cartooned him either as a dove bearing an olive branch or as an angel carrying a barrel of Pullman money.[17]

On June 18, about one hundred Republicans, led by James R. Cowley and B. F. Shaw, convened at the Hotel Nelson in Rockford to serve warning on the rest of their party that northern Illinois must have its just share of the nominations in 1904. Although Lowden stayed away and his name did not appear in the press release of the meeting, everyone knew that its purpose was to help him and William H. Stead of Ottawa, who wished to be the attorney-general of Illinois. If, as the *Tribune* declared, the Hotel Nelson conclave signified that Lowden's Chicago boom had collapsed and downstate support was his only remaining hope, he refused to admit it.[18] Not unmindful of the Negro wards or the example of President Roosevelt, he gave a dinner at the University Club in honor of Booker T. Washington and spoke before the Hamilton Club on Negro political rights.[19] On Labor Day, 1903, he told the Associated Building Trades workmen of Chicago at their picnic in Ogden Grove that the state government could help them lessen the amount of cutthroat competition in the labor market. Even more than low labor costs, he added, an employer wanted workmen upon whom he could rely to stick to their jobs at a definite wage. To effect this, there should be mutually inviolable contracts between employers and the unions. In his customary fashion, he included in his remarks an inventory of federal and state legislation for which labor could take much of the credit.[20]

Although he complained that his political advancement was at the high cost of a separation from Mrs. Lowden for most of the summer, he had no

16. Entry of July 25, 1903. In the main, FOL's visitors were of the "federal crowd."

17. *Freeport* (Ill.) *Bulletin,* June 18, 1903; *Chicago Post,* Oct. 19, 1903.

18. *Chicago Tribune,* June 19, 1903; *Rockford Republic,* June 18, 1903; *Rockford Gazette,* June 18 and 19, 1903. At the time of the meeting, FOL and Senator Cullom were visiting Congressman Hitt at Mount Morris, about 30 miles away.

19. Mrs. Lowden's diary, May 9 and Nov. 9, 1903.

20. MS of FOL's speech, Sept. 7, 1903. For efforts to portray FOL as labor's enemy see *Springfield Register,* Oct. 7, 1903; and John W. Hayes, Knights of Labor, to K. M. Landis, Feb. 1, 1904.

doubt of his progress. He assured her in mid-September that if the nominating convention were then in session, he most probably would be its choice.[21] Congressman Hitt staunchly supported him, perhaps in some measure because he knew that to make Lowden governor would eliminate a potential rival for his seat in the House of Representatives. Headed by Cowley of Freeport and Hughes of Dixon, a somewhat amorphous organization worked for "the Squire" in the Thirteenth Congressional District. Cowley, who was equally at home in journalism and politics, supplied "boiler-plate" material in praise of Lowden to an increasing number of rural newspapers.[22] Illinois's two Senators, Cullom and Hopkins, and the influential congressman, Joseph G. Cannon, soon to be speaker of the House of Representatives, manifested a benevolent neutrality toward his candidacy. Perhaps they might persuade the President to offer Governor Yates a federal position sufficiently attractive to make him forego his desire for re-election. Cullom could not help wondering whether his own place in the Senate would be secure in 1906 if the ambitious Deneen attained the governorship. Lowden seemed to be less grasping in his drive for political power.[23]

"You have no idea," Lowden assured his wife in September, 1903, "how many people one must see, how many letters one must write, who gets into this predicament of mine."[24] The "predicament," of course, was of his own making, and he felt happy to be in it. At this time he was about to leave on a friend-making trip through the southern counties. Thanks to the *St. Louis Republic*, owned by a company in which a friend of Mrs. Lowden held a controlling interest, an influential newspaper voice had been proclaiming his merits in the western portion of the "Egypt" area for several months before his arrival.[25] His principal address was at Carbondale, where, along with Yates, Warner, Deneen, and Hamlin, he spoke to a large audience of Civil War veterans. Mrs. (General) John A. Logan, one of Mrs. Lowden's oldest friends and very popular with the GAR, attended the meeting and let the old soldiers know where her sympathies lay. On the return journey Lowden and Deneen chanced to be on the same train. They talked together from one until four o'clock in the morning, but what they said is not of record.[26]

Both men were Springfield-bound to the annual state fair, always a favorite rendezvous of politicians. Any person searching for one of them would almost certainly find him at the Sangamo clubhouse on the fair grounds or in the lobby of the Leland Hotel, enveloped in cigar smoke and surrounded by a group of interested listeners. Lowden spent much time among the crowd

21. FOL to Mrs. Lowden, Sept. 18, 1903; also his letters to her of Aug. 18, 25, and Sept. 21, 1903.

22. Mrs. Lowden's diary, July 13, 1903.

23. *Chicago Chronicle,* July 20, 1903; *Springfield News,* July 21, 1903.

24. FOL to Mrs. Lowden, Sept. 22, 1903.

25. FOL to Mrs. Lowden, Aug. 28, 1903.

26. *Chicago Record-Herald,* Sept. 25, 1903.

as well as in conference with his workers. By the close of the fair, he felt
that he had added considerable strength to his candidacy.[27] But the cost to
his domestic life had been high, and even more strenuous days lay ahead. "I
begin to realize," Mrs. Lowden confided to her diary on October 4, "that I
am going to have to give up a great deal of my husband's society for the next
few months—a prospect that is anything but agreeable!"

All except one of the contestants for the gubernatorial nomination announced their candidacies immediately after the close of the Illinois state
fair.[28] The Ogle County Republican Central Committee arranged for Congressman Hitt to preside at a meeting in the courtroom at Oregon on the
afternoon of October 8. Visiting delegations attended from the other five
counties of the Thirteenth Congressional District, and Lowden's three young
children were also in the audience. Most of the stores in Oregon closed for
two hours in honor of the occasion. After brief addresses by Justice Cartwright and two politicians of local prominence, the gathering unanimously
requested Lowden to announce his candidacy.

Responding to this appeal, he mentioned his pledge to himself not to enter
the contest unless the Republicans of his congressional district favored him
and until more than a single faction urged him to come forward. These two
qualifications, he added, had now been met. He owed no political debts, and
he had been encouraged by friends in Cook County as well as in other areas
of the state. Therefore, he believed that his acceptance of the invitation of
the meeting would "stop the policy of extermination" within the Republican
party and help bring harmony.

For these reasons I can not resist your request, and I shall be a candidate for the
nomination until the Republicans in state convention assembled shall choose their
standard bearer for the next campaign. So far as lies within my power the campaign for the nomination will be free from personalities. I shall be a candidate *for*
the nomination; not *against* any aspirant for the office.

The rest of Lowden's short speech struck the keynote which he would
elaborate upon in many addresses during the seven months remaining before
the convention. If nominated and elected, he would keep in mind the too-
often-forgotten fact that the Illinois constitution provided for a separation
of powers between the three departments of government and that a governor
violated the letter as well as the spirit of this fundamental law when he used
his patronage power so as to dominate the judiciary and the legislature.
Merit, not service to party, must be the first requisite for every appointment
to office. Most of the work of the executive branch was of a business, rather
than a political, nature. Consequently, after naming the best available men
to the managing boards of the various state institutions, the governor ought
to leave them wholly free from interference as long as they performed their

27. Mrs. Lowden's diary, Sept. 27, 1903. He had prepared for his stay at Springfield by
writing in advance to local political leaders throughout the state, inviting them to meet
him during the fair or later in Chicago.

28. Vespasian Warner delayed his announcement until December.

duties efficiently. Nor should they or the other state appointees be expected to leave their offices for weeks at a time to help in a political campaign. "It is my ambition," declared Lowden, "to be Governor of Illinois and not a party manager."[29]

Evidently he was expanding into a state-wide platform the principles for which he had battled in Chicago. Theoretically, much could be said in their favor, but whether he or anyone else could be a successful governor by practicing a laissez faire policy toward his party and the administrative officers of the state is most doubtful. American political history at both national and state levels suggests that any chief executive, to make a distinguished record, must head his party and lead the legislature. Lowden's rivals quickly pointed to his stand on these matters as the best of proof that, having held no public office, he was wholly unqualified to occupy the highest in the state. They ridiculed his efforts to pose as a "goody-goody" "nice little man" when in truth he was the tool of William Lorimer and his corrupt Chicago machine.[30]

Whether Lorimer dominated Lowden was the most important issue in the contest with Deneen for the support of the Chicago delegation to the nominating convention. Before that contest had reached its height in the early spring of 1904, Lowden carried his cause into many of the 102 counties of Illinois. He kept almost continuously on the road during the autumn and winter, accompanied by two secretaries to handle his mail and arrange the details of his itinerary. To fend off the cold, he bought a fur coat and a pair of felt-topped boots. This outfit provided his rivals with much amusement. Down to his knees a plutocrat, his lower limbs and feet were those of a farmer. Lowden retorted that no man merited the governorship who lacked enough common sense to keep a cool head and warm feet.[31] When "Farmer" Lowden was asked whether he really could milk one of his famous Shorthorns, he replied:

I never have supposed that the ability to milk a cow was one of the qualifications prescribed for a governor. I am still of the opinion that there is nothing in the Constitution or laws of this state that makes cow-milking one of the duties of the Governor. But I want to say to you here and now that if I am mistaken and if this contest is to be settled on that issue, I hereby challenge each and all of the other candidates to a milking contest, and I agree to abide by the result.[32]

As the campaign progressed, it became clear that his audiences demanded, above all, to be entertained by sallies like this one rather to be instructed by a serious analysis of issues. When he made his listeners stretch their mouths with laughter, he was more likely to enlist their support than when he wrinkled their brows in thought.

29. In this speech, FOL also said: "I have never been a politician. I am a business man and will be business-like in politics."

30. Speech by C. Deneen at Grand Crossing Turner Hall, Chicago, Apr. 28, 1904, as recorded by FOL's stenographer.

31. Davis, pp. 91–94, 139. Mrs. Lowden's diary, Oct. 17, 1903, to Feb. 1, 1904, *passim.*

32. *New York Herald,* May 1, 1904.

His immediate purpose in canvassing the Illinois countryside so thorough-ly was to persuade Republicans to vote for him in the primary where they elected delegates to the party convention in each county. Because the date of this primary varied from county to county, he often could visit one of them on the crucial eve of its election without neglecting his interests in another. After choosing a delegation to go to the state nominating convention, the members of the county convention might instruct it to back the candidate who had received a majority of the votes cast in the primary. Sometimes the county convention split its delegation so as to reflect the proportionate vote polled by each candidate. On the rare occasions when a county convention refused to follow the popular will as expressed in the primary, the adherents of the aggrieved candidate dispatched their own contingent to the state con-vention, hoping that its committee on credentials would award it the con-tested seats.

With Yates, Hamlin, Sherman, and Warner in the field against him, Low-den did not expect to harvest more than a small minority of the nearly one thousand delegates from the counties exclusive of Cook, but he aimed to be the second choice of many who would be pledged to one or another of these four rivals. Above all, he wanted unanimous backing from the six counties comprising the Thirteenth Congressional District—namely, Ogle, Lee, Car-roll, Whiteside, Stephenson, and Jo Daviess. In this he was disappointed. On January 23, 1904, in subzero weather he carried his own county of Ogle by more than a two-to-one majority over Governor Yates. Before the end of the winter, he won the delegates from Lee and Stephenson and a minority of those from Whiteside, but lost all of those from Carroll and Jo Daviess.[33] Although Deneen did not campaign vigorously in most of the downstate re-gion, he was looked upon by many of the Yates delegates as their second choice. When the returns were all in, Lowden controlled about 125 delegates outside Cook County, Yates 505, Hamlin 120, Sherman 85, and Warner 45. Nearly 115 seats remained in dispute.[34] Lowden completed his country can-vass without offending any of his rivals. Hence he felt confident that when the vote-shifting began after the early ballots in the convention, he would be one of its principal beneficiaries.

Campaigning the length and breadth of Illinois in all sorts of winter weath-er brought many discomforts. The little county-seat hotels were usually of indifferent quality at best. Traveling sometimes necessitated long waits in shedlike stations at isolated junction points for under- or overheated trains. Lowden recognized from the outset that farmers would laugh derisively if he came to them in a luxurious private Pullman car to tell about his humble, rural upbringing and the blacksmith shop of his father. Late to bed, up be-

33. The vote in Oregon was 621 for Lowden to 33 for Yates; in Ogle County, 3,287 to 1,548.

34. Deneen campaigned in only about fifteen counties outside Cook. In southern Illinois the contest was mainly between Yates and Hamlin, except in seven counties, where it was principally between Hamlin and Warner. Probably to the surprise of his downstate rivals, FOL won the delegation from Perry County in southern Illinois.

times, and eating poorly cooked food at irregular hours in hotel dining rooms or at lunch counters of dubious cleanliness comprised a part of the cost of winning his 125 delegates. Treating to drinks was another commonplace. The colds to which he was susceptible irritated his throat and made him hoarse. To keep as fit as possible, he frequently sought the ministrations of a masseur and a throat specialist. Toward the end of the campaign Dr. Frank Billings warned him that unless he gave up smoking cigars for a while, his voice would sink to a whisper. He thereupon reduced his daily ration of tobacco but could not end it altogether because the aroma of his own cigars dispensed as largess to friendly politicians continuously tantalized his nose. During his between-trips stopovers at his home in Chicago or at "Sinnissippi," he often spent a day or two in bed, resting his body while he dictated letters, made telephone calls, and conferred with his campaign committee.

Heading his list of "hardships," however, was his lonesomeness when away from Mrs. Lowden. In the autumn of 1903 he regretted his absences the more keenly because his wife was confined to her home most of the time. When their third daughter was born on December 16, she was named Frances Orren in his honor. Before the winter ended, Mrs. Lowden occasionally accompanied him on his downstate forays. She helped him keep a balanced outlook upon his activities by often reminding him that their happiness did not hinge upon his nomination and election to the governorship. She had almost completely reconciled herself to his absorption in politics, but she sometimes wearied of so many politicians at her dinner table or in conference in the library.

Although Lowden enjoyed campaigning, he could not understand why Republican newspapers in Chicago, owned and edited by gentlemen, refused to admit his sincerity when he spoke of farming with knowledge and affection or when he advocated civil service and other governmental reforms. It humiliated and maddened him to have to deny so often that he was a tool of corporate interests or of Lorimer or that he remained in the contest merely in the hope of trading his delegates for a controlling voice in Cook County patronage. Every dollar spent in his campaign came from his own pocket, but his opponents charged that, if elected, he would be under embarrassing obligations to sinister interests. During the dozen years when he merely made an avocation of politics and fought for the same measures which he now supported as a candidate, he had usually been portrayed as an honest and civic-minded gentleman. By some perverse magic, running for office suddenly transformed him into a crook. Tormented by this abuse, he once declared somewhat self-pityingly that, although his home was Chicago, he had to turn to the New York newspapers for a fair account of his candidacy. He entered the contest, he continued, to find out whether ability and frankness were qualities appreciated in politics as in business, but the old-line politicians interpreted his candor as cunning and claimed that whatever talent he had was yoked to an evil purpose.[35] Little wonder that, before the campaign was

35. MS of FOL's speech at McVicker's Theatre, Chicago, May 5, 1904.

over, he assured rural audiences that, although his office and polling place were in Chicago, his heart reminded him that his true home was in the Rock River Valley. Its residents might question his right to style himself a farmer, but when they did so, they impugned only his accuracy of judgment rather than his morality.

The Chicago phase of the preconvention campaign rapidly gained momentum after mid-January, 1904. Although Lowden made many trips about the state between then and May 6, the date of the Cook County primaries, he devoted his main attention during that period to the city. Shortly after formally announcing his candidacy, he opened his Chicago headquarters in the Great Northern Hotel and put Kenesaw M. Landis in charge. Except for preparing pamphlets, badges, and news releases and encouraging precinct workers to form Lowden clubs, Landis did little to counteract Deneen's Chicago boom until the opening of the new year.[36] Lowden spent most of the last week of November at the International Live Stock Exposition at the Stock Yards, but his presence there was as much to gratify his liking for thoroughbred farm animals as to advance his political prospects by meeting important stock-raisers from all over the state. A big Lowden rally in the Masonic Temple on the evening of December 30 was diverted from its main purpose by the appalling news of the Iroquois Theatre holocaust. Under the circumstances Lowden declined to make a political speech and led the audience in adopting resolutions of sympathy for the families of the six hundred victims of the fire.[37] About three weeks later, nearly four hundred of his city workers assembled at the Hotel Sherman to take counsel together. This gathering officially launched his active Cook County campaign. A similar meeting in the Auditorium on the bitterly cold evening of January 25 was mainly intended to impress Illinois Republican leaders, about to assemble for their quadrennial "love feast" in Springfield, with the many Chicago elite supporting his candidacy.[38]

On the following morning, his forty-third birthday, he went with a trainload of his followers to the state capital. There, two thousand Republican politicians, mostly wearing the badges of their favorite candidates, assembled in the new armory. They fixed May 12 as the date of their nominating convention and listened to a plethora of short speeches by representatives of each congressional district, by each of the rivals for minor state offices, and by the half-dozen contestants for the gubernatorial nomination. Lowden had a carefully written fifteen-minute address. When he discovered that the occasion did not invite so much formality, he spoke extemporaneously on be-

36. In September, 1903, Volney W. Foster, of Evanston, Illinois, began the FOL movement in Cook County by soliciting signatures to an open letter asking him to run. From FOL's headquarters in the Great Northern Hotel, 200,000 pieces of printed matter were mailed (Davis, p. 97).

37. *Chicago Chronicle*, Dec. 31, 1903.

38. FOL's speech, in substance, is on pp. 9–18 of the Frank O. Lowden's Business Men's Committee's leaflet, *Why Chicago Business Men Favor Frank O. Lowden for Governor of Illinois*.

half of party harmony and against compelling office-holders to help pay the expenses of the campaign. All moved along merrily until Lawrence Sherman struck a discordant note by bluntly attacking Governor Yates and his "payroll brigade." For weeks past, the anti-Yates newspapers had accused the governor of swelling his campaign "slush fund" by assessing the wages of state employees and of arbitrarily dismissing those who opposed his renomination. However justifiable Sherman's charges may have been, they were unpalatable at a "love feast" meant to demonstrate the unity of Illinois Republicans in a presidential election year.[39]

Before Lowden left Springfield, he and Yates talked confidentially several times. What they said is unknown, but obviously neither persuaded the other to withdraw his candidacy or to agree upon a concerted plan of action in the nominating convention. After these powwows, the newspapers remarked with increasing frequency that many Yates delegates expected to transfer their votes to Deneen rather than to Lowden if their own man could not win. Perhaps this trend merely reflected the fact that Deneen, unlike Lowden, did not seek instructed delegates from the downstate counties.[40]

The Deneen-Lowden battle reached its climax in Cook County. Deneen's strength lay principally in the north and northwest wards of Chicago and in his own home neighborhood on the South Side. With Deans Harry P. Judson and Francis W. Shepardson of the University of Chicago and T. N. Jamieson, the boss of the Seventh Ward, supporting him, Lowden hoped to garner a few delegates near his opponent's residence. He relied mainly, however, upon the mill area farther south, the Lorimer-controlled West Side, and his own Prairie Avenue district just south of the main business section of the city. Volney W. Foster and Gordon Ramsay, a young lawyer whose early career was to be much shaped by Lowden, worked for him in Evanston and other northern suburbs.[41] The sudden death of John H. Hamline in the midst of the campaign lost him an influential friend, but he had the aid of such business leaders as John A. Lynch and W. T. Fenton, president of the American Trust and Savings Bank, Alvin II. Sanders, editor of the *Breeder's Gazette*, Charles A. Stevens, hotel owner, and the attorneys Joseph H. De-Frees, Noble B. Judah, and William J. Calhoun.

These men and some eighty others of like prominence formed the Business Men's Lowden Campaign Committee of Cook County. Elliott Durand and Marvin A. Farr were its chairman and vice-chairman, respectively.[42] In a printed letter they urged every man to vote for Lowden in order to have a governor who recognized Chicago's dire need for a new charter. To send a

39. *St. Louis Democrat,* Jan. 27, 1904. FOL's never-delivered speech had been released to the press and could not be recalled (see *Galesburg* [Ill.] *Register,* Jan. 29, 1904).

40. *Decatur* (Ill.) *Review,* Jan. 29, 1904; *Chicago Tribune,* Jan. 31, 1904.

41. Interview of author with G. Ramsay, Dec. 6, 1950.

42. Before his death, Hamline issued a statement indorsing FOL. "He is the only man," said Hamline, "who ever conducted an election in his and my home ward who did not allow a dollar to be spent in buying votes."

Chicagoan to the Executive Mansion, the appeal continued, was no longer "merely a matter of local pride . . . but a clear cut business necessity," because

municipal administration has broken down . . . and municipal bankruptcy stares us in the face. We are without sufficient revenues to carry on the ordinary functions of municipal government, and the taxes paid by our citizens are so frittered away between a multitude of independent tax-spending bodies that the city does not secure enough money to properly administer the affairs of 2,000,000 people. The fault lies in a defective charter. . . . [It is at Springfield that we must combat] all the wild schemes and vagaries of the socialistic, communistic and impractical theorists we have among us. . . . Chicago must have a governor or take the chance of error and misgovernment for another generation.

Deneen, they admitted, could represent Chicago as well as Lowden, but Deneen lacked even one pledged delegate outside Cook County and therefore had "absolutely no chance to be nominated." On the other hand, Lowden ran second to Yates downstate. Therefore, it became "the duty of every man interested in Chicago's welfare to sink his personal preferences and support Mr. Lowden as the only Chicago man who could win."[43] The business men's committee asked Democrats to take advantage of their legal right to vote in the Republican primary. The Democrat-controlled City Hall, however, was friendlier to Deneen than to Lowden. For a decade or more Lowden had been more scathing than his rival in his attacks upon the Carter Harrison administrations and their party machine."

In early April, Deneen refused to accept a challenge by Lowden to a series of public debates. Lowden wished to ask Deneen face to face whether he, too, did not owe much of his political advancement to Lorimer and Jamieson; whether he would not welcome their support now; whether during his seven years as state's attorney he had not pocketed $196,000 in fees, including some of doubtful legality; and whether he was not bossed by Victor Lawson of the *News* and Robert W. Patterson of the *Tribune*.[44] Unable to draw Deneen into a joint discussion, Lowden posed these questions anyway at his Thursday noon meetings in the Loop and before many precinct and ward clubs.[45]

Deneen justified his refusal on the grounds that debates served only to promote party discord and that most of his opponent's queries were as unrealistic as "Who Killed Cock Robin?" He still counted Lorimer and Jamieson among his friends and admitted without apology that he was a "machine politician," if that meant a believer in a strong party organization. Every fee

43. Printed letter of the Business Men's Lowden Campaign Committee to "Dear Sir," May 2, 1904.

44. Two articles by FOL on the issues of the campaign in the *Chicago Tribune*, Apr. 25 and 27, 1904. The usual editorial "line" of the *Tribune* and *News* was that FOL was an excellent person in very bad company. Victor Lawson also was suspicious of FOL's wealth and corporate affiliations.

45. Mrs. Lowden's diary, Apr. 14–May 6, 1904.

collected by him as state's attorney had been duly authorized by law. As for the "genial farmer's" assertion that Deneen believed "to the victor belongs the spoils," the "accused" candidly stated, "I am not a civil service reformer or civil service agitator. Not at all. I believe that positions ought to be held out as inducements for political work." Since Lowden, added Deneen, "wants me to say something about his record," I am obliged to agree that it

is clean in the sense that there is nothing on it. I can't say something about nothing. . . . If Lowden were elected governor whom would he, as a member of the Pullman Company, appoint to the Railroad and Warehouse Commission? Wouldn't he be embarrassed? Could he serve two masters? He seems to think that all a governor has to do is sit in his chair and obey the Constitution, but the governor has immense power and must exercise it. . . . I haven't a big fortune and so have only been able to make a fight in about fifteen counties outside of Cook. But I will have 350 delegates supporting me in the Convention.[46]

Lowden and Deneen each overestimated his own strength in Cook County. While Lowden declined to accept Deneen's proposal that the loser in the city primary withdraw from the contest, he confidently declared that, unlike his rival, he could become the first Republican governor of Illinois from Chicago if half or more of its delegates voted for him in the nominating convention.[47] His wife knew, however, that he did not expect to win more than 35 or 40 per cent of them. "We hope for victory," she wrote on the eve of primary day, "but are prepared not to allow defeat to be too great a disappointment."[48] Upon counting the 95,000 ballots, the tally was "not very satisfactory." He could rely upon the support of between 185 and 200 delegates, but Deneen had approximately 325. Of the thirty-five wards in the city, Deneen carried sixteen solidly and Lowden only five. Most Chicago newspapers joyfully hailed the outcome as still another blow to Lorimer's prestige. Helped by his downstate bloc, Lowden at least might have more votes than Deneen on the first ballot in the nominating convention.

This gathering was one of the most memorable in the political history of Illinois. Although its sessions convened in the new Springfield armory, where each contestant had an office, much of the significant activity centered at the Leland Hotel. There the rivals had "secret" conference places as well as reception rooms equipped with campaign literature, easy chairs, cuspidors, and free cigars. The hall at the armory accommodated many spectators in addition to the 1,502 delegates. The rostrum stood on a raised platform, sufficiently large to seat several hundred favored guests. These, during most of the sessions, included Mrs. Lowden and Mrs. K. M. Landis. Mrs. Lowden was quickly caught up in the excitement of the proceedings, although she

46. Typed extracts from various speeches of Deneen as recorded by FOL's stenographer.

47. Cook County had 529 delegates. Before the primary, Roy West claimed "over 400" for Deneen; Landis forecast 300–325 for Lowden.

48. Mrs. Lowden's diary, May 5, 1904.

regretted the reek of tobacco smoke in her clothing and the infrequency with which she saw her weary husband.[49]

"Uncle Joe" Cannon, the chairman of the convention, equipped with a hard-worked megaphone and gavel, as well as much homely wit and an easy familiarity with the duties of a presiding officer, could rarely enforce the rule against smoking. Chewing did not fall under his ban, and he enjoyed sampling the cut-plugs offered by the press reporters seated near his rostrum. Upon demand, he was as ready to lead in the singing of "Illinois" as to decide a moot point of procedure. Three brass bands waited upon his signal to play. When the tension mounted, he found it much simpler to evoke music than to produce quiet among the excited delegates and spectators. And yet, in view of the duration and keenness of the competition among the seven rivals for the gubernatorial nomination, the good humor normally pervading the prolonged sessions was more remarkable than the occasional confusion and outbursts of anger. The delegates could not have selected a more popular and skilful chairman.[50] Before the opening of the convention, everyone knew that on the first ballot no candidate would have anywhere near the 752 votes necessary to win. This was not ominous. Earlier conventions with a similarly divided field had reached a majority consensus within two or three days. As always, many delegates and their wives brought only enough clothing and cash for a brief stay. Being farmers or businessmen they could not afford to be long away from their occupations.

The proceedings started in the usual manner. The committee on credentials, headed by Judge Hanecy, decided most of the contested seats at Hamlin's expense and in favor of Yates or Lowden. The customary quota of cheers greeted each name as it was put in nomination. Even after tabulating the first ballot, the delegates had no premonition of trouble ahead. On this poll, Yates received 507⅔ votes; Deneen, 386⅔; Lowden, 354⅔; Hamlin, 121; Sherman, 87; and Warner, 45.[51] Except that Deneen received somewhat more and Lowden somewhat less support than expected, the outcome warranted no surprise. Without recessing for lunch or supper, fourteen more ballots were taken before, in the late evening, a majority of the tired delegates carried a motion to adjourn. After spending much of the day on the floor of the convention talking with friends and being introduced to those delegates whom he had not met before, Lowden had reason to feel encouraged. The only noteworthy trend in the balloting was his gain of about 50 votes and Sherman's decline in strength. Almost at the outset, the latter made known that he would release his followers to the first candidate receiving 700 or more votes. To the party

49. Mrs. Lowden's diary, May 6, 12, 15, 16, and 21, 1904. On May 9, she wrote in her diary: "I will be satisfied whatever the outcome if only Frank can cease this frightful work that he has been doing so many months."

50. Davis, pp. 192–314, *passim.*

51. Of the 112 contested seats, FOL gained 34 and Yates 78. Exclusive of those from Cook County, only about half the delegates were pledged by their instructions to vote for a particular candidate.

leaders, the adjournment meant only an uninterrupted opportunity to devote the rest of the night to discovering how the deadlock might be broken.

This deadlock had several keys if the holders wished to use them. If either Deneen or Lowden transferred his delegates to Yates or if Deneen or Lowden combined forces behind one or the other of them, the door to a nomination would open. If, however, the four downstate candidates, exclusive of Lowden, united in favor of one of them, he would still be about 35 votes short of a majority, unless, under those circumstances, Lowden's rural delegates deserted him. These obvious solutions were by no means so simple as they appeared at first glance. Although Lowden's supporters, for example, might be loyal enough to stand by him to the last ditch, they were disunited either by their instructions or by their personal preferences on the subject of their second choice. For this reason he could not—and, indeed, would not —promise to deliver all his strength to any one of his competitors. A Lowden-Deneen entente was probably the most unlikely of all possibilities because of the nearly irrepressible conflict between the Chicago factions which they represented. And, too, Lowden's country delegates would be most loath to share in a bargain of that kind.

The art of politics being what it was, no one at the convention doubted that the dilemma would finally yield to a "deal" involving some state and federal offices. Senators Cullom and Hopkins, as well as many congressmen, sat in the armory either as delegates or as influential onlookers. They naturally stood on guard against any bargain being made at their expense. The members of this "federal crowd" were not as one in their preference for the governorship, but most of them would unite to keep their jobs from going on the auction block in order to produce a nominee. In this connection, the senatorial office of Shelby Cullom was often mentioned, since his term would end in 1907, or two years before that of Hopkins. But the aged Cullom gave no hint that he planned to retire. Indeed, he declared that his toga never would be worn by any candidate who, being promised it, consented to withdraw from the gubernatorial sweepstakes. Like most of the other federal office-holders, he favored Lowden for the governorship. Hardly had the convention assembled, when a rumor went the rounds that President Roosevelt, wishing Lowden to win, had promised to appoint Yates United States ambassador to Mexico if he agreed to release his delegates. In all probability this "bribe," as the governor indignantly called it, was never offered. There is fairly strong evidence, however, that Roosevelt and the cautious Hopkins were on Lowden's side.[52] Almost everyone liked Yates personally, but he surprised many by his tenacity as a fighter and his success in holding the steadfast loyalty of his followers even when his opponents

52. In a letter on July 11, 1906, to L. A. Coolidge, Washington, D.C., FOL wrote that Roosevelt told him after the convention, in the presence of two of his cabinet, that he had wanted him (FOL) to win. But, as an offset, see Roosevelt to N. M. Butler, May 17, 1904, in E. E. Morison (ed.), *The Letters of Theodore Roosevelt,* IV (Cambridge, Mass., 1951), 799–800.

strongly tempted them to desert his cause. Since a merger between Lowden and Deneen was virtually out of the question, the governor confidently believed that no one could win without his help. As the undoubted choice of a majority of Illinois Republicans outside Cook County, he had more claim to the nomination than any of his rivals. For this reason he insisted that they should not expect him to be the one to surrender.

On the evening of the sixth day, after hearing the indecisive result of the forty-seventh ballot, Mrs. Lowden wrote in her diary: "No one is wise enough to have a solution. . . . Many delegates have had to go home and everyone is tired to death. I have only had glimpses of Frank."[53] The exhausted leaders had attempted fruitless combinations of all sorts during that week of balloting. Conferences between the rivals or their boards of strategy, behind the jealously guarded doors of hotel rooms or in the Executive Mansion, filled the late hours of every night. No sooner was the rumor of one "deal" afloat than it gave way to the contradictory news of another. The convention drew nation-wide attention, and hourly bulletins appeared outside newspaper offices in many Illinois towns.[54] Visitors came to Springfield to witness "the greatest political battle of the young century." For good reason, the merchants and hotelkeepers of the capital city wanted the deadlock to continue indefinitely. Springfield was in a holiday mood, with its store fronts gay with bunting and flags. Vendors hawked balloons, sandwiches, and souvenirs. Brass bands led marching men on their way to the armory, flaunting "Lowden Forever" banners or others bearing the equally uncompromising watchword of a rival candidate. The paraders often sang campaign doggerels, much better calculated to impress a listener by their enthusiasm than by the quality of their lyrics:

> The candidates are worried
> All over Illinois.
> They're getting awfully frightened
> About this Country Boy.
> He's got them all stampeded
> With his two-headed calf.
> They all are sad and somber now,
> You never hear them laugh.
>
> Oh, Oh, Frank, Oh, Oh,
> Our own Frank, you know,
> The Colonel is honest, brave and true.
> Oh, Oh, Frank, Oh, Oh,
> In the State House you will go.
> The people are crying now for you.

A procession with banners, bands, and songs of this variety sometimes inaugurated an effort to stampede the delegates into uniting upon one candi-

53. Entry of May 19, 1904.

54. Davis, pp. 268, 285; *Chicago Examiner*, May 17, 1904.

date. During the first week the Yates, Lowden, Deneen, and Hamlin blocs each tried to sweep the convention by a whirlwind demonstration. The lines of division bent under its impact but always snapped back as soon as the gale blew itself out. During the initial fifty-seven ballots, the fortunes of the three leading contestants—Yates, Lowden, and Deneen—seesawed continually, but never across a very wide arc. Following the first half-dozen ballots, no one of the rivals received over 500 votes. Lowden's maximum was 473 on the thirty-first.[55]

After several conferences, with Lorimer sometimes present, Lowden and Yates concluded that neither of them wanted anything which the other could or would concede. Thenceforward the governor confined his negotiations to the rest of the candidates, especially to Deneen. By Friday morning, May 20, almost everyone admitted that the delegates were too bone-weary to reach a sensible decision by remaining longer in the depressing atmosphere of the convention hall. On that day, when the fifty-eighth ballot showed no conspicuous change of alignment, a motion to recess until the afternoon of May 31 carried by a vote of 1,414 to 88. In Mrs. Lowden's phrase, they were a "tired and disgusted lot of people," all sharing her husband's and her own eagerness to get back to the quiet of their homes as soon as possible.[56]

After fourteen hours of sleep and a visit to Dr. Capps for cough medicine, Lowden felt sufficiently recovered to go delegate-hunting into the Yates territory of southern Illinois. The governor countered by making several speeches in Chicago and conferring there with Hamlin, Sherman, and possibly Deneen.[57] If the recess produced any bargains, they did not immediately become evident when the convention reassembled. Lowden and his managers arrived in Springfield on May 29, determined to take the aggressive in a big way. A special train carrying about five hundred of his delegates and other friends reached the state capital late on the afternoon of Memorial Day. They marched in noisy procession from the station to the Leland Hotel and a headquarters annex which Lowden had recently opened on the opposite side of the street.[58] But all this financially expensive effort had no effect upon the outcome of the ten ballots taken between May 31 and noon on June 2.

On June 1 Graeme Stewart proposed to the convention in the name of Lowden that its members request each candidate to release his delegates. After the motion went to the committee on resolutions, the meeting adjourned until the following morning. Before then, everyone knew that Yates and Deneen alone opposed the Stewart resolution—one more bit of evidence that they were working in conjunction. Their combined forces, however, could not prevent its passage in amended form on June 2. One by one the

55. Davis, p. 275.

56. *Ibid.*, pp. 299–304; Mrs. Lowden's diary, May 20, 1904.

57. The *Chicago Chronicle*, May 24 and 26, 1904, charged that Yates was in Chicago making a deal with Deneen and the "newspaper trust" backing him; see also *Chicago Examiner,* June 4, 1904.

58. Mrs. Lowden's diary, May 29–31, 1904; Davis, p. 311.

rival candidates, led by Lowden, arose and freed their delegates. As soon as the convention reached a completely "fluid state," in which, theoretically, every member could vote for whomever he chose, Cannon made a brief plea for compromise. "We have been trying," he said, "for two weeks to make one-half, and one vote more, out of a third. Nobody but God can do it, and He won't do it, because He never violates His universal law. . . . Nominate someone . . . and do it today."[59]

But even the respected chairman could not produce a decision. Permitting a delegate to vote as he pleased did not end his loyalty to a candidate or nullify the binding force of the instructions from his county convention. During seven ballots (the sixty-seventh through the seventy-third) on June 2, after the adoption of the Stewart resolution, the votes for Lowden mounted from $400\frac{1}{2}$ to $631\frac{1}{2}$. By the seventy-third, Yates's strength had dropped to 362 and Deneen's to $345\frac{1}{2}$. Although Lowden thus received greater support than any of his rivals up to that time, he still needed 120 more votes to clinch the prize. They were unavailable. He had climbed as far as he could go. Thereafter, in response to an enthusiastic demonstration for Yates, the Lowden count sagged, until on the seventy-eighth ballot, the last for the day, he was down 100 from his crest and the governor had recovered about 45. Lowden felt the more disappointed because he had been assured of votes which remained undelivered.[60]

During the evening his followers seemed confident that the next morning would see the victory, but his own mood probably was better reflected in a note from his wife written at 11:00 P.M.:

It has occurred to me tonight that perhaps I have not let you know how absolutely in sympathy I am with you in every move you are making in this wonderful struggle. I want you to win, of course, because you deserve and are entitled to the victory, but if you are defeated, I can't help confessing that my first thought will be that I shall have my blessed husband back again all to myself, and just at this moment that seems to me the very best thing that this life can give me.

I know it is all coming out for the best . . . whatever the outcome, that we have nothing to regret, and that you have made a name and a place for yourself in this State that will be a proud heritage for your children . . . the governorship seems to me tonight to be a matter of small importance compared with your loving companionship.

A persistent rumor told of Deneen, Yates, Sherman, and Hamlin agreeing to force a recess the following morning if the Lowden tide resumed its rise. A break of this sort might allow the ardor for him to cool and give them a chance to follow up their nocturnal negotiations by a further effort to frame an entire state ticket.[61]

59. Davis, pp. 332–40, 346–47; Mrs. Lowden's diary, June 1, 1904. In releasing their delegates, the candidates each made a grandiloquent little speech.

60. Davis, pp. 321–31, 351–61; *Chicago Examiner,* May 31 and June 1, 1904.

61. Davis, pp. 361–70. Deneen testified in the *Dillingham Committee Hearings,* II, 1082, that Yates took the initiative because his forces were disintegrating.

No sooner had the convention come to order on June 3 than their delegates overbore the opposition of the Lowden phalanx and carried a motion to recess until two o'clock. The quadrumvirate met at once in the Executive Mansion. There Yates finally consented to throw his strength to Deneen. Sherman admitted that he could not draw the vote of most of Yates's followers. He also pointed out that, in view of Chicago's demand for a governor, the Cook County delegates, whether for Lowden or for Deneen, would not vote for Yates. Facing these realities, Sherman reportedly said, "The logic of the situation suggests that Mr. Deneen is the only candidate among us whom we can nominate. Governor Yates can deliver to him and so can the rest of us." If the candidate had to be from Chicago, a better case could be made for Deneen than for Lowden, because the former had defeated the latter in the Cook County primary. With considerable plausibility, Yates could claim that, by leaguing with Deneen, he made effective the will of a majority of Republicans in both the country and the metropolis. In the future, Yates, Deneen, Hamlin, and Sherman would justify their action in this way and also by calling to mind that, unlike Lowden, Deneen was an experienced public official. Furthermore, Lowden's defeat would be a salutary lesson to the Lorimer-Jamieson machine, to the "federal crowd," and to the candidate's corporation backers. "At last," wrote Dawes far too optimistically in his diary, "the era of primary corruption, assessment of State employees and the prostitution of the State Civil Service is at an end. . . . The old machine, I think, is irrevocably gone in both [Cook] county and state, having lost both power and public respect."[62]

Bright in his armor of righteousness, Yates withdrew his candidacy as soon as the convention assembled on the afternoon of June 3. To an accompaniment of loud cheering and the waving of hastily prepared placards bearing the invitation, "Deneen for Votes—Come On In, Boys—the Water Is Fine," Hamlin and Sherman called upon their henchmen to follow the governor's lead. The decisive results of the seventy-ninth ballot, tabulated against the background of a heavy electrical storm, therefore came as no surprise—957½ for Deneen, 522½ for Lowden, 21 for Warner, and 1 for Yates. During the count Mrs. Lowden sat on the platform, while her husband, Landis, and several of their friends stood together close by. As soon as the results were announced and Mrs. Yates had presented Deneen with a huge bouquet of roses, Lowden mounted a chair to propose that the nomination be made unanimous. This motion carried by a thunderous voice-vote and was fittingly acknowledged by Deneen. Thereupon, Lowden assured the delegates that in the autumn he would make speeches in support of the state and national tickets. After asking his 522 "stalwarts" "not to look so depressed and melancholy and unhappy," he concluded by saying:

When the result of the last roll call was announced I began to think of the beautiful quiet I would enjoy on my farm and was happier than I have been at

---

62. *Dawes Journal, 1893–1913,* p. 372.

any time in the last nine months. And so, cheer up, because we will all meet again in a very short time, fighting shoulder to shoulder for a common cause.[63]

He received much applause both then and later for his good sportsmanship. Neither he nor his followers could reproach themselves for not trying hard every inch of the way from the auspicious start to the disappointing finish. He had gained much political experience, made hundreds of friends throughout the state, and demonstrated so much strength as a vote-getter that the winning Republican coalition could hardly afford to overlook him. In so far as he was concerned, his failure to attain the nomination did not mean economic disaster. Many of his unwavering backers, however, were glum and fearful lest their wing of the party be overlooked in the distribution of appointive jobs. Lowden's main political task in the days ahead would be to prevent neglect of his "die-hards" by the victors of the Springfield convention. The pro-Deneen newspapers in Chicago reinterred William Lorimer, as they had done unsuccessfully several times in the recent past. They expressed delight when his lieutenant, Dr. T. N. Jamieson, withdrew from all political activities after twenty years of South Side leadership.[64]

Although Lowden never publicly reversed his June 3 statement to the press—"It was a fair fight and I am beaten"—he knew that the verdict of his followers embodied much less tolerance. They insisted that their man would have been the victor if he had been as unscrupulous as Deneen in conniving with Yates. As proof positive of "a corrupt bargain," they pointed to the slate of candidates devised by the confederates. The Lowdenites had wished Frank L. Smith of Dwight to be the choice for lieutenant-governor, but Sherman was "paid off" with this place. Yates named his friends state Senator Len Small for state treasurer and James A. Rose for secretary of state. Edward D. Shurtleff, one of Hamlin's political managers, was rewarded with the speaker's chair of the Illinois House of Representatives. Roy O. West, Deneen's manager, and Bernard A. Eckhart, a leading Deneenite of Chicago, ensconced themselves as chairman and treasurer, respectively, of the Republican State Central Committee.[65] Only for the office of attorney-general were Lowden and the Republicans of northwestern Illinois given recognition by the inclusion on the ticket of the Ottawa lawyer, William H. Stead. According to report, Yates and Deneen expected to divide between themselves the awarding of appointive jobs throughout the state and strip the Lorimerites of all patronage power. The victors would try to have Yates rather than Cullom lead the Illinois Republican delegation to the national nominating convention and Hamlin become the Illinois member on the Republican Na-

---

63. Davis, pp. 374–85; Mrs. Lowden's diary, June 3: "This has been a day of great importance to us and has been filled with excitement and disappointment. Despite conferences Frank held till 4 A.M. with various leaders who told him they would back him, a combination was made." FOL's wire to his seven-year-old son, Pullman, June 4: "Tell Harriet her desire someone else be governor has been gratified."

64. *Chicago Examiner*, June 4, 1904; *Chicago Daily News*, June 4, 1904.

65. *Dawes Journal, 1893–1913*, pp. 373, 377.

tional Committee. If the Deneen-Yates-Sherman-Hamlin coalition succeeded, this convention would choose Congressman R. R. Hitt to be President Roosevelt's running mate, thereby freeing a seat in the House of Representatives as a consolation prize for Frank Lowden.[66]

Most controversial, in the light of future events, was the question whether Deneen pledged himself in regard to Cullom's senatorship and, if so, whether he had agreed to back Sherman or Hamlin for that office. Because this "deal or no deal" issue was of high emotional voltage, speeches and editorials threshed it over repeatedly during the next three years. And yet, granting the existence of such a bargain, what made it discreditable or unlike hundreds of other "deals" which dot the course of political history? In this instance, furthermore, an especially urgent need drove reasonable men toward a compromise. Without some understanding of this kind, the convention deadlock might have continued indefinitely. All in all, there is good cause for accepting Lowden's own judgment that he went down in a fair fight. On the other hand, the victors missed an opportunity to lessen party factionalism by sharing more of the appointive offices with his bloc. And the question remains unanswered, Did Deneen break his promise of 1904 during the senatorial battle two years later?[67]

After three weeks of almost uninterrupted rest at "Sinnissippi" following the ordeal at Springfield, Lowden took his seat in the Republican national convention at Chicago as a delegate from the First Congressional District of Illinois. Although Elihu Root's keynote speech greatly impressed him, he probably shared Mrs. Lowden's opinion that the sessions were "cut and dried" when compared with those in which he had been a principal a short time before. Following President Roosevelt's nomination by acclamation, Senator Charles Fairbanks of Indiana received so much support for the vice-presidency that the Illinois delegation scarcely had a chance to cast a complimentary vote for its candidate, Congressman R. R. Hitt.[68]

However dull the convention, its close meant for Lowden the beginning of four months of interesting political activity. Contrary to most predictions, the Illinois delegation chose him rather than Hamlin to be the national committeeman. His duties included the managing of Roosevelt's campaign in Illinois and serving on the four-man executive committee appointed to organize and direct the western headquarters of the Republican National Committee in Chicago. He much enjoyed two of his colleagues on this committee—David W. Mulvane of Kansas and Harry S. New of Indiana. Equally pleasant was his close association with Graeme Stewart, Charles G. Dawes, George B. Cortelyou, Cornelius N. Bliss, and Congressman James A. Tawney

66. *Chicago Inter-Ocean,* May 24, June 4, 19, and 21, 1904; *Chicago Post,* June 4 and 6, 1904; *Chicago Chronicle,* June 4, 1904.

67. Davis, pp. 386–89; *Dillingham Committee Hearings,* I, 268–70; II, 1082.

68. Mrs. Lowden's diary, June 21–23, 1904. In the contest for the chairmanship of the Illinois delegation to the convention, Cullom won over Yates, 29–25 (*Rockford Republic,* June 21, 1904).

of Minnesota. By good fortune, Lowden retained, as his chief assistant, James R. Cowley of Freeport, upon whose political skill he had relied heavily in the contest for the gubernatorial nomination.[69]

Besides helping the national ticket, Lowden shared actively in the state campaign. Eager to allay factional strife, he took extra pains to befriend Deneen and see that they were photographed arm-in-arm leaving a political conference.[70] He successfully resisted pressure from the state and national committees to begin his speech-making before the close of September. Confident that his party would win easily, he determined to stay with Mrs. Lowden and their four children as much as possible during the summer. "I would be perfectly happy," he assured her on August 19, "if I could spend the rest of my life with you—whatever else might betide—whether poverty, obscurity, or what not. After this election we will try it anyway." Sincerely meant no doubt, but written without heed to his political ambition!

When he finally took to the road in early October in the private Pullman, "The Oceanic," he campaigned all over Illinois with as much vigor as though he headed the state Republican ticket. He spoke at least forty times before the November 8 election, sometimes alone, sometimes with Deneen and Sherman, and sometimes with Fairbanks. Once again, as in the campaign of 1900, Lowden's speeches exhibited little originality. He followed very closely the standard Republican arguments being used everywhere in the country. According to Lowden's description, Judge Alton B. Parker of New York, the Democratic presidential nominee, was an unaggressive and wholly "lovely old gentleman," excellent in a judicial robe but entirely unfitted to be an executive.[71] Except for this fundamental fault, he deserved no criticism. It was a tribute to his common sense, if not to his candidacy, continued Lowden, that the worthy judge acknowledged the wisdom of almost all the Republican accomplishments at Washington during the past eight years. But why should anyone vote for him when, by his own admission, the party in power had made a fine record? It was also a feather in Parker's top hat that his fellow Democrat, William Jennings Bryan, disliked him. No Republican needed to speak against Parker because the Nebraskan could do it much more eloquently. "The Democrats," Lowden quipped, "have the peculiar habit of abusing their living Presidents like Cleveland and deifying their dead ones like Jefferson and Jackson."

After beginning his speeches in this light vein, he devoted most of the rest of them to defending Roosevelt's action in Panama, praising the protective tariff, and pointing to the prosperity which always attended a Republican regime in Washington.[72] In supporting the state ticket, Lowden did not

69. At the last moment, Hamlin's name was not brought forward for the national committee by the Yates-Deneen combine, and FOL reluctantly accepted as a "compromise candidate."

70. *Chicago Daily News,* Aug. 2, 1904.

71. Parker was then fifty-two years of age, or only six years older than Roosevelt.

72. MSS of FOL's speeches at Decatur, Illinois, Oct. 12, 1904, and at Marley, Taylorville, Gibson City, Mansfield, Bement, and elsewhere in Illinois on Oct. 12 and 13.

mainly stress the abilities of Deneen or the meager achievements of the Yates administration but the need of Chicago for a new charter and therefore the obvious wisdom of having a governor from that city. With doubtful accuracy he portrayed the Illinois Republicans as a harmonious band which had enlivened its recent nominating convention at Springfield by much good-humored rivalry between the best of friends.[73]

Although he had never feared that the Republicans might lose the election, he was much surprised by the magnitude of their victory. Helped by the popularity of President Roosevelt, the party carried normally Democratic Chicago as well as the downstate area. Also gratifying was the fact that the western office of the party terminated its activities without a deficit. Its executive committee commemorated its labors and its cordial relationship with the Republican National Committee by giving suitably inscribed loving cups to Cortelyou and Bliss.[74] As a national committeeman, Lowden occasionally conferred with Roosevelt at the White House and with leading members of his administration. At the President's request, the members of the national committee agreed not to encroach, as formerly, upon the patronage domain of the United States senators and senior congressmen. This self-denying action decreased Lowden's power in state politics, but it also spared him much embarrassment. It enabled him to say to competitors for an appointive position in the federal service: "I was frequently reminded during the campaign [of 1904] that a member of the National Executive Committee was a devil of a fellow until election was over, and then there was no U.S. Senator so small or insignificant that he did not have more influence than the entire national committee combined."[75]

If, in his role as a national committee member, he had pledged not to write to Washington to indorse his office-seeking friends, he at least could do so as one of Illinois's influential Republicans. He directed most of his patronage letters to Senator Cullom or Speaker Cannon. In January, 1905, when he declined the President's invitation to be the judge of a federal district court in Illinois, he pressed the qualifications of Kenesaw Mountain Landis in his stead and eventually gained his end.[76] Thus, for the second time, he refused an appointive position in the national service. Turning down a place on the bench signified how irrevocably by 1905 he had given up the legal profession. Several years earlier a federal court judgeship, with its security of tenure, would have strongly attracted him.

Election day, 1904, was often recalled by Lowden as the occasion when he cast his first ballot in Ogle County. By this change of polling place, he made known that his principal home was at "Sinnissippi" rather than on Prairie Avenue, Chicago. From this time forward, when asked to specify his

73. *Stanton* (Ill.) *Herald*, Oct. 28, 1904.

74. Mrs. Lowden's diary, Nov. 8 and 9, 1904; *Dawes Journal, 1893–1913*, p. 387.

75. FOL to F. H. Smith, Peoria, Illinois, Dec. 8, 1904.

76. Mrs. Lowden's diary, Feb. 12, Mar. 2–4, 18, Dec. 7 and 11, 1905. FOL attended Roosevelt's inauguration in March, 1905, partly to press further for Landis' appointment.

vocation, he replied "farmer." Mrs. Lowden assured him that she was willing to be "a farmer's wife" for the rest of her life.[77] Seventeen more years, however, would go by before agriculture rather than big business became the chief fashioner of his political views.

Among those for whom Lowden voted in the autumn of 1904 was Robert R. Hitt, then making his eleventh successful bid for re-election to Congress. He was chairman of the Foreign Relations Committee and had been in the House of Representatives for over twenty years. Owing to his advanced age and parlous state of health, he teetered on the verge of retirement. Lowden may have been somewhat disappointed by the veteran's confidence that he could outlast another term. Although the *Chicago American* erred when it declared that a seat in Congress had principally impelled Lowden to buy "Sinnissippi," his ambition unquestionably veered in that direction by late 1904. Hitt already viewed him as his likely successor.[78] The transfer of his place of voting to the Daysville crossroads, near his farm, was a necessary step toward his new goal. Although he told his friends that he sought no office and was so pleasantly absorbed in livestock-raising that he might never again enter the political arena, he convinced neither them nor himself. To be congressman from a "rock-ribbed" Republican district, where the biennial contest for re-election would not be severe, held out an appealing prospect, especially since he could spend much of every year on his farm. When his supporters urged him to oppose Hitt's renomination, he told them of his pledge to the congressman not to resist him as long as he wanted to serve. In exchange, so it would seem, Hitt agreed to do all in his power to make Lowden his political heir. [79]

During the winter and spring of 1905, Lowden discovered how difficult it was to keep out of state politics. Even before he returned from witnessing the "very simple and unostentatious" ceremonies attending Deneen's inauguration as governor, many of his staunch supporters in the Springfield convention embarrassed him by asking him to find them jobs in the new administration.[80] He hesitated to seek its favors until it gave some sign of friendliness. On the other hand, Attorney-General William H. Stead acknowledged his debt to Lowden and hastened to grant his request that the firms of Herrick and Ramsay and Gemmill and Foell handle much of the state's legal business in Chicago. When friends sought his backing for offices which only Deneen or one of his faction could grant, he sent a statement of their qualifications to the appropriate Springfield office and then wrote the applicants, saying he "would explain more particularly when I see you" why any intervention by him in their behalf would probably work more to

77. Mrs. Lowden's diary, Nov. 7, 1904.

78. R. R. Hitt to FOL, Nov. 10, and FOL's reply, Nov. 19, 1904.

79. FOL to H. A. Cunningham, Salem, Illinois, Aug. 2, 1904; to O. L. Mann, Danville, Illinois, Jan. 11, 1905; and to S. Cullom, Apr. 18, 1905. He told Cullom: "I am inclined to believe that I am better fitted for agriculture than for statesmanship."

80. Mrs. Lowden's diary, Jan. 8–9, 1905.

their injury than to their advantage. One of them complained in characteristic vein that "ever since we fought for you at Springfield the whole weight and power of the Chicago Post Office is [*sic*] wielded against what they call 'the Lowden gang.'" If he did not know either the office-seeker or his indorsers, Lowden returned the file to the suppliant with the suggestion that he channel his request through the Republican central committee of his own county.[81]

Without mentioning Deneen's name, Lowden told reporters late in October, 1905, that a constitutional amendment limiting a governor to one term, of perhaps six years instead of four, would be in the public interest. When a state executive, said Lowden, hoped for re-election, he spent too much time during his first four years in campaigning and building a machine to support him in the next nominating convention. Lowden also wished to change the year of the gubernatorial election in Illinois so that it would not coincide with the presidential campaign. As it was then, a candidate for the governorship, irrespective of his merit, won largely because his name appeared on the same ticket with a strong presidential aspirant. Finally, he believed that the state government would be more responsive to the rank and file of the majority party if more of its high administrative officers were made elective rather than appointive and were chosen in the mid-year of a governor's term. By this change, the party in control of the executive branch would have to come back to the people oftener than once in every four years. Deneen could hardly have viewed these proposals as a friendly gesture. Lowden would always cling to the first of them, soon forget the second, and, within a dozen years, completely reverse himself on the third.

The issue of Senator Cullom's re-election, even though it would not come up for decision until January, 1907, subjected the Deneen-Yates-Sherman-Hamlin coalition to severe strain as early as the summer of 1905. If Deneen attempted to pay his great debt to Yates by backing him instead of Cullom, he would need extraordinary skill and good luck not to wreck the alliance to which he owed his office. Whatever he did in the situation was almost certain to weaken his influence. By supporting Yates for the senatorship, he would offend Sherman and Hamlin—both eager to have the position—and also alienate some of his Chicago supporters, including Fred A. Busse and several newspaper editors, who desired Cullom to win again. If these were the only considerations, neutrality clearly would be the best policy for Deneen to follow. But neutrality meant that Yates's large downstate following would accuse him of ingratitude or even of breach of promise. How could he hope to have a successful administration or be renominated at its close unless he held the Yates faction to his banner?

Deneen was left in no doubt where Lowden stood on the issue of Cullom. He venerated the aged statesman as one of his mentors in politics and had ap-

81. C. E. Cruikshank, Chicago, to FOL, Nov. 20, 1905; FOL to W. H. Stead, Ottawa, Illinois, July 2, and Stead's reply, July 12, 1904. In his reply, Stead wrote: "There is nobody to whom I owe more and for whom I would go farther than yourself."

preciated his support in the recent Springfield convention. He talked about his political future to Senator Cullom with the same frankness that he confided in Congressman Hitt. Efforts of hostile editors to break this friendship by picturing Lowden as ambitious to supplant Cullom in the Senate completely failed.[82] Cullom regarded him as his possible successor but at the same time could not understand why he sought a political career. "I do not desire," he wrote to Lowden on April 22, 1905, "to make any remark that might discourage you in wanting to come to the Senate, or any other great office, because I am for you for anything you want, no matter what it is; but if I had your farm no one could run fast enough to catch me to make me run for the best office in the country."[83] Lacking an independent fortune, Cullom's decision to seek re-election at the age of seventy-six partially reflected his financial need. When his campaign organization took shape in the summer of 1905, with Charles P. Hitch, the United States marshal for the southern district of Illinois at its head, Lowden was on its executive committee and list of speakers.[84]

Being in a quandary about what to do, the forces of Yates and Deneen made no open move against Cullom until the close of the year. At that time, in the midst of an eloquent silence from the governor, Yates formally announced his candidacy for the Senate and declared that before the April primaries he would speak forty-six times downstate and forty-eight in Chicago. This manifesto, in the view of the *Chicago Inter-Ocean*, marked the opening of a great battle between the federal and the state Republican factions, with all the state offices as the prize for the victor. The reporter prophesied that Deneen would come out unwillingly for Yates, knowing that, if his ally did not win, their coalition would be ruined and Lowden would emerge as the gubernatorial nominee in 1908. Events soon demonstrated how completely erroneous a political forecast could be.[85]

In so far as Lowden was concerned, the columnist assumed a situation which had disappeared about a month before he published his article. Beginning in early November, 1905, Lowden encouraged his friends to discover a tactful way of persuading Congressman Hitt to retire. James R. Cowley, Judge Richard S. Farrand of Dixon, and "Cal" M. Feezer, the *Mount Carroll Democrat* editor who recently had experienced a remarkable conversion from Yates to Lowden, believed that they could ease Hitt out without hurting his feelings or those of his politically powerful friend, Colonel B. F.

82. Mrs. Lowden's diary, June 21, 1905, and Jan. 9, 1906.

83. Cullom to FOL, Apr. 22, 1905.

84. Cullom's money worries were reflected in an effort made by FOL and Judge J. Otis Humphrey of Springfield, Illinois, in 1908–9, to raise about $23,000 to provide the senator with a $3,000 annuity for life. FOL promised $5,000 if the judge could raise the balance among Cullom's other friends.

85. *Chicago Inter-Ocean,* Dec. 17, 1905, and Jan. 28, 1906; *Chicago Tribune,* Dec. 15, 1905; *Dillingham Committee Hearings,* I, 233. According to Yates's testimony here, he called Deneen a liar to his face in 1906 for denying that he had promised in 1904 to help Yates replace Cullom in the Senate.

Shaw.[86] Although Lowden declined to join actively in the plan, he was willing to be its beneficiary. Governor Deneen's co-operation, or at least his neutrality, appeared to be a prerequisite to success. Cheered by the outcome of Cowley's scouting expedition to Springfield, Lowden assured Deneen by letter on November 15:

I want to tell you how much I thank you for the kindly words you have spoken of me to Mr. Cowley and many others of my friends. I would hate to feel that our friendly personal relations were going to be broken on account of politics, and it will give me the very greatest pleasure if you will let me see you some time when you are here.[87]

Thus the ice was broken, and a channel of communication reopened between the two men. For the moment, nothing more needed to be done in the Springfield sector.

The friends of Congressman Hitt, who were also solicitous about Lowden's future, warned the elder statesman that he would be ill advised to subject his precarious health to the strain of another campaign. They arranged for a number of papers in the congressional district to print editorials similar in tone to the one in the *Mount Carroll Democrat* of January 23, 1906. "Many of Congressman Hitt's friends," Feezer wrote, "feel that his health is such that he should not, for his own sake, cling to his office. They are in an embarrassing spot when asked to oppose Senator Cullom on the grounds of his age but to support Mr. Hitt who is even older. The unanimity for Frank Lowden is unique."[88] To climax this unwonted concern about Hitt's physical welfare, Feezer and others apparently paid the travel expenses of the congressman's doctor to Washington so that he could advise his patient to retire "for the sake of his life." After being reminded so often for over two months about his dangerous condition, Hitt capitulated by wiring to Lowden on January 27: "I send to you, this the first news to anyone, that I shall not be a candidate for Congress. My best wishes to you for it." The Lowdens and the Culloms were then in St. Augustine, where Lowden sought renewed strength and ambition after a stubborn attack of the grippe and facial blotches, attributed by his physicians to nervous exhaustion.

Quick changes of mood characterized Lowden during his entire career. A cold or other minor ailment made him irritable and depressed. At times early in the winter of 1905–6 he must have wondered whether he or the congressman had the more cause to complain. But the Florida sunshine and Hitt's telegram quickly improved his condition and revived his good spirits. On

86. Letters to FOL from J. R. Cowley, Freeport, Illinois, Nov. 17, 1905; R. R. Hitt, Nov. 22, 1905; and C. M. Feezer, Jan. 1, 1906; FOL to Hitt, Dec. 4, 1905, and to C. M. Feezer, Jan. 4, 1906. In the autumn of 1905, FOL began his long-continued practice of sending to his friends calendars illustrated with a "Sinnissippi" farm scene. For 1907, for example, he distributed eight thousand and for 1910 ten thousand.

87. The contrast between the tone of this letter and the one which he wrote to Mrs. Lowden about Deneen in 1898 (see p. 111) is striking.

88. The editorial was in error. Cullom was seventy-six, or four years older than Hitt.

February 2 he assured Feezer and his other friends, "I am regaining my health fast." Although in this letter he hedged by saying that he "had not positively decided" whether he would run for Congress, he already had wired Hitt in a more decisive vein. After expressing "great surprise" over his friend's determination to retire, he added: "If the people wish me to be your successor, I shall be glad to serve them to the best of my ability. I would rather represent this great district in Congress than to hold any other office in public life." He soon followed up this telegram with a letter, humbly thanking Hitt for sending advance notice of his decision: "If there is anything in the world I can do for you, even to running an errand, command me."[89]

Now that he had marked time for a year and more, his doubts about his political future suddenly evaporated, and he felt eager to be up and doing. Much of his life was similarly punctuated by alternating periods of inaction and strenuous effort. After driving himself almost to the point of complete exhaustion in a campaign, he wearied of politics altogether and seemed ready to spend the rest of his days in retirement at "Sinnissippi." His lands and cattle were the best of restoratives. But no sooner had they banished his tiredness than the isolation of his farm bred a feeling of frustration. As a release, he plunged once again into the main stream of life. Thereupon the characteristic cycle began anew.

Three days after Hitt's wire to Lowden, the members of the Republican Central Committee of Ogle County held their regularly scheduled meeting in Oregon. They adopted a resolution calling upon him to announce his candidacy for Congress. Cowley simultaneously circulated petitions throughout the district and easily collected enough signatures to satisfy the legal prerequisite for Lowden's name to appear on the ballot at the August primary. Alvin Sanders, editor of the widely read *Breeder's Gazette* of Chicago, wrote to all important livestock farmers in the Thirteenth District, requesting them to help send a man of their own occupation to Washington.[90] Still in Florida, Lowden asked Cowley to use his own discretion about releasing to the newspapers a statement that "because of letters and telegrams received from all over the district I feel impelled to announce my candidacy for Congress to succeed the Honorable Robert R. Hitt." Cowley was in the more haste to give out the news because, to his annoyance, R. R. Tiffany, a Freeport attorney, had already declared that he was the choice of Deneen and Yates to be Hitt's successor.[91]

In view of Tiffany's claim, it was high time for Lowden to resume his amicable interchange of mid-November with Deneen. He refused to become

89. FOL to R. R. Hitt, Feb. 7, 1906; wire of C. Feezer *et al.*, of Carroll County, to FOL, Jan. 31, and FOL's wire in reply, Feb. 2, 1906; *Mount Carroll* (Ill.) *Democrat*, Jan. 29, 1906.

90. *Dixon* (Ill.) *Telegraph*, Jan. 30, 1906; *Chicago Chronicle*, Jan. 31, 1906; J. R. Cowley to FOL, Jan. 30 and Feb. 5, 1906.

91. FOL to J. R. Cowley, Feb. 2, 1906, appointing him manager of the campaign and sole almoner of its funds.

a party to a "deal," but common sense dictated that he ascertain the governor's attitude as soon as possible. Lowden's membership on Senator Cullom's campaign committee added a complicating factor. However silent Deneen might be about Yates's senatorial striving, he was not Cullom's friend. The majority of the Republican voters of the Thirteenth District, unlike Lowden, favored Yates for the Senate. Both Cullom and Senator Hopkins advised Lowden that he need not placate Deneen in order to win the congressional primary and election. But, as always, Lowden preferred to play safe. He had lost in 1904, and, if he were ever to have a political career, he could not afford a second defeat.

When he arrived in Chicago from Florida on February 10, he found that Cowley had carried negotiations with the governor dangerously close to a "deal." As early as January 29, both the *Chicago Post* and the *Chicago Chronicle* surmised that if Deneen entered no candidate in competition with Lowden, the latter would agree not to campaign actively for Cullom except in the Thirteenth Congressional District.[92] At the suggestion of Roy O. West, Cowley conferred at length with the governor in Springfield on February 1. He discovered that Deneen was "very kindly disposed," but labored under the misapprehension that Lowden controlled the *Chicago Evening Journal,* which was attacking the governor's policies. Cowley arranged for Deneen and Lowden to talk together as confidentially as possible at the Union League Club in Chicago on February 10. This appointment brought him home from Florida and obliged him to decline a White House invitation to dinner on the preceding evening.[93] Deneen, Lowden, Cowley, and Chief Grain Inspector W. Scott Cowen, an intimate of the governor, conferred for three hours. If anything was decided upon except that Deneen would keep hands off the congressional race after encouraging Tiffany to withdraw, it was not revealed to the press. Although Lowden always denied having made a bargain, the fact remains that he did not campaign for Cullom outside his own congressional district and that the *Springfield Evening News,* of which he was the principal owner, suddenly shifted from a warmly pro-Cullom position to one of almost complete neutrality. Probably Deneen also felt compensated by knowing that if Lowden reached Congress, he would not be a gubernatorial aspirant in 1908.[94]

For several months every circumstance indicated that he could coast into the House of Representatives with no difficulty whatsoever. After Tiffany withdrew, it seemed unlikely that any other Republican rival would enter the lists. The friendly reception accorded to Lowden on his trips over the congressional district with Cowley encouraged him to believe that its tra-

92. A. J. Hopkins to FOL, Feb. 2, 1906. The next day the *Rockford Republic* suggested that if FOL had made no bargain in 1904 when he needed to, he certainly would not do so in 1906 when one was unnecessary.

93. Mrs. Lowden's diary, Feb. 8, 1906; J. R. Cowley to FOL, Feb. 2, 1906; *Chicago Post.* Feb. 14, 1906.

94. Mrs. Lowden's diary, Feb. 10, 1906.

ditional Republicanism would continue. Most of the important local papers were on his side. In mid-March he filed with the county clerk of Ogle County his "declaration of intention to run" and paid the $16.67 fee required in order to have his name appear on the primary ballot. So confident was he of easy sailing that he went to Iowa in late February to purchase a champion Shorthorn bull, "Cumberland's Last," and shortly thereafter enjoyed a two weeks' vacation with Judge Landis at Hot Springs, Arkansas.[95] When Deneen declared his neutrality in the Senate race, Cullom's prospects of re-election so greatly brightened that, outwardly at least, he showed no annoyance because Lowden refrained from making a state-wide canvass in his behalf. Cullom told him:

You know I made a proposition to you once to swap places, you taking my senatorship and I your farm? I am satisfied however that I would not now be able to trade with you because you not only will soon have a seat in the Congress of the United States without opposition, but your farm as well. That is an ideal way to live. I do not know any man in Illinois who has as nice a layout for the future as you have. You can represent your district in Congress as long as you please, if you once get your footing, and live like a fighting cock on your farm besides. I wish you all sorts of success and good health.[96]

When Cullom wrote this letter, however, the halcyon days of Lowden's candidacy were over, and a long spell of stormy weather had begun. On May 22 William Pierce Landon, a Rochelle lawyer who had once been a Kansas farmer and more recently a Presbyterian clergyman, started a remarkable campaign of oratory, showmanship, and slander to defeat Lowden for the nomination in the August primary. Alphabetically, the name of Landon would precede that of Lowden on the ballot, where their similarity would further work to the latter's disadvantage. Landon was an appealing speaker, with no scruples against using tactics and types of argument which his opponent neither would nor could employ. Traveling over his district in a covered wagon, he was accompanied by a trumpeter, who summoned the people to come and give ear. The horn also signified how Landon, a modern Joshua, intended to crumble the "walls of privilege" protecting his rival so as to expose to the public gaze the sinister interests which he represented. To illustrate these interests, Landon equipped himself with a box of "Uneeda" biscuits, a Pullman ticket, and various other easily understood symbols of Lowden's directorships and high-toned clubs, which were listed at impressive length in *Who's Who in America.*

Inconsequential to Landon was the fact that his opponent had resigned most of his offices in corporations before he filed his "intention to run." In his view, Lowden was "a carpetbagger," an alien to the simple, rural life of the district, a tool of Lorimer, an opponent of organized labor and of trust regulation, a plutocrat branded with the dollar sign, and a man who was toadied to by almost every local postmaster and by the many country news-

95. *Ibid.,* Feb. 26, Mar. 15 and 28, 1906.
96. Cullom to FOL, May 24, 1906.

papers which he had subsidized. All these epithets must have reminded Lowden of his own alliterative blasts against Bryan six years before. In the course of his harangues, Landon quoted what purported to be an extract from an article by Albert J. Beveridge in a recent issue of the *Saturday Evening Post*. In this the senator supposedly made a covert attack upon Lowden for using his wealth to forge for himself a political career. Landon also praised Theodore Roosevelt fulsomely and declared that Lowden's defeat was undoubtedly desired by a President who had said: "It is time for the man with the patch on his breeches to come to the fore, and for the man with the dollar to go to the rear." Landon asked the Rock River Valley farmers whether the multimillionaire daughter of George M. Pullman and her husband could really represent their interests in Washington.[97]

Although Lowden and his supporters refused at first to accord their strange opponent serious attention, they soon changed their minds. By late May, Mrs. Lowden noted that her husband was "a good deal troubled." Two months afterward, with the primary close at hand, he felt "tired and depressed over the political situation and no one can foresee the outcome." In his *Mount Carroll Democrat*, "Cal" Feezer labeled Landon "a mountebank who deserves a horse whipping" for bringing Mrs. Lowden's name into the canvass.[98] But Landon escaped a "hiding," and the size of his audiences grew. His antics apparently more favorably impressed the voters than Lowden's oft-published photographs of his family, his farm, and his thoroughbred animals. Evidently few of his constituents found time to read the copies he circulated of his 1901 speech at the State University of Iowa on trust regulation or his 1903 remarks in praise of unions at the Labor Day workingmen's picnic in Chicago.

More effective in demonstrating that he had the "common touch" was his initiation that summer into the fraternal orders of Masons and Elks.[99] Equally to the point was Senator Beveridge's letter to him expressing the hope that he would win and categorically denying that the *Saturday Evening Post* article had been directed against his candidacy. Although Roosevelt declined to mix in a local political contest by openly favoring either side, he directed his secretary, William Loeb, to say that "not only has the President never used the expression referred to [the sentence mentioned above and attributed by Landon to Roosevelt], it is diametrically opposed to everything he ever has said."[100] Given wide publicity over the district on the eve of the primary, this note took some of the wind out of Landon's sails.

Late in July, Lowden also circulated a broadside stating simply and tersely

97. FOL to R. R. Hitt, May 31, 1906. When Landon announced his candidacy, he said: "Lowden is a multimillionaire who spent pin money on a country seat so as to make it his pocket borough." The Beveridge article is in the *Saturday Evening Post* of June 10, 1906.

98. Mrs. Lowden's diary, May 24 and July 17 and 24, 1906; *Mount Carroll* (Ill.) *Democrat,* June 9 and 28, 1906.

99. Mrs. Lowden's diary, July 11 and 24, 1906.

100. FOL to A. J. Beveridge, June 20 and July 6, 1906; Beveridge to FOL, June 25, 1906; W. Loeb, Jr., to FOL, July 27, 1906.

his views on trust and railroad regulation and on a sliding scale of maximum and minimum tariff rates to be so administered by the President as to increase the foreign market for American agricultural products. "If anyone," he declared, "proves that I lobbied against the [railroad] rate bill or for any bill on behalf of a corporate or private interest, I will withdraw from the race." Lowden told how he had admired Theodore Roosevelt ever since the late 1880's, when the New Yorker had worked for civil service reform. "I have often said," he added, "that Theodore Roosevelt's elevation to the presidency was as providential as was Lincoln's election in 1860." In this brochure Lowden devoted considerable space to setting the record straight about his corporation directorships. "I do not own," he affirmed, "one share of Pullman stock or a share of any stock of any company which by any possibility can be the subject of legislation by Congress." He also denied that he aimed to build a political machine. "I will resign from the race," he promised, "if it can be shown that I have tried to dictate the vote of any man in the District, including that of my own employees."[101]

During the entire preprimary campaign he made no political speeches. He relied upon circulars like the above and, what probably was far more effective, upon traveling back and forth over the district, meeting people in their places of business and talking with them as a neighbor. When Landon challenged him to a series of joint debates on the subjects of "Purity and Politics" and "The Control of Corporations," Lowden explained his refusal to accept in these words:[102]

There are some who have thought that I ought to enter into personal competition with those who are going up and down the district heaping abuse upon me. If, in order to get this office, I must detract from the ability and integrity of some other man, if I must build myself up on the ruin of another, I prefer the quiet and decency of private life. I shall so deport myself in this campaign, regardless of results, that, at its end, I shall be in good company, even when alone.

Although the campaign seemed to arouse much popular interest and the weather on primary day, August 4, was pleasant, only about 25 per cent of the electorate bothered to go to the polls. Lowden carried all six counties in his constituency, but his majority in Carroll was only thirteen votes and in Jo Daviess only seventy. In the district nominating convention at Freeport he controlled sixty-three delegates to Landon's twenty-four. In the same primary Lorimer won renomination to Congress in his district, and Cullom defeated Yates in the state at large.[103]

101. Broadside of July 23, 1906, entitled *Frank O. Lowden Makes a Statement to the Republican Voters of the Thirteenth Congressional District.*

102. Open letter of W. P. Landon to FOL in *Pearl City* (Ill.) *News,* July 26, 1906; printed single sheet, entitled *Statement of Frank O. Lowden, Candidate for Congress from the Thirteenth Congressional District.*

103. FOL's total vote was 11,265 and Landon's 8,285. FOL's acceptance speech before the Freeport convention on August 16 was a paean of praise for all major Republican policies, foreign and domestic, since 1896. It lauded Roosevelt as "the foremost man of all the world" and the "greatest peacemaker in history."

Lowden's hard fight against Landon warned him that he could not expect an easy victory in November over his Democratic opponent, "Honest" James P. Wilson, of Polo, Illinois. Wilson, a native son of the district, was a farmer who had served for a decade in the state Assembly. He made clear from the start that he was Landon's apt pupil. Landon had taught him where Lowden was vulnerable and had stirred up so much emotion by his demagogic oratory that his own followers might bolt from their party in the election.[104]

By late September, after enduring for over a month a barrage of ridicule and insinuation about his wealth, his family, his ability as a farmer, and his honesty, Lowden concluded that outside help alone might save him from defeat. Thanks to influential friends and his membership on the Republican National Committee, he could summon aid of a sort not available to his opponent or, for that matter, to most congressional candidates of his own party. He wrote for assistance, in the form of a speech or two, to Vice-President Fairbanks, Secretary of the Treasury Leslie M. Shaw, Postmaster-General George B. Cortelyou, Governor Cummins of Iowa, Speaker Joseph G. Cannon, and Senators Beveridge, Dolliver, Cullom, and Hopkins.[105] Most of these top-flight Republicans regretted their inability to help, but Shaw spoke three times in the district, and Fairbanks praised Lowden in a speech at nearby Peoria. The Republican National Committee sent Frank B. Sargent, United States commissioner of labor, to Savanna in Carroll County to bear witness to Lowden's friendliness toward organized labor. Although Yates pleaded his mother's serious illness as the reason why he could not hasten to the Thirteenth District, Deneen and Sherman cheered Lowden greatly by canvassing for him in northwestern Illinois. Also among his zealous supporters in the campaign were Attorney-General W. H. Stead, former Senator "Billy" Mason, and H. J. Hamlin.[106]

In spite of this battery of impressive allies, Lowden grew more anxious as the weeks passed by. He felt driven to speak much oftener than he had planned to do. By late October he was excessively tired, almost voiceless, suffering from nervous indigestion, and weighing only 160 pounds. The campaign exhausted him the more because he still felt obliged, in speech and newspaper interviews, to devote much attention to his wife's Pullman Company stock, her financial help to him in the campaign, his rural upbringing in a poverty-pinched home, his prowess as a dirt farmer, his freedom from enslavement by "John Barleycorn" and the wicked trusts, and the slanderous

104. FOL worried lest his supporters decline to be conciliatory toward the Landonites and thereby drive them into the Wilson camp. Whether correctly or not, the *Galena* (Ill.) *Gazette* on Aug. 16 said that Landon would vote for Lowden.

105. Letters of FOL to Cortelyou, Sept. 20; Cullom, Sept. 23; Cannon, Sept. 21; Beveridge, Sept. 18; and Dolliver, Sept. 20, 1906.

106. John F. Smulski of Chicago, fellow law student with FOL, banker, lumber company president, alderman, editor of a Polish newspaper, and state treasurer, came to FOL's district to help him. Deneen spoke at Mount Carroll, Freeport, and elsewhere and put FOL, as he wrote R. O. West, Oct. 20, "under great obligations."

charge that he was buying votes by hiring political workers at ten or fifteen dollars a head. He found his faith in popular government severely tested by being called upon so often to say, in effect:

If I am elected I will represent the people of this District and nobody else on earth. I did not move out here to go to Congress. I never expect to live in Chicago again. I grew up on a farm and I bet I could beat any man under thirty with an old Marsh harvester right now. Some think it's up to me to decide whether I want to go to Congress or give up my wife. I need no time to decide that. I have got enough to support my wife and would be able to do it better if I am not elected than if I am. I am sorry I am not nearly as rich as I am credited with being. I do not believe that the history of this country has so far proven that virtue, honesty, and integrity are only consistent with poverty. If you are going to beat me this fall, I hope you will do it so thoroughly that I will have sense enough to stay home, run my farm, and not get mixed up in politics again.[107]

He wrote in confidence to his best friends that if he were defeated, he would be through with politics for good and all. Indeed, to barely squeeze through to victory would be almost as bad as a defeat because his congressional district customarily favored its Republican candidates by a thumping margin of from eight to ten thousand votes. "If I can be elected by a fair majority this time," he wrote to Landis on September 30, "I am quite sure that it will be easy in the future." The big question then, however, was whether he would be elected at all.

Ten days before the date of this letter, Congressman Hitt died at his summer home at Narragansett Pier, Rhode Island. The Thirteenth District Republican Congressional Committee at once brought Lowden forward as its candidate to fill out Hitt's unexpired term. His name would therefore appear twice on the election ballot. In other words, because Congress would not be in session during the seven weeks before election day, the special election usually held to fill a vacancy was merely merged with the regular election. Since the Democrats did not bother to nominate Wilson for this "fill-in" office, Lowden was certain of a seat in Congress for at least one short session.

The turnout of voters on November 6 was the smallest in a by-election year since 1890. Lowden edged through to victory by a margin of only about 2,000 ballots in a total of 31,372. Of the six counties in the district, Wilson carried Jo Daviess and Stephenson and ran dangerously close to his opponent in Lee. In acknowledging his defeat, he expressed to Lowden the hope that "you will be an efficient servant and that your record may be replete with an earnest effort in the interests of the people.[108] "I believe," wrote Governor Deneen to him in a belated but gracious note, "that nearly everybody in public life has had the experience of a severe contest. I have

107. Summary of portions of FOL's speeches at Pawpaw, Amboy, and Ashton, Illinois, Oct. 2–4, and at Polo, Oct. 31, 1906.

108. Exchange of telegrams between FOL and J. P. Wilson, Nov. 7. Hitt had carried the district in 1902 by nearly 10,000 majority and in 1904 by 16,400. Cowley forecast a 5,000–10,000 majority for FOL. FOL wrote F. H. Smith, Peoria, Nov. 19, 1906: "Everything was against me at the time of Mr. Hitt's death, and under all the circumstances, I am very well satisfied with the result."

had two. I think that you have fought all your battles at one time, and that has made it a little harder."[109]

Thus a political career finally opened to Lowden but at a considerable drain upon his health and purse. In widening his friendships, often by converting enemies to his side, the two arduous campaigns of 1904 and 1906 had been highly rewarding. He demonstrated that he was a hard, clean fighter, one who could lose in good spirit and win without taking revenge upon those of his own party who had tried to defeat him. Amid a faction-ridden party he worked continually for harmony. No Republican leader in Illinois had tried harder to heal the schisms, even though his therapy had been largely unavailing. Lorimer and Deneen remained at daggers drawn not only in Chicago politics but as champions of rival plans for a deep waterway across Illinois from Lake Michigan to the Mississippi. Deneen had well-founded suspicions that Lorimer, while touring Illinois in the interest of the project, hobnobbed with politicians of both parties about ways and means of defeating him for re-election. Then, too, the senatorial campaign had split asunder the Deneen-Yates entente. Yates, smarting from defeat and anxious to retaliate against his former ally, was ripe to be enticed once more into Lorimer's camp.

From the meager foundation of a political apprenticeship confined largely to Chicago politics and before holding any elective office whatsoever, Lowden leaped for the governorship in 1904 and missed it by inches in a dramatic contest. From the standpoint of the circle of society and the expensive manner of living to which Mrs. Lowden and he were accustomed, they should be happier in Washington than in Springfield, even though a congressman usually had much less prestige than the chief executive of a state. Whether his wealth was more of a political asset than a liability was difficult for him to decide. It kept him free from obligations to those who otherwise would have had to finance his campaign; it enabled him to employ generously every legitimate means to advance his candidacy; and it indirectly won him influential friends upon whom he could call for help, but it barbed his opponents' shafts and had been mainly responsible for the arduousness of his road to victory. On this road, he accommodated his views on national issues almost without exception to those of the leader of his party, Theodore Roosevelt.

Rid of his former dependence upon Chicago politicians, Lowden now represented a rural constituency and could emerge, at long last, from William Lorimer's shadow. If he did not do so, he would clearly be within it by choice and not by necessity. Whether he would be merely one more millionaire in Congress or would stand out above the ruck of senators and representatives and develop into a statesman was by no means clear in the autumn of 1906. At least, he determined to try hard to be a national leader. Winning the opportunity to show what he could do, however, had taken such a toll of his strength that he still felt nervously tired when the short session of the Fifty-ninth Congress convened on December 3, 1906.

109. C. S. Deneen to FOL, Dec. 26, 1906.

CHAPTER VII

A "FARMER" IN CONGRESS, 1906–11

Few men's prospects of a long legislative career have been brighter than Frank Lowden's when Congressman Henry S. Boutell, of Chicago, escorted him down the aisle of the House of Representatives on December 3, 1906, to be sworn into office. Of more than ordinary ability and coming from a district with a half-century record of unswerving Republicanism, he could reasonably hope to gain the prestige of extended tenure and the chairmanship of some important committee. The longer he served, the more secure he probably would be, because his growing influence in the counsels of his party would become a matter of pride to his constituents and guarantee him aid from its national leaders in case of need. Although he disclaimed any wish to be a "boss" or to build a "machine," he could not help creating an organization if he performed his official duties successfully. Postmasters and other federal job-holders in his district would owe their appointments largely to him. An increasing number of its citizens and communities would feel under obligation for his favors.

But by no means all his unusual advantages depended upon the future for realization. His success as a businessman and a lawyer and, above all, the fact that his wife was Florence Pullman had made his activities national news for a decade before his election. Unlike many fledgling congressmen, he had close political friends not only in his district but also throughout his state and at Washington. As a member of the Republican National Committee, he spoke for his party in Illinois in its external relationships. As one of the executive subcommittee of that committee, he shared in planning political strategy on a national scale. Although Senators Cullom and Hopkins, Speaker Cannon, and Congressman Lorimer of the powerful Rivers and Harbors Committee were his close acquaintances, no one of them had been able to put the yoke of faction securely over his neck. Known favorably to President Roosevelt, Vice-President Fairbanks, and several members of the cabinet and the Supreme Court before he came to Washington, he associated with them from the outset not merely as a political colleague but as a friend.

His sociability and his wealth enabled him rapidly to broaden his range of acquaintanceship among men whose influence counted heavily in national affairs. During even a short session of Congress, Mrs. Lowden and he entertained elaborately at a cost far exceeding his annual salary of five thousand dollars. Invitations to teas, dinners, and theater parties multiplied by a figure nearly equal to the number of their own guests. An overloaded social calendar, however, might become as harmful to Lowden's health as it was helpful to his political position.[1]

Leaving the children at "Sinnissippi," the Lowdens made their home at the New Willard Hotel during the final session of the Fifty-ninth Congress. Besides the small office provided to every congressman, Lowden ensconced his private secretary, James R. Cowley, and several stenographers in two rooms of the Colorado Building, not far from his hotel. With the aid of this staff he tried to make more than perfunctory replies to his heavy incoming mail, praising or censuring his actions, asking all sorts of favors, or expounding, often at wearisome length and sometimes with complete irrationality, the "correct" solutions of public issues. Like other congressmen, he soon discovered that some of his constituents expected him to be their messenger boy in Washington, a quick source of factual knowledge about manifold subjects, a conjurer able to work a legislative miracle or provide excellent positions in short order, a scapegoat to blame for their troubles, and a Santa Claus eager to join their societies, help their churches, and contribute to the cost of old settlers' picnics, veterans' "campfires," county-fair premiums, and Fourth of July celebrations. Many of his correspondents lacked even a foggy notion of the difference in jurisdiction between the national and state governments. For fifteen years after he ceased to be a congressman, he received letters from people who believed that he was still their representative.

For answering the questions of some of his constituents and complimenting others of them, he found government documents and his annual quota of seeds and bulbs of considerable usefulness. The leaflets of the departments of interior and agriculture, especially, furnished expert replies to many inquiries, and he had bundles of this printed material mailed to the public libraries in his district. The historical society at Sterling welcomed the volumes of the Smithsonian Institution. Judges and prominent lawyers of the Rock River Valley professed delight over his gift of John Bassett Moore's *Digest of International Law*. One of his annual perquisites was ten thousand packages of vegetable seeds, five hundred of flower seeds, thirty of lawn-grass seed, twenty of narcissus, tulip, and hyacinth bulbs, ten strawberry plants, and eight grape vines. He increased this allotment and his share of agricultural bulletins by trading with congressmen from urban constituencies who gladly exchanged theirs for most of his quota of printed matter on ocean shipping or some other topic of no great interest to the people in northwestern Illinois. Under government frank, he distributed the seeds throughout his district early each year and, in due season, sent out follow-up letters asking how they had grown. On one occasion the superintendent of schools at Freeport received from him twenty-five hundred packages ac-

---

1. See pp. 189 ff. In addition to his salary, FOL received $100 a month for a clerk.

companied by Lowden's suggestion that each child plant his own plot and write an essay about his experiences as a gardener.[2]

Although he lived expensively in Washington, he never forgot that most of his constituents were farmers or residents of farmer-supported small towns.[3] As long as he stayed in the House of Representatives he listed himself in the congressional directory as a farmer. On his first arrival in the capital city he made good copy for the press by simulating a rural innocence about the ways of a metropolis, even though he was altogether urban in his attire and manner of living. The reporters continued to call him "Farmer" Lowden, partly in jest but also to acknowledge his familiarity with the needs of the American countryside.[4] The Washington newspapers always treated him and Mrs. Lowden generously. On his first day in the capital city the *Herald* quoted him as saying:

I am too new a man in Washington to have any views, at least any that will do for publication. Besides, I am a farmer, and what can you expect of a horny-handed tiller of the soil but to take a back seat till he learns the ropes? I can tell you all about growing corn and oats, and raising Shorthorn cattle, Percheron horses, Shropshire sheep, and Poland China pigs, but as to grave governmental questions give me a little breathing time.[5]

A week later the *Post* reported that he was "making some progress. I can now find my way from the hotel to the Capitol without the aid of a guide, and I can also make my way around the building very well. I have been told that about the hardest thing to locate in Washington is the Speaker's eye. They tell me if I can once get a line on that, that my future will be assured."[6] The newspapers of the Rock River Valley relayed banter of this sort to his constituents.

"Uncle Joe" Cannon favored him with a seat advantageously situated in the center of the House but disappointed him by assigning him to the Committee on Foreign Affairs rather than to the one on agriculture. The appointment was appropriate in the sense that it permitted him to fill out the term of Robert R. Hitt, who had been the committee's chairman.[7] Once in

2. *Freeport* (Ill.) *Standard*, Feb. 22, 1907. He paid a clerk $2.00 a thousand for addressing 17,000 packages of seed.

3. The *South Bend* (Ind.) *Tribune*, Mar. 14, 1908, listed twenty-nine millionaires in the Senate and fourteen in the House. It estimated FOL's fortune at $5,000,000, making him the fourth richest man in the House—topped by J. E. Andrus (N.Y.), W. B. McKinley (Ill.), and George F. Huff (Pa.).

4. *Washington* (D.C.) *Times*, Dec. 5, 1906.

5. *Washington* (D.C.) *Herald*, Dec. 2, 1906. On Jan. 9, 1908, the *Washington* (D.C.) *Star* showed a cartoon picture of FOL with this jingle:

> "Representative Loudon [*sic*] has money;
> So much that really 'tis funny.
> Every maid that he greets
> Hands him linguistic sweets
> And insists upon calling him 'Honey.' "

6. *Washington* (D.C.) *Post*, Dec. 9, 1906.

7. On Feb. 16, 1907, FOL spoke at the House memorial exercises for Hitt (*Congressional Record* [59th Cong., 2d sess.], XLI, 3157–58).

the swing of its work, moreover, Lowden enjoyed it as long as he remained in Congress. Furthermore, his membership provided a social passport into Washington's diplomatic circle and brought him into close touch with people and problems of importance. Anomalously, although he continued to insist that agriculture was his primary concern, he found international issues the most fascinating of all. Probably this attraction largely reflected his happy companionship with his committee associates in both political camps. Among these, Nicholas Longworth of Ohio, Edwin Denby of Michigan, James B. Perkins, J. Sloat Fassett, and Francis B. Harrison of New York, Robert G. Cousins of Iowa, Charles B. Landis of Indiana, and John N. Garner of Texas became his special friends.[8] He used the resources of the Library of Congress to familiarize himself with the background of current international questions. There, too, he enjoyed an occasional luncheon at Dr. Herbert Putnam's "round table," where he shared in discussion with J. Bassett Moore, J. Franklin Jameson, John Barrett, Frederic Bancroft, and university scholars engaged in research.

By the time he reached Congress, Lowden's belligerent imperialism of 1898–1900 had cooled considerably. The best defense for the nation, as he now viewed it, was a financially solvent government with a surplus in its treasury. He opposed the construction of additional battleships because they cost too much money and might entice the country into war. Most surprising of all, he ventured the opinion that, but for the big-navy policy of a decade before, the United States would have been spared the conflict with Spain and the embarrassing possession of the Philippines. Now that the Stars and Stripes flew over the archipelago, to relinquish it would be a "national crime," but its security demanded that the United States and Germany make common cause in the Far East. An understanding between them would serve to offset Japanese, French, and English encroachments upon the coastal areas of China and adjacent islands. England, said Lowden, "fears us as a competitor and despises us as a rival." On the other hand, the Germans, "from the Kaiser down," like Americans better than do the English. For this reason, a treaty between Germany and the United States, pledging mutual support against aggressor nations in the Far East, would be in the interest of world peace. On this point Lowden quoted with approval the Columbia University historian, John W. Burgess, whose pro-Germanism would bring him under fire after 1914. To strengthen the position of the United States in the Pacific, Lowden also favored a bill to extend and deepen the naval base at Pearl Harbor.[9]

Along with participation by the United States in a Far East balance of power, Lowden advocated patient reliance upon the Department of State to

8. Lowden's admiration for Secretary of State (later a senator from New York) Elihu Root was second only to that for President Roosevelt.

9. See pp. 90–91, 96, and 490. *Chicago Examiner,* Jan. 6, 1908. FOL was a member of the Committee on Naval Expenditures. On Apr. 16, 1908, he and other congressional members of the Illinois Old Guard dutifully voted to pass the Naval Appropriation Bill (*Congressional Record* [60th Cong., 1st sess.], XLII, 3195, 4447, 4838, 5454).

ease international tensions by friendly negotiations. San Francisco's discrimination against Japanese children in its public schools posed the general problem of the constitutional curbs, if any, upon the government of the United States in the field of foreign affairs. President Roosevelt's success in 1907 in temporarily settling this thorny school issue by means of executive understandings with the San Francisco authorities and the Japanese minister to the United States freed the Foreign Relations Committee from a prolonged discussion of the matter but, at the same time, aroused a controversy over the constitutional powers of a state in relation to a treaty. After much study, Lowden declared that "where a treaty is made, the only proper subject of inquiry is whether the subject of the treaty was a proper subject for international negotiation, and that, if so, it was of course the law of the land whether or not it pertained to matters reserved to the states."[10] In other words, the United States government may by treaty take jurisdiction over subjects which are beyond its constitutional competence to regulate in domestic affairs. This was the same position for which Senator George Sutherland received much acclaim when he stated it in an article in 1910, elaborated it further in lectures at Columbia University eight years later, and, finally, as an associate justice of the United States Supreme Court, brought a majority of its bench to adopt in the memorable Curtiss-Wright case of 1936.[11] Eighteen years later the Bricker Amendment debates once again threshed over this same general issue.

In early 1908, when many congressmen wished to lecture the czar sharply for refusing to let Russian Jews divest themselves of their allegiance to him and become American citizens, Lowden recommended nothing more drastic than a continuation of diplomatic interchanges on the subject. Eventually, so he believed, if bad temper could be avoided, the right of expatriation would become a universally acknowledged rule of international law. Nearly a century before, he admitted, the United States had failed after three years of war to force from England an acceptance of that principle. But reason ultimately would gain what conflict could not compel; and when reason triumphed in this instance, America would win her greatest victory in foreign affairs.[12]

He felt sanguine that the prospects for an enduring peace between nations were brightening. After visiting the old battlefields around Metz in the autumn of 1909, he wrote to his wife, "I hope and believe that such battles will become less and less frequent as the years go by." He was sufficiently realistic, however, to assure Richmond P. Hobson in early 1911 of his readi-

10. FOL to F. B. Kellogg, Nov. 22, 1913.

11. G. Sutherland, "Internal and External Powers of the National Government," *North American Review,* CXCI (March, 1910), 373.

12. *Congressional Record* (60th Cong., 1st sess.), XLII, 25–28, Appendix. As early as Jan. 21, 1907, FOL lectured Congress briefly upon the several ways whereby a United States citizen could divest himself of his citizenship (*ibid.* [59th Cong., 2d sess.], XLI, 1467; [60th Cong., 2d sess.], XLIII, 172).

ness to support a bill to create a Council of National Defense for the purpose of co-ordinating all federal activities relating directly to the protection of the country against a foreign enemy.[13]

Although and because Lowden trusted the State Department to maintain national prestige abroad, prevent war, and extend American commercial opportunities, he wished to effect a marked improvement in its facilities and personnel. To the achievement of this end he probably devoted more of his energies than to any other task. His qualified success after five years of effort was one of his few contributions of national importance while in Congress. The wonder is why, when he was backed by Presidents Roosevelt and Taft, by the Department of State, by the foreign relations committees of both houses, and by important business interests, he had to work so long and hard to win a majority of his colleagues to his side.

To his membership on the Foreign Affairs Committee, Lowden brought little knowledge of international relations but a long-sustained interest in civil service reform. At that time, poorly qualified men and not a few aliens often comprised much of the staff of American consulates. Lowden was by no means the first public official to call attention to these shortcomings. Following the emasculation by the Senate and House foreign relations committees of Henry Cabot Lodge's proposals for reform, President Roosevelt, by executive order on June 27, 1906, temporarily established an examination and classification procedure to weed out unfit applicants for consular positions and promote whatever able men already held them. This new system needed to be sanctioned and extended by law. Early in 1907, Lowden submitted to the House of Representatives a petition from the National Business League of America for a reform of the consular service.[14] The next year this same organization sent him the draft of a bill spelling out a method of improvement. The league had its main office in Chicago. Among its members were Lowden, La Verne W. Noyes, Samuel Insull, Philetus W. Gates, and Frederic W. Upham. It aimed, above all else, to promote American commerce and industry at home and abroad. Cullom and Hopkins in the Senate and Lowden in the House were among its principal spokesmen in Congress.[15]

The league's bill, which Hopkins and Lowden simultaneously introduced in December, 1907, required any applicant for consular appointment to be a United States citizen between twenty-one and forty years of age and to demonstrate by written examinations, prepared and scored by a non-partisan commission, his familiarity with one modern foreign language and the general

13. FOL to his wife, from Paris, Oct. 23, 1909, and to R. P. Hobson, Feb. 27, 1911.

14. *Congressional Record* (59th Cong., 2d sess.), XLI, 1190. As finally enacted, all examination and promotion-for-merit provisions had been deleted from the Lodge Bill.

15. A. A. Burnham, general secretary of the National Business League of America, to FOL, July 18 and Nov. 30, 1907; FOL to Burnham, July 20, Nov. 26, and Dec. 3, 1907; *Congressional Record* (60th Cong., 1st sess.), XLII, 116, 1436. On Jan. 31, 1908, FOL presented a petition of the league to have the Consular Bureau transferred from the Department of State to the Department of Commerce and Labor.

conditions and needs of American industry and commerce. The grades of the candidates, assessed comparatively, would determine their ranking for appointment on indefinite tenure. Applicants of equal merit were to be prorated geographically in order to fix their priority for assignment. When judging an appointee for promotion, the board of examiners would give weight to his service record filed in the office of the chief of the Consular Bureau. The Hopkins-Lowden measure, as it was called, also strengthened the section of the Lodge Bill providing salaries rather than fees for many of the consular agents. By the spring of 1908, the measure included a section authorizing the establishment of a government training school for consuls. This provision sought to confirm in law and elaborate the arrangements for training which Secretary of State Elihu Root had instituted the year before. By 1909 Lowden and the rest of the Committee on Foreign Relations embodied it in a separate bill and limited the original measure to "permanent consular improvement and commercial enlargement."[16] The latter was the Cullom-Sterling Bill. Beginning in the spring of 1908, Lowden and Nicholas Longworth sponsored still another measure known as the "Embassy Bill." This, in its first form, provided not more than one million dollars annually for the purchase of embassy and consulate buildings abroad, with Yokohama, Shanghai, Berlin, and Mexico City to be given preferred consideration when spending the appropriation for the first year.[17]

Lowden introduced and spoke on behalf of these measures in session after session. So completely did he make them his own that the newspapers often called each of them the "Lowden Bill" without making clear to which one they referred. Although their most voluble opponents were Democrats—Underwood of Alabama, and Sisson of Mississippi—the measures were not party legislation and had supporters on both sides of the political fence. To vote for their passage never constituted a test of Republican orthodoxy. Perhaps for this reason Lowden's road to even a partial victory was long and rugged. Many congressmen, who already felt pinched in dispensing jobs by the extensions of the classified civil service, no doubt opposed the consular bills as a further curtailment of their patronage power. In debate, however, they took the higher ground that the measures would create an "un-American bureaucracy" far removed from the people. Furthermore, they attacked the Embassy Bill as financially extravagant at a time when "economy" should be the watchword and as stimulating ambassadors of the United States to compete with those of foreign governments in an "un-American" contest to find out who among them could live in the greatest luxury. Champ Clark and Underwood went even further and questioned whether the time had

16. *Congressional Record* (60th Cong., 2d sess.), XLIII, 53, 1344, 2828. The National Business League opposed the National Consular School Bill on the grounds that United States colleges and universities already provided adequate training for the consular service (see National Business League's pamphlet, *American Universities, American Foreign Service and an Adequate Consular Law* [2d ed.; Chicago, Ill., 1909], esp. pp. 54–55).

17. *Congressional Record* (60th Cong., 1st sess.), XLII, 5566; *House Reports* (60th Cong., 1st sess.), Vol. II, No. 1564 (Apr. 20, 1908); *Congressional Record* (60th Cong., 2d sess.), XLIII, 497, 1199.

not come to abolish the United States diplomatic corps altogether and rely in the future upon special envoys during emergency situations. Much was also said about the unconstitutional curb which the consular bills would place upon the exclusive power of the President to appoint consuls by and with the consent of the Senate.[18]

In countering these arguments, Lowden declared that the enhanced international prestige of the United States and its growing dependence upon foreign nations for certain vital raw materials and for purchasers of the increasing domestic surplus of agricultural and industrial commodities required that it have a larger number of able and professional representatives abroad, fully as expert and well housed as those of any country in the world. Lacking a corps of this caliber, America would be unable to win its needed share of foreign trade or to maintain its rights and dignity by peaceful negotiations instead of war. Under present conditions, he continued, the field of choice of ambassadors narrowed down to very rich men who sometimes seemed more eager to advance their own social status than to promote the welfare of their country. If there were in each principal foreign capital a government-owned building large enough to house both the chancellery and the ambassador's residence, the work of the embassy would gain in convenience, dignity, and efficiency. Above all, an able man of moderate means could then afford to accept a diplomatic post. To provide him with a palatial mansion was not the intent of the bill.

National prestige, moreover, suffered when the size of the American envoy's purse determined whether his country's banner waved in Paris, for example, from the window of a dingy apartment building far distant from the Quai d'Orsay, or over a residence similiar in grandeur to the embassies of Great Britain and Russia. Lowden cited the remarks of Andrew D. White in his *Autobiography* to the effect that the accommodations of the American minister at St. Petersburg, compared with those of the ambassador from Great Britain, worked adversely to the interests of the United States during the Bering Sea seal-fisheries negotiations of 1888. If, as Lowden would not admit, it was un-American to house United States diplomats where they could perform their business and social obligations effectively, it was clearly as un-American to be obliged to confine ambassadorial appointments to men of great wealth. And yet his opponents probably spoke to the point when they queried whether a man of modest fortune could afford to be an ambassador even if the Embassy Bill became law. Were not the backers of the measure making an "unholy" attempt to provide rent-free residences for rich men with diplomatic aspirations?[19]

18. *Congressional Record* (60th Cong., 1st sess.), XLII, 5805; (61st Cong., 2d sess.), XLV, 2641–49. In the Lowden MSS is an undated note from President Taft to Attorney-General Wickersham, reading: "Dear George: Help Bro. Lowden as to consulate bill and diplomatic appointments and the Constitution. W. H. T."

19. *Congressional Record* (61st Cong., 2d sess.), XLV, 2641–49; (61st Cong., 3d sess.), XLVI, 2097–2104. In 1910, the only residences for diplomats owned by the government were those in Bangkok, Constantinople, Pekin, and Tokyo. In addition, the United States owned five consular buildings, all in the Pacific area except the one in Tangier (see

When Lowden and his supporters failed to persuade either session of the Sixtieth Congress to pass the bill, they tried to win more votes for it in the next Congress by reducing the proposed annual appropriation and stipulating that the secretary of state must gain legislative approval before purchasing any embassy building. After visits in the autumn of 1909 to the chancelleries of the United States in London and Paris, Lowden felt better prepared than before to speak authoritatively on the subject. But all in vain. On March 2, 1910, a motion carried to strike out the measure's enacting clause, and, as Mrs. Lowden recorded in her diary, her husband was "so entirely exhausted tonight that I was obliged to send word to Mrs. McCormick at 6 o'clock that we could not dine with her."[20] Regretfully, he tried to make his proposals more palatable by moving an amendment to limit the cost of any building to $150,000. Thereby, in effect, their application would be confined to the Orient, Latin America, and the smaller countries in Europe. Even this watering-down of the original provisions could not save them from defeat. On March 4, by a vote of 150 to 134, the House decided that under its rules the amendment was not sufficiently thoroughgoing to convert the measure rejected two days earlier into a new bill. Therefore, he could not re-introduce it during that session of Congress. Some of his close friends, like Cannon and Tawney, professing alarm about the state of the Treasury, voted with the opposition.[21]

Eventually his persistence won out, although by no means to the full extent of his original hopes. On February 7, 1911, a thinly attended House, by a standing vote of 141 to 39, passed the Embassy Bill with its $150,000 limitation. Approval by the Senate and President had never been in doubt. Why enough opponents of the measure in the House of Representatives were converted, or at least absented themselves, to assure its passage is not clear. Thirty-six Democrats were listed among the "Ayes."[22] Many prominent citizens, including Charles M. Schwab, Archbishop Ireland, Samuel Gompers, and William Jennings Bryan, had made public statements urging its adoption. Influential newspapers like the *New York Times*, the *New York Commercial*, and the *Boston Transcript*, repeatedly spoke in its favor.[23] Perhaps a few of Lowden's colleagues, realizing that his congressional career was

American Embassy Association, *American Embassies, Legations, and Consulates Mean Better Foreign Business* [New York, n.d., but probably 1911], pp. 59–65, quoting from FOL's speech in Congress, Mar. 2, 1910).

20. The motion carried, 160 to 84 (*Congressional Record* [61st Cong., 2d sess.], XLV, 246, 1894, 2641–49; *House Reports* [61st Cong., 2d sess.], Vol. II, No. 438 [Feb. 14, 1910]). In American Embassy Association, *Homes for Ambassadors* (New York, 1910), are statements or reprinted speeches by seven contributors, including Lowden.

21. *Congressional Record* (61st Cong., 2d sess.), XLV, 2757, 2872, 2960–62, 2966–67; *House Reports* (61st Cong., 2d sess.), Vol. II, No. 697 (Mar. 7, 1910).

22. *Congressional Record* (61st Cong., 3d sess.), XLVI, 707–8, 2097–2104; *House Reports* (61st Cong., 3d sess.), Vol. II, No. 1876 (Jan. 9, 1911).

23. *New York Times*, Jan. 23, 1911; *New York Commercial,* Jan. 23 and Mar. 23, 1911; *Boston Transcript,* Jan. 23, 1911.

about to end, voted out of compliment to him for a bill known to be near his heart.

The enactment of the Consular Bill also brightened his last days in the House. The President and the Department of State had always backed it more vigorously than the embassy appropriation measure. On January 14, 1911, Secretary of State Philander Knox wrote to Congressman D. J. Foster:

I can not overstate my belief that Mr. Lowden's bill is exactly what is demanded by the best interests of the foreign service. . . .

Several bills have in recent years been introduced for the purpose of making the foreign service more stable and efficient . . . in response to a really wide demand . . . particularly on the part of business men and organizations who realize that a good foreign service is essential to the promotion of foreign trade . . . each previous bill failed on the single ground that it had the effect of seeking to curtail the constitutional power of the President to appoint ambassadors . . . and consuls. . . .

Mr. Lowden's bill obviates this sole objection. It simply makes mandatory the annual holding of serious impartial examinations, the reporting of the results to the Secretary of State by duly constituted boards of examiners and the keeping of careful efficiency records. . . . The Secretary of State . . . [must] transmit to the President the data . . . [but] the President . . . [is] . . . still quite free to proceed as he likes.

The whole fabric of the modernized Diplomatic and Consular services, and to a considerable extent the efficiency of the department itself, now rest upon the executive order[s] of June 27, 1906 and November 26, 1909. This bill . . . embodies the substantial principles of both of these orders. . . .

I am now authorized to emphasize . . . that the President earnestly recommends such legislation . . . the President and the department charged with the foreign service believe . . . [the Lowden Bill] to be a fundamental necessity to its efficiency and usefulness to the nation.[24]

Having passed Congress, the bill went to the White House on February 14, 1911, assured of the signature of President Taft.[25]

Lowden further made known his stand on foreign issues by opposing bills to curtail immigration and to subsidize the United States merchant marine by more liberal mail-carrying contracts. His views about incoming aliens were shaped by the stereotyped picture of "Columbia stretching out welcoming hands to Europe's poor and oppressed," as well as by his conviction that American industry and agriculture needed a larger pool of inexpensive labor.[26] Spokesmen of big business probably took him more severely to task for his adverse votes on the subsidy measure than for any other of his actions as a congressman. He insisted that even a liberal bounty from the government would not offset the high operating costs of the merchant marine sufficiently to permit it to compete successfully with the cheaply run cargo vessels under foreign flags. In his opinion, eastern business interests too much dominated Congress, and the subsidy bill glaringly illustrated their proneness

24. *House Reports* (61st Cong., 3d sess.), Vol. I: *Miscellaneous,* Part I, No. 2007, pp. 12–13.

25. *Congressional Record* (61st Cong., 3d sess.), XLVII, 2564.

26. *Ibid.* (59th Cong., 2d sess.), XLI, 3232, 3949; (60th Cong., 1st sess.), XLII, 2756.

to raid the national Treasury. Neither Speaker Cannon nor the National Association of Manufacturers succeeded in convincing him that these bounties would promote the general welfare.[27]

His refusal to follow blindly the dictates of his party was more importantly illustrated by his course during the lengthy debates upon the Payne-Aldrich tariff bill. In the presidential election campaign of 1908 the Republicans seemed to pledge that after victory they would lower the rates of the Dingley Law. Immediately following his inauguration Taft summoned a special session of the Sixty-first Congress to enact a new tariff measure. Although Lowden supported the nebulous view that whenever a foreign-made article in the domestic market undersold a similar commodity of American origin, the import duty on the former should be raised so as to equal the difference between its lower production cost and the higher production cost of the latter, he rarely spoke of the protective tariff as a device for procreating unborn American industries or for nursing infant ones into lusty strength.

His dislike of the "political horse-trading" connected with rate-making also blunted his enthusiasm. This haphazard method of doing what only an impartial investigation should accomplish led to almost wholly bad results. Besides signifying that pressure groups really wrote the tariff laws, the resulting "unscientific" rates fostered international ill-feeling and often discriminated heavily against American farmers, whose voice was far less compelling at Washington than the lobbies of manufacturers. By working to remove some of the inequities and secure advantages from the tariff schedules for his rural constituents, Lowden invited the charge that his own views of the problem were as selfishly provincial as those which he opposed. He frankly admitted that "it is a most difficult matter . . . to revise the tariff on anything like satisfactory terms. Every community . . . desires a reduction of the duties on everything not produced by that community, but is in favor of a high protective tariff on its own peculiar productions."[28]

He had agreed with President Roosevelt that the Republicans should sidestep the explosive issue of the tariff until after the elections of 1908. In the meantime he studied the subject, canvassed the views of men prominent in his district, and wrote for advice to friends such as Clarence M. Woolley, president of the American Radiator Company. Lowden regretted that Congress did not prepare for the day of tariff-tinkering by having a commission of experts collect data for the use of the Committee on Ways and Means. This squared with his hope, called merely a pipe dream by most of his friends, that eventually a business matter like the tariff could be removed altogether from the realm of politics. By the time of the special session, he had made up his mind about the changes needed to render the Dingley Law more ben-

27. This was the Littauer Ship Subsidy Bill. FOL to J. M. Glenn, secretary of the Illinois Manufacturers' Association, Chicago, Apr. 10, 1909; *Congressional Record* (59th Cong., 2d sess.), XLI, 153, 4376–77; (60th Cong., 2d sess.), XLIII, 3694.

28. FOL to T. H. Hodson, Galena, Illinois, June 14, 1909.

eficial to agriculture, more "scientific" in its rate levels, and more flexible administratively.[29]

In almost every instance where his views about particular rates are known, they apparently mirrored the majority opinion of his constituents. As many of their letters requested, he advocated duty-free coffee, tea, spices, oil, hosiery, shoes, and gloves. Coming from an area producing almost no marketable timber, he also urged that foreign lumber be untaxed at its port of entry. Newspaper publishers insisted, and he agreed, that print paper and wood pulp should enter the United States without duty. So, too, books and all other publications. In his view, rate reductions were much needed on a great number of basic commodities, especially on iron, steel, and sugar. On the other hand, he echoed the request of Galena citizens for a higher impost on lead and zinc. His friend, John R. Morron, president of the Diamond Glue Company, convinced him that imported adhesives paid too low duties. As a resident of the Rock River Valley and a member of the National Wool Growers' Association and the American National Live Stock Association, he naturally strove for higher rates on foreign wool and hides and no tariff at all on thoroughbred breeding animals from overseas. If he estimated accurately, he and Speaker Cannon were more often at odds than in concert about rates. "Uncle Joe," for instance, desired duty-free hides and a high impost on imported lumber; Lowden exactly the reverse.[30]

Although he claimed some credit for obtaining rate reductions upon certain commodities, he contributed to the Payne-Aldrich debates mainly by working for a permanent tariff commission and, above all, for flexible and reciprocal minimum and maximum imposts. He had advocated a non-partisan commission for several years. Veteran congressmen warned him of its impracticability, but he was cheered by the support of the National Business League and the powerful National Association of Manufacturers. The constitutionality of the sort of commission he desired could hardly be doubted. It would have no rate-making or rate-changing powers. Its functions would consist solely of investigating costs of production at home and abroad and recommending tariff levels to the House of Representatives. To what extent his earnest and persistent advocacy of a commission contributed to the passage of the Tariff Board Act by the House on January 30, 1911, cannot be known.[31]

Although he believed that many rates in the Payne-Aldrich Bill were excessive, he voted for it because he wearily concluded that further wrangling

29. FOL to C. M. Woolley, Chicago, Nov. 25, 1907, and Dec. 30, 1908: "I believe personally that the time has come to make substantial reductions in the tariff upon the products of old and substantial companies."

30. For petitions addressed to FOL concerning the tariff see *Congressional Record* (61st Cong., 1st sess.), XLIV, 815, 1123, 1184, 1239, 1293, 1295–96. Although FOL, 54 other Republicans, and about 125 Democrats tried to put lumber on the free list, they failed to have their way.

31. *Ibid.* (60th Cong., 2d sess.), XLVIII, 2828; (61st Cong., 3d sess.), XLVI, 1696 ff. and 1709.

between the Senate and House during the oppressive heat of a Washington summer would produce no better measure. Furthermore, the statute embodied in somewhat diluted form the provisions for which he had fought the hardest during the entire course of the five-month-long debate. A tariff law, in his opinion, should aim as much to enlarge the markets for American commodities overseas as to protect domestic manufacturers from harmful foreign competition. He wished to open more European outlets for United States agricultural products and, above all, to persuade Germany and France to discard their sanitary regulations against American meat and cattle on the hoof. Convinced that reciprocity rates were "a settled and wise Republican policy since the day of McKinley," he wanted them included in the Payne-Aldrich Bill to a greater extent than ever before.[32]

In a half-hour-long speech in Congress on March 30, 1909, he pointed out the advantages to be expected from the system of maximum and minimum rates pledged in the Republican platform of 1904 and utilized by every principal European country except Great Britain. Because no general tariff law could reflect the particular trade relations existing between the United States and a foreign nation, Lowden moved to amend the proposed bill by adding a section establishing flexible imposts on a few principal commodities. He would empower the President to suspend the minimum rates on these articles from any country discriminating against American trade and to restore them whenever the offender abandoned its harmful policy or balanced it with some concession of benefit to United States exporters. If his amendment was adopted, continued Lowden, American industrialists would not need to open branch factories overseas and thus injure American labor. What he advocated would introduce into the administration of the tariff law a realistic degree of elasticity and "a human element of personal negotiation," without which the United States would never receive a fair return for its minimum rates in the form of enlarging foreign markets. In his view, many of the imposts stipulated in the bill were overly high because they topped those levied by America's chief customers abroad. Unless his motion carried, the growing agricultural surpluses would find no market in foreign lands. If, moreover, a threat of maximum rates induced those countries to admit American meat and cattle, it would encourage the farmers of the Mississippi Valley to produce more livestock. This was highly desirable because excessive grain culture depleted their soil. Increasing the number of their animals meant a salutary diversification of output and an important step toward restoring the fertility of their arable land. To increase the productive capacity of American farm lands should be the prime purpose of any general program for conserving the nation's natural resources.

Ten days after Lowden's speech, the Committee on Ways and Means reported out his amendment. He again spoke in its favor, but it failed to car-

32. *Ibid.* (61st Cong., 1st sess.), XLIV, 611–15.

ry by a vote of 73 to 126.[33] On the other hand, the Finance Committee of the Senate viewed his plan with favor when he explained it to them in late April, and the upper house quickly adopted it. In that body Senator Nelson Aldrich had the tariff bill in his particular charge. He was also influenced by conferences with Lowden's collaborator, Alvin H. Sanders, president of the American Reciprocal Tariff League. During late July when Lowden felt anxious to exchange torrid Washington for the cool breezes of "Castle Rest," he worried lest the joint conference committee of Senate and House discard his proposal as one means of reaching a mutually acceptable compromise. To his great relief, its essentials survived the shuffling and formed part of the Payne-Aldrich tariff measure signed by President Taft on August 5.[34]

Believing that in this manner he had rendered an important service to agriculture, he was the more deeply shocked two years later by the introduction of the Canadian Reciprocity Bill. In her diary entry of February 14, 1911, Mrs. Lowden noted that he had been "frightfully stirred up" that day by the discussion preceding the passage of the measure by a decisive 321-to-92 vote. Among the better-known Illinois stalwarts, only Cannon and Fred Lundin joined him in defying the President by opposing a bill calculated to deal "a crushing blow" to upper Mississippi Valley farmers. During the sharp debate he bluntly charged many of his fellow Republicans with deserting their party's traditional stand of preserving the domestic market primarily for American producers.

The provision of the bill, he continued, embodied the injurious Democratic policy of limited free trade and of a pseudo-reciprocity applied to commodities native to both Canada and the United States. Truly non-competitive reciprocity, on the other hand, meant a free exchange of articles which only one of the two countries had in excess of its domestic needs. Furthermore, the bill was eminently unfair because the free list comprised mainly farm and forest commodities rather than those of the factory. In short, American industrialists were taking care that this effort to bring about closer economic relations with the good neighbor to the north would not cost them money. "If the preservation of the American market," Lowden asked, "is desirable for the manufacturer, is it not desirable for the farmer as against his most formidable rival?" If the bill became law, the American market would be at the mercy of the Canadian farmer, not vice versa, because the latter's land values and production costs were much lower than those prevailing generally in the United States. As a result of this measure, warned Lowden, the prices of American farm products would fall, thereby stimulating the regrettable migration of country youth to the cities. Through the agency of the Reciproc-

33. *Ibid.* (61st Cong., 1st sess.), XLIV, 313, 611–15, 1285. "The world's way to trade peace," said FOL, "is through trade agreements in which reciprocal concessions are given and received."

34. *Ibid.* (61st Cong., 1st sess.), XLIV, 4755. Mrs. Lowden's diary, July 29–30, 1909. In a speech at Freeport, Oct. 25, 1912, FOL asserted that he was the "proud" author of the reciprocity provision "in the form in which it was finally cast."

ity Bill, the industrial East virtually nullified the benefits conferred upon farmers by the agricultural schedule of the Payne-Aldrich tariff. Except for that schedule, Lowden reminded his listeners, the congressmen from rural constituencies would never have voted to levy excessively high imposts on many basic manufactured articles. "If protection is not to be a general policy," he exclaimed with unwonted emotion, "but is to be extended only to the favored few, away with it. . . . The business of America is so complex and so interdependent that you can not strike a blow at one great industry of this country that will not be felt by all other industries."[35]

On this occasion Lowden would not have relished a reminder that some of his thoughts about agriculture echoed those of William Jennings Bryan. Although he failed to convert most of his conservative Republican colleagues and disappointed the liberal ones by not moving into the camp of the insurgents, he heard with grim satisfaction in September, 1911, that the Canadian electorate had ousted the Laurier ministry which favored the treaty embodying the provisions of the Reciprocity Bill.[36] Nevertheless, he must have asked himself why, if he had correctly portrayed its great advantages to Canadians, they had rejected the pact.

Lowden's memories of his youth, his reading, and his experiences at "Sinnissippi" led him to accept as true certain fundamental propositions about agriculture in its relation to the general welfare and to suggest definite ways whereby the federal government might foster rural life without violating the Constitution. Some of his assumptions were Jeffersonian, even though at this time he rarely mentioned the Sage of Monticello in other than disparaging terms. He believed that the continuance of American democracy, of "law and order," and of a sound national economy depended, above all else, upon the maintenance of a happy and prosperous rural citizenry.[37] With President Roosevelt, he deplored as dangerously un-American the growing tendency of publicists and politicians to speak of "classes" and "class-conflicts" in a land where the well-being of every honest person, no matter how he made his living, was inextricably bound up in the long run with the well-being of everybody else. He felt comforted to note that more and more city folk went to the country for their recreation or to establish their homes. This intermingling helped to keep American society unified. Better roads, more telephones and moving pictures, a larger circulation of books, magazines, and newspapers, and improved facilities for agricultural education were also breaking down the ominous wall which rapid urbanization and industrialization had been erecting during the previous half-century between the farmer and his neighbor in the city.

35. *Congressional Record* (61st Cong., 3d sess.), XLVI, 133–34, 2563–64; Mrs. Lowden's diary, Feb. 14, 1911.

36. For an excellent analysis of the whole matter see L. Ethan Ellis, *Reciprocity, 1911: A Study in Canadian-American Relations* (New Haven, Conn., 1939).

37. MS of FOL's speech, "The Relation of Agriculture to the Progress of the Nation," delivered on Mar. 9, 1907, before the Swedish-American Republican convention at Rockford, Illinois.

One of the great problems of the future, as Lowden foresaw them, would be to provide enough food for the world's fast-growing population. Less frequent wars and the yearly advances by medical science marked the progress of civilization, but they also signified a heavier drain upon the available food supply. Technological improvements in farm machinery would not cheapen the cost of production of food and fiber for clothing or accelerate the rate of their output fast enough to keep pace with the growth of urban population. "The statesman of the future," he told a farmers' picnic in his home neighborhood in 1907, "must deal with the problem of feeding mankind."[38] "If the crops of the Mississippi Valley were to be lost for one year, there would be a panic in this nation and the world."[39] During the preceding seventy-five years, according to his estimate, more new acreage had probably been brought under the plow than in all the earlier centuries of man's history. The world's supply of virgin arable land was about exhausted.

Posing the old problem of Malthus, Lowden believed that if the English economist had lived in the twentieth century, he would have been somewhat less pessimistic. Modern science could be the savior. Thanks to it, the intelligent farmer could double his acreage production and improve the quality of his livestock. Scientists and government officials, both federal and state, must join forces to do everything possible to conserve and increase soil fertility, apply modern methods to all aspects of agriculture, make rural life attractive enough to halt the surge cityward, and convince urban folk that farming, far from deserving a social stigma, brought financial and spiritual rewards. Confident that farming "was just coming into its own," Lowden predicted that in twenty-five years it would "be the most learned of all the professions."[40] Even in 1907 he incautiously remarked that "agriculture is the only learned profession left, the others having been swallowed up by the commercial spirit of the age."[41]

In characteristic fashion he garbed his reasoning in a cloak of emotion and portrayed life on the land in mystical terms. God intended farming, said he, "to be the most independent, happiest, freest and all-rounded occupation of man." "Mother Earth," he continued, "is a phrase as old as the ages, and it is good to feel as we are going along that this bountiful Mother is not the worse for our having lived." By improving the quality of livestock, "you feel that in some way you are in sympathy with the divine law of life, that all living things to justify themselves must constantly take a higher form." To be a farmer was to share in the work preferred by the Creator. Improving the yield of seeds and livestock brought the spiritual satisfaction of harmonizing with the highest law of the universe. Once shown this vision, farm youth would be better able to resist the lure of the city. Rural life, further-

38. *Freeport* (Ill.) *Standard,* June 21, 1907, reporting FOL's speech of the day before to the Stephenson County farmers' picnic.

39. Speech cited in n. 37.

40. MS of FOL's speech of Aug. 24, 1908, to the Stephenson County old settlers' picnic.

41. FOL to F. W. Cushman, Tacoma, Washington, Oct. 9, 1907.

more, was the ideal "natural" life for children. "Reared in the open air," declared Lowden, "with the birds and flowers their fellows, with the colts and the calves, and the lambs and the puppies for playmates, they grow up in God's way, not man's. The great, yet simple, ways of Nature shame out of the human heart all pretense and affectation."[42]

On this foundation of ethical, economic, social, and political assumptions Lowden built his program of definite federal aids to agriculture. Most important of all were the maintenance and, if possible, the increase in the quality and extent of arable land by means of flood control, reforestation, forest reservations, crop diversification, and the greater use of fertilizers carefully adapted to varying types of soil; the encouragement of the Mississippi Valley livestock industry and of better breeds of livestock; the widening of foreign markets for agricultural surpluses and the protection of American farmers from foreign competition; the study and control of plant and animal diseases; the appropriation of more public money for agricultural experimentation and education; and the co-ordination of governmental and private efforts to bring science to the aid of husbandry.[43] His visit to the rural areas of France, Germany, and Switzerland in 1909 opened his eyes to the meaning of truly intensive and efficient agriculture. What he saw convinced him that Americans had much to learn about tillage. He wryly told his wife of his doubt whether the cession of the eastern Mississippi Valley by France to England in 1763 had been a blessing.[44] He deeply believed that all commonsense expedients for persuading children to stay on the farms must undergird any realistic conservation policy. Country youth, he insisted, were the most valuable human resource of the nation, corresponding to fertile soil in the realm of its physical assets. With the hope that he might have some influence in halting the flight from the farms, he accepted membership on the National Committee of the Boy Scouts of America.[45]

Although he sought to demonstrate at "Sinnissippi" that forestation was practicable on marginal lands in northern Illinois, he recognized that if experiments of this kind received public aid, it must come from the state rather than the federal government. He voted, however, for a bill to set aside a large national forest at the headwaters of the Mississippi on the United States public domain. On the other hand, for reasons of economy and to forestall opportunities for widespread frauds, he opposed a measure to purchase timber reserves from private owners in the White Mountains of New Hamp-

42. All quotations are from one or another of the following letters of FOL: to P. C. Ellis, Quincy, Illinois, June 7, 1909; to H. B. Puterbaugh, Lanark, Illinois, Dec. 13, 1909; to J. Small, Polo, Illinois, Jan. 29, 1910; and to Dr. C. G. Hopkins, Urbana, Illinois, Oct. 25, 1910.

43. *Congressional Record* (59th Cong., 2d sess.), XLI, 4494.

44. FOL to his wife from Paris, France, Oct. 6, and from Basel, Switzerland, Oct. 10, 1909.

45. FOL to Dr. C. G. Hopkins, Urbana, Illinois, Oct. 25, 1910, and to J. E. West, Boy Scouts of America, New York, Jan. 16, 1911.

shire and the southern Appalachians.[46] The constitutional aspects of a national conservation policy puzzled him greatly. Beyond any doubt, in his judgment, the interstate commerce clause furnished ample warrant for the government to reforest along the banks of navigable streams, but to appropriate public funds for the purchase of timber in private hands seemed of such questionable legality that he asked Edgar Bancroft to prepare a brief upon the subject. He gladly voted for bills creating the National Forest Commission and Inland Waterways Commission and helping the International Institute of Agriculture at Rome with government money.[47] Because the work of the Forestry Bureau under his friend Gifford Pinchot aroused his enthusiasm, he opposed its transfer from the Department of Agriculture to the Department of the Interior. Any bill to furnish more than the usual amount of financial support to the Department of Agriculture and agricultural experiment stations or to assist in co-ordinating their work with that of farmers' institutes and agricultural colleges could count upon his vote.[48] In 1910 he staunchly backed the Dolliver-Davis measure to extend monetary assistance to any state willing to use its own funds for high-school extension courses in agriculture, the trades, and home economics, under the aegis of its state university.[49]

Two bills which he made particularly his own and introduced in every session from early 1908 until they became law two years later related to "relief from disease." This he once called "the biggest thing that could be done for agriculture."[50] One of these measures appropriated ten thousand dollars for the use of the Bureau of Animal Industry for the study and eradication of hog cholera. As the sponsor of this proposal, he received many letters offering, for a price, to furnish "sure-fire" methods of wiping out the scourge. Much more gratifying was his correspondence with animal husbandry experts at the state universities.[51]

His second and probably the more important measure mirrored the Pure Food and Drug Act of 1906. It prohibited the manufacture, sale, and trans-

46. *Congressional Record* (59th Cong., 2d sess.), XLI, 4489; (60th Cong., 1st sess.), XLII, 6098, 6103, 6430, 6870, 6925; (60th Cong., 2d sess.), XLIII, 3566. He voted against enlarging the size of homesteads on the public domain in the Rocky Mountains and Pacific Coast states. He supported a bill to permit any group of not over 16 persons, each with a claim to 160 acres of Alaskan coal lands, to unite into a company to develop those lands.

47. In a letter on Aug. 16, 1933, to H. C. Taylor, United States representative at the International Institute of Agriculture in Rome, FOL said that in 1908 he had "saved" from defeat the bill to appropriate money for this newly established institute (*Congressional Record* [59th Cong., 2d sess.], XLI, 1190; [60th Cong., 1st sess.], XLII, 4246–47; [61st Cong., 2d sess.], XLV, 4918.

48. *Congressional Record* (60th Cong., 1st sess.), XLII, 6424, 6705; (61st Cong., 2d sess.), XLV, 383 ff., 404–5, 838, 840–41.

49. FOL to Senator J. P. Dolliver, Fort Dodge, Iowa, Aug. 25, 1910.

50. FOL to Dr. L. Pearson, University of Pennsylvania, Philadelphia, Jan. 16 and 23, 1908.

51. *Congressional Record* (60th Cong., 1st sess.), XLII, 4811; (61st Cong., 1st sess.), XLIV, 199.

portation in interstate commerce of adulterated or misbranded insecticides and fungicides. This bill also sought to standardize the materials customarily used for dusting or spraying food plants, vines, and trees. "It is," said Lowden in a speech of April, 1910, "as though the physician in prescribing for his patients had no pharmacopoeia which insured the standardization of the drugs." He reminded his fellow congressmen that, in days when the problem of an adequate food supply loomed so large for future generations, insects and fungi every year destroyed food to the value of a billion and a half dollars in the United States alone. Proper preventive measures, in his opinion, would reduce this waste by at least one-third.[52]

He called the venerable Secretary of Agriculture, James Wilson, "the father of the new agriculture."[53] At the close of Roosevelt's second administration, a widespread but baseless rumor foretold that Taft would appoint Lowden to this cabinet post. His own choice for the position was Alvin H. Sanders of Chicago. More than placidly receptive, Sanders asked influential stock-raisers and editors of agricultural journals to boost him for the appointment by writing to his friend Lowden. Thereupon, he forwarded these indorsements with a strong one of his own to his close acquaintance, Charles Norton, Taft's private secretary, and to Frank Hitchcock, chairman of the Republican National Committee.[54] Probably the incoming President never gave serious consideration to Lowden's or Sanders' name for the portfolio of agriculture. He reappointed Wilson and eventually pleased Sanders by naming him to the United States Tariff Commission.[55]

The Thirteenth Congressional District of Illinois was not wholly rural. The factories in Rockford, Freeport, Dixon, and Sterling, for example, made these communities more than banking, shipping, and marketing centers for the neighboring farmers. The commerce-busy Mississippi formed the western border of the district, while transcontinental railroads and potentially navigable streams traversed it. Even if its economic life had been exclusively agricultural, Lowden's business experience would have drawn him into debates on measures affecting wage-earners, bankers, distributors, and manufacturers. He believed that "to promote the general welfare" meant to harmonize their legitimate expectations from the federal government with those of agriculture.

He voted for a half-dozen bills desired by organized labor. These included the measures limiting the number of hours of continuous work by railroad employees in interstate commerce, providing a maximum eight-hour work-

52. *Ibid.* (60th Cong., 1st sess.), XLII, 5318; (61st Cong., 1st sess.), XLIV, 199; (61st Cong., 2d sess.), XLV, 1954, 4917–18.

53. *Ibid.* (60th Cong., 1st sess.), XLII, 4247.

54. FOL to A. H. Sanders, Dec. 8, 1908, and Jan. 21 and 29, 1909; and to W. H. Taft, Dec. 8, 1908; Sanders to FOL, Jan. 18, 1909.

55. H. M. Pringle, *The Life and Times of William Howard Taft,* I (New York, 1939), 384–86.

day in factories producing under government contract, making employers liable for injuries suffered by their workers on common carriers moving across state borders, restricting child labor in the District of Columbia, and creating the Bureau of Mines in the Department of the Interior.[56]

Although he did not see eye to eye with organized labor in its advocacy of a federal income tax, he joined the rest of the Republican Old Guard from Illinois to support the joint resolution proposing an income tax amendment to the Constitution. If a choice had to be made between an income and an inheritance tax, he preferred the latter. As he saw it, a graduated income tax exempting all persons with incomes under five thousand dollars a year was "class legislation," "the most insidious and dangerous of all perils to a republic."[57] For a similar reason he opposed the corporation tax recommended by President Taft as an equitable offset to some of the financial benefits conferred by the Payne-Aldrich tariff act of 1909. Lowden believed it discriminatory to tax corporations but not partnerships and to require the former but not the latter to open their records to public scrutiny.[58]

At first glance his dislike of this inspection requirement ran counter to his long-held view that a federal law should compel corporations in interstate commerce to make known their assets and liabilities. This had been the theme of his address at the State University of Iowa in 1901 and also of his maiden speech in the House of Representatives on February 16, 1907. To "let in the light," as he phrased it, would go far toward protecting small investors who wished to purchase stocks and bonds. By discouraging dishonest financial manipulations, public confidence in big business would revive. Here, however, unlike the case of the corporation tax act, the publicity requirement had no connection with taxation by the government. If taxation were the end in view, partnerships as well as corporations should be required to open their books; if investor security were the sole aim, partnerships could fairly be exempted because they issued no stock for the public to buy. Said Lowden:

Make it possible for the owner of a single share of stock to feel the same security and share on equal terms with the largest stockholder the privileges of the corporation, and the money of the people will go, not into savings banks, but into the business of the country. . . . Isn't it time for the senseless war between the corporations and the public to end? . . . Open and unchecked warfare between them must finally result in one of two things: Either the supremacy of the corporations over the Government, which means the passing of the American democracy, or the acquisition by the public of the means of production and distribution which equally signifies the triumph of socialism. . . . Corporate ownership is upon trial. So far, in the main, it has proven a beneficent influence in the development of our country. If, however, the good it brings . . . shall be exceeded by the evils it bears

56. *Congressional Record* (59th Cong., 2d sess.), XLI, 3252, 3761, 4625; (60th Cong., 1st sess.), XLII, 2325, 4438–39, 5396, 5968, 6034, 6723, 7009; (61st Cong., 2d sess.), XLV, 1216.

57. *Ibid.* (61st Cong., 1st sess.), XLIV, 4440. FOL to P. S. Post, Chicago, May 22, 1909.

58. FOL to H. H. Antrim, Freeport, Illinois, July 22, 1909; to W. B. Brinton, Dixon, Illinois, Dec. 22, 1909; and to Rockford Home Telephone Company, Jan. 13, 1910.

in its train, it is doomed to perish. . . . Who can rightfully object to this publicity?
. . . To protect and to limit property rights are the dual office of the state.[59]

This maiden speech, delivered by Lowden after ten days of nervous tension
while waiting for the opportunity to give it, brought him many congratulatory
letters and press notices in papers as diverse in viewpoint as the *Wall Street
Journal* and the *Washington Trade Unionist*. Although his remarks were those
of a man wholly sympathetic with big business honestly operated, they illustrated what he meant by the duty of a public servant to treat with an even
hand every element in society and not to talk or legislate in terms of economic classes. Some wealthy men did not understand his purpose and accused
him of playing to the gallery and breaking faith with people of his own
kind.[60] In his almost illegible penmanship, Judge Landis assured Lowden
after reading the speech:

> You said it just right. Of course you appreciate that you will be slandered for it.
> Eminent capitalists will agree at the Chicago Club that you have turned demagogue
> as they agree I have become an anarchist. But you will have the consciousness that
> honest men will do you justice. The people you and I have trained with . . . think
> the Federal Court is charged with the duty of giving "the little fellow" the limit
> and of finding some way out for the big fellow who would scorn to steal less than
> a million dollars. I guess you and I can both get along whatever may be their views
> of our official demeanor.[61]

Lowden also followed a middle course on questions relating to banking
and currency. Monetary problems fascinated and puzzled him all his life. On
these difficult issues he remained always the learner, certain of the general
goals to be aimed for but never dogmatic about how to attain them. He believed economic panics could not be prevented—at least by any governmental
action not destructive of democracy itself—but he hoped that Congress could
find constitutional means to lengthen the intervals between depressions, to
lessen their severity, to prevent eastern money centers from dominating the
nation's currency and credit facilities, to render the supply of currency more
elastic in terms of the varying seasonal volumes of business, and to provide
farmers with as favorable opportunities to borrow money as those enjoyed
by men whose assets were mainly in the form of stocks and bonds.[62] He deplored the fact that small investors in corporate securities often lost their

59. *Congressional Record* (59th Cong., 2d sess.), XLI, 3138–39. In a letter to President
Roosevelt on Mar. 15, 1907, inclosing a copy of this speech, FOL said: "In my judgment,
the corporations have mainly themselves to blame for the plight in which they find themselves today. History will record that, in the course you have taken, you have really been
the best friend that what is called 'vested rights' has had in these momentous years."

60. Congressman F. W. Cushman to FOL, Feb. 17, 1907: "I do not recall any man in
the House in recent years whose first speech in that body was as decided a success as
yours has been." *Prophetstown* (Ill.) *Echo,* Feb. 21, 1907: "We are so proud of Frank O.
Lowden that every time we think of Whiteside County's vote for him last fall we feel
like stepping higher than a boy with his first pants."

61. K. M. Landis to FOL, Mar. 1, 1907. On Feb. 4, 1907, FOL had written Landis in
high praise of his memorable Standard Oil Company case decision.

62. FOL's speech at Morrison, Illinois, as reported in the *Morrison Record,* Nov. 8, 1908.

savings during the ruthless and mysteriously complex, but usually legal, "reorganizations" by a small inside group owning a majority of the stock.

Lowden also expressed dissatisfaction because the nation's currency consisted mainly of notes issued by privately controlled banks. And yet the obvious alternative—a government monopoly enveloped in politics—seemed equally repellent. The money supply, like the tariff, was vital to the nation's economic life and hence must be isolated from the emotional ups and downs of partisan majorities.[63] He viewed skeptically the proposal to extend governmental supervision of national banks sufficiently to warrant a pledge from the Treasury to redeem every banknote at need. In the light of experience within his own congressional district, this degree of paternalism appeared unnecessary. If he were correctly informed, not a single depositor in any of its ninety national, state, or private banks had lost a penny since 1865 because of a bank failure. Partly for this reason he opposed Bryan's demand that Washington insure every depositor against loss.[64] Furthermore, Lowden's reading of American history convinced him that a monopolistic central bank, operating under a federal charter of limited duration, was open to serious criticism. In Madison's and Jackson's day the business world suffered for an extended period from the acrimonious political bickering aroused by the issue of renewing the institution's charter. Evidently, concluded Lowden, the banking and currency enigmas admitted of no perfect solutions. But of one fact he was certain. "Wall Street" dominated the money and banking situation in 1906 and "loaded" it against the interests of rural America. Some form of compromise between governmental and private control would eventually emerge, but, to be satisfactory, it must end the existing discriminations against farmers, planters, and stockmen.[65]

Seeking enlightenment upon these baffling matters, Lowden kept in touch with the bankers in his district and also with three Chicago bank presidents —Charles G. Dawes, John A. Lynch, and George E. Roberts. Shortly after reaching Washington in late 1906, he pleased Lynch by inducing the secretary of the Treasury to increase from $225,000 to $475,000 his deposit of public funds in the National Bank of the Republic.[66] At Samuel W. Allerton's suggestion, Lowden later introduced—and was gratified to see enacted— an amendment to the banking act of 1882, barring any group controlling a national bank from going through a nominal reorganization, including some slight change in the institution's name, for the sole purpose of squeezing out the small stockholders.[67]

63. FOL to W. B. Brinton, Dixon, Illinois, Jan. 23, 1908.

64. MS of FOL's speech at Centralia, Illinois, Sept. 16, 1908.

65. FOL to W. T. Rawleigh, Freeport, Illinois, Nov. 25, 1910.

66. Letters of FOL to the secretary of the Treasury, Dec. 10, 1906; to J. A. Lynch, Dec. 14, 1906, and Nov. 25, 1907; to G. E. Roberts, president of the Commercial National Bank, Nov. 25, 1907; to C. G. Dawes, Jan. 21 and 28, 1908.

67. *Congressional Record* (60th Cong., 1st sess.), XLII, 5456; (61st Cong., 1st sess.), XLIV, 199; (61st Cong., 2d sess.), XLV, 8549–50. In a letter of Feb. 17, 1910, to E. C. Jones of Palm Beach, Florida, FOL declared that commercial banks should be barred from dealing in stocks and bonds.

The Aldrich-Vreeland Banking and Currency Bill occupied more of Lowden's attention than any other law passed during the long session of Congress in 1907–8. The measure sought to prevent a recurrence of the currency famine and Wall Street panic of 1907. The terms of the bill failed to satisfy Lowden, even though they had the sanction of Roosevelt, Dawes, and other men whose opinions he respected. In spite of his misgivings, he eventually voted for it on the score that it was "the best that could possibly be passed at this session. I think it will meet any emergency pending the time when a more comprehensive measure" can be formulated.[68] His chief objection, one which he tried unsuccessfully to remove by an amendment, was the bill's failure to permit the issuance of legal-tender notes on the security of commercial paper, such as warehouse receipts for cotton, small grains, and corn. These receipts, he believed, constituted as sound a basis for currency as industrial bonds. Until they were so recognized in law, the nation's supply of currency and its elasticity would continue unfairly to depend almost wholly upon business in the large cities. Not only did the measure continue this discrimination in favor of "Wall Street" and against rural America, but it failed to adjust the supply of currency and credit to the major fluctuations of demand for them. In a word, concluded Lowden, the Republicans had little reason to take pride in the new law. Its benefits would not be evident to the constituents of congressmen from the Mississippi Valley farm lands.[69]

Many voters in northern Illinois, however, did not gauge the worth of their representative by his stand on abstruse financial problems but by his success in supplying them with jobs, pensions, federal buildings, and inland waterways. On these down-to-earth matters they had much cause to applaud Lowden's record. For years he had insisted that "nothing was too good" for the old soldier, his widow, or his dependent children. While in Congress he let it be known throughout his district that he always had time to help the veteran, even to the extent of running errands for him to the Bureau of Pensions. Although death had cut a wide swath through the ranks of the GAR by 1906, he refused to accept this fact as justification for abolishing local pension agencies and thus concentrating their work in Washington. To do this, he said, would cause delays and other inconveniences, introduce cold, long-armed formality into the relationship between the government and its heroes, and incidentally oust his friend, Colonel Charles Bent, from the headship of the Chicago pension office. "There is nothing which appeals so much to my sympathies," Lowden wrote, "as the unhappy condition of so many soldiers' widows," even of those young ones whom "love" had led to marry aged veterans. Stirred by this emotion, he enthusiastically supported a bill to give twelve dollars a month to every widow whose husband had been in uniform for ninety days or more.[70] A private bill granting twice

68. *Congressional Record* (60th Cong., 1st sess.), XLII, 7077; FOL to Charles Bent, Chicago, May 28, 1908.

69. *New York Tribune*, Feb. 12, 1908; FOL to J. V. Farwell, Jr., Chicago, May 11, 1908.

70. *Congressional Record* (60th Cong., 1st sess.), XLII, 3687. A bill to abolish all eighteen pension agencies in the United States passed the House, 94–76, on Mar. 26, 1910. FOL

that amount to one Noah Perrin of Lena, Illinois, was the first bit of legislation which Lowden piloted successfully through Congress. It heralded his sponsorship of dozens of similar measures. Headlines such as "Lowden Secures Many Pensions" left him with no sense of raiding the Treasury. On the contrary, he felt highly complimented when the GAR Post at Oregon made him an honorary member in recognition of his assistance to veterans.[71]

Post-office employees and especially the pitiably paid rural mail carriers were second only to old soldiers as objects of his solicitude. He explained his opposition to raising congressmen's salaries on the ground that he could not in good conscience take more money when mailmen in his district received only $720 a year. Before the close of 1907 he happily voted for a bill increasing the wages of most grades of postal workers, including rural carriers.[72]

Nominating men for postmasterships within his district comprised almost the full extent of his patronage power as a junior congressman. Indeed, he would willingly have relinquished even this limited prerogative, because its exercise obliged him to decide between rival candidates whose abilities and records of service to their party made them equally deserving of recognition. He was certain to aggrieve someone by his choice. Whenever he looked back upon this minor phase of his activities as a congressman, three episodes probably stood out above all others. The death of his aged friend, B. F. Shaw, postmaster of Dixon, Illinois, imposed the unwelcome duty of recommending a successor.[73] On the other hand, he derived pleasure from the reappointment of General Smith D. Atkins as postmaster at Freeport, Illinois. Besides holding this job for fifty years, Atkins owned the *Freeport Republican* and hence was a close business friend of Lowden's private secretary, J. R. Cowley.[74] Finally, Lowden must have long remembered the flood of criticism from temperance advocates when he had two former saloonkeepers named as postmasters of Fulton and Rock Falls in Whiteside County, Illinois. These indiscretions might have lost him its support in his re-election campaign if he had not counterbalanced them by securing an appropriation for a new post office at Sterling, its largest town. He also managed to increase the original sum

---

opposed it, among other reasons, as increasing the "bureaucracy" centered at Washington. And yet in the same session he favored creating a Department of Health of cabinet rank and a Children's Bureau.

71. *Congressional Record* (59th Cong., 2d sess.), XLI, 161, 233, 324, 799, 860, 1122, 1303, 1400, 4608. During his five years in Congress he introduced at least one hundred private pension bills.

72. *Ibid.*, pp. 389–90.

73. FOL to W. E. Enright, Aurora, Illinois, Feb. 4, 1907: "I find that everything worth having down here is under Civil Service. I have been looking diligently for places, but have as yet failed to locate any."

74. *Rockford* (Ill.) *Star,* Feb. 10, 1910.

allotted for a similar building in Dixon, Illinois, even though unable to help Savanna and Rochelle in this regard.[75]

Among the congressional measures of liveliest interest to his constituents were those to create postal savings banks and a parcel-post system, to raise second- and third-class mail rates, and to prohibit the government from printing on its prestamped envelopes the names of private firms or other matter relating to business. As a member of the Committee on Post Offices and Post Roads, Lowden shared in the heated discussions aroused by these bills. His attitude toward them exhibited his characteristic dislike of the government's entering any field of economic activity hitherto in private hands. The obvious benefits of postal savings banks to small depositors led him to except them from his usual opposition to similar proposals.[76] He did not need the many petitions and letters of protest from individuals and companies in the envelope-printing field to range himself on their side against government competition. Congress and the President finally removed their grievance. The blast of hot protest from newspaper and magazine publishers, manufacturers, literary circles, and ordinary folk against the move to "curb a free press" for the profit of the "corrupt railways" withered the attempt to increase postal rates on printed matter. One of Lowden's constituents told him bluntly that if he voted for that bill, "you may as well go to Africa and hunt lions. . . . I think the people will be through with you."[77]

The parcel-post bill, however, gave Lowden the most pause. Probably he felt lucky because the measure did not reach a vote until after he left Congress. No other issue so crowded his mail with petitions. They mostly supported his own inclination to oppose the bill. Not only would it make the government a competitor of the express companies, but it would injure the small merchants in his district for the benefit of the big-city mail-order firms and department stores. On the other hand, the farmers generally wanted parcel post because they foresaw its usefulness in marketing light-weight fruits and vegetables. Even more persuasive was the prospect of lower prices for what they had to buy. Parcel post would break the monopolies of the express companies and local tradesmen. Lowden had often made known his wish to bridge the social and economic gap between urban and rural America. Parcel post would help to do it. And yet the parcel-post measure was "not only an economic question but a political question of the highest importance. The security of this country resides largely in the hundreds of local communities where the people know one another and discuss matters

75. *Fulton* (Ill.) *Journal,* Dec. 25 and 28, 1906; *Sterling* (Ill.) *Gazette,* Feb. 2, 1907, and Jan. 10, 1908; *Mount Carroll* (Ill.) *Democrat,* Dec. 20, 1907; *Dixon* (Ill.) *Telegraph,* Mar. 1, 1909.

76. *House Reports* (61st Cong., 2d sess.), "Hearings on Postal Savings," pp. 98 ff., 107, 113–17, 144; (61st Cong., 3d sess.), Vol. III, No. 1586 (June 14, 1910).

77. W. Heath, Jerseyville, Illinois, to FOL, Feb. 10, 1910. The surprising number of protests in the Lowden MSS reveal more hostility toward railroads than concern about "freedom of the press."

between themselves."[78] The problem also had a moral side. What had the local storekeepers in his district done to deserve the punishment of parcel post? On concrete issues Lowden found that his "general principles" sometimes ran afoul of one another. This was more than the dilemma of a congressman.

From the standpoint of immediate interest to his neighborhood, waterway development stood near the top of the list. When he ran for re-election in 1908 he mainly pointed to his record on this issue in support of his bid for votes. Carroll, Whiteside, and Jo Daviess counties had the Mississippi River on their western edge. Many people in Jo Daviess looked for federal aid to make the Galena River of greater consequence.[79] With somewhat better reason, the residents of Whiteside, Lee, Ogle, and Winnebago counties hoped that Washington would deepen and in other ways render navigable the Rock River, a stream of considerable size. Not to be outdone, many citizens of Stephenson County, having neither the Mississippi nor the Rock to attract a government bounty, wondered whether their Pecatonica River might not have a bright commercial future.[80]

Most of Lowden's constituents readily indorsed any waterways program giving promise of forcing a reduction of railroad freight rates. When he entered Congress, the completion of the Hennepin Canal was in sight. It ran from Rock Falls on the Rock River to the Illinois and Mississippi Canal. The latter connected the Mississippi at Moline with the Great Lakes at Chicago via the Illinois River and the Illinois-Michigan Canal. By dredging a 7-foot-deep channel in the Rock River from Janesville and Beloit, Wisconsin, through Rockford, Oregon, Dixon, and Rock Falls, Illinois, to make junction with the Hennepin Canal, barge traffic could flow diagonally across Lowden's congressional district. As a result, many farmers would be able to move their produce to market at less expense than by rail. Furthermore, the water power created at the locks and dams gave promise of cheaper electricity for their houses and barns. The deepening of the Rock River and the control of its flow also meant less damage from floods to the fields and towns along its course. All this was especially attractive in a day when the good-roads crusade in Illinois and the auto-trucking age had scarcely begun. Moreover, the making of hard-surface highways appeared to spell higher taxes for all Illinois property owners. In contrast, when the federal government deepened a river, built a canal, or constructed a dam, it seemed to be conferring a gift for which the local citizenry paid nothing.

Lowden's enthusiasm for the development of inland waterways was not limited to those within his own district. Believing that America's interstate trade had outgrown the railroad net, he warmly favored "the improvement

78. FOL to Postmaster-General G. von L. Meyer, Washington, D.C., Nov. 6, 1907.

79. In 1909, FOL became the toast of Galena, Illinois, because he won a $14,200 appropriation from Congress to remove snags from the Galena River, mainly used by pleasure craft.

80. *Galena Gazette,* Nov. 30, 1906. The Pecatonica flows into the Rock River.

of every river in the United States which is capable, at a reasonable expense, of bearing commerce." In fostering the lakes-to-gulf deep waterway, Congressman Lorimer had no more wholehearted ally than Lowden. Perhaps, in some degree, his championship of water-borne traffic was intended to disprove the dire prophecies of his opponents that, as the husband of Florence Pullman, he would speak with the voice of the railroads. After collaborating with the Upper Mississippi River Association and congressmen from the river districts of Illinois, Missouri, Iowa, Wisconsin, and Minnesota, Lowden could tell his constituents in 1907 about the authorization from Washington to dredge a channel 6 feet deep at low water, from St. Louis, Missouri, north to St. Paul, Minnesota.[81] Thereafter, his main concern about the Mississippi was to discover ways of speeding up the work of the army engineers as the only effective reply to the growing volume of complaints because the project went forward so slowly. To this end he early won the friendship of Major C. S. Riche, U.S.A., the officer in charge, by catering to his pipe-collecting hobby and making gifts to his two sons.[82]

Lowden's most valued associate in stimulating interest in waterways development was William A. Meese, a Moline lawyer and a vice-president of the Upper Mississippi Valley Improvement Association. He ranked as an authority on the history of internal improvements in northwestern Illinois. Fifteen hundred copies of his pamphlet entitled *Abraham Lincoln: Incidents in His Life Relating to Waterways* were printed at Lowden's expense and presented with his compliments to locally important men. He also paid for Meese's many trips over the congressional district and to Springfield and Washington on behalf of river improvements. Meese justified these peregrinations by often reminding Lowden how much they helped his political fortunes.[83]

After Meese laid the groundwork, Lowden invited to "Sinnissippi" in the summer of 1908 the mayors and town-board presidents of the principal Rock River communities between Janesville and Sterling. The chief outcome of the gathering was the formation of the Rock River Improvement Association.[84] At its subsequent meetings, representatives of water and electric power interests discussed their needs in terms of the river. They listened while Lowden, Lorimer, Riche, Meese, or Deneen described his dreams of a teeming commerce plying from Janesville to Rock Falls and thence through the

81. FOL to W. A. Meese, Moline, Illinois, Mar. 28, Oct. 5 and 31, and Nov. 27, 1907. FOL addressed the banquet of the Upper Mississippi River Improvement Association at Moline on Oct. 22, 1908 (*Rock Island Union*, Oct. 25, 1908).

82. FOL secured an appropriation to enlarge the harbor at Savanna in Carroll County (*Congressional Record* [60th Cong., 1st sess.], XLII, 3504).

83. Meese's essay was printed at Moline in 1908. On Dec. 14, 1907, FOL wrote him: "You can not realize how much your interest in this river improvement is helping me in my district."

84. Mrs. Lowden's diary, Aug. 29 and Oct. 6, 1908; FOL to W. A. Meese, July 1, 1908.

completed Hennepin Canal to the Great Lakes or the Mississippi.[85] Much remained to be done before this vision could become a reality. Although, upon Lowden's request, Congress took a first step toward its realization, most stretches of the Rock River are still of little importance as arteries of commerce. To complete the vast project would have required the conversion of the Horicon marsh, at the source of the stream in Wisconsin, into a reservoir to regulate the river's flow. Besides this costly enterprise, there were a deep channel to dredge for many miles, a discouraging number of small wooded islands to remove, and several dams and locks to construct. The chief dam would have had to be at Sterling, near the northern outlet of the Hennepin Canal. Of these expensive undertakings, Lowden succeeded only in gaining appropriations for this dam and for a survey by army engineers of the river from Janesville to Sterling. By persistent effort he finally secured federal sanction for private water and electric power concerns to build and operate dams at Lyndon and Byron. In the first flush of enthusiasm, a Sterling, Dixon, and Rock Falls Packet Company appeared, and Lowden bought some of its stock. After a few barge trips to Peoria it ceased operations because Sterling had no convenient dock and breaks in the Hennepin Canal made it too shallow to be navigable.[86]

Looking forward to a government survey of the Rock River, Lowden commissioned Meese to co-operate with the army engineers in assembling data about the stream from the communities along its course. He also hoped that the citizens of these towns would willingly assess themselves enough to enable the Rock River Improvement Association to lobby in Washington and engage in a more active publicity campaign. Meese's difficulty in securing either information or money made clear that most residents of the valley cared nothing for the project if it were to involve them in work or expense. Realistically viewed, in the light of the fast-approaching era of automotive transport, their apathy accorded more nearly with what was soon to be than did Lowden's strivings on behalf of his favorite stream. By bringing to pass all that he and Meese had proposed, much valuable property would have been protected from floods and soil erosion, but the resulting commercial traffic could hardly have been large enough to justify the huge cost.

Lowden's attention to the needs of his district, his prominence in national politics, and his impartiality in dealing with local Republican leaders led to his unopposed renomination in the summer of 1908. Until the autumn he mainly confined his speech-making to old settlers' picnics, veterans' reunions, county fairs, and the fiftieth anniversary commemoration of the Lincoln-Douglas debate at Freeport. Beginning in late September, he canvassed his

85. FOL was one of the speakers when the Hennepin Canal was formally opened in October, 1907. A year later he addressed the Rock River Improvement Association, meeting at Dixon, on "The Improvement of Our Waterways: A National Problem."

86. N. E. Shontz, president of the Packet Company, Sterling, Illinois, to FOL, Apr. 1, 1908; FOL to J. M. Stager, Sterling, Dec. 4, 1908. The *Freeport Bulletin,* Apr. 22, 1909, reported the first trip of the packet boat "City of Henry" from Sterling to Peoria and said it hoped to make two round trips a week.

district thoroughly, traveling much of the time by auto. He spoke so often and drove himself so hard that a fortnight before election day he was almost voiceless and completely exhausted.[87] He ran a little ahead of the national ticket, carrying every county in his district and defeating his Democratic opponent, William C. Green, a merchant of Fulton in Whiteside County, by 24,757 votes to 13,274.[88] Scarcely waiting long enough to hear the returns, he and Judge Landis hurried to Atlantic City for several weeks of relaxation before Congress convened in early December.[89]

Participation in the national campaign added to Lowden's extreme weariness that autumn. With Frederic W. Upham of Chicago, he persuaded the national committee to select Chicago for the meeting of the Republican national convention.[90] Early in 1907 the Republican Old Guard in Illinois picked Speaker Joseph G. Cannon as the state's "favorite son" for the presidency. While visiting Lowden at "Castle Rest" in the summer of that year, Cannon told reporters about his "availability." Although meaning to be complimentary, Lowden called the Speaker "just a Republican," neither radical nor conservative, and thus compressed into very few words his limited qualifications for the office he wished to hold.[91]

Lowden admired Theodore Roosevelt except for his efforts to subordinate Congress to his will and dictate the choice of his successor. Hardly had he entered Congress when he introduced a resolution proposing a constitutional amendment to limit every future President to one term of six years.[92] Many of his constituents opposed Cannon's candidacy, and Lowden well realized its feeble chance of success. On the other hand, he could not afford to offend Cannon or run counter to the will of the state Republican convention.[93] To his embarrassment, the party convention of his own county indorsed Taft rather than Cannon, while other similar gatherings in his congressional district adjourned without declaring in favor of any presidential aspirant. Thus the local Republican leaders let Lowden know that he was not their "boss," even though they supported him for re-election to Congress.[94] A month before the convention opened, Lowden confided to a friend that, although

87. Mrs. Lowden's diary, Sept. 27–30, Oct. 6–20, 22–25, 1908.

88. *Dixon Star,* Nov. 7, 1908.

89. Mrs. Lowden's diary, Nov. 4–26, 1908. FOL had planned to go to Panama, but Dr. Billings recommended a less strenuous vacation.

90. Chicago businessmen guaranteed to pay the convention's cost; Denver offered $100,000 and Kansas City, $75,000.

91. In the autumn of 1907, FOL was a member of the Cannon-for-President executive committee. On Oct. 28 he presided at a meeting in Chicago of fourteen congressmen for the purpose of formally launching the "boom" for Cannon.

92. *Congressional Record* (59th Cong., 2d sess.), XLI, 231; (60th Cong., 1st sess.), XLII, 364; (61st Cong., 1st sess.), XLIV, 37.

93. FOL warned his constituents that if they failed to support Cannon, they might find him unfriendly toward legislation desired by them.

94. At least the Republican convention of the Thirteenth Congressional District, on Apr. 16, indorsed Cannon.

in his public utterances he would continue to back Cannon, he recognized that Taft would and should be the nominee.[95]

As a member of the Republican National Committee and of its executive committee, he had the usual nuisance of parceling among his many political friends his limited allotment of tickets to, and his appointments of sergeants-at-arms in, the convention. There was also the tedious and unpleasant business of judging between the opposing claims of contesting delegations from a number of states. The preparation of the official roster of those to be seated depended upon the outcome of these hearings. On June 15, 1908, after repeated rumors that Roy O. West and Frederic W. Upham would try to displace him, the Illinois delegation chose him to serve another four-year term as national committeeman.[96]

The convention itself was an anticlimax. The nominations of William Howard Taft of Ohio for the presidency and James S. Sherman of New York for the vice-presidency encountered little opposition. At his own request Lowden had not been named a delegate, but shortly after the convention adjourned he met with Myron T. Herrick, Frank B. Kellogg, William E. Borah, Sherman, and several others at Taft's home in Cincinnati, to confer about the chairmanship of the Republican National Committee. So much opposition developed there against Frank Hitchcock of New York, whom Taft favored for the post, that further discussions at Virginia Hot Springs became necessary before the presidential nominee had his way.[97] Soon afterward, T. Coleman du Pont resigned from the executive committee of the Republican National Committee "for the good of the cause." The rank and file of the party had shown their displeasure because so many "big capitalists," including Lowden, comprised its inner council. Du Pont appeared to be an appropriate sacrifice, since his firm was then being sued by the United States government for alleged violations of the Sherman Anti-Trust Law.[98] All this bickering, as well as Lowden's obligation to make speeches on behalf of the national ticket during the same weeks that he conducted his own campaign for re-election, convinced him that his eagerness to serve again as national committeeman had been ill advised. The rewards in patronage and prestige were much too meager to compensate for the labor.[99]

Although with complete sincerity he could denounce the Democratic presidential candidate, William Jennings Bryan, as "a grasshopper," who, since 1896, had jumped from one "drivelish issue" to another, he could not

95. FOL to L. N. Littauer, New York, May 25, 1908.

96. On June 12 Upham declared that he was not a candidate. West continued as chairman of the Republican State Committee and Upham became assistant treasurer of the Republican National Committee.

97. Mrs. Lowden's diary, June 16–19 and 21, 1908; *New York Herald,* June 20, 1908; *Chicago Evening Post,* July 8, 1908.

98. *Philadelphia North American,* Sept. 26, 1908; *Philadelphia Record,* Oct. 2, 1908.

99. Mrs. Lowden's diary, Sept. 1, 1908; FOL to J. C. Hooe, Washington, D.C., Sept. 19, 1908.

support Taft with unqualified enthusiasm. Compared with his praise of Roosevelt in 1900 and 1904, his complimentary references to the new Republican standard bearer were little more than perfunctory. The apathy of Illinois voters disturbed him, and yet he could hardly expect to arouse them to emotional fervor by describing Taft tritely as "big mentally and physically," and as "an able, clean candidate who will make an excellent President." In ill-health and certain by mid-October that only the size of the Republican majority in his state and the nation remained in doubt, he looked forward to election day as a release from an onerous duty. Following the easy victory, he assured Taft that "his manly and candid campaign" had given everyone "a new confidence in self-government."[100] In truth, Lowden felt much disturbed by the omens of his own decline in physical vigor and of an imminent schism within the Republican ranks in Illinois, if not in the nation at large.

100. FOL's wire to W. H. Taft, Nov. 4, 1908.

CHAPTER VIII

CHOOSING A SENATOR AND CLOSING
A CONGRESSIONAL CAREER

The growing Republican factionalism alarmed Lowden during his first two years in Congress. Newspapers in Illinois nourished the dissension by giving currency to many unconfirmed stories about deals and "double crosses." The erroneous report in 1906, for example, of Lowden's desire for Cullom's seat in the Senate had its parallel two years later in the rumor about his determination to displace Hopkins in the same body when the Illinois legislature made its choice in January, 1909.[1] Much closer to the truth was the gossip concerning Richard Yates's willingness to march his "downstate legion" into Lorimer's camp in exchange for aid from the "Blond Boss" in supplanting Hopkins. Yates continued to denounce Governor Deneen as an "ingrate" and "pledge-breaker" for not helping him reach the Senate at Cullom's expense as a *quid pro quo* for Yates's essential assistance in the deadlocked convention of 1904. To all outward appearances, Deneen and Lorimer continued to be irreconcilable foes. In company with his Democratic congressional colleague, Henry T. Rainey, Lorimer toured Illinois ostensibly on behalf of a lakes-to-gulf deep-waterway project which ran counter to Deneen's views on the same subject. Deneen correctly surmised that the "traveling statesmen" devoted their journey mainly to promoting opposition to his renomination in 1908.[2]

For over a year before the meeting of the Republican state nominating convention, speculation was rife as to whether Lorimer would bring Lowden or Yates forward as Deneen's rival for the governorship. To Lowden, this merely signified another idle discussion by press reporters. As long as he remained a congressman and a national committeeman, he declined to seek a state elective office for himself or anyone else. The wisdom of this policy became manifest when Yates, after announcing his gubernatorial candidacy with Lorimer's blessing, expressed gratification to Lowden because "in the present contest the closer men are to you, the closer they are to me."[3] Lowden did not rise to this bait. Nor had he authorized the *Springfield*

1. The *Chicago Evening Journal*, Dec. 12, 1907, ran an editorial entitled "Lowden Out for Senator." The next day's issue printed his emphatic denial.

2. *Dillingham Committee Hearings*, II, 1213–16, 1220–23.

3. FOL to F. H. Smith, Peoria, Illinois, Oct. 7, 1907; R. Yates to FOL, May 18, 1908.

Evening News, which he financially controlled, to promote Judge Landis as the "man of the hour" for the governorship. Surprised by the release of this trial balloon in his behalf, the judge commented to his friend: "I have the best position in the whole world. I would not give up the judicial work for three times Mr. John D. Rockefeller's money. This is my estimate of the place you got for me, old fellow."[4]

Several years later, Lorimer charged that Senator Hopkins and Mayor F. A. Busse of Chicago, after persuading him to back Yates for the governorship, had failed to do so themselves. According to the congressman, if they had remained true to their promise, Yates would have defeated Deneen in the bitterly contested advisory primary and hence would have become the nominee of the Republican state convention early in September, 1908.[5] In retaliation for this breach of faith, Lorimer determined to prevent Hopkins' re-election to the United States Senate. Although the preferential primary had shown that a majority of Illinois Republicans wanted Hopkins to serve a second term, its verdict could not legally bind the action of the state legislature.

In the nip-and-tuck gubernatorial election in November, Deneen apparently defeated his Democratic opponent, Adlai E. Stevenson, although the latter formally protested to the legislature against an allegedly dishonest count of the ballots. This protest would add to the troubles of the Assembly in electing a senator.[6] During the autumn, newspapers charged Lorimer with behind-the-scenes activity in Stevenson's behalf. He subsequently declared that he had voted for Deneen, although a prolonged attack of vertigo had barred him from helping the governor in the campaign.[7]

Few political battles in Illinois have been longer or more complex than the legislative contest over the senatorship during the first five months of 1909. Even in Lincoln's day the Republicans of that state had divided into factions; but the deep cleavages revealed by this senatorial deadlock were a forewarning and a contributing cause of the complete split three years later. Unlike 1912, however, disagreements over principles and legislative measures counted for little as compared with the rivalries between ambitious men for high office and the control of the party machine. Probably one experienced observer erred only by being somewhat too pessimistic when he commented to Lowden: "The politicians here in Springfield in the main have no love of party or fealty to principle. They are moved by sordid seeking for money—legitimate and illegitimate."[8]

Before the legislature convened early in January, 1909, newspaper re-

4. Landis to FOL, Oct. 29, 1907.

5. *Dillingham Committee Hearings,* I, 226, 228, 280; V, 4514; VIII, 7674–77, 7689. Hopkins denied that he had promised Lorimer to support Yates (*ibid.,* I, 360–62).

6. *Journal of the House of Representatives of the Forty-sixth General Assembly of the State of Illinois* (Springfield, 1909), pp. 26, 307–13; see also below, p. 183.

7. *Dillingham Committee Hearings,* II, 1109–11; V, 4367–68; VIII, 7553, 7674–77.

8. John A. Corwin, Springfield, Illinois, to FOL, undated but probably Jan. 31, 1909.

porters declared that Governor Deneen, Congressmen George E. Foss, Henry S. Boutell, Lorimer, Lowden, and William B. McKinley coveted Hopkins' senatorial seat. Friends assured Lowden that many Hopkinsites in the legislature favored him as their second or even as their first choice. He was told that, better than any other leader, he could unite the discordant factions. Therefore, even though he did not wish to be a senator, his sense of duty to his party should induce him to seek the office. "This is your chance of a lifetime," exclaimed one of his followers.[9] But to Lowden the situation at Springfield and his honorable relationship to it were by no means so clear-cut and simple.

The Republicans in the Assembly fell into five main groups on the subject of the senatorship. One looked to Deneen for guidance; another backed Hopkins; a third attuned its ear to Lorimer's commands; E. D. Shurtleff led a fourth; and a small bloc voiced the will of Mayor Busse of Chicago. Busse's importance stemmed largely from the fact that his coterie, including the able Edward J. Brundage, held the balance of power between the rival metropolitan machines of Deneen and Lorimer. The mayor's henchmen in the legislature would vote for Hopkins as long as they did not count for enough to re-elect him. The vulnerable record of the mayor warned him against inviting a retaliatory investigation of it by drastically alienating any large group in the Assembly, such as the Lorimerites.[10] Shurtleff's small band, joined by many Democrats, was satirically called the "Holy Alliance" and worked with Lorimer's followers against Hopkins. Governor Deneen controlled a majority of votes in the Senate but not in the House.

Within these five groups, of course, some legislators were less ready than the others to stand by their leader to the last ditch. As Ira Copley remarked later about the party factionalism: "Well, sometimes they are enemies and sometimes they are friends. You know the checkerboard is moving all the time . . . and the men who are strong enemies today, may be friendly six months from now."[11] Several assemblymen, priding themselves upon their independence, voted without regard to the will of any "boss," but they could not affect the over-all picture.

Although Hopkins' adherents, some eighty or ninety strong, numbered too few to bring him victory, they could go far toward deadlocking the legislature. Hopkins' support by Theodore Roosevelt was a weak reed to lean upon, since he would soon leave the White House. President-elect Taft refused to influence the contest by using his patronage power. Senator Cullom evidently intended to be neutral or perhaps to bend in Lorimer's direction. Among Hopkins' chief assets, besides the verdict of the primary, was the aid of federal officials who owed him their jobs and of railway interests centering in Chicago.[12] On the other hand, Hopkins had no foe

9. A. J. Lester, Chicago, to FOL, Jan. 29, 1909.

10. *Dillingham Committee Hearings,* I, 367; V, 4587; VIII, 7400–7401; 7411–12.

11. *Ibid.,* V, 4403; see also 4517 ff.

12. *Ibid.,* II, 1921–22; VI, 6106.

more implacable and powerful than his fellow townsman of Aurora, Ira C. Copley, a wealthy newspaper publisher and public utilities owner of northern Illinois.

The Democrats could not agree upon their proper strategy. Some followed the advice of Roger C. Sullivan of Chicago, their national committeeman, and threw away their votes upon a downstate member of their own party. Others, led by Lee O'Neil Browne of Ottawa, Illinois, joined the Lorimer-Shurtleff coalition against Hopkins. Still a third group strove merely to maintain a deadlock, thus embarrassing their opponents and perhaps forcing the issue back once more to the people. On at least one matter these three blocs agreed. Heartily disliking Hopkins for his rigid partisanship and arrogance, they would never assist in his re-election.[13]

As soon as the legislature convened, about sixty Democrats joined twenty-five anti-Deneen or anti-Hopkins Republicans to make Edward Shurtleff of Marengo, Illinois, the speaker of the lower house. In this position he could largely control the committee assignments and order of business.[14] When Judge Landis heard this news on January 6, he at once wrote to Lowden in Washington: "This means that 'hell has broken loose' . . . everybody seems to regard Hopkins' election as seriously jeopardized. I am not advising you to get into it now, *but the situation should be closely watched*." Landis probably meant that if a deadlock developed, his friend might become its beneficiary with the help of Lorimerite and some Hopkinsite votes.[15] Alert to this possibility and also perforce interested as Republican national committeeman, Lowden arranged for John A. Corwin, an expert political observer, to be his "eyes and ears" in Springfield. Others among his staunch supporters, including James Cowley and Gordon Ramsay, also kept him abreast of the senatorial news. Their letters and telegrams between January and March furnish almost a daily—and at crisis moments even an hourly—account of the contest.[16]

Lowden's quick decision to have a "scout" on hand by the time that the balloting began in Springfield, on January 19, soon paid off. On the initial poll, W. W. Gillespie of Lowden's congressional district voted for him. When his count rose to five the next day, Lowden felt "disturbed." Being pledged not to oppose Hopkins, he worried lest the latter charge him with breaking a promise. At his request his friends in the legislature, with the exception of Gillespie and occasionally one or two others, ceased to vote for

13. J. A. Corwin, Springfield, Illinois, to FOL, probably on Feb. 6, 1909: "I haven't found a man in the General Assembly who at heart loves A. J. Hopkins."

14. *Journal of the House . . . of the Forty-sixth General Assembly,* pp. 9, 13.

15. FOL to Landis, Jan. 12, 1909. FOL tried to keep in touch with Lorimer in Washington but found him elusive.

16. Corwin's many and long letters from Springfield are vivid and informative but are rarely dated with more than the hour and day of the week. Dating them is a nice problem, not certainly solved in all cases by the author. FOL wrote Corwin on Feb. 6, 1909: "I don't know what in the world I would have done if you hadn't gone to Springfield. Your information has been about two days ahead of any other information I have received. This means everything."

him during the ensuing months of deadlock. His inconsequential strength in the balloting, however, is an inaccurate measure of his prominence in the contest.

Although he declined to announce his candidacy and repeatedly said that the legislature should honor the result of the primary, he did not deter his friends from working in his behalf behind the scenes. They haunted the corridors of the Capitol and spent money freely for cigars and drinks in a patent effort to win the good will of reporters and Hopkinsite assemblymen.[17] In short, Lowden was playing a delicate game, posing difficult problems of ethics, strategy, and timing. He relied upon his adherents to be sufficiently subtle to distinguish between activities which would make him the second rather than the first choice of the legislators. Nor was it easy for him in Washington to control ardent well-wishers in Springfield, who, as day after day of the deadlock went by, became more and more impatient because of his refusal to proclaim his availability. Some had stood by him loyally to the last roll call in the memorable convention of 1904. Their steadfastness on that occasion had probably denied them remunerative jobs in Deneen's administration. They naturally worried lest history repeat itself in 1909 to their detriment. In their opinion, Hopkins fully realized the hopelessness of his cause but stubbornly or spitefully refused to concede defeat in time for Lowden to benefit.[18]

Recognizing his dilemma, Lowden wrote to Corwin on February 20: "Of course I am in an unfortunate position, but I have not felt nor do I feel now that I should under any circumstance consider this thing as long as Hopkins has a chance." This was playing fair, but Corwin cautioned him:

He'll [Hopkins will] *hang on to death, but don't let him keep such a strangle hold on you that he drags you down with him.* . . . The undercurrent of talk is all for you. The drift is that way. . . . *Don't let Hopkins keep you out too long.* If Lorimer is for you we can make it. . . . Consider well the time to come here—the psychological moment—not too early and above all not too late.[19]

In this situation, where choice had to be made between what his political ambition tempted him to seek and what faithfulness to a promise obliged him to do, he did not hesitate. "If it shall finally appear," he wrote Landis, "that Hopkins can not be elected, there may be an opportunity; if so we ought to seize it. That is about all there is or has been in the whole matter."[20]

17. J. A. Corwin to FOL, probably on Feb. 20, 1909: "I am nice with newspaper people without any great expense. . . . This will have good results if we need them later on."

18. Hopkins' strange mixture of doubt and confidence is revealed in his wire of Jan. 23, to FOL. It reads in part: "Its [*sic*] man Larimer [*sic*] favors will be my successor. . . . I have the votes and shall win." If this makes any sense, it is that he was warning FOL not to be a candidate, inviting him to influence Lorimer to his (Hopkins') side, and expressing confidence that Lorimer would eventually come there.

19. J. A. Corwin to FOL, "Two A.M., Thursday"—probably Feb. 11, 1909.

20. FOL to Landis, Feb. 6, 1909. Landis' affection for and sense of obligation to FOL were so great that he offered to resign his beloved judgeship in order to work for his friend in Springfield.

Journals hostile to Lowden, however, accused him of trying to knife Hopkins, even though ill-health made his connivance for the senatorship "absurd."[21] A brief spasm of excitement over the prospect of an impending "break" to him led newspapers on February 20 to carry headlines such as "Lowden Is the Dark Horse" and "See Lowden Senate Boom."[22] After futilely casting a thirty-seventh ballot six days later, the legislature recessed until March 10. Rumor had it that Illinois Republican leaders would discover a key to the deadlock while in Washington for Taft's inauguration. Perhaps the new President would place enough patronage at Hopkins' disposal to enable him to win. During the inaugural festivities, Congressman and Mrs. Lowden welcomed about three hundred guests to their home at an evening reception in honor of Governor and Mrs. Deneen. Although socially a success, it contributed nothing toward resolving the impasse in Hopkins' or the host's favor.[23]

Expectations ran high, however, that the continuous negotiations during the recess would bear fruit as soon as the legislature reconvened on the tenth. Lowden reached Chicago on that day after reinforcing his band of workers and observers at Springfield. Newspaper articles boosting him for the Senate were prepared for immediate release in case the situation veered in his favor. But Hopkins, who had become an ex-senator on March 4, refused to throw in the sponge. Lowden soon returned to Washington after advising his friends to "lie low" for a few more days of inconclusive balloting.[24] Mrs. Lowden suggested his tenseness when she noted in her diary on March 15: "Frank unexpectedly left for Chicago at 10:45 P.M." During his week there, newspapers told of his banners, canes, lithographs, and stationery in readiness for a "coup" and of his campaign headquarters soon to open in Springfield. Editors predicted a millionaires' duel over the senatorship between him and William B. McKinley, the public utilities king of central Illinois.[25]

Although these reports were mostly untrue, Lowden's senatorial hopes rose to their crest during the last two weeks of March. On March 28, Mrs. Lowden wrote somewhat cryptically: "Frank thought he would have to go to Chicago but he phoned Lorimer and finds it isn't necessary." This probably means that he asked Lorimer, then in Springfield, whether Hopkins showed any signs of raising a white flag, and his friend replied in the negative. In retrospect, however, the call seems to have marked the end of Lowden's dream of becoming a senator in 1909. Thereafter, his correspondence

21. *Springfield Evening Journal*, Feb. 20; *Chicago Examiner*, Feb. 27; *St. Louis Globe-Democrat*, Feb. 28; *Chicago Record-Herald*, Mar. 23, 1909. FOL took care to assure his Illinois friends that his health was "improving rapidly."

22. *Chicago Daily News* and *Springfield Evening Journal*, both of Feb. 20, 1909.

23. Mrs. Lowden's diary, Mar. 2, 1909; *Chicago Inter-Ocean*, Mar. 1, 1909.

24. H. B. Ward, Du Quoin, Illinois, Mar. 12; FOL's reply, Mar. 15, 1909.

25. *Chicago Journal*, Mar. 20; *St. Louis Post*, Mar. 21; *Chicago Daily News*, Mar. 20, 22, and 23—all dates, 1909.

seldom mentions the matter. During April the newspapers usually said—probably correctly—that he could not win because the Deneenites refused to join the Lorimerites in backing him. Until that month neared its close, however, he still faintly hoped that "the unexpected might happen."[26]

The puzzling maneuvers of Deneen and Lorimer help to explain the rise and fall of interest in Lowden and why he felt more sanguine in late March than at any other time. Deneen mildly favored Hopkins, even though the latter had declined to aid him during his recent campaign for re-election. In that hard-fought contest, Deneen promised to press the legislature to enact a series of reform measures in the event of his victory. If he sided openly with the Hopkins faction in the Assembly, he would lessen his chances of fulfilling this pledge. Furthermore, he lacked enough legislative strength to "make" a senator. The most he could do was to control sufficient votes to prevent a choice without his help.[27] Up to mid-March, another important circumstance deterred him from trying to break the deadlock in Hopkins' favor. As mentioned earlier, Adlai Stevenson lodged a formal protest against the allegedly fraudulent count whereby he had been kept out of the governorship. This cloud hung over Deneen's title until March 18. Before that date he and his followers in the legislature had worked to maintain the deadlock over the senatorship.[28] While it continued, each Republican and bipartisan faction, seeking his indorsement of its "favorite son" for the Senate, took care not to alienate him by questioning the legality of his re-election.

Although Hopkins understood Deneen's predicament and apparently expected no active help from him until he was firmly seated, the delay of over two months in freeing Deneen's hands worked greatly to Hopkins' disadvantage. By mid-March, not only had about forty-five joint ballots failed to demonstrate his capacity to win, but they had also revealed his inability to add to his initial strength. Some of his adherents grew restless when they discovered that they were most likely backing a loser. Although the angry senator blamed his troubles principally upon Lorimer, he could not hide his increasing annoyance over Deneen's failure to help. Lorimer may not have exaggerated when he later testified that Hopkins would have won on the first ballot if Deneen had used his full resources to that end.[29] But Deneen as well as Lorimer preferred to have a senator whom he could dominate. Hopkins did not fit this specification.

With the Lorimer-Shurtleff bipartisan coalition controlling the House and the Deneenites the Senate, an entente between the congressman and the governor would break the deadlock. A reconciliation between them, however, seemed hardly within the range of possibility. One was known as the

26. FOL to F. H. Smith, Peoria, Illinois, Apr. 14 and 24, 1909; *Chicago Daily News,* Apr. 8, 1909.

27. *Dillingham Committee Hearings,* V, 7414–15.

28. *Ibid.,* II, 1096, 1242–47; *Journal of the House . . . of the Forty-sixth General Assembly,* pp. 310, 317.

29. *Dillingham Committee Hearings,* I, 372; II, 1087; VIII, 7416, 7684.

leading spoilsman among the Illinois Republicans; the other as a moderate liberal who favored civil service reform and primaries. Deneen headed the "state crowd," while Lorimer was an influential member of the "federal crowd." For over six years they had fought each other unceasingly for the control of the Cook County Republican machine. Neither had wholly gained it by 1909, but Deneen probably held the lead. Since 1904 they had met only by chance or when political conventions brought them to the same hall. And yet, if Deneen can be believed, no personal enmity kept them apart.[30] A truce between them would go far toward reuniting their seriously divided party. If they effected this at Hopkins' expense, his followers, of course, would be alienated. But most of them, so it was said, supported him for reasons of self-interest rather than affection and would not long remain estranged by his defeat.[31]

In January, 1909, Roy O. West brought Lorimer and Deneen together at the Executive Mansion in Springfield. Thereafter the two men met at least fifteen or twenty times, frequently at night. They reminisced about Illinois's political history, discussed the deep-waterway project, and sought a mutually agreeable solution of the senatorial problem. Several years later, Deneen and Lorimer could not agree over what each had said to the other about the senatorship. According to Deneen, he always wanted and expected Hopkins to win, although he was anxious, as stated previously, to delay the victory until he was securely in office for a second term. Not wishing to go to the Senate, he had not been tempted by Lorimer's offer to send him there.[32] Rather than see Lorimer or a Lorimer-dominated man take Hopkins' place, Deneen would have preferred the Assembly to adjourn without electing anyone. Neither the Roosevelt nor the Taft inner circle ever pressed him to use his influence in any candidate's behalf. From start to finish of the deadlock his chief aim had been to find a solution which would heal the party schism as completely as possible. This was Deneen's tale.

Although Lorimer insisted that he, too, wished above all else to use the situation to rebuild Republican solidarity, he charged that Deneen always opposed Hopkins' re-election and did not rebuff the repeated suggestion that he exchange the mantle of a governor for the toga of a senator.[33] Deneen, added Lorimer, asked that no open effort in his behalf be made until Hopkins' term ended on March 4. Thereafter for about three weeks, the governor hesitated to make his senatorial candidacy public only because he feared that Victor Lawson, Frank Noyes, and Medill McCormick, the newspaper "czars" of Chicago, would disown him if he turned over his

30. *Ibid.*, II, 1209, 1220–21; VIII, 7424.

31. *Ibid.*, I, 365; II, 1093, 1106; VIII, 7399–7400, 7409.

32. *Ibid.*, I, 308, 364, 367; II, 1113–15, 1136, 1246; VIII, 7407, 7412, 7416. According to Deneen (*ibid.*, II, 1118–19), the forces trying to "exile" him to the Senate were the Peoria liquor interests, the electric light companies along the Illinois and Des Plaines rivers (Copley), a Chicago gas company, and the Illinois Central Railroad.

33. *Ibid.*, V, 4515, 4521, 4578–79, 4923; VIII, 7407, 7412, 7414, 7423.

office to Lieutenant-Governor John G. Oglesby. The latter was no Deneen-ite and allegedly followed Lorimer's lead.[34] For this reason and because a reconciliation between Deneen and Lorimer would probably enhance the latter's power in Chicago politics, the triumvirate of the press emphatically opposed the suggestion that "their man" Deneen become a senator with Lorimer's help.

Perhaps John Corwin also chanced upon some part of the truth when he told Lowden that Deneen dreamed of achieving so much during his second term that he would either be presidential timber by 1912 or be able in the following year to succeed Shelby Cullom in the Senate. Whatever the cause, Deneen told his supporters on March 28 that under no circumstances would he be a senatorial candidate. For the next six weeks, according to Lorimer, he tried to persuade Deneen to change his mind.[35] As mentioned previously, the preparations for a Lowden "boom" were most active at just the time when Lorimer exerted the most pressure on the governor. Lowden evidently expected the senatorial road to open for him if Deneen gave a decisive "No" to Lorimer's overtures. But Hopkins' never-say-die policy destroyed Low-den's chance at that juncture, and no second opportunity appeared during the remainder of the contest.

From late March until early May, Lorimer suggested name after name to Deneen in an effort to find someone upon whom they could unite for the senatorship. They discussed at least nine men, including Lowden, but the governor raised more or less weighty objections against each of them.[36] If Lorimer can be believed, Deneen rejected Lowden on the grounds that "he didn't want to build up men. . . . If they did not have political strength, he was not in favor of giving it to them by giving them high and important office with a lot of patronage attached to it." Lorimer decided that the governor would favor no one whom he could not control or use to his own political advantage.[37]

Deneen probably believed that Lowden was too much "Lorimer's man" or too nearly in the "middle of the road." From the beginning of the deadlock, Lowden's emissaries had tried unsuccessfully to convince the governor of his mistaken judgment in this regard. Lorimer also "talked Lowden" to Deneen for about three weeks but got nowhere.[38] For this reason Lowden reluctantly concluded by early April that he had little chance of winning, even though Hopkins withdrew from the competition.

Lorimer later testified sardonically that during his negotiations Deneen

34. *Ibid.*, II, 1116; VIII, 7418 ff., 7717.

35. *Ibid.*, II, 1118; V, 4578–79; VIII, 7419–21, 7594.

36. The nine were A. C. Bartlett, H. S. Boutell, W. J. Calhoun, G. Foss, Lowden, McKinley, W. Rodenberg, Shurtleff, and West. West told the author on Jan. 6, 1951, that he could not have stood the financial cost of a senator's social life in Washington in 1909, having just built an expensive home in Chicago.

37. *Dillingham Committee Hearings*, VIII, 7428.

38. *Ibid.*, I, 335–39, 347.

repeatedly offered to help make him the senator. This the governor categorically denied.[39] There is ample evidence, however, that both before and after the legislature convened, Shurtleff, Copley, and other locally prominent Republicans urged Lorimer to declare his own candidacy. He resisted their appeals until mid-May. Made wary by many earlier rebuffs in Illinois politics, he preferred to stay in the House of Representatives until it passed his lakes-to-gulf waterway measure. On the other hand, his foreign birth obliged him to view a senatorship as the summit of his political career. If he were in the Senate and Deneen in the Executive Mansion at Springfield, harmony should reign within the party because its two principal factions would be equitably provided for. Furthermore, after March 4, leading Republicans in Washington, including President Taft and Senators Aldrich and Penrose, pressed to have the vacant seat filled. The protectionists needed to rally their full strength behind the Payne-Aldrich tariff bill.[40]

Early in May, Lorimer convinced himself that only his own candidacy could end the impasse. As late as May 6, Lowden probably had no inkling of this decision, because he wrote on that day that he was "absolutely unable to see how the deadlock could be broken."[41] Two days later he left Washington for a ten-day vacation at French Lick and at "Sinnissippi." With Judge Otis Humphrey he was in Arkansas inspecting some cotton plantations on May 26, when the Illinois legislature on its ninety-fifth joint ballot ended eighteen weeks of deadlock by easily electing William Lorimer.[42] In Lowden's words, written seven years later: "Just before the election when it was rather apparent that Lorimer would be elected, he phoned to ask me if I wouldn't get hold of one or two members in my district in his behalf and I told him I could not do that even for myself, if I were a candidate; that I had taken the position that the primary vote should control as long as Hopkins was a candidate."[43] In another letter, Lowden aptly summarized his own relation to the entire episode: "There never was a situation, of course, where either my friends or myself could consistently do anything for me, and, therefore, I have no regret. As you have often remarked, chance has much to do in these matters."[44]

In his brief speech of acceptance before the joint session of the legislature immediately following his election, Lorimer declared that he would remain a Republican and a high-tariff advocate even though, contrary to all precedent in Illinois, a senator had been chosen by a bipartisan vote. That evening while two brass bands, allegedly paid for by Ira Copley, marched through the

39. *Ibid.,* I, 369, 835–36; II, 1124, 1134; V, 4577.

40. *Ibid.,* I, 813, 816, 823 ff.; II, 1649, 1652, 1668, 1792–97.

41. FOL to W. A. Meese, Moline, Illinois, May 6, 1909.

42. *Journal of the House . . . of the Forty-sixth General Assembly,* pp. 1057–62. The final vote was Lorimer, 108; Hopkins, 70; Stringer, 24. Of those who voted for Lorimer, 53 were Democrats (*Dillingham Committee Hearings,* VIII, 7429).

43. FOL's memorandum, dated July 4, 1916.

44. FOL to F. H. Smith, Peoria, Illinois, June 3, 1909.

streets of the capital in noisy celebration of Lorimer's victory, the Democrats of Aurora rang its bells and made merry with a parade in jubilation over Hopkins' defeat.[45]

Amazement, occasionally tinged with suspicion that the surprising vote could not have been honestly come by, also greeted the news of Lorimer's election. Many editors, misinterpreting its cause and effects, wrote about an imminent reshuffling of factional lines with Lorimer's cohorts exchanging their alliance with the Yates Republicans for a tie-up with the Deneenites. As a consequence of this "incredible" pact between the spoilsmen and the reformers, Lorimer would become "top dog" again, with the Hopkinsites ousted from appointive state and federal jobs, Mayor Busse and his Chicago balance-of-power group relegated to insignificance, and the packing and public utility interests of northern Illinois once more "riding high."[46] Perhaps these predictions would have come to pass if Lorimer's enemies, both within and without his party, had not harassed him relentlessly after his election and if the rising progressivism in American political life had not soon forced many conservatives in the North and West to fight a desperate battle for survival.

Whether Lorimer owed his senatorship to the bribery of state legislators cannot be answered with complete certainty because the primary sources are in conflict. After listening to much testimony, an investigating committee of the state senate decided that his election "would not have occurred had it not been for bribery and corruption."[47] On the other hand, two investigations by committees of the United States Senate, of which one was unusually thorough, resulted in clearing his name, although not by a unanimous vote. Following the report of the second of these committees, however, the Senate by a fifty-five to twenty-eight margin, on July 13, 1912, excluded Lorimer from his seat.[48]

Among the many witnesses who gave their versions of what had happened during the months of deadlock, Lowden was conspicuously absent and his name rarely appears in the voluminous printed testimony.[49] Deneen affirmed that, although he had no direct knowledge of bribery, he believed sinister interests hovered about the Capitol in Springfield in 1909. Lorimer, however, declared that he purchased no man's vote, and, in so far as he knew, no one had done so in his behalf. The confessions of several legislators that they had been bribed were, in his opinion, fairy stories concocted by, or at the instiga-

45. *Dillingham Committee Hearings,* III, 3013–14; VI, 6084.

46. *Chicago Inter-Ocean* and *Chicago Tribune,* both of May 27, 1909.

47. *Helm Committee Hearings,* pp. 9, 11, 158.

48. *Senate Reports* (62d Cong., 2d sess.), No. 769, Part I, pp. 87, 91. After amassing eight large volumes of testimony, this committee by an 8-to-5 vote concluded that Lorimer's election was not due to bribery.

49. The index volume (Vol. IX) of the *Dillingham Committee Hearings* lists only four page-references opposite FOL's name. The indexer missed a few, but the true total is small.

tion of, the editor of the *Chicago Tribune,* who had paid them generously for their perjury.[50]

The welter of contradictory testimony leaves its reader almost completely baffled. From the outset of the contest, representatives of powerful economic groups worked for Lorimer, and others only less influential backed Hopkins. This warranted no surprise. For ten years or more there had been frequent mention of a "jackpot" at Springfield kept filled by "interests" desiring to have certain legislation either passed or repealed or to defeat bills deemed injurious. As at other state capitals, a few Illinois senators and assemblymen may occasionally have sponsored "blackmail" measures in the hope of being compensated for quashing them. In May, 1909, the payment of money probably induced one senator and three representatives to be enthusiastic Lorimerites, but the source of this cash is still unknown. In all likelihood, Lorimer did not need these four bribed votes in order to win. Granting the dishonest use of cash, there is no conclusive proof that he sanctioned it or even knew about it at the time.

Although exonerating no one, Richard Yates recalled an important aspect of the setting in which the decisive ballot was polled. The legislators, said he, were

absolutely tired out [by late May]. It had gotten to be an absolute joke. Everybody voted for everybody. I think there were 150 of us that got about one vote apiece at a time. It got to the point where the papers had cartoons representing senators as saying: *"I vote for that bald-headed man up in the gallery. I vote for that messenger boy coming down the hall."* It was all a good argument for election [of Senators] by the people.[51]

And more besides. It helped to cause a popular revulsion which in due season eased the path of the political progressives. Some of them cited the Lorimer affair as evidence that a conservative policy or politician usually meant a dishonest one. During the course of the deadlock, any citizen wishing well for his country must have been shocked to note how very seldom the contestants mentioned the public weal or shaped their actions with it in mind. Editorial comments and private letters rarely viewed the election as more than a selfish scramble for a choice political plum.

In May, 1909, Lorimer's success pleased Lowden because neither he nor Hopkins had been able to win. Knowing nothing of the imminent scandal and assuming that Deneen was satisfied, Lowden concluded that the outcome of the battle had lessened party factionalism. Lorimer seemed sincere when he made known his readiness to let bygones be bygones. Overly optimistic about the depth of good feeling between the state and federal wings of his party in Illinois, Lowden soon informed President Taft and the chairman of the Republican National Committee that he was giving Lorimer his proxy as

50. *Ibid.,* II, 1155; VIII, 7391, 7578–82, 7804, 7931 ff. For further evidence of *no* bribery see *ibid.,* I, 202, 768 ff., 843; V, 4526–29, 4585, 4931; VI, 5417. For further evidence that there had been bribery see *ibid.,* I, 431, 436–38; II, 1593, 1881 ff.; III, 2840–41, 3005.

51. *Ibid.,* I, 262.

a member of that body.[52] When this action made the headlines in the Chicago papers on August 1, Lowden quickly discovered the shallowness of the entente between the governor and the new senator. The Deneenite press excoriated him, while the Lorimerite editors praised him. Unwittingly, he had tossed a new apple of dissension into the ranks of his party. Unless he had the consent, so it was said, of the Illinois delegation to the 1908 convention which had re-elected him to the national committeemanship, he could not delegate his powers to anyone, even for a brief time. But more serious than the technical issue was the accusation that by giving his proxy he had paid his political debt to Lorimer, helped him become the Republican "czar" of Illinois, knifed Deneen, injured his already weak party on the eve of the important mid-term elections of 1910, and bent his knee to Lorimer in the hope of being helped by him four years later into the senatorial seat of the ailing Shelby Cullom.[53]

The vehemence of this assault took Lowden by surprise. By ill chance he had pointedly reassociated himself with Lorimer only a few months before the latter fell under grave suspicion of bribing or consenting to bribery. Viewed from whatever standpoint, his proxy grant was a serious mistake. That he could have made it after fifteen years of training in a hard political school can be accounted for plausibly only on the grounds of sickness and extreme fatigue. This condition had increased his quandary during the senatorial deadlock and would largely shape his career for several years thereafter. For this reason his poor health needs more than a passing mention.

Although before entering Congress he drove himself unsparingly for months on end without ill effects, he tired easily during his first winter in Washington and often suffered from insomnia. These symptoms were the harder to account for because he had resigned most of his business positions and his congressional duties seemed far less strenuous than his previous regimen. He was inured to public speaking, and yet in Washington he worried for days before delivering carefully prepared remarks in the House of Representatives. During the week preceding his first address to that body he was "miserable" and hard to live with. Once past his ordeal, Mrs. Lowden noted in her diary with relief, "I'm sure he will now feel better."[54] His improved state of mind and body verified her forecast for a time, but during the spring of 1907 he twice subjected himself to the French Lick course of treatments, once in Washington and once at their source in Indiana. Even his physician, Dr. Frank Billings, after cheering him for some months with the word that

52. Copies of FOL to Taft and to F. Hitchcock on July 31, 1909, are not in the Lowden MSS. That these letters were written, however, is made clear by Taft to FOL, on Aug. 2, and FOL to Taft, Aug. 16, 1909.

53. *Chicago Inter-Ocean,* Aug. 1 and 2; *St. Louis Globe-Democrat,* Aug. 1; *Chicago Tribune,* Aug. 2; *Chicago Examiner,* Aug. 3—all dates 1909. In a letter to Charles Bent, Chicago, Aug. 16, 1909, referring to the proxy, FOL wrote: "Of course, my health was partly responsible, but there were other reasons as well." He did not explain the "other reasons."

54. Mrs. Lowden's diary, Feb. 7–16, 1907.

he was fundamentally in sound health, sternly ordered him in July to take a complete rest for the balance of the summer. Much discouraged because of his nervousness, sleeplessness, loss of appetite, and tired eyes, he frequently obliged his wife to sit with him in his room at "Castle Rest" and leave the numerous guests to their own devices. All in all, as she confided to her diary, it "has not been a very happy season here."[55]

By October, after a long motor trip in New England and short excursions in his congressional district to visit friends, Lowden felt improved in body and mind. All went well until early February, 1908, when he contracted a heavy cold on the eve of his elaborate dinner at the New Willard Hotel for the members of the Gridiron Club and other guests.[56] Although the volume of praise accorded to this banquet exceeded his fondest expectations, his exhaustion at its close compelled him to recuperate for some days at Atlantic City. He had been there once before during that winter, and he would return twice again before Congress adjourned on May 30, in the midst of a heat wave which almost prostrated him. Earlier that month the critical illness and death of his mother, necessitating two trips to Iowa Falls in quick succession, added to the strain upon him.

During the ensuing summer and autumn he had little opportunity to rest, because the presidential, state, and congressional election campaigns followed closely upon the Republican national convention in June. Even by mid-September, before the pressure of the canvass had reached its crest, Mrs. Lowden noticed with alarm that her husband was completely worn out. "Tired, nervous and with a bad cold," he and Judge Landis, as already mentioned, vacationed at Atlantic City immediately after election day. As usual when away for more than a few days, he became so homesick and depressed that Mrs. Lowden had to join him or else expect his immediate return to "Sinnissippi." He was half-sick when Congress convened in December for its short session. Frequently during the next three months, illness kept him from going to the Capitol. When there, he often waited for Mrs. Lowden to come in the landau or victoria so that they could take a relaxing late-afternoon drive through Rock Creek Park before dinner. On January 8, 1909, at the opening of the senatorial battle in Springfield, Mrs. Lowden made note that her husband was "coming down with a very heavy cold." In less than a week a painful eczema, covering him from head to foot, necessitated trained nurses and calls by physicians several times a day. Two weeks later he felt sufficiently recovered to spend the rest of his convalescence in Atlantic City. Thereafter for a few months he seemed to be so much improved that he viewed the severe attack as both the end and the climax of his cycle of ill-health.

That attack, however, came as a puzzling surprise. For years he had been unusually susceptible to sun and wind burn, accompanied occasionally by a rash on his face and hands known as "sun eczema." To guard against it, he

---

55. Mrs. Lowden's diary, Aug. 28, 1907. Much strong wind and rough water at "Castle Rest," spoiling fishing and cruising, did not improve FOL's humor that summer.

56. *Ibid.*, Feb. 2–8, 1908.

often dispensed with shaving during the summer. But his skin affliction in the midst of a Washington winter patently stemmed from some other cause, and one which would not yield permanently to Pluto Water, drugs, and bran and cornstarch baths. Nor had he hit the mark when he concluded that his years of overwork in Chicago were finally taking their toll.[57]

For a man of his nervous temperament, accustomed to prominent participation in important civic and business projects, it was singularly frustrating to be only a junior congressman, spending hours in committee meetings debating petty matters and rarely "making the news" except in its society columns. He wrote with a touch of dry humor:

It is very difficult, as you say, for one to get used to the seeming waste of time down here . . . in a representative government it is apparently necessary to waste this time. One of the first things that surprised me was a discussion over whether or not certain copies of the President's Panama Message should be printed with or without the illustrations. The difference in cost would have been trifling. I made a hasty calculation which convinced me that, if the Spartan advocates of economy had succeeded, for every dollar saved it would have cost the Government ten dollars to print the speeches in the Record. But there was doubtless an economy hidden in this somewhere, for something else might have passed during that time involving a needless large expenditure.[58]

On another occasion he complained that he had devoted an entire morning to a discussion about the proper design for a postage stamp. After his phenomenal rise in Chicago, this was slow going, especially for an ambitious politician, already forty-five years of age.

Mrs. Pullman may well have contributed to his feeling of unease. Restless, dynamic, and heedless of practical considerations, she apparently dreamed of at least a senatorship for her beloved son-in-law, and that speedily. While he attended Congress, she also stayed in Washington, usually at the Arlington Hotel. For years she had lived exclusively in an environment where wealth and assured position were taken for granted and where the high station of public officials was far more evident than the hard fight whereby they had attained it. Entirely beyond her ken was the nature of the democratic process, with its requirements of influencing voters, compromising issues, dispensing patronage shrewdly, taking one's turn up the political ladder, and winning elections. From her experience she naturally believed that the principal avenue to political preferment was a social one. Let her build for the Lowdens an impressive mansion in a fashionable district of Washington; let them entertain the great and the near-great in a manner befitting their large income, and Frank might easily reach the highest office in the land.[59]

This prospect tempted neither Mrs. Lowden nor her husband. Although eager to move ahead, he knew from bitter experience that wealth furnished no open sesame to the favor of most American voters, whether rural

57. FOL to F. M. Hoyt, Milwaukee, Wisconsin, Mar. 16, 1908, and to C. Bent, Chicago, Aug. 16, 1909.
58. FOL to W. Reeves, Streator, Illinois, Feb. 2, 1907.
59. *Washington Post,* Feb. 2, 1908.

or urban.[60] Mrs. Pullman, nevertheless, built a $360,000 mansion at 1125 Sixteenth Street, N.W., and furnished it expensively. Neither she nor the Lowdens ever lived in it. In 1913 she sold it to Mrs. John Hays Hammond, who shortly thereafter resold it to the czar of Russia as the residence for his ambassador. Ironically, Mrs. Pullman's dream house was fated, some twenty years later, to become the home of A. A. Troyanovsky and his Communist successors.[61]

During their last three years in Washington the Lowdens leased for their own use the Wayne MacVeagh residence at 1710 Massachusetts Avenue, N.W.[62] Although they resolved not to make entertaining and being entertained the main aspect of their stay in the capital city, they also believed that the families of public officials who could afford it should contribute to the social life there while Congress was in session.[63] Mrs. Lowden's diary and the Washington newspapers bear witness to how extensively they participated. She and her mother often gave a tea or musicale for one hundred and fifty or more guests. Once each session Mr. and Mrs. Lowden invited to a reception or dinner the entire Illinois delegation in Congress, their wives, and any other prominent citizens of the home state who happened to be in the city. Dining in or dining out with a score of guests was a routine item on their social calendar. These formal affairs ranged in impressiveness from White House or embassy banquets or one of Mrs. John B. Henderson's famous vegetarian dinners to a meal at a club with a half-dozen intimate friends or a big-game movie at the White House with running commentary by Theodore Roosevelt.[64] Fritzi Scheff in *Mlle Modiste*, David Warfield in *The Music Master*, Blanche Bates in *The Girl of the Golden West*, Julia Marlowe in *Gloria*, Margaret Anglin in *The Great Divide*, and Maude Adams in *What Every Woman Knows* suggest some of the Lowdens' theater parties. To enable them to take friends on Potomac River outings, they had their steam yacht "Venice" brought from Alexandria Bay to Washington in late 1908. After the vessel had run aground on one occasion and been rammed by a fishing boat on another, Mrs. Lowden concluded, "It has been a costly and unsatisfactory experiment."[65]

Not a little of her time in Washington during 1908 and for the next three

60. In 1907, as an investment, Mrs. Lowden purchased for about $70,000 five large lots near the intersection of Massachusetts and California avenues (Sheridan Circle) in Washington and still owned them thirty years later.

61. Mrs. Lowden's diary, Apr. 12 and Dec. 5, 1909; Nov. 18, 1912; and May 16, 1913.

62. After staying at the New Willard Hotel during the winter of 1906–7, the Lowdens rented the house of Mrs. John A. Logan on Columbia Heights for the period of the 1907–8 session of Congress. At about the time when they leased the MacVeagh property for $10,000 a year, they sold their own house in Chicago for $69,200.

63. *Washington Post*, Feb. 2, 1908: "She [Mrs. Lowden] shares with Miss Helen Cannon the prestige of elevating the congressional contingent of the Middle West in general, and that of Illinois in particular, into the circumscribed area called 'exclusive officialdom.'"

64. In view of their strenuous social schedule, Mrs. Lowden's diary entry of Feb. 28, 1908, comes as no surprise: "I have declined all invitations in March. We are both very tired."

65. *Ibid.*, Dec. 6, 1908; Apr. 3, 16, 18, May 2 and 4, 1909.

years was devoted, in company with Mrs. James Breck Perkins and several other women, to organizing, finding and furnishing a building for, and planning the annual social activities of the Congressional Club. Either Mrs. Lowden or her husband probably was the first to suggest the creation of this society for the wives of congressmen. It still plays a significant role in the life of official Washington.[66]

In addition to the social engagements of Mrs. Lowden alone and those shared by her husband, he was often either a guest or the host at stag luncheons, dinners, and other evening gatherings. With some of his many friends he frequented the Chevy Chase, Metropolitan, and Valcour clubs. His dinner for over two hundred men at the New Willard on the evening of February 8, 1908, was his most elaborate offering to the social festivities of Washington during his congressional career. To the music of a portion of the Marine Corps Band, his guests enjoyed their martinis, caviar, oysters, brook trout, filet of beef, terrapin, squabs, sauterne, champagne, parfait Neapolitan, black coffee, and much else besides. Among those at the banquet were Nelson Aldrich, Frederic Bancroft, John Barrett, Albert Burleson, Murray Crane, Charles Curtis, Edwin Denby, Chauncey Depew, John Garner, Herbert Putnam, Norman Hapgood, Truman Newberry, Oscar Straus, Philander Knox, and John Weeks. Observing the rule that "ladies are always present, reporters never are," there were remarks after the banquet by Vice-President Fairbanks, Mr. Justice Brewer, Speaker Cannon, Congressmen Champ Clark and Nicholas Longworth, former Secretary of the Treasury Leslie Shaw, President Henry Hall of the Gridiron Club, and Lowden. The Gridiron Club Chorus led in the singing of pieces especially written for the occasion. A sufficient sample ran in this wise:

> Everywhere he goes, everybody knows
>> All about him, all about him.
> Out upon his farm, surely 'tis no harm
>> He works the "Rubes" and "Hayseeds" to a charm.
> He has a humble cot on a thousand acre lot,
>> It's got a mansard and a hundred rooms.
> The games he loves best and enters with a zest,
>> Are raising corn and Presidential booms.

> *Chorus*
> Lowden you are a daisy
> You are the man for us;

> .   .   .   .

> We're mighty glad to greet you
> As our old farmer friend.
> If there's anything loose that you may want
> On us you may depend.[67]

66. Incorporated by Congress in May, 1908, the club inaugurated its social life in the following December by giving a reception for President-elect and Mrs. Taft in its clubhouse at Vermont Avenue and K Street.

67. Printed menu and program of the banquet, in Lowden MSS. The only evidence of an effort to promote FOL for the presidency was *The Sage of Sinnissippi,* a book of over

This one banquet cost Lowden about half his annual salary as a congressman. But the financial expense meant little when compared with the toll which these affairs levied upon his health.

Cause and effect by 1908 were revolving with an ever accelerating speed which Lowden found himself less and less able to control. Although his lengthening list of social appointments signified the making of more and more friends in high places and a "release" for his growing feeling of frustration, it also meant late hours night after night, clouds of tobacco smoke to which his own panatelas contributed not a little, and too much liquor. The *Peoria Star* in the summer of 1909 erred only in not giving a full explanation of his ill-health when it charged that "his stomach is worn out with too much champagne and eating of soft shelled crabs."[68] Time and again he resolved to curtail his drinking and smoking. Although he mastered his desire for a few days at a stretch, he could not hold himself to an extended observance of his pledge. The more tired and nervous he became, the more reason he had to abstain, the more desire he felt to partake, the less will he could muster to resist.

Late in the summer of 1909, after the cool weather, golf, and good fishing at "Castle Rest" had failed to quiet his nerves or restore his spirits, he suddenly decided to follow his physician's oft-given advice and go to Europe for six weeks. With four young children to look out for, his wife could not accompany him, but Mrs. Pullman, always eager to shop in Paris, was easily persuaded to go. Following a conference with Lorimer in New York City and a glimpse of the Hudson-Fulton celebration, they sailed aboard the "Cincinnati" on September 24.

When he arrived back on the "Lusitania" seven weeks later, his improved appearance pleased Mrs. Lowden, even though he felt little benefited by the excursion. While abroad, he forgot his troubles when he studied the agricultural methods of the French and Swiss and inspected the buildings occupied by the embassies of the United States in Paris, Bern, Berlin, and London. But he tired of Paris far sooner than Mrs. Pullman and decided "to kill time" by having a chauffeur drive him through eastern France, Switzerland, and the upper Rhine Valley. Day after day he tried to visit every historic spot along his route. Every night he felt fagged out and "desolate," wholly failing to appreciate "the far-famed charm of the country inn." He whiled away the evenings playing "500" with Reiman, his chauffeur, and writing or cabling to his wife.[69] From Basel: "I never was so homesick in my life, and I have

---

300 pages, designed for that purpose. It was written and published in the autumn of 1907 by K. A. Ostewig of Lee County in FOL's congressional district. Apparently, FOL neither encouraged the author to write it nor helped meet its publication cost. The reference in the lyric quoted in the text is probably to FOL's share at that time in "booming" Speaker Cannon for the Republican presidential nomination in 1908.

68. *Peoria* (Ill.) *Star,* Aug. 4, 1909.

69. FOL to Mrs. Lowden, from Paris, Oct. 6, 10, 23, 27, and 30, 1909, and an undated one from Basel.

vowed a hundred times a day, I would never leave home again without you." From Heidelberg: "I prefer your benevolent despotism to all the liberty in the world. . . . You may count me thoroughly subjugated now." Back in Paris and cheered by the prospect of an early departure for home, he commented with rueful good humor that he hoped "our children will none of them be handicapped as their father is in this matter of foreign languages." By then he could even give an optimistic report on his health. "The terrible nerve depression, which was well nigh constant two years ago has come but seldom on this trip and then has been of short duration. My appetite has been good and my sleep of the refreshing kind." But when he disembarked in New York two weeks later, he felt much less sanguine.

Early in December he greeted without enthusiasm the opening of the long session of the Sixty-first Congress. The familiar grind of committee work and the equally demanding social life of Washington once more began to wear upon his nerves. The Christmas festivities of 1909 at "Sinnissippi" would have been happier if the master of the house had not had a heavy cold. Hardly was this conquered than eczema on his face kept him out of his seat in the House for nearly a week. Even a few days in Atlantic City in late January and again in mid-March afforded only brief respites from his discomforts of mind and body. His failure to gain a majority for his Embassy Bill added to his feeling of depression. For several weeks the severe illness of Mrs. Pullman drew Mrs. Lowden away from home during most of every day. The fight in Congress at that time to reduce the speaker's power meant little to Lowden, whatever might be its results, but it left him nervously exhausted.[70]

As early as the spring of 1908, the *Des Moines Register and Leader* suggested that an able, younger Republican of progressive leanings, such as Frank Lowden, should supplant the ultra-conservative "Uncle Joe" Cannon as speaker.[71] Some of Lowden's constituents indorsed this recommendation and urged him to seek a revision of the House rules so that the speaker would have less power to determine the order of business and the personnel of committees. But he made known at once that he was on Cannon's side. In March, 1909, when the new (Sixty-first) Congress convened in special session, he not only voted for his colleague from Danville but also for a continuation of the old rules defining the speaker's power.[72] He deplored the widening splits between the Republican progressives and standpatters and the party's leaders in Congress and President Taft. According to Lowden's theory of government, the chief executive should hold himself aloof from the "family" quarrels within Congress and acquiesce in the will of his party as expressed in legislation. The Democrats and certain Republican malcon-

70. Mrs. Lowden's diary, Mar. 17–19, 1910.

71. *Rockford* (Ill.) *Republic,* May 23, 1908, quoting from the *Des Moines* (Iowa) *Register and Leader.*

72. *Congressional Record* (61st Cong., 1st sess.), XLIV, 18, 20, 22, 23; also (60th Cong., 2d sess.), XLIII, 3572.

tents no doubt exaggerated the seriousness of Taft's conflicts with both the liberal and the conservative wings of his party on currency and tariff legislation, but his leadership was inept. Lowden noted with alarm the many omens presaging Republican defeat in the by-elections of 1910.[73]

As always, he sought a formula of compromise, a middle-of-the-road solution that might preserve his party's unity. Although observers usually numbered him among the Old Guard, a few of them called him a progressive or a "regular" moving toward insurgency. This doubt about the camp to which he properly belonged accurately reflected his own quandary. On most issues dividing the liberal and conservative segments of his party, he aligned with the standpatters. At the same time, he came from the upper Mississippi Valley, a stronghold of progressive leaders who advocated unorthodox political remedies for the ills of agriculture. Although he lagged well behind such thoroughgoing innovators as George Norris, Victor Murdock, and some forty other Republicans in the House, he favored civil service reform and tariff, banking, and currency changes in the interest of the farmer. Merritt Starr, a leading Chicago advocate of civil service reform, congratulated him upon being "not exactly a wild-eyed insurgent and by no means a stupid standpatter."[74]

He agreed that theoretically the speaker should not control committee memberships, but he could think of no practicable way to eliminate Cannon's overweening power without so complicating the problem of organizing the House that public business would suffer. If a rules committee determined when and what bills should come up for debate and if a committee on committees appointed the committees, he foresaw as the only result the substitution of a small oligarchy for a one-man dictatorship. In reply to President Harry Pratt Judson of the University of Chicago, who favored the progressives' program for curbing the speaker, Lowden wrote:

> We know now in the House where to place responsibility if improper appointments are made, but would we if a committee . . . named the committees of the House? Wouldn't corruption be made easier with the proposed change? . . . I know that the sentiment of the country is against us with reference to the rules, but I don't think it is fair to the people for a Representative to favor some change, urging that it will be effective, when he knows in his heart that it will not. If anyone can help me to find a path that will be effective and yet will not make it impossible to transact public business, I shall be more grateful to him than to anyone I know.[75]

In March, 1910, when this letter was mailed, Lowden voted three times with the Old Guard in its unsuccessful effort to defeat the Norris motions to change the membership of the Committee on Rules and to bar the speaker from a place on it. Some days later, the Republicans met in caucus to select their members on the reconstituted rules committee. Over the determined

73. FOL to J. W. Dwight, Dryden, New York, Sept. 20, 1909.

74. M. Starr, Chicago, to FOL, Apr. 5, 1910.

75. FOL to H. P. Judson, Mar. 23, 1910.

opposition of the progressives, the Cannonites had their way, choosing, among others, Lowden's warm friends, Tawney (Minnesota), Boutell (Illinois), Fassett (New York), and Dalzell (Pennsylvania). Although Lowden was among those nominated, he received only fourteen votes, far short of the eighty-five necessary for election.[76]

In mid-April, about three weeks after this caucus, Dr. Billings and Dr. Hardin told him that "his health demands that he take a complete rest for a year at least." This had been their advice for many months, but now he decided to follow it. As early as January, 1909, while he was bedridden with eczema, he had informed a friend:

Since I have been lying here it has seemed to me that I would lead quite as useful a life by giving all my energy to the Farm, and I am sure it would be better for me physically. It is not at all improbable that when I have served my next term here, which will end on March 4, 1911, I shall entirely withdraw from politics and give the rest of my life to the interesting problems which relate primarily to the soil.

Whenever he felt depressed during the next fifteen months, he had written in this vein.[77]

Newspaper comment about his decision was most diverse in tone. Almost every editor in his own constituency, however, whether Republican or Democrat, expressed regret. Although several opposition journals in Chicago and elsewhere assured their readers that fear of defeat rather than the doctors' orders accounted for his retirement, there can be little doubt of his success if he had stood for re-election in 1910. Many of his constituents were anti-Cannon Republicans, moving toward insurgency, but few of them classified Lowden as a dyed-in-the-wool standpatter beyond all hope of salvation.

When he reached "Sinnissippi" in late September, after spending a pleasant summer at "Castle Rest," he found his congressional district locked in battle over the election of his successor. His declaration of retirement had been the signal for several local Republican leaders to declare their candidacies. He remained neutral until state Senator John C. McKenzie of Elizabeth won the nomination. Although McKenzie opposed Cannonism, Lowden respected his ability and rejoiced over his success in November.[78] This victory, however, and John Dwight's re-election in New York provided nearly all the grains of comfort he could garner from the nation-wide returns. Mrs. Lowden's diary entry of November 9 probably echoed her husband's feelings: "The Democrats have won great victories everywhere. I am sure Frank has been more than reconciled during the past three weeks to the fact that he was out of it all and had no campaign to make. He is particularly sorry that Mr. Fassett and Mr. Denby have both been beaten."

She probably limited her observation to the "past three weeks" because, on

76. *New York World,* Mar. 24, 1910.

77. FOL to Charles Bent, Chicago, Aug. 16, and to John Campbell, Denver, Colorado, Nov. 22, 1909.

78. J. C. McKenzie to FOL, Apr. 25, and FOL's reply, Apr. 27, 1910.

October 19, their two older daughters, Florence and Harriet, were stricken with infantile paralysis at "Sinnissippi." Lowden rushed home from a visit to Arkansas, accompanied by such exaggerated headlines as "Lowden Wins Death Race to Children," "Two Lowden Children near Death with Infantile," and "Grim Death Fights against Millions." The Rockefeller Institute for Medical Research felt obliged to wire that "no specific treatment is available at present," but the Lowdens received scores of telegrams, telephone calls, and letters—some even from abroad—suggesting and occasionally sending allegedly remedial powders, ointments, and liquids, as well as directions for therapeutic exercises and comfortable leg braces. Happily the three Chicago doctors in attendance soon assured the parents that they could confidently expect almost a complete cure after long and patient treatments, although Harriet, who had suffered the more severe attack, would probably be left with a slight limp. Lowden deemed it a lucky circumstance, in view of the strain to which his daughters' illness subjected him during the two weeks before election day, that he had not been involved in the hectic climax of a political campaign.

All was again good cheer at "Sinnissippi" when he and Mrs. Lowden left it in early December for the short "lame-duck" session of the Sixty-first Congress. Since they returned to the farm for three weeks during the Christmas season and for a shorter visit a month later, their last winter in Washington passed quickly. Now at the end of his career as a representative, with congratulations flooding in because of his "wisdom" in withdrawing from politics during a "hurricane season," he was at his congenial best.[79] After he followed his usual practice of giving each of the forty page boys of the House a five-dollar gold piece for Christmas, they reciprocated with a much appreciated parchment expressing their thanks for his generosity and regret because of his imminent departure. Late in December he sent a "confidential" communication to eighteen of his closest friends in Congress, informing them that he would reach the half-century mark on January 26 and inviting them to dinner that evening. In tune with the jovial spirit of the occasion, Mrs. Lowden gave him "a very old and rare book—Cicero's *Discourse on Old Age*, printed by B. Franklin and translated by Justice Logan." Entertaining the Illinois delegation at a banquet, attending the vice-president's Charity Ball and a reception at the British Embassy, and dining with the Foreign Affairs Committee, the Gridiron Club, the Fassetts, the Weekses, the Longworths, Mr. Justice Day, and Mrs. Hanna marked their last weeks in the capital. To Lowden's great delight, his Embassy Bill finally became law. Even his stormy opposition to the Canadian Reciprocity measure was more exciting than depressing in view of his early release from all congressional wrangles.

With the weight of responsibilities slipping from his shoulders, he felt like a schoolboy just before his graduation. The Republicans in Washington,

79. Although FOL was absent from his seat in the House on 20 of its 68 working days, he was not away more than the average for the Illinois delegation. For example, McKinley was absent 24 days, Lundin 46, Boutell 10, etc.

about to lose control of the House of Representatives for the first time in nearly fifteen years, enveloped themselves in an autumnal sadness, lightened by the mellow glow of sentimental good fellowship among comrades in a lost cause. Lowden reveled in it. Sitting with Miss Helen Cannon on the speaker's bench while the Sixty-first Congress drew to its close on March 4, Mrs. Lowden noticed that Uncle Joe's words of farewell caused many members to wipe tears from their eyes. She felt sorry "on some accounts" to leave Washington, but she rejoiced "for Frank's sake since I believe that getting away from this life will mean restoration to health for him."[80]

80. Mrs. Lowden's diary, Mar. 4 and 5, 1911.

CHAPTER IX

SPECULATOR AND PLANTER

Although the fall of the speaker's gavel in early March, 1911, could not end Lowden's lively interest in the fortunes of his party, it signified that his participation in politics would yield place, for a while at least, to his primary tasks of recovering good health and managing his increasingly complicated business affairs. Three years before the closing scene of his brief congressional career he had declined "a wonderful opportunity" extended by Charles G. Dawes to invest in a public utilities company. "As long as I am in politics," he wrote at that time, "I am really in no position to do much in a business way." The following pages will show how greatly this statement minimized the scope of his economic activities during his five years in Washington. Resigning his directorates and disposing of his Pullman Company securities before his first election to Congress did not mean, of course, the sale of his many other stocks and bonds. His own and Mrs. Lowden's surplus income each year demanded remunerative investment in enterprises not prejudicial to his political reputation. Mrs. Pullman, furthermore, often sought his counsel about her intricate affairs, even though he was not her financial manager. As long as he stayed in Congress, politics necessarily overshadowed business, but the demands of the latter were both continuous and insistent.

Among these concerns was one born of Illinois politics in 1904. J. McCan Davis, Springfield lawyer, political reporter, and chronicler of the deadlocked Republican state convention of that year, persuaded Lowden to join him in the purchase of the *Springfield Evening News* for $50,000. Of this sum, he contributed $40,000 and Davis the balance. After organizing a company, they took over the ownership of the journal on December 1, with Davis as editor at a $3,500 annual salary. Although the troubled and profitless career of the paper since its birth in 1880 gave no grounds for optimism, they expected to have before long the most influential Republican daily in downstate Illinois.

Lowden's liking for new ventures partially explains why he joined in an enterprise entirely foreign to his previous business experience. If he had bought the *News* during the months of his gubernatorial striving, a plausible reason for its acquisition would be apparent. In late 1904, however, a seat in Congress was the sole object of his immediate political ambition. To its attainment a newspaper published far outside his own district would be of little help. If political considerations lay behind this investment—and it is difficult to believe that they did not—they must have embodied a hope of becoming governor or a senator in the not distant future and of aiding the Republican cause in central Illinois.

His decade of effort to make the *News* self-supporting was complimentary to his persistence in the face of repeated and costly misadventures but not to his business acumen. During the first year under Davis' editorship, Lowden had to lend the paper over $6,000 to keep it alive and was soon forced to advance it as much more because many subscribers and advertisers failed to pay what they owed. These "bills receivable" mounted so high by January, 1906, that Lowden asked an accounting firm to go over the books. Commenting that it rarely had seen financial records "so ignorantly and unsystematically kept," it recommended the employment of a business manager.[1] Over Davis' protest, Lowden followed this advice in March by placing Walter F. Dumser in charge of the paper's financial income and outgo. He and Davis were soon at odds. The latter accused his associate of economizing to the extent of banning ice from the water coolers in the office and staging a "silly and damaging" contest, wherein an automobile rewarded the woman who "blackmailed" the merchants of Springfield into furnishing the most lines of advertisements. If Davis can be believed, the tradespeople so much resented this pressure upon them that the outcome of the stunt was the reverse of its purpose. By ill chance rather than chicanery, the winner of the car turned out to be a close friend and neighbor of the Dumsers.[2] Lowden, however, chose to rely much less upon Davis' complaints than upon the year-end balance sheet, which showed a small increase in number of subscribers and lines of advertising over the corresponding figures of the preceding twelve months.

As 1907 opened, Orville P. Bassett, a political acquaintance of Lowden with long journalistic experience on the *Sterling* (Ill.) *Standard* and *Sterling Gazette*, took Davis' place as editor of the *News*. Davis was also replaced as president of the company by Brode B. Davis, a Chicago lawyer and Lowden's close friend. During the next four years, J. M. Davis frequently threatened to sue for alleged breach of contract, for arbitrary dismissal, and for not being notified of meetings of the company in which he still held stock representing his original $10,000 investment. Finally, in early 1911, after financial need obliged him to release his securities to one of his creditors, Lowden bought them from the assignee for $3,000.[3]

Early in 1907, Lowden declined an offer of $50,000 for his controlling interest in the company and a cancellation of its debt to him.[4] During the

1. Report of Wilkinson, Reckitt, Williams and Company, Chicago, Feb. 10, 1906.

2. Unsigned and undated report to FOL, but undoubtedly written in September, 1906, by Davis.

3. G. D. Sutton to W. Burroughs, Chicago, Feb. 3, 1911; FOL to V. E. Bender, Springfield, Illinois, Feb. 18, 1911.

4. FOL to J. F. Jones, Springfield, Jan. 4, 1907.

months ahead, he probably often regretted forgoing this opportunity to withdraw from an enterprise which became ever more bothersome and costly. Bassett worked in harmony with Dumser and Archibald Bowen, the able chief reporter, but the monthly deficits continued. At least they were not so large as during Davis' regime. Although Lowden chafed under the repeated calls upon him for "advances" in $2,000 lumps, he stubbornly hung on and even declared in the summer of 1908 that he would not sell out for less than $75,000.[5] For what sound reason he could be so sanguine is by no means clear.

In February of that year Bassett gladly relinquished his position to Charles H. May, the editor of the *Peoria* (Ill.) *Herald-Transcript*. Eight months later Arthur D. Mackie, well versed in the economics of gas-heating but not of newspaper publishing, succeeded Dumser as business manager. By delegating his voting rights in the company to May, Lowden was enabled to say that he had severed his previous connection with the *News*, but many persons accurately surmised that he still controlled it.[6] Being Governor Deneen's friend, the new editor gained for the journal a few lucrative state printing contracts, including one to publish the names of all delinquent property-tax payers. Circumstantial evidence alone suggests that Lowden's willingness to be a senatorial candidate, if Hopkins withdrew, helps to explain May's appointment. On the other hand, May had to be cautioned in early 1909 to moderate his praise of his chief lest he completely alienate the Hopkinsites in the legislature.[7]

For some months after May took charge, Lowden's optimism about the prospects of the *News* mounted high. He supplied the funds needed to provide it with larger quarters, a new press, and rebuilt linotype machines. He even seriously considered following May's suggestion to buy a 75 per cent interest in the *Springfield State Journal* for $55,000 or $60,000. By doing so, he would gain an exclusive Associated Press evening franchise, a monopoly of the Republican newspapers of the state capital, and a leading morning journal as well as an afternoon one.[8] At May's invitation, Lowden invested and subsequently lost $2,000 in the New Associated Farmer Company, a concern which published agricultural material for insertion in country dailies and weeklies. Perhaps May's assurance that "Sinnissippi" would not be overlooked in the articles and illustrations inveigled Lowden into supporting this project.[9]

5. J. R. Cowley to O. P. Bassett, Apr. 13, 1907.

6. C. H. May to FOL, July 7, 1908; FOL to A. A. Lindstrum, Galesburg, Illinois, Aug. 12; to F. M. Mills, Benton Harbor, Michigan, Dec. 2; and to C. H. May, Dec. 9, 1908.

7. See pp. 177–78 and 180.

8. According to the Dec. 1, 1908, balance sheet, the *News*'s assets, including a $20,000 plant and $60,000 "good will," totaled $93,000. Its liabilities, including $50,000 in stock and $62,665 in debts, amounted to about $113,400.

9. C. H. May to FOL, July 3, 1909, and June 18, 1914; FOL to May, July 10, 1909, and June 20, 1914.

By the summer of 1909, however, with the senatorial deadlock broken, Charles May in poor health, and a succession of gloomy financial reports from the *News* office, Lowden again sought a new manager. Autumn was far advanced before he met Victor E. Bender, "a brilliant newspaper man" who for long had been in charge of the *Council Bluffs* (Iowa) *Nonpareil*.[10] Lowden felt the more eager to give his own paper a fresh start after being reminded at the year's end that he had advanced about $15,000 during May's regime. By then, May was calling the *News* a costly "damned nuisance," saying that the sooner his successor took over, the happier he would be.

With Bender and Mackie working in team, Lowden became so confident of pulling his paper out of its bog of chronic troubles that he reorganized the company for their benefit. Over a period of years the two men were to have the "privilege" of investing a total of $20,000 in the enterprise. To enable Bender to purchase a block of stock, Lowden loaned him $5,000, taking *Nonpareil* bonds as his security. By this time—January, 1910—Lowden had amassed seven hundred shares of stock in the *News* company, representing his original stake of $40,000 and subsequent loans of about $30,000.[11] Not one cent of dividends or interest had come to him, and the end was still far in the future.

Under the Bender-Mackie management during 1910–11, the annual average deficit declined, and the paper gained in readers and advertisers. A summer campaign in 1911, during which pianos, diamond rings, and watches served as premiums for the most successful solicitors, enrolled over fifteen hundred new subscribers. Bender called the *News* not only the best but also "the fastest growing paper in central Illinois." Notwithstanding the frequent calls upon him for more money, Lowden momentarily shared this enthusiasm and agreed that he felt "more comfortable about the *News* than ever before."[12] Additional lines of advertising alone were needed, so Mackie assured him, to make the journal a profit-maker. But these could not be found. Evidently there were too few newspaper readers in Springfield, even when supplemented by several thousand subscribers from the neighboring countryside, to support four dailies. Although the *Springfield Record* ended its tottering career by going bankrupt in the summer of 1912, the balance sheets of the *News* showed little improvement thereafter. Under their contract with Lowden, Bender and Mackie agreed to advance needed cash in proportion to their holdings of stock, receiving one share for every hundred dollars paid in. By October, 1911, with eighty-six shares, Mackie had reached the end of his financial resources. Although Lowden would not and Bender could not take over these securities, Mackie resigned in good spirits, feeling "highly

10. Congressman W. I. Smith to FOL, Nov. 10, and E. E. Hart, First National Bank, Council Bluffs, Iowa, to FOL, Nov. 15, 1909.

11. FOL to V. E. Bender, Dec. 11, 1909, and Apr. 3, 1910; to J. L. Schaeffer, Oregon, Illinois, Jan. 11 and 16, 1910. When the company was reorganized, FOL exchanged his "IOU's" for their equivalent in stock.

12. FOL to V. E. Bender, Aug. 21, 1911.

complimented at having been associated with you [Lowden] in business."[13]

Lowden's unwillingness to buy out Mackie signified that, at long last, he was beginning to doubt whether the *News* would ever become a financial success. During 1912 he manifested a growing reluctance to advance more money, although he frequently gave Bender a verbal pat on the back when the editor sadly wrote of "letting his own salary ride" in order to have some cash in the till. In fact, the paper lost only about $5,500 that year, its smallest annual deficit while under Lowden's control. By then, however, his eleven hundred shares of sterile stock painfully reminded him of his many thousands of dollars locked up in the venture.

When the ill fortunes of the paper took a turn for the worse during 1913, he cautioned Bender: "I do not expect to put more money in the *News* and so you will have to get on as best you can until you can effect a sale. . . . We must bring this matter to a close. I can not go on with it longer."[14] Although he relented somewhat during the early months of the following year, his refusal to respond to every call for funds forced Bender to borrow from a Springfield bank up to the $10,000 limit of the paper's credit there. The gloom deepened when the editor fell ill. The sudden death of his wife a few months later brought him temporarily to a state of almost complete collapse.[15] Long before this new misfortune, Lowden and he had been searching for someone who wanted to publish a journal badly enough to offer a fair price for the *News*. As Lowden sardonically commented to Bender: "There must be someone, somewhere, who wants a paper, and we certainly, under the circumstances, could afford to make such a man a better proposition than anyone else I could think of."[16] Congressman William B. McKinley was one of the wealthy men upon whom Lowden tried unsuccessfully to unload his journal.

Finally, on October 1, 1914, he disposed of his interest in it for an unknown sum to J. David Stern, the owner of the *New Brunswick* (N.J.) *Daily News*. Stern soon bought the plant of the bankrupt *Springfield* (Ill.) *Record* and, still later, two Camden, New Jersey, papers and the *Philadelphia Record*. If, as appears likely, Lowden did not receive more than $30,000 from Stern, his decade as a newspaper owner cost him at least $75,000, and

13. Letters to FOL from V. E. Bender, Oct. 5 and Dec. 14, and from A. D. Mackie, Oct. 26; letters from FOL to Bender, Oct. 13 and Dec. 23, and to Mackie, Oct. 28, all in 1911.

14. FOL to V. E. Bender, Nov. 20, 1913. FOL wrote him, Aug. 19: "I absolutely agree . . . that the paper is a much more valuable property than it was when you took hold of it, and I don't think that we ought to sacrifice it. . . . I appreciate, of course . . . what it means to the Republican party and therefore . . . [to] . . . good government, to have a real Republican paper down the State, and particularly in view of the fact that there is but one in Chicago, but I cannot alone be expected to do much more in this cause."

15. FOL to Bender, Feb. 12, and Bender to FOL, July 31, 1914.

16. FOL to Bender, Mar. 2, 1914.

probably more.[17] The *Springfield News* was one of his most unprofitable business ventures and as unrewarding in political benefits as in dividends. Well might he comment long afterward: "If there is one subject upon which I know less than any other, it is what goes to make a newspaper, or in fact a periodical of any kind."[18]

During these same years he and many of his friends found speculation in mining stocks an exciting diversion. Among those who refused to indulge was Charles G. Dawes. "I thank Heaven," he wrote in his diary on August 6, 1904, "that the pernicious mining microbe has never gotten into my vitals." He had just come back from a trip with several other Chicago businessmen in Lowden's private Pullman car to Tipton, Missouri. There they had inspected a lead and zinc mine in which their host owned a financial interest. Dawes's fervent expression of gratitude also reflected his safe return in a bucket after descending its shaft, 160 feet deep, and groping around on its flooded bottom amid "pitfalls and dynamite."[19] With somewhat less emphasis, Lowden confided to his wife, "We weren't at all pleased with the mine but believe there is a lot of ore there if it can be got at."[20] The complete silence of his later records suggests that neither he nor his money ever again disturbed whatever metal was hidden in that tunnel.

By coupling hope with disappointment when summing up his Tipton expedition, he perhaps revealed why so many similarly risky speculations attracted him. A few yielded more than enough profits to offset the collapse of those which left him nothing except ornately engraved stocks and bonds. To own or share in owning a mine of potentially precious ore, especially if it had an alluring name, was sheer romance and a suspenseful gamble as well.

J. D. Hubbard, president of the Chicago Exploration Company, with an imposing letterhead bearing a cable address and mentioning four codes from which his foreign correspondents might select, was one of the biggest promoters in the Middle West during the early twentieth century. In 1906, when treasurer and general manager of the Western Mines Development Company, he persuaded Lowden to subscribe over $50,000 to various gold- or silver-mining enterprises of this concern or its affiliate, the Colombian Exploration Syndicate. These ventures included the "Aurora" mines in Calaveras County, California, the "Top" and "Last Chance" mines in the Mogollon district of New Mexico, and gold-dredging in the Nechi River near Zaragoza in Colombia, South America. According to custom, Lowden did not pay his total stake all at once, but in instalments when called for. Before he sent the full $50,000, the company's officers decided to reorganize the

17. *Philadelphia Public Ledger,* Oct. 1, 1914. In a letter to Bender on Feb. 12, 1914, FOL had offered to sell for $30,000 cash; so it seems unlikely that Stern paid him more. At the time of the sale, the *News* had a daily circulation of about 7,200—about 40 per cent in Springfield and 60 per cent outside that city.

18. FOL to F. A. Koenig, Chicago, Aug. 20, 1932.

19. *Dawes Journal, 1893–1913,* p. 379.

20. FOL to Mrs. Lowden, Aug. 5 and 7, 1904.

business in order to provide a much larger fund of capital. Frequent transformations of this kind were almost as characteristic of the life-cycle of a mining company as of a butterfly—and there were other obvious parallels between the two.

At the same time Lowden and a group of about a dozen prominent Chicagoans, including John S. Runnells, general counsel of the Pullman Company, and Frederic A. Delano, president of the Wabash Railroad, owned most of the stock of the Combination Mines Company, another Hubbard development. This firm focused upon Nevadan mines and was an exceedingly profitable enterprise from the start. In December, 1906, after distributing several large dividends, it sold out to Senator George S. Nixon of Nevada and his partner, George Wingfield of Goldfield in that state, for over $2,600,000 in cash and 175,000 shares of Goldfield Consolidated Mines Company stock. Lowden's return from this deal was nearly $125,000. Of this he took $49,000 in cash and the balance in the form of about 18,200 shares of stock in Nixon and Wingfield's company. For some years this speculation rewarded him with immense gains.[21] Referring to it in a letter to former Congressman Robert G. Cousins of Iowa a few years later, Lowden commented, "We have had so much prosperity that it has been difficult to keep our heads."[22]

Profits such as these led him to invest more heavily in and join the directorate of the Chicago Exploration Company, as the Western Mines Development Company was called after undergoing several reorganizations in 1907 and early 1908. Holding $25,000 worth of its stock, he eagerly followed its "exploratory" work in gold, silver, copper, and lead mines in California, Utah, and Nevada and in Mexico and Colombia as well.[23] Expectations ran high, but assessment notices rather than dividend checks were all that came to its stockholders.

On an unlucky day in 1909, Hubbard decided to concentrate most of the company's resources upon the "Mina Mexico" silver property in the state of Sonora, about thirty miles from a railroad. He believed the 215 acres could be acquired for about $200,000. And then, continued the promoter, after installing $50,000 worth of new machinery, the mine should earn between $40,000 and $45,000 a month for perhaps two years or more. In his opinion, it was "the best mining opportunity ever presented to our company." Lowden felt privileged when Hubbard permitted him to invest $25,000 in the Mina Mexico Company, organized as a subsidiary of the Chicago Exploration Company.[24] So eager were the speculators to buy Mina Mexico stock that they oversubscribed for its total issue by more than 50 per cent.

21. In 1907, FOL was a trustee of the Goldfield Consolidated Mines Company and received $10 a share dividend monthly on its stock. By the close of 1907, he owned 20,000 shares.

22. FOL to R. G. Cousins, Tipton, Iowa, Jan. 31, 1910.

23. FOL to J. D. Hubbard, Mar. 12, 1907, and to H. S. Derby, secretary of the Chicago Exploration Company, Feb. 21, 1910.

24. FOL's initial subscription was $12,500, but he doubled it on Jan. 15, 1910.

Thereafter for another year the Chicago Exploration Company followed up many "leads" to alleged mining opportunities ranging from Mexico to Canada but discovered nothing which yielded aught except expense. Late in February, 1911, Hubbard reported that the stockholders had voted to liquidate the company because its business had been "too speculative and hazardous" and for three years "disappointing and unsatisfactory in the extreme." Its only potential assets were twenty-five hundred shares of Mina Mexico Company stock. Upon the demise of the Exploration Company, Lowden as owner of 17½ per cent of its stock received that percentage of these securities.[25]

By then the Mexican venture was in serious straits. In 1910 no construction work started at the mine until autumn because of the rainy season and a delay in deciding what type of reverberatory furnace to use. Hubbard had told the stockholders that the smelter would probably be completed by July, but late March of the following year arrived before it was ready. Although on-the-spot reports of the ore's richness continued to be cheering, a steady flow of complaints also reached Chicago about the inefficiency of the furnace mechanism, the slowness and lack of skill of the Mexican laborers, the scarcity of mules and firewood, the poor quality of the iron pyrites used for the flux, and the occasional work-stoppages because of political disturbances.[26] These latter became more frequent and prolonged as the year advanced, forcing the Southern Pacific to discontinue most of its rail service in the state of Sonora. As 1911 closed, however, the Mina Mexico balance sheets indicated that the company had made a little profit from the year's sporadic operations. Nevertheless, the net income failed to cover stockholders' loans to the company of nearly $50,000 and its $2,500 overdraft at the Banco Sonora in Hermosillo.[27]

In March, 1913, just after the company authorized a bond issue of $150,-000 in order to provide operating capital, the long-smoldering political unrest in Sonora burst into flame. Smelting at the mine abruptly ceased. The ore and matte, ready for shipment or smelting and said to be worth over $60,000, could not be moved. The superintendent dared hope only to keep a small force at work extracting ore and manning the pumps so that water would not flood the new equipment in the mine.[28] In the face of this somber news, subscribers to the full amount of the $150,000 bond issue, at par, failed to come forward and about one-third of it had to be negotiated at 75 cents on the dollar. Lowden invested $8,000 in these securities. Reports from the

25. J. D. Hubbard to stockholders, Chicago Exploration Company, Feb. 27, 1911; J. D. Hubbard to FOL, June 22, 1911.

26. H. S. Derby to stockholders, Mina Mexico Company, Dec. 8, 1910; J. D. Hubbard to stockholders, Chicago Exploration Company, Feb. 27, 1911; copies of letters of H. L. Hollis to J. D. Hubbard, Apr. 20 and May 5, 1911.

27. J. D. Hubbard to stockholders, Mina Mexico Company, Dec. 2, 1911; *Mina Mexico Company Report, Submitting Statement of Receipts and Disbursements, etc., for Period to 31 December 1911,* by Arthur Young & Co., C.P.A.

28. P. Palmer, Jr., president of Mina Mexico Company, to stockholders, June 12, 1913.

mine by late summer told of over $100,000 worth of ore or matte lying in heaps on the surface. Until the company could realize upon this large asset, it would be unable even to pay interest on its bonds. Consequently, by late 1913, the creditors rather than the stockholders wielded the whip hand over the enterprise, although with few exceptions they were the same persons. In effect, therefore, when the bondholders threatened to foreclose within ninety days unless they received their overdue interest at once, they merely were warning themselves as stockholders or, rather, themselves and a few "little people" who, owning no bonds, would soon be squeezed out of the company altogether.[29]

Thus the time was at hand by late 1913 for another reorganization—a complicated procedure whereby a new corporation of identical name, but with a Delaware charter instead of one from South Dakota, arose like Phoenix from the ashes of the old. As a part of this transformation, by a mathematical legerdemain too intricate to analyze here, Lowden turned in his old stocks and bonds and a check for $4,000. In exchange he became in the new company the owner of $4,000 worth of 6 per cent first series trust bonds, $8,000 of 6 per cent second series trust bonds, 467 shares of stock with a par value of $4,670, and a promissory note for $400.[30]

By this administrative and financial maneuvering, the bondholders gained complete control of the mine and also raised enough money among themselves to protect their property from damage until, as they fondly hoped, the return of peace in Mexico would permit operations to be resumed. The treasurer explained matters in this wise:

There is at present in ore, on cars at Tonichi, and on the surface at the mine, which [*sic*] as soon as it can be delivered to the smelter will give us a return in gold of about $110,000. There is also additional ore in the mine, blocked out and exposed, amounting to $130,000 or $140,000. The indebtedness . . . now aggregates about $75,000 to $80,000. . . . The bondholders have now to consider an additional advance of money to protect this nearly a quarter million dollars worth of ore. . . .

The operating expenses [will be] about $3,000 to $4,000 a month, gold, . . . to keep a superintendent and some miners at work . . . for the purpose of guarding the property. . . .

Should we flood the mine it would mean a loss . . . of about $60,000. . . . With the disturbed condition of the country, everything of conceivable, and even inconceivable, value is stolen if not protected. You are as good a judge as the rest of us as to how soon . . . peace will be restored. . . . So far we have not been disturbed at our mine . . . but we have been unable to ship any ore for over six months.

The status of the Mina Mexico Company has for a long time been exasperating almost beyond endurance, but it seems unwise . . . to abandon a property [which now promises to be] . . . of greater value than ever before.[31]

29. Bryant to FOL, Oct. 23, and FOL's reply, Oct. 25, 1913.

30. Printed leaflet entitled *Mina Mexico Bondholders' Reorganization Agreement,* dated Nov. 1, 1913.

31. E. F. Bryant to FOL, Oct. 30, 1913.

The new Mina Mexico Company survived for eight years. Every January its managing director provided the assembled stockholders with a new tale of woe. When United States troops landed at Vera Cruz in April, 1914, the American employees at the mine withdrew north of the border on half-pay, and the Mexican bookkeeper watched over the virtually abandoned property. After the "Yanqui" workers returned in July, they succeeded in holding on for almost a year before a warning from the State Department at Washington caused them to leave for what proved to be the last time. The bookkeeper kept the pumps working for another twelve months. By then the drying-up of the company's funds obliged him to let water flood into the tunnels and shafts of the mine. During this entire period only a few tons of silver ore reached market on muleback. The Southern Pacific Railroad showed no sign of rebuilding its line within the near future.[32]

With 1917 came the presidency of General Carranza and a new constitution providing for the nationalization of subsoil mineral deposits. The manager of Mina Mexico Company urged its stockholders to point out to President Wilson and members of his administration "the serious situation that would result if our government recognized Carranza . . . without reservation for the protection of American interests."[33] Although Washington exchanged ambassadors with the Carranza regime, a decade of pressure from the State Department upon the Mexican authorities availed little to encourage the investment of American capital in Mexico.

In April, 1918, after the Mina Mexico Company defaulted upon the interest due to its nine first-mortgage bondholders, including Lowden, it turned over its assets to them. Without hope of reopening the mine, they agreed to pay its carrying charges for two years while they sought a buyer. The two years of futile search lengthened into five. Lowden evidently wrote his final word about the hapless speculation when he inquired of the trustees for the bondholders in 1924: "What ever happened to the Mina Mexico Company? Are the securities worthless? If so, I would like to know it for income tax purposes."[34] The answer is missing, but it probably made clear that his investment of about $40,000 was a total loss.

During these same years, mining ventures in British Columbia, the isthmus of Tehuantepec, and the American Southwest yielded virtually no returns upon his $60,000 stake in them. He engaged in one of these gambles, as well as in several others almost as costly, to accommodate friends in need of financial aid. They rarely sought his help in vain.

Among Lowden's many boon companions, none was more stimulating and venturesome than Leigh S. J. Hunt. Of inexhaustible energy and imagina-

32. Copy of letter of H. L. Hollis, managing director, Mina Mexico Mining Company, to P. Palmer, Jr., Chicago, Jan. 9, 1918. Typed report of Palmer to the stockholders, undated, but probably January, 1918.

33. H. L. Hollis to FOL, Apr. 23, 1917.

34. FOL to E. F. Bryant, Nov. 26, 1924. The charter of the Mina Mexico Company was annulled by Delaware on Jan. 17, 1921, for two years' non-payment of taxes.

tion, his enterprises ranged around the globe, from the Oriental Consolidated Mines of Korea to the first cotton plantation (so he claimed) in the Anglo-Egyptian Sudan.[35] Anyone wealthy enough to risk a long financial shot counted his association with Hunt almost a sufficient recompense, even though he missed the target altogether. Shortly after Lowden's brief stay at Iowa State College in 1878, Hunt became its president. But the tameness of campus life irked him, and within a decade he was the owner and editor of the *Seattle* (Wash.) *Post-Intelligencer.* From then until 1909, when Lowden first joined him in a business venture, Hunt traveled far and wide seeking opportunities for quick profits. He found many of them and derived much fun from the search. He felt equally at home in a Brazilian jungle, on a bleak mountainside in Korea, on a blooded hunter in a steeplechase, or in the exclusive Metropolitan or Chevy Chase Club in Washington. Lowden thought of him as "a very old and particular friend," "of unusual character and ability," "one of the best and ablest men I have ever met."[36]

Between 1909 and 1913, Lowden and others, sometimes including Bernard M. Baruch, Nelson W. Aldrich, J. Sloat Fassett, John S. Runnells, and Robert D. Clarke, enlisted under Hunt's leadership in a variety of exciting but unremunerative enterprises. Among these were an exploration of the "American Girl" mines in Arizona, a search for undeveloped agricultural and mineral lands in Brazil, a survey of a twenty-thousand-acre tract in Panama as a possible site for citrus-fruit orchards, the establishment for two years of an experimental farm in connection with Princeton College, and the production of a new type of turbine. Lowden's participation in all this cost him about $10,000. He finally recovered a little over 10 per cent of it.[37]

The expense of his involvement in Hunt's Latin-American ventures was small when compared with his $25,000 loss in an organization formed earlier in the century to construct and operate bonded warehouses in Vera Cruz.[38] Furthermore, under the aegis of Lowden's old commanding officer, Colonel J. B. Sanborn, a group known as the Orizaba Rubber Plantation Company acquired over six thousand acres of dense jungle near El Salto, Mexico, not far from the Guatemalan border. After eight years of effort, made the more arduous by unreliable overseers, unpredictable laborers, unexpected expenses, and delinquent subscribers to the stock of the company, about one-third of the tract came under cultivation. With no dividends in sight, the owners tried to dispose of their holding without financial loss. In Sanborn's words: "The Company almost sold all its property at a handsome profit in

35. *Who's Who in America*, XII (1922–23), 1619.

36. FOL to A. H. Sanders, Chicago, July 27, 1911.

37. In the winter of 1911–12, Hunt and the well-known Brazilian promoter, Percival Farquhar, made a 6,000-mile trip into the Brazilian back country. Upon his return, Hunt advised FOL against investing in land there. After a ten-day test of the turbine by the Navy at Annapolis in October, 1913, it was found to be unsatisfactory.

38. File of correspondence in the Lowden MSS entitled, "Almacenes Generales de Deposito de Mexico y Vera Cruz at Mexico City."

1910 to a British Syndicate but then the rubber boom collapsed. We are trying to sell our surplus lands. We need a competent manager. Our present one was absent so much, the tapping operation of the current year was not satisfactory, but our outlook is good."[39] The coming of the revolution speedily changed this prospect to one of deep gloom. By the close of 1913, with empty coffers and no sign that Mexico would soon be at peace, the company reached the end of its road. Thereby Lowden chalked up another loss of $15,000 or $20,000.

Although Charles Dawes shared the financial caution of most bankers and shied away from mining stocks, he laid much of the foundation of his considerable fortune and increased it after becoming president of the Central Trust Company of Chicago by promoting and operating public utilities corporations in the fields of gas and electric lighting and heat. Usually in association with his brothers, Rufus C., Beman G., and Henry M. Dawes, his interests of this kind ranged westward by 1906 from Ohio to Seattle, Washington, and southward from Wisconsin to Texas. Five years later they formed Dawes Brothers, Inc., to manage these diverse companies and merge many of their securities into a single stock. Charles Dawes and Lowden often differed over which wing of the Illinois Republican party to support, but their relations were always cordial. Lowden helped his friend launch his trust company in 1902, and Dawes reciprocated with opportunities for profit-making in public utility and oil company securities.[40] Unlike the instances mentioned earlier where personal friendships led to monetary losses, the association of Lowden with the Dawes brothers for over forty-five years was financially as well as socially rewarding.

Between 1907 and 1921 he invested more than a quarter of a million dollars in their enterprises. None utterly failed, and several became exceptionally remunerative. Well might Charles Dawes tell him in 1907 that the earnings of the Seattle Lighting Company were "enormous."[41] Seven years later, as another example, Lowden received a bonus of six hundred shares of common stock on his one thousand shares of Union Gas and Electric Company stock, in addition to a 60 per cent cash dividend. On an earlier occasion, Dawes, Lowden, and W. I. Osborne formed a syndicate to buy and sell public utility securities. During its brief existence, Lowden's investment of $70,000 returned him his principal and nearly a 25 per cent profit.[42] Such a way to wealth lacked the glamour and excitement of speculating in mining properties, but it led in the long run to fewer disappointments and larger profits.

As the years went by, Lowden's interest centered more and more upon

39. Statement of J. B. Sanborn to the stockholders, Orizaba Rubber Plantation Company, Feb. 6, 1911.

40. FOL's correspondence with R. C., B. G., and H. M. Dawes about his securities in their companies between 1907 and 1917 is much too bulky to detail here.

41. C. G. Dawes to FOL, Feb. 21, 1907.

42. Union Gas and Electric Company, Chicago, to FOL, Dec. 24, 1914; C. G. Dawes, FOL, and W. I. Osborne, syndicate managers, to FOL, Oct. 7, 1911.

the purchase and development of farm and timber lands. Clipping coupons, indorsing dividend checks, dealing with brokers, reinvesting profits, writing off losses, and filling safe deposit boxes in several Chicago banks with bond and stock certificates were normal occupations of any wealthy man. But Lowden disliked their impersonal quality and his isolation from the businesses represented by the engraved paper. He preferred, as he once wrote, to control any enterprise in which he invested much money.[43] For this reason, real estate was his favorite form of property. Not city lots with buildings on them, although Mrs. Lowden owned many in Chicago, Washington, Memphis, and elsewhere,[44] but farm land which he could walk upon, ride over, experiment with, and sow to crops. Alone among all his enterprises, it engaged his heart as well as his purse. He confessed to a friend, "I do not feel that I am at all fitted for buying lands and then selling them again. It is too hard for me to let go of real estate when I have once purchased it."[45] During the seven years preceding the outbreak of World War I, he found land so irresistible that he was obliged to sell some of his securities and borrow heavily from Dawes's bank in order to meet his commitments for country properties.

These included a huge ranch in west Texas as well as large tracts in Idaho and Michigan which he and his co-owners mistakenly believed to be suitable for growing fruit. In 1907, for reasons now wholly forgotten, he and two Texans, who were united in a separate partnership, acquired 17,414 acres of Panhandle land near the New Mexico border.[46] This expanse lacked both trees and water, except for several windmill-operated wells and an arroyo near its southwest corner. At about the center of the range was a dwelling flanked by a few flimsy outbuildings and a corral. Some twenty-two miles to the north a number of rail lines converged at Dalhart, while some six miles southeast of the property there was a depot at Middlewater.[47]

When the partners defaulted on their instalments of the purchase price, Lowden stepped into the financial breach and eventually came to own the entire property. It cost him more than $140,000.[48] Wire fences and other improvements added another $10,000 to the outlay. In the autumn of 1908, on one of his very infrequent visits to the ranch, Mrs. Lowden accompanied him. They noticed coyotes, "prairie chickens," antelope, and a few longhorn steers, but "fortunately . . . no snakes." Following this expression of relief,

43. FOL to R. C. Dawes, Apr. 3, 1912.

44. In 1908, FOL owned at least twenty lots in Chicago subdivisions, not counting Mrs. Lowden's 99 buildings in Pullman, which she had taken in exchange, in 1907, for 1,875 shares of Pullman Company stock. This exchange was a part of the process of bringing to an end G. M. Pullman's model village there. In May, 1908, after selling 600 shares of Pullman stock at 158½, Mrs. Lowden still owned 4,477 shares.

45. FOL to C. B. Landis, Wilmington, Delaware, Nov. 14, 1914.

46. Mrs. Lowden's diary, June 14, 1907. J. R. Cowley went to Texas to look at the land. The Texas partners were E. C. Reed and Charles Allen of Dalhart.

47. Memorandum describing Texas lands, Apr. 11, 1913.

48. FOL had acquired 14,000 acres of it by 1910, and the total by 1916.

she commented in her diary, "Frank is puzzled to know what to do with the property."[49] She might have written this succinct summary of her husband's quandary at any time during the next twenty-five years.

Occasionally, as at the close of 1908, when he received $2,600 for his share of the sale price of cattle on the ranch, he felt much encouraged. But he preferred crops to Texas steers, and, although he believed that water underlay some of the property at no great depth, he declined to incur the expense of making it available unless he were first shown that grain could be grown there. Below-average rainfall in 1909 nourished his caution and warned him to be less hasty in developing the land than he had been in acquiring it. He foresaw, however, a bright future for the holding, even though he neglected it completely for a decade or more. The population of the Panhandle and the annual demand of city meat packers for beef cattle were bound to grow. Under these circumstances and without any effort on his part, the value of his property should rise. In the meantime he could lease grazing rights to a portion of it for more than enough to pay the taxes and use some of the reserved acreage as plots to experiment with various grasses and grains.[50] If an attractive offer to purchase came his way, he would gladly accept it.

In 1918, when Dalhart realtors told him that $12 an acre was the most he could expect, he replied that $15 was the least he would take. To sell at their figure would have netted him a $50,000 profit, but he trusted that another ten years' wait would bring him twice as much. In his more optimistic moments he wrote of the gas and oil that might lurk beneath the mesquite and of the possibility of growing cotton there. The fall in beef prices at the close of World War I put his grass-lease tenant "in a hard hole," but Lowden then estimated that his ranch was worth at least $20 an acre. In 1929, after an absence of eighteen years, he took another look at the property and came away more sanguine than ever before.[51] But the onset of the general economic depression quickly blasted his optimism and forced him to supplement his much reduced income by unloading unprofitable investments for whatever cash they would bring. Under these circumstances in April, 1933, he sold the ranch for about $47,000, or less than one-third its original cost.[52]

Complex incentives spurred Lowden in his pursuit of land. His love of good soil and the open countryside, his faith in the bright future of the American farmer, and his conviction that the producer of food and fiber rendered a patriotic service have already been mentioned.[53] Dr. Cyril G. Hopkins, distinguished soil conservationist of the University of Illinois, was,

49. Mrs. Lowden's diary, Sept. 21–27, 1908.

50. The taxes were less than $450 a year. FOL leased grazing rights in 1910 for $1,000 a year; in 1916 to a much larger acreage for $1,300 for six months; in 1919 for $7,000 a year; and in 1921 for $5,225. D. C. Reynolds of Dalhart was the lessee.

51. Mrs. Lowden's diary, Sept. 30 and Oct. 4, 1929. According to the *Dalhart Texan,* Oct. 18, 1929, FOL told D. C. Reynolds, "this country has the greatest possibilities of any section of North America for power-farming."

52. Miss Nell Hanley, "Sinnissippi Farm, Inc.," to the author, July 11, 1955.

53. See pp. 72, 74, and 160–61.

in Lowden's judgment, "the most useful citizen" of his state, and his work merited "the heartiest congratulations of the country."[54] No field of study so fascinated Lowden as the application of science to agriculture in all its aspects. Soil chemistry, the development of better seeds and hybrids, the elimination of insect pests, the cure of animal and plant diseases, the discovery of more efficient systems of field drainage and cultivation, the adaptation of electricity and gasoline motor-driven implements to agricultural uses, and the drive for hard-surface roads and improved rural schools all meant better days for the farmer.[55] Lowden enjoyed reading of these developments in scientific books, in farm and livestock journals, and in the bulletins of the United States and state departments of agriculture. But, above all, he liked to experiment with a tract and thereby contribute, if possible, new ideas and methods. To do this he needed land—all sorts of it, ranch, plantation, and farm—to furnish the variety required for diverse tests under diverse conditions.

The gratification of a strong personal desire to indulge in agricultural experimentation on his own acres, with the hope that it might benefit farmers everywhere, supplied reason enough for his extensive purchases, but he anticipated financial profit as well. The agricultural hard times of the late nineteenth century had ended, land values were rising, and a growing demand for grains and livestock could be expected at rewarding prices. If agricultural tariffs warded off foreign competition and if high imposts on finished goods spurred domestic manufacturing sufficiently to enlarge the home market for all products of the soil, the farmers of America stood at the threshold of an age of prosperity, the like of which they had never known before. On a West Indian cruise with Lowden in 1912, Dr. Harry Pratt Judson expressed amusement at his friend's eagerness to own as much arable land as possible. He, in Judson's words, had

become a thorough farmer, and wherever I happen to go with him he at once begins to wonder whether he can't invest in a new farm in that part of the world. As you know, I went down to Panama with him last January. He thought seriously of buying a farm in Panama. Then he was impressed with the desirability of buying land in Cuba when we sailed by that lovely island. We crossed over Hayti, and if only life and property were safe there, he I think, would buy a plantation in Hayti.[56]

A number of Lowden's friends, including Robert D. Clarke, J. Sloat Fassett, J. Otis Humphrey, Leigh Hunt, William Lorimer, and John W. Dwight, shared his financial interest in, if not his idealism about, undeveloped lands. Clarke, a plantation owner as well as a big Peoria distiller, encouraged him to

54. FOL to Hopkins, Urbana, Illinois, Oct. 25, and Nov. 9, 1910, and Oct. 18, 1913.

55. MS of FOL's speech, Sept. 24, 1913, at Plano, Illinois, before the thirty-third annual session of the Farmers' National Congress of the United States.

56. H. P. Judson to F. L. Gates, Aug. 16, 1912; in "Presidents' Papers" (University Archives, Harper Memorial Library, University of Chicago).

make his first purchase of Arkansas real estate. Quickly becoming enthusiastic about this property, Lowden tried unsuccessfully to have Lorimer, Fassett, Hunt, Dwight, and others buy plantations near his own. For a time in 1911 he and Lorimer seemed ready to acquire together a huge tract near Belhaven on Pamlico Sound in North Carolina. Before the senator made up his mind, however, Lowden changed his own and decided to use his money to enlarge his properties in Arkansas.[57] Although he shared in some of Leigh Hunt's enterprises and bought stock in the timber land companies of Fassett and Dwight, he had less success in persuading friends to join his ventures than they had in drawing him into theirs.

Between 1909 and 1911 he traveled many miles throughout the seaboard South and the Mississippi Valley, scouting for fertile acres at bargain prices. A soil chemist usually and an oil geologist occasionally accompanied him on these expeditions. In the spring of 1911, after receiving a discouraging report from an expert whom he had engaged to look for agricultural opportunities in Florida, he toured the Mississippi delta country south of Memphis for ten days on a similar quest. As a result of this trip and an earlier one to North Carolina, he was finally convinced that, on the score of comparative costs, fertility, and all other relevant considerations, Arkansas bottom lands would best repay his attention.[58] He came to this conclusion the more readily because the productivity of the plantation he had purchased there two years before was exceeding his highest expectations.

"South Bend" plantation stretched along the Arkansas River some sixty miles below Little Rock and twelve miles from the railroad village of Varner. In the summer of 1909, when Lowden bought it for $75,000, it contained about 5,450 acres.[59] During the next five years twelve separate purchases, totaling approximately $170,000, enlarged it by over 15,000 acres. Of these, a considerable portion was pasture and virgin timberland both outside and inside the levee.[60] By 1913, on this tract lived 150 tenant families, comprising 250 adults and 204 children, and, in addition, 21 employees ranging in status from managers and assistant managers to house servants. The homes of everyone working on the plantation, except the tenant farmers, clustered about the gin building, the cotton and cottonseed storage structures, the implement and mule barns, and the large plantation store built by Lowden.

57. Mrs. Lowden's diary, Jan. 6, 8, Mar. 5–8, Apr. 15 and 17, 1911.

58. S. Everly Simonson of Luxora, Arkansas, was FOL's principal agent in the search for land. In FOL's interest he scouted in 1910 in Kansas, Nebraska, Colorado, Wyoming, Idaho, Washington, Oregon, and parts of Canada (affidavit of Simonson, made about Apr. 1, 1925).

59. Mrs. Lowden's diary, May 26–30, 1909.

60. The $170,000 did not include over $15,000 paid for the personal property on the Langdale tract. According to an auditor's sheet headed "F. O. Lowden's South Bend Investment Account, 1914," he then had $280,041.70 tied up in the property. Even though financially pinched at that time (see pp. 212 and 219, n. 74), he was seriously thinking of buying another Arkansas plantation for $70,000. Not until the close of 1915 was he satisfied that he owned enough land.

Overlooking the big bend in the river and separated from it by the levee and a "park" of lofty trees, stood the plantation house, erected in 1848 by a kinsman of Henry Clay. Leading to its front door was a long and wide flight of steps flanked by balustrades of intricate ante bellum iron work. At the top of its ascent a broad porch stretched almost across the width of the house, guarded by an ornamental wrought-iron railing and covered by a roof resting upon four tall, fluted columns in the customary southern plantation style. Opening off the big central hall, which extended from front door to back, were eight large rooms, with fireplaces in four of them. Many windows let light into the basement kitchen whose ceiling was nearly ten feet above ground level.[61]

When Lowden first became its owner, this house needed much renovation. Counseled by his wife, he supplemented its several pieces of antique mahogany furniture with additions from the attic of "Sinnissippi." By 1913 he had transformed it into a comfortable place to live during his regular visits in spring and autumn, thanks to a new furnace and electricity generator in the basement, bathrooms on the main floor, and lace curtains at the windows. He liked to relax there for a week or ten days with one or two friends who would enjoy accompanying him on horseback during his daily inspection trips over the broad acres.

Mrs. Lowden rarely joined him on these visits. Even though obligations to one or another of her family had not held her at home, she did not relish surroundings where the means of gracious living were limited, whether at her husband's "fishing camp" on the Rideau or at the much less primitive "South Bend." No one could like creature comforts and a smoothly running household more than Lowden. If there was no one to shave him, he grew a beard; if there was no one to cook for him or keep his room in order, his life became almost intolerable. But a barber, cook, and housemaid were available at "South Bend." With these, a saddle horse or two, and someone with whom to talk and play cards when he felt so inclined, he could be happy on his plantation, at least for a brief stay. Nevertheless, he exaggerated when he remarked in 1914, "I would really like to live and work there six months of every year."[62]

The usual cost of operating "South Bend" was about $50,000 a year. Even so, as long as his cotton crop of from seven hundred to a thousand bales brought from 12 to 18 cents a pound, he could net annually some $12,000–$15,000 in profits. Although this return was small in proportion to the size of his investment, it looked big when compared with his ranch and "Sinnissippi" balance sheets. Above all, however, "South Bend" offered challenging opportunities to try out crop diversification. This appealed to him the more because he believed it basic to any thoroughgoing reform of southern agriculture.

61. Katherine Watson, "Old Home at South Bend," *Little Rock* (Ark.) *Gazette,* Feb. 12, 1933. This includes a photograph of the house.
62. FOL to C. B. Landis, Wilmington, Delaware, Jan. 22, 1914.

In this work, as in the growing of cotton, he relied heavily upon the supervision of his competent, on-the-spot manager, J. D. Crockett, and the advice of S. E. Simonson of Luxora. During his many years of service, Crockett wrote to his employer every week or two about the state of affairs at "South Bend." As long as he lived, Lowden had no stauncher champion and no more indefatigable correspondent than Simonson. A native of Illinois and undeviatingly Republican in his politics, he seemingly possessed inexhaustible energy and optimism. If Lowden did not often invest in Simonson's manifold projects for making huge gains quickly in land, oil, bauxite, or cotton, he at least enjoyed hearing about them and was pleased when his friend named a son for him. Simonson's fortunes fluctuated erratically, but his high spirits never deserted him. Apparently, he could be as happy when working as a foreman in the construction of the Guntherville dam in Alabama as when pocketing large gains from the sale of Arkansas lands. In 1942, at the age of seventy, he wished to help rebuild and expand the Pearl Harbor naval base in Hawaii.

For a time after his initial purchase of "South Bend," Lowden moved cautiously because "this is absolutely a new enterprise to me."[63] But from the outset he resolved that cotton would never monopolize all his arable land. This was the more advisable because the frontiers of boll-weevil and army-worm infestation advanced ever closer to his plantation. By means of soil analyses, by corresponding with Dr. Hopkins of the University of Illinois and experts at the universities of Arkansas and Wisconsin, and by occasionally having one of these authorities or a successful Illinois farmer go with him to the plantation, he gathered much wise counsel about rotation cycles and crop diversification. He experimented with rice, corn, wheat, cowpeas, timothy, red clover, alfalfa, and lespedeza. Of these, the latter three especially pleased him by their rapid and luxuriant growth. If he was correctly informed, they never before had been sown on Arkansas River bottom lands. By 1912 he concluded that producing big cuts of alfalfa at "South Bend" was easy, but the crux of the problem, unsolved by the bulletins of the United States Department of Agriculture and state experiment stations, was how to cure the crop before the frequent summer showers and humid heat spoiled it. Raising pigs was also a simple matter, and cattle could be fattened for market more economically on his plantation than at "Sinnissippi."[64] In 1914, of the 4,650 acres directly under Crockett's supervision, exclusive of the tenants' holdings, 700 were devoted to alfalfa, lespedeza, and cowpeas; 800 to pasture; 900 to corn; 350 to rice; and 1,900 to cotton.[65]

63. FOL to S. E. Simonson, Feb. 21, 1910.

64. Raising cattle at "South Bend" required 9½ miles of fence.

65. FOL systematized his seeding so as to have one-half of his arable land in cotton each year and the balance in corn, alfalfa, lespedeza, and cowpeas. He directed Crockett to plant four acres of corn for each mule and horse. He must not seed the corn on poor land but on fields which had been sown to cowpeas the year before. At least two or three hundred acres, needing restoration, should be annually devoted to lespedeza.

Inexperienced in plantation economy and living far away from "South Bend," Lowden had to rely heavily upon Crockett's honesty and efficiency. During the course of a year he occasionally advanced as much as $75,000 before the crops were sold. He treated his manager generously and was repaid by devoted service. Besides providing Crockett with a rent-free new house, he paid him in 1913, for example, a salary of $2,400 and 25 per cent of the net profits. Before arriving at the latter, Lowden deducted from the gross income $15,000 land rent and 6 per cent interest on all money which he had advanced for plantation use, including the cost of the goods sold at the store.[66]

With this concentration of responsibility went a concentration of power. Whenever Lowden sent a farmer to experiment at "South Bend" with a northern crop under plantation conditions, he let Crockett know that his authority controlled the newcomer. Although, by 1915, Lowden wondered whether he might not be foisting too much work upon his accommodating manager, he did nothing to lighten it. "I've had a feeling for some time," he wrote, "that I was loading Crockett up with more than he can carry—a common failing of mine. I will study the situation and suggest changes in organization that will relieve him."[67] By then their business association had ripened into a friendship. When Crockett confessed to his employer, "Owing to . . . the Dry Condinition [*sic*] of the State I have used the little store of the Col's boose [*sic*] and now appeal to you to replenish the stock before you make another visit," Lowden replied, "I will certainly order the whiskey and wine and some ale, as I think you are entitled to all the liquid stuff you had on the place."[68] Although Lowden kept a small stock of liquor at "South Bend" for his own use, he was glad when prohibition came to Arkansas because he deplored drinking by his tenants. In order to hold his labor force, he had been obliged to follow the custom of the country and sell intoxicants as well as groceries, tobacco, clothing, and tools at the plantation store.

From Crockett's reports, Lowden knew his tenants only "as so many Negro families" rather than as individuals. They worked their holdings under contracts which were neither better nor worse than on other plantations,[69] but their living conditions and their chances of making a good crop exceeded the average. Many of the cabins at "South Bend" were new. Its store was unusually large and well stocked, although this may have tempted the tenants to overbuy and go into debt. Lowden's insistence upon rotation and cover crops in order to maintain soil fertility probably worked to their advantage.

66. FOL to J. D. Crockett, May 3, 1913.

67. FOL to Mrs. Lowden, Oct. 17, 1915.

68. J. D. Crockett to FOL, Feb. 13, and FOL's reply, Feb. 16, 1916.

69. In a letter to A. Gray, Evansville, Indiana, July 5, 1912, FOL wrote: "The present method of either renting land to tenants or receiving a share of their crops, is very demoralizing. In good years it frequently happens that the tenant receives compensation out of all proportion to his efforts; this is followed by extravagance and riotous living, and very little, if anything, of the large returns to the tenant is saved for a possible lean year."

Thus in 1917, at his suggestion, each tenant planted half his acreage in cow-peas and received an equivalent amount of cotton land elsewhere. During the following year he seeded the other half with the same legume. Under this system Lowden hoped that, by the third season, the tenants' cotton yield would double.[70]

In 1912, when boll weevils threatened to make serious inroads at "South Bend," he offered a cash bonus to his tenants for an extra-hard assault upon the pest. During July he authorized Crockett to pay each child 5 cents for every two weevils he destroyed and 1 cent for every weevil-punctured boll which he picked. Hearing that twins had been born to one of the few white families on "South Bend," Lowden sent "a porringer and spoon and plate for little William, and a cup and spoon for little George." "These are the only white children born on the place so far as I know since I owned it," he continued, "and I wish to commemorate the fact in this way."[71] Based upon an admittedly limited observation of the labor force on southern plantations other than his own, he believed that Negro tenants were usually treated with "much kindness and fairness." In his opinion, Booker T. Washington understood how to unlock the door of opportunity for his people. He wrote in 1914: "I am more and more persuaded that Washington's industrial education . . . is doing more toward the solution of the race problem than any other force . . . I know. The small negro farmer of the south has as good an opportunity as the poor white man of the north, and is really making progress."[72]

The outbreak of World War I that year and the momentary sharp decline in cotton prices led Lowden to store most of his pick in a Pine Bluff warehouse. Hoping that the cotton market would revive in "a year or two," he directed Crockett for 1915 "to put every available acre in corn, alfalfa, lespedeza, oats, rye or even pasture. We can not hope to make much on cotton . . . so let's restore the land with legumes, and experiment a little with wheat."[73] The price of medium-grade short-staple cotton had sagged to $10\frac{1}{2}$–$12\frac{1}{2}$ cents a pound in late 1913 and was still lower the next year. Unlike Lowden, his tenant farmers needed to turn their bales into cash at once. For this reason he paid them $12\frac{1}{2}$ cents a pound and 50 cents a bale to haul it to Pine Bluff for storage in his name.[74] A glutted market, more than the usual

70. FOL to J. D. Crockett, Dec. 4, 1916. In this letter he told Crockett to pay each assistant manager a premium of 10 cents a bushel for all corn in excess of an average of 20 per acre, and a premium of $5.00 a bale when more than 200 pounds of lint cotton per acre were picked.

71. FOL to B. A. Stone, "South Bend," May 17, 1914.

72. FOL to Professor T. H. Macbride, Iowa City, Iowa, Jan. 19, 1914.

73. FOL to J. D. Crockett, Oct. 22, 1914.

74. FOL to J. W. Dwight, Sept. 30, 1914: "Poor South! Just as it had begun to emerge from the ravages of our own war, it is plunged into gloom by this one. A week before the war I thought we would have a cotton crop this year which would sell for from $125,000 to $150,000. Now I don't know that I shall be able to sell it at all. In the meantime we have got to take care of our negroes. . . . The situation is anything but comfortable."

loss to insects, and considerable damage from spring floods and seepage made the next two years lean ones also. Thanks to an excellent cotton crop and rising prices, Lowden offset these losses by pocketing a huge profit in 1916. From then until the end of the war "South Bend" enjoyed great prosperity.

Mrs. Lowden came to share her husband's faith in the rich agricultural future of eastern Arkansas. In 1911 she purchased nearly ten thousand acres of timbered and cutover land on the St. Francis River near Luxora in the northeastern corner of the state.[75] This stump- and brush-covered expanse, swarming with mosquitoes and threatening malaria to any trespasser, eventually was named "Florenden." It offered Lowden the kind of challenge he had been looking for—to make a plantation where none had been before. "I do not expect any substantial returns for five years," he told Sloat Fassett:

> I do expect to have the star plantation of the South when I get through with it. There are no bayous through the tract and every foot of it can be put under cultivation as soon as it is drained, and a drainage district has recently been established there that will begin operations very shortly. I have never developed, agriculturally, a virgin tract of land, but I know I can avoid a lot of mistakes which have been made in the development of all the plantations I have seen. In the first place none of the old plantations have had the slightest respect for a right angle, and right angles and land in square or rectangular form mean economical agriculture. . . . Mississippi County is developing very rapidly and will be one of the show spots of the continent, I have no doubt.[76]

By a "star plantation" he meant one of fertile soil, so well drained and cultivated, and, above all, so expertly managed that it would produce four hundred pounds of short-staple cotton to the acre rather than the more usual yield of about two hundred and fifty. "It is possible," he wrote, "to develop managerial competency [in agriculture] just as railroads and great industrial organizations have done . . . but . . . [it] . . . will be rather tardy."[77]

Lowden's ambitious plans for "Florenden" matured more slowly than he had anticipated. He built a barn, sawmill, and about twenty cabins for Negroes and assembled mules, horses, machinery, and tenants, but the drainage work lagged.[78] As a result, he had to use his labor force for wood-cutting and brush-burning rather than for farming. When the account sheets of late 1912 told a story of inefficient management and considerable wasted money, he suspended most of the operations and transferred many animals and much

75. The price was between $200,000 and $210,000. FOL believed that it was a bargain because the neighborhood had not been "invaded" by many northerners; hence land prices were still low.

76. FOL to J. S. Fassett, May 19, 1911.

77. FOL to A. Gray, Evansville, Indiana, July 5, 1912. In a letter of Apr. 18, 1914, FOL congratulated J. D. Crockett for averaging three-fourths of a bale per acre at "South Bend" in 1913. This would be about 375 pounds.

78. *Little Rock Gazette,* Mar. 26, 1926, noted that the tenants' houses at "Florenden" were in straight lines, one-half mile apart, with double and single units alternating. Thus each family lived in the center of its own cotton patch and "not too close to the store."

equipment to "South Bend." About a year later, on her first visit to her property, Mrs. Lowden was impressed by the fine timber and the cotton growing among the stumps.[79] A few months later the work of dredging and draining began in earnest, and conditions at "Florenden" improved rapidly.

On Crockett's recommendation, Lowden named J. D. Hightower to be its manager and never had cause to regret his choice. At the outset, Hightower could do little except plant corn, raise pigs, and keep the sawmill busy, but by the fall of 1915 he had nearly five hundred acres under crop, including one hundred in cotton, twenty in alfalfa, two hundred in corn, and some in sorghum and cowpeas. A barn for fifty mules had been completed, his own two-story house was nearly ready for occupancy, and work on the big gin was about to start. "All this interesting and desirable transformation," reported the *Osceola* (Ark.) *Times,* "is taking place in what has always until lately been regarded as an almost hopeless wilderness and swamp. Mississippi County is certainly fortunate in having Mr. Lowden interested so fully in her great development problems." Delighted with Hightower's progress, Lowden reassured his wife that "in a few years Florenden will be the most wonderful farm I know anything of."[80] Thereafter, the plantation came rapidly under crop just in time for its heavy yield of cotton to catch the high prices of the war years.

79. Mrs. Lowden's diary, Oct. 7–Nov. 4, 1913.

80. *Osceola Times,* Oct. 15, 1915; FOL to Mrs. Lowden, Oct. 13, 1915.

CHAPTER X

THE "SQUIRE OF SINNISSIPPI"

When Lowden was in Arkansas under the spell of "South Bend" and "Florenden," he sometimes described them in terms so glowing that they seemed to eclipse "Sinnissippi" in his affection. When on his Rock River farm, however, or after a few weeks away from it, he knew there could be no other spot on the globe where he would be so happy. It called forth a continuing depth of feeling which his plantations only occasionally aroused, even though a long spell of rainy or humid weather at the farm or anywhere else made him irritable, taciturn, and eager to leave.[1] To his great satisfaction, by the time of his retirement from Congress and always thereafter, friends and representatives of the press linked his name inseparably with "Sinnissippi."

Its transformation from one of the homes of the Lowdens into *the* home, with all the sentimental overtones connoted by that word, had taken place rapidly. The Chicago residence, once the source of so much pride, became little more than a cumbersome property to be sold, even at a considerable financial sacrifice, if necessary.[2] Although strong Pullman ties drew Mrs. Lowden to "Castle Rest," she viewed it mainly as a family rendezvous, beginning usually in late July and lasting at least until the traditional tree-planting ceremony in mid-August.[3] Nor did she or her husband desire to build or buy a house in Washington. Christmas without the hearth fire at "Sinnissippi" was almost unthinkable. Spring in Washington was often pleasant but could not compare in its beauty with the same season at the farm. "What a joy it would be to us," wrote Lowden in April, 1908, "if we could be at home and witness the new birth of flowers and foliage on the Rock River."[4] From then until October its blossom-studded meadows and woods harbored many varieties of birds. Bass and pickerel waited to be caught in the river at the rim of the front lawn. There were wild raspberries, strawberries, and blackberries for the gathering in the summer, and hickory nuts,

1. For example, Mrs. Lowden's diary, June 5 and Oct. 16, 1911, and Dec. 18, 1912.

2. FOL to C. M. Dawes, Chicago, Nov. 21, 1906: "I never expect to live in Chicago again." See p. 192, n. 62.

3. "Memorial Day" at "Castle Rest" was Aug. 14. During the Pullman reunion on that day the family history for the year was read, a tree was planted, and one of the children put a ring on it bearing the date.

4. FOL to R. S. Farrand, Freeport, Illinois, Apr. 9, 1908.

hazel nuts, and black walnuts in the autumn. The fall coloring of the hardwoods, interspersed with evergreens, was breath-taking in its beauty. Even before 1915, when the property became a state game preserve, it gave shelter to quail, pheasants, squirrels, rabbits, deer, and occasionally an unwanted wolf. By 1911, a road led through the timber along much of the river frontage, while other lanes circled up the hills or followed the edges of the fields. Although these were essential to the operation of the farm, they often had an aesthetic justification as well. Along their route in the woods, openings were cut to disclose the more attractive vistas. From the pergola atop Wolf Hill, the highest point in the entire neighborhood, Mr. and Mrs. Lowden often enjoyed the wide sweep of countryside or the colors of a sunset.[5]

The children shared their parents' enthusiasm for "Sinnissippi." With their nurses and tutor, with the youngsters of the farm families for playmates, and ponies, dogs, rabbits, croquet, tennis, and much else besides, their life seemed idyllic. In 1909 the parents provided a commodious playhouse, its walls gay with fairy-tale scenes and its furniture scaled down to appropriate size. There the young people served tea to their elders and romped when it rained. By then, in addition to the weekly Sunday school and the family birthday parties, the children looked forward to a regular series of red-letter days. When the lilac bloom along the river signified that spring was at high tide, they crowned one of their number as queen and danced around a maypole. On Memorial Day they helped decorate the graves in the Daysville cemetery. Two weeks later on Flag Day, they dressed in costumes reminiscent of America's past and marched up Flagpole Hill to the base of the staff. Lowden sometimes accompanied them and talked about love of country and the meaning of the Stars and Stripes. The Fourth of July was always memorable. Besides entertaining some celebrity whom he had persuaded to deliver an oration in the courthouse square in Oregon, he arranged for a parade and picnic, abundant food and fireworks, and races both serious and humorous in which the members of the farm families competed for the "Squire's" gold pieces.

As a part of the Christmas festivities after the children reached their teens, Coachman William Hewitt occasionally staged a barn dance in the big carriage house. On Christmas morning the family gathered in the library to open their presents. Lowden allowed his packages to accumulate until the last, enjoying the pleasure which his gifts brought to his wife and children, but always finding it hard to express his own thanks gracefully and without self-consciousness. In the afternoon, fifty or seventy-five of the farm folk assembled at the "big house." Carols were sung, recitations given, a magician from Chicago astounded the children, and a Santa Claus distributed toys, fruit, and sweets. Much of all this was English country living with an American flavor.

The Lowdens first occupied their "big house" in September, 1906. Several

5. The pergola was built in 1911 and replaced by a larger one in 1935.

years earlier they had enlarged its predecessor, the Hemenway homestead, to the limit permitted by its old foundations but still found it too small for their needs. Unwilling to give up the wide vista of river and farm lands afforded by its front windows, they had no choice but to tear it down and erect a larger dwelling on the same site. This Tudor-style residence cost nearly $100,000. Its twenty rooms, supplemented by a guest house constructed several years before, assured the hospitality of "Sinnissippi" to their many friends during the years ahead.[6]

In its large, walnut-paneled library Lowden shelved his several thousand volumes and catalogued them on Library of Congress index cards. For light reading he liked, above all, certain nineteenth-century novels such as Thackeray's *Henry Esmond* and the Waverley cycle of Scott. But he also pored over many weighty volumes with pencil in hand, underlining a sentence here and there, and sometimes adding his own comments in the margins. Besides treatises on farming, he greatly enjoyed biographies of statesmen and studies of American history and government. Not a little impressed by the weight of his own reputation, he liked to compare his qualities of distinction with those of past worthies. He subscribed for most of the scholarly periodicals in the field of the social sciences and was a patron of the Mississippi Valley Historical Association and Illinois State Historical Society.[7] Collecting volumes on Lincoln and the early history of Illinois remained one of his hobbies. Any living author whose works appealed to him could count upon receiving his note of comment and congratulation.[8]

At his expense, markers appeared along the route followed by Lincoln from Beardstown to the Rock River on his way to the Black Hawk War. Lowden read all he could find about Black Hawk and was proud to preside on a very hot July day in 1911 at the unveiling of Lorado Taft's monumental statue in the warrior's honor on a hill near Oregon.[9] As an expression of

6. In 1903, FOL bought 320 acres across the river from his residence, largely in order to protect its outlook. Probably the best description of the house, including floor plans and a dozen photographs, is by William Herbert in the *Architectural Record* (New York), XXII (October, 1907), 299–310. Herbert was especially impressed by "a certain rhythm to its irregularity" of design, its "sturdy simplicity of treatment," its "convenient and compact" arrangement, the way in which the big upstairs and downstairs halls served as a "clearing house" for all rooms except the appropriately isolated library, and the skilful utilization of the outside angles for porches. See also Wilhelm Miller, "A New Kind of Western Home," *Country Life in America* (Garden City, N.Y.), XXIII (April, 1913), 39–42. This house was razed in 1949.

7. He was one of the original guarantors of the *Mississippi Valley Historical Review* and a member of the Lincoln Centennial Association. Among the journals which he read as well as accumulated were the *Political Science Quarterly*, the *American Political Science Review*, the *American Economic Review*, the *Illinois Law Review*, and the *Annals of the American Academy of Political and Social Science*.

8. FOL liked to correspond with other Lincoln students, including William Meese of Moline, Illinois, and Clark E. Carr of Galesburg, Illinois.

9. *Springfield* (Ill.) *News,* May 14, 1909. The markers were put up under the aegis of the Illinois State Historical Society. At the unveiling of the statue on July 1, 1911, Edgar Bancroft gave the principal address, Taft spoke briefly, and Hamlin Garland and Mrs. Elia Peattie read poems. To have the statue was Taft's own idea, and he did the work without charge. FOL and Wallace Heckman shared the expense of getting it into place.

friendship for Taft and his art-loving associates in their "Eagle's Nest" colony, he paid most of the cost of an illustrated pamphlet of one hundred pages telling about the Indian, the statue, its unveiling, and its sculptor. The spell cast by the chieftain remained potent in the Rock River Valley. Local poets celebrated his fame, while a Boy Scout troop, a woodland trail, and a highway took his name.[10] Lowden's eldest daughter, Florence, greatly pleased him on Christmas in 1915 by reciting her own verses in praise of the talented red man whose tribe once claimed the land of "Sinnissippi."[11] Charles Francis Browne, a well-known Chicago artist who summered at "Eagle's Nest," painted a frieze of Rock River vistas in the library of the "big house" and provided landscapes of the farm in oils. Ralph M. Pearson, another member of the artists' colony, used a gnarled old white pine, growing from a rock near the house, as his inspiration for Lowden's bookplate.

Before the close of his years in Congress, Lowden convinced most of his neighbors of his genuine concern for the welfare of the Rock River Valley and his determination to live there the rest of his days. Sarcastically humorous jabs at "Farmer" Lowden appeared less frequently in the rural press. In their stead were friendly references to "the Squire" and to "the gracious lady" or "Lady Bountiful" who was his wife. The dirt farmers of the area never wholly accepted him as one of themselves, but they recognized the sincerity of his interest in agriculture and came more often to "Sinnissippi" to admire than to scoff. Week-end sightseers in the summer increased to the point where Lowden's eldest daughter in 1917 found the size of the crowd "perfectly appalling. I don't see how to lessen the number except to lock the farm gate. They trample the grass and sometimes even ask if they can eat lunch on the porch. Can you beat it?"[12]

The agricultural organizations in the vicinity of "Sinnissippi," such as the Ogle County and Lee County farmers' institutes, the Ogle County Soil Improvement Association, and the Rochelle and Polo poultry clubs, drew Lowden's support. Each year he donated prizes and paid the expenses of an Ogle County boy and girl while they attended the short course in agriculture or domestic science at the University of Illinois. In Oregon he provided medals for the winners of the high-school oratorical contest, as well as scarf pins for the boys and brooches for the girls when they graduated in June. He contributed liberally to the town's public library and its annual Chautauqua and harvest festival and bought the instruments for its cornet band.

In 1913 Mrs. Lowden erected two buildings and laid out a well-equipped playground on a ten-acre tract of high ground along the Rock River at Daysville, adjoining "Sinnissippi." To "Hilltop," as this project was known, were brought every summer a few underprivileged children, either crippled

10. For several years FOL was president of the Black Hawk Trail Improvement Association.

11. To his daughter's embarrassment, FOL released her poem to the press (*Centralia* [Ill.] *Review,* Dec. 31, 1915; *Cairo* [Ill.] *Herald,* Jan. 1, 1916).

12. Florence Lowden to FOL, July 8, 1917.

or recuperating from illnesses.[13] The staff of this convalescent home comprised two trained nurses, a kindergarten teacher, a cook, a houseman, and a handyman. With the advice of the social service departments of several Chicago hospitals and the Visiting Nurses Association, youngsters from six to twelve years of age were selected for a stay of at least two weeks. They came in groups of twelve or fifteen, alternating between girls and boys.[14]

Soon after settling in the Rock River Valley, Lowden became a leader of the movement for good roads. Although he built nine miles of them at "Sinnissippi," he discovered later that the increasing automobile traffic wore them out quickly. Following the National Good Roads Convention of 1903 in Chicago, attended by delegates from thirty states, he served on a committee which sought $20,000,000 from Congress for highway construction. In so far as the national government was concerned, this effort was premature. He thereupon asked for financial aid from the local authorities "to pull his county and township out of the mud."[15] Constitutional as well as fiscal issues complicated the problem. "The subject of good roads in Illinois," he wrote in 1905, "is one of the most important and, at the same time, one of the most delicate questions before us. What might be a fine scheme for Massachusetts or New Jersey might be impracticable and inequitable here."[16] The next year he warmly congratulated Governor Deneen for pushing good-roads legislation through the Assembly. This law guaranteed instruction and materials at state expense to any township willing to pay the labor and other costs of improving its turnpikes.[17] If the state highway commission would send a representative to tell him how, Lowden offered in 1907 to build a mile of "model road" as a salutary lesson for his neighbors. He fulfilled this promise two years later, but he found the Nashua Township folk far more inclined to praise his generosity than to approve of higher taxes for a continuation of the good work.[18]

Mrs. Lowden had to wait until 1913 before she could note happily in her diary, "The road improvement election went our way, 84–14." Even this victory did not assure sufficient funds to lay down much "bituminous macadam" at $6,700 a mile. After long hesitation the Oregon Township fathers agreed to construct a pike twelve feet wide toward "Sinnissippi" to the limit of their jurisdiction. On the eve of an April day in 1914 dedicated to the cause of better highways, Lowden spoke at a rally in the courthouse. The next day townsmen and farmers toiled on the roadbed in holiday spirit from

13. Entry of May, 1913, in "Real Estate Record: Frank O. Lowden," a book in "Sinnissippi" farm office; Mrs. Lowden's diary, Oct. 12, 1913.

14. Anonymous, undated document, probably written in 1916, entitled "Hilltop: The Lowden Country Home for Convalescent Children."

15. FOL's wire and letter to A. N. Johnson, Springfield, Illinois, Apr. 1, 1907, and his letter to C. Bemis, Oregon, Illinois, Apr. 9, 1907.

16. FOL to R. N. Crawford, Mendota, Illinois, Apr. 29, 1905.

17. FOL to Gov. C. Deneen, Dec. 29, 1906. FOL overpraised the governor for "starting this most desirable movement." Its origins dated back to the 1890's.

18. FOL's "model road" was 5,346 feet long and cost $5,544.

sunup until dusk. "We sent them a huge milk can full of coffee for their dinner," Mrs. Lowden recorded, "and Frank was out with them for awhile shoveling gravel!"[19] Of much more practical assistance than his labor, however, was his gift of a little over two miles of hard-surface road, including two small bridges, from "Sinnissippi's" gate to the junction of the three miles of new highway coming out of Oregon.[20] When these twin projects were completed in October, three hundred people gathered in the "Daysville Pasture" of "Sinnissippi" to express their appreciation to the "Squire" and listen to informal talks about all-weather highways. However useful all this had been in arousing local enthusiasm, it could not often be repeated. The general problem remained wholly unsolved.[21]

Between 1900 and 1919 "Sinnissippi" grew from less than six hundred to about forty-four hundred acres. "Any time I get a little money," Lowden remarked to Frederick Landis in 1907, "I buy a farm adjoining mine somewhere and turn myself loose upon it." The expansion comprised some three-dozen purchases of contiguous land, costing about $265,000 in all.[22] Considerably less than half was arable and not much of that was unusually fertile. Hundreds of acres were in meadows or pasture infested with hazel brush, a timbered fringe of river bank three or four miles long, several small wooded islands, and hills covered with hardwoods. The thin soil of the slopes, as well as of many level stretches, invited grazing or silviculture rather than agriculture.[23] Outcroppings of rock here and there along the river rose high enough to be called bluffs.

Shortly after acquiring the original property, Lowden began to supplement its extensive stands of timber with plantings of evergreens. Although he hoped to demonstrate in the distant future that Illinois farmers could profitably harvest merchantable lumber annually, his initial purpose was to increase the beauty of "Sinnissippi" and experiment with conifers on sandy soil and steeply pitched hillsides unfit for cultivation.[24] He also wished to

19. Diary, Apr. 15, 1914.

20. FOL's road was finished on Aug. 27, 1914. It is described in *Illinois Highways* (official publication of Illinois State Highway Department, Springfield), II, No. 11 (December, 1915), 170–71.

21. Mrs. Lowden's diary, Oct. 9, 1914, and Oct. 1, 1915. With FOL's encouragement, an Ogle County Good Roads Association was formed in 1915.

22. FOL to F. Landis, Logansport, Indiana, Mar. 30, 1907; "Real Estate Record: Frank O. Lowden." Including the original purchase of 576 acres for $27,500, the average cost per acre was about $63.60. All but about 700 acres of the total was acquired before 1908. After 1919, when 239 acres were added, no more was bought except about 7 acres in 1943. The 4,400 acres do not include 28 lots and 5 blocks in the village of Daysville, near the farm. Taxes, real and personal, on "Sinnissippi" in 1916 were $3,811.42.

23. In a letter of July 9, 1914, to A. G. Smith, Elm Grove, West Virginia, FOL stated that he had 1,250 acres of arable land, not counting several hundred acres of blue-grass pasture.

24. H. T. Morgan, MS, "Practical Reforestation on a Corn Belt Farm," July 20, 1916. Here FOL was quoted as saying that the cost of planting pines was $8.00–$10.00 an acre; that in 15 years they would be 15–17 feet tall and 10 years later would produce 10,000 board feet an acre and 10 years after that, 30,000. This harvest forecast was overly optimistic.

give evidence of his sincerity when urging reforestation in Cook and Ogle counties and elsewhere in Illinois. He resolved to prove to his own and his neighbors' satisfaction that tree planting retarded erosion and gullying, so bothersome and costly to farmers with tilted land. Evergreens were scarce in northern Illinois, but he believed they would thrive there as well as deciduous trees. During the rest of his life he urged the state legislature to encourage silviculture by tax-exempting land newly devoted to trees.

Between 1902 and 1910, beginning on Flag Pole Hill near the farmhouse and continuing from there to other partially timbered hills or brush-covered fields, he planted nearly 130,000 seedlings. Over 70 per cent of these were white pines, with larch, spruce, firs, and red, Scotch, Austrian, and mountain pines making up the balance.[25] Finding many of these trees growing well in 1910, he thereafter increased the yearly planting to over 50,000. Hardwoods and young evergreens soon covered about one-third of the entire estate. Before long his oldest seedlings required transplanting, and this work, in turn, necessitated a thinning-out of the hardwoods. As a result, he had much lumber and firewood to sell. All this activity and the need to protect his pines against saw flies and blister rust started Lowden upon his long search for a competent forester. Thus what had begun as an interesting experiment became by World War I an important aspect of "Sinnissippi's" business life. But the Lowdens derived much pleasure from driving through their evergreens in early autumn and noting the lighter-green needles marking the amount of the year's growth. By 1917 they could walk erect beneath the pines on Flag Pole Hill, although fifteen years earlier they had been scarcely a foot in height.

Soon after being dubbed the "Squire of Sinnissippi," Lowden recognized that this gratifying title carried with it a considerable responsibility. To be identified so closely with his farm meant that he could not afford to have it fail.[26] "Sinnissippi" must become more than a place of quiet beauty where well-groomed flower beds, lawns, cattle, and up-to-date equipment elicited "Oh's" and "Ah's" from the sightseers. It must also be a model of scientific agriculture and, if possible, a profitable enterprise bearing witness to the practicability of whatever its owner advocated about farming. The complexity of its operation as a business naturally increased as its size grew. Except by occasional semihumorous remarks in his political speeches, he never pretended to do the manual labor expected of a farmer, but he wanted his hearers to know that he was not merely a city man living in the country. By trying his best to make his property a "going concern" financially, by experimenting with field crops, stock-breeding, and forestry, and by applying methods of business efficiency to problems of farm management, he set out to show that he was indeed a practical husbandman.

25. J. Roy West, Chicago, to FOL, June 24, 1910, with sheet inclosed itemizing the varieties planted each April from 1902 through 1910; also the 1906 list entitled "List of Trees, Shrubs and Ornamental Plants on Sinnissippi Farm." This included about 60 varieties of deciduous trees, 12 varieties of evergreens, 62 of shrubs, and 25 of other hardy plants.

26. FOL to Mrs. Lowden, Sept. 26, 1904.

In searching for the secrets of successful agriculture and trying to list them in the order of their importance, his superlatives occasionally canceled one another out, depending upon the particular issue holding his attention at the moment of writing or speaking. Sometimes the "key" was soil conservation through the use of a rotation system, appropriate fertilizers, and cover crops; sometimes it was skilful cultivation and field drainage; and often it meant "wise management."[27] This term, as used by Lowden, frequently embraced all his other recommendations. He hoped to run his farm with the same degree of efficiency that an industrialist insisted upon in the operation of his factory. Whether a farmer realized it or not, he was a capitalist and therefore should not expect a profit unless he had a thorough knowledge of his resources. Among the most important of these was the fertility of his soil, a prime asset to be gauged at the outset by soil analyses and then husbanded or restored. Whatever printed materials recorded the field or laboratory experiences of hardheaded experts, rather than the musings of theorists, should be a much-studied part of every farmer's library. For his benefit departments of agriculture and experiment stations had been created, and he should gratefully welcome, rather than cynically spurn, their services.[28] If he was an up-and-coming farmer, he would visit the property of men who had succeeded in doing what he aimed also to do. For his own good and that of his fellows, he should always experiment with a few of his acres or animals. If the results of these tests seemed important as either a success or a failure, he ought to let his state experiment station or an agricultural editor know about them.

Lowden stressed careful bookkeeping as an important aspect of wise management. Ideally at least, the ledgers would let a farmer know at the end of his fiscal year which crop, animal, and implement had been remunerative and which should be abandoned or sold. Lacking this information, he could not rationally plan his next season's operations, and luck alone would determine whether he made a decent livelihood and a fair return upon his investment. Although the vagaries of weather and prices, insects in the grain, or illness in the herd often vitiated the most thoroughgoing financial planning, they must not discourage farmers from seeking, in so far as possible, to replace guesswork by tested data about what he could and could not do with a reasonable expectation of profit. Furthermore, various kinds of insurance would protect him against the costly disasters which no amount of prudent foresight could prevent.

In 1904, at Lowden's request, Walter Burroughs of the George M. Pull-

27. On Nov. 21, 1910, Dr. C. G. Hopkins, of the University of Illinois Agricultural Experiment Station, recommended to FOL for his bottom lands a rotation cycle of peas, sweet corn, small grains, and fallow. "I should like especially to see you produce the great staple farm crops of the country, and to demonstrate upon a large farm that you can sell wheat and maintain the fertility of the soil without purchasing manure or feed produced on other farms."

28. In 1913, when Dr. C. G. Hopkins published his *The Farm That Won't Wear Out* (Champaign, Ill.), FOL distributed a dozen copies to his superintendent and tenant farmers. Whether they ever read it is not revealed by the evidence.

man Estate recommended a bookkeeping system for "Sinnissippi." During the next several years, he audited the farm accounts every month and made a more elaborate check after the annual inventory in February. Neither his experience nor Lowden's reading and thought produced a wholly satisfactory method of recording the daily financial life of a large property devoted to diversified agriculture. No method was practicable if it had to be so intricate and time-consuming that the ordinary farmer, unable to hire a bookkeeper, would lose patience with it from the start.

Reducing life at "Sinnissippi" to figures on financial balance sheets necessitated the omission of many real but intangible assets. To the Lowdens it meant a more pleasant home, greater happiness, and perhaps better health than they would have had in Chicago. Unlike recreation in that city, much of theirs when at the farm was without obvious financial cost. Furthermore, they sometimes declined to give up the comforts of "Sinnissippi" for the sake of an expensive excursion to the mountains, seashore, or abroad. Lowden's farm office served as the center from which he managed all his business and political affairs, not merely his Rock River property.[29] As long as he stayed in public life and sought the favor of rural voters, "Sinnissippi" had great political value, but he could not equate it in dollars and cents.

Under these circumstances his only recourse in bookkeeping was to exclude from considerations of profit and loss a "Park Department," made up of the residence and its surrounding grounds, the gardens and orchard, the guesthouse, the children's playhouse, the cottages of the household staff, the laundry building, and the coach barn. When this department needed milk, eggs, firewood, black earth, labor, or anything else available on the rest of the property, its fair market value was credited on the books of the supplying department. Some account was kept of what the "Park" cost each year, but very little of its outgo affected the figures representing the operation of the farm as a business. Thus, when newspaper editors frequently commented to the effect that "we would much rather have in our pocket what Lowden puts into his farm than what he gets out of it," they mainly had in mind the family's expensive style of living at "Sinnissippi," although the "Squire" gave it almost no financial weight when viewing the property as a going concern.[30]

Even after solving the Park Department's bookkeeping problem by largely eliminating it, he ran against many other thorny questions when he tried to transmute the farm operations into columns of figures. How, for example, could the cost of labor and equipment, common to all the departments, be apportioned between them with even approximate accuracy? What was a fair scale of annual depreciation or appreciation for the various buildings, implements, and animals? What debit should be entered for the reduced

29. FOL had a room fitted up as an office at "Sinnissippi" in 1905. In 1911 a separate office building was erected there.

30. *Ogle County* (Ill.) *Republican,* May 21, 1903; *Freeport* (Ill.) *Journal,* July 25, 1903. In an effort to counteract the widespread impression that FOL farmed extravagantly, the *Sterling* (Ill.) *Gazette* on Dec. 17, 1908, included a column entitled, "Sinnissippi Farm Is a Model of Thrift."

fertility of a field after its crop had been harvested, and what credit for the fertility added to a tract by fallowing it or plowing under its crop of legumes? Apparently these last two questions remained unanswered, but an undated memorandum in Lowden's hand, written in 1904 or 1905 and entitled "Rules for Depreciation," include these:

Cows (after 5 years old) write off in 6 years; Bulls (after decline of bulls, commencing at 4 years) 20% per annum; Harness (Life 5 years) 20% per annum; Machinery (Binders and Mowers) 6 years; Wagons 20 years—charge off 5% per annum; Horses (Life 16 years) from 6 years, 10% per annum; Calves—Price of calves born within the year, $100.00; the year before, $125.00; 2 years before, $150.00; Sheep—at what they cost, adding $1.00 per head.

This table, as well as the budget of expected income and outgo which the foreman of each department submitted for his approval at the beginning of each fiscal year, furnished him with at least a more accurate knowledge of "Sinnissippi's" business than most other farmers could exhibit about their operations.

Although these elaborate computations stemmed mainly from his conviction that a successful farmer must be a businessman, they also expressed his penchant for juggling figures and wrestling with a new problem. As will be shown later, he did not always move in the directions pointed out by his mathematics. He sometimes ruthlessly eliminated an unremunerative phase of the farm's operations, but he also continued projects of interest to him even when they stood out in red ink on his balance sheet. Whether "Sinnissippi," exclusive of its Park Department, made money between 1900 and 1917 cannot be answered with certainty. Particular departments in one year or another showed a profit on the basis of the book value of the investment, but, all in all, it seems unlikely that "Sinnissippi" was a successful business. However this may be, no other of Frank Lowden's large enterprises returned him as much satisfaction in so many ways.

The entries in his farm ledgers helped him to weigh the honesty and efficiency of his superintendent and the several department heads. He soon discovered that personal integrity was a more usual virtue than unflagging energy and managerial skill. By 1917 he ruefully concluded that the head man who perfectly fitted his prescription had not yet been born. He had searched in vain for a paragon possessed of all the moral virtues, including a willingness to work with equal zeal no matter whether his employer was looking over his shoulder or touring in Europe. Among his qualifications should also be expertness in livestock-raising, general farming, forestry, gardening, fruit-growing, and keeping accounts. Furthermore, he needed force and tact in dealing with department foremen, tenants, and hired hands; an eagerness to stay abreast of the new developments in scientific agriculture; and sufficient education to write clear and frequent reports about the farm's operations.[31]

31. In a letter of Sept. 28, 1915, to W. D. Hoard, *Hoard's Dairyman,* Fort Atkinson, Wisconsin, FOL listed what he believed to be the needed qualifications of a dairy-farm manager.

With the acreage of "Sinnissippi" multiplied by eight within a few years and the focus of its economy shifting several times during this same period, the job of managing it successfully was unusually difficult. Simultaneously, its owner's political and other business obligations expanded so rapidly that he could not concentrate for long upon its needs, even when he was at the farm. Hence he stood ready to pay a qualified superintendent liberally, although the salary between 1900 and 1917 did not rise in proportion to the growth of the estate. In 1906, for example, James B. Davidson received $100 a month, a house, fuel, milk and cream, and enough land for a garden and chicken yard. Three years later, Walter D. Mack's salary was $125 a month and similar perquisites. By 1915, however, with living and labor costs tending upward and with more tenant farmers to supervise, Delos L. James was paid $3,500 a year in addition to a house and small plot of land, rent-free. Following the appointment of each superintendent there came, characteristically, a more or less brief "honeymoon" period of complimentary exchanges between him and Lowden, succeeded by an ebbing of enthusiasm on the part of each man. Thus in 1909 Lowden wrote to Mack, the new superintendent, "You haven't any idea of what a load your management has taken off my shoulders. I never expected to see the place run so satisfactorily as it already is."[32]

After much of the land was under lease to tenants, a superintendent operated the remainder with the help of several department heads. Customarily, these numbered three—one each for the Park, Livestock, and Farm departments. Lowden prepared typed memoranda for their guidance. In "Circular No. 1" he explained in considerable detail what he meant by "full obedience to modern business and scientific methods" in "the noblest and most ancient of all industries." "Order, system and neatness," said he, comprised the prime requisites for successful management. A department chief should know at all times the whereabouts of the material under his charge "from a feather to a steam roller." Any worn-out or useless implement "must be sold if sellable"; otherwise it must be disassembled for its spare parts. To keep these from rusting, they should be sorted out, labeled, and put under cover.[33]

Although Lowden probably set his standards of performance somewhat higher than he expected his subordinates to attain, he kept tab on them as best he could. Occasionally he was up and around by seven o'clock in the morning to find out how many of them and of his tenants were already at work. He combined this supervision with exercise by riding horseback almost daily over some part of his property. Explosive in anger when he discovered laxity, he was as quick to apologize if he found out later that he had blamed the wrong person. But the turnover of foremen continued to be surprisingly large. Although Mrs. Lowden gave primary attention to the land-

32. FOL to W. D. Mack, Aug. 23, 1909.

33. FOL's letter of May 28, 1916, to D. L. James is a fair sample of his detailed instructions to the superintendent.

scaping and gardening, she also helped to ameliorate the relations between her husband and his employees. Her judgment of personnel often seemed to be more reliable than his.

In 1903 she expressed much interest in the short-lived Poultry Department of "Sinnissippi." If the *Rockford Republic* did not exaggerate, "chicken cottages" spread over nearly forty acres, including many incubators for the hatching of Plymouth Rocks, Leghorns, Wyandottes, and Pekin ducks.[34] The Lowdens counted upon finding a host of customers who would prefer to buy fowl direct from them rather than from middlemen. For economy's sake, they had the poultry crates made on the farm. Although Aaron G. Baker, the head of the department, went East to observe the methods used by profitable hatcheries on the Atlantic Coast, he failed to convince Lowden that his study had been rewarding. Worse still, he could not find enough buyers of chickens and eggs to justify his salary and the heavy outlay for up-to-date hygienic equipment. Completely disillusioned about hens and chicks by 1906, Lowden sold all of them and the attendant paraphernalia at bargain prices.[35] In his own words: "My own experience in the chicken business, in a large way, was not satisfactory. I found that the competition of a million or more housewives all over the country whose chickens simply ate what otherwise would have been wasted, and who did not figure on labor, was too much for one who had to buy feed and employ help."[36]

Meanwhile, in 1903, he had terminated his partnership in the cattle business with W. G. and Aaron Baker and had put Thomas Stanton in charge of the animals at "Sinnissippi." Although the Livestock Department usually included sixty or seventy Poland China and Berkshire hogs, about one hundred Shropshire sheep, some two dozen work horses together with a few thoroughbred Percherons, and up to five hundred Angora or "tin-can" goats assigned the job of clearing the meadows of hazel brush, it was known principally for its Shorthorns. In contrast to the poultry, Lowden's interest in these cattle remained at a high pitch for nearly ten years. Besides reading whatever he could find on their breeding and care, he visited and corresponded with Shorthorn experts, attended sales, and searched the country for champion bulls, almost regardless of their cost.[37] He made his annual sale a nationally known event in the livestock world. Few awards during his lifetime brought him greater satisfaction than the blue ribbons won by his bulls at the Inter-

34. *Rockford* (Ill.) *Republic*, May 15, 1903. Mrs. Lowden's diary for Apr. 10, 1904, mentions 5,000 brooder chicks ready for market and 200 dozen eggs to be shipped "next week." Davis, p. 52, states that the Lowdens had 25,000 chickens and shipped an average of 300 a day to Chicago buyers.

35. Mrs. Lowden's diary, Mar. 31 and Apr. 11, 1906.

36. FOL to H. B. Puterbaugh, Lanark, Illinois, Apr. 27, 1915.

37. In 1904, FOL toured livestock farms in central Illinois with Professor C. F. Curtiss, of Iowa State College. For years they visited the International Live Stock Exposition together. Alvin Sanders, editor of the *Breeder's Gazette* and FOL's close friend, wrote a volume on Shorthorns upon which FOL placed great reliance. Sanders, in turn, published illustrated articles about "Sinnissippi's" livestock.

national Live Stock Expositions at the Chicago Union Stock Yards. "Ceremonious Archer," "Cumberland's Last," and "Valiant" were among the best of their generation anywhere.[38] After extensively advertising his first annual cattle sale, Lowden held it at "Sinnissippi" in June, 1906. In spite of the rain, three or four thousand people attended, including Professor Charles F. Curtiss, director of Iowa's Agricultural Experiment Station, former Senator William A. Harris of Lawrence, Kansas, whose Shorthorns were well known among cattle men, and Alvin H. Sanders, editor of the *Breeder's Gazette*. Lowden sold forty-one head for nearly $18,000. His elation was the greater because Curtiss told reporters that "Sinnissippi" had the best herd in the United States and Harris called the farm "the most valuable experimental station in agriculture and stock raising" in the country. No wonder Lowden wrote exultingly to Laenas Weld: "This, of course, is very gratifying, and I think I now may call myself a successful farmer."[39]

Before the two auctioneers at the sale began asking for bids, he shared his views on cattle with the assembled crowd. More Mississippi Valley farmers, he said, should be breeders and feeders because soil fertility declined alarmingly when fields were overcropped with grain. The growing cities called for a larger supply of beef at the very time when the open range of the Great Plains had disappeared. Since land prices were higher in the valley than in the West, an Illinois farmer must choose his livestock with care and "push the calves to quick maturity." Furthermore, the breed should be able to yield a profit from milk as well as beef. The purebred Scotch Shorthorn filled the bill; but whatever the type of herd, the owner needed to keep a careful record of each beast and cull out mercilessly every one not paying its way. "I am aiming for a low, smooth, blocky animal," said Lowden, "possessing a good milking strain . . . by a constant process of elimination I believe I have now got so good a herd that I can not afford to use any but the best herd bulls obtainable."[40]

Mixed with his pride was a feeling of annoyance that his cattle were more productive of expense than income. Hoping to remedy this, he decided in 1907 to stage his annual sale in the Pavilion at the Chicago Stock Yards. Under careful chaperonage, sixty-two of his Shorthorns reached Chicago in a special freight train of the Burlington Railroad. On the day of the sale Judge Landis adjourned court, and Lowden's pastor, Dr. Frank Gunsaulus, deserted his study. The auction was another triumph, with the cattle bringing over $39,000.[41] Following the sale, Stanton resigned in order to manage a stock farm in Wisconsin, and the "Sinnissippi" herd was held down to fifty

38. After "Ceremonious Archer" won the grand championship in 1903, FOL bought him for $5,000 and thereafter mentioned him on "Sinnissippi's" letterhead. "Cumberland's Last," which had been the Junior Champion in 1905, cost FOL $3,000.

39. Seventy-nine-page pamphlet, *Public Sale of Sinnissippi Shorthorn Cattle, 1906;* FOL to L. Weld, Iowa City, Iowa, July 5, 1906.

40. Preface of FOL's pamphlet for his 1906 sale.

41. Mrs. Lowden's diary, June 5 and 11, 1907.

or sixty head. Its owner's long absences in Washington largely accounted for this retrenchment. Once again, he found confirmation of his view that a large farm could not operate successfully without able management. Mrs. Lowden frequently noted in her diary that many on the staff at "Sinnissippi" worked hard only when her husband was on the property.

His Shorthorns reached the peak of their reputation in 1908. One of his bulls then attained the Grand Championship and one of his heifers the Junior Championship of their breed and sex at the International Live Stock Exposition. He minimized the full measure of his gratification when he admitted that he felt a "little puffed up over these honors."[42] By that year, however, tuberculosis was rife among Illinois cattle, and he had to slaughter some of his most valuable animals. The smaller amount of pasturage on the "home farm," resulting from leasing so much acreage to tenants, also inclined him to reduce the number of his Shorthorns. However expert the new superintendent, W. D. Mack, might be in some aspects of farming, he lacked skill as a herdsman. At a vendue in early 1910, Lowden disposed of most of his Percherons and Shropshires, a few of his remaining Shorthorns, and a considerable number of farm implements. For seven years thereafter, with only a small herd and no famous bull, "Sinnissippi" held little interest for breeders of pedigreed cattle.[43] Even in their heyday they had not paid their way except in terms of the reputation gained by Lowden and his farm in livestock circles.

By 1917, about three-fourths of the total "Sinnissippi" property was included in nine tenant holdings, varying in size from sixty to six hundred acres. The remaining twelve hundred acres, of which much was woodland, made up the Park and home farm. All the tenants engaged in diversified agriculture, but their financial resources and farming preferences were so various and their holdings so unlike in size, topography, and fertility that the terms of the leases had to be kept flexible. Otherwise an honest, hardworking, and progressive young farmer, difficult to find under the best of circumstances, might choose to locate elsewhere.

By 1914, however, Lowden had drawn upon the experience of C. D. Etnyre and Company, farm operators of Oregon, and reduced his leasing options to three in number. These were known as the "Joint Crop–Pasture Rent Agreement," the "Joint Dairy–Joint Crop and Joint Stock Agreement," and the "Joint Stock–Joint Crop Agreement," respectively. The lease year in all of them began on March 1. In the first, Lowden mainly promised to supply the house, barn, windmill, fences, and firewood and half the seed and binder twine. The lessee could keep "a reasonable number of chickens and turkeys" and use land enough for a vegetable garden. He agreed to pay $5.50 an acre

42. FOL to W. Reeves, Streator, Illinois, Dec. 26, and to H. O. Hilton, Rockford, Illinois, Dec. 30, 1908.

43. George E. Martin, "Sinnissippi Farm: What It Contributed to Shorthorn History," *Breeder's Gazette,* July, 1915, p. 148. This article was widely reprinted in Illinois papers. FOL disposed of the last of his Shorthorns in 1914.

rent for pasture and meadow, to plant from ten to fifteen acres in clover and timothy, furnish half of all grain and grass seed, half of the binder twine, and give Lowden half of his crop. In addition, he pledged to ring his hogs, mow the sides of his roads, and keep his holding clear of "burdocks, yellow dock, cockle burs, morning glories, velvet and ragweed." The kinds of grain sown were to be mutually decided upon, and either party could end the contract after giving at least seven months' notice. In the second type of lease, it was stated, in addition to the foregoing, that Lowden would lend as many cows as the premises would support and pay half their maintenance cost. He reserved the right to prescribe how they were to be fed and otherwise cared for. These cows must be bred to his bulls only, and half of their offspring would be his. The same proportion of the surplus milk belonged to him. This and the tenant's half must be sold only to the Pacific Coast Condensed Milk Company at Oregon. In the third form of contract, if the tenant supplied half as many cows, sheep, and hogs as his leasehold could support, Lowden would furnish as many more. The proceeds of the sale of these animals and their offspring were similarly divided. The lessee, however, must provide his own horses, wagons, and machinery. The clauses covering ground rent, weed clearance, etc., duplicated those in the joint crop–pasture rent agreement cited previously.

The drafting of equitable leases proved to be simple compared with finding satisfactory tenants or keeping a tactful check upon their operations. The desirable kind of lessee was one who had enough ambition to view his tenancy as an unsatisfactory, although necessary, step on his road to land-ownership. A contented renter had the virtue of permanence, but Lowden sometimes complained that they did not return him more than 2 or 3 per cent a year on his investment.[44]

As early as 1909, Lowden pondered the advisability of shifting from beef-strain to milk-strain Shorthorns. Ogle County farmers, attracted by the vast Chicago milk market as well as the demand of smaller cities closer at hand, were acquiring dairy herds. In an effort to persuade Libby, McNeill, and Libby to build a condensed-milk factory at Oregon, Lowden helped to canvass the cattle owners within a seven-mile radius of the town to find out how much milk a condensery could count upon. The amount proved to be insufficient to warrant a favorable response from the firm. Two years later a branch of the Pacific Coast Condensed Milk Company, which had recently been established in the town, found it hard to operate at full capacity because of the short supply of milk.[45] By then the conflict between his own advice and his lack of action disturbed Lowden. Owning no milch cattle, he nevertheless often portrayed northern Illinois as exceptionally well fitted for dairy farming. "I am thinking," he wrote late in 1912, "of putting in a little dairy

44. FOL to J. B. Davidson, Feb. 23, 1909.

45. C. S. Haas of Oregon wrote FOL on Feb. 12, 1909, that the owners of 2,408 of the 2,741 dairy cows within seven miles of the town had pledged to sell milk to a condensery, if built there.

simply for my own use at present, but I like to begin small upon any new enterprise, so as to give me a chance to learn for myself."[46] Probably he recalled his hasty plunge into poultry-raising and wished to avoid a similar fiasco.

Having decided to make the change, he substituted *Hoard's Dairyman* for the *Breeder's Gazette* as his favorite agricultural journal, looked for a young man who knew milch cows, and gradually assembled a mixed herd of Holsteins, Guernseys, Jerseys, and milk-strain Shorthorns. After a two-month tour of dairy farms and co-operative creameries in the Netherlands, France, and England in the summer of 1913, he came back singing the praise of European methods and Holstein-Friesian cattle.[47] And yet he decided to experiment a year or so longer before selecting one breed for his own. To help him arrive at a decision, he engaged A. F. Laity, allegedly an expert in managing a dairy herd.

Thus began a costly transition at "Sinnissippi," involving the building of a creamery and an additional silo, the purchase of milking machines and other equipment, and the refitting of the big barn as a home for a hundred milch cows. Characteristically, Lowden devoted much time to devising a satisfactory dairy-farm accounting system. Long before he had milk to sell to the Oregon condensery, he sent a short article about figuring profit and loss on milch cattle to *Hoard's Dairyman*. He also made its publisher his friend by frequently exchanging letters with him and admiring his model dairy farm at Fort Atkinson, Wisconsin. This acquaintanceship illustrates how Lowden's congeniality, in alliance with his social and economic standing, enabled him to garner expert advice on almost any subject merely at the cost of a postage stamp or a visit.

After carefully watching the milk output of each of his cows for two years and judging between the several breeds in his mixed herd from the standpoints of quantity and quality of milk, their sturdiness, intake of food, and other traits, he decided that the Holstein-Friesians were making the best over-all record.[48] Therefore, in 1917 he disposed of his other cows and soon joined the Holstein-Friesian Association of America.

While "Sinnissippi" underwent this change in emphasis, its owner was again deep in politics and unable to give his property more than incidental attention. Probably for this reason, he found especially appealing the fluent tongue and pen of Judson T. Williams, the proprietor of a successful Holstein dairy enterprise near Sterling, Illinois, known as the Woodlawn Farms

46. FOL to F. Carlton, Winslow, Illinois, Dec. 28, 1912.

47. He visited a model dairy at Broek, two farms at Arnhem, three at Leeuwarden, a livestock show on the Champ de Mars, Paris, farms near Caen, and the Rothamsted Agricultural Experiment Station in England.

48. In November, 1916, the herd comprised 80 head, including 40 Guernseys, 19 Jerseys, and 10 Holsteins. In April, 1917, it numbered 73 head. By the next month the butter yield was at 758 pounds, plus 111 of cheese. Butter sold for about 40 cents a pound and cheese for 20 cents. Milk was sold on the farm at 5 cents a quart, but it retailed in Oregon at 10–12 cents.

Company. If Williams had been no more than an able dairy farmer, he might never have won his way, but he early divined that Lowden was vulnerable to an approach of straight-from-the-shoulder frankness combined with flattery. As a Bull Mooser, Williams took no pains to conceal his dislike of Lowden's standpattism, but he also complimented "the Squire" repeatedly upon his political acumen and prophesied his eventual residence in the White House.[49]

Subjected to this barrage of letters and conversation and realizing that 1916 had been a "lamentable" year at "Sinnissippi" because of "wicked waste" by his superintendent and slovenly agriculture by his tenants, Lowden invited Williams to inspect "Sinnissippi" in the following summer. After his visit, Williams proposed an operational partnership covering all the property except the home farm. Even its manager was to be under his eye and amenable to his advice. In Williams' words, he offered Lowden a contract embodying "one hundred thousand dollars worth of experience."

Judging from the outcome of their association, he was saying euphemistically that his partner should pay the entire cost of this "experience." In return, Williams would provide "Sinnissippi" with as "much press publicity . . . as possible" and make its proprietor half-owner of some expensive and pedigreed Holsteins.[50] Lowden eagerly accepted this offer and on March 1, 1918, turned over to Williams' management several large pastures and the nine tenant holdings, totaling about thirty-three hundred acres. Lowden guaranteed to spend up to ten thousand dollars to have silos built on these farms and remodel their barns for dairy use. Each renter must be an expert dairyman and accept the lease form prescribed by Williams. Although his property at Sterling and Lowden's remained distinct financially, they were merged for purposes of advertising, management, and sale of products. Lowden pledged to furnish sixty-five thousand dollars by June, 1918, for investment in a fine herd of Holstein-Friesians and advertisement of their quality. Williams frankly told his partner that breeding Holsteins was a highly competitive, "wealthy man's game," and he would probably need five years to "get out in front" as far as he once had been in the Shorthorn world.[51] In exchange for this large outlay, Lowden would have a first lien on the annual

49. J. T. Williams to FOL, Dec. 21, 1916, and Oct. 10, 1917. In 1916 FOL was a candidate for the gubernatorial nomination and may have regarded a business tie-up with Williams, an influential Roosevelt Republican of northern Illinois, as desirable politically as it might be remunerative economically.

50. J. T. Williams to FOL, July 24, Aug. 9, Sept. 1 and 12, 1917. Williams guaranteed to "keep Sinnissippi Farm in the headlines" and to make its herd, unlike those owned by other wealthy men, "show a profit."

51. J. T. Williams to FOL, July 24 and Sept. 24, 1917; FOL to Williams, Sept. 27, 1917. Holstein bulls of first quality cost $35,000 and up. "We are in a stiffer game than with any other breed," Williams wrote. He went to the East Coast in August and September and hired Ray L. Williams to begin work in November. He was considered one of the top Holstein breeders in the United States; his $10,000 salary was divided between "Sinnissippi" and the Woodlawn Farms. FOL was much pleased.

net receipts of "Sinnissippi" up to ten thousand dollars for rent and 7 per cent on the money he spent for Holsteins. Of the remaining yearly profits, he could pocket one-third and Williams two-thirds until the latter amounted to fifteen thousand dollars; thereafter they would share equally. At the termination of the partnership, if ever, the assets would be divided equally, but only after Lowden's prior lien upon them, up to the amount of his investment, had been satisfied.[52]

Lowden gave his partner a free hand in leasing the tenant farms to "cowmen," stipulating only that if his present lessees were unqualified or unwilling to come under the new regime, they would be reimbursed for any seed they had sown. This represented no large concession because the agreement with Williams did not take effect until the close of the fiscal year of 1917. When one of the tenants protested that the altered lease form was unfair, Williams curtly replied:

I am out to correct the old notion that because Frank O. Lowden is rich he can be gouged at Sinnissippi. I intend to get tenants loyal to him. . . . Under the old arrangements Lowden was not receiving his due. To be sure a poor man will not be so well off as a tenant under the new as under the old lease but a man who can do his part will be better off. Live stock and farm papers have editorially praised our new plan.[53]

Although he offered a choice of three lease forms, each to run for a year and to be terminable by either party on six months' notice, he found that most tenants, having little money of their own, chose the one known as Plan 3. This complicated document ran for five closely typed pages, divided into twenty-eight separate "clauses." The main provisions of the "McKenney Farm" (229 acres) lease, for example, were that the partners would charge no rent to the lessee and would furnish him with half of all seed, horse feed, binder twine, thoroughbred hogs and sheep, and half the cost of threshing. They would also allocate to his care a herd of twenty-five registered Holstein-Friesian cattle. On his part the tenant must supply all labor and devote his entire time to tillage and to caring for the animals, except that he might have a vegetable garden and a maximum of fifty chickens. Furthermore, he must furnish at his own cost—although the partners offered to lend him money at 7 per cent interest—all necessary work horses, machinery, and wagons, and the other half of the seed, feed, livestock, and twine mentioned previously. The lease limited him to one carriage horse only. He must ring his hogs, prevent all weeds from going to seed, forgo having any ducks, geese, or turkeys, and pledge to keep a careful record of the weight and quantity of the milk produced by each cow in his charge. The partners' instructions were to be law in the care of his herd, in the sowing and cultivation of his grain, and in determining the use to which each of his fields should be put. In return for faithful adherence to these and other regulations, the

52. J. T. Williams to FOL, July 27 and Aug. 1, 1917.

53. J. T. Williams to J. E. Fissel, Oregon, Illinois, Sept. 28, 1917.

tenant was assured of 50 per cent of the marketable produce of his farm, except the cattle. In addition, he was guaranteed certain incentive payments, such as 5 cents a pound for every pound of milk added by each cow in his care. On the other hand, he would be docked at that rate for any animal whose yield declined.[54]

Whether such meticulous supervision could yield either harmony or profits would be for the coming years to make clear. As always when beginning a new venture, Lowden in 1917 was most sanguine about what the answer would be. "I feel very comfortable," he told Williams, "about the future of Sinnissippi Farm under your direction" and "think you are getting along better than reasonably could have been expected."[55] By that time, indeed, this whole matter as well as his other business enterprises had passed virtually beyond his control. Holding a public office whose responsibilities had multiplied because America was at war, he looked back upon his years in Congress as a period of comparative leisure. Necessarily, his private affairs receded into the background until the return of peace.

54. Lease of Lowden and Williams to J. E. Fissel, Aug. 22, 1917. The several lease options are summarized in J. T. Williams' memo entitled, "Sinnissippi and Woodlawn Farms, August, 1917." See also FOL, "Tenant-and-Landlord Partnerships," *Breeder's Gazette,* Dec. 25, 1919.

55. FOL to J. T. Williams, July 31 and Aug. 31, 1917.

CHAPTER XI

RECOVERING GOOD HEALTH AND POLITICAL AMBITION, 1911-15

The adjournment of Congress in the spring of 1911 enabled Lowden to make a search for good health his primary occupation. His physicians prescribed little medicine but generous amounts of relaxation and exercise and a drastic curtailment of tobacco and liquor. He gradually reduced his daily ration of cigars and shifted within a few years mainly to cigarettes—about twenty a day. Although he continued to relish a tumblerful of Bourbon, taken neat in the late afternoon, and wine with his dinner, he stopped excessive drinking once and for all. Horseback riding at "Sinnissippi" and golf at "Castle Rest" provided plenty of exercise, while reading, fishing, and card playing remained his favorite forms of diversion. His unofficial doctor was the self-appointed Edgar Bancroft who chided him whenever he broke his good resolutions about tobacco and liquor, bantered him about exaggerating his ailments, and persuaded him to undergo a two-week course of treatments at the Battle Creek (Michigan) Sanitarium. By September, 1911, Mrs. Lowden believed her husband felt "remarkably well," but he refused to concur with her judgment. Although he admitted to some improvement, he was still underweight and lacked zest for either work or food.

His physicians suggested travel as a way to gain a new "lease on life." With Harry Pratt Judson he visited Jamaica, the Panama Canal Zone, and Haiti for three weeks as 1912 opened and spent ten days near its close with John W. Dwight in Cuba. He liked Jamaica especially, while Panama long reminded him of Colonel William Gorgas' hospitality. During most of February, March, and April of that year he and Mrs. Lowden lived in hotels in Pasadena, in San Francisco, and at the Grand Canyon. He improved his time there by having experts coach him in golf and bridge and by sometimes playing poker for considerable stakes.[1] At the Raymond Hotel in Pasadena he met John Tracey, the head bellboy, who for long periods during the next eight years served as his valet and masseur.

After twenty months of these varied efforts to make himself feel better, he was still greatly depressed in mind and body when 1912 reached its close.[2]

1. It was about 1913–14 that FOL's former sporadic interest in bridge changed into a habit which he indulged thereafter for an hour or so every evening, whenever possible.

2. Mrs. Lowden's diary, Nov. 10, 1912.

Almost as a last resort he yielded to the coaxing of John W. Dwight and consulted Dr. W. Gerry Morgan, of Washington, D.C. With Mrs. Lowden close at hand to visit him every day in Morgan's sanitarium, he underwent a two-week stint of dieting, exercising, relaxing in bed, and being massaged. He responded amazingly. At the end of his stay he had recovered ten pounds and a keen appetite. By adhering to Dr. Morgan's regimen upon his return to "Sinnissippi," he added another five pounds within a short time and felt eager to be up and doing. "It is so delightful," Mrs. Lowden commented, "to see him interested and enthusiastic again."[3] When they went back to Washington in March, Dr. Morgan deflected Mrs. Lowden from her wish to try the "cure" by suggesting as her most needed tonic the "diversion and amusement" of a European trip with her husband.

Their seven weeks in the Netherlands, France, Belgium, and England during the early summer of 1913 allowed him, as already mentioned, to study European methods of dairying and tillage. Since he was always eager to stand on the site of great events, his most exciting experience on this trip was a visit to the battlefield of Waterloo. Following his return to the United States, the "bounce" of his letters written from "Castle Rest" leave no doubt of his marked improvement in health.[4] Upon persuading Mrs. Lowden to accompany him to his fishing camp at Brewer's Mills on the Rideau River, he commented to J. Sloat Fassett:

I am treating her with real liberality . . . and allow her two sheets for her bed, a concession never yet made to any one. In other respects she will live just as I do. I am sure that she will enjoy some features of camp life, but I must admit that her training and predilections hardly fit her for roughing it; but, on the other hand, she was always a good soldier. She appeared to be in some doubt as to whether or not to take her maid, but I explained to her that it wasn't usual . . . as the accommodations were hardly good enough for a lady's maid. . . . I am very much attached to this camp. The quiet and independence of the thing, and the beauty of the environment all appeal to me, and if, when the revolution comes, I am exiled, I shall take my family to a camp somewhere and laugh at the reforming patriots. I will say, however, in fairness, that I don't believe so much in this talked-of revolution.[5]

After four days at the camp, Mrs. Lowden gladly went back to "Castle Rest," but she had been "interested to see how little is really necessary to make one comfortable."[6] Far more important to her, however, were the many evidences of her husband's return to good health. "This has been a much happier Christmas than I have had for years," she confided to her diary as the year ended, "due largely to the fact that Frank has been so well and is ready to enjoy it all with us." To his political friends, his good spirits signified that he might again be willing to seek a public office.

3. *Ibid.,* Jan. 12–28 and Feb. 11, 1913. FOL's praise of Dr. Morgan was unqualified and long-lasting. As late as 1926 he thought that he owed the prolongation of his life to the doctor's ministrations thirteen years before (FOL to Dr. G. Morgan, Mar. 3, 1926).

4. FOL to C. G. Dawes, Aug. 12, and to J. W. Dwight, Aug. 14, 1913.

5. FOL to J. S. Fassett, Elmira, New York, Sept. 5, 1913.

6. Mrs. Lowden's diary, Sept. 6–9, 1913.

Indeed, he had never wholly isolated himself from politics. For a year after leaving Congress, his ill-health provided a valid and welcome reason for declining to make a political speech, but he took pains to retain his seat on the Republican National Committee and recover his proxy from Lorimer.[7] Even in 1911, when he felt his worst, his erect carriage and ruddy complexion belied the reports of his breakdown and bred rumors that prudent political considerations accounted for his retirement. Commentators in this vein could not agree upon the goal of his artfulness. Some concluded that a premonition of the stormy weather in store for all standpatters had led him to avoid defeat by running for cover until the gale of progressivism blew itself out. Others, equally mistaken, guessed that he wished to clear his desk in order to give his full attention, with Cullom's and Lorimer's help, to winning the Republican gubernatorial nomination from Deneen in 1912.[8]

On the contrary, Lowden desired no political office requiring an exhausting campaign for its attainment. "I have told every living being who has come to see me, or who has written me," he wrote, "that I was not a candidate for Governor."[9] If he had stood for re-election to Congress in 1910, he almost certainly would have won; if he had tried for the governorship two years later, he almost as certainly would have failed to receive the nomination or, gaining that, to win at the polls.

During 1911, progressivism within the ranks of his party in Illinois made rapid strides, and the *Chicago Tribune* served as its most influential mouthpiece. Burdened with old age and illness, Shelby Cullom had lost most of his influence, while his senatorial colleague, Lorimer, faced the mounting storm of indignation over the alleged bribery connected with his election. Even "Uncle Joe" Cannon often found himself at odds with President Taft.[10] The conservative members of the Republican party in Illinois derived some little comfort from knowing that their liberal brethren were also split into factions. Probably most of them felt well enough satisfied with Governor Deneen's mild progressivism, in spite of Senator La Follette's denunciation of him, to support him for re-election.

When signs multiplied that the Republican liberals in 1912 would secede from their party unless they could control it, William Hale Thompson, Lorimer, and Congressman Fred Lundin called upon Lowden repeatedly to come out for the governorship. In their opinion "sentiment from one end of the state to the other" favored him, and only he could prevent a schism. Lowden told Harvey Ingham: "I've had more pressure brought to bear on me to be a

7. See pp. 188–89. Probably because of its doubtful legality, Lorimer never used the proxy. FOL asked for it back in October, 1911, at the urging of Cullom and other Illinois Republican leaders.

8. Roy O. West, chairman of the Republican State Central Committee in 1911–12, told the author on Jan. 6, 1951, that he scotched FOL's gubernatorial ambitions because Lorimer seemed to control him. FOL's own correspondence of 1911–12 makes clear that West was unnecessarily alarmed, although there is no doubt that Cullom and Lorimer, separately and for different reasons, pressed FOL to announce his candidacy.

9. FOL to W. A. Meese, Moline, Illinois, July 1, 1911.

10. See pp. 187–88 and 195–97. Cullom was defeated in the 1912 primary.

candidate . . . than I ever had for anything in the past." In view of the gloomy political outlook, he was almost reconciled to his ill-health because it supplied him with an unanswerable reply to every plea that he throw his hat into the ring. Thus, while he assured Lorimer that if he felt better he would "hardly have the heart to refuse what so many" asked of him, he confided to Fassett: "I would rather develop a good sized tract of land for five years than be President of the United States in these days. . . . I think you and I are in luck that we are out of it [politics]."[11]

The *Chicago Tribune* included him among the "unhappy Tories."[12] His unhappiness, however, stemmed less from fear that the rising tide of progressivism would split the Republican organization than from the conviction that the malcontents in both major parties worshiped strange and dangerous gods. A rereading of several scholarly works on the Constitutional Convention of 1787 and some of James Ford Rhodes's volumes on United States history confirmed him in his belief that "the Fathers" had recognized the perils of the "pure democracy" now being sought through the use of direct primaries and the initiative, referendum, and recall. Lincoln, he was certain, had also looked upon representative rather than direct popular government as the chief bastion of the Republic against "rule by the inexpert."[13]

Although Lowden had advocated the use of primaries in his younger days, he henceforward criticized them caustically. If it made him a "Tory" to line up with Washington, Hamilton, and Lincoln, he gloried in the title. Even Thomas Jefferson, who never before had been one of his favorite American statesmen, deserved to be held in grateful remembrance. With his contribution of $100 to the Jefferson-Monticello Association he included a note remarking that "may be if, as a Nation, we had more respect for the tombs of the Fathers of the Republic, we would have more respect for their teaching."[14] Often during these months, he sounded the note struck in his comment to J. Sloat Fassett:

These new fads have got to run their course, which means hard times for everybody, before our people will be willing to listen to such old fossils as the gentlemen who framed the Constitution. I do not despair of the future, because I believe that the country will have enough of direct nominations, initiative, referendum, and recall, and other so-called progressive policies in the next few years, and that they [*sic*] will be mighty glad to come back to representative government. In the meantime, let us look after our lumber and farming operations, and give the news-

11. W. Lorimer to FOL, Aug. 6, and FOL's reply, Aug. 25, 1911. In April, W. H. Thompson had come to "Sinnissippi" to urge Lowden to run. In late August, Lorimer sent Lundin to "Castle Rest" to renew the pressure while they fished together. FOL to J. S. Fassett, Elmira, New York, May 19, 1911, and to H. Ingham, Des Moines, Iowa, Jan. 29, 1912.

12. Editorial, Nov. 28, 1911.

13. FOL to J. S. Fassett, Sept. 14, 1911: "Never before were our people so indifferent, as now, to constitutional government."

14. FOL to Mrs. M. W. Littleton, Port Washington, New York, May 14 and Sept. 26, 1912.

papers and magazines an opportunity to rule the country for a while. That is all there is needed for a return of sane thinking.[15]

Views such as these, expressed candidly to newspaper reporters as well as in confidence to his friends, explain why the progressive wing of his party wished to oust him from the Republican national committeemanship or at least to pressure him into advocating a presidential preference primary in Illinois in the spring of 1912.[16] As the liberals no doubt expected, he refused to resign his position or to favor a plebiscite of that sort. He bluntly declared that direct primaries had not had "the slightest favorable influence toward the elimination of Bossism or machine politics in Illinois." "If the people," he added, "cannot select delegates among their neighbors, men . . . who will not betray them, what possible chance have they of selecting, directly, a long line of officials, most of whom they do not know, who will not betray them?"[17] In other words, he believed that the Republican voters in each precinct could choose, if they wished, a committeeman pledged to support a particular presidential candidate. These committeemen in their county convention would then send similarly pledged representatives to the convention of their congressional district and thus, under the existing Illinois law, assure that the Republican delegation to the national nominating convention accurately voiced the will of a majority of the party's voters in the state.

Some of the Illinois progressives, moreover, wanted, above all, a preferential primary as a means of repudiating Taft rather than of eliminating bossism and political corruption. They insisted, so they said, upon defeating the President because he supported Lorimer. Leading in this fight was the *Chicago Tribune*, long accustomed to oppose any Republican leader in the city and state who refused to bow to its will. It was no less of a "boss" because it was a newspaper. It had the good fortune at this time to be able to reinforce its drive for greater power by blasting the vulnerable Lorimer and indorsing measures of political reform which were enlisting more and more popular support.

To supplant the congressional district convention system by a state-wide preferential primary as a device for selecting delegates to the national nominating conventions would also result, if Lowden were correct, in a lamentable transference of the power balance in politics from the countryside to the cities of Illinois. "We know," he declared, "that it has been the rural districts, in all our history, which have saved our institutions."[18] This assertion suggests the gradual shift then under way in the quality and focus of his political conservatism. Whether he realized it or not, he was no longer primarily concerned to protect urban business corporations from meddle-

15. FOL to J. S. Fassett, May 19, 1911.

16. *New York Sun,* May 29, 1911, reporting over fifty Republican progressives on their way to Oyster Bay to enlist Theodore Roosevelt's aid in obliging FOL to resign as national committeeman.

17. FOL to D. C. Busell, Lanark, Illinois, Nov. 14, 1911.

18. FOL to H. Ingham, July 27, 1912.

some legislation not clearly in the public interest but rather to resist reformers who would brush aside the old methods and institutions upon which, in his opinion, the governing power of the farmers depended. In the earlier phase of his political career he championed a minority of the people owning a majority of the wealth against the untrammeled will of the majority. Now, on the contrary, he was alert to prevent a majority of the people (the city folk) from depriving a minority, possessing a minority of the country's wealth, of their means to defend themselves politically. In opposing direct primaries and the initiative, referendum, and recall, he summoned early United States history to his aid. However irrelevant this type of argument may have been in view of the marked changes in American life since 1789, Lowden returned to it time and again.[19]

Progressive Republican leaders accused him of defying the majority will of his party in Illinois, "facing backwards," pursuing a policy of "rule or ruin standpattism," and outraging their "sense of justice." Victor Murdock, outstanding Kansas liberal, hastened to defend his friend by declaring that he had always been "on the square."[20] Outwardly, Lowden remained calm, but he felt hurt by the criticism of prominent Republicans who hitherto had been his staunch supporters. Besides working to make Chicago the Republican convention city in 1912, he promised to judge impartially the contested-delegations cases which would come before him as a member of the party's national committee. Deneen also helped him by declaring that Illinois could not legally hold a presidential preference primary. Thereupon the Assembly rushed through a bill to authorize one and the governor signed the measure.

For a time in the autumn of 1911, Lowden seemed sanguine of Republican victory in the presidential election of the following year. Although the cordial relationship between Taft and Roosevelt ended in June, the latter appeared willing to have Taft renominated. La Follette's precarious health had weakened the punch behind his drive for the nomination. Because the Wisconsin senator had attracted little firm support on the Atlantic seaboard, Lowden believed that, if Roosevelt remained tractable, the Republicans might carry New York State and with it the presidency. At best, however, the outcome would be nip and tuck. With election day still a year in the future, Lowden hoped that the Democratic-Republican insurgent coalition controlling the House of Representatives would make enough mistakes to react strongly in favor of the conservative wing of his party. Within the Democratic ranks the dissension between the Bourbons, Bryanites, and Wilsonian liberals gave reason for good cheer.[21] He was further encouraged by

19. FOL to Senator H. C. Lodge, Washington, D.C., July 10, 1912: "What a pity that, as a people, we do not study history more and sociology less!" Lodge replied on July 12: "If we abandon representative government and try direct democracy, we shall come to a bad end."

20. *Dixon* (Ill.) *News*, July 18, 1911. Murdock and FOL had served on committees in Congress together, and both were interested in purebred cattle.

21. FOL to J. S. Fassett, Elmira, New York, Sept. 14, 1911, and to H. S. Boutell, Bern, Switzerland, Nov. 26, 1911.

the "very satisfactory" meeting of the Republican National Committee in Washington in mid-December. Bearing a certified check for $100,000, he and Frederic W. Upham of Chicago succeeded in persuading the committee to name Chicago as the site of the forthcoming convention.[22]

Anticipating that the use of presidential primaries for the choice and instruction of state delegations to this convention would be an important subject of discussion by the national committee, Lowden consulted with Fassett about what the wording of the committee's call for the election of delegates should be.[23] Reaching Washington with a resolution on this subject in his pocket, Lowden was named one of a subcommittee of three to talk with the President about the matter. To the anger of the few progressive Republicans on the national committee, including William E. Borah of Idaho and Lucius N. Littauer of New York, Taft agreed in the main with Lowden's draft. Subsequently, the national committee delegated to him and two other members the task of putting "the call" in final form. By its terms, convention delegates could not be chosen by a preferential primary unless a state law and the Republican committee of that state authorized its use. Borah countered with a proposal to compel the party's central organization in every state to provide a primary unless the law explicitly forbade one. The national committee sided with Lowden by a vote of forty-four to seven.[24] It further alienated the progressives by naming an undeviating standpatter, Harry S. New of Indiana, as chairman of the Committee on Arrangements for the national nominating convention. This powerful group, with only a small minority of progressives among its personnel, would nominate the temporary officers of the convention and prepare a preliminary roster of its qualified delegates.

As mentioned earlier in this chapter, Lowden spent most of the winter and early spring of 1912 outside Illinois.[25] During his absence, he had the pro-Roosevelt James R. Cowley speak and act for him on matters of national committeeman business. He cautioned his friend to show no favoritism between the several Republican factions when he parceled out Illinois's quota of convention jobs and tickets. This even-handedness, of course, did not halt the rising wave of progressivism, especially after late February when La Follette faded out and Roosevelt announced his candidacy for the nomination. At that time, Walter D. Mack, the manager of "Sinnissippi," warned Lowden that the progressives would probably carry his own county and congressional district in the presidential preference primary on April 9. "I do not think," concluded Mack, "that you personally, if you were here, could change conditions, without a hard bitter fight . . . and I think it is fortunate for you, that you are away."[26] Apparently the Republican national com-

22. *Chicago Inter-Ocean,* Dec. 10, 1911.
23. FOL to J. S. Fassett, Dec. 21, 1911.
24. *Chicago Record-Herald,* Dec. 10, 1911.
25. See p. 241.
26. W. D. Mack to FOL, Pasadena, California, Mar. 13, 1912.

mitteeman from Illinois would not even be able to guarantee that Taft delegates would come from his own neighborhood.

Fresh from his reading of Lord Rosebery's *Napoleon: The Last Phase* in which the author concluded that flattery weakened the emperor's character, Lowden wondered whether excessive adulation had not launched Roosevelt upon his dangerous course. He thought that the "end of the Republic" would be hastened if his party decided to sponsor the radical measures advocated by the former President in his Columbus, Ohio, speech.[27] He was shocked when a large majority of the Republican voters of Illinois, including those of the Thirteenth Congressional District, expressed their preference for Roosevelt in the April primary. The Republican state convention at Springfield later that month echoed this verdict by instructing the delegates to the Chicago convention to vote for the Colonel. The Springfield gathering extolled him for his "great work . . . in arousing the public conscience and mind to the necessity . . . for protecting the people against predatory interests." After somewhat vaguely repudiating Lorimerism, it devoted a brief and perfunctory paragraph in the state platform to praise of the Taft administration for "its judicious progressiveness and . . . remarkable record of achievements." In the primary, Deneen won renomination for the governorship. The convention named him a Roosevelt-pledged delegate at large to the national convention.

Thus, by summarily brushing aside some of the cherished political principles of Lowden and his choice of a presidential nominee, the Illinois Republican party in effect repudiated him as its national committeeman. Under these circumstances, he naturally looked forward with much distaste to his job of helping to weigh the claims of conflicting delegations to the national convention. No matter how he voted, he was certain to be condemned. "If I can get through this Convention alive," he confided to Harry S. New over a month before the committee began its hearings, "I shall be very grateful. Isn't this a devil of a campaign?"[28]

Lowden foresaw that the conduct of this Taft-dominated committee might determine whether the progressives would secede from the party in June or support the nominee of the convention. For this reason he urged that each disputed-seat issue be decided after an impartial examination of the evidence and not on factional grounds. In late March he asked Congressman William B. McKinley, the leader of the Taft forces, to have the President exert his influence upon the committee to that end. Taft did so by mid-May, and Victor Rosewater, acting chairman of the national committee, also pleased Lowden by declaring that every contest must be dealt with "intelligently and judicially."[29]

27. FOL to H. Ingham, Des Moines, Iowa, Mar. 15, and to W. D. Mack, Oregon, Illinois, Mar. 18, 1912. Roosevelt's Columbus speech in February, entitled "A Charter of Democracy," advocated the initiative and referendum, the recall of elective officers, and, most shocking of all to FOL, the recall of judicial decisions. This last was, in his view, as bad as an elective judiciary, which was one of the "worst of evils."

28. FOL to New, May 2, 1912.

29. FOL to McKinley, Mar. 29, 1912; V. Rosewater to FOL, May 6, 1912.

If "judicially," however, meant an application of the strict letter of the Republican rules regulating the choice of delegates to the national convention, no more certain way of embittering the progressives could be found. By such a gauge, pro-Roosevelt contingents elected by extra-legal methods in the many states not specifically authorizing preferential primaries would be automatically disqualified, even though they, rather than the Taftites chosen by legal state conventions, clearly voiced the majority will of their constituents.

Judging each case on the basis of what had occurred, the terms of the "call" by the national committee, and the law of the state in question, Lowden voted time and again against seating the pro-Roosevelt contestants. Occasionally, as in the much-publicized dispute from the Ninth Congressional District of Alabama, he concluded that the progressives had right on their side and futilely tried to seat them. Such staunch Roosevelt men on the committee as Frank B. Kellogg and William E. Borah congratulated him upon his fairness and joined him in denying admittance to some dubiously selected delegates favoring their own candidate.[30]

Illinois progressives, nevertheless, bombarded him with letters, telegrams, and petitions demanding that he reflect in his votes the "undoubted will" of the rank and file of his party rather than an adherence to the national committee's "outworn rules." Some of these angry liberals charged him with conniving to "steal the nomination for Taft by any means" and warned him that they would keep green the memory of his "dishonesty" even though he should live for another fifty years.[31] The pro-Roosevelt forces in a number of states probably sent rival delegations to Chicago merely to create an exaggerated impression of their strength and would have been amazed if they had been seated. On the other hand, it seems clear that the committee should have barred about forty of the Taft delegates from the convention.[32]

Whether the committee excluded enough Roosevelt adherents, legally chosen, to make all the difference between victory and defeat for the progressives in the choice of a presidential nominee and in the content of the platform was a question hotly debated by politicians and columnists in 1912 and one which has baffled historians ever since. The more important consideration, however, is beyond dispute. By ratifying most of the decisions of the national committee, the convention afforded Roosevelt and his cohorts an eagerly grasped opportunity to cry "fraud" and "gross disregard of the

30. Victor Rosewater, *Back Stage in 1912* (Philadelphia, 1932), pp. 93 ff. The *Freeport (Ill.) Standard,* Nov. 10, 1914, reported a statement by F. B. Kellogg praising FOL for his impartiality in the contested-delegations cases. On Feb. 8, 1933, after Mark Sullivan sent to FOL for criticism the *Our Times* MS chapter on the 1912 convention, FOL commented that it was "fair and accurate" and added: "My chief feeling in many of the contests was that I should have liked to vote to unseat both sides."

31. C. Ferguson, Chicago, to FOL, June 13, 1912. Telegrams to FOL from L. K. Wynn and about one hundred others of Sterling, Illinois, June 10, and from about two hundred voters of Rockford, Illinois, June 10, 1912.

32. This especially refers to the inconsistent handling of the Indiana, Washington, and Texas disputes and the arbitrary decisions concerning delegates from certain California districts. Of the 254 contested seats, Roosevelt delegates received only 19.

will of the great American people." This issue, so potent in emotional voltage, became the principal immediate cause of the progressives' "bolt" and subsequent formation of the "Bull Moose" party, with Roosevelt and Governor Hiram Johnson of California heading its ticket.

The ten days of wrangling over the contested seats, followed by the dramatic sessions of the convention, left Lowden completely tired out and with a bad cold.[33] Watching with her mother from the gallery of the Coliseum, Mrs. Lowden was shocked by the unruly conduct of the excited delegates. She viewed politics as a man's game from which women of culture ought to remain aloof. For this reason she disliked the forwardness of Mrs. Medill (Ruth Hanna) McCormick and others of her sex and social standing on behalf of Roosevelt. In her diary entry for June 19, after boredom caused her to leave the Coliseum early that afternoon, she remarked: "There is much disorder and the crowds are hard to handle, and I am not sorry to be going home tonight as I am not interested in the proceedings." Almost two weeks before, a Chicago paper had quoted Lowden as saying that his main wish had been "to get back to his farm."[34] He was on hand, however, on June 22, when Taft and J. S. Sherman won renomination and the disgruntled Old Guard delegates, foreseeing defeat, scattered to their homes. With a feeling of great relief, he turned over the position of national committeeman for Illinois to Roy O. West. In reply to Lowden's dutiful telegram of congratulation, President Taft interestingly commented: "It has been a hard fight, and the taste of victory would be sweet even without the added appreciation of what it means for the constitution, the judiciary, and the country at large."[35] Although recognizing the importance of the issues at stake in the campaign, Lowden felt happy because his party's headquarters did not expect him to make more than three speeches before the election in November.

Aided by his physicians and relaxation at "Sinnissippi," "South Bend," "Florenden," and the Battle Creek Sanitarium, he finally mastered his "dreadful cold." Early in the campaign he believed that Taft's stock was rising and that the nomination of the liberal Woodrow Wilson by the Democrats on July 2 might restrain the Roosevelt bolters from forming a third party. As the summer advanced, he repeated in many letters his earlier warnings that direct government of either the Democratic or the Bull Moose variety would endanger the nation. In his view, government by popularly chosen representatives, disciplined by their political organizations, had the saving virtues of assuring definiteness of program, concerted action, and a compromise of seriously divisive issues. History taught that "pure democracies" always succumbed to factionalism and class struggles. These ill omens, Lowden lamented, were already discernible in American life. The "Fathers," he wrote, "studied government more profoundly than we of this age. . . .Those who now seek indirectly to repeal the work of the Fathers are the real reaction-

33. Mrs. Lowden's diary, June 11, 1912.

34. *Chicago Record-Herald,* June 6, 1912.

35. W. H. Taft to FOL, June 24, 1912.

aries, for they would return to a form of government which has always failed."[36]

Although he sounded this alarm with the utmost sincerity, he expressed no personal dislike of those who espoused the "perilous" doctrines. Roosevelt remained "that wonderful man." When a would-be assassin wounded him in Milwaukee, the Lowdens were "horrified." In his own bailiwick, Lowden extended the due date of his loan to the Bull Moose Congressman, J. C. McKenzie, offered to contribute to his campaign fund, and helped as much as he discreetly could to assure his re-election. When Oscar S. Straus became the Progressives' nominee for governor of New York, Lowden warmly congratulated him.

Except for letter-writing and counseling with prominent Republican politicians, he confined his active share in the campaign to speeches at DuQuoin, Pontiac, and Freeport, Illinois, in late October. His contribution of $1,000 to the campaign fund brought a querulous letter from the Republican National Committee's treasurer, reminding him that headquarters had ticketed him for a donation twenty-five times larger.[37] His public addresses seemed scarcely more generous in their support of the national ticket. In his one speech, repeated twice over, he mildly chided Roosevelt for denouncing the Republican party as "a failure and a fraud" after trying to be its nominee. He half-heartedly complimented the Taft administration upon its legislative record, including the Payne-Aldrich tariff, strongly defended the decisions in the contested-delegations cases, and emphatically warned against pure democracy and the economic collapse to be expected from tariff-tinkering if the Democrats should win. In its stress upon the high tariff and "full dinner pail," much of what he said was of 1896 vintage.

Although usually an effective speaker, his efforts in this campaign suffered from his continued ill-health, his lack of enthusiasm for Taft, and his premonition of Republican defeat. The re-election of Congressmen Mann and McKenzie went far toward offsetting his depression over the extent of the Democratic victory in Illinois and the nation at large. In his customary fashion he at once wired his congratulations or condolences to friends in both parties. Surprised to find himself among the vanquished, "Uncle Joe" Cannon commented that his party was only "in Purgatory" rather than in the "hotter place" and accurately predicted that he would live to see it again in power. When Lowden attempted to cheer the defeated Illinois governor by mailing him one of his farm calendars for 1913, Deneen graciously replied that it would remind him daily of their "long and pleasant friendship."[38]

Political as well as personal considerations prompted Lowden's exchange

36. A sentence each from FOL to R. S. Dow, Boston, Aug. 27, and to M. F. Girten, Chicago, Sept. 26, 1912.

37. Wires of W. H. Wilson to FOL, Oct. 11 and 14, and letter to FOL of Oct. 14, 1912; FOL to Wilson, Oct. 12 and 15, 1912. Wilson reminded FOL that "we could win with money," but $1,000 "from such men as you . . . is like throwing money in the wastebasket, it simply does no good."

38. C. S. Deneen to FOL, Jan. 15, 1913.

of amenities. Republicans everywhere recognized that, to regain power, they must close up their ranks, settle their factional differences, and open their door at least a crack for the return of the Progressive prodigals. Soon after the election, a few of the Bull Moose leaders indicated their willingness to "forgive and forget." Lowden believed that, by 1916 at the latest, the Progressives and the Republicans, chastened by defeat and aided by a popular reaction against Wilsonian "radicalism," would reunite "into a militant and successful party."[39] In this optimistic mood and feeling much improved in health, he often visited Washington in early 1913, conferring with President Taft and other Stalwarts about how to rehabilitate their party. From what he saw in the capital, he probably concurred with a congressional friend's comment that "it is a mess here . . . more broad rimmed hats and Kentucky Colonels, Sah! than we have had since Cleveland."[40]

With party harmony as his foremost objective, Lowden felt obliged to quash a move by his supporters to run him against Lawrence Y. Sherman for the unexpired portion of Lorimer's term in the United States Senate.[41] When Frank Funk of Bloomington, the Progressive aspirant, seemed likely to defeat Sherman, Lowden in a blunt public statement scotched the persistent rumor that he stood ready to came out as a compromise candidate if the two rivals would withdraw. He could not resist adding, however, that his health was better than it had been for ten years in the past.[42]

As he perhaps expected, many people interpreted this irrelevant comment to mean that he would soon be a receptive office-seeker. Friends at once urged him to make ready for either a senatorship in 1915 or the gubernatorial race in the following year. Although he remained noncommittal, he clearly was pleased. Aware that Lorimer's power had collapsed except in Cook County, Lowden looked for new allies in the Sherman and Deneen camps. In this search he fostered party harmony and his own political advantage at one and the same time.

During these months he counseled his fellow Stalwarts that the continued life of their party depended upon an unshaken adherence to its old but still vital principles. If it moved toward the "radicalism" of the Democrats and Progressives, it would no longer have a valid reason for being.[43] This theme ran through his speech to his fellow alumni of Northwestern University Law School at their banquet in April, 1913. After expressing regret that able lawyers with their useful knowledge of precedents were avoiding public office more than in the past, he criticized any President who tried to dictate

39. FOL to C. H. Potter, Elgin, Illinois, Dec. 12, 1912, and to W. F. Stone, Baltimore, Maryland, Feb. 1, 1913.

40. Congressman B. McGuire (Okla.) to FOL, Feb. 5, 1913.

41. FOL to H. B. Ward, DuQuoin, Illinois, Feb. 14 and 26, 1913.

42. *Chicago Inter-Ocean,* Mar. 5, 1913. Sherman was elected by the legislature on its fourteenth ballot on Mar. 26, 1913. The Democrat, J. Hamilton Lewis, succeeded Cullom in the Senate in 1913.

43. FOL to H. O. Hilton, Rockford, Illinois, May 8, 1913.

a program of legislation to Congress. Obviously, he meant Woodrow Wilson. Lowden's devotion to legislative leadership accorded with sound Republican doctrine of Whiggish ancestry. He also deplored the current fashion of deprecating rather than extolling the time-tested political institutions which had conferred so many blessings upon the American people for one hundred and twenty-five years. "There is nothing which is so arresting our orderly progress today," he added, "as the assumption that there are no means for the redress of grievances under existing constitutional forms." "From the way a majority of our men are voting today," he quipped acidly, "I would almost be in favor of enfranchising the women and disenfranchising the men." In view of his usual lack of enthusiasm about women in politics, this sally signified only that wives of alumni were present at the banquet.[44]

His advice against conceding an iota of Republican "principles" in order to lure the Progressives back into the old party gained in persuasiveness with every passing month in 1913. The Bull Moosers were in financial straits and torn by factional strife between westerners and easterners, trust-busters and trust-regulators, high- and low-tariff advocates, and co-operationists and isolationists. The latter insisted upon holding aloof from Democrats and Republican liberals who had not seceded from their party in 1912. As early as February of the following year, Frank A. Munsey, one of the chief financial backers of the Progressives, desired to reunite his party with the Republicans if an amalgamation did not oblige an abject surrender to the standpatters.[45] Led by the President and without much help from the Progressives, the Democratic majority in Congress forged into law some of the reforms which Roosevelt and his co-workers had advocated during the recent campaign. Although the Progressives had helped greatly to create the ground swell for reform and the political situation assuring a Democratic victory, they were mostly overlooked by the new administration in its allotment of offices. For these reasons Lowden felt confident that many of the Bull Moosers of Illinois would soon be ready—nay, eager—to return to the Republican fold. Time was working strongly in his party's favor.

In this sanguine mood he spent "a vacation from politics" during the summer of 1913 in Europe and at "Castle Rest."[46] Although the Illinois state fair at Springfield in early October featured a separate day for each of the three political parties, some of the Progressives and many of the Stalwarts seemed less interested in maintaining the distinction between them than in finding a way to wipe it out. The downstate Roosevelt men, led by Frank Funk, discussed unification the more willingly because they resented the recent capture of their state central committee by the Chicago wing, headed by Medill McCormick, Raymond Robins, and Harold Ickes. Robins and Ickes, however, were still too greatly at odds with most of the old-line Republi-

---

44. *Chicago Inter-Ocean*, Apr. 23, 1913; see also pp. 280 and 322–23.

45. *Munsey's Magazine*, XLVIII (February, 1913), 729–33; XLIX (April, 1913), 16–17.

46. See pp. 237 and 242.

cans to permit a merger of the two state central committees. Lowden heard much talk at Springfield about running him in 1916 as a "bridge" candidate for the governorship, but, if the *Chicago Inter-Ocean* reported accurately, he "declined to get excited" over the prospect.[47]

By this time, Edward J. Brundage had founded in Cook County the "1916 Club" and a little magazine entitled the *Reflector* to serve as its voice. Lowden helped it with money after it printed his widely discussed speech before the club in which he told the Republicans and Progressives how to close the chasm between them.[48] His remarks drew faint applause from the Bull Moosers because he attributed their bolt in 1912 almost solely to a quarrel over party leadership rather than to a disagreement over issues. Most of the Progressives would gladly have accepted the Old Guard platform if the convention had nominated Roosevelt for the presidency. The fact that nearly all of them in Congress had voted against the Wilsonian measures was, in Lowden's view, excellent circumstantial evidence supporting this interpretation.

This interpretation, however, is far from satisfying. The voting records of the dozen Progressive congressmen and one senator in the sessions of 1913–15 show no uniformity of pattern either for or against the "New Freedom" program. Furthermore, had the delegates for Roosevelt been numerous enough to nominate him, they probably would also have controlled the platform committee and produced a document quite unlike the one adopted by the convention. Perhaps, too, if the Progressives had dominated that assemblage, the Old Guard Republicans, including Lowden, would have "bolted" as the Gold Democrats did when Bryan was nominated in 1896. Moreover, by calling "archaic and unjust" the method whereby his party determined how many delegates each state might send to the national convention, Lowden nearly admitted that this inequitable distribution formula accounted for Roosevelt's defeat by that body in 1912. He wished each state's quota of delegates proportioned to the number of Republican votes cast in that state in the presidential election last preceding the convention. Thereby the greatly overweighted vote of the ineffective southern Republicans would disappear. By recommending that "this reform take effect before the next presidential campaign," Lowden implied that, by rejoining the Republican party, the Progressives might nominate Roosevelt in 1916. On the other hand, he opposed a reunion at the price of accepting the presidential preference primary or the initiative, referendum, and recall. Fortunately, the Republicans and Progressives differed hardly at all on foreign affairs, currency, and the tariff.

Lowden believed any worthwhile merger must arise from a spontaneous demand by the rank and file of both parties and not be imposed by their leaders. To initiate a "grass-roots" movement of this kind, he suggested that, when local committeemen were next elected, the Progressives and Republi-

47. *Chicago Inter-Ocean,* Oct. 11, 1913.

48. FOL's speech appeared in full in the *Reflector: A Chronicle of Politics,* Vol. I, No. 10 (November, 1913), and in the *Peoria Herald Transcript,* Nov. 6, 1913.

cans in each precinct unite upon one man "without inquiring how he voted in 1912." Thus they would provide the basis for a real amalgamation. Upon these district leaders rested the whole superstructure of party organization, even up to the national committee and national nominating convention.

In late April, 1914, in an address on this subject to a large audience at Peoria, Illinois, he pointed to the falling prices as a warning of the need for Progressives and Republicans to come together quickly in order to win the mid-term elections. Otherwise, the recently enacted Underwood Tariff might remain in force long enough to precipitate a severe economic depression. If the tariff wall were rebuilt, he continued, prosperity would return, and the labor legislation advocated by the Progressives in their 1912 platform would become superfluous. He insisted, furthermore, that the Republican party had always been truly liberal. It "has learned in its long and eventful life," he exclaimed, "that motion is not always progress, any more than noise is always music or words always oratory. In its program of a half a century it has heeded Paul's admonition—'Prove all things; hold fast that which is good.' . . . The united wisdom and patriotism of all Republicans . . . are needed now as they never were needed before."[49]

In his private correspondence, however, Lowden manifested less confidence about the readiness of Progressives to rejoin their old party at no price except a share in the offices. The popular demand for direct primaries and other political reforms appeared to grow rather than diminish. Theodore Roosevelt gave no evidence of a willingness to parley with the Old Guard about reunion. Nevertheless, the outlook was not wholly dark. The party in power at Washington usually lost some of its congressional seats in a mid-year election, and 1914 gave promise of running true to form. Business lagged, and unemployment increased. The President could be effectively charged with ineptitude in his policy toward Mexico.[50] By "Pan-Americanizing" the Monroe Doctrine, repealing the Panama Canal tolls discriminating against England, and appeasing Colombia with a grant of money for the United States seizure of the Canal Zone a decade before, the Democratic administration might well make Roosevelt angry enough to lead his insurgents back into the Republican camp merely to increase the likelihood of Woodrow Wilson's defeat for re-election in 1916. Fusion movements between the Progressives and Republicans in California and New Jersey were already well advanced. After listening to the Panama tolls debate in Congress, Lowden candidly admitted that the President's strong moral position on that issue gave Senator Lawrence Sherman of Illinois good reason for voting with the Democrats. But he also knew that Sherman's action had offended the Pro-

49. FOL's speech before the Xanthor Lodge, Peoria, Illinois, Apr. 27, printed in full in the *Peoria Star,* Apr. 28, 1914: "The indispensable condition of successful self-government is the existence of two parties so nearly equal that each must inevitably act as a corrective of the other." The reunion of Progressives and Republicans was "natural, logical, inevitable."

50. FOL to J. W. Dwight, Washington, D.C., Dec. 5, 1913.

gressives in his state and inclined them against merging with the Republicans
to support the senator's bid for re-election.

During these same months, a half-dozen local Republican leaders quietly
promoted Lowden in their downstate neighborhoods as the man best qualified to be the next governor.[51] He knew about this scouting but apparently
had not prompted it. He continued to state publicly and even in letters to
some of his closest friends that he was in no sense a candidate for any office.
Nevertheless, he engaged in exploratory talks with Frank L. Smith of Dwight,
Len Small of Kankakee, and other main cogs in the state machine. By means
of frequent trips to Washington and letters from John W. Dwight of that
city, he kept in close touch with Senator Sherman and the Republican congressmen from Illinois. At Shelby Cullom's funeral in Springfield in late
January, 1914, Lowden found a large gathering of important men of his
party who were able to honor the dead without neglecting the political fortunes of the living. Newspapers soon mentioned his unusual activity. His
Peoria address, already mentioned, seemed like the speech of a candidate.
Although he told reporters that enjoying "the peace of 'Sinnissippi' " marked
the summit of his desires, he sent a copy of his Peoria remarks to Harvey
Ingham with the suggestion that the *Des Moines Register* might find them
acceptable for publication.[52]

Contrary to his hopes, no merger of the Progressive and Republican parties
either in Chicago or in the state at large took place during 1914. On the same
day in mid-September each party met in convention and drafted a platform.
Both documents denounced the Democrats for extravagant spending, for
failure to extend the classified civil service and to create a federal tariff commission, and for pledging to pay Colombia $25,000,000 as "conscience
money." Both favored woman suffrage. The Republicans, however, charged
the Democrats with "sectional and destructive experiments and legislation,"
while the Progressives called for more economic, social, and political reforms, including an anti-child-labor law, an eight-hour-day law for women
in industry, a social insurance measure, and the initiative, referendum, and
recall. Above all, their platform demanded a convention to revise Illinois's
outmoded constitution. If they came to power in Springfield, they promised
to investigate the traction "monopolies" of William B. McKinley and Samuel Insull, in order to find out whether they were paying their due share of
taxes. They unjustly charged Senator Sherman with being "smirched by
franchise grabbing and taint of legislative corruption" and called upon all
honest men to vote for their senatorial nominee, Raymond Robins, "who is
against Lorimerism and all it connotes."[53] In the light of their platforms, the
Illinois Republicans and Progressives remained far apart.

51. These chiefly were H. B. Ward of DuQuoin in southern Illinois, R. F. Bradford of
Pontiac in central Illinois, and J. R. Cowley of Freeport in northern Illinois. Congressman
Loren E. Wheeler was doing "gumshoe" work in FOL's behalf at Springfield among the
legislators.

52. FOL to H. Ingham, May 3, 1914.

53. Illinois Legislative Reference Bureau pamphlet, *Illinois Party Platforms, 1914* (Springfield, Ill., 1914).

Judging from the silence of these two documents, the leaders believed either that the European conflict was of no political concern to the voters of Illinois or that prudence counseled an avoidance of so divisive an issue. Hardly had the opposing armies begun to march than Lowden commented: "It is unthinkable that in some way this war should not speedily be stopped . . . it will take even the nations which conquer fifty years, at least, to repair the losses." By late September Lowden concluded somewhat bitterly: "The only person in the whole world, as far as I can see, who can derive any benefit from this war, is Wilson. Because of it he has been able, in large measure, to rehabilitate himself."[54] With so many voters of German and Irish backgrounds in Illinois and especially in Chicago, it behooved any pro-English office-seeker to guard his tongue. Until 1916, Lowden's speeches and letters gave no hint whether he favored the Allies or the central European powers. In late 1914, moreover, politicians complained that the war news drove their own activities from the headlines and that it was necessary to pay advertising rates in order to reach the public through the press.[55]

Lowden's four or five campaign speeches that autumn, ranging in location from Cairo at the southern tip of Illinois to the Cort Theater in Chicago, mainly pointed out the faults of the tariff and war-tax legislation of the Wilson regime and the absurdity of the Democratic warning that a vote for the Republican congressional candidates meant a vote for involvement in the war. He handled the Progressives gently and commended them for agreeing with the GOP that low tariffs injured the American farmers. Accepting the counsel of his friends, he talked informally to downstate audiences about his horses and cows, as well as about Wilson's highhandedness in dealing with Congress. Although he journeyed over the state to help the Republican candidates, he obviously used that opportunity to rebuild his own political fences.

The weakness of his party in Cook County on election day disappointed him, but he found much reason for good cheer in the general outcome of the voting in Illinois and the nation. Senator Sherman won re-election, and a number of Republican congressmen from Illinois, including Cannon and Foss, either retained their seats or regained those which they had lost in 1912. The little band of Progressives in the House of Representatives dwindled to one man. "As it is," Cannon chortled, "the result of the election . . . is sufficient to serve notice upon our Democratic friends to vacate on the 4th of March, 1917." "I hope," former President Taft wrote to former Secretary of State Knox on November 17, 1914, "the late election satisfied your desires. I am able to endure it with Christian resignation."[56]

In Chicago, however, William Lorimer lamented his financial reverses, his political eclipse, and the sorry showing made by Republican congressional

54. FOL to J. W. Dwight, Aug. 4 and Sept. 30, 1914.

55. E. C. Wetten, Chicago, to FOL, Aug. 31, 1914.

56. The Taft letter is quoted by George Mowry, *Theodore Roosevelt and the Progressive Movement* (Madison, Wis., 1946), p. 303. J. G. Cannon, Danville, Illinois, to FOL, Nov. 7, 1914.

candidates in Cook County. He blamed the outcome upon the bungling of Deneen and his "masters," the owners or publishers of the influential newspapers of the city. In one of the few long letters written by Lorimer during his career, he summoned Lowden to come forward "now," rally the faction-torn party about his flag, and

authorize your friends to pass the word down the line that you *are* a candidate for governor. . . . The situation awaits the *man* to give force and direction. . . . You are he. . . . I won't come out publicly for you for it would do you more harm than good . . . but . . . no one would hail your triumph with greater joy than I. Our party is in chaos all over the state due to lack of a leader. . . . "There is a tide in the affairs of men which if taken at the flood leads on to fortune."[57]

What Lowden replied to this appeal is unknown. Unaware that he merely echoed the words of a politician whom he heartily disliked, Charles G. Dawes a few days later also urged his friend to announce his candidacy. If he appeared in the arena as soon as possible, Dawes advised, he would discourage other Republicans from entering it as his rivals for the nomination. Furthermore, a quick entry would help foil Deneen's usual tactics of dividing the opposition within his own party by appearing to welcome its leaders as candidates and then defeating them all with the solid bloc of his own adherents.[58]

By late 1914, with many downstate leaders working quietly for his cause, with Senator Sherman on his side, and with Brundage, Dawes, Lorimer, Lundin, and Thompson ready to back him in Cook County, Lowden knew of no major resistance within his own party except possibly the enigmatic Deneen and his able co-worker, Roy West. Moreover, there was a strong rumor that Deneen would much rather go to the United States Senate than re-enter the Executive Mansion at Springfield. Here, then, might be the basis for an "understanding," although the next senatorial election in Illinois would not occur until 1918, when J. Hamilton Lewis' term neared its close. Encouraged by these favorable signs, Lowden assured his political intimates that he probably would seek the governorship, although he was not yet ready to announce his candidacy.

Characteristically, he hesitated to commit himself publicly and irrevocably to a course which would curb his freedom of action, subject him to renewed abuse, and perhaps endanger his newly found good health. If Illinois law had not obliged an aspirant to survive a primary campaign during the heat of a corn-belt summer and then move with scarcely a break into an equally strenuous election campaign, he might have been less reluctant to toss his hat into the ring. He and other political leaders vainly requested the legislature to shift the gubernatorial primary date from mid-September to early April.[59] Slow-moving local trains, roads often hub-deep in dust or mud, breathless

57. W. Lorimer to FOL, Nov. 6, 1914.

58. C. G. Dawes to FOL, Nov. 14, 1914.

59. Contrary to FOL's wish, the legislature in June, 1915, set Apr. 11, 1916, as the presidential preference primary date, and Sept. 13, 1916, for the gubernatorial primary.

nights in small hotels, and open-air speaking many times a day for weeks on end were inescapable circumstances, giving pause to men less concerned than Lowden about their personal appearance and creature comforts and less prone than he to wilt in torrid weather.

Every state-wide campaign in Illinois took place on two dissimilar fronts, scarcely less unlike in attitudes than in geographic extent. Cook County, comprising only a little more than one-sixtieth of the state's area, contained almost half of its six million people. A satisfactory downstate electioneering technique was unsuited to the metropolis, and the two electorates did not see eye to eye upon several important issues. An office-seeker was tempted either to sidestep these issues or to accommodate his stand upon them to the place where he happened to be canvassing for votes. Unlike most Chicagoans, downstate folk mostly favored prohibition but opposed woman suffrage. In the election of a governor or President, the big Republican outpouring downstate usually snowed under the Democratic majority in Chicago. The Progressive defection of 1912 had temporarily wiped out this advantage of the GOP and helps to explain why it earnestly wished for reunion.

The primary campaign began at the moment when a politician informed his friends about his "receptivity." The intra-party battle with his rivals was always longer and often as bitter, expensive, and exhausting as the election campaign itself. Perhaps the primary provided a more democratic way of choosing nominees than a party convention, but it cost so much that a candidate either had to be rich or willing to place himself under financial obligations to the persons or "interests" supplying the necessary cash. To reach every Republican before primary day by direct appeal from the platform or by leaflets required thousands of dollars. As a rule, no comparably expensive canvass faced a candidate after he had won the nomination. The state committee then bore much of his outlay, and he could count upon the support of most members of his party who had opposed him in the preprimary battle.

Early in a contest for the gubernatorial nomination, anywhere from a half-dozen to a dozen politicians customarily appeared in the arena. A number of the congressional districts and several of the larger downstate cities had "favorite sons," while the Republican factions in Chicago usually trotted out two or three. Probably most of these candidacies were not bona fide; at least their endurance was weak. Sometimes a local "machine" wished to compliment its leader and bring him evanescent fame by "booming him" for the governorship. A gesture of this sort occasionally paid a big political dividend if a major candidate felt sufficiently impressed by the upstart to promise, in exchange for his withdrawal, to back him for some lesser elective office or to allocate to him patronage in the event of his own election. When the members of a city or a regional Republican organization found themselves in hot disagreement over which one of the rival candidates for the nomination to support, their boss might quiet the dissension by entering the race himself. He continued to run until he and his coterie were "bought off" by one of the leading contestants or until it became fairly clear who would win in the primary. For obvious reasons, a local machine tried to be on the side of the victor or, better still, to have its support of some candidate make all the difference between his success and defeat.

Partly because its much smaller battle front fostered infighting and competition between newspapers for increased circulation or for domination over one or another of the rival candidates, the internecine war in Cook County exceeded the simultaneous downstate contest in bitterness and heedless violations of the laws against libel and slander. The political machines in Chicago were often more closely knit than those in the country districts. Furthermore, the city leaders showed a greater reluctance to compromise because more numerous and remunerative jobs awaited the victors. Noting the scandalous charges hurled back and forth between rival Republican bosses in Chicago, a downstate member of the party had good reason to conclude, even though his conclusion erred, that Cook County politicians were always incompetent and often dishonest.

No one Republican faction in Illinois had enough strength to fill all the state elective offices with its own members. The winning slate emerged from a coalition between one or several of the Chicago machines and one or several of those downstate. When, for example, a leader announced his wish to be the party's gubernatorial choice, he customarily declared that he was the puppet of no faction whatsoever. He really meant that he would welcome help from Republicans outside his own organization and, in exchange, would have it support their candidate for another office. From these "give and takes" a complete ticket eventually appeared, ready to test its strength in the party primary against other slates similarly evolved. While this contest was under way, the candidates paid homage to the folklore of American politics by avowing that, if elected, they would enter office free of entangling alliances or embarrassing pledges of any kind. Why it always seemed necessary to make a statement so greatly at variance with reality is hard to explain.

Like any other experienced politician, Lowden knew that even a highly qualified candidate courted defeat unless he built an organization to work for him. Unlike many professional politicians, however, he did not make the contriving and operating of his machine an end in itself but merely a necessary means whereby he might eventually have the planks in his platform enacted into law. This outlook lifted him above the common ruck of office-seekers. Furthermore, his involvement in many enterprises always kept him from feeling "dedicated" to a political career to the extent of letting it monopolize his thoughts and making him regard success at the polls as essential to his happiness.

Between 1913 and 1916 he said repeatedly that he was loath to re-enter politics.[60] Besides being absorbed in the development of his farm lands and

60. Letters of FOL to H. Ingham, May 25 and June 9; to Dr. E. Poppe, Burlington, Iowa, June 16; and to J. W. Dwight, July 31, 1915: "I am pretty well weaned from public life, and I shrink from giving up my independence."

the management of his other investments, he recognized that Mrs. Lowden would probably be more content if he did not seek public office. Denied vigorous good health, she could not look forward with keen anticipation to the social demands upon a governor's wife. By 1915, on the other hand, he liked to believe that, because many Wilsonian liberals and Bull Moosers were demonstrating how a man could be rich, progressive, and honest at the same time, the old prejudice against a wealthy office-seeker had considerably lessened. One of his campaign workers wrote: "The only thing they can say against him [Lowden] is that he is rich. . . . One thing is sure, he will not have to use the office to make money, but can devote his time to giving a high class administration and leave the record of it as a legacy to his children."[61] True enough, but his fortune inclined him to forget that most politicians could neither regard the salary attached to a public office as inconsequential nor count as sufficient remuneration the success of the cause for which they labored. Stated differently, Lowden might not conclude that the men who mainly assisted in his nomination and election were also the ones best fitted for appointment to top appointive posts. Persons excellently qualified for administrative offices often shunned the rough-and-tumble of practical politics. In 1915, however, Lowden did not yet have to choose between rewarding his supporters and serving his state.

During this entire year and until the spring of the next his statements to the press about his candidacy merely mentioned his probable willingness to yield to the "pressure of his friends" if a widespread demand for him became evident.[62] This coyness fooled no one. To the newspapers he was no less a candidate because he declined to accept that label formally. Everyone alert to the political undercurrents knew how he was working with might and main throughout the state—and at Washington at well—to create the favorable sentiment whose extent he professed to be waiting to determine. His correspondence files bulge with letters from his "stalking horses" among the legislators at Springfield and in the little rural county seats and from his well-wishers in the cities. They advised him whom to visit or write to and what to say when he spoke in some town or district in Illinois. Many farmers, they warned him, still refused to concede that he understood their needs. Hence he should portray in words and pictures his activities at "Sinnissippi." For the same reason, he invited local political leaders to conferences there or in a Chicago, Springfield, or St. Louis hotel room. His field workers sounded his praises to editors of county-seat newspapers and, by the spring of 1915, had persuaded the Republican central committees in several downstate counties to proclaim him their choice for the governorship.[63]

61. W. H. Stead to E. F. Achard, Ottawa, Illinois, Nov. 3, 1915.

62. FOL to C. W. McCall, Morrison, Illinois, Feb. 28, and to M. J. McGowan, Dixon, Illinois, May 12, 1915.

63. For example, R. F. Bradford, by letter on Apr. 10, 1915, urged FOL to write Omer N. Custer, former mayor of Galesburg, Illinois, and editor of the *Republican-Register* of that city. Thus, in so far as the MSS reveal, began the long and politically important friendship between Custer and FOL.

At the same time, Fred E. Sterling of Rockford, one of his most effective backers, sought to convert the waning enthusiasm of the *Chicago Tribune* for the Progressive party into an indorsement of Lowden. With an eye to Progressive support, Lowden addressed the state assembly in late March and urged it to call a convention for the purpose of revising the outmoded Illinois constitution. The new document, he said, should avoid detailed provisions inappropriate to an organic law. "I believe," he added, "we might learn much from Big Business which would help in conducting the business of the state of Illinois."[64]

Unknown even to most of his close associates, by March, 1915, and probably earlier, Lowden had arranged with William H. Stead of Ottawa to be his campaign manager. Stead accepted unwillingly but felt under deep obligation to Lowden for help in winning the attorney-generalship of Illinois eleven years before.[65] While Stead was clearing his desk preparatory to working full time in Lowden's interest, he wrote to all the county clerks and other locally prominent Republicans throughout the state. In this way he gathered the names of the precinct committeemen and everyone else who should receive campaign material. Like Lowden, he believed that business methods made for efficiency in politics as well as in government. Honest, loyal, thorough, and tireless, he commanded respect but not enthusiasm. To the exuberant and imaginative Gordon Ramsay, who soon took the lead in organizing Chicago businessmen behind Lowden's candidacy, Stead was a dour automaton. But he had Lowden's complete confidence, and fully deserved it.[66]

As always, the Republican party in Chicago was a complex institution with a structure and leadership difficult to understand. It, or rather several factions within it, elected Fred Busse as mayor in 1907. Thereafter for four years, much of his record in City Hall did little credit either to him or to his party. In 1911, over strong opposition from bipartisan reformers led by Charles E. Merriam, the Democratic former Mayor Carter Harrison, Jr., regained control of the city's administration. Badly shaken by this defeat, as well as by the expulsion of Lorimer from the United States Senate and the loss of many members to the Progressive party, the Republican organization needed skilful rebuilding. Both Deneen and Lowden turned to this task, but they worked at cross-purposes. Lowden's appeals to the Progressives, already mentioned, were not sufficiently generous to attract them back into the old party. When the governorship of Deneen ended in early 1913, he returned to Chicago and had better success. He drew many of the Progressives into an alliance with his bloc for the purpose of running a "fusionist" candidate for mayor. At the same time, Lowden helped produce an accord between the several anti-Deneen Republican groups and hoped that the coalition would dominate the party by the time of the mayoralty election of 1915.

64. MS of FOL's speech at Springfield, Illinois, Mar. 23, 1915.
65. See pp. 130 and 134.
66. G. A. Ramsay to FOL, Dec. 14, 1914.

During Busse's administration, Sherman's and Dawes's close friend Edward J. Brundage was corporation counsel of Chicago. After Busse's death in 1914, many in his faction turned to Brundage for leadership. He thereupon appeared willing to hitch his political wagon to Lowden's rising star. In terms of Chicago politics, this meant a *rapprochement* between the Brundageites and Lowden's old Cook County friends, the Lorimerites, who were grooming the popular alderman, William Hale Thompson, for the mayoralty race. After defeating his fusionist rival in the primary, Thompson soundly trounced his Democratic opponent in the April, 1915, election. "What a victory it was!" Lowden exclaimed in a wire to "Big Bill," "My heartiest congratulations." Thompson's success damaged Deneen's prestige and boosted Lowden's political fortunes. On the other hand, if Deneen's candidate had won, the Progressive party in Chicago most probably would have disbanded as a separate organization.

The new mayor quickly added to his popularity. His skilful settlement of a streetcar strike, his pungent oratory, dramatic attire, and readiness to act decisively in emergencies led many good citizens to condone his close ties with Lorimer. Even Dawes came momentarily to agree with Lowden that "Hizzoner" seemed to be "a coming man" whose friendship would be well worth having.[67] Not until some years later would the "Thompson gang" remind many shocked Chicagoans of the Tweed Ring in New York City a half-century before. But, even from the outset of his administration, Thompson made clear that he did not include party harmony among his aims. Revenge against the Deneenites, neglect of the Brundageites and Progressives, and everything for the Lorimer wing comprised his patronage policy. With ample financial backing and plenty of jobs to dole out, he made the "poor Swede," Fred Lundin, his chief almoner. A good friend of Lundin from their congressional days together, Lowden had invested $13,000 in one of his business ventures.[68] Probably few men in American urban history have been his equal in building and operating an intricate political machine and keeping it well oiled. Politics to him signified a business in which the managerial staff deserved to pocket most of the gains. Any favor conferred must return at least an equivalent from the beneficiary.

Firm in the saddle at City Hall, the Thompson organization was clearly in a position to give, while Lowden was as clearly in a mood to receive. For years the cordial good fellowship of Thompson had elicited from Lowden a warmth of response which Deneen's aloofness never invited. Although Thompson encouraged his friend's ambition, Deneen fostered it with no gesture of approval. If Lowden entered the gubernatorial primary, he obviously would need the votes of many Cook County Republicans. On the other

67. Copy of letter of C. G. Dawes to Senator L. Y. Sherman, July 1, 1915.

68. In 1912 and 1913, FOL purchased 300 shares each of preferred and common stocks, as well as some bonds, of Lundin and Company, a mail-order drug and soft-drink concern. On Jan. 12, 1916, FOL asked Lundin to give him in cash whatever these securities were then worth. The sum received is not known.

hand, he had assured his downstate workers and Senator Sherman that he would be beholden to no man or group for monetary aid and would remain apart from the squabbles of rival factions.[69] The time was ripe for the "Squire" and the mayor to talk business. In all likelihood the discussion would be wholly amicable. The danger lay in the future, when, if Lowden reached the Executive Mansion, he would have to confront the Thompson-Lundin policy of rewards and punishments. The mayor and he might then be surprised to discover that their similar apprenticeships in Chicago politics had taught them very different lessons.

69. FOL to H. B. Ward, DuQuoin, Illinois, Dec. 16, 1914.

CHAPTER XII

WINNING THE GOVERNORSHIP, 1915–17

On a week end in mid-May, 1915, at Eagle Lake, Wisconsin, in the country home of former state Senator Albert C. Clark of Chicago, Lowden discussed politics with Thompson, Lundin, and other members of the mayor's staff. No record of the conversations survives. Occurrences shortly thereafter suggest that Lowden promised to back "Big Bill" for national committeeman against the Deneenite incumbent, Roy O. West, while the mayor agreed to support Lowden for the governorship. Thompson's precinct committeemen would circulate petitions asking Lowden to declare his candidacy, and Lundin apparently guaranteed at least three or four hundred thousand signatures.[1] No certain evidence exists that at this conference or at the longer one at "Castle Rest" three months later the participants came to any clear-cut understanding about patronage.

Immediately after the Eagle Lake discussions, Thompson made public his decision to help Lowden win the governorship. At the same time, Brundage and Dawes formally launched Sherman's campaign for the Republican presidential nomination. Thompson's refusal to commit himself in Sherman's favor angered Brundage. He and the mayor were also at odds over patronage, and Lowden feared lest their quarrel seriously injure his own cause.[2] Working with equal vim for Sherman and Lowden, Dawes bluntly reminded the senator that Brundage was disregarding an elementary rule of politics by failing to isolate his local squabbles from his endeavors in Sherman's behalf. To alienate Thompson so that the Illinois delegation to the national nominating convention would not be solidly for Sherman would blast his hopes.[3]

Dawes, however, was too pessimistic. After Congressmen Martin Madden and James R. Mann of Chicago discovered that few Republicans wished to make either of them the "favorite son" of Illinois for the presidency and after Thompson had conferred with Lowden in late August at "Castle Rest," the

1. Leslie P. Volz, who was Lundin's secretary in 1915, told the author on Dec. 6, 1950, that it was Lundin's guaranty of so much Cook County support that ended FOL's indecision about running for governor. In view of FOL's activities before May, 1915, Volz's view exaggerated Lundin's influence.

2. On Feb. 21, 1916, FOL wrote Sherman: "I realize thoroughly the risk I run of being badly injured in this organization fight, but how in the world to settle it, is beyond my wits."

3. C. G. Dawes to L. Y. Sherman, June 17 and July 1, 1915; Dawes to FOL, July 6, and FOL's reply, July 7, 1915.

mayor finally announced that he would rally his cohorts behind Sherman. By then, however, Thompson's ruthless exclusion of Brundageites from city jobs had driven some of them into Deneen's camp. Until the late winter of 1916, Lowden, Dawes, and Sherman tried in vain to effect even a partial reconciliation between Brundage and Thompson.

Among Lowden's supporters by the summer of 1915, the aggressive Thompsonites had by far the most efficient and best-disciplined organization. They sought to rebuild the old Lorimer entente with downstate Republicans so as to reach up for the control of the state administration. Their will to rule imperiled Lowden's candidacy. His supporters in rural Illinois naturally wanted to back a winner and hence welcomed his tie-in with Thompson as long as it did not become a yoke. When Frank L. Smith, the Dwight banker and realtor who had managed Taft's state campaign for re-election in 1912, announced his candidacy for the gubernatorial nomination, he stressed that he was as much a successful businessman as Lowden and had the added virtue of freedom from Chicago's City Hall. Smith also pointed scornfully to the rural camouflage whereby his competitor tried to disguise the fact that he was really a city man, heavily interested in many big corporations and much more at home on La Salle Street than on a country road. Although both these lines of attack had been followed *ad nauseam* and with more justification ten years before, when Lowden first tried to be governor, they still carried weight in all of the downstate area outside his own congressional district. They put him on the defensive in rural Illinois by obliging him once again to undertake the wearisome task of demonstrating his right to call himself a farmer.

He never completely solved the problem of how to maintain his own independence without offending Thompson. The two men took care not to appear together at the same downstate rallies, fish fries, barbecues, old settlers' picnics, and harvest homes. Lowden had the more reason to be cautious in this regard because many of his own "die-hards" of 1904, as well as the followers of Richard Yates, stood ready to support him if he made clear that he was not simply the tail of Thompson's political kite. At the outset, Stead sharply warned Lowden against seeming to be Fred Lundin's puppet and even threatened to step wholly from the picture unless he could control the downstate campaign absolutely. His insistence upon a complete concentration of responsibility in his own capable hands meant efficient management, but it caused Lowden's workers in Chicago to writhe. They charged that the Ottawa lawyer was ready to antagonize the Cook County bloc if, by doing so, he could gain more downstate support for his candidate. Perhaps Mayor Thompson had really jumped on Lowden's band wagon rather than the other way around, but Stead was indiscreet to declare this publicly and with such evident relish.[4]

He and his two assistants slowly constructed a smoothly operating organization downstate. Joseph C. Mason, who had served Deneen at Springfield

4. W. H. Stead to G. Ramsay, Dec. 9, and Ramsay's reply, Dec. 10, 1915.

during his governorship, was an excellent director of publicity. James Cowley spread the good news about Lowden among the publishers of Illinois local newspapers and prepared biographical material in leaflet form for mailing broadcast whenever Stead gave the signal. Many unpaid workers and a few on salary, including at least one assemblyman, drummed up enthusiasm for Lowden in their own neighborhoods, made scouting trips into other areas, and kept Stead in touch with the activities of the opposition. Each of the following quotations refers to a different person, but they together illustrate the nature of these agents' reports:[5]

A swede lawyer who is quite a fellow in the county except for his occasional sprees, however, the political fellows all like him. If I were you I would send Palmer Anderson over there to see him.

An old time republican who has nothing to do but live and talk politics. . . . Give him a good letter.

Give him a good letter as they tell me he makes a lot of noise—he is a peg-legged blacksmith at a mine.

C—— is County Judge and a brother of Circuit Judge C——. . . . You better give the judge the glad hand in good language.

These scouts often took the lead in forming clubs to work for Lowden, distributing pledge cards, initiating petitions begging him to run for the governorship, and gathering the names of all Republicans and Progressives who had voted in each precinct in the 1914 primary. These names, supplemented by many others sent in by county clerks, eventually comprised Stead's mailing list of over 250,000 persons. He gave special attention to all veterans' organizations and to his and Lowden's "brothers" in their many fraternal orders. Stead's accordion-like filing case for each downstate county soon became swollen with his correspondence to his field workers and local bigwigs. To his considerable annoyance, the Cook County canvass largely eluded his control. It could not be centralized because of the frequent lack of harmony between the four pro-Lowden groups—those who kept in direct touch with either Lowden or Stead, the businessmen organized by Dawes and Ramsay, the many Republicans looking to Lundin and Thompson for orders, and the comparatively small remnant in Brundage's camp who still cheered enthusiastically for Lowden.

Recognizing that the candidate's wealth would be a favorite target of his rivals, Stead took pains not to give them just grounds for accusing him of spending lavishly to "buy up" Republican newspapers or supplying Lowden clubs with extravagant amounts of buttons, banners, and printed materials.[6]

5. R. F. Bradford to W. H. Stead, Dec. 13, 1915.

6. Up to mid-August, 1915, Stead paid nothing for advertising except $1,650 for three articles in the *Breeder's Gazette*. The full cost of Stead's operations up to April, 1916, is not known. From July 1 to Oct 1, 1915, he spent $7,125. This included the $1,650 mentioned above, $850 for an automobile, $300 for lapel buttons, $600 salary for an assistant, etc. On August 17, Stead reminded FOL that he was losing $3,000–$3,500 legal fees a year by managing the campaign and hoped that he would not have to pocket this loss. FOL probably assumed it, but the sources are silent.

If he subscribed to their papers and furnished them with text and "cuts," he found most editors willing to publish gratis an occasional article about farming, stock-raising, wild flowers, wild animals, or silviculture at "Sinnissippi" or about the Black Hawk Trail, the "Hilltop" home for convalescent children, or Lowden's avocations.[7] The several newspaper publishers on Stead's board of strategy sent him extra copies of their best political editorials whenever their tone was not too belligerently pro-Lowden. Stead mailed these to friends, who undertook to have them reprinted in their local newspapers. When editors grumbled about being asked to do a lot for nothing, they received tactfully phrased notes from Stead assuring them of Lowden's readiness, once he announced his candidacy, to pay advertising rates for publishing all material sent them from the headquarters office. He continuously cautioned his office staff and field workers against building up Lowden by pulling down his rivals. In so far as possible, the opposition Republicans must be kept in good humor so that, if their favorite candidate withdrew, they might come over to the "right" side.

Some of Stead's correspondents, including a few newspaper editors, wanted to know what would be "in it for them" if they worked for Lowden or pledged to vote for him in the primary. Letters of this sort ranged from blunt demands for "a good job" or invitations to invest in the writers' businesses to a host of requests for donations to worthy projects. These *quid pro quo* Republicans often simulated a lively interest in building a church or paying off its mortgage. "I have been misrepresented . . . so often in the past, in the use of money," Lowden informed a Danville pastor, ". . . I want to be in a position to say that not one single dollar has been contributed by me either for philanthropic or religious purposes with a view to influencing any support in my favor."[8]

If this correspondence accurately mirrors the ethics of the Negro leaders in Illinois politics forty years ago, they stood on the auction block ready to support the candidate offering them the largest gift of money for some social or religious enterprise. Lowden and Stead rarely joined in the bidding and never, in so far as the records reveal, promised a job in return for help. On the other hand, neither man ever offended a suppliant by calling his offer of assistance, in exchange for a reward, insulting and dishonest. Throughout the entire campaign, Stead worked to bring Negro voters downstate and in Chicago to the side of his candidate. The seven thousand Pullman porters declared in his favor almost at once. Paid agents organized Lowden Colored Clubs, and Negro newspapers received generous amounts of advertising. Later in the contest, when the manager of Chicago's Great Northern Hotel barred Negroes from using the elevators to go to Lowden's

7. An *American Forestry* (Washington, D.C.) article on FOL's pines was copied in 38 Illinois newspapers in a single week of January, 1916, at a cost to Stead's office of only $25 for 100 reprints.

8. FOL to Rev. E. L. Krumreig, Danville, Illinois, Apr. 12, 1916.

eleventh-floor headquarters, Stead quickly forced a cancellation of the order by threatening to move elsewhere.[9]

Lowden's efforts to prove that he was an Illinois farmer and not a city "dude" with an agricultural hobby shaped most of his few speeches during 1915, as well as the downstate publicity emanating from Stead's office. W. E. Taylor, director of the Soil Culture Division of Deere and Company of Moline, and R. M. Patterson on the Illinois Board of Livestock Inspectors also worked to this end. At the close of 1915 Lowden distributed 25,000 calendars bearing an attractive picture of his purebred cattle. Although the hope of political advantage mainly determined his course at this juncture, he was not posing. His long hesitation in formally announcing his candidacy arose in part from his doubt whether he would be happier and could render greater public service in the governor's chair or by continuing with voice, pen, and practice at "Sinnissippi" and on his plantations to advance the cause of better agriculture. As in the early 1900's, when he teetered for a time between the law and politics and between a city and a country home, he now wavered between yielding once more to the lure of politics and dedicating the remainder of his life to the farmers' welfare. Perhaps he would find that the one pursuit did not exclude the other.

His headquarters confidently summarized his congressional voting record on measures desired by labor unions. Many wage-earners, however, continued to view him skeptically because of his wealth, his corporation directorships, and, above all, his allegedly close affiliation with the Pullman Company and its open-shop policy. The opposition even resurrected the old canard about his support of George M. Pullman during the Pullman strike.[10] For these reasons Stead and his staff took extra pains to inform union leaders that the candidate had risen from the poverty of an Iowa blacksmith's home, that he probably had not even met Pullman by 1894 when the strike occurred, and that he had severed most of his ties with big business. How many converts he made from the ranks of labor is unknown, but at least several Illinois workingmen's journals supported him, including the *Bloomington Trade Review*, the *Peoria Labor Gazette*, the *Decatur Labor World*, and the *Union Advocate* of Chicago and Quincy. Although several leaders of the conservative railroad brotherhoods favored his nomination, they could help him but little in the coal counties of southern Illinois, where Frank Farrington, the president of the United Mine Workers of America, stoutly backed Frank L. Smith.[11]

The rising prohibition forces in Illinois, spoken for mainly by F. Scott Mc-

9. W. H. Stead to R. Townsend, Oct. 6, 1916.

10. J. H. Walker, president of the Illinois AF of L, to Mayor Thompson, Sept. 21, published in *Belleville* (Ill.) *Democrat*, Sept. 23, 1915. In mid-March, 1916, there were disturbing rumors of the injury being done to FOL's candidacy by a strike of 400 Pullman Company workers for a pay increase from an alleged 23 cents an hour to 28 cents (J. C. Mason to FOL, Mar. 27, 1916).

11. See pp. 284–85.

Bride and his Anti-Saloon League, also viewed Lowden with distrust. Robert Clarke, a large Peoria distiller, carefully kept his support unobtrusive, lest it work to his friend's injury. Stead received an occasional letter charging that Lowden had been drunk in 1904 after failing to win the gubernatorial nomination and also at Governor Deneen's inaugural reception early in the following year. Stead's replies flatly denied the truth of these stories or somewhat inconsistently gave assurance that the candidate had long since become a temperate drinker or, what was untrue, that he did not drink at all. Since his face flushed in hot weather or when he was tired, his appearance sometimes led people to conclude that he had been imbibing. Justice J. H. Cartwright of the Illinois Supreme Court appealed to McBride to treat Lowden more fairly by stopping the assaults made upon him in the Anti-Saloon League's organ, the *American Issue*. In his unsatisfactory reply, McBride disclaimed any personal ill will toward Lowden but deplored his help from the "liquor interests."[12]

Seeking support from the "wets" and "drys" alike, Lowden declared that he belonged in neither camp. He recognized the trend of public opinion toward absolute prohibition, but he believed that it should not come at one fell swoop. When Mayor Thompson in October, 1915, surprised many Chicago saloon owners by enforcing the Sunday-closing law against their places of business, he drew a quick indorsement from Lowden, together with a pledge that, if elected governor, he would "perform this duty without fear and without favor."[13] "Your courageous and manly stand," Dawes assured him at once, "brought everybody else into line, but it is only what I expected of you and always shall expect under similar circumstances. Just such chances to do the right thing courageously are what make public office worth having."

How many of the "drys" would follow the behest of the Anti-Saloon League and whether they would injure Smith or Lowden the more were two of the campaign's imponderables. As the months went by, the league's opposition intensified, and its representatives spoke in many downstate Protestant churches.[14] If the mounting number of queries in Stead's mail about Lowden's drinking habits reflected the activities of the league, it no doubt cost him some votes. At the same time a whisper went the rounds that Mrs. Lowden was a Catholic. With reluctance she finally answered an inquiry about her religion by affirming that she was a Presbyterian and, when in Chicago, attended Dr. Gunsaulus' church.[15]

12. *American Issue* (Illinois ed.), July 30 and Aug. 20, 1915.

13. FOL's wire to the *Chicago Tribune,* Oct. 6, 1915; FOL to A. W. Rosecrans, Ashton, Illinois, Oct. 21, 1915: ". . . absolute obedience to the law is more important under a republic or democracy than under any other form of government. For in a republic or democracy law is the only supreme thing, and in every form of government there must be something supreme . . . or the result is anarchy."

14. *American Issue,* Aug. 11 and Sept. 8, 1916; printed letter of F. S. McBride to "Dear Friend," Aug. 22, 1916.

15. Mrs. Lowden to G. W. Sargent, Meredosia, Illinois, July 6, 1916.

Several clergymen did all in their power to counteract this harmful gossip. Dr. Gunsaulus and Dr. Johnston Myers, of the Emmanuel Baptist Church of Chicago, and the Rev. I. P. Berry, pastor of the Methodist Church in Oregon, authorized Stead to mention them to his correspondents as ministers eager to testify to Lowden's sobriety. His posters declaring his stand on local option bore the indorsements of the Rev. Frank O. Sheets, superintendent of the Aurora District of the Methodist Episcopal Church, and of the Rev. Fred D. Stone, pastor of a Methodist church in Elgin. More than any other clergyman, Dr. Myers put his pen and his influence at Lowden's disposal. Ministering to a large church on South Wabash Avenue in Chicago, he had for years furnished breakfasts to "down-and-outers" in his section of the city. Lowden often contributed generously to this charity. In gratitude, Dr. Myers wrote many letters to downstate clergymen telling about his friend's character and kindness and urging them to use their influence in his behalf.

In the summer of 1915 a Chicago newspaper aptly characterized Lowden's policy as one of "watchful waiting." Although Thompson and Lundin pressed him to announce his candidacy boldly and at once, he declined because he believed that Frank L. Smith had tossed his hat prematurely into the ring. A boom, once launched, was difficult and expensive to maintain for long under a full head of steam. Farmers would not come in large numbers to the Republican "roundups" until they had harvested their crops. News about the European battle fronts and Wilson's foreign policy crowded Illinois politics out of the headlines. Lowden refused to let his informal candidacy keep him and his wife from going in late summer for a seven weeks' stay at "Castle Rest." He even directed Stead to forward no Chicago newspapers unless something of particular importance occurred. When Thompson and Lundin spent a week in August as his guests, they told him that over two hundred thousand Cook County voters had signed petitions asking him to run for governor and that the number of indorsers was increasing daily.[16]

To offset the unfavorable impression made upon downstate Republicans by this visit, Lowden asked Stead to come to "Castle Rest" for four days in September. He brought little except encouraging news. Indeed, he feared lest the fast-rising tide might ebb before primary day, still a year in the future. For this reason, he counseled the willing Lowden to hold back announcing his candidacy, at least until the state fair opened in Springfield, and to delay his return to Illinois until after the earlier Kankakee fair, where the Thompson forces wished to monopolize the political spotlight. In preparation for the fair at Springfield, Stead framed a letter for Lowden's signature, to be printed on "Sinnissippi" stationery and mailed from Oregon, inviting the five or six thousand Republican precinct committeemen, members of the legislature, judges, and county officials to call upon "the Squire" at the Leland Hotel. "We must make clear," added Stead, "that your *country* friends as compared with our Chicago friends occupy seats in the main tent." He

16. Mrs. Lowden's diary, Aug. 16–24, 1915.

reserved three connecting rooms at the Leland, close to the main stream of traffic in that favorite rendezvous of Illinois politicians. Prudently, he also engaged two bedrooms on an upper floor, "where we can get a rest, after midnight at least."[17]

Mayor Thompson and over five hundred of his stalwarts, carrying no Lowden banners but decked out with ten-gallon hats, bamboo canes, and "$2 badges" bearing "Big Bill's" photograph, went to the state fair on a special train on September 21.[18] Lowden had reached Chicago three days before, talking "a lot about fishing but nothing about politics as he tip-toes his way around the 'Loop' " to confer with Stead and Homer K. Galpin of the Brundage forces.[19] The next morning he left for Springfield, attended by about two hundred members of the "Young Men's Frank O. Lowden Club." At the Leland Hotel he found Frank L. Smith's headquarters already open, with its leader announcing a platform upon which he would run if he became the choice of the Republican party for the governorship.

The *Chicago Herald* prophesied that "the most thrilling spectacle" at the fair would be "the chariot race of the governorship candidates," with many downstate politicians on edge because "Lundin is trying to kidnap their Ben Hur."[20] This forecast failed of fulfilment. Although Thompson and his lieutenant carefully avoided Lowden, the benefits conferred by their discretion were more than offset by the mayor's harangue against Deneen and West for alleged "treason against Taft" at the nominating convention of 1912. After this ill-advised attack upon their chief, the Deneenites felt even less inclined than before to support " 'Big Bill's' candidate" for the governorship. His diatribe helped to thwart Lowden's efforts to foster harmony within his party's ranks and draw the Progressives back by friendliness rather than by offering them any important concession on issues.[21]

Lowden made no speech at the fair but released a statement disappointing to many of his followers because he omitted an unqualified promise to be a candidate. He said:

I came to Springfield Tuesday afternoon. Since then I have met hundreds of Republicans from different parts of the state, and have frankly discussed the situation with them. If the sentiment which I have found continues, I will be a candidate for governor, without pledges or promises of any kind whatsoever, and at the proper time will enter upon and conduct a vigorous campaign of which W. H. Stead of Ottawa, former attorney-general, will have entire charge. I shall welcome the support of every Republican in the state, but I will not be the candidate of any faction.

In a concluding paragraph he partially justified his delay in arriving at a decision by saying that the presidential primary of the coming April must take

17. W. H. Stead to FOL, Aug. 19; FOL to Stead, Aug. 22, 1915.

18. *Chicago Daily News,* Aug. 28 and Sept. 21, 1915.

19. *Chicago Post,* Sept. 18 and 20, 1915.

20. *Chicago Herald,* Sept. 21, 1915.

21. *Chicago Journal,* Sept. 23, 1915. FOL reported to his wife: "The thing that pleased me most was the way I stood it physically . . . a cruel test of three terrible days."

precedence over the gubernatorial primary five months later. He referred favorably to Senator Sherman's presidential ambitions but made no mention of Thompson's wish to be Republican national committeeman. He obviously had so worded the statement as to reassure downstate Republicans that he was not "Lundin's man," that he had not agreed upon a "slate" of state officials, and that he was not then, and never would be, in bondage to Chicago's City Hall.

From the close of the fair until the following spring, he left the advancement of his campaign largely to his headquarters staff. Besides visiting the Panama-Pacific Exposition at San Francisco, he spent about three weeks "politicking" in Washington, inspected his Arkansas properties, and stayed a fortnight with Mrs. Lowden and her mother at Ormond Beach, Florida. To the frequent inquiries about his candidacy he answered vaguely that he "supposed he would have to enter the race eventually but was finding it most difficult to decide."

During these same months, however, not the slightest doubt plagued Stead about what the decision would be. He and his co-workers extended the size of their mailing list, prepared pamphlets, postcards, and other material for distribution, and made contracts with union-shop firms to supply "Lowden Forever" banners, lapel buttons, pins, and posters.[22] He stayed severely away from districts where rivals for the gubernatorial nomination lived, even though their congressmen assured him that they were covertly for Lowden but dared not declare openly for him until after the primary. Mason gathered weekly statistics showing the number of newspaper columns of helpful publicity which had appeared during the preceding seven days, the number of Illinois Republican editors friendly to Lowden as compared with those for his rivals, and a summary of the latter's arguments and activities.[23] Thanks to these analyses and frequent reports from his field workers and other political friends, Stead kept his finger continually on the public pulse.

He tried to have one Republican and one Progressive take the initiative for Lowden in every downstate precinct. The precinct leaders within a county became its Lowden committee. Whenever possible, each committee included representatives of all Republican cliques. Its presiding officer and secretary maintained liaison with Stead's office and encouraged the organization of Lowden clubs in their locality. Membership entailed merely the signing of a printed card reading, "I Favor the Nomination of Frank O. Lowden of Ogle County as the Republican Candidate for Governor of Illinois in 1916." The "Creed" on the card's reverse side began by evoking the shades of Lincoln, Grant, and Logan, then pointed with alarm at the economic hard times attending "Democratic misrule" in state and nation and closed with a

22. FOL lapel buttons cost $5.75 per thousand; posters cost $1,275 per hundred thousand, and a 12-foot-long muslin banner in colors, about $8.00. The "Lowden Forever" slogan harked back to the 1904 deadlock.

23. In February, 1916, a sixteen-page pamphlet, containing a biographical sketch and pro-Lowden editorials from thirty Illinois papers, was mailed to 35,000 persons distributed by residence in almost every precinct.

forecast that, if Lowden were nominated, "an overwhelming victory will be achieved at the polls and the welfare and prosperity of the people of this state will be assured." The club members constituted the preferred mailing list in Stead's office. By comparing the signatures from any one county with the names on the polling list in its county clerk's office, he could easily discover which local leaders still needed to be converted to Lowden's cause.

Although, by the winter's end, Stead viewed the downstate situation with confidence, he felt uneasy about Chicago. As soon as the campaign shifted into high gear there, Gordon Ramsay's Business Men's Club would do effective work, but the Young Men's Cook County Frank O. Lowden Club was merely a cog in the Thompson-Lundin machine. Stead reluctantly recognized the need for pro-Lowden downstaters to keep in friendly touch with Thompson, but he firmly opposed giving the mayor sole charge of Lowden's fortunes in Cook County. Should "Big Bill" acquire such a monopoly, Deneen and his powerful city bloc would never support Lowden's candidacy. If the former governor decided to run again or bring out a strong candidate for the position—and rumors persisted that he would do so—the result might be catastrophic.[24] Following the aldermanic primary in late February, when the Thompson forces polled less than half the total Republican vote, Stead threatened to resign unless Lowden broke the grip of City Hall on his Cook County campaign and put it in charge of a twenty-man committee drawn from all factions. Eventually, Lowden yielded, but he wondered how completely he could isolate himself from Thompson and Lundin without alienating them. On the other hand, Stead felt certain that they needed Lowden more than he needed them, at least until after the national committeeman issue was decided in June.[25]

Beginning in the late winter of 1916, Lowden accepted more invitations to speak than for several years but centered his remarks almost wholly upon national issues. In the opinion of Will Hays, chairman of the Indiana Republican State Central Committee, Lowden delivered a "wonderful speech" on February 12, before the Lincoln League of Terre Haute. Declaring that Washington must uphold America's neutral rights to their fullest extent against England and Germany, he denounced any move to involve his country in a foreign alliance, even in the guise of President Wilson's Pan-Americanization of the Monroe Doctrine, and spoke out for universal military training and other preparedness measures short of conscription. He thought, however, that there was less danger of involvement in the European conflict than in 1914.[26]

24. Fred Smith of Peoria, Illinois, wrote FOL on March 6, 1916: "I have never been so confident of anything as I am of your winning. I wish we had Deneen. His is the only name I am afraid of as a candidate."

25. S. A. Ettelson, Chicago, to FOL, Mar. 3, 1916; W. H. Stead to FOL, Apr. 8 and 11, 1916. FOL conferred with Thompson on April 9. Stead's threat to resign in his letter of the eighth may have been merely to strengthen FOL's hand when he talked to the mayor.

26. W. H. Hays to FOL, Feb. 15, 1916.

President Wilson's Mexican policy of "meddling" and his refusal to recognize Huerta also drew Lowden's fire, but he aimed it mainly at the Democratic tariff policy. After expatiating at length about the differences between a revenue and a protective tariff, he declared that the low rates in the Underwood Law would have caused even greater economic miseries if its power for evil had not been weakened by the "artificial protection" provided by the war. Farmers and businessmen alike, Lowden contended, needed a nonpartisan tariff commission. The Underwood tariff was of mongrel breed—a measure tossed together mainly at the behest of southern Democrats without regard either to the revenue or to the protective principle and hence a prime illustration of the sort of monstrosity to be expected from a Congress unguided by a commission of experts. Being a hybrid measure, even a commission could never administer it successfully.

A few days after his Terre Haute address, Lowden spoke before the Union Club of Belvidere, Illinois, and had a speech read for him at Knox College.[27] In these he elaborated his views about foreign affairs and military preparedness. Although he extolled the Monroe Doctrine, he advocated its abandonment as preferable to Wilson's scheme for enforcing it in concert with the Latin-American governments. People in the United States, native to one or another of the European belligerent countries, could not comply with the President's admonition to be neutral in thought, but they undoubtedly would be loyal to their adopted nation if it were drawn into the maelstrom. While carrying through the military preparedness program, so necessary to national security, Americans should not forget to gird themselves for the tasks of peace. Basic to the achievement of security against both foreign and domestic dangers was a "religious awakening." "There never was a time in history," he warned, "when God was more often on the lips of men and so seldom in their hearts."

Not until the Swedish-American Republican Clubs' annual "love feast" at Princeton, Illinois, on March 9—and then only because overly long orations by his predecessors on the program forced him to substitute a few extemporaneous remarks for his prepared speech if he were not to miss his train—did he shift from national issues and plead earnestly for an end of factionalism within his party in Illinois and a "return home" by the Progressives. Although he felt gratified by the attention bestowed upon him at Princeton, including a seat beside Senator Sherman in the lead automobile of the parade, he returned to "Sinnissippi" exhausted by the day's crowded festivities, disgruntled because he had been almost pushed off the banquet program, and determined to make no more speeches until the Republican state convention assembled at Peoria six weeks later. To ward off further invitations, he left almost at once for his Arkansas plantations and subsequently for a vacation in Florida.

To his annoyance, state Senator Medill McCormick obliged him to break

27. *Belvidere* (Ill.) *Republican,* Feb. 19, 1916; *Galesburg* (Ill.) *Mail,* Feb. 22, 1916.

his silence in late March by asking the gubernatorial aspirants to reply publicly to four questions. McCormick believed that the voters should know whether Lowden and his rivals favored mayor-and-council control of all Chicago's public utilities, a state-wide plebiscite on the calling of a constitutional convention, a consolidation and centralized control of the state's administrative agencies, and a concentration of responsibility for the state's financial affairs by means of an executive budget. Except to the first, Lowden's answers were unqualified affirmatives. Chicago's City Hall, said he, should oversee all public utilities operating wholly within the city, but the Public Utilities Commission of the state should regulate those serving several municipalities.[28] His competitors for the nomination answered approximately in the same way.

During these weeks, Stead and his staff worked to gain as many friends as possible in the Republican state convention scheduled to meet in Peoria on April 21, so that the platform drafted there would uphold what Lowden had been saying in his speeches. In line with this purpose and under pressure from Stead, he reluctantly agreed to advance the time of formally announcing his candidacy from late June, after the national ticket had been named, to April 13, or just before the party's county and congressional district organizations chose their delegates to the Peoria gathering. Further to influence the platform-makers, Stead and Lowden prepared a statement of issues for release to the press simultaneously with the declaration of candidacy. They twice consulted Mayor Thompson while drafting this document. Newspaper readers in Illinois knew well in advance of the primaries on April 11 that Lowden's months of hesitation had come to an end.

These primaries were for the selection of congressional district delegates and their alternates to the national nominating convention and of a state central committeeman from each of the twenty-five congressional districts. The Progressive party as well as the Democrats and Republicans put up nominees in every district. The outcome in the Republican camp dispirited both Lowden and Thompson because it portended continued Deneenite control of the state central committee.[29] On the other hand, the prospect was not wholly bleak. The Deneen forces let it be known that they would not oppose the candidacy of Lowden's backer, Fred Sterling, to head that committee. Furthermore, because of the rebuff to the Thompsonites in the primary, no one could fairly charge Lowden with hinging his decision to run upon the ability of the mayor to become master of the state Republican organization.

Thus, on April 12, Lowden mailed notes to about 250,000 Illinois Republicans, making known his gubernatorial candidacy and that his "vigorous state-wide campaign" before the September primaries would be managed by Stead from new headquarters in the Lumber Exchange Building in Chicago. On the following day, Justice Cartwright asked Lowden at a meeting in Oregon to bow to the heavy popular demand by becoming a candidate.

28. *Chicago Examiner,* Apr. 10, 1916.

29. Leaflet compiled by L. G. Stevenson, secretary of state of Illinois, *Official List of Candidates for the Primary Election, April 11, 1916* (Springfield, Ill., 1916).

In accepting the call, he guaranteed to make his campaign "fair and free of abuse," to hold himself aloof from all factions and their quarrels, and to support for the governorship whichever candidate won in the September primaries. He pledged that "a committee of well-known Republicans, selected regardless of past or present factional alignments," would have charge of his campaign in Cook County under Stead's guidance. In closing, he pledged "not [to] be a party to any 'slate' ticket." "I shall make no promises, either express or implied, and shall have no alliances, either direct or remote, which will embarrass the free exercise of my best judgment in discharging the duties of governor, should I be nominated and elected."[30] What Thompson and Lundin would think of these commitments if they should prove to be more than empty eloquence remained for the future to disclose.

Business-like as always, Stead had reminded Lowden late in March of the soaring expenses to be expected, of the immediate need for ten thousand dollars to pay for mailing announcements, and of other costs. Probably with a sigh, Mrs. Lowden confided to her diary on the evening of April 13 that "from now on there will be little peace or quiet for any of us."

The rural setting in which Lowden launched his candidacy underlined his declaration of independence from City Hall and his determination to give a downstate focus to his campaign. Moving its office to Chicago merely carried out a common-sense decision to center his operations where the railroad net converged and whence "Sinnissippi" could be easily reached. Most downstate Republican newspapers enthusiastically welcomed his announcement of candidacy. The Chicago editors, however, having been mostly anti-Thompson and therefore anti-Lowden, pretended to be amazed because he dared to try for the prize after Thompson's setback in the city primaries. They attributed his pledge to remain his own master either to insincerity or to political naïveté. By not taking him at his word, many good citizens of Illinois were readying themselves for a big surprise.

Just before the opening of the Republican convention at Peoria, an all-night conclave in one of its hotels produced a sufficiently strong Lowden-Thompson-Sherman-Brundage coalition to assure its control of the party's state organization. As a result, the hitherto dominant Deneenites became a minority on the new state central committee and recognized that they could not re-elect Roy O. West to the post of Republican national committeeman from Illinois. The Peoria convention decided to delay drafting a state platform until after the national nominating convention and the gubernatorial primary.

Mayor Thompson had played his cards skilfully. Upon arriving in Peoria, he strengthened his bargaining position by feigning coolness toward Sherman's presidential ambitions and Fred Sterling's wish to be the new chairman of the state central committee. To gain Thompson's support for both men,

30. FOL wrote W. H. Stead, Feb. 13, 1916: "I am going to send to you before mailing, all the letters which might be considered by any possibility as committing me to any proceeding in this campaign."

the downstaters promised to back him in June for national committeeman. Having thus appeased his apparent ill humor, the convention easily passed a resolution proclaiming Sherman the "favorite son" of Illinois for the presidency. Before he left Peoria, Lowden may have promised to back Brundage if he decided to seek election as attorney-general of Illinois.[31] At the same time, John G. Oglesby, who from his six-thousand-acre estate near Springfield had worried Lowden for over a year by threatening now and again to enter the gubernatorial sweepstakes, declared with some condescension that he wished only to be lieutenant-governor and would gladly help his old friend attain the higher office. Little wonder that Lowden described the Peoria convention as "a regular old time . . . love feast," where "everybody seem[ed] willing to work and bring about Republican success this fall."[32]

Frank L. Smith and Charles Deneen by no means subscribed to this comment. The exuberant enemies of the former governor believed that they had pushed him "down and out." His friends among the editors, however, talked about "the hog combine" at Peoria which left him no choice but "to fight fire with fire" by launching his own ticket for the principal state offices. No matter in their view whether Lowden was puppet or master plotter, he had selfishly underwritten a "slate" of candidates including no Deneenite whatsoever.[33] How could he reconcile his action at Peoria with his many pleas for party unity or his promises to keep clear of bargains when advancing his candidacy? Even newspapers working in his behalf, like the *St. Louis Globe Democrat*, referred to "his ticket" of nominees for every major executive office at Springfield.[34] When he continued to insist that he had no "slate" and had not limited his freedom in exchange for help, the hostile press pilloried him for being incredibly childlike or full of guile. Indeed, it knew as well as he did that, within any party made up of many ambitious leaders and local machines, the degree of unity necessary for successful political action rarely emerges except from an accommodation reached by some of its rival parts.

As a gesture of friendship toward the Progressives, the Peoria convention chose state Senator Medill McCormick to be its temporary chairman, and he used the occasion to announce his return to the GOP. But the domination of the state Republican machine by its more conservative wing blasted whatever hope most other Progressive leaders may have had of resuming their old allegiance without losing their self-respect. Consequently, the Progressive State Central Committee made known that it would continue in business with Harold Ickes of Chicago as chairman and Frank H. Funk of Bloomington as treasurer.[35] They probably expected the disgruntled Deneen to pro-

31. *St. Louis Globe Democrat,* Apr. 22, 1916; see also pp. 281–82.

32. FOL to H. J. Spurway, Washington, D.C., Apr. 28, 1916.

33. *Chicago American,* Apr. 21; *Chicago Tribune,* Apr. 23, 1916.

34. *St. Louis Globe Democrat,* Apr. 22, 1916. Besides Oglesby and Brundage on Lowden's "slate," this paper added Len Small of Kankakee for state treasurer, Louis L. Emmerson of Mount Vernon for secretary of state, and Homer J. Tice of Greenview for state auditor.

35. *Chicago Journal,* Apr. 21, 1916.

duce some liberal Republican aspirants whom they also could support for the state offices. Professor Charles E. Merriam was their first choice as gubernatorial candidate. He was also Deneen's friend, but the former governor hesitated to sponsor a scholar in politics whom he could not control. Commentators generally agreed in the spring of 1916 that Deneen wanted a somewhat left-of-center Republican, who would draw both the Progressive vote and the indorsement of the Anti-Saloon League. Neither Lowden nor Frank Smith fitted these specifications. And yet, unless Smith consented to withdraw from the race, he would poll enough votes to prevent any candidate brought out by Deneen from winning in a three-cornered contest. In other words, the preprimary battle clearly pitted Lowden against the field. Recognizing this fact, Deneen decided in late May to delay his decision about entering a candidate until after the national nominating convention. Simultaneously, the Illinois Progressive party resolved not to share in the gubernatorial fight as a separate party unless it found the Republican presidential nominee unacceptable.

In the meantime, on May 12, Lowden told a large audience in the armory at Ottawa what his policy would be if he were elected governor. It was by far the best, as well as the most important, speech of his campaign. Without "perfervid oratory or flowing rhetoric," he presented "solid facts in plain language" for over an hour to the attentive crowd. Even several of the opposition papers faintly praised the address, and Stead soon sent it in pamphlet form to everybody on his huge mailing list.[36] After once again affirming in unqualified terms his determination to be an "unbossed and unbossing" governor of all the people of Illinois and not merely of its Republicans, he turned to his main theme with the statement: "One of the gravest dangers today is the constantly increasing cost of government." He quoted figures to demonstrate how Illinois government by 1916 had become seven times as costly as in 1876 and how the rate of rise in its operating costs during the most recent ten years had been quadruple that of the national government.

Turning from diagnosis to prescription, he recommended two types of remedies. He pledged to submit to the legislature a series of measures to eliminate much of the waste and inefficiency and introduce business methods into state administration. These measures included a centralized budget, a consolidation of the sprawling bureaus, boards, and commissions into a few departments with responsibility concentrated in the director of each under the governor, and an extension of the classified civil service. Toward the same end, he would lessen the cost of elections and heighten public interest and intelligent participation in them by shortening the ballot and confining the annual election days to one in the spring and another in the autumn. To increase the revenue from taxes and make them more equitable, he proposed to classify personal property for assessment purposes so that the main tax burden would no longer fall upon owners of real estate. In other words, the tax structure would be drastically remodeled so as to reflect the growth of cities

36. *La Salle* (Ill.) *Tribune,* May 13; *Chicago Tribune,* May 13; *Chicago Herald,* May 15, all dates in 1916.

and industries in Illinois and the fact that most wealth was no longer in farms and city lots. Lowden recognized that some of these reforms exceeded the scope of legislative or executive power and would necessitate constitutional amendments. If elected, he promised to seek legislative authorization for a plebiscite on the calling of a constitutional convention. Once assembled, he hoped that among its revisions of the fundamental law, it would grant Chicago home rule over its public utilities and other matters "essentially local."

In his Ottawa speech Lowden did not spell out his other main type of needed reforms. It stemmed from his conviction that the progressives, whether Bull Moosers or Democrats, looked to government for certain services destructive of individual initiative and not within the proper scope of welfare legislation. "A paternalism," as he expressed it, "which considers only the weaker members of society to such an extent as to impair the rugged independence of these men and women would ultimately defeat its own ends." "These men and women" were the "great mass" of citizens who paid the taxes and yet asked of government only that they be allowed "to earn their livelihood under favorable conditions." In this same address, on the other hand, he called for the formulation of constructive policies by the state to aid the good-roads movement, develop "a broad and permanent scientific agriculture," and protect wage-earners against industrial hazards. As for woman suffrage in state elections, he favored it; and as for prohibition, he was ready to support whatever county-wide option bill the legislature might enact.[37]

He had much reason for good cheer on the eve of the Republican national convention. The widespread and complimentary attention accorded his Ottawa address, the patent quandary of Deneen and the Progressives, and the many evidences that Smith was having tough going justified Stead in reporting on May 18: "The sentiment throughout the state is now friendly to you. The problem is to keep it that way." Smith had recourse to abusive speeches charging Lowden with stealing his platform, dancing to the tunes of "Big Bill" and big business, and conniving in a dark plot "incubated in the City Hall, matured in the wilds of Canada, and hatched at the Peoria Convention."[38] Lowden declined to reply in kind. Even Mayor Thompson was in too optimistic and expansive a mood to turn his well-filled arsenal of invective against Smith.

No doubt for the purpose of helping toward his election as national committeeman but avowedly in order "to do everything in my [his] power to further Sherman's [presidential] candidacy," Thompson entertained many

37. In a letter of May 2, 1916, to W. A. Peterson, immediately multigraphed and widely distributed, FOL wrote that woman suffrage was so nearly an accomplished fact, "it is hardly worth while to discuss it." If women are to vote for presidential and vice-presidential electors, it is "absurd" not to let them vote in state elections also. "I know of no reason why the women of Illinois should not have full suffrage."

38. *Chicago Herald,* May 18, 1916.

of the senator's friends, together with the Illinois delegates and their alternates to the nominating convention, at a La Salle Hotel luncheon in Chicago on May 20. Lowden sat at Thompson's right hand next to Deneen.[39] Everything rolled along merrily. If Stead can be believed, harmony within the party measurably increased during the repast. "Whatever faults the mayor may have," he commented to Sherman, "and whatever mistakes he may have made, one thing is plain to me, and that is he is playing the game on the square so far as you are concerned and so far as Lowden is concerned."[40] In like manner, Sherman "played square" by having his supporters among the Illinois delegates join Lowden's in the mayor's behalf. By a vote of over two to one, they substituted Thompson for West on the national committee. Deneen's fortunes thereby reached a low ebb.

Sherman's presidential dream quickly faded after the nominating convention opened. All except two of the fifty-eight Illinois delegates supported him on the first and second ballots, but he attracted only about ten votes from seven other states.[41] Although Theodore Roosevelt probably would have accepted the Republican nomination with as much alacrity as he declined to head the Progressive party ticket for a second time, he gained prolonged applause from the convention rather than votes. Nor was his presidential choice, Henry Cabot Lodge, awarded the prize. On their third ballot the delegates named Chief Justice Charles Evans Hughes, a somewhat liberal conservative, to head the ticket. The standpatter, Charles W. Fairbanks of Indiana, became his running mate. The Lowdens witnessed these proceedings in the Chicago Coliseum and felt satisfied, but not enthusiastic, over the outcome. Fairbanks was a respected and well-liked friend, but Lowden would have preferred Elihu Root as the presidential nominee.

By combining recreation with business for ten days immediately after the convention adjourned, Lowden readied himself for the last and most strenuous phase of his own campaign preceding the Illinois primaries on September 13. The political news greeting him upon his return from his Arkansas plantations was wholly encouraging. Mayor Bennett of Rockford, once known as the Anti-Saloon League choice for the governorship, withdrew from the contest and announced his preference for Lowden.[42] Even more gratifying was the word that, after weeks of wrangling over the leadership of the Cook County Republican committee, the Brundage and Thompson factions had agreed to have Homer K. Galpin, a Brundageite, as chairman and Congressman Martin Madden, a Thompsonite, as vice-chairman. Thus ended an impasse which had already thrown some of the Brundage group into the arms of Deneen. Madden, furthermore, was a vigorous and

39. W. H. Thompson to FOL, May 16, 1916.

40. W. H. Stead to L. Y. Sherman, May 22, 1916.

41. *Official Report of the Proceedings of the Sixteenth Republican National Convention Held in Chicago, Illinois, June 7, 8, 9, and 10, 1916* (New York, 1916), pp. 181, 184, 196.

42. *Rockford* (Ill.) *Register-Gazette*, June 15, 1916.

influential supporter of Lowden. At the same time, and certainly to Lowden's satisfaction, if not with his advance knowledge, Brundage formally declared his candidacy for the attorney-generalship of Illinois. Nor did Lowden and Stead grieve because Deneen's long run of political ill luck continued. The former governor urged Edmund J. James, president of the University of Illinois, to come out for the gubernatorial nomination. After ten days of indecision, he declined on June 21, on the plea that the board of trustees refused to accept his resignation. Much sunburned and in fine fettle, Lowden reached Chicago on that day from "Florenden" and "South Bend."

Deneen refused to admit defeat. He soon persuaded state Senator Morton D. Hull, a wealthy Chicagoan and former Progressive, to compete for the nomination against Lowden.[43] Although Hull's legislative record won for him the backing of the Anti-Saloon League and several important labor leaders, many of the principal downstate Progressives or former Progressives, like Ira Copley of Aurora, B. F. Harris of Springfield, and Frank H. Funk of Bloomington, chose to support Lowden. Ickes, Merriam, and other Chicago Bull Moosers, however, rallied with as much enthusiasm as they could muster behind Deneen's cold and somewhat colorless candidate. At least the City Hall did not rule him. By dividing between Lowden and Hull and nominating no candidate of their own, the Progressives reached the end of their road as a distinct party in Illinois politics.

The press described the Republican gubernatorial race as a competition between three millionaires, running on approximately the same platform.[44] Deneen recognized that, because Lowden was so far in the lead in both popularity and strength of organization, the "trotting-out" of Hull amounted to little except a gesture of defiance toward Thompson. No sooner had Hull announced his candidacy than he and Smith concentrated their oratorical barrages on Lowden rather than against each other. In their view, Lowden was a "good fellow" who pretended to be a farmer and who never could say "No," especially to "Big Bill."

Stead seemed much more worried lest Lowden wilt under the intense heat in downstate Illinois than under the verbal assaults of Hull and Smith. For a month following June 25, Lowden kept on the move almost continuously, speaking to large audiences in southern and central Illinois from Cairo north to Joliet. If his own comfort had been the prime consideration, he would have traveled by special train. The rear platform of a private Pullman car, however, was hardly a persuasive vantage point from which to ask sweat-soaked farmers and miners for their votes.[45] After a strenuous day of speaking and handshaking, he resigned himself to the care of Tracey, his masseur. Equally indispensable was a supply of biographies and war reports, such as

43. *Chicago News,* June 29 and July 1, 1916.

44. *Chicago Journal,* July 5, 1916. It commented that, with so much wealth in the field, "the politicians should clean up."

45. Stead planned to have FOL spend three days in each congressional district and the last three weeks before primary day in Cook County.

Frederick S. Oliver's *Alexander Hamilton* and *Ordeal by Battle*. Wearing a light-weight suit and a broad-brimmed Panama hat, Lowden felt confident at first that he could outlast the heat wave, especially since the cordiality of his reception had a tonic effect. But after the temperature rose to 100° or more day after day in early July, he necessarily curtailed his original speaking schedule. When he returned to "Sinnissippi" on July 20 for a two-day respite, he was so "exceedingly tired" that Mrs. Lowden induced Stead to provide longer rest periods between his remaining oratorical forays into one congressional district after another.

These speeches, in so far as they dealt with needed state reforms rather than farming, the tariff, and President Wilson's foreign policy,[46] resembled those of Hull and Smith. For this reason, a thoughtful Republican voter had to select between men rather than opposing viewpoints. Which of the three candidates was the most sincere, the ablest, the least dominated by "predatory interests," and the most likely to defeat the Democratic nominee after the primary? Each one of the rivals counted among his adherents some former Progressives, some leading "drys," some union labor leaders, and some influential farmers and businessmen. However much they might stress the importance of their rivalry, they well knew that many Republicans would not bother to vote in the primaries. Since it was a presidential election year, the gubernatorial race attracted less popular interest than the battle between Wilson and Hughes for the White House.

In late August, Lowden shifted the center of his campaign efforts from downstate to Chicago. Thereupon, the Frank O. Lowden Business Men's Association, organized by Dawes and Ramsay and numbering nearly one thousand members, swung into vigorous action. Although Lowden welcomed the support of these bankers, lawyers, brokers, merchants, and manufacturers as a refutation of the charge that he spoke merely with the voice of the Thompson-Lundin machine, he had grave doubts whether the wide publicity given to the enthusiastic indorsements of so many wealthy men would add to his strength at the polls. Hull, Smith, and a number of labor leaders seized at once upon the activities of the association as proof positive that Lowden kowtowed to undemocratic La Salle Street and the "Gold Coast" of Chicago as well as to City Hall.[47]

The indefatigable Gordon Ramsay took pride in the moving picture prepared under his direction, showing his champion emerging from the sunrise (Sunrise City, Minnesota!) and by his own talents and persistence mounting the steep ladder from a humble cabin in the north woods to the Executive Mansion of the governor of Illinois. Having been competently made, the film

46. The cost of his trips was not high. For example, J. S. Baldwin of Decatur, Illinois, on July 24 sent him a bill for $313.58, incurred during his three days in the Nineteenth Congressional District, for printing, music, advertisements, hotel, and stamps. R. Bradford of Pontiac, Illinois, on July 24 told Stead that a man in a car would "decorate telephone poles" with FOL's picture for $10 a day.

47. Hull's mimeographed press release, Sept. 2, 1916.

was in much demand for Lowden rallies downstate as well as in Chicago. With it went copies of the *Frank O. Lowden Song Review*. The imperfect rhymes of these songs needed no rehearsal because they were tailored to fit some of the popular melodies of forty years ago.[48]

In Chicago Lowden carried through his hectic schedule of crowding nearly seventy speeches within less than three weeks. For the first time during his campaign, he had to confront an unbroken rank of hostile newspaper editors. If they can be believed, his boom faltered everywhere, and his audiences were humiliatingly small, whether at his noonday meetings in a Loop theater, at the Labor Day workingmen's picnic in Riverview Park, at the evening rallies in the wards of the metropolis, or in the suburban towns. According to these commentators, the crowds at the Kankakee fair in early September showed far more eagerness to shake hands with Hull or Smith than with him. Mrs. Lowden, however, accompanied her husband to some of his speaking engagements, and her diary entries leave an entirely different impression. So, too, do the accounts of his Cook County campaign appearing in friendly downstate dailies. His wife's terse record is sprinkled with such phrases as "splendid ovation," "huge noonday meeting," and a "tremendous" final rally in the Columbia Theatre on September 12, with "an overflow crowd of 2,000 outside" the building.[49] The press of Chicago usually allocated its front pages to Hull and Smith and to the meager wages of Pullman porters as compared with the allegedly huge sum of money being used by Lowden to win the nomination. Hull's quip, "The voice is the voice of Lowden, but the hand is the hand of Lundin," caught the fancy of political reporters, and they repeated it again and again.[50]

During these closing days of the preprimary campaign Stead prophesied an easy victory and worried only because overly sanguine Lowdenites might not bother to go to the polls. How the labor vote would divide among the three contestants furnished a favorite subject for his speculation. Many southern Illinois miners pleased him by repudiating Smith when they discovered that he had paid $1,000 to their union leader, Frank Farrington. Even though the latter spent the money legitimately in Smith's behalf or distributed it to needy miners, he blundered seriously by using the stationery of the United Mine Workers of America for political letter-writing.[51] In the midst of the

48. For example, the lyric to be sung to the tune of "Hello Hawaii, How Are You?" went as follows:

> "Hello, Frank Lowden, how are you?
> We will stick together just like glue
> To put you there.
> You're on the square.
> Governor's chair
> For you, Frank."

49. Mrs. Lowden's diary, Aug. 24–Sept. 12, 1916.

50. Hull's mimeographed press releases of Sept. 2 and 9, 1916.

51. F. Farrington's wire to F. L. Smith, July 10, and Farrington's open letter to members of the UMWA, July 26, 1916.

flurry in labor circles caused by Farrington's indiscretions, Stead mailed broadcast, on September 1, a little pamphlet showing how Lowden had voted in Congress on measures of particular interest to union members. The brochure also included passages from his forthcoming Labor Day speech in which he guaranteed that, if elected governor, he would accord organized labor "fair and impartial treatment."[52] As expected, most of the Republicans on the Pullman Company payroll backed him in the primary, but he derived special pleasure from the news that the miners of Herrin, in the center of the Illinois soft-coal area, preferred him by a large majority to either Smith or Hull.[53]

On the eve of primary day, Mr. and Mrs. Lowden traveled in their car "through fearful mud" from Chicago to "Sinnissippi." "All are excited over tomorrow's events," she recorded, "and it will be difficult to wait in patience for the election returns!"[54] However that might be, Lowden slept until noon on the fateful day. After voting at the Daysville polling place, he took a long horseback ride with his daughter Florence. By late afternoon the first returns began to reach the farm. "We have sat in the library where phones have been installed," Mrs. Lowden commented that evening, "and have listened with growing amazement to the ever-increasing vote Frank has received throughout the State. . . . We know enough to be sure that it has been a veritable landslide. . . . We are naturally very happy."

Since the Republican primary votes totaled scarcely half of those which would normally be cast in a regular election, "landslide" was too strong a word. But more ballots had a cross opposite Lowden's name than those for Hull and Smith combined, and he carried Cook as well as 91 of the other 101 counties. "His" counties added up to 6 more than Stead and Mason in their most optimistic moment had ventured to claim.[55] Although hundreds of congratulatory messages poured in, none seemed to please the Lowdens as much as the hearty welcome given them by the gatemen and "redcaps" at Chicago's Union Station when they arrived there from "Sinnissippi" on the morning after the primary.[56]

To recover from the strain of the one campaign and prepare for the other equally demanding one soon to begin, Lowden would have preferred to go at once with Stead to his fishing camp on the Rideau. Politics demanded, however, that he appear with his wife and four children at the Republican state convention at Peoria on September 19 and with Charles Evans Hughes the next day at the state fair at Springfield. Probably his enthusiastic recep-

52. *Union Labor Advocate* (Chicago), September, 1916, p. 2.

53. *Herrin* (Ill.) *News,* Oct. 12, 1916. The vote in Pullman, Illinois, was FOL, 354; Hull, 54; and Smith, 8.

54. Mrs. Lowden's diary, Sept. 12, 1916.

55. The official total was: FOL, 227,443; Hull, 117,229; Smith, 76,287. In his own county, FOL polled 3,455 votes; Hull, 544; and Smith, 138. In the GOP primary of 1912, 439,662 votes were cast, and Deneen had a 64,168 plurality.

56. Mrs. Lowden's diary, Sept. 14 and 17, 1916.

tion at both places was even more exhilarating than catching bass. Most of the planks in the state platform adopted at Peoria voiced his desires, although, for strategic reasons, he regretted its terse forthrightness in favor of woman suffrage. In his view it was impolitic to be so blunt about a reform which found little support in southern Illinois and among citizens of German background. Furthermore, the "wets" opposed it because they feared lest votes by women impose prohibition upon the state.[57] The platform's silence about a lakes-to-gulf deep waterway also displeased him. He had favored the project for years. Besides offending Lorimer and Deneen, the failure to mention it might be construed to mean that railroads dominated him.

While he and Stead caught their breath along with numerous bass in Canadian waters, Mason gathered speech material at the Chicago headquarters for use against Governor Edward F. Dunne, who had won an easy victory in the Democratic primary. Mason also co-operated with the Republican State Central Committee in arranging an itinerary for Lowden's October tour throughout Illinois. Now that the primary was over, his political fortunes passed largely under the aegis of this committee and its friendly chairman, Fred E. Sterling. He kept in close liaison with the western headquarters of the Republican National Committee and arranged for a correspondence committee of five men in each precinct of the state. Almost as an afterthought, he made some little effort to organize the Republican women in the same way.

The outstanding feature of the downstate campaign was a three-week-long and nearly six-thousand-mile jaunt by the Republican special train through all except four of the 101 counties. The traveling politicians had the use of a library-buffet car, diner, Pullman sleeper, coach, two private Pullman cars, and a platform car in the rear, from which they made speeches. Each day's schedule for this de luxe Republican caravan was prepared in advance in elaborate detail. A small segment of the itinerary for October 9 ran as follows:

> Arrive Thompsonville (Franklin)   11:35
> Leave Thompsonville   11:40
> Arrive Galatia (Saline)   12:00
> Speak from car 5 minutes
> Leave Galatia   12:05 P.M.
> Arrive Raleigh (Saline)   12:25
> Speak from car 5 minutes
> Leave Raleigh   12:30
> Arrive Eldorado (Saline)   12:55
> I.C. Station; speak 20 minutes
> I.C. deliver train to L & N.   1:15

57. Leaflet entitled *Platform of the Republicans of Illinois, Adopted by the State Convention in Peoria, Sept. 19, 1916.* FOL informed Judge W. W. Duncan of Marion, Illinois, on Sept. 20 that the suffrage plank had been inserted at the behest of "Hughes' representatives" at Peoria.

Train accepted by L & N.   1:25
Leave Eldorado   1:30
Arrive Shawneetown (Gallatin)   2:30
Speak from car 15 minutes

Even though unexpected delays often threw out of kilter so meticulously tight a program of voice and voyage, Lowden had to hold forth a dozen or fifteen times daily from the rear platform of the train in all sorts of weather and be wide awake and affable at some county seat each evening for a dinner, a reception, a torchlight procession, and a long speech. To share in this ordeal with fifteen or twenty other Republican candidates, he returned from "Castle Rest" to Chicago at the close of September.

In the train's baggage car was "Chin Chin," a docile baby elephant on loan from Ringling Brothers' circus. In its coach was the Fife and Drum Corps of the GAR Post at Rockford. In its Pullmans were the candidates, varying somewhat in number from day to day but always including Lowden, Oglesby, Emmerson, Brundage, Small, Russel, McCormick, and Mason. They were the aspirants, respectively, for the offices of governor, lieutenant-governor, secretary of state, attorney-general, state treasurer, state auditor, and two seats as congressman at large. Former Senator "Billy" Mason was always "raring" to deliver a "rip-roaring old-fashioned G.O.P. speech," although his companions endeavored to moderate his anti-Democratic invective in nip-and-tuck neighborhoods where a conciliatory approach might entice enough of the opposition into the Republican column to allow the local candidates to win.

Knowing the schedule of the "Campaign Special," the party's committee in each town assembled an audience at the station a few minutes before the train arrived. When it puffed to a halt, the fife and drum corps played, the candidates appeared on the platform car, one or more spoke briefly, and "Chin Chin," wearing a Republican saddle cloth, trumpeted and stomped in response to the applause. "Aerial bombs" from the train scattered "Lowden for Governor" leaflets over the crowd. The engine's bell signaled time to leave, the candidates leaned over the side of the rear car to shake a few hands, and a speaker occasionally kept on with his oratory as the gap widened between him and his listeners. This was the way of politics in rural America—strenuous, hearty, and peppered with enough humor and showmanship to make every voter a willing captive while the candidate expounded the issues of the campaign.

After two weeks of meandering through southern and central Illinois, the train pulled into Oregon late on the afternoon of October 17. Mrs. Lowden wrote in her diary that evening:

I was most disturbed to find that Frank's voice was bad, that he had a cold and the other members of the party thought he either ought to go home to rest or I must go with him. I had of course made no preparation for a trip but as it seemed necessary, I came on just as I was, and will stay with him for two days at least. We have persuaded him to go to bed and not attempt the Rock Island meeting tonight and I hope my remedies will have had effect by morning. The trip is frightfully exhausting . . . and I don't see how the men can stand another week of it.

For several days before reaching Oregon, his laryngitis had obliged him to wave and bow rather than speak to the people gathered at the way stations.[58] The weather turned unusually cold for October, with brisk winds, rain, and occasional snow flurries. Helped by the ministrations of his wife, he was able to make himself heard for fifteen minutes at Peoria on the evening of October 18. By the next afternoon he felt sufficiently improved to permit Mrs. Lowden to return to "Sinnissippi." Thereafter for another week, except for a Sunday spent at home, he kept up the grueling schedule, talking briefly at fifty or sixty more "whistle stops," and making full-length addresses at Dixon, Rockford, Aurora, Joliet, Bloomington, and Decatur. Thus ended the Republican downstate campaign, with Lowden "very tired" but with his cold "somewhat better" when he rejoined his wife at the Blackstone Hotel in Chicago, early in the morning of October 26.[59]

On that day the high-pressure drive for votes in Cook County opened with almost hysterically enthusiastic receptions extended to Theodore Roosevelt at the Coliseum and Stock Yards Amphitheatre. The campaign closed nine days later with an impressive, but far less exuberant, parade of twenty thousand people on Michigan Avenue in honor of Charles Evans Hughes. Besides sharing prominently in these affairs, Lowden spoke every noonday in the Loop and a half-dozen times every night in various halls of the city and its surrounding communities. Upon reaching his home town on the evening of November 6, he found at the station a brass band and "what was said to be a bigger crowd in Oregon than ever before." Before his admirers permitted him to go to the peaceful haven of "Sinnissippi," they obliged him to speak not once but thrice—in the central square, the Star Theatre, and the courtroom of the County Building. Mrs. Lowden and some of his closest friends expressed amazement over how well he withstood the rigors of the campaign. Evidently he had regained the good health which had been his when he first sought the governorship in 1904.

During the campaign, Governor Dunne attacked his friend Lowden on the same grounds and sometimes in nearly the same words as those that Hull and Smith had used before primary day. This embarrassed them and Deneen more than Lowden because, as good Republicans, they now canvassed the state asking voters to support the man they had so recently opposed. Lowden, on the other hand, found that by giving his speeches of the primary campaign a somewhat sharper edge, they served admirably as replies to Dunne. Nor was it difficult for him to take the offensive. The Dunne adminis-

58. On Oct. 13, FOL opened his remarks at Springfield, Illinois, by saying that he was "travel stained, unshorn, and weary," because he had made between 150 and 200 speeches in ten days. He still had enough voice to address the audience at Canton, Illinois, the next day.

59. Mrs. Lowden's diary, Oct. 18–26, 1916.

tration had been the most expensive in Illinois peacetime history. Employees in some of the state's mental and penal institutions wrote to Stead, mentioning instances of mismanagement or worse. Feeling that Dunne and Lowden represented a choice between evils, the Anti-Saloon League took little part in the contest. Organized labor generally favored the Democratic candidate, mainly because the unions distrusted Hughes and viewed Woodrow Wilson as a friend.[60] The speeches of the dignified Hughes lacked punch and decisiveness. Lowden referred to him with respect but little enthusiasm and probably shared the view of other Republican leaders in Illinois that he was "a drag on the state ticket."[61]

Although studiously avoiding personalities in his speeches, Lowden indicted the regime at Springfield the more unsparingly because the Democrats pointedly attacked him in their state platform. Under the heading "Invisible Government," they labeled him the candidate of the large corporations "which control the cattle, grain and railway interests of this state and practically of the country." Echoing this theme in his keynote speech, Dunne declared that his opponent won in the Republican primaries because he had spent more money than either of his millionaire rivals. "The most important issue before the people today is," Dunne continued, "Can Money Buy the Governorship of Illinois?" In late October William Jennings Bryan visited his native state to denounce Lowden as "a tool of the corporate interests."[62] Day after day the Democratic newspapers harped on this theme. Dunne's headquarters even republished some of the 1904 cartoons of the *Chicago Tribune* showing Lorimer, a Pullman porter, and a bewhiskered personification of corporate wealth shedding bitter tears because Lowden, in the form of a very dead Cock Robin, failed to win the gubernatorial nomination in that year.

The opposition also stressed his tie-up with City Hall and predicted that if he won, he would pack the regulatory commissions with his big-business friends and follow Mayor Thompson's iniquitous practice of circumventing the civil service laws by ensconcing his cronies in office by a succession of temporary appointments. The Democrats pounced upon the GOP special train as a prime object of their ridicule and as irrefutable proof that ruthless wealth supported Lowden and his "slate." If some Democratic commentators could be believed, his "menagerie," "side show," or "vaudeville troupe" washed down their terrapin with champagne and sometimes became too drunk to stand erect on their platform car without clinging to its rail. It "is a collection," sneered the editor of the *Gillespie* (Illinois) *News* on October 18, "that would beat any dime museum ever put on the road by P. T. Bar-

60. FOL, pamphlet entitled *The Record of Two Public Officials: Facts Show Governor Edward F. Dunne Failed To Enforce Remedial Laws. In Congress, Colonel Frank O. Lowden Voted for Important Labor Legislation.*

61. *Rockford* (Ill.) *Republic,* Oct. 7, 1916.

62. *Chicago Herald,* Sept. 27; *Cairo* (Ill.) *Herald,* Oct. 20; and *Chicago American,* Oct. 27, 1916.

num." The passengers, declared the *Chicago Journal*, shrewdly left their silk shirts and top hats at home when they talked to Illinois farmers, and voters should note that Governor Dunne traveled only in the public conveyances used by ordinary folk.[63]

The Democratic state platform, except for its praise of the Wilson administration, its denunciation of the corporations alleged to control the party out of power, and its support of the Lake Michigan–Mississippi deep waterway, resembled the Republican. For this reason Lowden could not oppose much of what the Democrats stood for at the state level but centered his fire upon the vast gap between their professions and their performances. In other words, he emphasized the harm they had done at Washington by their tariff-tinkering and inept Mexican policy and the good they had neglected to do while in power at Springfield. Although the Dunne administration, said Lowden, had talked about consolidating 120 state agencies into a few departments for the sake of efficiency and economy, it had in reality increased the number of board and commissions. Instead of fulfilling his promise of instituting a single biennial budget for appropriations and expenditures, the governor had raised taxes by 50 per cent and administrative costs from the $30 million under Governor Deneen in 1911 to $46⅓ million in 1915. Stung by the accusation that he was dominated by big business, Lowden exclaimed at Sullivan, Illinois: "It is time for someone who has had some experience in even what is called big business to introduce some things into the form of our state government, if we are going to have an efficient administration." Instead of prating so much about civil service reform, the governor should admit that the Democratic machine "unjustifiably and immorally" ordered state employees to neglect their duties in order to campaign for its ticket and compelled him to violate the spirit of the civil service laws by appointing many party hacks to "temporary, emergency positions."[64] Lowden further charged that the Dunne administration without competitive bidding awarded contracts to companies owned by prominent Democrats. Neglect by its inexpert Live Stock Commission had resulted in a loss to Illinois farmers of over a million dollars from the ravages of hoof and mouth disease. Having improved only six hundred of the state's seventy-five thousand miles of road, the governor nevertheless boasted of "pulling Illinois out of the mud." Quite on the contrary, said Lowden, the credit for starting the good-roads movement rightfully belonged to Governor Deneen. He had created the State Highway Commission and laid down the first four hundred miles of improved experimental highway.

There was much exaggeration in many of these claims and counterclaims. No doubt the cost of state government had risen alarmingly under Governor Dunne, but the increased appropriations applied mostly to projects of which Lowden thoroughly approved, such as schools and the state university, road

63. *Chicago Journal,* Sept. 28, 1916.

64. MSS of FOL's speech at Jacksonville, Sullivan, and Canton, Illinois, in October, 1916.

construction, public charitable institutions, and aid to agriculture. Furthermore, a Republican-controlled legislature had made the grants. Nor could Dunne be fairly charged with doing nothing to reform the state's administrative and financial machinery. He had created a Legislative Reference Bureau, which, for the first time in Illinois history, presented the Assembly with a scientific budget, although, to be sure, its coverage of appropriations and expenditures was far from complete. The blueprint which Dunne's Efficiency and Economy Commission prepared for the reorganization of the administrative offices had been rejected by the legislature. As for bringing pressure upon state employees to hustle in their party's interest during an election campaign and as for evading the civil service regulations by awarding deserving henchmen "temporary" or "emergency" appointments, only an uninformed citizen would believe that the Republican record was innocent of these almost routine practices.

Mrs. Lowden wrote on the evening of November 7:

The fateful day has come and nearly gone, and Frank has received so large a plurality over Dunne that his election as Governor by over 100,000 was settled quite early in the evening. Hughes' election has been conceded by many Democratic papers, tho' Wilson refuses to concede it as yet. We have had a private telegraph and telephone service . . . and our evening has been spent in the library getting returns. . . . Frank has been very calm on this important day in spite of the excitement in the air.

The bright sunshine of election day yielded on November 8 to weather "dismal beyond description"—the more so for the Lowdens because they were "horrified beyond words" to learn that the election returns from California would probably assure Hughes's defeat. Their one consolation was the widespread report that Illinois also would have given its electoral votes to Wilson if it had not been for Lowden's popularity.[65]

He viewed the outcome in his own state as a vindication as well as a triumph. Notwithstanding the two years of drumfire about his subservience to "predatory interests" in politics and business, many thousands of men and women evidently had faith in his integrity and independence. His majority was nearly 150,000 in a total of about 1,260,000 votes cast. He carried seventy-nine counties, including Cook County, and thirteen out of fifteen downstate congressional districts. Three out of four of the voters in his own county and four out of five of those in its county seat marked their ballots for him. In the state as a whole he ran ahead of the national Republican ticket.[66]

Immediately after the election, Lowden conferred in Chicago with W. H.

65. Mrs. Lowden's diary, Nov. 7 and 8, 1916.

66. Typed and bound volume entitled "Votes Cast for Governor at General Election, Tuesday, November 7, 1916." Hughes and Fairbanks carried 64 counties against Wilson and Marshall. Lowden polled 696,535 votes as compared with 621,000 cast for Deneen (Republican) and Funk (Progressive) together in 1912; but Dunne polled about 114,000 more in 1916 than he had four years before. Although Lowden ran well, two of his colleagues on the ticket, E. J. Brundage for attorney-general, and Andrew Russel for auditor of public accounts, each received more votes.

Stead and General Frank S. Dickson, commanding officer of the Illinois National Guard, about the forthcoming inauguration ceremonies. During his few hours in the city, reporters and importunate office-seekers so closely beset him that he was heartily glad to board a train for his Arkansas plantations. Accompanied by his friend Andrew J. Lester, he rested there for over two weeks and gave much thought to the course he would follow as governor. While he was gone, Mrs. Lowden spent a rainy but very pleasant day in Springfield with Mrs. Dunne, making herself acquainted with the Executive Mansion and finding out what she "must do before moving down in January."[67] She noted the dilapidated condition of the old house and the shabbiness of many of its furnishings.

Upon Lowden's return, he found his desk at "Sinnissippi" piled high with messages of congratulation. None pleased him more or seemed more significant than the note from Theodore Roosevelt. "Let me heartily congratulate you," he wrote on November 14, "I earnestly hope you will now assume a position of leadership. We need leadership! What I most desire is that you shall help to bring the Republicans far enough forward to enable us to hold the progressives far enough back to keep a substantial alignment." On the same day the *Aurora Beacon-News* advised its readers to "Keep Your Eyes on Lowden" for the Republican presidential nomination in 1920.

67. Mrs. Lowden's diary, Nov. 22, 1916.

CHAPTER XIII

STATESMANSHIP AT SPRINGFIELD

While astride his horse at "South Bend," Lowden reached an important decision. Immediately upon his return to Chicago, he confided to John Dwight: "My mind is firmly fixed upon the proposition to make as creditable an administration as I can without reference to the future, and get back into private life at the end of this four year period. I suppose I could go to the Senate if I wanted to, but I do not want to."[1] If he made known his determination to serve for a single term only, he would lose one of his chief controls over his lieutenants. But, by dismissing from his mind all thought of re-election or even of partisan advantage, he could shape his policies solely in terms of the public welfare and thus fulfil his pledge to be the governor of Illinois and not merely of its Republican voters. Furthermore, he would be able to appoint the best-qualified men to public office, regardless of their political usefulness to him in the future.

Realizing the great influence which any executive can wield through his patronage power, he decided to withhold its use until he had submitted his proposals to the legislature. Senators and representatives would be more willing to favor his recommendations if they were competitors for his bounty.[2] Could he be successful as a statesman without rewarding the principal politicians who had helped him reach the Executive Mansion? If he declined to divide the spoils of office with Thompson and Lundin, would not they and their henchmen in the Assembly retaliate by opposing him at every turn? Was it statesmanlike to burn his political bridges so that, if his public service made him worthy of higher honors and he became willing to seek them, he would find that he had destroyed a prime means for their attainment?

Having resolved to lift his program above partisan politics and make it center upon a thoroughgoing reform of the state administration, he devoted much time during the month before his inauguration to familiarizing himself with the maze of state committees, boards, and commissions. He sought to discover how and to what extent they might be rearranged as quickly as possible into an orderly system without amending the constitution. He recognized how difficult in practical politics it was to abolish any long-established

1. FOL to J. W. Dwight, Washington, D.C., Nov. 29, 1916: "When I am at South Bend, I wonder why the Devil I got into this . . . trouble."

2. W. H. Stead to FOL, Dec. 18, 1916: ". . . Your only safety lies in sitting on the jobs until you get something accomplished."

office or even to reduce its prestige by subordinating its occupant to the direction of a superior. The statutes creating some of the overlapping commissions obliged them to be bipartisan in membership. For this reason, any change in their status invited resistance from Democrats and Republicans alike. Probably, too, they would be supported by interested groups of citizens, not usually in politics, who believed that a particular board selected for extinction had contributed to their economic welfare or even catered to their own hobbies, as, for example, the trustees of Fort Massac or of the Lincoln homestead. Factory, mine, and railroad owners, whose businesses were regulated by one or another of these commissions, might resist any reform which would put them under a stricter curb.

During December, 1916, therefore, Lowden also pondered matters of strategy and frequently consulted men who were wise in the ways of Springfield politicians. By good fortune, influential legislators like Richard J. Barr and Medill McCormick of the Senate and David Shanahan and Edward Shurtleff of the House assured him of their support. Stead and Lowden worked together in complete harmony. They agreed to make administrative reorganization the almost exclusive goal of their first year in office and, in fact, to count the governor's entire term a failure if it failed to reach this objective. As compared with it, even a constitutional convention to rewrite the antiquated organic law of the state was to be of secondary importance.

Besides stressing administrative reform in his inaugural address, Lowden planned to draft a special message on the subject. By means of newspaper articles prepared by J. C. Mason, he gave advance notice during December of what he had in mind and asked every voter, whether a Democrat or Republican, to urge his representative and senator to support the proposed reorganization. He planned to have the reform impressively introduced as an administration measure and, by using every device of parliamentary tactics, to prevent the bill from being lost in committee, emasculated by amendments, or debated to death. By deciding to press for one law at a time, delay his distribution of patronage, and appeal for help from the public in bringing reluctant legislators to heel, Lowden adopted the tactics which had enabled President Wilson to drive much of his domestic program through Congress during his first term. This forceful executive leadership was a far cry from Lowden's earlier pronouncements that he would not dominate his party or the state Assembly.[3]

Notwithstanding the obvious hurdles, he had good reason to count upon surmounting them by persistence and political finesse. The party platforms and the gubernatorial candidates in the recent primary and election contests had all emphasized the desirability of a drastic reformation of the executive branch. Prolonged discussion in the press and from the hustings, as well as rising tax rates, had kept Illinois citizens informed of the mounting cost of state government. The need to make it more amenable to the people's will, to sharpen the responsibility of appointed public officials, and to use state powers to harness more effectively the new economic and social forces born

3. See pp. 116–17 and 279.

of the industrial age had been dominant themes of the progressives in both political parties for a decade or more.

However "standpat" most businessmen might be in politics, they recognized in their own affairs the inseparable tie between sound administration and profits. As the new regulatory legislation brought them into more frequent touch than ever before with government boards, they had been shocked by the slipshod fashion in which these agencies often functioned. Red tape, delays, lack of decisiveness, and "passing the buck" were commonplace, while favoritism and downright dishonesty were not unknown. To Lowden and other men of affairs, government itself constituted a business, one of the biggest businesses in Illinois. Although it spent $25,000,000 a year, no one really controlled its vast organization. Its financial income and outgo reflected little planned foresight, and its manifold parts usually lacked coordination. Its operating staff from top to bottom was seldom chosen for its expert knowledge of the job to be done. Clumsy administrative methods, sometimes unchanged for nearly a century, were unnecessarily costly and confusing. Lowden liked to say that if any private concern operated as inefficiently as government, it would be bankrupt within a few weeks. Irrespective of party, there was a widespread demand that he convert his words into action.

Nor would his action have to wait upon a diagnosis of the existing situation or a long discussion of how to abolish the evils. Three years before, on Governor Dunne's recommendation, the Illinois legislature had named four senators and four representatives as an Efficiency and Economy Committee to prepare reformative bills after a thorough study of the existing administrative structure and procedures. Aided by investigatory powers and an expense fund commensurate with the difficulty of its assignment, it worked diligently for two years before making known its findings in a volume of over one thousand pages.[4] Its recommendations carried the more weight because they had been formulated after many public hearings and a review of administrative practices in several states besides Illinois.

During its inquiry and for the drafting of its report, the committee had the invaluable assistance of Dr. John A. Fairlie, secretary of the Legislative Reference Bureau and professor of political science at the University of Illinois. Associated with him were other experts from this university and elsewhere. Although the committee purposely restricted its recommendations to changes requiring no constitutional amendments and no extensive revisions of statute law, the last legislature of Dunne's term adjourned without taking action upon them. Instead of trying to thin out the administrative jungle and effect the saving of a million dollars a year, which, according to the committee, would result from the adoption of its proposals, the Assembly did nothing except to create several new boards and commissions.

Charles E. Woodward, Stead's law partner in Ottawa, had helped the com-

4. *Report of the Efficiency and Economy Committee, Created under the Authority of the Forty-eighth General Assembly, State of Illinois* (Chicago, 1915), p. 12; hereafter cited as "*E. and E. Comm. Report.*"

mittee. At his suggestion in the late autumn of 1915, Stead requested Lowden to examine its report carefully and "get it into your system."[5] Nearly a year before, Lowden had written to the secretary of state of Minnesota for information about the "Civil Administrative Code" bill, about to be submitted to its legislature. In the same month Harvey Ingham sent him the report of Iowa's Committee on Efficiency and Reform. Neither the Minnesota "Code" nor the "Des Moines Plan" was thoroughgoing enough to satisfy Lowden, and both assumed the existence of practices and institutions not found in Illinois. For this reason he concluded that the report of the Illinois Efficiency and Economy Committee furnished a sounder guide and a more realistic point of departure.

With this volume's painstaking analysis of what was wrong, Lowden almost completely agreed. During the campaign he criticized nothing of consequence which had escaped attack in its pages, and he also accepted many of its constructive suggestions. Among these was one to regroup most of the hundred or more bureaus, boards, and commissions into ten departments. This reshuffling included the abolition of about fifty of these agencies or their consolidation with others. Immediately above the department heads would stand the governor, charged with the ultimate responsibility for their conduct. Non-partisanship rather than bipartisanship would be the guiding principle in choosing the administrative personnel. In some cases the head of a department might also serve as the chief of a division or the chairman of a commission within his department. Each department would depend for its origin upon a separate bill, so that if the legislature adopted only a part of the recommendations of the Efficiency and Economy Committee, it still would effect a considerable reform.

Although instructed "to secure a more perfect system of accounting," the committee had decided at its first meeting to make this aim secondary and concentrate upon improving administration. Consequently, its report included no provision for a more consolidated and comprehensive budget than that created in 1913. The committee, however, asked for a Department of Finance directed by a commission whose regular members would be the comptroller, a tax commissioner, and a revenue commissioner, with the auditor of public accounts and state treasurer as members ex officio. Until the state constitution could be amended, it barred much-needed reforms in the tax structure of Illinois. Fearing lest the legislature refuse to act at all if too much were asked for, the committee confined its recommendations to appointive officials only. Hence its report made no mention of the elected dignitaries, such as the secretary of state and the attorney-general.[6]

With several of the basic and many of the detailed recommendations of the committee, Lowden could not concur. He favored a much more centralized

5. W. H. Stead to FOL, Nov. 12, 1915. Woodward later became a U.S. district court judge in Chicago.

6. *E. and E. Comm. Report*, pp. 33–37, 76–77; pamphlet, *The Legislative Reference Bureau: Its Work and Functions* (Springfield, Ill., 1916).

administrative structure than the Fairlie proposals envisaged and asked Woodward to prepare a reorganization bill for submission to the legislature in late January, 1917.[7] In every instance where the committee designated a commission to head a department, Lowden insisted upon having one man only. In his view a group of co-equals could best exercise legislative or judicial powers but was wholly unfit to direct an executive office.

His main specific objection to the committee proposals, however, arose from their silence about an executive budget, the one indispensable component of any workable administrative reform. This budget, according to Lowden, must be prepared by an expert, but only after every money-spending and money-collecting agency had adopted an identical accounting system. The consolidated budget should include careful estimates by each department of its financial income and outgo during the next biennium and of the legislative appropriation needed to carry it through that period. Almost as essential in the interest of economy was a central purchasing agency, empowered to buy at wholesale and for cash all the manifold materials required to operate the state government, including its educational, charitable, and correctional institutions as well as its administrative offices. Thereby the purchasing contracts resulting from open, competitive bidding would assure standardized articles of the desired quality at rock-bottom prices.[8]

Finally, he believed that the Efficiency and Economy Committee had been ill-advised in preparing a separate bill for the creation of each department. Far better strategically would be an omnibus measure, embracing the entire reform and called the "Civil Administrative Code of the State of Illinois." This statute must not be cluttered up with compilations of laws for the guidance of the departments. Such codifications would make a complex matter even more intricate than necessary, hamstring the directors, and encourage bureaucratic red tape. The code bill would merely include an outline of the new administrative structure, general definitions of the powers and duties of each of the principal officials, and a list of the superseded bureaus, boards, and commissions and of the statutes necessarily repealed.

By the close of 1916, besides thinking through the method and content of administrative reform, Lowden had substantially completed his inaugural address to the satisfaction of his friendly critic, Stead. As usual, the Lowdens spent Christmas at "Sinnissippi" with gift-giving and other exercises at the Daysville School, at the Children's Convalescent Home of "Hilltop," and at the farm. Snug in his new seal-lined coat, Lowden soon returned to Chicago to resume his weary round of conferences with office-seekers. After superintending the crating and packing at "Sinnissippi" preparatory to their four

7. C. E. Woodward, "The Civil Administrative Code," in Louis L. Emmerson (ed.), *Blue Book of the State of Illinois, 1917–1918* (Danville, Ill., 1917), p. 62.

8. *State of Illinois: First Administrative Report of the Directors of Departments under the Civil Administrative Code . . . July 1, 1917, to June 30, 1918* (Springfield, Ill., 1919), p. 174; Louis L. Emmerson (ed.), *Blue Book of the State of Illinois, 1919–1920* (Springfield, Ill., 1919), pp. 39–43.

years' stay in Springfield, Mrs. Lowden joined her husband at the Blackstone Hotel in early January. Although she hoped to ease his crowded schedule by persuading him to accompany her to symphony concerts, she found his days so filled with appointments that she occupied their box at Orchestra Hall alone. On Sunday, January 7, they and their four children traveled in the private Pullman car "Olympia" to Springfield, where Adjutant General Frank S. Dickson guided them to their suite in the Leland Hotel. In the evening they called upon Governor and Mrs. Dunne.

There was scarcely a cloud in the sky on Inauguration Day. In their own car and with the Dunnes as their guests, the Lowdens were escorted by a civic and military parade shortly before noon through the flag-draped streets to the State House. Standing between the portraits of Lincoln and Douglas and before an overflow audience in the House chamber, Lowden took the oath of office. Following Dunne's valedictory, the new governor delivered his inaugural address.[9] The *Chicago Tribune* called the speech a "knock out" and "a smashing message for state reforms." Judging from the prolonged applause frequently interrupting the reading, Lowden's many listeners agreed. Men prominent in the public life of the state declared the address to be "the strongest document of the kind ever submitted to the General Assembly of Illinois by an incoming governor."

"The Government of Illinois in the New Industrial Age" would be an appropriate title for the address. Politically viewed, it was an appeal or, perhaps more accurately, a manifesto from the chief executive to the legislature to join him in enacting the Republican state platform into law. "Party pledges," he declared, "must be held as sacred as obligations incurred in other fields. The time is past when one rule of ethics applies to an individual's word and another to a political party's word, if parties are to survive." The people and their representatives must accept the fact that the old days of laissez faire and unbridled individualism had gone beyond recall. A commercial, industrial, and agricultural revolution had rendered them obsolete. Economic and social change necessitated political change. Unless government adjusted itself to the requirements of the new age, democracy would die. "Our public business," said Lowden, "is the most important of all our business. We too often say that our private affairs will not permit us to interest ourselves in public affairs. We seem to forget that if government were suspended for a single day, our private affairs would be of no moment and that ruin would rule all about us."

Among his many specific recommendations, he underlined the imperative need for a constitutional convention. Without a revision of the organic law, which had been framed for a predominantly rural society forty-five years before, some of the most-needed reforms could not be achieved. The long Illinois constitution was cluttered up with specific limitations and directives wholly out of place in any fundamental law and preventing public officials

9. *House Debates, Fiftieth General Assembly, State of Illinois, 1917* (Springfield, Ill., 1917), pp. 60, 62, 64–69.

from serving the people with maximum effectiveness. "They [the framers] labored under the delusion," he declared, "that they could shackle the legislator's power for evil and still give his virtues full play. . . . A constitution which seeks to legislate will inevitably be outgrown. This is our situation today."[10]

Even under the outmoded constitution, however, the state government could be considerably modernized within a short time if a few amendments were adopted, certain hampering statutes repealed, and several new ones passed. His program of immediate action called for measures to extend the area of public regulation and assistance, to enlarge the electorate and shorten the ballot, and, above all, to assure better and less expensive administration and law enforcement. He spoke in favor of legislation to encourage soil conservation, farmers' co-operatives, and the reforestation of waste lands; to limit the length of the working day of women in industry; to curb private banking; to oblige employers to pay the full cost of injuries incurred in line of duty by their employees; and to abolish, in so far as possible, whatever hazards to life and limb still existed within factories and other places of work. He insisted that the unfortunate people in state hospitals and other charitable institutions receive more humane and expert care and that scientific research seek to discover why the number of mentally ill persons had risen so ominously in recent years. The amazing increase in the use of automobiles, he said, demanded a speed-up in hard-surface road-building. Only in one particular did he qualify his call for wider state operations and control. He once again urged, as so often in the past, that the legislature empower Chicago to regulate its own public utilities with little or no interference from Springfield.

He asked that the democratic base of political action in Illinois be broadened by amending the constitution to allow women to vote for state and local officials. After requesting that absentee voting be legalized, he added:

Elections have been multiplied . . . [and] the burden of expense which elections impose is becoming unbearable. But this is not the most important consideration. The lengthening of the ballot and the increasing frequency of elections . . . have caused interest in public affairs to flag. The stay-at-home vote is becoming ominous. The ballot has been cheapened. Decrease the number of elections and public interest will be quickened.

Earlier in his inaugural address he voiced the earnest hope of having the constitution amended so as to reduce the number of elected officials. Students of government, he said, were agreed about the necessity of this reform "if democracy is to be made workable."

But nearest to his heart and primary in his emphasis was a radical improvement in the composition and performance of the executive arm. As he phrased it:

10. "To withhold necessary power from a public official because he may abuse it," Lowden said, "is to confess the failure of our form of government."

Something goes wrong, and we enact a law and there the matter rests, as though the law were an end in itself. We are confronted with a problem requiring solution, and then we pass the problem on to a commission and felicitate ourselves that we have solved the problem. . . . The progress needed most now is progress in administration.[11]

To this end he asked the legislature to extend the classified civil service and, above all, to provide for a budget system and the consolidation of the many administrative agencies into a few principal departments. Under the present "vicious" method, the head of each office had no knowledge of, or concern about, the over-all picture but was merely eager to enlarge the sphere of his own activities. With this purpose in mind, the ambitious official submitted his request for money to the legislature. "He very often asks for more than enough and he usually gets it." By establishing a Department of Finance, this blind and expensive procedure could be scrapped. The director of the new department would initiate a uniform bookkeeping system in all state offices and gather from them the information needed for compiling a centralized and scientific budget. Thereby the governor, for the first time in the history of Illinois, could obey his constitutional mandate to submit to the legislature, at the beginning of each regular session, intelligent "estimates of the amount of money required to be raised by taxation for all purposes." With so many overlapping bureaus, boards, and commissions he necessarily failed in his duty to supervise and control all executive functions of the government. To enable him to abide by his oath was "one of the imperative needs of the State." Lowden forewarned the legislature that within a few days he would "submit a special message covering this entire subject."

Thus, from the moment of his induction into office, he made clear that he would be a vigorous governor. Patriotic platitudes, characteristic of so many inaugurals, found almost no place in his address. His courage and evident sincerity more than atoned for his lack of eloquence. No hint of partisanship marred his words. Many of the recent Bull Moosers expressed much surprise to hear him speaking with their voice. "It is a truly progressive message," said Medill McCormick. "It is perfectly candid, the ablest, the most important delivered by an Illinois governor within my recollection." The *Chicago Tribune* reported agreement within "legislative circles" that Lowden had "laid down a program of forward-looking legislation which can never be ignored nor defeated in this general assembly."[12]

Following the inauguration, the Lowdens lunched in their new home with ten of their close friends. Later in the afternoon the governor attended a Hamilton Club party in his honor at the Sangamo Club House. The tradi-

11. "Upon the whole, the people have governed honestly. In the main, the people have acted wisely, so far as they have acted at all. It remains to inquire whether or not we have governed efficiently."

12. *Chicago Tribune*, Jan. 9, 1917; "Governor Lowden's Program for Illinois," *Survey*, Jan. 20, 1917, p. 466. There were 33 Republicans among the 51 senators, and 85 Republicans among the 153 representatives.

tional inaugural reception in the Executive Mansion, amid a profusion of smilax and pink roses, filled the evening until nearly midnight. At its close, Adjutant General Dickson, the master of ceremonies, told the Lowdens that they had shaken hands with six or seven thousand people. Unless they averaged twenty-five handshakes a minute during a four-hour stretch, he exaggerated the total. Nonetheless, the crowd was unusually large. Many people who ordinarily would have avoided the throng felt drawn to the reception by the perfect weather and a desire to see the socially elite Mrs. Lowden and her mother, Mrs. George M. Pullman. The representatives of the press as well as other guests paid homage to the "First Lady's" graciousness, her cloth-of-silver evening dress, and her rope of large pearls. As for her, it was "altogether a day never to be forgotten!"[13]

The acclaim accorded to the inaugural address did not necessarily signify that the legislature would readily adopt Lowden's recommendations. Hoping that administrative reorganization could take effect at the beginning of the new fiscal year on July 1, he worked long hours with the Efficiency and Economy Committee during the rest of January and early February, hammering out the code and talking with heads of executive agencies and delegations of citizens who feared lest their prestige or purse be in peril. After ten days of this regimen he felt sufficiently weary to agree with Mrs. Lowden's suggestion that, whenever possible, they walk together for forty-five minutes before lunch and go for a drive in their new limousine in the late afternoon. The people of Springfield soon looked to this daily walk for assurance that all was well with the governor and his wife.

On February 9 the committee submitted the Civil Administrative Code or Consolidation Bill, as it was often called, to the House of Representatives. With considerable reluctance, Lowden had agreed to a deletion of all references in the bill to the elected administrative officers, hence limiting its coverage to those subject to his appointment. The press erroneously forecast strenuous opposition from many assemblymen. What resistance there was in the lower house took the form of a few minor amendments and protests against the speed with which the Republicans "railroaded" the bill through to a final vote. It reached its second reading on February 13 and passed the House two days later by the huge margin of 143 to 2. Mrs. Lowden listened to some of the debates and joyously called the outcome "a great triumph for Frank!"[14] Once again Theodore Roosevelt wrote to him, expressing a lively interest in the reforms and inviting him to "Sagamore Hill" on his next trip to the eastern seaboard. "I might be able," Roosevelt added, "to use your example to point to as a moral in some of my writings." Unable to leave Springfield until the legislature adjourned, Lowden sent him copies of his inaugural address and the Administrative Code. After examining them, the

13. Mrs. Lowden's diary, Jan. 8, 1917.

14. *Ibid.,* Feb. 13–15, 1917; *House Debates, Fiftieth General Assembly, State of Illinois, 1917,* pp. 104 ff., 123–24, 126, 152–61. The debate often reduced itself to a duel between M. L. Igoe (Democrat, Cook County), and E. Shurtleff (Republican, McHenry County).

former President seemed even more eager than before to have Lowden come to see him.[15]

The Illinois Senate required only six days to have the bill considered in committee, reported out, debated, and carried through its three readings. Neither its thirty-six amendments nor the cursory discussion did more than peck at details. As soon as the Senate adopted the bill by a unanimous vote and learned that the lower house refused to accept its revisions, the Assembly recessed for a week after appointing a joint conference committee to iron out the differences. On March 1, upon the recommendation of this committee, the Senate withdrew thirteen of its amendments, and the House accepted the other twenty-three. The final vote came also on that day. It showed the upper chamber 100 per cent for the measure and the lower house with only two members in dissent.[16]

During the debate Lowden kept in close touch with the leaders of the Assembly and with the joint conference committee. Following the enactment of the code, the legislature recessed until after the inauguration ceremonies in Washington. The governor took advantage of the break to spend five quiet days on his Arkansas plantations. The *Chicago Tribune* reported on March 2 that he seemed "entirely worn out with the strain . . . was up until 3 o'clock [on the morning of the 1st] digesting the final conference report sentence by sentence, having the advice of experts. . . . It is conceded that no legislature in the last twenty years has responded so readily to a governor's suggestion."

The passage of the Consolidation Bill brought him face to face with difficult problems of patronage. The measure created nine departments with a total administrative staff of about seventy persons, not counting some ninety members of advisory and non-executive boards and a clerical force for each office.[17] The machine politicians naturally clamored to hold or to have the disposal of the more remunerative jobs, but Lowden refused to use most of them as rewards for campaign services. The wonder is not that he fell somewhat short of achieving his ideal but that he could draw so many able and politically disinterested men about him, in spite of intense pressure from rival Republican factions.

Even during the closing weeks of 1916, Lowden had been so beset by place-seekers that he disliked to go to his office in Chicago or even to venture on the streets. His telephone rang almost continuously, and his mail overflowed with envelopes made weighty by dozens of letters of indorsement

15. T. Roosevelt to FOL, Feb. 7 and 20, 1917; FOL to Roosevelt, Feb. 15, 1917.

16. *Journal of the Senate of the Fiftieth General Assembly of the State of Illinois* (Springfield, Ill., 1917), pp. 368–69, 381–86, 388, 394, 398, 414–17, 428; *House Debates, Fiftieth General Assembly, State of Illinois, 1917,* pp. 152–61. One amendment explicitly stated that the classified civil service would not be affected.

17. The nine departments were divided into a total of 96 divisions, offices, commissions, etc. As a result of the reform, about 125 boards, bureaus, or commissions were abolished, consolidated, or regrouped.

attached to applications from worthy citizens anxious to render public service in well-paying positions. After examining some hundreds of these missives, the reader can surmise the phraseology of all the rest with considerable assurance. "His appointment would meet the hearty approval of Republicans all over the state." "He will reflect much credit on your administration." "His appointment will be applauded by the boys who do things in Kane County." "The fellows over in Lake County at Waukegan have been inquiring very seriously about a position for" X. "Judge L—— has made more speeches and done more real work for the Republican Party in Southern Illinois than any other one person." "No man has ever responded more cheerfully to the party's call in fair weather and in foul than" Y. "His activities in the interest of the party have been such that they ought not to militate against him." Mr. J. has "worked unceasingly for you" and is a "true friend of the Negro race." "As Mr. L—— and Mr. C—— are both constituents of mine, I am very free to say that I should be pleased to see them recognized as their merits deserve." Judging from this voluminous correspondence, the reservoir of political talent in Illinois was full to the brim. No appointive job, however petty or meager in salary, seemed too inconsequential to be overlooked by the throng of job-hunters. No doubt the pressure mounted the higher because the Republicans had recovered control after four years out of office.

Although not a few of these applicants frankly demanded a reward for their work during the campaign, most of them used a more oblique approach. Bankers wished to be custodians of the public funds, lawyers to be state attorneys or public administrators, doctors to be on the staff of state hospitals, and social service workers to be public guardians or associated with the state charities. State senators and chairmen of county Republican committees sought conferences about the jobs in their respective bailiwicks.[18] One or another member of the Thompson-Lundin organization hovered close to Lowden's office whenever he visited Chicago. To each of these importunate people, whether a high and mighty business executive or a humble citizen ambitious to be merely a "rabbit shepherd," as Senator Sherman called a game warden, Lowden replied in much the same fashion. He would give the application "his best consideration" but would make no appointments or promises of appointments until after the legislature acted upon his proposals for administrative reform.

The salaried jobs ranged from $7,000 for each of the five members of the Public Utilities Commission and $5,000 for the chief grain inspector of Illinois to $780 for a chaplain at a reformatory. A few positions like that of the state architect carried with them a salary and also a percentage of the cost of each project supervised. Other appointive officers, of which the state inspector of apiaries and the five state examiners of horseshoers were examples,

18. The letters in the Lowden MSS from preachers, industrialists, bankers, senators, representatives, mayors, county chairmen, college professors, etc., asking for, or indorsing someone for, a job are far too numerous to cite here.

received per diem compensation instead of yearly stipends. Certain assignments, such as membership on the Art Commission and the Charities Commission, were honorary posts, repaying their occupants with the prestige derived from the title. Because many advisory boards and commissions had bipartisan personnel, Democrats as well as Republicans competed for the governor's favor. Until the Civil Administrative Code became law, the rivalry within each political party sometimes centered upon a position destined to be abolished by that measure.[19]

Its enactment early in March, 1917, caused a second flood of applications to descend upon the governor from federal and state officials on behalf of friends "who must be taken care of." Since the new administrative machine would not begin to operate until July 1, he had nearly four months in which to choose his subordinates. Nevertheless, the coming of the war in April, with its many extraordinary demands upon his time and thought, made this period of grace seem very short. By reducing the number of appointive offices in the interest of economy and efficiency, he had correspondingly increased the number of candidates for each surviving position. Some of the most influential Republicans in the state impatiently charged him with disregarding their personal letters, allotting too few offices to Germans, Bohemians, Scandinavians, Jews, women, or former Progressives; with failing to apportion patronage fairly throughout the state; and with overlooking many local leaders who had worked valiantly for his election.

On April 30 the *Chicago Journal* reported that, in order to get anything else done, the governor was limiting his patronage interviews from 10:30 A.M. to 12:30 P.M. and had told a representative of the press that "another two weeks like the last two" would put him "in his grave." On July 2 when the worst was over except reading the bitter letters from applicants not favored with positions, Lowden confided to John Dwight:

I am disappointing scores of my political friends. . . . A lot of men, and good men too, like to hold an office which pays a salary and requires only a day or two of time a month, and we no longer have any of these positions. Some days when I leave the office I think I shall not have a friend in the State when this whole thing is over. The people, however, generally, who are not interested in office, I think are with me.

His critics were the more numerous because he had recently signed a bill which invited attack as a glaring example of spoils politics. In the interest of greater administrative efficiency he had encouraged the Republican-dominated legislature, over shrill protests from the opposition and several good-government societies,[20] to amend the Civil Service Law of 1905 so as to

19. Typed sheets in Lowden MSS entitled "Exempt Positions Appointed by the Governor." "Exempt positions" meant not under the classified civil service. The governor's salary was $12,000.

20. *Assembly Bulletin of the Legislative Voters League of the State of Illinois* (Mount Morris, Ill., 1917), Vol. II, No. 19 (May 19, 1917); *Civil Service News* (Chicago), May 24, 1917; *Senate Debates, Fiftieth General Assembly, State of Illinois, 1917* (Springfield, Ill., 1917), pp. 442, 455, 457, 459, 470–71; *House Debates, Fiftieth General Assembly, State of Illinois, 1917*, pp. 278–83, 411, 414, 687–93.

enable state officials to discharge without a hearing any classified civil service employee deemed to be incompetent. An aggrieved job-holder had no redress unless he could prove that his dismissal resulted from political, religious, or racial discrimination. Obviously, he rarely could demonstrate that partisanship rather than inefficiency had prompted his ouster, even though some Democrats appointed during the Dunne regime became the immediate targets of the amendment. The measure also removed a considerable number of jobs from the classified list. Although Lowden welcomed these additional niches for place-hungry Republicans, his passion for efficiency and for permitting the department directors to choose their subordinates with almost complete freedom mainly explains his willingness to expose the sincerity of his oft-voiced support of civil service reform to assault.

On this issue, moreover, Edgar Bancroft, who had championed an examination and classification system for many years, upheld the governor. "The true friend of the civil service reform movement," Lowden told him, "is he who stands squarely against the spoils system, and equally strongly for efficiency under civil service reform laws." "The inevitable tendency of all reform organizations," Bancroft agreed, "is to become technically expert and theoretically critical, and to forget that all the laws for the improvement of the public service have one sole object . . . an increased efficiency."[21] Some months later, on the other hand, he warned the governor that the removal-without-a-hearing amendment had sometimes been used to dismiss Democrats rather than incompetents of both parties. Lowden's reply did not meet this charge squarely. He merely answered that the war was increasing the difficulty of finding high-grade men for civil service jobs.[22]

Although the directors of the nine new departments were all Republicans, only two of them had conspicuously advocated Lowden's election. Two others were fairly active in the political life of the state. Several of the nine were not Lowden's first choices. Indeed, he often felt discouraged before he succeeded in filling these key positions with men in whom he had confidence.[23] The appointment of Stead as director of the Department of Trade and Commerce surprised no one. Charles Adkins, a farmer and stock-raiser of Bement, accepted the directorship of the Department of Agriculture after Dean Eugene Davenport, of the University of Illinois, declined. Adkins, a good friend of Congressman William B. McKinley, had been speaker of the House during one of his four terms in the assembly. After deciding not to run for the gubernatorial nomination, he strongly backed Lowden. He and Stead were both well qualified for their posts, but their help during the campaign weighed heavily with Lowden in appointing them.

For over twenty years, Leslie D. Puterbaugh, the director of the Department of Public Works and Buildings, had served as a judge in the courts of

21. E. A. Bancroft to FOL, Dec. 27, 1917, and Jan. 4, 1918; FOL to Bancroft, Jan. 2, 1918.

22. Bancroft to FOL, Mar. 20, 1918, and FOL to Bancroft, Apr. 4, 1918.

23. A biographical sketch of each of the nine directors is in *Blue Book of the State of Illinois, 1917–1918*, pp. 322–26.

Illinois. More recently he had engaged in banking at Peoria, where he staunchly supported the Bradley Polytechnic Institute. Lowden and he were acquaintances of long standing within that Peoria circle which included Mayor E. N. Woodruff and Robert D. Clarke. Friendship and the advisability of having a representative in his cabinet from the second largest city of Illinois probably counted more heavily with Lowden than Puterbaugh's limited help during the campaign.

For the directorship of the Department of Finance, which Lowden considered the key post among the nine, he selected Omar H. Wright of Belvidere, president of a national bank and of an insurance company. Although Wright had favored Lowden's election, he had done little to help effect it. They had been casual acquaintances for at least ten years, and their work together at Springfield quickly made them warm friends. Lowden assured Wright's son in 1941 at the time of his father's death: "No one outside your family mourns . . . [his] passing . . . more than I. . . . I visited him oftener than any other member of my Cabinet and I enjoyed these visits greatly. There never was a finer man, I think."[24]

Although Puterbaugh's and Wright's names appear infrequently in the massive correspondence relating to the campaign of 1916, the five other men who became department heads had been scarcely mentioned at all. Dr. C. St. Clair Drake of Chicago, who took over the directorship of the Department of Public Health, brought more than twenty years' experience to his new position. At the time of his appointment, he was secretary and executive head of the Illinois State Board of Health. Barney Cohen of Chicago, the director of the Department of Labor, and Evan D. John of Springfield, director of the Department of Mines and Minerals, were naturalized citizens like Dr. Drake, and for long had worked within the general areas covered by their assignments. Cohen had been the president of the Cigar Makers' Union of Chicago, president of the Association of Government Labor Officials of the United States and Canada, and president of the Illinois State Federation of Labor. As a state factory inspector he had lobbied at Springfield on behalf of bills desired by union labor. When eight years of age, Evan John began work in a Welsh coal mine. In America he slowly forged ahead until he acquired part ownership of the Carterville and Big Muddy Coal Company in Williamson County, Illinois, and had served several earlier Republican administrations as a mine inspector.

For director of the Department of Registration and Education, Lowden selected Francis W. Shepardson, a history professor at the University of Chicago. Shepardson was a Doctor of Philosophy of Yale, an honorary Doctor of Laws of Denison, and a senator of Phi Beta Kappa. Lowden probably was less impressed by his friend's academic honors than by his skill in public relations and his prominence in the Beta Theta Pi fraternity. For Lowden this "bond of brotherhood" was occasionally a compelling one.

24. FOL to O. B. Wright, Sept. 15, 1941.

The cabinet appointment causing the most public comment was that of Charles H. Thorne of Chicago as director of the Department of Public Welfare. In a day when big businessmen rarely entered state service and often regarded any political office except at the top national level as unworthy of their talents, Thorne's willingness to accept a $7,000 post at Springfield three years after resigning the presidency of Montgomery, Ward and Company, came as a real surprise. Lowden had never met him, but Gordon Ramsay wisely judged that he would be an excellent choice. In a lengthy conference at Springfield, the governor finally persuaded the reluctant Thorne to accept. Interested for many years in numerous public welfare movements, he brought sympathy, imagination, and much-needed business skill to the task of supervising the state's twenty-three charitable and penal institutions. His impatience with all considerations of practical politics sometimes drew him into acrimonious controversies, but it was at least as much a virtue as a fault.[25]

These nine men comprised Lowden's inner council or cabinet. Thanks to them, he could perform his executive duties with more up-to-date information at his command than any of his predecessors in the governorship. He selected the directors with great care, because he recognized that the success or failure of his administration would hinge largely upon their performance. He held each of the nine to a strict accountability for the efficient operation of his department. In his formal charge to Stead, he wrote:

The Public Utilities Commission is an absolutely independent body so far as the administration of law is concerned; still it is in the Department of which you are the head. That means that you are to exercise exactly the same supervision over it that the Governor himself could properly do. I shall, therefore, hold you responsible for results, and to that end I shall act upon any recommendations you may make with reference to the personnel of the Commission. In other words, whatever powers I have in the premises, I am expecting you to advise me how to exercise.[26]

Professional politicians, already aggrieved because so few of their own number entered the governor's cabinet, took further offense when the men and women they indorsed for less exalted positions lost out to better-qualified persons who had not worked in the campaign. And yet the long list of appointees included many a tried and true Republican. For example, Joseph C. Mason and John G. Gamber, Stead's chief lieutenants in managing Lowden's campaign, became administrative auditor and fire marshal of Illinois, respectively. Gordon Ramsay gained the lucrative post of public administrator of Cook County. Ralph F. Bradford was named chief fish and game warden, Omer N. Custer and James A. Culp, members of the Industrial Commission,

25. Thorne's forward-looking policies are excellently summarized in his first report as director: *State of Illinois: First Administrative Report of the Directors of Departments under the Civil Administrative Code . . . July 1, 1917, to June 30, 1918;* also *Blue Book of the State of Illinois, 1917–1918,* pp. 311–12, 321. In 1918 there were about twenty-seven thousand persons in the state's charitable and penal institutions.

26. FOL to W. H. Stead, July 13, 1917.

William L. Sackett, supervisor of waterways; Will Colvin, superintendent of pardons and paroles; James S. Baldwin, assistant director of the Department of Trade and Commerce; and Fred E. Sterling and Frank H. Funk, members of the Public Utilities Commission. These men and as many other appointees had actively supported Lowden for the governorship.

With the exception of Herman Goda, the governor's favorite Chicago barber who was named to the State Board of Examiners for Barbers, Lowden apparently made no appointment solely because of friendship. Those critics, however, who had warned that he would give the rich and socially elite too much voice in the state's government liked to point to the membership of some of the advisory commissions as evidence of their foresight. On these non-salaried boards, leading Chicago manufacturers, merchants, artists, and lawyers were conspicuous, as well as professors from the three largest universities in Illinois.

No one of the prominent Republicans except those named to high executive offices at Springfield greatly influenced Lowden on matters of patronage. Among well-known politicians, he probably listened to Senator Sherman the most and to Mayor Thompson the least, in proportion to the number of men whom they recommended for jobs. An indorsement from Thompson seemed almost equivalent to a blackball, notwithstanding the help given by the City Hall in the primary and election campaigns.[27] Deneen and West urged few of their own friends for positions, but Lowden so favored their wing of the party that Congressman Madden writhed. Among the congressmen, only Edward E. Denison, William A. Rodenberg, and Burnett M. Chiperfield seemed to be well satisfied by the positions allotted to their constituents, while Congressmen Madden, McKinley, and Copley felt that their wishes received too little attention. Former Governor Richard Yates, in high dudgeon because his membership on the Public Utilities Commission was not renewed, accepted the assistant attorney-generalship with poor grace.[28]

When Attorney-General Brundage sent Lowden the names of seven men for appointment as the Board of Commissioners of Lincoln Park in Chicago, he added that "from time immemorial" Republican governors had conformed to the wishes of the North Side machine in filling these posts.[29] Regardless of custom, the governor followed these recommendations in only two instances. On the other hand, after Gordon Ramsay mentioned two men whom he wished on that board, Lowden accepted his suggestions with alacrity. Ramsay's own appointment as public administrator of Cook County thwarted

27. In the vast mass of patronage correspondence, only one letter from Lorimer (Feb. 14, 1917) was found, and that recommended a woman for a clerical post. Lorimer visited FOL at Springfield for an hour on Apr. 7. L. P. Volz, Lundin's secretary in 1917, told the author on Dec. 6, 1950, about how dissatisfied his boss and Thompson had been by FOL's practice of listening to Brundage rather than to them. But Brundage also was dissatisfied.

28. R. Yates to FOL, June 29, and FOL's reply, July 2, 1917.

29. E. Brundage to FOL, Dec. 15, and FOL's reply, Dec. 29, 1916; *Chicago News,* June 9, 1917.

Brundage's hope of having his chief henchman, Homer K. Galpin, occupy that coveted post. The attorney-general's pique would have been even greater if he had known that, in naming the seven members of the West Chicago Parks Commission, Lowden accepted five of the six nominees of their chairman, John F. Smulski, the Polish-American banker. On several occasions, when asked by the governor, Harold Ickes suggested former Progressives whose appointment would "assist thoroughly to reunite the Republican Party." Very few of his preferences, however, were honored. Lowden's subordinates averaged high in quality, but many machine politicians wondered whether he really had appreciated their help during the campaign.

After witnessing the induction of the department heads into office on July 2, 1917, Mrs. Lowden commented in her diary: "It was a fine body of men that assembled in the governor's office and a new and interesting experiment in government is now beginning." It worked so well in practice that Lowden proudly told the Assembly eighteen months later:

It amounted to a revolution in government. . . . It has more than justified all the expectations that were formed concerning it. . . . Unity and harmony of administration has been attained, and vigor and energy of administration enhanced.

It seems to me almost Providential that it should have been enacted into law before war actually came. . . . Illinois, through the greater elasticity and efficiency of her new form of government, was able to meet every emergency of the war without an extraordinary session of her Legislature.[30]

Probably in some measure because partisan bickering virtually ceased during the war, the ominous predictions that the legislature of 1919 would cut the code to ribbons and disregard the figures in the executive budget did not come true. On the contrary, the Assembly accepted the governor's financial estimates almost without change and seemed more inclined to extend administrative reform than to curtail it.[31] Since the code was frequently inquired about, complimented, and advocated by state officials and students of government outside Illinois and since its operation helped to bring tax reduction and a virtual end to calls upon the legislature for extra appropriations to cover administrative deficits, many office-holders and office-seekers of both parties realized that political wisdom counseled them to accept it with good grace.[32]

30. FOL's message of January 8, 1919, in *Journal of the House of Representatives of the Fifty-first General Assembly of the State of Illinois* (Springfield, Ill., 1919), p. 14. In his message of January 5, 1921 (*Journal of the House of Representatives of the Fifty-second General Assembly of the State of Illinois* [Springfield, Ill., 1921], p. 13), he called the Civil Administrative Code "a distinct contribution to political science." For an excellent description and evaluation of the code see John M. Mathews, "Administrative Reorganization in Illinois," *National Municipal Review* (Baltimore, Md.), IX, No. 11 (November, 1920), suppl., pp. 739–56.

31. FOL, "Executive Responsibility in Illinois," *Proceedings of the Academy of Political Science in the City of New York,* VIII (New York, 1920), 1–6, and "The Budget System in Illinois," *American Review of Reviews* (New York), LXI (March, 1920), 299–300.

32. FOL, "The High Cost of Business Inefficiency in American Government," *Current Opinion* (New York), LXVIII (May, 1920), 618–21.

Once the new machinery was in operation, the governor discovered virtues in it which he had not recognized before it took effect. As the years went by, he also tended in his speeches to take somewhat more than his just share of credit for its invention. The silence of those men who had been members of Governor Dunne's Efficiency and Economy Committee or who had actually drafted the code suggests, however, that they found no reason to complain because he personalized it in his own name. Indeed, he probably had been indispensable. Without his vigorous and persistent backing and his skilful handling of the legislature and patronage during the first months of his administration, the reform could hardly have been enacted into law at that time. Furthermore, he helped assure its successful operation by eliminating important weaknesses in the Dunne committee's blueprint and by filling the directorships with men more interested in rendering unselfish public service than in their own political futures.

Indisputably, he merited praise for including among the nine departments a Department of Finance with the power to systematize and supervise the financial operations of the other eight and to prepare a biennial executive budget. As he foresaw, this department soon became the keystone of the entire structure, and its director the most important of the code officials. Lowden wrote later: "The Department of Finance was a new conception in our state government—and in that of the government of any American state, I think . . . I put into effect the first executive budget in any State."[33] When this budget quickly proved its worth, Lowden urged the federal government to establish one of its own. In late 1919, while explaining its operation and merits to the relevant committee of each house of Congress, he recommended that the director of the national budget be made accountable to the secretary of the Treasury rather than independent of all control except that of the House of Representatives. Failing to provide for this, the Budget Act of 1921 seemed to him to fall far short of the ideal. Here again he demonstrated how completely he had been converted from a belief in legislative leadership to an advocacy of executive power and responsibility.[34]

When he reflected upon the problems of state administration, he discovered a philosophic as well as a practical justification for the new order of things at Springfield. Before his election his favorite argument had been that government was a big business and hence must be conducted like one. Although he continued to speak and write in this vein after his inauguration, he shifted his emphasis to the theme that political democracy could not func-

33. When introduced to the Massachusetts lower house on Feb. 13, 1919, FOL was called by its speaker "the pioneer and originator" of "the very budget system on our calendar today." See also MS of FOL's speech at the University of Virginia, Aug. 5, 1930.

34. MS of speech by FOL to American Bankers Association, Chicago, Sept. 26, 1918; see also FOL, "Problems of Civil Administration," *North American Review* (New York), CCX, No. 765 (August, 1919), 186–92; and "Reorganization in Illinois and Its Results," *Annals of the American Academy of Political and Social Science,* CXIII (May, 1924), 155–61. In 1933 Murray Seasongood, president of the National Municipal League, announced that sixteen states had followed Illinois's lead by adopting executive budgets.

tion, if, indeed, it could even survive, without sound administrative practices. A government was no longer democratic when it became so complicated that the sovereign people neither understood it nor knew whom to blame when something went wrong. The leviathan government made necessary by the new urban-industrial age could not elude their control if its structure were systematized and the responsibility for its action were centered in one or a few elected officials.

Furthermore, World War I taught the sharp lesson that the continuance of democratic government depended upon its equaling an autocracy in its efficiency. Efficiency involved something more than a logical division of functions between the several components of the executive branch, a clear chain of command running up to the governor, and economical operation. The governor must also be able to act quickly and decisively to the limits of his constitutional powers, upon the basis of accurate and up-to-date information always available for his use. To help toward this end, Lowden clustered the nine directors' offices closely about his own in the Capitol at Springfield. The resulting ease of communication also made unnecessary much time-wasting correspondence and red tape. "Without the organization furnished by the Administrative Code," the governor wrote later, "it would have been humanly impossible for me to have exercised any real supervision over most of the activities of the state government."[35] Thanks also to an orderly administrative structure, every citizen could readily determine to which state office he should direct his inquiry or take his problem.

In a word, Lowden championed a new type of representative government for the new American society of the twentieth century. Just as he stressed that boards or commissions were unsuited for executive tasks because "individuals . . . do things and not bodies of men,"[36] so also he held that the authority of a public official must be commensurate with his responsibility. "I am a good deal of a monarchist when it comes to execution," he admitted. "I believe as a rule one man accomplishes a little more than ten men. . . . Great bodies of men don't execute anything."[37] By the provisions of the Civil Administrative Code each director as well as his chief subordinates had a term of office identical with that of the governor and a tenure unprotected by civil service regulations. Not only did they serve at his pleasure, but he could check them through his virtual control of the executive budget.

Lowden, however, probably did not sufficiently foresee what several of his successors in the governorship would make abundantly clear. An administrative structure which centralized so much power in the chief executive could become a mighty engine of spoils politics. Of course, his reply would have been that the voters had the responsibility of nominating and electing

35. FOL to Leonard D. White, Chicago, Oct. 26, 1922.

36. FOL, "Executive Responsibility in Illinois," p. 3, and "Problems of Civil Administration," p. 189.

37. Typed MS entitled "Conference on the Constitutional Convention Proposition. Governor's Office, Springfield, April 8, 1918."

honest and able governors. Self-government would break down completely if necessary authority were withheld from any public official through fear that he would abuse it. "The ingenuity of man," he wrote, "could never work out any scheme by which you can tie men's hands for evil and leave them free for good."[38]

From his reading of history he recognized the "progress made in America in the last century in everything except the science of government."[39] One phenomenon attending the rapid social and economic changes had been the enhancement and concentration of power. This resulted from the application of electricity to manufacturing, transportation, communication, and agriculture; the amassing of capital by colossal banks and other corporations; and the uniting of like-minded people into organizations of all kinds for the purpose of achieving their diverse purposes through co-operative action. Since these competing centers of power were "natural," they must not be crushed. On the other hand, their growth had thrust upon federal and state governments the unfamiliar role of guarding the commonweal against mighty and often conflicting forces. Power alone could check power. Authority conferred cautiously in meticulously detailed statutes inevitably fell short of the need. In a complex urban-industrial society, where conditions might alter importantly from month to month, the problems requiring prompt governmental action were of almost infinite variety. For this reason a state legislature should merely define the general areas of control and expenditure and then intrust the governor with ample discretion and funds to perform his manifold duties effectively.

Americans of the new century must rid themselves of the notion inherited from long years of English history before the American Revolution that the progress of human liberty could be measured by the number of statutory limitations placed upon executive power. A highly qualified governor with an expert administrative staff under his sole direction knew better than two hundred legislators how much money was needed and how it could be spent so that the taxpayers would receive maximum service for every dollar. When a legislature accepted the informed estimates in an executive budget, it avoided such wasteful and largely blind actions as were taken by the Forty-eighth General Assembly just preceding Lowden's administration. That body enacted ninety-four separate appropriation acts without adequate debate in the hectic closing hours of its session and in response to conflicting pressures from the unco-ordinated administrative officers and commissions. In Lowden's view the old lesson from English history that an executive usually exceeded a legislature in financial extravagance had become outworn and harmful in modern America.

Whether the Civil Administrative Code saved Illinois one million dollars a year, as prophesied by the governor, cannot be determined with certainty.

38. "Executive Responsibility in Illinois," p. 3.
39. FOL, "The High Cost of Business Inefficiency in American Government," pp. 618–21.

Although the first legislature of his regime based its appropriations upon prewar prices and conditions, the 1917–19 biennium ended with a deficit in only one of the nine departments. The original allotments to the Department of Public Welfare had to be supplemented in the face of the rising costs of the food, clothing, and fuel required by the charitable and penal institutions. Its deficit, however, amounted to less than the total surplus of money in the possession of the other directors as the biennium closed.[40] Lowden took pride in this record, even though the extraordinary war expenses of the governmental branches outside the code caused the total cost to rise above the record high of $46,000,000 reached by the Dunne administration.

Lowden deplored this continuing upward trend. "You cannot reduce the high cost of living," he said, "until you reduce the high cost of government." Besides being subject to heavier taxes, every adult citizen paid more than before for essential commodities in limited supply because public officials, who had to have them for state use, drove up their selling price by competing for them in the open market. This rise in the cost of government, however, could be measurably retarded by making it operate more efficiently.[41]

Deferring to Lowden's insistence, the joint legislative committee which had worked on the code conferred upon each department head all powers hitherto vested in the separate agencies united under his supervision. Furthermore, the Assembly left him free to devise the operational rules to apply within his own jurisdiction. In this way the code avoided the mistake which Lowden summed up later in these words: "Democracy has been afraid of itself and has hemmed in its officials by a multitude of laws which result in red tape." By the terms of the code, every director had a non-salaried advisory committee to consult at his option. Eminent men who would have scorned to hold a paid job at Springfield gladly shared their expertness with the state government by accepting membership on these boards. Also helping toward flexibility of operation was the governor's power to shift a civil service employee from one department to another whenever any position tended to become a sinecure.[42]

40. *State of Illinois: First Administrative Report of the Directors of Departments under the Civil Administrative Code . . . July 1, 1917, to June 30, 1918,* pp. 5, 21–22, 171–73, 227–28, 238: "Food prices have increased 78 per cent since the war, fuel 106 per cent and general supplies an average of 91 per cent." The deficit of the Department of Public Welfare was about $1,500,000. The other eight departments, after covering this, had a total unexpended balance of $290,508 at the end of the biennium. The surplus, however, was due in large part to the fact that the unexpected coming of the war, with the resulting shortage of men and materials and the higher prices, made it impossible or unwise to proceed with certain building construction and repairs which had been contemplated when the appropriations were made.

41. FOL, "The High Cost of Business Inefficiency in American Government," p. 621.

42. FOL, "Business Government," *Saturday Evening Post,* Mar. 13, 1920, pp. 5, 165–67, 169. Under legislative authorization, FOL appointed a thirteen-man commission in 1919 to recommend, after investigation, a job-classification system so that the salaries of public officials might be standardized. In its report of June 30, 1920, it admitted that the task was too vast for it to complete.

Practical considerations restrained Lowden and his co-framers from making the code as comprehensive as they would have liked it to be. If they had asked the legislature for too much, it might have balked at doing anything in the way of administrative reform. They did not try, for example, to have the laws repealed which granted financial powers to elected officials such as the secretary of state, the attorney-general, and the Board of Trustees of the University of Illinois. These, together with the adjutant general, the National Guard, and the state librarian, remained completely immune from supervision by the Department of Finance. The extraordinary postwar pressures probably explain why the governor declined, except in two particulars, to urge the new legislature in 1919 to extend the scope of administrative reform. Following his lead, that session required the non-code officers to clear with the director of the Department of Finance before disbursing their funds, although he gained no control over their requests for appropriations.[43] In the same year a tax commission of three men under the Department of Finance supplanted the elected State Board of Equalization. "This marks the successful end of Frank's entire program of legislation as planned two years ago," Mrs. Lowden noted in her diary on June 10, 1919. "Great triumph for him!"

Political leaders of both parties and numerous civic organizations viewed this latter change as a forward step toward modernizing the state's tax structure and improving its administration. There could be no thoroughgoing reform of the decentralized and cumbersome machinery at the county and township levels, however, as long as the constitution remained unamended. Nevertheless, much could be done by statute to distribute the state tax burden more fairly and render the assessment work more expert. Illinois depended in part for its revenue upon indirect taxes like corporation and other license fees. The legislature raised many of these upon Lowden's recommendation. For this reason and because of his stricter enforcement of the laws, they produced much more income than ever before. The new franchise tax on corporations yielded nearly $3,000,000, while the return from the tax on the gross premiums of insurance companies not chartered by Illinois but doing business within its borders rose from $600,000 to about $2,300,000. Although heavier indirect taxes helped to shift a somewhat larger proportion of the cost of government upon wealthy individuals and companies, this desirable easing of the burden upon the poor could better be accomplished in the realm of direct taxation.

Direct taxes theoretically varied in amount, depending upon the assessed value of real and personal property. Much of the privately owned wealth in Illinois by 1917 consisted of "intangibles"—stocks, bonds, and other securi-

43. Appropriations for wages and salaries were hereafter made in a lump sum, not a specific amount for each employee and officer. As a result, the director of a department could often get the needed work done for less money or raise the pay of a valued staff member so as to prevent his resignation. The legislature further provided that the director of finance should control the only contingency fund ($250,000) available to the nine directors.

ties. These forms of personal property could be easily hidden. Even when a diligent assessor ferreted them out, he needed to be a highly trained expert to estimate their value accurately. If a "uniform" tax, as required by the Illinois constitution, were levied upon all personal property without prior classification, it would be confiscatory in some instances and inconsiderable in others. For these reasons most intangibles went scot-free. Consequently, direct taxes upon land and buildings still provided most of the state's revenue, just as they had fifty years before when the wealth of Illinois was mainly agricultural. Lowden told an audience of Chicago businessmen in September, 1918: "There was not anybody in Illinois who did not know that we had been violating the constitution in Chicago and throughout the state from the time it was adopted, with reference to the assessments of property. . . . If [the constitution were] enforced . . . I think I am safe in saying that bankruptcy would come to Chicago within a year."[44]

The replacement of the State Board of Equalization by the Tax Commission was a notable reform, long urged and long overdue. The twenty-five elected members of the old board had met briefly each autumn and in some fashion accomplished their task of "equalizing" the separate valuations of real and personal property sent in from the several districts of the state. Rarely skilled in what Lowden called "the very difficult science of property evaluation," they were "helpless" when confronted by the "legal experts" of big business with whom they frequently had to deal.[45] After they estimated the value of the intangibles or real estate of a corporation, they could not convincingly, if challenged, justify their findings by citing accurate facts and figures.

Although the board had "outlived its usefulness," as Lowden said, it had many defenders. In their opinion its inexpertness was offset by the facts of its origin in a democratic election and its representation of every congressional district in Illinois. Because a majority of its members came from rural downstate, they regarded corporations with hostility. The expiring board had a vehement and even a vindictive champion in the person of its chairman, William H. Malone of Park Ridge. At his urging in 1918, the board increased by about $50,000,000 its valuation of certain public utilities and of the Pullman Company. According to Malone, it was for this reason that Lowden, "the servant of all tax-dodging corporations and a large shareholder in many of them," used extreme political pressure to have the board abolished. In its stead, Malone added, the governor obtained a small, appointive Tax Commission which he could control in the interest of his wealthy friends.[46] Early in 1917 Harold Ickes had strongly warned Lowden

44. MS of FOL's speech to Mid-Day Club, Sept. 17, 1918.

45. FOL's speech to Illinois State Bar Association, Feb. 4, 1919.

46. W. H. Malone to G. A. Ramsay, Aug. 25, 1919. Undated pamphlet entitled *W. A. McKee, Chairman* [of W. H. Malone's] *Public Defense Committee.* For a defense of FOL, see *House Debates, Fifty-first General Assembly, State of Illinois, 1919* (Springfield, Ill., 1919), pp. 152–58. After hearings, at which both Wright, director of the Department of

against gratifying Malone's wish to be the superintendent of state highways.[47] Perhaps his failure to receive either this position or a place on the new Tax Commission helps to account for his enmity toward the governor.

Nothing in Lowden's papers during or after his governorship lends support to Malone's charges. He had spoken in favor of abolishing the State Board of Equalization many months before it increased the taxes of the Pullman Company. In fact, he wished for an expert Tax Commission in order to bring a greater amount of corporate property within the range of taxation and thus compel the rich to contribute more nearly in proportion to their wealth. If this were done, he hoped that the tax rate on real estate could be lowered. Caustic critics like Malone mistakenly thought of Lowden not as a farmer but as a big businessman whose affections still centered wholly in La Salle Street. Larger and new sources of public revenue, a more equitable apportionment of the tax load, more efficient tax administration, more control by the governor over that administration, and a lower rate of direct taxation were Lowden's five chief aims in destroying the State Board of Equalization. Its abolition, the new taxes already mentioned, and the Civil Administrative Code comprised a single pattern of reform. If he had had his way, rural landowners would have been the only considerable group whose taxes would decline, unless the return of peace and lessened costs because of more efficient administration warranted an across-the-board reduction.

The new Tax Commission began its work on July 1, 1919. Its three members, unlike the personnel of the old board, gave full time to their task and had a permanent office in Springfield. Their first objective was "to establish a scientific basis for making assessments." To attain this, after ascertaining the methods used by a similar commission in Wisconsin, they amassed statistics on the sale price of all land transfers in Illinois during the preceding five years and compared them with the assessed values of these plots. The commission, furthermore, prepared a card file of all corporations doing business in the state and, through public hearings, consultation with corporation tax agents, and a study of the records of the Interstate Commerce Commission and Illinois Public Utilities Commission, computed the real value of the property of railroads and public utilities.

Lowden followed this work with intense interest. Quite apart from his recognition of its importance, he was always fascinated by statistics and any problem which could be reduced to mathematical terms. The commission discovered, for example, that, of 1,232 corporations in Cook County, only 726 had ever paid any property tax whatsoever to the state. When the commission completed its survey and added up its valuations of taxable property, it had increased by over $332,000,000 the total arrived at by the old board of

---

Finance, and Malone were represented by counsel, the Illinois Assembly's joint committee of investigation declared that Malone's charges had been wholly unsustained and that he had done FOL and Wright "a grievous wrong" (*House Debates, Fifty-first General Assembly, State of Illinois, 1919*, pp. 433–37; *Journal of the Senate of the Fifty-first General Assembly, State of Illinois* [Springfield, Ill., 1919], pp. 1662–65).

47. H. Ickes to FOL, Apr. 10, 1917.

equalization in its last year of operation. Most of this increase was from property owned by corporations. Of the 102 counties in Illinois, the Tax Commission raised the assessed valuation of real and personal property in 56, decreased it in 9, and left it unchanged in 37. Having made a thorough and unbiased study before reaching its conclusions, it could reply convincingly to most of the petitions for "review and correction" which challenged the fairness of particular valuations.[48]

Knowing the assessed value of all private property in Illinois, the approximate amount to be expected from indirect taxes, and the appropriations made by the legislature, Governor Lowden, the state treasurer, and the state auditor decided each December what the property tax rate for the coming year would have to be in order to produce the required income. As a result of the larger revenue from indirect taxes, the uncovering of a third of a billion dollars more of taxable wealth, the increased valuation of much property, and the reduction of administrative costs by means of the code, the state tax rate fell from 90 cents per $1,000 valuation in 1917 to 60 cents in 1919. To William Malone's horror, certain conspicuous corporations like the Pullman Company, which under the regime of the board of equalization had been heavily mulcted, while many less prominent companies escaped altogether, now had the assessed worth of their property lowered by the Tax Commission. In spite of this fact and the slash in the tax rate, the state treasury, empty when Lowden was inaugurated, had a surplus in its general revenue fund of over $5,000,000 on January 1, 1918, over $13,000,000 one year later, and over $15,000,000 at the opening of both 1920 and 1921. During these same years, the appropriation for schools more than doubled and for the University of Illinois rose about 33 per cent.[49]

This financial achievement was the more extraordinary because it had been carried through in years of rising prices and abnormal expenses due to the war. Thus the new tax administration, directed by a few experts and centrally controlled by the governor, amply justified itself. Lowden was convinced that taxation must be the chief instrumentality for maintaining democracy in a capitalistic society where wealth tended to concentrate more and more in a few hands. Furthermore, as he told the legislature on January 5, 1921, "there is no question but that the whole industrial structure of the future of our country is directly related to the question of taxation." On its proper handling hinges "our getting back to a normal basis."[50]

48. Typed report entitled "Division of Tax Commission, Frank F. Noleman, Chairman, Joseph B. Sanborn, Charles C. Craig," undated but about July 20, 1920; pamphlet, *Third Annual Report, The Department of Finance, July 1, 1919, to June 30, 1920, Omar H. Wright, Director.*

49. O. H. Wright to FOL, Dec. 1, 1920, and memorandum of Wright to FOL, Dec. 10, 1920. In 1917 about 71 cents of every tax dollar collected went into the general revenue fund, 17 cents for schools, and 11 cents for the University of Illinois. In 1920, these figures were 35, 41, and 17 cents, respectively. By 1920, 7½ cents of each tax dollar was allocated to waterways improvement.

50. *Journal of the House of Representatives of the Fifty-second General Assembly of the State of Illinois,* p. 25.

As in the case of the Civil Administrative Code, the provisions of the Illinois constitution prevented these tax reforms from going to the full length desired by Governor Lowden. Except by giving advice and information, the Tax Commission had no check whatsoever over the valuations made by the township and county assessors. By raising rates during the war, the latter offset much of the reductions effected by the authorities at Springfield. Among the many reasons why Lowden urged a radical revision of the constitution of 1870, the obsolescence of its Article IX, entitled "Revenue," was one of the chief. He wished to dispense with township assessors and other local taxing officials in Illinois. By abandoning the "uniformity" stipulation, personal property could be subdivided into a number of realistic categories, each subject to its own assessment rate. He recommended a centralized tax structure for all of Illinois, focused in the governor and the Tax Commission. Such a system, together with a more comprehensive executive budget and the Civil Administrative Code, would enable the state administration to operate with all the economy, expertness, and smoothness of a big business office.

Although administrative reform in Illinois was far from complete, more had been accomplished there than in any other state up to that time. Lowden viewed the code as his greatest contribution to "the science of government" and as probably his most notable public service. Forward-looking politicians, political scientists, and better-government associations acclaimed his work and pressed him for articles or speeches describing it. He discovered that he suddenly had become a national figure, mentioned as a presidential possibility, referred to frequently in Congress when national administrative reform was under discussion, and called upon to address joint sessions of state legislatures and associations of scholars.

This widespread interest in what he and his co-workers had accomplished in Illinois was not transitory. It continued as long as he lived.[51] In his own state the general principles of the code of 1917 still undergird the form of the executive branch, even though Lowden was often distressed after his governorship by the creation of new autonomous boards and commissions and the prostitution of the centralized administrative structure to the uses of spoils politics. Six new departments have been added to the nine, and several of the latter have undergone a change of name and a reshuffling of agencies

51. In the Lowden MSS the correspondence about the code is very heavy. Furthermore, in the MSS of Professor John A. Fairlie, according to Dr. L. J. R. Herson, of Northwestern University, there are about a thousand letters of inquiry about the code. FOL referred many of the questions to C. E. Woodward or W. F. Dodd for reply. Dodd had helped Woodward prepare the code bill and headed the Legislative Reference Bureau during FOL's governorship. Between 1919 and 1922 official inquiries came from at least sixteen states and Hawaii. Relying more or less heavily upon the Illinois model, Idaho, Nebraska, and Massachusetts revised their central administrative structures in 1919; Washington, Ohio, and California in 1921; Maryland in 1922; Pennsylvania, Tennessee, and Vermont in 1923; Minnesota and New York in 1925; and Virginia and Georgia before 1930. Stiff, but largely unsuccessful, fights to achieve reform took place in Iowa and North Carolina.

under their jurisdiction. In spite of these and other modifications, the imprint of Lowden's work is still deep and clear at Springfield.[52]

Ever since his early days as a lawyer in Chicago, Lowden had advocated a revision of the Illinois constitution to extend to his city more control over its government. With a widened political horizon by 1917, however, he wanted, above all, a constitutional convention to open the way for a more equitable tax structure and more efficient state administration. Furthermore, by the time of his governorship, he no longer believed that separate amendments could effect the many alterations needed in the organic law. In accord with the letter of the constitution, any amendment must propose a change in only one of its articles, pass each house of the Assembly by a two-thirds majority, be submitted to the electorate, and win a majority vote in a general election. The constitution needed so much revision before it would square with the facts of twentieth-century economic life that the one-amendment-at-a-time requirement would spin out the work of reform for a generation or more. By then, new conditions would oblige the weary process to begin all over again. Competition for priority between equally urgent amendments, moreover, made it unlikely that the legislature could ever muster a two-thirds vote for any one of them. A stalemate of this kind was the more probable because the oft-discussed amendments, including those providing home rule for Chicago, woman suffrage, and prohibition, were bound to run afoul of Cook County–downstate sectionalism. Furthermore, most legislators were not qualified to frame constitutional amendments or to give them adequate thought and discussion during their crowded biennial session.

An obvious way out of the impasse was merely to amend the amending section of the constitution so as to permit the legislature by a simple majority vote to submit any number of changes to the people at a single election. Although often talked about by Lowden and others, this expedient seemed to be "too abstract a proposition" to arouse public interest.[53] The governor pointed to the procedure used by the federal Constitutional Convention of 1787 as a model for Illinois to follow. Unlike then, however, the delegates to a similar assemblage in his own state would have to be elected amid the heat of party strife rather than appointed by the legislature. The drafting of a fundamental law was a task for experts, deliberating unhurriedly and undistracted by political clamor. The product of their work should resemble the federal Constitution, by being concerned almost wholly with general principles of government and a delineation of fields of power.

Following the governor's inaugural address in which he asked for a plebiscite on the calling of a constitutional convention, a joint resolution to this effect was introduced in the state legislature. After a senate committee re-

52. The bienniel *Blue Book of the State of Illinois* during the last thirty-five years records the changes made in the original code.

53. In 1892 and 1896 futile efforts had been made to amend the amending clause. Although 871,500 votes were cast in the 1892 election, only 178,000 voters took the trouble to express their opinion on the constitutional issue, and in 1896 only 230,000 out of over a million.

duced the four prefatory "whereases" to two—namely, that the constitution was inadequate to the present and prospective needs of the people and was too difficult to amend—the resolution passed on January 24, 1917, by a vote of 46 to 1.[54] To interpret this near unanimity as evidence of great enthusiasm for the proposal would probably be an error. The platforms of both parties spoke for a constitutional convention. In all likelihood, however, many senators supported the resolution as an easy means of demonstrating their party regularity and belief in "progress" but expected, even if they did not hope, that the House would kill the measure or the electorate would reject it. Most of the legislators gladly favored a convention "as an abstract proposition" and as long as a revision of the fundamental law worked no injury to their constituents. This view finds support in the content of the two deleted "whereases." They declared that constitutional change should "secure a satisfactory revenue system" and empower the enactment of laws demanded "by the rapid increase in the wealth and population of our cities and the vast amount of capital invested in commercial enterprises."[55] If these fairly definite and controversial purposes had been retained in the joint resolution, it certainly would not have passed by so large a majority, and possibly not at all.

The main debate, moreover, occurred in the lower house in the presence of crowded galleries and with Mrs. Lowden frequently sitting "on the Speaker's sofa." Here, too, the motion finally carried with apparent ease (112 to 30), even though the governor had doubted whether it would pass. Unfriendly newspapers attributed the outcome in large measure to the crack of his "party whip over the Republican House."[56] The division was principally between the Cook County delegation and many assemblymen from downstate. The City Council of Chicago and various political, professional, and civic organizations of that city worked vigorously for the adoption of the resolution. To some of the assemblymen from rural Illinois, this pressure meant that "sinister interests" backed the drive for a new constitution. They identified these lobbyists as spokesmen for the big manufacturers, bankers, public utility magnates, mine owners, and newspaper "czars," who sought to control the proposed convention and have it make them even more immune from high taxes than before. Some who fought the resolution in the Assembly professed to believe that jury trial and the privilege of the writ of habeas corpus would be abolished or greatly curtailed in the new fundamental law. With much greater plausibility, other legislators pointed to the advocates of a shorter ballot as among the most vehement champions of a constitutional convention. Fewer elective officers, these opponents insisted, would mean undemocratic government, executive dictatorship, and corruption in high places. Finally, they could not find many "men in the street" dissatisfied with the existing constitution. If they were correct, the demand

54. *Journal of the Senate of the Fiftieth General Assembly of the State of Illinois,* p. 251.
55. *Ibid.,* p. 251.
56. *Chicago Tribune,* Mar. 3, 1917; *Chicago Journal,* Mar. 3, 1917.

for its discard came mainly from selfish pressure groups, political theorists, and "radical" reformers like the suffragettes.[57]

Shortly after March 14, when the lower house concurred with the Senate by adopting the joint resolution, the United States entered the war against Germany. Since there would be no general election in Illinois that year, the convention plebiscite could not take place until the autumn of 1918. Somewhat persuasively, the opposition argued that it could not fairly be held when so many voters were overseas. Drastic constitutional changes should await the return of peace. In Lowden's view, on the other hand, the civilians of his state should provide it with a better government as a merited reward to their sons fighting overseas to make a better world.[58] He tried unsuccessfully to gain the War Department's consent to poll the Illinois soldiers in Europe.

The war and the long interval of eighteen months between the passage of the joint resolution and the election hampered the supporters of a constitutional convention. Public interest naturally lagged. To revive it was difficult in days when battles on the western front monopolized the headlines. For this reason the governor called a meeting in his office as early as April 8, 1918, to plan a campaign on behalf of the resolution.[59] The conferees chose Mr. Justice Orrin N. Carter as chairman of an executive committee. It undertook to direct the publicity and serve as a clearing house for the "general committee" made up of workers in every congressional district. Silas H. Strawn and Walter H. Wilson of Chicago agreed to raise the necessary funds. Many influential newspaper publishers stood ready to assist in the drive for votes, and Barney Cohen seemed certain that union labor would favor the proposed convention.

The governor suggested that the publicity material avoid highly controversial matters like woman suffrage and point out that any new constitution would include much of the old. The people could be won over, he felt confident, by appealing not to their selfish interests but to their patriotism and their desire for a business-like government, honestly administered. "If," he said, "we must make democracy safe for the world, we must make it efficient at home. . . . We must get ready to meet the new problems which will arise as an aftermath of this war." The beginning of Illinois's second century in the Union was an appropriate moment in the history of the state to rewrite its fundamental law. One constitutional convention had signalized its admission to statehood; another would be a fitting climax of its Centennial Celebration. With partisan politics submerged under the united war effort, the

57. *House Debates, Fiftieth General Assembly, State of Illinois, 1917*, pp. 91, 197–219. Strangely, in view of the action of the legislature and the known attitude of FOL, the official *Blue Book of the State of Illinois, 1917–1918*, pp. 63–64, contains an unfriendly article by George B. Gillespie entitled "The Constitutional Convention Proposition."

58. MS of FOL's speech at Leland Hotel, Springfield, Illinois, Oct. 2, 1918.

59. *Chicago Tribune*, Apr. 9, 1918; *Blue Book of the State of Illinois, 1921–1922* (Springfield, Ill., 1921), pp. 216–17.

time seemed unusually propitious for accomplishing the difficult task of drafting a new organic law.[60]

Lowden spoke frequently during the summer and autumn of 1918 on behalf of a convention and chided the businessmen of Chicago about their lethargy. "No democracy can survive," he warned, "with a most important class in a community despising politics, taking no part in politics, criticizing those who are in politics. . . ." The multitude of elective offices, requiring so many names on a ballot that no one could vote intelligently, was a favorite target of the governor's attack. "You might just as well," he told the Chicago Association of Commerce, "send your people to the polls with a city directory and ask them to make up a ticket to suit themselves."[61] In a press release in late October, he called for a new constitution on the grounds that it would "mean writing the progress which Illinois has made in every other line during a half century into the fundamental law of the State."

In his public utterances Lowden took care not to mention, or at least not to be dogmatic about, several of the most divisive issues which a constitutional convention would have to face. "I haven't urged many of the things that I think are important," he confided to a friend, "because it seemed to me that we might arouse opposition by going too much into detail in what it is desirable to accomplish."[62] To clear the way for the convention was the great task of the moment, trusting that its 102 members would have sufficient wisdom and forbearance to bridge the deep cleavages. Thus he gladly joined Strawn, Wilson, and Roger Sullivan, a Democratic "boss" in Chicago, in winning the coveted support of Victor F. Lawson and his newspapers, by pledging to use his influence to have the proposed convention submit the most controversial articles in a new constitution for separate approval or rejection by the voters of Illinois. Satisfied by this assurance, Lawson ceased to write editorials opposing a convention unless the amending clause of the old constitution were first of all altered. "I shall therefore," he wired the governor on October 25, "do all I can to further the effort at the election." On the other hand, the Hearst-owned *Chicago Journal* uncompromisingly fought against assembling a convention as long as Illinois had a governor whose "sympathies are too obviously and completely with corporations and with his very rich personal friends."[63]

One of the emotion-ridden issues to which Lowden rarely referred in his speeches was woman suffrage. In his correspondence, however, he declared somewhat halfheartedly that he favored giving the ballot to women, especially since their war service showed "no field of human endeavor in which

60. Typed MS of 57 pages, entitled "Conference on the Constitutional Convention Proposition, Governor's Office, Springfield, April 8, 1918"; Charles E. Woodward, "The Constitutional Convention," *Blue Book of the State of Illinois, 1919–1920*, pp. 306–8.

61. Speeches of FOL on June 1 and Sept. 17, 1918, to the Mid-Day Club of Chicago, and on Nov. 2, 1918, to the Hamilton Club of Chicago.

62. FOL to H. A. Hollister, Urbana, Illinois, Nov. 2, 1918.

63. *Chicago Journal,* Nov. 2 and 5, 1918.

they can't work successfully."[64] Organizations of women campaigned with might and main for a constitutional convention, although their fervor stemmed principally from a determination to win the ballot for themselves. Some prominent citizens downstate, where opposition to the crusade centered, reminded the governor that the suffrage problem was too hot to handle. In September, 1918, for example, Mr. Justice Warren W. Duncan of the Illinois Supreme Court warned Lowden of the fate of Governor Deneen six years before when, toying with progressivism, he "made a leap for the Roosevelt band wagon and landed squarely and firmly on the hearse." The irate Judge threatened to help split the party again if the governor led the Republicans "to violate their oath to uphold the Constitution of Illinois" by declaring their willingness to add the Susan B. Anthony amendment to their fundamental law. In his reply Lowden refrained from suggesting to the jurist that his warped outlook upon an issue which might come before his court was far from judicious, but merely promised to send his letter to the Committee on Resolutions of the Republican state convention.[65] Heedless of Duncan's empty threat, that body declared itself unequivocally in favor of the Nineteenth Amendment. In the following year the governor recommended its speedy ratification by the Illinois legislature. He liked to say that, because his state had been the first to approve the Thirteenth Amendment giving freedom to the slaves, it should also lead the way in making women the political equals of men. The Assembly quickly followed his advice.[66]

He also was much pleased when the voters of Illinois in the November elections of 1918 authorized a constitutional convention. The ensuing session of the legislature provided for an election in November, 1919, of two convention delegates from each senatorial district. The voters did not fully achieve the governor's ideal of choosing only "broad-vision men," but they averaged high in quality. When they first assembled on January 6, 1920, in the state capital, Lowden welcomed them in a brief address. This, he said, "is the most remarkable meeting having to do with government which has occurred in Illinois for fifty years. . . . I am sure that no body of men . . . has ever met in a finer spirit or purpose than the spirit and purpose which actuate you today."[67] He was further cheered when the delegates chose his respected friend, Charles E. Woodward, to be their presiding officer.

The governor's initial optimism soon vanished. Divided by conflicting

64. FOL's public statement of Oct. 3, 1918, declaring that "women have been meeting the new demands of industry upon them in fine spirit and with entire satisfaction. They have earned the right to have exactly the same rewards as men, when they render the same service. This is simple justice."

65. W. W. Duncan to FOL, Sept. 17, and FOL's reply, Sept. 20, 1918.

66. *Journal of the House of Representatives of the Fifty-first General Assembly of the State of Illinois,* pp. 10–11 and 1003.

67. He was highly pleased with the personnel of the convention. Its 85 Republicans and 17 Democrats included 56 lawyers, 5 bankers, and 4 manufacturers, but only 5 farmers and 1 labor-union official.

economic blocs and downstate versus Chicago sectionalism, the convention
deliberated at intervals for over two years before agreeing almost in desper-
ation to a document which Lowden could not support enthusiastically.[68]
Along with Deneen, Brundage, Medill McCormick, McKinley, and other
leaders, however, he believed that its merits were sufficient to justify its ratification. In several speeches he tried to persuade his hearers to accept this
view. He praised the proposed constitution for authorizing a state income
tax and for encouraging reforestation by tax-exempting land devoted to silviculture. Furthermore, it had the special virtue of being easy to amend. But
Lowden and his co-workers were opposed by most Democrats, Mayor
Thompson, Governor Small, and many liberals in both parties. The voters
rejected the document by an overwhelming majority on December 12,
1922.[69] To this day, Illinois manages somehow to get along under a constitution mostly eighty-seven years old.

Lowden believed that law in a democracy exceeded its rightful limits
when it ran counter to widely accepted norms of personal conduct or morality. Crusading sentimentalists and humanitarians who shut their eyes to
every cause except their own severely taxed his patience. He disliked the
company of professional reformers and deplored fanaticism of any kind. He
shrank from "do-gooders," who sometimes seemed anxious to have the state
supplant the family, the school, and the church as the chief agent of individual betterment. Utopias born of meditation or cloistered research attracted him not at all. He insisted that the new in government must evolve
naturally out of the old, square with facts carefully ascertained, be limited
in scope to what was workable, and be intrusted in its operation to men of
common sense and successful experience in conducting public affairs.

The governor conceded somewhat reluctantly that, as an inevitable aftermath of the Nineteenth Amendment, at least a few women politicians would
have to be admitted to the inner council of his beloved Republican party.
These, perforce, he would learn to work with, especially if they were attractive, flattered him a bit, and were witty and teachable rather than humor-
less zealots determined to have their own way. Probably the men should
feel thankful because their wives had decided to remain within the Republican or Democratic ranks and not form a new party of their own. But he
never wholly convinced himself that a career woman in politics maintained
her full social standing by entering an arena which traditionally had been a
masculine monopoly.

Far more distasteful than a suffragette, moreover, was a "dedicated" prohibitionist. Here, in Lowden's view, was a reformer at his worst—intolerant,

68. C. E. Woodward to FOL, July 12, 1922. Woodward admitted that the constitution
was a compromise between conflicting agricultural, manufacturing, and transportation
interests.

69. The vote was 921,398 against and 185,298 for. The vote in Cook County was 541,206
against and 27,874 for (*Blue Book of the State of Illinois, 1923–1924* [Springfield, Ill., 1923],
pp. 284–85).

swayed by emotion much more than by reason, scornful of the golden mean, and ready to employ slander or libel in his reckless effort to gain his end. Having been a favorite target of the "teetotalers," he could not judge their crusade impartially; but, even though they had never injured him, he would have opposed them as misguided theorists who expected a law to accomplish the impossible. On the other hand, statutes restricting the sale of liquor and taxing it heavily were legitimate and wise uses of the state's police power. In view of the growing "dry" sentiment, he regretted that the "wets" in the legislature of 1917 voted down mild regulatory measures which might have kept many temperance folk from allying with the uncompromising Dr. McBride and his Anti-Saloon League. Thus, by refusing to yield a little, the "wets" had hastened the coming of the Eighteenth Amendment.[70]

The war emergency spurred Lowden's willingness to occupy an extraordinary range of executive authority. Force of circumstance and popular demand thrust it into his extended hands. Following the example set by his recent predecessors in the governorship, he exercised his veto power frequently.[71] He struck down the unexampled total of one out of every six bills passed by the first Assembly of his regime. In some instances the legislators probably welcomed his courage in quashing measures of questionable merit which they had introduced against their better judgment in order to please influential people back home.

The usual grist of the legislative mill in Illinois forty years ago amounted to four or five hundred bills during the life of any one Assembly. Most of these measures reached the desk of the governor shortly before the lawmakers finally adjourned. The constitution obliged him to explain every veto in writing and record his dissent within ten days after the close of the session whenever he wished to prevent any of these last-minute bills from becoming a law.[72] For this reason he had to work under high pressure every day and much of every night during the week before the biennial Assembly disbanded and for ten days thereafter. In this hectic period he frequently called upon Attorney-General Brundage for written opinions concerning the constitutionality of some of the measures. He held many hasty conferences with his administrative staff and interested outsiders before reaching a decision about bills of doubtful merit. Whenever he vetoed them, he held that they were unconstitutional, contrary to sound public policy, financially extrava-

70. *Chicago Tribune*, May 11, and *Chicago Examiner*, May 12, 1917. As a war measure, Congress banned the manufacture of whiskey after Sept. 9, 1917. The Illinois legislature ratified the Eighteenth Amendment in January, 1919 (*House Debates, Fifty-first General Assembly, State of Illinois, 1919*, p. 37).

71. Niels H. Debel, *The Veto Power of the Governor of Illinois* (Urbana, Ill., 1917). Debel found that Illinois governors had vetoed 7 per cent of all bills between 1870 and 1916, or 12 per cent if only the years 1900–1916 are considered. Of the bills passed by the 1919 session of the legislature, FOL vetoed only about 1 in 12.

72. Seventy of the 407 bills passed in 1917 and 23 of the 468 passed in 1919 became law without FOL's signature; that is, he neither vetoed nor signed them within ten days (Sunday excepted) after the legislature adjourned.

gant, or too loosely drafted to be intelligible or enforcible. Fortunately, the constitution empowered him to reject separate items of appropriation bills. In June, 1917, for example, he struck out appropriations totaling over a million dollars.

Although the lessening of interparty strife and factionalism within the Republican party during the war helped to make Lowden a well-liked and forceful governor, he demonstrated after the Armistice that his ability to lead did not depend upon the existence of a political truce or a national crisis. Individual assemblymen sometimes chafed under his tight rein. Opposition newspapers hopefully predicted that he would stir up a rebellion in Springfield. Most of the legislators, however, appeared to follow his guidance gladly. The popularity of his regime illustrated the general truth that Americans prefer executive to legislative leadership if the executive is honest and able, not narrowly partisan, and willing to take them into his confidence. Newspaper editors and good-government associations praised him for his achievements, and he in turn thanked the members of the Assembly for their co-operation.[73] Thus everyone concerned seemed to be satisfied except a few of the bosses, who equated government with spoils politics. Even they were usually restrained in their hostility as long as the people of Illinois looked chiefly to Governor Lowden to give voice to their patriotism and their hatred of the Kaiser.

73. *Assembly Bulletin of the Legislative Voters League of the State of Illinois,* Vol. II, No. 24 (July 5, 1917), said: "No General Assembly in recent times has made so good a record for constructive legislation.... Much of the credit ... is due to Governor Lowden."

CHAPTER XIV

THE WAR AND GOVERNOR LOWDEN
ECONOMIC AND SOCIAL ISSUES

America's war effort during 1917 and 1918 tested the leadership of all governors, but especially of those in states like Illinois with ethnically diverse populations, many miles of trunk-line railroads, and hundreds of factories producing essentials for the armed forces. The making and maintenance of "national unity" at home were basic to the military defeat of the Central Powers overseas. Springfield had to work in close and harmonious co-operation with Washington, even though presidential proclamations and emergency legislation by Congress seemed often to encroach upon the rightful domain of the state's constitutional powers.

In a period of rising prices and remunerative contracts for suppliers of war goods Governor Lowden was expected to prevent profiteering and hoarding, help labor get a fair deal, and see to it that the factories of Illinois received an equitable share of government contracts. As the executive head of a leading grain- and stock-raising state, he was obliged to encourage maximum production and, to that end, guard against an overdraft of farm labor into the armed services. New organizations of all kinds dedicated to the winning of the war looked to him for his indorsement and often an inspirational talk as well. Either he or Mrs. Lowden must take the lead in buying Liberty Bonds and war-saving stamps; preparing soldiers' knitted wear and kits, surgical bandages, and service flags; opening canteens; sponsoring drives for the collection of everything from peach pits to tinfoil; offering and conferring prizes to stimulate warwork; and visiting camps, soldiers' hospitals, and urban vegetable gardens. On April 6, upon hearing that President Wilson had signed the joint resolution of Congress declaring the existence of a state of war, Mrs. Lowden sadly noted in her diary: "None of us yet realize what it will really mean but Frank appreciates the many added responsibilities which will fall upon him, and we all will have our part to do." Ten days later she saw more clearly that "the problems facing men in public life are appalling."

The timely enactment of the Civil Administrative Code greatly eased Lowden's executive tasks. There was little friction within his official family, and Lieutenant-Governor John G. Oglesby helped him on many occasions. In days when willingness to serve the state became the prime test of loyalty, business leaders usually responded with alacrity to his calls for aid.

As a Republican governor during a war directed by a Democratic administration in Washington, Lowden felt called upon to point out, by precept and example, how far a constructive opposition could go without injuring the common cause. He faced this issue squarely and made known his position without hedging. He and most of the other Republican leaders in Illinois welcomed the President's call for a political truce and observed it in good faith until Wilson's appeal for the election of a Democratic Congress in the autumn of 1918. "If the president of the United States," Lowden declared, "were a Prohibitionist or a Socialist, I would consider myself a traitor to my country if I did not support him with the same ardor and energy and enthusiasm . . . which I am showing the president now. There is only one test of patriotism in a war like this. Either we are for the government or we are against it."[1]

"Win the War Lowden," as he was sometimes called by 1918, insisted with almost monotonous frequency that every proposal of significant public or private action must be measured, first and foremost, against the question "Will it help to bring the victory?" This singleness of purpose, unblemished by partisanship, helps to explain why he could command the support of the 1917 Assembly for an extensive program which almost certainly would have run afoul of factional politics in peacetime. Moreover, he felt lucky because most of the war took place in the interval between two meetings of the Assembly. Thus, amid the unusual demands upon him, he was spared the time-consuming chores of preparing the long biennial message and many shorter messages, attending legislative hearings, worrying about the constitutionality or expediency of several hundred pending bills, and fulfilling the host of other obligations, social as well as political, which a governor could not avoid when the lawmakers were in session. In their absence and with the Supreme Court unobtrusive, Lowden was virtually the central government of Illinois from June, 1917, until January, 1919.

Although he rarely spoke or wrote about the European conflict until Germany began its unrestricted submarine attacks in the late winter of 1917, he surpassed most Illinoisans for six months thereafter in his wholehearted support of the national administration. When diplomatic ties with Germany were severed on February 3, he at once called upon the citizens of his state to forget their political party affiliations and give the President unstinted support. Upon Lowden's request three days later, the legislature unanimously adopted a joint resolution assuring Wilson that the people of Illinois stood shoulder to shoulder with him in the crisis. Recalling Stephen Douglas' memorable speech to the same body in early 1861, Lowden told the joint session:

If war is to be averted, it will be averted only through our presenting such a united front to the world that no nation will lightly incur our armed enmity. . . . And let us, whatever our sympathies . . . remember only that we are Americans. We all have foreign blood flowing in our veins and our sympathy with one or an-

1. MS of FOL's Labor Day address at Ottawa, Illinois, Sept. 3, 1917.

other of the belligerent peoples is but natural. . . . We may have many sympathies; we can have but one allegiance, and that allegiance is to the United States.[2]

For the next few days Lowden's mail pouch overflowed with letters from organizations and individuals offering their services in case of war.

At the same time he had sharp reminders that the national emergency would require from him more than patriotic speeches and correspondence with citizens eager to rally to the colors. The diversion of unprecedented amounts of Appalachian coal to East Coast navy yards and ports threatened Chicago with a fuel famine. The city's Renting Agents' Association informed him on February 8 that, unless the embargo on westward-moving coal was speedily lifted, Chicago's gas supply would cease, all plumbing freeze, and the city suffer "the greatest calamity" in its history. After the governor wired the Interstate Commerce Commission in Washington to this effect, it acted quickly to avert a crisis. In early March at a Preparedness Meeting in Chicago he recommended that the governors of Mississippi Valley states devise a plan for mobilizing and utilizing their regional food resources to the maximum, so as to ward off the necessity of rationing in the event of war.[3] These threats of a fuel famine and food rationing were a forewarning that war against Germany would not revive on the home front the lighthearted, flag-waving days of 1898.

At the request of Newton Baker, secretary of war and chairman of the Council of National Defense, Lowden asked the legislature in April, 1917, to authorize him to appoint an unsalaried State Council of Defense. It would keep closely in touch with the national body and gear together and stimulate all phases of warwork in Illinois, so that they could function speedily and economically. By unanimous votes the two houses of the Assembly followed the governor's bidding.[4] Since Lowden and the Senate quickly agreed upon its membership, it began to operate almost at once. By overseeing every conceivable war activity, collecting and disseminating information, and helping to "wake up Illinois" to the meaning of the war, the council rendered indispensable aid to the governor as long as the conflict lasted.[5] Samuel Insull of Chicago became its chairman, and ten others of the fifteen members resided in that city. Public utilities, manufacturing, meatpacking, union labor, agriculture, banking, law, medicine, the press, social service agencies, and the state government had representatives among its personnel.[6] Insull sup-

2. *Journal of the Senate of the Fiftieth General Assembly of the State of Illinois*, p. 321.

3. MS of FOL's Preparedness Meeting speech, Mar. 3, 1917.

4. *Journal of the Senate of the Fiftieth General Assembly of the State of Illinois*, p. 734; *House Debates, Fiftieth General Asembly, State of Illinois, 1917*, p. 509.

5. The complex work of the council is conveniently outlined in Marguerite E. Jenison (ed.), *The War Time Organization of Illinois* (Springfield, Ill., 1923) (Vol. V of Theodore C. Pease [ed.], *Illinois in the World War* [6 vols.; Springfield, Ill., 1921–23]), pp. 29–66.

6. For a full list of the members see *Journal of the Senate of the Fiftieth General Assembly of the State of Illinois*, pp. 801–2.

plied without charge a six-story building in Chicago as its headquarters. Its stenographers, clerks, and other helpers were wholly volunteers. When its operating fund of $50,000, provided by the Assembly, neared exhaustion, Chicago businessmen quickly contributed twice that sum, so that its activities could continue.

The council functioned through numerous committees, subcommittees, and boards whose membership totaled over fifty thousand people. Their diverse activities are suggested by the names of some of these committees—food production and conservation, industrial survey, labor law and legislation, publicity, manpower survey, women's organizations,[7] military affairs and state and local defense, and sanitation, medicine, and public health. Under the council's aegis a Volunteer Training Corps organized and drilled as a pool for the recruitment of the Reserve Militia. The council also rendered conspicuous service in systematizing the work of many volunteer war-service organizations so as to eliminate duplication of efforts and the solicitation of money from the public for useless or fraudulent purposes. It worked in team with the American Red Cross, the Four-Minute Men, the National War Service Committee, the American Protective League, the National Security League, the United States Boys' Working Reserve, and other similar organizations. In conjunction with the United States Committee on Public Information, the council staged in Chicago during early September, 1918, a Government War Exposition attended by nearly two million people. It netted over $300,000 for the use of the Creel Committee, as the national Committee on Public Information was usually called.

Although much waste motion and considerable intolerance almost inevitably characterized a vast organization hastily created and manned by volunteers amid the tensions of wartime, the Council of Defense of Illinois made an impressive over-all record.[8] Its shortcomings dwindled into insignificance when compared with its services in producing, collecting, and conserving food and other essential commodities; making inventories of human and material resources; selling bonds; sustaining morale; arranging for patriotic meetings; providing recreation and amusement for men in uniform; educating youth in skills needed on the home front; and encouraging the saving of records essential to the preparation of a war history of Illinois. As Samuel Insull, Jr., remarked to Lowden twenty years later about his father, "I think the recollections he would have his family cherish most of his career are those in connection with war service in Illinois under your leadership."[9]

7. Pamphlet, *Report on the Work of the State Council of Defense of Illinois to July 1, 1918*. This official report called the Women's Committee "the Council's right arm." This committee, with Mrs. J. T. Bowen at its head, was the stimulator and co-ordinator of over 300,000 women working in one or another of 22 "departments." These included women and children in industry; employment; food production; motor corps; training farm; child welfare; thrift and conservation; Americanization; liberty chorus and community singing; Liberty Loan; Allied relief, etc. Among its aims in community singing was "to standardize the National Anthem."

8. Samuel Insull, "Civilian Achievements of Illinois in the War," in Louis L. Emmerson (ed.), *Blue Book of the State of Illinois, 1919–1920* (Springfield, Ill., 1919), pp. 97–103.

9. S. Insull, Jr., to FOL, Aug. 12, 1938.

Although Lowden found the State Council of Defense an invaluable ally in guiding civilian warwork in Illinois, he necessarily had to shoulder the ultimate responsibility for what was done or not done. Crises or near-crises involving conflicts between federal and state jurisdiction, employers and employees, Negroes and whites, war-heated patriots and pacifists or lukewarm persons of German ancestry occurred frequently. Rarely a month went by that he was not called upon to act decisively in some sudden emergency. Although the existence of the conflict went far toward determining the course and outcome of these disturbances, many of them were not peculiar to a war period. Much less industrial unrest, moreover, characterized Illinois during the eighteen months of war than would have been normal in days of peace. Illinoisans were justifiably proud of their war record, whether assessed in terms of their loyalty, their purchases of Liberty Bonds, their production of crops and manufactured goods, or their number and performance in the armed services. The untoward episodes are stressed here only because they added to Lowden's burdens as war governor.

If complete harmony between the federal and state authorities had not been vital in wartime, Lowden as a lawyer would probably have been more interested than alarmed by the dispute climaxing in the late spring of 1917 between the Interstate Commerce Commission and the United States District Court at St. Louis, on the one hand, and the Illinois railroad passenger-fare law, the Superior Court of Cook County, and the United States District Court at Chicago, on the other. Caught in the middle of the constitutional snarl were about two dozen railroads engaged in intra-state and interstate commerce in Illinois.

Some years earlier, without giving the railroad companies an opportunity to be heard, the Illinois legislature directed the Public Utility Commission to enforce a passenger rate of 2 cents a mile between all stations within the state. After prolonged hearings before the United States Interstate Commerce Commission, that body empowered these railroads to charge a rate of 2.4 cents a mile. Thereupon, the roads running between Chicago and St. Louis and other cities outside Illinois advanced their fares to that level, but in deference to Illinois law retained the lower rate for shorter trips, on the same trains, beginning and ending within the state. This, in the opinion of St. Louis and Keokuk (Iowa) businessmen discriminated against them by enticing Illinois buyers toward Chicago. The Interstate Commerce Commission took these complaints under advisement for over a year. Finally, in October, 1916, it appeared to order the railroads to standardize their fares on or before January 15, 1917.

Although the commission declared 2.4 cents a mile to be a reasonable rate, it neither commanded Illinois to repeal its 2-cents-a-mile law nor made clear what areas and roads were affected by its order. The carriers naturally chose to infer from the ruling that they should advance their intra-state rate wherever their lines ran in Illinois. They vainly sought from Judge K. M. Landis in the United States District Court at Chicago an injunction to restrain Illinois from suing them for violating its law. Landis held that the Interstate

Commerce Commission's order was too vaguely worded to be accepted as an annulment of the state's rate-fixing statute. Less plausible, in view of several recent decisions of the United States Supreme Court, was Governor Lowden's doubt whether a dictum of a federal administrative agency, no matter how specific it might be, could supersede the control of a state legislature over intra-state commerce. Having been rebuffed by Judge Landis, the carriers also failed to gain an injunction from the United States Supreme Court. That tribunal agreed, however, to entertain at its October term an appeal from Landis' ruling in the form of a suit by the Illinois Central Railroad Company against the Public Utilities Commission of Illinois *et al.* Pending the outcome of this case, the railroads resigned themselves to a compliance with the state law.[10]

This was the situation when Lowden became governor. But the Interstate Commerce Commission, its order flouted, responded quickly to renewed pressure from the impatient merchants of St. Louis and Keokuk. On May 1, 1917, Judge D. P. Dyer of the United States District Court at St. Louis backed up the commission by enjoining the railroads from continuing their intra-state 2-cent fare beyond the end of that month, under penalty of being in contempt of court. Squeezed between a federal injunction and a law of Illinois, they chose the course promising the greater financial return.

The time had come for the governor to act decisively. On May 26, he wired Attorney-General Brundage:

The rights of the State must be asserted with vigor and at once. You are requested to take any and all actions or proceedings which you may deem are necessary or advisable to assert and protect the rights of the State and the people, to the end that the present rates or such rates as may be authorized by the General Assembly may be sustained.

Two days later Brundage filed bills of complaint in the Superior Court of Cook County against twenty-five railroads with offices in Chicago and secured an injunction restraining them from raising their passenger fares. All the lines bowed to the mandate. Judge Dyer, however, upon the petition of the Interstate Commerce Commission and without permitting Brundage to be heard in his court, notified the state authorities on June 7 that if they tried to enforce the county court's injunction to prevent the carriers from collecting the higher fare, they would be haled before him and imprisoned for contempt. In like manner, if the railroads did not institute the advanced rate by mid-June, they, too, would be guilty of contempt of court.

Thus the issue reached a complete impasse. The governor was under oath to obey the federal Constitution, the highest law of the land, but he also had solemnly pledged to uphold the constitution and laws of Illinois. Under circumstances where two federal district courts could not agree, he held that the constitutional right in the matter was too obscure to be determined fairly by a decree of Judge Dyer issued after an *ex parte* hearing in which Illinois

10. For the background of the controversy see 245 U.S. 493–510.

had not been represented. Since the controversy would be decided by the Supreme Court of the United States within a few months, he believed that the Interstate Commerce Commission and Judge Dyer had acted with unreasonable haste, especially in wartime, when the national and state governments and the railroads must work together in concord.

It was this aspect of the dispute which Lowden regretted the most. As soon as he heard of Judge Dyer's ultimatum, he arranged for a conference in Washington between Brundage and the assistant attorney-general of the United States.[11] In long identical letters to Senators Sherman and Lewis, after detailing the factual background of the issue, he urged them personally to apprise the attorney-general of its seriousness and the need for him to intervene so as to preserve the status quo until the Supreme Court rendered judgment. In the governor's words: "The state authorities have no option in the matter. Their right and duty to uphold the State law has been vindicated in every court, both State and Federal, in which they have been heard. . . . They must and they will, if necessary, go forward in the performance of their duty."

The members of the Illinois legislature unanimously indorsed his action and counseled him to stand firm. He was the more heartened by this support because Silas H. Strawn, a prominent railroad attorney of Chicago, E. P. Ripley, president of the Atchison, Topeka, and Santa Fe Railroad, and George R. Thorne, of Montgomery, Ward and Company let him know that his constitutional position was untenable. Ripley tartly expressed the hope that "your Administration will be marked by a broader and saner spirit than has been shown by your immediate predecessors."[12] It was ironic that Lowden, so often attacked for being a tool of the railroads, should now be chided by a railroad president for unfriendliness to them. Thorne solemnly reminded him:

A great many of our troubles are due to the efforts to maintain state rights in the face of the trend of events which tends to reduce them. The trend of events should be recognized and followed, because defeat will be the result of resistance. . . . I think that the State should abandon its contentions *in toto*. . . . I take the liberty of writing because I am keenly interested in having your administration adjudged progressive and constructive. . . . Adherence to the unfair 2¢ rate is reactionary . . . and will end in defeat.[13]

Thanks to the good offices of the attorney-general of the United States, Judge Dyer did not cite either the railroads or the state authorities for contempt. The counsel of all parties in interest agreed by late June that the railroads might sell tickets, with coupons attached, at the 2.4-cent rate for fares

11. FOL's wire to the attorney-general, June 8, 1917: "I can see no escape from grave consequences except through action of your Department. At such a time as this I felt sure you would co-operate with us to avoid these consequences."

12. E. P. Ripley, Chicago, to FOL, June 13, 1917; S. Strawn to G. R. Thorne, Chicago, June 8, 1917; *House Debates, Fiftieth General Assembly, State of Illinois, 1917*, pp. 1227–28.

13. George R. Thorne to FOL, June 9, 1917.

between stations within Illinois until the Supreme Court rendered its decision. If it should be adverse to the railroads, they would reimburse the coupon holders for the overcharge. On January 14, 1918, this tribunal, with Mr. Justice Holmes abstaining, unanimously upheld the main contention of the state authorities. Speaking through Mr. Justice Van Devanter, the court stated that the Interstate Commerce Commission apparently had not intended the 2.4 cent rate to apply to a larger area than between intra-state points on the rail lines in Illinois serving St. Louis and Keokuk. An act of Congress or an order of a "subordinate agency" like the commission, continued the Justice, "should not be given precedence over a state rate statute otherwise valid, unless, and except as far as, it conforms to a high standard of certainty."[14] On the contrary, the commission's mandate had been ambiguous in its intended scope. Thus the Supreme Court affirmed Judge Landis' ruling, which Ripley had called "preposterous," and impliedly sustained Lowden in his refusal to obey Judge Dyer's injunction. Although Lowden called the outcome "a very notable triumph," the court made plain that if the commission's order had been clear-cut in its intent, it would have superseded Illinois's 2-cent law to the degree that they overlapped.[15]

About two weeks before the announcement of this decision, the federal government by presidential proclamation took control of the railroads for the duration of the war, and in March, 1918, Congress defined the method and scope of their operation. Two months later the director-general of railroads decreed that coach passengers pay 3 cents a mile and those in parlor or sleeping cars, $3\frac{1}{2}$ cents a mile. The Illinois authorities grudgingly acquiesced. The increased rates became effective for intra-state as well as interstate travelers, but the Public Utilities Commission declined to violate the law of Illinois by approving the new fares. The 2-cents-a-mile law remained unrepealed during Lowden's governorship, but it became a dead letter when a federal court injunction forbade the Public Utilities Commission to hear complaints that intra-state rates exceeded the maximum set by the statute.

Other public utilities also caused the governor much concern during the spring and summer of 1917. Columnists like Carl Sandburg doubted whether Lowden could resist his influential friends among the gas, electrical power, and traction magnates of Chicago.[16] Their skepticism increased when he made Insull the chairman of the State Council of Defense. At the same time a bill before the Assembly to enable the City Council of Chicago to grant thirty-year franchises to the elevated- and trolley-line companies embarrassed the governor. By nearly a two-to-one majority the aldermen signified their liking for this act. For many years Lowden had actively supported the

14. 245 U.S. 493–510.

15. FOL to J. H. Wilkinson, Jan. 19, 1918.

16. *Chicago Day Book,* May 12 and June 1, 1917. Sandburg, however, mixed sugar in his acid. He admitted that FOL was "one of the best political surprises Illinois has had in many years" but added, "there is, of course, plenty of time yet for him to slip and play the game of the Insull and railway interests."

efforts of Chicagoans to gain more "home rule" over their public utilities, but he also had opposed long-term franchises. After the Senate passed the Franchise Bill on June 6, the lower house pleased the governor by adjourning ten days later without acting upon it. Unless he summoned a special session, the issue would wait at least two more years for a decision. During the remainder of his term, however, the opposition press often needled him for subservience to the public utilities because the state commission, reflecting the rising costs of operation, authorized many of these companies to increase their rates.

Closely connected with the rates charged by railroads and other public utility companies was the price of coal. About eight hundred soft-coal mines in Illinois employed approximately seventy-five thousand men. Bituminous lump coal, selling at the mine for approximately $3.50 a ton, cost about $6.75 in Chicago.[17] Lowden emphatically declared that this was too big a "spread," especially when mine owners pocketed an "unpatriotic profit" of from $1.20 to $1.50 a ton. Besides calling this a grossly exaggerated estimate of their gains and insisting that miners' wages would have to fall if the price of coal went down, the owners plausibly argued for national rather than state regulation, since their output was in interstate commerce and well over half of the bituminous coal used in Illinois came from outside its borders. If the price within the state fell below the national level, the domestic coal would all be exported to the more profitable markets. Probably the mine owners were the more willing to advocate federal control because they believed that Washington would keep hands off.

If a drastic move by Lowden served no other purpose, it at least might spur the Wilson administration into taking over the mines "for the duration." This action would benefit house owners, result in an equitable allocation of the output, and, above all, provide the national government with a sufficient coal supply for war needs at a fair price. In midsummer, 1917, however, he still hoped that the State Council of Defense could induce the mining companies to lower their rates. Failing that, he was ready as a last resort to call a special session of the legislature to fix the price of coal. In late July a conference between the council and the mining companies helped not at all. Besides urging delay until the completion of a nation-wide survey of the coal situation, they charged that the "public" pressure for lower coal prices came mainly from Chicago manufacturers avid for higher profits and from a governor equally avid for popularity.

Although Levy Mayer, chairman of the law committee of the State Council of Defense, advised that if the owners refused to lower their prices, Lowden could legally seize and operate their mines for the duration of the war, he preferred the more moderate course of conferring with the chief executives of the neighboring states. In this way he and his fellow governors might

17. In 1916 Illinois was third among the states in the production of soft coal. Its output was 62,000,000 tons, at a human cost of 165 miners killed and 1,305 seriously injured. The average yearly wage of a miner was less than $600.

either devise a uniform plan of coal-price control or else, through united action, induce Washington to intervene to that end. After consulting together in early August, he and Governor Goodrich of Indiana invited twelve other midwestern governors to assemble in Chicago to talk about the fuel situation.

At this juncture on August 8, Congress passed the Food and Fuel Control Bill. Although it did not specifically empower President Wilson to fix coal prices in intra-state commerce, it had that effect, since he was given the option of taking over the mines. The "coal barons" had no recourse but unconditional surrender. To make this doubly clear to them, Lowden appointed Chief Justice Orrin N. Carter of the Illinois Supreme Court to be the fuel director of Illinois. By a prearranged plan he would fix the price of coal at the mines after consulting on August 17 with three representatives of the operators and three of the miners.

When the Federal Trade Commission in Washington heard of what Lowden intended to do, it asked him to delay until the national Fuel Control Law became operative. Simultaneously, a "wildcat" strike of some miners in the Springfield area complicated the picture. Rumor was current that the owners had encouraged the walkout because they wished to forestall price-fixing by Illinois in the hope of receiving better terms from Washington. In pursuit of this same end they stormed out of the public hearing before Mr. Justice Carter.[18] Replying to this defiance, the governor publicly called undue profits "blood money" and threatened to take over the mines, but he privately hoped that the federal government would relieve him of the whole problem. His main purpose was to force a speedy reduction in Illinois coal prices, and he counted upon his evident impatience to drive the authorities at Washington to a quick decision.[19]

Most of the delegates from thirteen states meeting in a coal conference in Chicago on August 17 shared Lowden's views. After adopting eight bluntly worded resolutions, they recessed for five days without taking steps to force an immediate fall in the prices of coal. Branding these prices "unreasonably excessive and in many cases extortionate," they admonished mine owners to give up profiteering and increase their output. To relieve the hard-pressed railroads, they talked hopefully about more coal-carrying ships on the Great Lakes. The conference urged the governors and state councils of defense to determine a fair price of coal immediately. Copies of the resolutions were sent to President Wilson accompanied by a pledge to co-operate with the central government in enforcing the congressional fuel and food control measures.

18. The Carter hearing was on Aug. 17, 1917. Mrs. Lowden noted in her diary the previous evening: "Frank is much concerned over the coal situation as the signed agreement between the leading operators and himself made last Fri. [Aug. 10] isn't considered binding by them."

19. MS of speech by FOL to a chautauqua at Jacksonville, Illinois: "The time has come when American business men must decide whether they will put their country or their fortunes first. It is essential for business to proceed on normal lines at a fair profit. All else is blood money."

Before Mr. Justice Carter completed his fact-finding inquiries to determine a just selling rate for coal within Illinois, Woodrow Wilson proclaimed a national schedule of coal prices and soon appointed President Harry A. Garfield of Williams College to be the United States fuel administrator. Carter's assignment thereby became superfluous, and Lowden immediately wired his thanks to Wilson "for saving the United States from a situation which would have greatly embarrassed us in the conduct of the war." Many newspaper editors credited the governor with hastening the action of the authorities in Washington.[20] The price of Illinois bituminous lump coal fell as much as $1.30 a ton at the mine, and a considerable share of this reduction filtered down to the retail buyer. Amid the exchange of congratulations, no one foresaw that a severe coal famine by early 1918 would oblige Garfield to decree "heatless days" as well as other days when all manufacturing plants, except those producing goods essential to the war effort, had to suspend operations.

The shortage of factory labor in Illinois during the war accelerated the migration of southern Negroes to that state. Since they were willing to work for a lower wage than the whites and were thronging into already overcrowded Negro districts in the larger cities, their presence aggravated interracial tensions to the point where only an "incident" was needed to cause a serious outbreak. Convinced that lurid pictures often fostered race hatred, Robert R. Jackson, an assemblyman from a Negro constituency on Chicago's South Side, introduced a bill in March, 1917, to forbid the manufacture, sale, advertisement, or display of any lithograph, moving picture, photograph, play, or painting which tended to incite race riots or depicted the hanging, lynching, or burning of any human being. The measure occasioned little debate and quickly passed both houses by large majorities.[21] While agreeing with the laudable intent of the bill, the governor vetoed it because of its obvious ambiguity, fixing no clear-cut standard whereby an artist or producer could possibly know in advance whether his work would be blameless or subject him to a heavy fine. "If it should become a law," continued Lowden, "it would simply add another to the long list of laws, promoted and passed with the best of intentions, but unenforced, or . . . invoked indiscriminately against presentations, publications, . . . that are meritorious, as well as against those producing the evils aimed at by the . . . bill."[22]

On the last day of the session, however, the legislature adopted a measure of much the same tenor, and the governor let it become a law without his signature. This statute, making it a criminal offense "to incite race or religious prejudice" by means of a picture or a book, was virtually a "group libel" law, but the United States Supreme Court upheld its constitutionality

20. *Chicago American*, Aug. 20; *Chicago Tribune*, Aug. 21; *Chicago News*, Aug. 23, 1917.

21. *House Debates, Fiftieth General Assembly, State of Illinois, 1917*, pp. 267–70; *Journal of the Senate of the Fiftieth General Assembly of the State of Illinois*, p. 648.

22. *Journal of the House of Representatives of the Fiftieth General Assembly of the State of Illinois* (Springfield, Ill., 1917), pp. 766–67.

by a five-to-four decision as recently as May, 1952.[23] Near the close of the 1917 session Lowden vetoed a bill designed to prohibit the owner of any hotel, theater, restaurant, school, resort, etc., from advertising, or from replying to a letter of inquiry, that he would not admit persons of a particular race, creed, sect, class, denomination, or nationality. In Lowden's judgment— and Attorney-General Brundage concurred—this proposed statute would invade an individual's constitutionally guaranteed freedom of speech and press by penalizing him for expressing his preference.[24]

Even while this measure was before the Assembly, the long-smoldering fires of Negro-white enmity in southern Illinois burst into a consuming flame. East St. Louis, separated from its larger namesake by the Mississippi River, had been for some years a stark example of the evil brew which could result from mixing within a constricted area venal politicians split between rival machines, factories mostly owned by absentee investors, and wage-earners of diverse ethnic stocks viewing each other with suspicion, discontented with their economic lot, living in slums, and too often seeking to forget their troubles by patronizing the superabundant saloons and other dives. Many "solid citizens," scorning to reside in East St. Louis, regarded it only as the source of their profits and not as a community to which they owed any return in the form of parks, playgrounds, and social service institutions.

With the coming of the war, the hard feeling between the whites and Negroes in East St. Louis quickly increased. A number of its manufacturing concerns, anticipating lucrative war contracts or faced with walkouts by their white employees, imported from downriver some ten thousand Negroes as strike breakers or inexpensive refills for a labor pool which war enlistments or better wages elsewhere were fast depleting. Often living cheek by jowl in miserable hovels and tenements, the Negroes and whites clashed with alarming frequency. Neither group was guiltless, but the Negroes found no favor in the eyes of the police and usually suffered more in these brawls than did the whites.[25] By May 28, 1917, the situation got out of hand so completely that the local authorities appealed to Governor Lowden for troops. He at once dispatched six infantry companies of the National Guard and a troop of cavalry.

As long as they bivouacked in the city, a sullen truce prevailed, but on July 1, ten days after the last company had left, renewed disorder swiftly mushroomed into sheer tragedy. That evening an automobile full of whites

23. Illinois Legislative Reference Bureau, *Legislative Digest* (1917), p. 206; *Time* (New York), May 12, 1952, p. 50. This was a suit against J. Beauharnais, founder of the anti-Negro, "White Circle League of America" (343 U.S. 250).

24. *House Debates, Fiftieth General Assembly, State of Illinois, 1917*, pp. 1081–85. The Assembly of 1919, however, passed a law forbidding hotels, theaters, etc., to discriminate against anyone because of his race, color, or religion.

25. "Report of the Division of East St. Louis Free Employment Office" in *State of Illinois: First Administrative Report of the Directors of Departments under the Civil Administrative Code . . . July 1, 1917, to June 30, 1918*, pp. 89–90; *Congressional Record* (65th Cong., 2d sess.), LVI, Part 9 (July 6, 1918), 8826–27.

drove through the Negro quarter, shooting indiscriminately into any home which took their fancy. Miraculously, they injured no one, but soon a church bell rang, and a group of armed Negroes killed two white policemen in a squad car.[26] Thereafter for the next twenty-four hours a considerable area of the city became a blazing and bloody battlefield. At least thirty-nine Negroes and eight whites died in the fighting, while some reports mentioned nearly one hundred as the true number of fatalities. Fire destroyed approximately two hundred and fifty buildings and over forty loaded freight cars. Panic-stricken Negroes streamed over the bridge into St. Louis, many never to return. During the carnage some policemen and firemen joined the white mob, while others fled the scene or stood idly by as spectators. The governor rushed twelve companies of militia to the city on July 2, but their inefficient commanding officer seemed unwilling to expose his own person to danger. The troops were poorly equipped, and some appeared content to let the rioting continue as long as the Negroes bore its brunt.[27]

On July 3, Lowden arrived on the scene with a troop of cavalry and seven more companies of infantry. After visiting the burned-over sixteen acres and conferring with the mayor and Adjutant General Dickson, who by then commanded the soldiers, he guaranteed to maintain peace "at whatever cost" and to have the militia treat Negroes and whites with absolute impartiality. Mrs. Lowden noted that her husband was "much depressed."[28] In his Independence Day address at Carrollton, he referred to the riots as "a blot on Illinois history which can never be erased" and demanded that all guilty persons be punished severely.[29]

After examining witnesses for three days in closed sessions at East St. Louis, a military board of inquiry confidentially reported to the governor about the misconduct of the troops. At the same time Attorney-General Brundage co-operated with a St. Clair County grand jury in a five-week-long investigation. This resulted in the indictment of 144 men, including 5 policemen, for crimes ranging from riot and conspiracy to arson and murder. The grand jury placed the immediate blame upon white and Negro agitators but held Mayor Mollman of East St. Louis and "a coterie of corrupt politicians" responsible for the "evil political conditions" without which the outrages would never have occurred.[30] A special committee of the national House of Representatives delayed for a year before making its report. It had much to

26. *Chicago News,* July 2, 1917; *Congressional Record* (65th Cong., 2d sess.), LVI, Part 9 (July 6, 1918), 8828.

27. Accounts of the number of killed and injured vary greatly. The figures in the text appear in the *Congressional Record* (July 6, 1918), pp. 8830–33; FOL to J. W. Dwight, Washington, D.C., July 6, 1917.

28. Mrs. Lowden's diary, July 3, 4, and 8, 1917; report of the adjutant general, 1916–18, in *State of Illinois: First Administrative Report of the Directors of Departments under the Civil Administrative Code . . . July 1, 1917, to June 30, 1918,* p. 628. Dickson arrived in East St. Louis, Illinois, on the evening of July 2; troops were kept there until July 24.

29. *St. Louis Globe Democrat,* July 5, 1917.

30. *Ibid.,* September 10, 1917.

say about East St. Louis as "a mire of lawlessness" and "a plague spot on the face of the earth," harboring "a low-grade gang of politicians," "corrupt justices," "criminal police," conscienceless mill owners, and "unscrupulous real estate operators," all of whom had "sowed the dragon's teeth of race hatred."[31]

The investigators showed more facility in the use of epithets than in devising ways to prevent other interracial clashes. Even the punishments meted out by no means reflected the number and heinousness of the crimes. The House of Representatives committee took Lowden to task for not bringing the accused National Guardsmen to trial. No adequate answer could be made. A few days after the riots many of the troops were inducted into the Army of the United States and scattered to distant camps or overseas. Soldiers would not testify against their comrades. Exciting news from the battle fronts soon pushed the riots out of the headlines.

The murder and arson in East St. Louis bequeathed a legacy of fear to all Negroes and their white neighbors who lived in a similar urban environment elsewhere in Illinois. Chicagoans warned the governor of the ominous situation on their near South Side, where some Negroes allegedly began to collect arms under the spur of inflammatory speeches. A delegation from the area, however, came to Springfield to assure Lowden that most of their people, if only because of their weakness, wished for nothing except to live in peace. They recognized its price and were willing to pay it. "We advise our people," they said, "not to sit by whites in the cars, to avoid white restaurants and theatres; not to intermarry or to live in white districts. . . . We appeal to the best conscience of the American people and to the Constitution." Former Governor Deneen and other leading Chicago citizens, seemingly blind to the fact that their remedy placed all blame upon the Negroes, called for the wiping-out of the "saloons, vicious cabarets and disorderly houses in Chicago's black belt."[32] Once again there was much talk but little action. Good luck rather than good management mainly explained why no race riot disgraced Chicago until after the Armistice overseas. All during the summer of 1917, the governor feared lest the news of an interracial clash anywhere in the United States would ignite the abundant tinder in that city. For this reason he hastened there in late September as soon as he heard of an outbreak in Omaha. By then, as a result of a prolonged strike in Springfield, he was almost ready to believe that German agents or "reds" lurked in the background whenever a serious disorder occurred on the home front.[33]

The month of the East St. Louis riots also witnessed the beginning of a prolonged deadlock between management and labor in Springfield. Refusal of the trolley-line company to permit its employees to unionize under the

31. *Congressional Record* (July 6, 1918), pp. 8826–34.

32. *Chicago Tribune,* July 4 and 7, 1917; *Chicago News,* July 7, 1917; *Chicago Journal,* July 10, 1917.

33. Mrs. Lowden's diary, Sept. 29, 1917.

American Federation of Labor was the crux of the trouble. By early August, when the police no longer could control the situation, Lowden called in troops from nearby Camp Lincoln to dispel "the rioters." Mrs. Lowden looked from her window upon guardsmen encamped on the lawn of the Executive Mansion. They jailed seventeen alleged disturbers of the peace without informing them of the specific charges justifying their detention. While their friends tried vainly to obtain writs of habeas corpus in their behalf, the governor did his best to negotiate a settlement of the labor dispute. "I have never seen him work harder over anything," his wife observed. "The atmosphere is tense with anxiety."[34]

Matters became even more serious when the state fair crowded the city with visitors, and workmen in many occupations struck in sympathy with the streetcar employees. The three hundred troops first summoned to Springfield grew to fifteen hundred by September 9. On that afternoon, after failing to prevent a parade by the strikers and their supporters, the soldiers dispersed it by force and severely injured several marchers while doing so. Although threatened with an imposition of martial law, the increasing number of laborers on sympathetic strike declared that they would never return to work until they had been allowed to parade. So many employees, both union and non-union, "took a vacation" that a food and fuel shortage threatened the city. When several sticks of dynamite, "capped for destructive use," were reportedly found in a cache near Oak Knolls, the "fashionable section of the city," the governor concluded that "pro-German propagandists" had instigated the disorders. He appealed to the strikers "to drive the traitors from their midst." "Whatever the merits of the controversy," he declared, "peace and order will be maintained at all cost. This I will do."[35]

Beginning to feel the pinch of what had developed into nearly a general strike, more and more citizens of Springfield accepted the governor's view that Germans or "radicals" lurked at the root of the trouble. Public opinion turned sharply against the workmen. With their funds exhausted by the long layoff and their families in need of money for rent and food, the strikers had no recourse but to capitulate. Sensing the change of mood, Lowden called upon the streetcar company to recognize the union and their employees' right to bargain collectively. Threatened with a strike of its streetcar labor force in Rockford, Illinois, it grudgingly complied with Lowden's request. The "vacationers" in Springfield thereupon agreed to go back to work, provided that they could parade without molestation. Mayor Baumann consented after the governor disclaimed any jurisdiction as long as the demonstration was peaceable. To Lowden's surprise, the labor leaders then asked him to review the procession, scheduled for Sunday afternoon, Sep-

34. *Ibid.,* Sept. 8–11, 1917. During these days FOL's many conferences with strikers, representatives of the employers, Springfield businessmen, city officials, and his adjutant general were in defiance of the orders of his doctor, who told him, "after a curious spell," to "stay at home and rest."

35. FOL to W. H. Stead, Sept. 13, 1917.

tember 16. Somewhat tactlessly, he designated Adjutant General Dickson to represent him after pleading a prior engagement with Senator Sherman at that time. Between five and eight thousand men and women marched along the principal thoroughfares of the capital without disorder. On the following day the two National Guard regiments ended their vigil by withdrawing to Camp Lincoln. In view of this long strike, Lowden asked by proclamation on September 20 for six thousand volunteers to enlist as a Home Guard for two years or until the National Guardsmen, then in the Army of the United States, returned to Illinois.[36]

Not strife, however, but harmony or an uneasy truce mainly characterized the relations between capital and labor within the state during the war period. In his inaugural address, delivered when the nation was still at peace, the governor had said: "The true test of a country's greatness is the lot in life of the . . . men and women of the shop, of the factory, and of the farm. These are they who carry on the work of civilization, and a nation is strong in proportion to their well-being. Whatever permanently improves their lot in life is best for all and best for the State." Following these generalizations, he advocated the establishment of a Department of Labor and the strengthening of the state's workmen's compensation law so as to compel the employer at his own expense to provide more certain financial benefits to an injured employee or to his heir. He also asked for legislation to limit the length of women's working days in industry and to better their conditions of employment so as not to "impair their vitality or prevent them from becoming the mothers of a hardy race."[37]

The Assembly readily acceded to the first of these requests. It assigned to the Industrial Commission under the newly created Department of Labor the duty of enforcing the Workmen's Compensation Act of 1911, as amended in 1917. By the terms of this law, employers in hazardous occupations, including mines, common carriers, and some types of manufacturing, had to submit all accident cases to the agents of the Industrial Commission for adjustment.[38] Most of its decisions were accepted as final, without appeal to the courts.

After prolonged debate, however, the lower house of the Assembly, by a one-vote margin, defeated a bill, desired by the governor, to amend the law of 1909 by reducing from ten to eight hours the maximum length of the working day for women in industry. The war came before the discussion had fairly started and greatly helped the legislators who opposed any change. They at once declared that every patriotic American must favor long work-

36. *Chicago News,* Sept. 17, 1917; *Chicago Tribune,* Sept. 20, 1917.

37. *House Debates, Fiftieth General Assembly, State of Illinois, 1917,* p. 68.

38. *State of Illinois: First Administrative Report of the Directors of Departments under the Civil Administrative Code . . . July 1, 1917, to June 30, 1918,* pp. 119–39. Before these amendments, an injured employee was often forced to institute court action and hire an expensive lawyer in order to extract damages from his employer. The amendments embodied the principle that these damages should be viewed as a part of the employer's cost of production.

ing days in many trades. In a special message to the legislature on June 4, 1917, Lowden tried to counter this argument by saying: "The purpose [of the proposed eight-hour law for women] is to safeguard the future of the Nation. War must of necessity impair the fatherhood of future generations. Doubly important is it then that we take every precaution to protect the mothers of the next generation. I believe that need for [this] legislation . . . is more imperative than if we were at peace."[39] But his plea was the less convincing because even he, at the request of the secretary of war, had asked the Assembly earlier in its session to empower him to "suspend or modify restrictions contained in . . . [the] . . . labor laws when such suspension or modification shall be requested by the [U.S.] Council of National Defense."[40]

After failing to have his way, he appointed a commission known as the Illinois Industrial Survey to investigate the problems of women employed outside their homes and make recommendations for the guidance of the legislature in 1919. On the basis of its report he again urged an eight-hour law in his biennial message of that year and also in a special appeal. "While all the world," he reminded the legislators with considerable exaggeration, "is moving toward shorter hours of labor, shall it be said of Illinois that she permits her women to be worked seventy hours per week?"[41] Once more, however, he could not bring a majority of the Assembly to his side, even though he signified his readiness to accept a watered-down version of the original measure and had the backing of an impressive number of civic and women's organizations throughout the state. Of these, the most persistent was the Department of Women and Children in Industry of the State Council of Defense, spoken for by its chairman, Mrs. Raymond Robins. Harold Ickes and Medill McCormick also vigorously advocated the bill.

No simple statement suffices to identify the opposition. In general, the big manufacturers and merchants of Chicago manifested almost no unfriendliness toward the proposed reform, but it ran afoul of their smaller competitors and especially the little factory owners and shopkeepers downstate. The latter often said that the enactment of the bill would place them at an unfair or ruinous disadvantage and that Illinois commodities would be priced out of the market by wares produced in states which had no similar law. Furthermore, tradesmen of modest size who had to meet Saturday night payrolls feared lest they be forced to the wall by family-operated stores exempted from the restrictions imposed by the bill. Owners of certain types of seasonal factories, like canneries, employed many women. For these manufacturers an eight-hour day during the hectic rush season in a rural area, where enough extra help was always hard to find, would probably mean bankruptcy. Other employers warned that if the measure became a

39. *Journal of the Senate of the Fiftieth General Assembly of the State of Illinois*, p. 1116.

40. *Journal of the House of Representatives of the Fiftieth General Assembly of the State of Illinois*, p. 403.

41. *Journal of the House of Representatives of the Fifty-first General Assembly of the State of Illinois*, p. 1378.

law, they would replace their female operatives with men. They often added that the women in their employ overwhelmingly opposed a reduction of hours. If these employees knew that their jobs hung upon the fate of the bill, they naturally resisted its enactment. Physicians disagreed among themselves. Some contradicted the members of their own profession on the Illinois Industrial Survey who held that women injured their health by working over forty-eight hours a week in particular industries.

When friends of the measure tried to make it palatable to many of the legislators by exempting more varieties of enterprises from the eight-hour day, the owners of mercantile establishments, not so favored, raised the cry of "discrimination." However divided the economic interests might be in vying for special favors from government, they coalesced sufficiently to defeat a governor and his allies who could not argue that a shorter work-week for women would be profitable but only that it would promote individual and social welfare and bring Illinois into step with enlightened opinion.

The Assembly also disappointed labor in 1917 and again two years later by failing to ban the injunction as an antistrike weapon, or at least to guarantee a jury trial to alleged violators of an injunction. Lowden neither recommended the passage of this bill nor came to its aid. Its defeat probably caused him no regret because he always hesitated to curb the power of the judiciary or lessen the legal safeguards of private property.

Two measures enacted by the Fiftieth General Assembly with his enthusiastic indorsement helped any laborer who needed a short-term loan or a safe place in which to keep his small savings. Fairly stringent laws regulated banking in Illinois by incorporated companies. On the other hand, over five hundred banks, operated by either an individual or an unchartered group, enjoyed complete immunity from state inspection. Although many of these private banks were financially sound and conservatively managed, a few speculated with their depositors' money and occasionally lost it all. For twenty years before Lowden's governorship, efforts in the Assembly by members of both parties to bring private banking under state regulation had been fruitless. He had said in his inaugural address:

> There is an urgent demand for the supervision of private banks. Indeed, it is difficult to understand why this demand should have been denied so long. . . . There is no reason why corporations exercising this privilege should be subject to supervision by the State, and not the individual. It is time that this exception to all the sound rules of government supervision should be wiped out.[42]

In 1916 the state platforms of both parties spoke for the regulation of private banks, but the legislators did not see eye to eye on the method and scope of the control or whether it should affect all institutions of that kind or merely those in Chicago. The downstate members of the Assembly feared lest a restriction upon the moneylending business of private banks would prevent farmers and stock-raisers from borrowing enough during the lean months of every year to tide them over until they could market their grain

42. *House Debates, Fiftieth General Assembly, State of Illinois, 1917,* p. 69.

and cattle. The debate in each house of the Assembly was long and at times acrimonious.[43] In early May, 1917, when agreement seemed unlikely, the governor sent a special message reminding the legislators of their party platforms. The proposed bill, said he, would divest private banks of no privileges except those which

the experience of this world has found to be unsafe for the public as well as for the bankers themselves. If there is danger in permitting an incorporated bank to make a loan to one individual, unlimited except in the discretion of the bankers, why does not the same reason apply to the private bank? . . . doubt should be resolved in favor of the thousands of thrifty but poor people who are now defenseless against the unscrupulous adventurers who hold themselves out to the public as bankers.[44]

About a month later, when both houses finally agreed upon a measure acceptable to Lowden, he was widely credited with winning "a notable victory." The law compelled all private banks to incorporate under a state charter within four years, stipulated a minimum capital proportioned to the size of the community in which the institution was located, and prescribed a liberal maximum limit on the amount of money it could lend to any person, firm, or corporation. The legislature was obliged by the terms of the Illinois constitution to submit this law to the voters. They ratified it in the autumn of 1918.

The governor was also pleased by the passage of a "small-loan" bill designed to drive the "sharks" out of business by establishing 3½ per cent as the maximum interest which could be charged on short-term advances not exceeding $300. Many avaricious moneylenders had been preying upon needy people by requiring them to pay a monthly interest rate of from 15 to 25 per cent. "The operation of the law . . . ," wrote Lowden ten years later, "has justified its enactment. I am informed from reliable sources that the loan shark has practically disappeared from Chicago and from the small industrial cities. . . .The problem is not a rural one."[45]

Labor leaders in Illinois co-operated to the full with the governor and the State Council of Defense in endeavoring to settle the grievances of wage-earners without recourse to strikes. John H. Walker, president of the Illinois Federation of Labor, and Frank Farrington, president of the Illinois branch of the United Mine Workers of America, had opposed Lowden's election, but they became his staunch supporters before the war ended. "To me," Walker admitted in December, 1918, "he was an exceedingly agreeable surprise."[46] Lowden liked to believe that the patriotic considerations impelling

43. *Ibid.,* pp. 764–68, 826, 839–43, 897 ff., 991–1002; *Senate Debates, Fiftieth General Assembly, State of Illinois, 1917,* pp. 625–26, 648–56.

44. *Journal of the Senate of the Fiftieth General Assembly of the State of Illinois,* pp. 876–77; *Chicago Journal,* May 3, 1917; *Chicago Post,* May 9, 1917; *Chicago Herald,* June 3, 1917.

45. FOL to J. S. Baldwin, Decatur, Illinois, Jan. 3, 1927.

46. Speech of J. H. Walker on Dec. 4, 1918, to convention of Illinois Federation of Labor at Bloomington, Illinois. Walker and Victor A. Olander, secretary of the federation, were on the State Council of Defense.

employers and employees to keep the wheels of industry turning while they arbitrated their differences around the table of the state's new Industrial Commission heralded a new day which would continue after the war. During his administration this board under its able chairman, Charles S. Andrus, settled seventy-four disputes, or more than its predecessor, the State Board of Arbitration, had ironed out during its twenty-two years of existence. Apparently, however, the governor overlooked the fact that, by forgoing strikes, unions were making a heavier sacrifice than management on behalf of the war effort. In most industries wages failed to keep pace with the mounting cost of living, although its adverse effects were somewhat offset by steadier employment and more overtime pay than in days of peace.

On the many occasions when Lowden spoke to groups of laborers or businessmen during the war, he stressed the necessity of co-operation and compromise. Victory hinged upon a mighty outpouring of products from American farms and factories. Everybody would lose everything, according to the governor, unless the United States won, because under the Kaiser's iron rule neither capital nor labor was free. Furthermore, to assert that the conflict had come at the behest of businessmen was the "wickedest of lies."[47] In point of fact, continued Lowden, wage-earners stood to gain more from victory than did the capitalists. In justification of this statement, he and others of his day lifted the discussion into a realm of sheer fantasy. For some years before the opening of the war, according to the governor, democracy had functioned badly in the United States, with ominous class cleavages appearing along economic lines. The Civil War had served to restore the Union after it had split along a parallel of latitude. In like fashion the world war, by inspiring all sorts and conditions of people with devotion to a great cause, would re-create social wholeness. Before 1917, a growing spirit of materialism had menaced old American values and threatened the very existence of democracy. Providentially, the war made citizens as eager as in the day of the Revolution to subordinate economic gain to high principles and patriotism. Out of sacrifices would emerge a "rebirth of brotherhood" and out of victory, "a new, better and more humane civilization than the world has ever known."[48]

This all bore directly upon the relations between capital and labor. "If organized labor moves forward to the end of this war with the patriotism and the devotion and the unselfishness it has shown thus far," Lowden declared in September, 1918, "it will be found . . . that organized labor has made more progress during these few years than in any twenty in the past."[49] The key to this advance was the workers' willingness to co-operate with their employers; but, unless the latter continued to give ample recognition

47. MSS of FOL's speech to Illinois State Bankers Association, meeting at Quincy, Illinois, Sept. 19, 1917, and his address at Christopher, Illinois, Sept. 2, 1918.

48. MSS of FOL's speeches at Ottawa, Illinois, Sept. 3, 1917, and to the Illinois Federation of Labor at Bloomington, Illinois, Dec. 9, 1918.

49. MS of FOL's address at Johnston City, Illinois, Sept. 2, 1918.

to the rights of the wage-earners, the happy entente would not outlast the war. Besides guaranteeing wages high enough to provide the conveniences and many of the comforts of modern life, an employer should draw his operatives into a closer personal relationship and let them share in the management of his plant. Although the governor did not know how this might be effected, he warned that, unless it were done, democracy and industrial civilization could not coexist in the future.[50]

Having enfolded the subject in a cloak of idealism and patriotism, the governor characteristically turned to considerations of business efficiency and economic profit. During the postwar years, he told the Industrial Club of Chicago on February 21, 1918, "industrial peace in this country will be as imperative for the nation's welfare as international peace." A substitute for strikes must be found, because they are "the greatest factor of waste in American industry" both to management and to labor. If the wage-earner was made happy by giving him a larger share of the profits, the resulting increase in efficiency in factory operations would dispel its owner's fear that he could not compete successfully with foreign-made wares in the markets of the world after the war. Let there be co-operation at home to assure those remunerative sales overseas without which the staggering national debt could never be paid. Manufacturers' associations and labor unions should appoint joint committees to devise methods for attaining this requisite co-operation and efficiency. In his New Year's message of 1919 the governor voiced his hope in these words:

When I visualize industrial Illinois one hundred years hence, I like to think that all who then labor in the industrial plants may in some way be partners therein. . . . If we are wise we will begin now to restore the old relation between employer and employed that prevailed in simpler times. We shall see that children are no longer the victims of industrial greed.

Taken all in all, Lowden's speeches on the subject of capital and labor during the war were more pleasing to wage-earners than to manufacturers. The latter felt that he would concede too much to the worker and that he lectured them too often about the iniquity of high profits in wartime. Nor were they convinced that he was doing everything in his power to gain for them from Washington an equitable share of government war contracts.[51]

50. MS of FOL's speech to the Industrial Club of Chicago, Feb. 21, 1918. In his address to the Illinois Manufacturers Association on Dec. 10, 1918, FOL admonished employers to cease "bribing and spying on" their employees. He reminded his audience that laborers had as much right to unionize as capitalists had to form corporations, "but that violent strikes must cease."

51. In its pamphlet of July 1, 1918, entitled *Report on the Work of the State Council of Defense* the council claimed to have brought $35,000,000 worth of war business to Illinois and to have relieved "eastern congestion" by ending "western stagnation." And yet an editorial headed "Where Is the Hon. Frank O. Lowden?" *Manufacturers' News* (Chicago), Vol. XIV, No. 6 (Aug. 8, 1918), reminded him that the U.S. Department of Labor had shifted between 500,000 and 1,000,000 Illinois laborers to the East or West Coast, although much of the work they were doing there could as well have been accomplished by Illinois factories.

His friendliness toward co-operatives in industry and agriculture made them doubt his right to be labeled "conservative." They also disliked his implied answers to the following rhetorical questions in his letter of March 15, 1918, to Frederick Dixon of the *Christian Science Monitor:*

In the past we have measured a man's business success by the amount of wealth he has acquired. . . . Must there not be a new standard? Take a man at the head of a great industrial corporation. Will he not be adjudged successful in the future just in proportion to the well-being of the men employed in his industry? Must he not be held responsible for the moral and physical welfare of those engaged in that industry? Will not capitalism have to show not merely that it is best for the exceptional man but that it is also best for the average man? Must not the employer be charged with some of the duties of a statesman?

He had no patience, however, with the able-bodied workman who unpatriotically gave priority to his own grievances over his country's needs or bent his ear to radical doctrine. He gladly stood all morning in the cold rain reviewing a vast labor parade on Michigan Avenue in support of the Third Liberty Loan, but he refused to use his influence on behalf of a new trial for Tom Mooney in California.

Although Lowden improved the administrative methods used by the educational, charitable, and correctional institutions in Illinois, the exigencies of the war blocked him from carrying out much of his original program in the realm of social and humanitarian reform. The heavy demands from Washington for doctors, nurses, and psychologists reduced the trained staffs of the state hospitals and other welfare agencies.[52] A crime wave sufficiently severe even to shock Chicagoans led to an all-day conference in the governor's office, but nothing of moment resulted from the deliberations. Spokesmen for the metropolis blamed paroled prisoners for most of the offenses and asked the governor to have the state's parole commissioners hold a public hearing in Chicago before paroling any convict who had been imprisoned for a crime committed in that city. Lowden refused to agree. "I want to remind you gentlemen . . . ," he said, "that it is the hardest thing on earth to keep the capital of the state down at Springfield and if we didn't fight all the time, Chicago would be running the whole western country here in a short while."[53]

His insistence upon every possible economy in a period of soaring living costs meant that schoolteachers and employees in the state welfare institutions were even more underpaid than usual, although their salaries increased somewhat during the war years. For this reason, he became the target of mounting criticism from such organizations as the Southern Illinois Development Association, the Illinois State Teachers Association, and, above

52. MSS of FOL's speeches of Sept. 7, 1917, to the Women's Committee, State Council of Defense, and on Oct. 26, 1917, to the Conference on Charities, meeting in Joliet, Illinois.

53. Typed record in Lowden MSS of "Conference on Feb. 18, 1918, between Governor Lowden and Representatives of the Chicago City Council, Chamber of Commerce, the Bench and Bar."

all, the Chicago Teachers Federation, spoken for by the forthright and able Miss Margaret Haley. To the delight of the Hearst newspapers of Chicago, she and the gadfly, William H. Malone, reminded Lowden early in 1920 that, while teachers starved, his public utilities and tax commissions discriminated in favor of big business. They called upon him to summon a special meeting of the legislature to provide additional money for teachers' salaries.

This he refused to do, although he asked the regular session in 1921 to remedy the situation. He admitted in a speech before the Illinois State Teachers Association late in the preceding year that economists had misled him by predicting a rapid decline in living costs as soon as the war ended.[54] At the same time but in a more friendly fashion, President David Kinley, of the University of Illinois, importuned him frequently for added funds to enlarge its plant and raise faculty salaries. Lowden gained bigger legislative appropriations for these purposes but by no means the 100 per cent increase requested. The state university had a valid claim to more generous treatment. Its student enrolment was growing at an almost alarming rate, and the government at Springfield continually called upon the institution for more and more services. In his farewell message to the legislature in 1921, the governor mentioned these facts and recommended larger financial provision for public education at every level.

Except in the realm of teachers' salaries, Lowden could justly say in 1920 that his administration had brought "marked progress along educational lines." With even less restraint, the superintendent of the Department of Public Instruction boasted of achievements exceeding those of any earlier time in Illinois history "except in 1855 when the free public school code was first enacted."[55] Responding to the governor's prodding, the legislature in 1919 accepted the terms of the federal Smith-Hughes Act in aid of vocational training and continuation schools. By 1923 all children between the ages of fourteen and eighteen years who had dropped out of the regular schools would have to attend these continuation classes for at least eight hours a week, thirty-six weeks annually. Improved roads and faster means of transportation caused the legislators to authorize the consolidation of elementary and high schools in the rural areas. They doubled the yearly appropriation for the teachers' pension fund. Furthermore, they empowered the district school boards and local tax officials to maintain kindergartens, provide free textbooks, and raise more money for school support. By tightening the state's certification law, the Assembly sought to confine the recruitment of teachers to those who were well qualified.

Lowden thought of himself primarily as the farmer-governor of the state which led all other states in the value of its agricultural products. He never

54. MS of FOL's speech at Springfield, Illinois, Dec. 29, 1920.

55. F. G. Blair to H. G. Fuller, Pierre, South Dakota, Feb. 28, 1920. The 1919 legislature provided for county truant officers, increased county superintendents' salaries about 30 per cent and normal-school teachers' salaries about 15 per cent, and banned the use of a foreign language in the public schools, except in language classes.

doubted that the nation could furnish enough money, troops, munitions, and other war materials to assure ultimate victory on the western front, provided that the flow of food from American farms was sufficient to maintain soldier and civilian morale. "The last battle," said he, "between the forces of evil and the forces of righteousness will be fought, not on the battle fronts of Europe, but in the wheat fields, in the corn fields, in the gardens, and in the feed lots of Illinois" and the other states of the upper Mississippi Valley.[56]

He saw no reason to apologize for the contradiction between his long-run policy of conserving soil fertility in Illinois as a guaranty of its future well-being and his short-run policy of "conserving the flag" by abandoning crop rotation in order to furnish a maximum amount of meat and wheat as long as the war lasted. In proclamations and speeches he stimulated this greater production by appealing to the patriotism of farmers, to their desire for profits, and to their fear of what a victorious Germany would mean to them.[57] In February, 1918, for example, at the twenty-third annual meeting of the Illinois Farmers' Institute, he delivered separate addresses on the same day to the assembled men, women, and children. He warned the men that under the heel of the Kaiser the farmer could not freely choose his own crop; he reminded their wives of women's inferior status in Germany; and he portrayed for the youngsters the "goose-step" life of children in the Fatherland.

Even though emotional appeals of this kind ranged far beyond the facts, they assisted good weather and good soil to produce bumper crops—almost more, indeed, than the harried railroads could carry to the Atlantic seaboard.[58] Co-operating with the state and federal departments of agriculture, the State Council of Defense relieved a serious shortage of seed corn in early 1918 and incidentally cleared a financial profit by buying seed outside Illinois for sale to its farmers. War gardens dotted every urban area. In Chicago alone in 1918, over 240,000 of these vegetable plots, covering nearly three thousand acres, yielded a harvest said to be worth $3,500,000.

One continuing agricultural problem, never satisfactorily solved, was the shortage of labor. Lowden passed along to the War Department the frequent complaints made to him that the local draft boards conscripted proportionately more farm boys than wage-earners. This inequity, so it was said, prevented many farmers from carrying on even their routine operations, let alone increasing their output to meet the war demand. With considerable inaccuracy it was alleged that "any hobo or street loafer" could work effectively on a factory assembly line but was worse than useless when faced with the diversified tasks of a farm. Some critics believed that, because the draft

56. *Blue Book of the State of Illinois, 1919–1920,* p. 117.

57. MS of FOL's speech to Champaign County farmers, Sept. 22, 1917. The U.S. government fixed $2.20 a bushel in 1917 and 1918 and $2.26 in 1919 as the Chicago price of "basic grade" wheat.

58. In 1917 about 60 per cent more acreage was planted to winter wheat in Illinois than in 1916. The harvest of corn naturally declined greatly. In 1920, when Illinois agriculture was about back to normal, the 8,652,000 acres planted in corn totaled approximately the amount of land devoted to wheat, oats, and barley, taken together.

boards did not dare resist pressure from labor unions for the exemption of their members from military service, they made up their quotas by conscripting an undue number of young men from the rural areas.[59] The lure of high wages in the mills also helped to drain away the pool of hired hands available for farm use.

Lowden knew, of course, that the rush cityward merely continued an old drift which the war had accelerated rather than created. During the conflict he talked as much about long-range agricultural reforms needed in Illinois and elsewhere in America as about "sowing for Victory." Somewhat ironically, in the light of the immense crop surpluses so soon to come, he often declared that the rapidly growing population, combined with the near-exhaustion of the world's supply of virgin arable land, made a dearth of food the greatest danger of the years ahead. He apparently did not foresee that transporting food economically to hungry people and having them pay for it might become much more difficult problems than reaping abundant harvests.[60]

After comparing agricultural practices in America and western Europe, he concluded that his fellow citizens took legitimate pride in their efficiency as manufacturers and distributors but were far less expert as farmers than those across the Atlantic. If he were correct, the westward movement in United States history had been in considerable degree a flight from soil exhausted by wasteful tillage. Although the upper Mississippi Valley, with Illinois at its center, was one of the world's chief granaries, it would resemble New England by the year 2,000 in the number of its abandoned farms unless immediate steps were taken to preserve the quality of its soil. "No man," said Lowden, "has a good enough title to an acre of farm land . . . to bequeath it at the end of his life in any less fruitful condition than it was when he came into its possession."[61] The planting of legumes, the application of a crop cycle to every acre of arable land, the combining of livestock-raising with grain-growing, and the use of appropriate fertilizers comprised well-tested ways of maintaining fertility. For this reason he happily noted the increasing harvests of alfalfa and soybeans in Illinois. To follow his complete formula for better agriculture, however, required a considerable outlay of cash. Crop diversification obliged the purchase of additional machinery. A dairy herd represented a large investment, especially when made up of the purebreds

59. J. M. Page, editor of the *Jersey County Democrat* (Jerseyville, Ill.), to FOL, Mar. 6, 1918. In April, 1919, every member of the lower house of the Illinois Assembly voted for a resolution requesting the United States to discharge all Illinois farm boys from the armed services at once, so that they could reach home in time to help with the coming harvest (*House Debates, Fifty-first General Assembly, State of Illinois, 1919*, pp. 255–56).

60. FOL's fear of a food shortage in the quite near future probably reflected in part a great overestimate of the rate of population increase in the United States. He did not foresee the drastic curtailment of immigration within six years. Charles Adkins, director of the Department of Agriculture, wrote him on Aug. 23, 1918, that the U.S. population would likely be three or four hundred million within fifty years.

61. MS of FOL's speech on Feb. 28, 1918, to the Illinois Association of County Agricultural Fairs.

which he insisted were alone worth having. In short, the transition from hap-hazard to scientific agriculture would be far too expensive for most small farmers to undertake.

Every farm-journal editor and professor at a state agricultural college knew how to rebuild soils. They served as invaluable allies in the cause of better farming, but a vast chasm often separated what they taught from the actual practice in Illinois. The county and state fairs, in so far as they stressed rural education rather than horse-racing and sideshows, had slowly helped to bridge this gap. But the men who most needed instruction in scientific hus-bandry usually declined to avail themselves of the educational opportunities available. The small farmer, as the governor sadly commented, was a dyed-in-the-wool conservative who rarely changed his ways because of what he read or heard. He "had to be shown."[62] Perhaps he would listen if a teacher came directly to his farm.

Here and there in the United States during the first years of the present century, forward-looking landowners banded together into county-wide clubs or soil-improvement associations. They employed demonstrators or field agents recommended to them by the state universities or the United States Department of Agriculture. Prominent farmers in several of the lush northern counties not far from "Sinnissippi" led the way in Illinois. During Governor Dunne's administration, the legislature had authorized county governments to help these "farm bureaus" with money, and the state college of agriculture established a Cooperative Extension Service in Agriculture and Home Economics. This "Service" depended upon the federal Smith-Lever Act (1914) providing financial aid for county-agent work. By 1916 on the eve of Lowden's governorship, twenty-two northern Illinois counties had farm bureaus and county agents, and the number more than tripled within the next three years. Keeping in close touch with the University of Illinois Extension Service and Experiment Station and with the United States De-partment of Agriculture, the county agent used experimental plots and other "face-to-face" devices, including discussion groups, to teach improved farm-ing methods. In Lowden's opinion this farm-bureau movement marked "the most important step taken by agriculture in my time." As a part of the stride forward, he urged the county agents to stimulate co-operative buying and selling.[63]

In this congenial environment of wartime prosperity and increasing finan-cial aid from Washington, the drive for improved agriculture rapidly gained momentum. Herman W. Danforth, head of the Tazewell County Farm Bu-reau, worked effectively to bring the Illinois Agricultural Association into being and deservedly became its first president. Destined to develop into one

62. MSS of FOL's speeches to the farm managers of state institutions, Feb. 14, 1918, and to the Boys' Agricultural School at the state fair, Aug. 22, 1918.

63. Illinois's first farm bureaus appeared in De Kalb and Kankakee counties in 1912 (MS of FOL's speech at Libertyville, Illinois, Sept. 17, 1918, at the Commencement of the Women's Land Army). The standard volumes on the farm bureau are Orville M. Kile, *Farm Bureau Movement* (New York, 1921) and his *The Farm Bureau through Three Decades* (New York, 1948).

of the most powerful societies of its kind, it inaugurated its career by pressing the legislature to enact measures helpful to farmers. Viewed with much favor by the governor, by the dean of the College of Agriculture of the University of Illinois, and by influential farm-journal editors such as Clifford Gregory of the *Prairie Farmer* and Alvin Sanders of the *Breeder's Gazette*, it soon chalked up a considerable record of achievement. Although avowedly non-partisan, most of its leading spirits were staunch Republicans.[64]

During the halcyon days of the war, societies similar in form and function to the Illinois Agricultural Association appeared in other states. On the initiative of the one in New York, five hundred representatives of these statewide unions of farm bureaus, as well as other agricultural leaders, met in Chicago in late 1919 and agreed to establish the American Farm Bureau Federation. In his address of welcome Governor Lowden credited the movement with doing much to end "the awful isolation" of rural America from the rich fruits of research at state colleges of agriculture. Thanks largely to the farm bureaus, he added, the paradox of a nation with the most advanced agricultural science and the most inefficient farming in the world would soon disappear.[65]

During his administration Lowden initiated a study of tenant farming. He especially regretted its rapid increase because renters often depleted the fertility of their leaseholds. The best corn lands in Illinois had risen in value from $40 or $50 an acre in 1885 to about eight times those figures by 1918. As a result, many able young men, lacking enough money to buy land, had to choose between being hired hands, renting, or migrating to the cities. With good soil selling at such a price, its rental cost was correspondingly high. Lowden called the customary one-year lease "a conspiracy to ruin land." By its terms a tenant had every reason to work his holding mercilessly. The governor held that in every lease the state was or should be a third party in interest. It represented the general welfare and the future generations who must depend upon the richness of Illinois soil. For this reason he hoped that an aroused public opinion or, if need be, a law would compel the use of a lease-form calculated to spur a tenant to preserve or increase the fertility of his fields. This could be done by obliging him to plant legumes on certain tracts designated by the owner or by the latter's promising the tenant a rebate in rent, at the expiration of the contract, proportioned to the improvements he had made in the condition of the arable land. As Lowden at this time urged manufacturers to share their enterprises financially with their workmen, so he also advocated partnerships between farm owners and their lessees.[66]

64. MS of FOL's speech in March, 1917, at Champaign, Illinois, to fifteen agricultural societies and associations; William B. Storm, "An Analysis of the Illinois Agricultural Association as a Pressure Group for Farmers" (Ph.D. dissertation, University of Chicago, 1949).

65. MS of FOL's speech of Nov. 12, 1919, at Chicago.

66. FOL's biennial messages to the Fifty-first General Assembly, Jan. 8, 1919, and to the Fifty-second General Assembly, Jan. 5, 1921. See also FOL, "Tenant and Landlord Partnerships," *Breeder's Gazette,* Dec. 25, 1919. The Farm Tenancy Commission, author-

Equally desirable was a federal farm loan law, much more generous in its terms than the one of 1916, to encourage any upstanding young man to borrow enough government money at a nominal interest rate to buy a small farm. American ideals of liberty and democracy were as much the product of the rural areas as grain and milk. Spiritual as well as bodily sustenance must continue to come from the countryside. No more important task confronted the United States than to make farm life so attractive and rewarding that the movement of promising young people to the cities would decline.[67] "As the farmers of America," said Lowden, "helped save the world from military despotism, so they will save their country from anarchism." He liked to quote the aphorism allegedly first uttered by James J. Hill, the railroad magnate—"Land without population is a wilderness, and population without land is a mob." In a word, considerations of patriotism, of bequeathing good soil to the Americans of the future, and of providing food and fiber for the world's teeming population made scientific agriculture imperative.

Scientific agriculture also involved the adaptation of crops to the nature of the land. On this matter the Illinois Soil Survey confirmed Lowden's long-held view by reporting that 17 per cent of the state, or an area larger than Connecticut, was suitable for silviculture rather than tillage. Much of the seven southernmost counties, as well as the banks of rivers like the Mississippi, Illinois, Rock, and Sangamon, especially invited forestation. Trees would lessen the destructive runoff of heavy rains and the gullying of slopes. Grazing and forestry could often go hand in hand. Stands of pine and hardwoods would enhance the beauty of the countryside and might eventually make Illinois self-sufficient in timber. Trees, however, grew slowly, and few farmers would voluntarily set out many for the benefit of posterity. To encourage them to do so, the governor recommended the appointment of a state forester and the tax-exempting of tree-planted tracts until their timber was ready for market. In 1919 the legislature provided for a forester in connection with a natural history survey, but two more years went by before he had sufficient funds to begin a tree inventory of Illinois.[68]

---

ized by the legislature in 1919, found that tenancy and absentee ownership were increasing, especially in northern Illinois, and soils were deteriorating except in the livestock-farming area west of the Illinois River. Crop-sharing rather than cash-rent leases were normal. The commission discovered few discontented tenants but believed that many unhappy ones had stayed away from the hearings. To discourage land speculation, it recommended that a tax on the sale price of farm land be levied when it was sold within a year after its purchase. It also advocated a law to oblige lessors to reimburse lessees who improved their leasehold. It spoke for easier credit facilities for tenants and for a $25,000 appropriation to enable the University of Illinois to study tenancy further.

67. FOL to Mrs. H. R. Graham, May 18, 1918, praising the Country Home Improvement Association; MS of FOL's speech to The National Association of Real Estate Boards, June 19, 1918.

68. *State of Illinois: Third Administrative Report of the Directors of Departments under the Civil Administrative Code . . . July 1, 1919, to June 30, 1920* (Springfield, Ill., 1921), pp. 785–86; *State of Illinois: Fourth Administrative Report of the Directors of Departments under the Civil Administrative Code . . . July 1, 1920, to June 30, 1921* (Springfield, Ill., 1922), pp. 795 and 806.

By the mid-1920's Lowden's interest in reforestation led him to accept President Coolidge's invitation to be the chairman of a Citizens' Committee of about one hundred members to arrange for meetings throughout the nation on behalf of conservation during an annual National Forest Week. This movement was also sponsored by many private organizations, including the American Forestry Association, the Izaak Walton League, the National Lumber Manufacturers' Association, and the General Federation of Women's Clubs.[69] By calling attention to the rapid depletion of United States timber resources, the committee hoped to encourage better fire-precaution measures, more extensive reforestation, and the creation of additional state and national forests. In his speeches and articles on the subject Lowden sought to make Americans understand that the fast-declining supplies of fertile land, timber, and minerals would be the chief "limiting factors in our future national growth."[70]

All-weather roads had been slowly pushing out into rural Illinois from its larger cities for twenty years before Lowden became governor. As "Squire of Sinnissippi," he had tried repeatedly to convince his neighbors that better highways would bring them many economic and social benefits. Being "mud-bound" in their homes for days at a time lent force to his arguments, but he could not gainsay their reply that good roads meant heavier taxes, as well as pleasure-seeking city folk killing poultry and frightening horses with their cars. More and more farm families, however, yielded to the lure of the automobile and became converts to the cause of hard-surface highways. In the usual American fashion, they and their urban counterparts formed societies to influence public opinion and the legislature at Springfield. They could count upon the interested help of car manufacturers and suppliers of road-building materials. The latter, whether makers of brick, bituminous macadam, or cement-concrete, often confused the issue by their sharp competition for lucrative contracts. Among the societies, the Chicago Motor Club and, above all, the Illinois Highway Improvement Association, with the Chicago banker William G. Edens as its able head, were the most important. In the legislature, Homer J. Tice of Greenview was for some years the outstanding champion of hard-surface roads.

Governors Deneen and Dunne had laid a foundation of substantial achievement in highway construction before Lowden in his inaugural address called for "a comprehensive system of good roads" as a sound investment. During Dunne's term some four hundred miles of all-weather turnpikes had been completed under the Tice Law, whereby the state extended financial aid to any county which was willing, by means of a bond issue, to shoulder most of the cost of building and keeping good roads in repair within its borders. At the same time many townships and road districts, in accordance with long

69. Calvin Coolidge to FOL, Apr. 24, 1925.

70. FOL to M. L. Requa, San Francisco, California, Oct. 20, 1925. FOL's speech of Jan. 22, 1925, before the American Forestry Association was published under the title "The Challenge of Woodless Lands" in *American Forests and Forest Life* (Washington, D.C.), XXXI, No. 375 (March, 1925), 131–32, 172, 176.

practice, also levied taxes for the improvement of their local thoroughfares. Dunne did not exaggerate when he mentioned "the phenomenal growth of sentiment" in favor of better highways. He omitted to add, however, that a county-option statute would never produce an orderly state-wide road system. The constitution prohibited any county from incurring a debt exceeding 5 per cent of the assessed value of its residents' property.

At about the time of Governor Lowden's inauguration, several new circumstances gave added impetus to the drive for better highways. A federal law enacted in 1916 offered to match state and county appropriations for the construction of main thoroughfares of national importance. In Illinois these were chiefly the north-south Dixie Highway and the east-west Lincoln Highway, following, in part, the route of the Old National (Cumberland) Road.[71] With 340,000 automobile owners in the state by 1917 and the number certain to rise from year to year,[72] the Illinois Highway Improvement Association, in consultation with the Chicago Motor Club, chambers of commerce, and similar groups, drafted a bill authorizing the building of forty-eight hundred miles of road with the cash provided by a $60,000,000 bond issue. New taxes would amortize half of this huge sum, and car-license fees the balance. When the governor declined to sponsor any measure requiring heavier taxes, the association altered its bill so as to assess the entire cost against car-license fees and proposed a drastic increase in their rates. With the enthusiastic support of Lowden and most of the members of the Assembly, this plan was enacted into law.

Thus the first hurdle was successfully surmounted, but the remaining ones proved to be much more difficult to jump. The constitution stipulated that a financial measure of this kind could not become operative until a majority of the voters at the next general election signified their approval of it. The legislature scheduled this plebiscite for November 5, 1918, when the electorate would also vote for or against the bills providing for a constitutional convention and the abolition of private banks. In all likelihood the income from car-license fees would easily underwrite the proposed issue of twenty-year bonds, but the terms of the constitution left the legislature with no choice but to include in the highway-construction bill a provision for discharging the $60,000,000 debt with additional taxes. Even though this tax section merely signified a *pro forma* compliance with the fundamental law, the cost-conscious electorate might refuse to accept a big road-building project which apparently would take millions from their pockets. In a period of rising prices, when many voters were virtually disenfranchised by being overseas or in military cantonments outside Illinois, some opponents argued persuasively that the times were too much out of joint to embark upon so

71. A highway was also to go diagonally across the state from Chicago via La Salle, Peoria, and Springfield to East St. Louis. During Lowden's administration, Illinois received about $12,000,000 of federal highway-aid money.

72. The total number of motor vehicles in Illinois was 389,761 in 1918; 670,389 in 1921; 1,128,503 in 1924; and 1,642,628 in 1930. The income from licenses and drivers' fees increased from $2,762,568 in 1918 to $18,447,247 in 1930.

ambitious a venture. The bill empowered Lowden to decide when to offer the bonds for sale and begin construction. He stilled some of the criticism by guaranteeing to delay the start of the project until after the war and to prevent the road debentures from competing with Liberty Bonds for the money of investors.

He also used the national emergency as a strong argument in behalf of the highway plan. By speech and correspondence he reminded Illinoisans that a business depression often followed a major war. In justice to the veterans, jobs must be ready for them upon their return. If private industry could not provide them, the state must have a public works program to fill the void.[73] To this end, he shelved many of the state-aid projects under the Tice Law until victory came in Europe. In any event, the high prices and scarcity of labor and materials made work on local roads uneconomical, if not unpatriotic. Unlike Governor Dunne, Lowden refused to use large numbers of convicts in construction work. When the head of the Illinois Department of Public Works asked the director of the United States Office of Public Roads in March, 1918, whether he considered road-building an unjustifiable diversion from the main job, he sanctioned "construction of the most heavily traveled highways," provided that the work did not seriously deplete the supply of farm labor.[74]

Late in his administration, the governor arranged for the building of about two miles of experimental highway with the main types of hard-surface materials joined end to end. Thus they could be compared in terms of cost and speed of construction and resistance to summer's heat, winter's cold, and the wear and tear of heavy traffic.[75] The governor hoped that some of the state's engineers, then gaining much road-building and repairing experience in France, would bring home new ideas to help make Illinois highways the model for the entire Midwest.

As election day in 1918 drew nearer, the referendum campaign increased in tempo. Lowden proclaimed October 30 as "Good Roads Day" and spoke many times during the late summer and early autumn in support of the project. The Illinois Highway Improvement Association prepared at least eight different leaflets or pamphlets and distributed them by the thousands throughout the state. In them, Lowden's unqualified indorsement of the bond issue had a prominent place. "Looking at the question from all angles,"

73. MSS of FOL's speech at the Illinois Highway Improvement Association convention at Bloomington, Illinois, Oct. 24, 1917, and of his public statement, Dec. 18, 1917.

74. T. G. Vennum, acting director, Department of Public Works and Buildings, to L. W. Page, director, United States Office of Public Roads, Mar. 19, and Page's reply, Mar. 26, 1918.

75. *State of Illinois: Third Administrative Report of the Directors of Departments under the Civil Administrative Code . . . July 1, 1919, to June 30, 1920*, p. 215; *State of Illinois: Fourth Administrative Report of the Directors of Departments under the Civil Administrative Code . . . July 1, 1920, to June 30, 1921*, pp. 273–74. This road was at Bates, near Springfield. It was divided into sixty-four sections, each of different materials or made unlike the others. It was not completed until 1921. FOL was highly gratified by the lessons which it taught.

he wrote, "I am more than convinced that the failure of the bond issue at the polls in November would be a calamity." Former Governor Dunne's support also received wide publicity because many Democrats thought of him as the "father" of the good-roads movement in Illinois.[76]

Besides defending the highway project as an insurance against postwar unemployment, Lowden made much of its financial virtues. The car owners of Illinois, said he, were really offering a $60,000,000 gift to the people of the state. The income from license fees would pay the entire construction cost and also provide a surplus for upkeep and further road-building. The governor denied that road-material firms or Chicago banks, expecting to profit by floating the bonds, had initiated the bill. According to his estimate, over half the funds would be paid out for wages. The vast enterprise would demonstrate whether highways could be built as inexpensively and as durably by government as by private contractors. He warned the cement-making companies and others that the sooner they offered their products at reasonable prices, the sooner the construction work would begin. If they tried to profit exorbitantly, they would lose a big market of indefinite duration because the Department of Public Works would manufacture its own materials.[77]

Although advocates of the bond issue somewhat exaggerated the blessings which hard-top highways would immediately confer upon Illinois, they had common sense and the future on their side. Governor Lowden and his friends enthusiastically explained how the projected network of about forty-six new thoroughfares, traversing every one of the 102 counties at least once, would "aid the farmer, the laborer, the businessman and the housewife . . . lower the cost of living, help our schools, improve social conditions, add to the attractiveness of both farm and city life, increase land values, lead to enlarged business activities, and wonderfully promote the general prosperity of our State." "Pull Illinois Out of the Mud," the slogan of the Illinois Highway Improvement Association, was pictured as the sovereign cure for a host of ills. The railroad companies were by no means so lyrical, but with their lines under government control and their days beset by war-born problems, they could not offer much resistance. The *Chicago Journal*, always out of humor with the Lowden administration, denounced the bond issue as extravagant and declared that convict labor should build the highways of Illinois.[78]

On November 5, a decisive majority of the voters registered their ap-

76. *Blue Book of the State of Illinois, 1919–1920*, p. 129, estimated that newspapers donated 25,000 columns to the good-roads campaign. The Illinois Highway Improvement Association issued *Will the Bonds and Interest Thereon Be Paid from Motor License Fees?*, *The Road Question Answered by $60,000,000 State Hard Roads Bond Issue*, *Vote "Yes" for Good Roads*, *The Sixty Million Dollar Bond Issue Explained*, *Ten Leading Questions and Their Authoritative Answers*, *Good Roads Campaign Text Book for Illinois*, *365 Day Roads*, and *Governor Lowden's Statement*.

77. MS of FOL's speech of Dec. 11, 1918, to the Illinois Highway Congress; *Blue Book of the State of Illinois, 1919–1920*, p. 15.

78. The quotations are from the pamphlets and leaflets cited in n. 76. Another often heard statement was that "good roads, good schools, good churches, good citizens, and a good commonwealth go together." *Chicago Journal*, Nov. 2, 1918.

proval of the project.[79] Thereafter for the next two years adverse economic conditions hindered Lowden and his associates from taking much advantage of their victory. No bonds were sold during his governorship because the income from license fees covered the cost of the few roads built before the end of his term. Strikes by organized labor, a shortage of railroad cars to transport materials, and the unwillingness of many veterans to work on the roads contributed to the delay.

The high price of cement proved to be the principal deterrent. According to the original estimate, $32,000 would build a mile of road. To Lowden's surprise, the cost of materials increased sharply for some months after the Armistice. At the new levels the expense of construction rose nearly 80 per cent.[80] The governor charged that the Portland cement firms had upped their quotations as soon as they heard the result of the referendum vote. For this reason he asked Robert D. Clarke to determine confidentially the cost of making cement and of building a cement plant with a daily capacity of three thousand barrels. Clarke reported on January 30, 1919, that the latter would require an outlay of nearly a million dollars but that at $1.85 a barrel the private concerns were probably reaping a 75 per cent profit. He predicted—accurately, as it turned out—an early drop in price. The governor submitted Clarke's figures to a closed session of the legislative committee investigating the alleged "cement combine." During this probe the cost of cement fell 20 cents a barrel.

Resisting sharp criticism from influential editors who wanted many more road crews at work, Lowden decided to delay full-scale construction until the price of cement dropped at least another 20 cents. As a result, very little of the newly projected road net was built during the next two years, although there were much surveying, grading and filling, and bridge-making along the designated routes. By exercising the right of eminent domain, the state also acquired title to a large part of the land needed for roads. In addition, the Division of Highways pointed with pride to its accomplishments in federal- and local-aid construction and to the Bates experimental road, already mentioned.[81]

Motorcar owners, growing in number beyond all expectation, became more and more impatient when the state administration, on grounds of thrift alone, delayed improvements so necessary to the public welfare. Even the Illinois State Automobile Association, hitherto in tune with the gover-

79. The vote was 661,815 to 154,396. The vote in only two counties was adverse.

80. MS of FOL's speech to the Illinois Highway Improvement Association, Springfield, Illinois, Jan. 27, 1920.

81. By December, 1920, about 3,000 of the 4,800 miles of bond-issue roads had been "designated and located" (MS of FOL's speech at Mason City, Illinois, Dec. 21, 1920). On this date FOL shared in the brief ceremony at Mason City marking the opening of the hard-top road from Peoria to Springfield. Under public pressure and against its better judgment because of the high costs, the Department of Public Works completed about 550 miles of federal-aid and license-fee roads during FOL's administration. This was 150 miles less than it had expected to build in 1919 alone, if conditions had been favorable.

nor's refusal to pay excessive prices for cement, passed resolutions in the autumn of 1920 calling for greater activity in highway-building. This would come with feverish haste after Lowden's term ended.

His contribution cannot be fairly measured in terms of the few miles of thoroughfares completed during his governorship. By promoting a favorable public opinion, by devising a practicable financial plan, and by fostering experiments in construction methods, he prepared the way for the remarkable expansion of the Illinois road net during the rest of the 1920's and influenced the highway-improvement policies of other states. As he left office, he urged the legislature to create a state highway police force. This suggestion bore fruit a few years later. Still in the future, however, is the realization of his hope that representatives from the forty-eight states would assemble in convention and agree upon a nation-wide code of traffic regulations for motor vehicles.[82]

William L. Sackett, superintendent of the Division of Waterways, did not foresee track electrification, Diesel locomotives, and streamlined trains when he bluntly announced in 1919, "railroads have reached their highest state of development and efficiency and cannot handle the commerce of the nation. Development and use of the waterways and highways are essential."[83] His prophecy would be at least partially fulfilled even though the airplane did not come within the range of his vision. During the war the movement of men and materials strained the facilities of the railroads almost to their breaking point. For this reason Governor Lowden urged the federal government to rehabilitate the old Illinois and Lake Michigan Canal speedily and complete the trans-Illinois link of the lakes-to-gulf deep waterway. In his enthusiasm he pictured his commonwealth as the new "Keystone State" of the nation, with Chicago the hub of an arterial highway system radiating to all parts of the Union and of many inland waterways making that metropolis the busiest port of the Western Hemisphere. A channel already connected Chicago with Lockport, thirty-seven miles away. From Lockport, by dredging some sixty-five miles of the Des Plaines and Illinois rivers to Utica, tugs and barges could merge with the fifteen thousand miles of water-borne commerce of the Mississippi Valley.[84] Thereby the advantage enjoyed since the opening of the Panama Canal in 1912 by East Coast businessmen over those of the Midwest in their competition for Pacific seaboard markets would largely

82. FOL's biennial message of Jan. 5, 1921, in *Journal of the House of Representatives of the Fifty-second General Assembly of the State of Illinois*, pp. 30–31; MS of FOL's speech of Mar. 22, 1920, to Illinois Automotive Dealers' convention.

83. *State of Illinois: Second Administrative Report of the Directors of Departments under the Civil Administrative Code . . . July 1, 1918, to June 30, 1919* (Springfield, Ill., 1919), p. 219.

84. W. L. Sackett, "The Lowden Plan for the Illinois Waterway," *Blue Book of the State of Illinois, 1919–1920*, pp. 134–38; also see *Blue Book of the State of Illinois, 1921–1922*, pp. 337–42.

disappear. A deep waterway, furthermore, would act as a brake upon freight rates charged by railroads for carrying heavy articles.[85]

Provided with $150,000 by Congress, the Department of Public Works during 1918–19 repaired some of the locks on the Illinois and Lake Michigan Canal and deepened it to four and one-half feet. The drying-up of federal aid as soon as the war emergency ended blasted the plan to restore its original depth of six feet. After the Illinois legislature amended its Deep Waterway Act of 1915 to bring it into line with federal specifications, the secretary of war gave Governor Lowden clearance in January, 1920, to proceed at once with the Lockport-Utica project. Although the scarcity and high price of labor and materials delayed the beginning of the work until November, he felt confident that its completion would come within three years. Much too optimistic, he had to wait until 1933 and 1934 before sharing in the celebrations attending its opening to traffic.

The war affected old social and economic problems and created many new ones. To Lowden's surprise, he apparently gained in vigor as his work load increased. Although bothered, as always, by frequent colds, he suffered no recurrence of the nerve exhaustion which had forced his withdrawal from Congress some years before. He had no need to feign enthusiasm for the American cause; it completely engaged his heart. At times he even found the emergency exhilarating, as when he reviewed thousands of troops to the strains of martial music. The victory came too soon to oblige him to combat war weariness on the home front. Believing that his passionate speeches aroused many Illinois citizens from their initial apathy and knowing that what he said and did elicited much applause, he was continuously buoyed up by a sense of important accomplishment and the realization that he was fast emerging into national prominence.

85. FOL, "Illinois, the New Keystone of the Union," *American Review of Reviews,* LVII (March, 1918), 271–72.

CHAPTER XV

SOLDIERS, CENTENNIAL, AND SEDITION

Sobered or disillusioned by world events during the last forty years, some Americans recall with amazement today how readily they believed in 1917 that the Allied cause was unqualifiedly holy and that ever-lasting peace would be the reward of victory. Perhaps the crusading fervor of the progressive era prepared the way for this romantic enthusiasm, even though a few outstanding liberals like the elder La Follette refused to view the war either as a clear-cut contest between good and evil or as a path-breaker toward a happier world. On the other hand, Lowden and other members of the Republican Old Guard out-Wilsoned Wilson in their bellig-erence toward the Central Powers. Even among the members of his own party the President had no more staunch backer than the governor of Illi-nois. His refusal to criticize the regime at Washington during 1917 and 1918 is more remarkable than his fervent support of the war. Without apparent difficulty, he recaptured in his middle age the youthful ardor of his Spanish-American war days. In the cold light of the mid-century his public addresses during World War I are more impressive in number than in content. But they were enthusiastically received by his audiences and undoubtedly suited the temper of their time.[1]

Lowden's explanation of why the conflict began was as narrow in scope as his view of what hinged upon its outcome was sweeping. For fifty years the Hohenzollern dynasty, unknown to the rest of the world, had prepared for "Der Tag" when it would bring the Western Hemisphere, if not the whole globe, under its heel. German Christianity, philosophy, education, military science, and statecraft had been diabolically fashioned for the attainment of this goal. Wotan supplanted the God of the Holy Bible as the deity of the "Bosches," and Nietzsche, Treitschke, and Bernhardi served as his chief apos-tles. With every spiritual and material asset subordinated to the Kaiser's foul purposes, "the cruelest military autocracy the world has ever known" cen-tered along the Rhine and the Elbe. It embodied "all that civilization . . . thought it had conquered centuries ago." For proof of this, read the writings of the devilish triumvirate mentioned above, and let the German atrocities in Belgium and France bear witness.[2]

1. FOL's principal speeches on the war are in Marguerite E. Jenison (ed.), *War Docu-ments and Addresses,* published in 1923 as Vol. VI of Theodore C. Pease (ed.), *Illinois in the World War* (6 vols.; Springfield, Ill., 1921–23).

2. MS of FOL's speech of Jan. 28, 1918, to the Chicago Church Federation Council.

This being so, "all we are, and have, and all we hope for our children are involved in the issue of this strife." The governor portrayed it as a contest in which individual liberty was arrayed against slavery, democracy against autocracy, and, above all, righteousness against unrighteousness. The survival of freedom, nationality, civilization, and Christianity hung in the balance. Therefore, it was not only the greatest of all wars but also the "holiest cause" ever championed by the American soldier. Once again, as in all the nation's major wars, except possibly the conflict with Mexico, the United States armed forces could appropriately inscribe the Sermon on the Mount upon their banners. "We will win," Lowden exclaimed, "because there is still a God in His Heaven."[3]

He pointed out repeatedly that, although the United States had joined several European powers in the struggle, every American was defending, first and foremost, his own country and all the values consecrated by the heroes of its past. Indeed, the war marked the culmination of the struggle begun by the patriots when they threw off the tyrannical yoke of George III. The issues at stake should be of special moment to citizens of Illinois because their own Abraham Lincoln, "the greatest life since Calvary," had defined them in unforgettable terms and had become a martyr in their behalf. In his day the nation was "the house divided," and it had to choose freedom instead of slavery in order to endure. In 1917 the "house divided" encompassed the whole Western world, but it faced America's identical choice of 1861. If the North had lost the Civil War, there would still have been a United States, however limited in its area, dedicated to the advancement of human freedom. Defeat in the world war, however, would destroy the nation, with no refuge left for liberty anywhere on the globe. In the ensuing dark ages every true American would count as fortunate only those of his fellow citizens who had fallen in battle while fighting for the lost cause.[4] With "life, liberty, and the pursuit of happiness" in jeopardy, Lowden called upon Illinoisans on July 4, 1918, to read the Declaration of Independence and solemnly pledge "their lives, their fortunes, and their sacred honor" in support of the crusade against the new "Anti-Christ."

Besides presenting the meaning of the war in terms of world civilization and national survival, Lowden endeavored to make the attainment of victory seem especially vital to whatever audience he addressed, whether of businessmen, wage-earners, farmers, teachers, mothers, or children. Each of these groups, he insisted, had at stake its freedom, its dignity, its social status, and its property. "Buy Liberty Bonds or pay tribute to the Kaiser" was the option he extended to anyone with money in his pocket. He assured clergymen that they could appropriately open the churches to patriotic services because "all that the church stands for is challenged by our enemies."[5] He warned

---

3. MSS of FOL's speeches to the Zionists of Chicago, Dec. 30, 1917; to the Serbian Mission, Jan. 27, 1918; to the Chicago Culture Club, Jan. 28, 1918; and to the Fort Sheridan Association, Chicago, Apr. 23, 1918.

4. MS of FOL's speech at Hotel La Salle, Chicago, Jan. 29, 1918.

5. FOL's wire to Rev. E. J. Rose, Lockport, Illinois, Apr. 5, 1918.

women about the Kaiser's determination to reduce their role in society to housekeeping for men and bearing children—preferably male. As for American mothers, "we are fighting a war to vindicate the lessons which our Mothers taught us. . . . So, ladies, it is your war . . . even more than it is the men's war."[6]

But Lowden appealed to the hopes as well as to the fears of his listeners. God had always protected the American people, and he certainly would not forsake them when they fought on behalf of Christ's teachings. Although victory would preserve a priceless heritage, the common effort and personal sacrifices required to win the war would also be of great worth to America. Providence might well have sent the fiery trial in order to recall many errant citizens from the undemocratic paths of materialism, selfishness, and economic class exclusiveness. Whoever used the crisis to heap up profits for himself was as despicable as the foe because he betrayed American ideals and menaced national unity. In essence the war signified a struggle to the death between might and right, between brute materialism and man's higher spiritual self. In the winning of it, the patriot renewed his love of country, learned the worth of liberty, democracy, and self-discipline, and justified for all time Lincoln's faith in the value of the common man. Following the victory the world would be a happier dwelling place, with the cause of man's brotherhood vindicated and the fear of another great war removed.

Except for his stress upon the global importance of the conflict, Lowden rarely struck an international note in his speeches. The emotion of the moment, however, led him to assure the Zionists in December, 1917, that America was fighting for "the integrity and security of small nations everywhere in the world." Nine months later he informed the Bohemian National Alliance and Slovak League that "this war is revealing as was never revealed before, the fact that our liberties are safe only when the liberties of other peoples are also secure."[7] He naturally used the visit of Premier Viviani and Marshal Joffre to Chicago and Springfield early in the conflict to ring the familiar changes upon America's debt to Lafayette and upon France as the twentieth-century champion of humanity's cause. The governor rarely mentioned England. He indorsed the hope of the Irish Fellowship Club for a "united and independent Ireland" as one important outcome of the war.[8] Late in the struggle he finally declared publicly that the United States must lead in revitalizing the World Court of International Justice. Apparently he spoke only once in favor of a league of nations, and then very briefly. He doubted its ability to prevent all wars, "but that they will be reduced in number and extent, no one can doubt." In the same address he also suggested "a league of religions to insure the dominance of righteousness throughout the future of the world."[9] Winning the war was the supreme task of the mo-

6. MS of FOL's speech to the Chicago Culture Club, Jan. 28, 1918.

7. FOL's wire of Sept. 13, 1918, to Lieutenant-Governor Oglesby to be read to the league mentioned in the text.

8. MS of FOL's speech, Jan. 26, 1918, to Irish Fellowship Club of Chicago.

ment. Since idealism could help to that end, he eagerly contributed his share of it in all his speeches. Probably he best summarized his views about the whole matter when he remarked to the Illinois Federation of Labor a month after the Armistice:

Internationalism . . . is a beautiful word and within its proper limitations it is a very valuable word . . . and so we in America . . . are not any the less kindly disposed toward all the world because we first cherish our own country and put it first above all the world. . . . We . . . can best serve our time and serve humanity . . . if we give our first affection to America and trust that America may become the exemplar of all the world.[10]

Lowden's views changed but little during the war. At its outset he often said that America's foe was the ruling class in Germany and not its people. By 1918 he had abandoned this distinction. Early in the conflict the apathy of many citizens of Illinois, their dislike of the draft, and their evident wish to "sit it out" greatly disturbed him. Not a few of them quickly offered to defend the homeland but opposed the sending of American soldiers overseas. To these "yes and no" patriots, Lowden's admonition was strong and clear. The time for hedging had passed; loyalty to the flag admitted of no middle-of-the-road position. Far better to carry the war to the enemy and fight him on foreign soil than be obliged, unaided, to drive him from America's own shores after he had crushed England and France. Citing General U. S. Grant's maxim that the best defense was a smashing offense, Lowden frequently expressed regret before October, 1918, because so few American troops had reached the front lines overseas.

About six months earlier, he acknowledged for the first time that almost all the people of Illinois were fully aroused and working with might and main to win the war. But he feared lest Russia's withdrawal from the conflict and the subsequent massing of more enemy troops on the western battle line would lead the United States, England, and France to accept a truce offer from Germany. A negotiated peace, in Lowden's view would merely afford the Kaiser a breathing spell in which to prepare further aggressions. No victory would be worthy of the name, short of his unconditional surrender, accompanied by a confession of guilt and abdication. As for his momentary successes, said Lowden, they must serve only to spur America's determination to win. On June 2, 1918, when the German offensive seemed irresistible, he electrified his audience at Freeport by exclaiming:

If in this hour the wires should thrill with the tragic news that Paris has fallen, I still would say, "We will go on." And if, my friends, the armies of heroic France, those armies that have won the admiration of every true and valiant and generous heart in all the world, if those armies should be crushed, I still would say "We will go on." And if the soldiers of England are pushed into the Channel and fail to reach their own shores, there is but one thing for us to do if we are men who respect ourselves, who love our wives and children, and that is, we will still go on.

9. MSS of FOL's speeches of Sept. 20, 1918, to Republican state convention, Springfield, Illinois, and on Sept. 29, 1918, to B'nai B'rith, at Chicago.

10. MS of FOL's address on Dec. 9, 1918.

Three months later, after the tide of battle had definitely turned in favor of the Western powers, the governor sensed a slackening of the war effort in Illinois and cautioned its citizens against counting upon an early peace. "Nothing fights harder," he warned, "than a bankrupt concern."[11]

Convinced that the Allied cause was a crusade blessed by God, Lowden transformed every American soldier into a peerless knight locked in combat with a foe whose weapons were "robbery, murder and arson on a wholesale scale." No death could be more glorious and no life more rewarding than that of the man in uniform. The governor envied the Illinois troops in France and chafed because he was "chained to his desk" in civilian clothing. If the war had continued until 1919, he would probably have visited the Prairie and Blackhawk divisions at the front. Every doughboy, as he pictured him, was inspired by the highest ideals, exalted in morale, impeccable in morals, and more religious than before he enlisted. The armed services constituted the best of all schools for teaching Americanism, self-discipline, and true comradeship. The governor effortlessly extended his sentimental regard for all Civil War veterans to the "magnificent boys" of the world war. Among them was his own son.[12]

During his administration Lowden was never happier than when talking to troops, watching a sham battle, or riding a horse at a military review. The War Department disappointed him by declining his offer of "Sinnissippi" as the site of a mobilization center for an army division from Illinois. He and Mrs. Lowden often visited the cantonments, followed the federalized National Guard to its training areas in Texas and Kentucky, and bade it Godspeed upon its embarkation in New York harbor for France. Although the governor hobnobbed mainly with colonels and generals, he seldom visited a camp without gathering the enlisted men about him. They found him democratic and cordial and reciprocated his good will by cheering him to the echo when he favored them with an oration. In manuscript these speeches often seem longer and always more flowery than soldiers of today would willingly tolerate. "Happy, thrice happy," he exclaimed, "those men who were born at a time when they can become a part of the greatest hours of all history; and such are the hours that lie ahead of you, officers and men of the Black Hawk Division!" This grandiloquent peroration so impressed many in Lowden's vast audience that they repeated it time and again with wry humor as they slogged through the mud of France in heavy marching order.[13]

Brigadier General Charles G. Dawes and Colonel Robert R. McCormick of the Army and Sergeant Edwin Denby of the United States Marines wrote

11. MS of FOL's speech of Sept. 17, 1918, to the Women's Land Army, Libertyville, Illinois.

12. Pullman Lowden enlisted on Oct. 1, 1917, was sworn into federal service on Oct. 29, trained at Camp Logan in Texas with the Thirty-third Division, and embarked for France in May, 1918, in the division's Quartermaster's Office.

13. MS of FOL's speech to the Eighty-sixth (Black Hawk) Division, at Camp Grant, Rockford, Illinois, July 13, 1918.

occasionally to the governor about their experiences. Above all, however, he liked to hear from the privates and frequently quoted from their letters in his public speeches. Inquiries from the parents and wives of soldiers about their monthly pay allotments or war risk insurance received his personal attention. He wrote a note of condolence to the nearest relative of every Illinois soldier killed or severely wounded and indorsed the proposal to bring back to America after the war the bodies of the slain. "Blue stars changing to gold" in the service flags was one of his favorite oratorical themes.[14]

Convinced that the Selective Service Act was the most constructive measure enacted by Congress during the war, the governor gave short shrift to anyone who protested against it. He had no jurisdiction over the local draft boards, and his office was not the channel through which appeals from their decisions eventually reached the Provost Marshal General in Washington.[15] But, in 1918, when the United States Department of Justice, aided by the American Protective League, began its hunt for slackers, the federal agents found Lowden eager to co-operate in the chase.[16] He emphatically believed that all able-bodied men must either "work or fight." In peacetime every youth, nineteen years of age, should spend one year in uniform learning the rudiments of military science. If, added Lowden, there had been a universal military training law in force for several years before 1917, the Kaiser would never have dared to run amok. He also urged a continuation of conscription after the war as a device for reminding young men that Americans had duties as well as privileges. "Our citizenship has been too cheap," he declared in February, 1917. "We have acquired the habit of looking to the government for everything, expecting it to be a fairy godmother to whom nothing needs to be returned."[17]

Weeks before the Selective Service Act passed Congress on May 18, 1917, the authorities in Washington had been preparing a plan of registration dependent upon the help of state officials. Lowden and his competent adjutant general, Frank S. Dickson, upon whose shoulders most of the burden would fall, knew well what they had to do as soon as the draft law became effective. Less than two hours after receiving the go-ahead signal from Washington, Lowden wired to the War Department that he had already sent every mayor and sheriff in Illinois a telegram of instructions about the national registration on June 5. With almost no friction on that day the four thousand regis-

14. For example, MS of FOL's speech at Alton, Illinois, Centennial Celebration, Sept. 27, 1918.

15. So many letters came to FOL from fathers, usually farmers, asking draft exemption for their sons, that he prepared a form reply disclaiming any jurisdiction.

16. Marguerite E. Jenison (ed.), *The War Time Organization of Illinois* (Springfield, Ill., 1923), Vol. V of Theodore C. Pease (ed.), *Illinois in the World War* (6 vols., Springfield, Ill., 1921–23), pp. 76–77, 108–9. In Illinois, there were 16,193 deserters, 1,781 entrainment deserters, and 7,795 wilful delinquents. This startling total of about 25,000 was approximately as large as the number of Illinois National Guard inducted into national service.

17. MS of FOL's speech to the Advertising Association of Chicago, Feb. 23, 1917.

tration boards, each made up of the sheriff, county clerk, and county physician or their deputies, enrolled 672,498 men between the ages of twenty-one
and thirty years. Of these, approximately half claimed exemption from military service for various reasons, including their support of dependents and
employment in essential civilian occupations.[18]

On registration day the governor appeared before a joint session of the
legislature to ask the state senator and three assemblymen from each senatorial district for the names of two trustworthy and influential men, irrespective of their political affiliations, residing in each draft division of the senatorial district. Lowden nominated these to President Wilson for membership
on the local draft-exemption boards. If a county had a population of less than
45,000, it became a single draft unit; otherwise the latter embraced an area
containing about 30,000 people. Of the 227 exemption boards in Illinois, 95
were in Cook County.[19] Although chosen in a hurry, the personnel of the
draft boards averaged high in quality, and only ten members had to be dis-
missed during the war. The Army eventually inducted about 190,000 of the
1,575,000 Illinois registrants. Almost every allegedly unfair decision by the
exemption boards involved an issue of farm labor rather than of political partisanship. The governor had reason to feel gratified by Illinois's record in ad-
ministering the Selective Service Act.

However much he applauded the principle of compulsory military service,
he could not conceal his satisfaction because the state furnished almost as
many volunteers as draftees to the armed forces. After the Army of the
United States absorbed some 20,000 members of the Illinois National Guard
on August 5, 1917, and moved them for further training to camps outside the
state, Lowden took steps to remedy its defenseless condition in the event of
domestic disorder. He soon had three new National Guard regiments alerted
for home duty. A reserve militia, numbering over 6,000 men, and a Voluntary Training Corps nearly twice that size were also organized. The latter,
under the aegis of the State Council of Defense, constituted a Home Guard
and gave elementary military instruction to prospective draftees. The reserve
militia merged with it before the end of the war.[20]

Besides his many responsibilities in connection with home defense, the
federalization of the National Guard, and the administration of the Selective
Service Act, the governor was often called upon by Washington and various
official and semiofficial bodies to help with other war-born activities. Using
his proclamation power, he designated, inaugurated, or encouraged bond
sales, food conservation and other thrift measures, united warwork campaigns of various kinds, Red Cross drives, holidays and similar commemora-

18. Jenison, *The War Time Organization of Illinois,* pp. 4–5, 100.

19. *Journal of the Senate of the Fiftieth General Assembly of the State of Illinois,* pp.
1113–14; *House Debates, Fiftieth General Assembly, State of Illinois, 1917,* pp. 961–68; *Blue
Book of the State of Illinois, 1917–1918,* pp. 99–103.

20. F. S. Dickson, "The State Militia and Voluntary Training Corps," *Blue Book of the
State of Illinois, 1917–1918,* pp. 96–98; Jenison, *The War Time Organization of Illinois,*
pp. 5, 78–84, 86–91.

tive occasions, and the singing of patriotic songs in schools. The United States Fuel Administration sought his aid in reducing the use of coal and in rallying public opinion in favor of "gasoline-less" Sundays. He gladly lent his influence on behalf of the YMCA, the Salvation Army, the Boy Scouts, and the United States Boys' Working Reserve. At the request of the head of the Illinois Federation of Women's Clubs he publicly testified that its Soldiers' Clubs and "protective homes for girls" at Camp Grant (Rockford) and the Rantoul Flying Field contributed significantly to the maintenance of troop morale.[21] As a stimulus to the sale of Liberty Bonds and War Saving Stamps he made known that he and his family owned the full limit allowed by law but would buy more to offer as prizes in a bond-sale competition between the state's school children. He was a member of the cast of a film entitled *Soldiers and Sweethearts*, which the *Chicago Herald and Examiner* prepared to show during the 1918 Christmas festivities of Illinois troops in France.

Amid these manifold extra tasks, the burden imposed by the influenza epidemic came as a bolt from the blue. The first case occurred at the Great Lakes Naval Training Station, thirty-five miles north of Chicago, in September, 1918. By the end of the month the disease had invaded the metropolis, certain areas in southern Illinois, and Camp Grant.[22] Thereafter, throughout the autumn and winter, the scourge took an appalling toll. The extreme shortage of doctors and nurses heightened the crisis.

In mid-October, at the request of the United States Public Health Service, the governor was about to forbid all public meetings, when he received "the strongest kind of protest" from Archbishop Mundelein speaking for the million and a half Catholics in Illinois. To close the churches, the prelate warned, would be "like turning away from God in war and pestilence." "I have been haunted by a fear," he continued, "that to do so, would be opening the door to a long series of ill fortunes for our state, our city, or our country." The "boys overseas and their mothers' heartache find more relief in God's presence in church than anywhere else," and foreign-born Catholics especially would become restive if they were barred from the church buildings. "I could not take upon myself the responsibility," the archbishop concluded, "of absolving my priests from the duty of celebrating Mass on Sundays or my people from the obligation of hearing Mass on that day."[23] In response to this plea, the governor confined the scope of his proclamation to "public gatherings of a social nature." Faced with heavy financial losses, a few proprietors of dance halls and theaters threatened to sue him or the state for damages. Shocked by over thirty-two thousand deaths out of two hundred thousand reported cases of influenza and "complicating pneu-

21. FOL to Jessie I. Spafford, Rockford, Illinois, Sept. 30, 1918.

22. At Camp Grant there were about 10,000 cases and 1,000 deaths.

23. Archbishop G. W. Mundelein, Chicago, to FOL, Oct. 16, 1918; J. C. Mason's memorandum of a telephone conversation with the Chancery office, Oct. 16; Mundelein to FOL, Oct. 17, 1918.

monia," most citizens of Illinois eagerly supported all his precautionary measures.

Long before the "flu" invasion, the people of the state had greatly curtailed their social activities. Beginning in the spring of 1917, thrifty and simple living became a mark of patriotism. In full agreement with this emphasis, the Lowdens also recognized that their conduct in the Executive Mansion would be under ceaseless scrutiny. While the governor urged everyone else to use food and fuel sparingly, he guarded against providing any critic with a justifiable reason to accuse him of wasting them in his own home. The press remained the more watchful because the editors of its society pages had prophesied before his inauguration that the Lowden regime would be "brilliant," reflecting the wealth and prestige of his family.

During the first three months of his administration when the United States was at peace, these forecasts bade fair to be fulfilled. In January, Governor and Mrs. Lowden held a reception in the Mansion for all the members of the Assembly and their wives. On the eve of the declaration of war, they entertained at separate state dinners the justices of the state Supreme Court and the executive officials. By then, invitations were out for two stag dinners for the Senators and also for similar functions to which the Representatives were to come in groups, twenty-five or thirty strong. On still another evening the capital city's newspaper correspondents gathered around the governor's table. The Senators' banquet for the Lowdens at the Leland Hotel ended the "official season." By that evening the nation had been at war for over two months.

Mrs. Lowden quickly "won her way into Springfield hearts." She frequently attended the First or Second Presbyterian church and, with her husband, became a member of the former in February, 1920. Soon after coming to the Executive Mansion, she joined the city's Women's Club, YWCA, and chapter of the Daughters of the American Revolution. On almost every Wednesday afternoon during the winter and early spring she served tea to an unpredictable number of callers—sometimes a couple of dozen and occasionally five times that number. These "at homes" were the only regular appointments on her social calendar during the war. Following tradition, the Lowdens greeted state employees at the Mansion on New Year's morning and received anyone who wished to visit in the afternoon. The huge crowd at these affairs left enough litter to shock as careful a housekeeper as Mrs. Lowden.

When she first came to Springfield, the governor's residence belied its pretentious title of "Executive Mansion." Erected many years before, it badly needed repair. Rats and cockroaches disputed its possession with the state's "first family." Its roof leaked, and its heating system was far from adequate. Some of its fireplaces were unusable, its plumbing and lighting fixtures antiquated and insufficient, its closets few, much of its furniture worn and drab, and the sidewalks surrounding its grounds badly broken. Noting some of these defects when she had called on Mrs. Dunne late in 1918, Mrs. Lowden consulted a Chicago contractor about making improvements. Without including the value of the furniture brought from "Sinnissippi" and never taken back, the renovations and repairs cost nearly fifty thousand dollars. Of this sum, the legislature appropriated half, and the Lowdens paid the rest. In this way the governor made the Executive Mansion into a more comfortable home at a cost to him of his twelve-thousand-dollar salary for over two years. During the reconstruction in the summer of 1917, the Lowdens occupied the residence of John W. Black on Williams Boulevard in Springfield. Upon returning to the official residence in October, the governor found his new basement office a much quieter place to work in than his headquarters in the Capitol.

The Lowdens easily accommodated themselves to the wartime curbs on social life. The governor's favorite diversions had never included big dinners and receptions. On the other hand, he thoroughly enjoyed a noon-hour walk with his wife, a late-afternoon drive with her into the country or to the Oglesby home at Elkhart for tea, and an evening game of cards. Occasionally he went for a horseback ride or played nine holes of golf with Stead or Dickson at the country club. When opportunity offered after the evening meal, he listened to a piano and mandolin concert by his daughters Harriet and Frances. Vachel Lindsay sometimes dropped in to read a newly finished poem, and the many devotees of Lincoln in Springfield found the governor a sympathetic listener to their lore. It was a rare week when there were no guests for dinner, one or more state officials at luncheon to talk business, and a visiting dignitary from Washington or elsewhere to spend the night. Florence Lowden often helped her mother as co-hostess and did much of the shopping with a market basket over her arm. On the few occasions when official business seemed well in hand, Lowden asked Lieutenant-Governor Oglesby to stand in for him while he visited his Arkansas plantations for a week or ten days. A much-anticipated trip to his Canadian fishing camp in the late summer of 1917 fell short of his expectations. Unable to relax when out of quick touch with state affairs, he returned to Springfield earlier than planned and thereafter abandoned fishing until the war ended.

During 1917 and 1918 entertainment often merged with duty. The Lowdens attended many fairs, exhibitions, soldiers' athletic contests, amateur theatricals, and dances, mostly staged for the benefit of some enterprise connected with the war. Mrs. Lowden worked at Red Cross headquarters in Springfield, making bandages, packing kits, and teaching knitting. As the governor's wife, she judged knitting contests and donated prizes for, or conferred them upon, the winners of various warwork competitions among women and children throughout the state. When two pounds of wool, sheared from sheep grazing on the White House lawn, were bid in at auction by the governor for $250, she had it carded and spun, and then she fashioned the yarn into socks to be sold at a Red Cross fair. She made the comfort of the troops at Camp Lowden in Springfield her special concern and frequently attended meetings in Chicago of the Women's Committee of the State

Council of National Defense. She usually accompanied the governor on his speech-making and camp-visiting expeditions. Rarely in the best of health, she endured these exhausting trips for his sake and because she knew that the people expected to see her. To be closely surrounded by a gaping crowd, to spend a night in a small-town hotel, and to simulate interest in the conversation of rank-and-file politicians were not experiences which she relished, but she played her part courageously and with a graciousness which won her much acclaim.

Four years before Lowden's inauguration the Illinois legislature had created a commission to plan an elaborate series of celebrations in honor of the one-hundredth anniversary of the state's admission to the Union in 1818. The Centennial Commission, the state and local historical societies, and other groups within many of the counties and older towns worked diligently to arrange for a full year of festivities, punctuated by special commemorative exercises on high days such as Lincoln's Birthday, the Fourth of July, and the centenaries of the enabling act, the drafting of the state's first constitution, the inauguration of the state government, and the formal admission of Illinois into the Union on December 3. Statues of Lincoln and Douglas were to be unveiled at Springfield and a centennial shaft in Logan Square on Chicago's Near North Side. The legislature designated a site, hard by the Capitol, for a Centennial Building. The keynote of these observances, as originally planned, was to be lightheartedness and pride in commonwealth.[24]

The onset of war caused many Illinois citizens to urge that the entire project be abandoned. It would cost much in time, money, and labor and distract all who shared in it from their primary job of helping to defeat Germany. In the governor's view, on the contrary, the widely ramifying organization, already in being, could perform distinguished service by arousing the people to an enthusiastic support of the war. To accomplish this, let the dominant note of all the commemorative exercises be altered from carefree rejoicing to the sacrificial devotion of bygone Illinois civil and military leaders to democratic ideals and the federal Union. Hugh S. Magill, Jr., chairman of the Centennial Commission, stated later in his official report: "To him [Lowden] more than to any other one person belongs the credit for the lofty patriotic sentiment which pervaded the Illinois Centennial Celebration."[25] The governor called it "a great vehicle for patriotic propaganda," a most timely means of reminding Illinoisans that they would be unworthy of their famous ancestors if they did not respond nobly to the demands of the

24. In the *Blue Book of the State of Illinois, 1919–1920*, pp. 17, 127–28, 139–45, and 311–35, are separate accounts of the celebration by H. S. Magill, Jr., Edgar Martin, and Jessie Palmer Weber. Students of Illinois history will remember the anniversary longest because one of its "memorials" was the scholarly five-volume *Centennial History of Illinois* (Springfield, Ill., 1918–20), edited by Clarence W. Alvord. Another centennial project was Theodore C. Pease (ed.), *Illinois in the World War* (6 vols.; Springfield, Ill., 1921–23). Congress authorized the minting of 100,000 half-dollars, with Lincoln's head on one side and the seal of Illinois on the other. County or other centennial organizations bought these at face value and sold them for one dollar as a means of paying their expenses.

25. *Blue Book of the State of Illinois, 1919–1920*, p. 127.

instant crisis. By living up to their great heritage, they, too, would merit similar reverence by future generations.

The various commemorative meetings held from Chicago south to Old Kaskaskia added much to the governor's speech-making, traveling, and entertaining of distinguished personages. The centennial year opened on December 3, 1917, with Lowden serving as toastmaster at a banquet in Springfield, where three former governors—Fifer, Yates, and Dunne—were the orators. Following this curtain-raiser, nearly one thousand gatherings here and there throughout the state during 1918 paid homage to the anniversary. Of these, Lowden attended about a dozen of the larger ones and was usually one of the speakers.[26] In April he addressed a meeting in the Capitol, attended the exercises of the Chicago Historical Society in Orchestra Hall, and witnessed at Springfield a patriotic pageant entitled "The Sword of America," in which his daughter Florence had a prominent part. His Fourth of July oration was delivered at Chester, close to Old Kaskaskia. Late in August he introduced Theodore Roosevelt to an immense throng at the State Fair Grounds in Springfield, as "the greatest of all . . . partisans of the rights of the common man," dearer to "the hearts of the American people" than ever before in his career. That evening the former President and the Lowdens witnessed the first performance of "The Masque of Illinois." In this elaborate series of tableaux, Florence Lowden had the leading role of "Illinois." The praise showered upon her by Roosevelt and the press highly pleased her father.[27] In September he shared in the parade at Vandalia and headed its battery of centennial orators. Two days later he dedicated a memorial fountain in Alton and spoke at the site of Elijah Lovejoy's press.

By then the centennial year was nearing its climax. The fifty-one members of a special Invitations Committee, with Lowden as its chairman, had each signed a letter to President Wilson, written on hand-illuminated vellum and bound in red morocco, asking him to visit Illinois on October 5 and 6, the centenary of the inauguration of the state government, and speak at the Memorial Building cornerstone-laying and the unveiling of the Lincoln and Douglas statues on the Capitol grounds. After long hesitation, the President declined on September 30. "Every consideration," he assured Lowden, "disposes us to accept, most of all our deep personal interest, but apparently I am bound hand and foot by imperative duties which I should wholly dishonor Lincoln's memory by neglecting."[28]

Lord Charnwood, author of a widely read biography of Lincoln, agreed to come from England to make the address at the unveiling of the statue of the Great Emancipator. Besides appreciating the honor of the invitation, he remarked in his letter of acceptance that many of his fellow citizens felt highly pleased by this additional evidence of the growing friendship between the American and English people.[29] Secretary of the Navy Josephus

26. *Ibid.*, pp. 314–20.
27. *Ibid.*, pp. 321–22, 328–29; and *Centennial Bulletin,* No. 9 (October, 1918), p. 14.
28. W. Wilson to FOL, Sept. 30, 1918.
29. Lord Charnwood, Lichfield, England, to FOL, Aug. 3, 1918.

Daniels spoke at the base of the Douglas statue, and Governor Lowden delivered the oration at the foundations of the Centennial Building. Large crowds witnessed these ceremonies on October 5, as well as a repeat performance of "The Masque of Illinois." On the following morning the Lowdens, Lord Charnwood, and fifteen thousand other people attended an open-air Mass at the Sacred Heart Convent. In the afternoon two hundred descendants of former Illinois governors came to a reception at the Executive Mansion, and Charnwood spoke that evening at a union service of Protestants in Springfield. This was the largest cluster of celebrations in honor of the anniversary. Shortly thereafter, Lowden closed a five-day series of observances in Chicago by speaking at the dedication of the centennial monument in Logan Square.

The "Year of Remembrance" ended on December 3, 1918, with the Lowdens again sharing prominently in the meetings in Springfield. They held a reception at the Mansion and, with Dr. John H. Finley, attended a dinner given by the Centennial Commission at the Sangamo Club. In the evening at the Capitol the governor presided at the final gathering of the anniversary year. So long-continued had been the celebration and so conspicuous had Lowden been in it that many people thought of him thereafter as "the centennial governor."

Although he believed that the "inspiration from the past" evoked by the "Year of Remembrance" helped Illinois citizens fulfil "their high and solemn duties," he had to contend with radicals, pacifists, and alleged German spies during the entire war period. The posters, speeches, moving pictures, pageants, and organizations designed to promote a solidarity of purpose and action inflamed some people to the point of suspecting anyone of disloyalty who did not share their enthusiasm. Their patriotism became indistinguishable from intolerance, and their behavior revealed a misunderstanding of the very slogans whereby they tried to display their Americanism. Parading their allegiance to liberty and democracy and their hatred of the Kaiser, they equated criticism of the government at Washington with sedition or treason and denied to an accused person a fair trial or even protection of his person and property. While the governor did all in his power to stimulate everyone to give unsparingly for victory, he sometimes was obliged to prevent a misuse of the force he helped to generate. "Democracy is now on trial," he declared. "If it cannot secure a due and orderly government at home, how can it expect to win battles abroad?"[30]

By the winter of 1918 the increasing number of alleged disloyal acts and utterances somewhat offset the governor's satisfaction because the initial apathy in Illinois about the war had clearly ended. Although accusations against halfhearted patriots naturally multiplied with the mounting war excitement, they also reflected dismal news from the fighting front and the drive by federal authorities to round up draft-evaders and seditious persons.

30. *Chicago Herald,* Feb. 26, 1918.

The many Illinois residents of German descent included forty thousand enemy aliens. A concern for national security made their close supervision advisable, even though most of them discreetly held their peace.

Robert Paul Prager, however, a German-born socialist living at Collinsville, Illinois, could not remain silent. After haranguing the coal miners of his neighborhood about President Wilson's iniquitous policies, he was jailed in Collinsville on the charge of making disloyal speeches and probably being a German spy. Unrestrained, if not actually abetted, by its police, a mob of three or four hundred persons dragged him from his cell and hung him to a tree limb outside the village limits on April 5, 1918. This lynching aroused wide public attention, including a Cabinet discussion in Washington, a speech by William E. Borah in the United States Senate, an offer from Germany through the Swiss embassy to pay the victim's funeral expenses, and a running fire of press comment for over two months.[31]

"Patriotism will not be permitted to be used as a cloak for crime in Illinois if I can help it," declared the governor when he heard of the outrage." What will it avail us for our soldiers to win victories abroad if self-government breaks down in our very midst?"[32] He asked the attorney-general personally to prosecute the suspected leaders of the mob. After a lengthy investigation by a grand jury, it found true bills for murder against twelve civilians and four policemen. The former were tried first, but the lawyers had to question over seven hundred talesmen before discovering twelve "impartial" jurymen. Following the presentation of the evidence, they quickly decided that the night of April 5 had been too dark to permit positive identification of any of the defendants. The indictments against the policemen were soon quashed. Lowden denounced the outcome as "a lamentable failure of justice."[33]

He had little sympathy for Prager and men of his stripe who, by word or deed, gave "much provocation" for acts of violence against them. The lynching reinforced his request, made as early as February, 1918, that the federal authorities help him apprehend all disloyal persons in Illinois. Immediately after the Collinsville tragedy he sent the lieutenant-governor to Washington to press for the needed co-operation. By late April, thanks to the recruitment of about 12,500 Home Guards and help from the Department of Justice, Illinois had "one of the most far-reaching intelligence and espionage organizations to beat down sedition" and prevent mob assaults upon pacifists, pro-Germans, and Bolsheviks.[34] Furthermore, the Prager case apparently hastened the enactment of the Espionage Act by Congress. The more sternly Lowden repressed enemy sympathizers, the more frequently he praised loyal citizens of German descent for their many services to the nation throughout its entire history.

31. Illinois paid Prager's funeral expenses of $197.
32. Speech of FOL at Rock Island, Illinois, Apr. 6, 1918.
33. *Springfield Register*, June 4, 1918.
34. *Chicago Tribune*, Apr. 10, 1918; J. G. Oglesby, "The Volunteer Training Corps," in *Blue Book of the State of Illinois, 1919–1920*, pp. 103–8.

In Illinois, as in other states, citizen organizations urged the governor to forbid the teaching of German in the public schools and state university and its use in churches, newspapers, telephone conversations, and on the streets. According to these patriotic groups, the constitutional guaranties of freedom of speech and the press applied only to the English language. To these extremists, including those who demanded a ban on all German music, Lowden turned a deaf ear. In the interest of public tranquillity, however, he advised citizens of German background to recognize the "abnormality" of the times by holding "in abeyance the exercise of purely legal rights," such as the use of their language, in situations where it would give offense.[35] He agreed with the resolutions of the Council of the American Association of University Professors, asking that the teaching of German be continued as an elective in high schools and colleges but be eliminated from the curriculums of the elementary schools. Shortly after the Armistice, he told the National Education Association: "The idea and the printed word are closely allied. You do not get the true American spirit if you are educated in a foreign tongue. The English tongue is the language of liberty, of self-government, and of orderly progress under the law. Unless our children are compelled to learn to think in that language, we cannot expect them to come under the influence of American ideals."[36]

The governor wanted to prod unnaturalized persons toward citizenship and exclude them from suffrage but not from tax-paying while they remained foreigners. The crisis conditions revealed to him as well as to other leaders that "unassimilated aliens" should undergo more thoroughgoing Americanization. To determine what this meant, he created an Immigrants' Commission within the Department of Education and Registration. National in scope, the problem was really for Washington to handle, but he hoped that the commission's research might help to guide the action of Congress.

During the closing months of the war, Lowden decided that economic radicals posed as serious a danger to the United States as did enemy aliens. Shortly after the Armistice he urged General Dawes to return from France without delay to aid in the fight against the Bolsheviks, now that the menace of a military autocracy had been dispelled.[37] In common with many people of his day, the governor classified socialists merely as loyal or disloyal and made no attempt to differentiate between Communists and Industrial Workers of the World. By his definition the latter two were "traitors" because they fostered public disorder and preached war against the capitalists. Unaware of his own inconsistency, he demanded a fair trial for men like Prager even while he prejudged alleged Communists without a hearing. Probably the explanation lies in his hatred of mob action whether taken in the name

35. FOL to F. E. Demuth, Ellsworth, Kansas, Sept. 12, 1918.

36. MS of FOL's speech of Feb. 27, 1919, in Chicago.

37. FOL told C. G. Dawes in his letter of Nov. 26, 1918, that, until the radicals were repressed, the war to make the world "safe for Democracy was only half-won."

of patriotism or of Karl Marx. Prager or some other pro-German of his ilk generally stood alone, goading excited citizens to use lawless means in his repression. The Communists and IWW's, on the contrary, usually employed group action to impede the war effort.

Early in the conflict the governor probably overdrew his dire picture of what would befall America if the Central Powers won. By the late summer of 1918, after the tide of battle turned in favor of the Allies, he certainly overestimated the number and power of the radicals in the United States. He and his hearers easily shifted their focus of antagonism and fear from a humbled autocrat overseas to a supposedly vast underground conspiracy at home. Their high idealism during the early months of the war rapidly waned when they sensed that victory abroad had aggravated, rather than solved, many domestic problems. In their disillusionment they sought a scapegoat. The radical was conveniently at hand. With so many voters of German ancestry in Illinois, political expediency also counseled a transfer of public distrust to a new group as rapidly as possible after the Armistice. Every considerable economic and social component of the state's population viewed the bolshevists as its natural enemy. The Marxist, like the Kaiser, could serve as a foil to all the values embodied in the American democratic tradition and way of life.

Lowden's first brush with the "reds" came early in the war. Their offense at that time seemed the more flagrant in his eyes because they resisted the Selective Service Act. A hostile demonstration staged by the IWW's in Rockford marred an otherwise peaceful registration day in Illinois on June 5, 1917. Lowden applauded Judge Landis when he sentenced several "Wobbly" leaders of this outbreak to two years and about one hundred others to one year in federal prison. During the same summer the governor strongly suspected that the East St. Louis race riots and the prolonged streetcar strike in Springfield had been instigated, or at least aggravated, by disloyal persons. But he could not decide whether to blame enemy agents or radicals. In September, 1917, he indorsed the seizure by federal agents of "seditious material" in the Chicago headquarters of the Socialists and IWW's. He conceded that the loyalty of many Socialists was beyond reproach, even while he advocated the summary suppression of Victor Berger, Wisconsin Socialist Congressman, and everyone like him. At an Elks Club meeting in East St. Louis in the following month, Lowden stated bluntly that he would deny freedom of speech to any person in Illinois who misused his birthright by inciting treasonable acts. The same fundamental law which guaranteed liberty of utterance also made treason a crime.[38] In spite of the thoroughness of the 1918 search-and-seizure drive for saboteurs, seditious persons, enemy spies, and draft-evaders, at least a few escaped the dragnet of the federal and state authorities.

Now and again in Illinois, "Bolsheviks" furnished a ready explanation of

38. MS of speech of Oct. 27, 1917.

an explosion, fire, train derailment, or other baffling mishap. Thus in Chicago on September 4, 1918, a bomb explosion in the Federal Building killed a sailor and caused considerable property damage. The governor blamed the IWW's. He used the occurrence to warn his fellow citizens that the Germans employed radicals as agents and that "misguided and sentimental university professors" sometimes taught un-American doctrines in their classrooms. The lieutenant-governor, who was also the chairman of the Military Committee of the State Council of Defense, dramatized the danger by posting guards around public buildings and the Executive Mansion in Springfield. If Lowden read the *Chicago Post,* he may have agreed that the real culprit of the bomb explosion was Mayor William H. Thompson because he had been "preaching class war against men of wealth."[39]

Differences over the requirements of patriotism combined with differences over matters of patronage to cause a fateful break between the governor and the mayor even before the end of the war's first year. "Big Bill's" brand of loyalty seemed to be a close twin of disloyalty in the opinion of the governor and many other Illinoisans. In 1917 the mayor made no secret of his intense dislike of the Selective Service Act. His political enemies soon labeled him "Unser Bill" and "Burgomeister Bill."[40] As he availed himself to the full of his own right to freedom of speech, so he upheld others in the exercise of the same liberty, especially when they wished to exercise it by tirading against the war policies of the Wilson administration. On this issue he and the governor had their memorable clash. The mayor's constitutional position was strong, but he maintained it for questionable reasons. Contrariwise, Lowden was on weak constitutional ground, but his purpose was praiseworthy.

Late in the summer of 1917, the "People's Council of America for Democracy and Terms of Peace," or "a society of antiwar cranks" as Mrs. Lowden called it, found itself harried from city to city in its effort to halt long enough to perfect its organization and plan of action. Mayor Thompson assured its leading spirits, after Minneapolis drove them out, that "pacifists are law-abiding citizens" and hence "he could not deny them the right to meet in Chicago" on September 1.[41] Thereupon, H. H. Merrick of the National Security League appealed to Lowden to forbid the assemblage. Nothing loath and failing to reach the mayor by telephone, the governor ordered Chicago's chief of police to prevent the conference if it had not started or to disperse it if it was in session. Without questioning the right of Lowden to give him direct orders—as Thompson would do later—Chief Schuetter immediately sent twenty policemen to the West Side Auditorium. They took Seymour Stedman, a Chicago lawyer, into momentary custody for disobeying their command to stop speaking but otherwise dissolved the

39. Mrs. Lowden's diary, Sept. 7, 1918; *Chicago Post,* Sept. 5, 1918.

40. *Chicago Herald,* Aug. 13, 1917.

41. Mrs. Lowden's diary, Sept. 1, 1917.

gathering without trouble of any kind. The governor defended his action by citing his solemn oath as chief executive to maintain the public peace. Everyone knew, he added, that antiwar meetings often incited riots. In his view, pacifism differed little from disloyalty in wartime, especially when the pacifists included well-known Socialists, obviously of German ancestry. In his words:

There is a time to discuss, and a time to act unitedly on the lines finally approved as the result of discussion. . . . I shall employ the full power of the state in suppressing the meeting of this society or of any other similar society. . . . The People's Council is a treasonable conspiracy which must not find refuge under the guarantee of freedom of speech. If we lose this war the freedom of speech of all of us will be lost. Freedom of speech in Illinois can not be used as a cloak for treason. . . . The time has come in Illinois and elsewhere to find out who are for the government and who are against the government. This is the only classification which matters at the present time. . . . The Civil War would have been briefer if less tenderness had been shown to traitors at home, especially in the cities. The right of self-preservation is the first law of a Democracy. . . . When you are engaged in a battle to the death, you do not pause and take breath and begin to prate of peace.[42]

Having failed to complete their business at their first meeting because of police interference, the People's Council again sought the sympathetic ear of the mayor. Denouncing Lowden for unconstitutionally invading his own jurisdiction and for violating the right of freedom of speech, Thompson guaranteed the pacifists that they could meet the next day under police protection. Stedman would preside, while former Senator William E. Mason of Illinois, former Senator John D. Works of California, and Morris Hillquit, a leading New York Socialist, would address the delegates. When Merrick informed the governor that both the mayor and the pacifists intended to defy him, Lowden tried vainly to telephone Sheriff Traeger of Cook County and Major General Carter at Fort Sheridan. As a last resort he dispatched Adjutant General Dickson from Springfield by special train with several companies of the Illinois National Guard—the first time that troops had been sent to Chicago on riot duty since the Pullman strike over twenty years before. By noon of September 2, when they reached their destination, the four-hour-long session of the pacifists had adjourned. At this meeting they heartily denounced the governor, the President, and the war.

In this fashion "Big Bill" won his skirmish at the cost of much personal popularity. The cheers greeting the troops at the railroad station rose to an even greater volume when Governor and Mrs. Lowden arrived in Chicago the next day. There, in his wife's words, he was "overwhelmed with letters and messages of congratulation."[43] The Hamilton Club, the Chicago Association of Commerce, and other civic organizations adopted resolutions upholding his action and condemning the mayor. The Veterans of Foreign

42. The quotations are combined from references to the incident in several of FOL's speeches of September, 1917.

43. Mrs. Lowden's diary, Sept. 3 and 4, 1917.

Wars hung "His Honor" in effigy at the corner of Michigan Avenue and Randolph Street, and the National Security League appointed a special committee, with Clarence Darrow as one of its members, to discover a way to oust Thompson. In Minneapolis, Samuel Gompers gave his blessing to Lowden's stand by telling the American Alliance for Labor and Democracy that slackers and pacifists merited nothing but denunciation. Chicago newspapers reviled the mayor as a traitor. Protesting that he was the victim of a "plot," and that his telephone had been tapped, he began libel proceedings against the *Chicago Daily News*, the *Chicago Tribune*, and H. H. Merrick. Amid this excitement, the constitutional issue of whether a governor could lawfully send orders directly to the police of a municipality was almost forgotten. In a vague statement Attorney-General Brundage appeared to indorse Lowden's stand, but neither Lowden nor Thompson seemed eager to press the matter to a conclusion. The governor was content to declare that if Chicago were to have more home rule, it must demonstrate by the high quality of its administration in City Hall its ability and willingness to keep the peace without resort to the National Guard.

Of much more immediate importance than the jurisdictional issue were the political implications of the episode. The *Chicago Journal* of September 3 may have hit upon part of the truth by reporting that Lowden's resolve to cut loose from Thompson's Republican faction had shaped his course more importantly than his fear lest a pacifist meeting stir up a riot. Leading members of his party immediately ranged themselves on one side or the other of the controversy, while a few, like Len Small, the state treasurer, and Fred Sterling, chairman of the State Republican Central Committee, significantly remained aloof. The Deneenites rallied to the governor's support. So, too, did most of the former Bull Moosers, gratified not only by his administrative reforms but by his hard-hitting Americanism, well calculated to win Theodore Roosevelt's applause. Evidently an important realignment of Republican forces was under way in Illinois, as the governor's former City Hall friends exchanged places with his erstwhile enemies.

Notwithstanding his insistence that partisan politics within and between the two major parties must recess for the duration of the war and notwithstanding the non-partisan character of his legislative program and appointments to war-emergency positions, he exemplified certain ideals and policies by the close of 1917 which he could not wholly divorce from politics. He had identified himself with strong executive power, administrative and constitutional reforms, honest and economical government, road and waterway development, a moderate program of social service and prolabor legislation, militant patriotism, "100 per cent Americanism," and unqualified support of the war. What he did and said had come to be matters of interest beyond the borders of his own state.

Political pundits felt certain that he hoped to go either to the Senate or to the White House. However often he disclaimed this ambition, he failed to convince either his friends or his foes. Flattered by the widespread approval of his words and deeds, pressed by political supporters whose counsel he respected, and cheered by his continued good health under the strains of the governorship, he gradually came to doubt his own protestations that nothing except a farmer's life at "Sinnissippi" could attract him when he yielded his present office to his successor.